*Personal Perspectives on
Emotional Disturbance/Behavioral Disorders*

Personal Perspectives on Emotional Disturbance/Behavioral Disorders

Edited by
Benjamin Leigh Brooks
David A. Sabatino

pro·ed
8700 Shoal Creek Boulevard
Austin, Texas 78757-6897

pro·ed

© 1996 by PRO-ED, Inc.
8700 Shoal Creek Boulevard
Austin, Texas 78757-6897

All rights reserved. No part of the material protected by this copyright notice may be reproduced or used in any form or by any means, electronic or mechanical, including photocopying, recording, or by any information storage and retrieval system, without the prior written permission of the copyright owner.

Library of Congress Cataloging-in-Publication Data

Personal perspectives on emotional disturbance/behavioral disorders /
 edited by Benjamin L. Brooks, David A. Sabatino.
   p. cm.
  Includes bibliographical references.
  ISBN 0-89079-618-1
   1. Mentally ill children—Education—United States. 2. Mentally ill children—Services for—United States. 3. Emotionally disturbed children—Education—United States. 4. Emotionally disturbed children—Services for—United States. I. Brooks, Benjamin L. (Benjamin Leigh) II. Sabatino, David A.
LC4181.P47 1995
371.94' 0973—dc20   94-45064
                                                              CIP

Production Manager: Alan Grimes
Production Coordinator: Karen Swain
Art Director: Lori Kopp
Reprints Buyer: Alicia Woods
Editor: Tracy Sergo
Editorial Assistant: Claudette Landry

Printed in the United States of America

1 2 3 4 5 6 7 8 9 10   00 99 98 97

Contents

Preface • vii

Introduction • xv

About the Editors • xxi

Part One: Historical Perspectives • 1

1. Genesis to a Personal Perspective on Emotional Disturbance
   BENJAMIN L. BROOKS AND DAVID A. SABATINO • 2

2. A Brief History of How We Have Helped Emotionally Disturbed Children and Other Fairy Tales
   ELI M. BOWER • 24

Part Two: Personal Perspectives • 37

3. David B. Center • 38

4. Margaret Cecil Coleman • 50

5. William H. Evans • 72

6. Steven R. Forness • 84

7. Robert A. Gable • 96

8. Eleanor C. Guetzloe • 110

9. Norris G. Haring • 132
10. John L. Johnson • 152
11. Edward J. Kelly • 170
12. Nicholas J. Long • 196
13. Richard L. McDowell • 214
14. Thomas McIntyre • 232
15. William C. Morse • 250
16. Mary Beth Noll and Barbara A. Braaten • 272
17. James L. Paul • 290
18. William C. Rhodes • 320
19. Richard L. Simpson • 340
20. James R. Tompkins • 358
21. Brenda L. Townsend • 378
22. Jo Webber • 398
23. Frank W. Wood • 424
24. Mitchell L. Yell • 442
25. Robert H. Zabel • 464
26. Where Do We Go from Here? • 483

Additional Readings • 493

Preface

The field of educating children with emotional disturbance is a twentieth-century development still very much in a formative period with considerable transition taking place. Foremost in this ongoing change has been the search for an "inclusive" definition of the population to be served. General agreement in defining this segment of the disabled population is an essential initial step in establishing common ground for professionals across the helping disciplines. There must exist a basic understanding of what the problem is and where and under what conditions the problem exists. Once this has been accomplished, professionals then can proceed with the identification of children meeting the criteria for services.

The complexity of the problems in defining and educating youths with emotional disturbance is evident in the nonacceptance of what is currently in place and the desire to formulate a new, broader definition that will include those who have not been served previously (Forness & Knitzer, 1991). Currently, the field uses noninterchangeable definitions to address a common social phenomenon of behaviors that are difficult to understand in children: behaviors that interfere with self and others and that are inappropriate or draw undue attention to the child, thus presenting interpersonal and intrapersonal adjustment problems in home, school, and community. There is no single solution to this complex problem.

Educators must remember that the major role of any definition of emotional disturbance/behavioral disorders is to aid in decision making with regard to identification, programming, and placement. While there appears to be no "best" definition of the problem, the one that has gained widest acceptance in the educational field has been adopted for the Individuals with Disabilities Education Act (IDEA, 1990, formerly known as the Education of All Handicapped Children Act) and by most states' departments of education.

This definition states that a serious emotional disturbance in a child is behavior that is developmentally inappropriate or inadequate for educational settings and is indicated by one or more of the following characteristics:

- an inability to learn that cannot be explained by intellectual, sensory, or health factors
- an inability to build or maintain satisfactory interpersonal relationships with peers or teachers
- inappropriate types of behavior or feelings under normal circumstances
- a general, pervasive mood of unhappiness or depression
- a tendency to develop physical symptoms of fears associated with personal or school problems

The behavior must be of sufficient duration, frequency, and intensity to call attention to the need for intervention on the child's behalf to insure educational success. The term *emotionally disturbed* does not include children who are socially maladjusted, unless it is determined that they are seriously emotionally handicapped (Federal Register, 1977, p. 474).

This definition uses the social context, the school, as the environment in the evaluation of emotional disturbance or behavior disorders. Although deriving a common scientific definition of this condition is not the intent of this text, it presents an opportunity for the reader to read firsthand about the "road that has been traveled" thus far in an attempt to bring definition and perhaps some closure to a very real problem in the education of individuals who bear one of the following labels: emotionally disturbed, children with behavioral disorders, socially maladjusted, children with disturbing behaviors, children in conflict, troubled youth, norm-violating children and youth, children with mental disorders, chronic disruptive, seriously emotionally disturbed, mentally ill, and children with conduct disorders. This is by no means a complete list, as several other terms also are used depending on the observer's professional orientation and disciplinary background.

While we know that labels are not warranted in this day and age, unfortunately there is a need for a label in this instance. We are not going to take a stance on whether labeling is good or bad but rather will state that a label enhances the communication process. A label will allow communication among those who come in contact with individuals displaying the characteristics of this condition, whatever they may be. Once we have established an acceptable label for communication purposes, we then can move on to the important issues of identification, placement, and intervention. Redl and Wattenberg (1959) warned that "there is a tremendous gap between knowing what to call a particular type of behavior and having really helped the child who displays it" (p. 39).

Unfortunately, agreement does not come easy to an area that has several disciplines providing some type of intervention for the identified individual. In practice we often find ourselves relying on what we think the term means as opposed to relying on firsthand knowledge of what was actually meant when those terms were formulated or, for that matter, what the professional using the term meant to convey to us. The absence of consolidated meaning, meaning specific to a description of a behavior or emotion, creates massive disinformation. It appears that the old axiom, "he who defines classifies," is absolutely true in this field.

Rather than presenting a book on assessment or intervention techniques, this text examines the field in and of itself. Some of the most significant theorists and practitioners associated with various perspectives of emotional disturbance present their views and experiences in a brief, concise manner and offer the reader an opportunity to gain from the "road traveled."

Growth in most human endeavors results when a person acts or speaks out from beliefs. The strength of conviction occurring in a statement of belief frequently provides clarity for others. Those reading such a statement can accept or reject that stated position. In many cases reading why others have approached an issue in a certain manner brings added clarity to one's own thinking and often provides others the empathy to develop and the courage to state their own point of view. History has established that those who provide leadership are frequently prone to criticism. Certainly, there is a probability that in the process of communicating beyond what is currently accepted they will be misunderstood. This appears particularly true in areas of human endeavors that society might wish to be self-correcting or very possibly just remain out of sight and out of mind, sweeping it under the rug, so to speak.

Society today is being critically challenged by the constantly increasing number of children and young adults whose behaviors are unacceptable and draw unfavorable attention to them, those whose personal adjustment is a threat to themselves, interferes with positive adjustment, or is a threat to others. The number of children and adults incarcerated or on probation or parole speaks to one form of limited social adjustment. Most states find it difficult to build jails fast enough, realizing as they make these huge capital investments that additional jail cells are not the answer. Society desires protection, and our society believes in punishment more than it believes in rehabilitation. However, there are those whose leadership promoted and continues to promote a greater expenditure of society's resources on prevention and treatment. This text is written by those past, present, and future leaders.

The number of children and adults receiving outpatient services at mental health facilities or substance abuse centers, who additionally may be homeless while being maintained on medication with histories of hospitalization, is a very real, current social issue. The number of children displaying chronic disruptive and norm-violating street, home, and school behaviors, coming from homes with increasing patterns of domestic violence, is another issue that has reached epidemic proportions. The continuing increases in adolescent suicides and adult depression, and the plain and simple pain that exists far too frequently for too many people resulting from intrapersonal and interpersonal conflict, suggest that all is not well in this great society of plenty. Society today should be more aware than ever of the price its citizens, especially the young, pay for the absence of consistent nurturing, the tragedy of the cycle of emotional abuse and neglect within the home, and the promotion of self-serving social values. For many of our youth there is far more social learning and security offered by a gang than was ever offered in the home or in the classroom. The gap between what we know is necessary as a social order to do and what in fact gets done seems to be growing exponentially.

It has been 250 years since Charcot entered French jails to separate the insane from the criminal. It has been 225 years since Pinot instituted treatment instead of isolation or punishment for those with mental illness. It has been almost 200 years since Howe designed the first institution in this country founded on cure, not custodial isolation. It has been nearly 70 years since the founding of Judge Baker Child Guidance Clinic in Boston. Compulsory school attendance, child labor laws, and the continuing enactment of law after law to protect children and families from forces that would reduce or remove basic human rights are in place in this country. How can it be that with so much having been done that we find ourselves still needing to do so much more?

The answer to that question is not an easy, unidimensional one. The complexities of our social order do appear to be increasing. The more we tend to do, the more we see that needs to be done. Twenty years ago the literature on the effects of child abuse was scant and written principally in the medical journals, focusing on the recognition of physical symptoms seen in emergency rooms of hospitals. Today, we are more concerned with the relative and nebulous effects of emotional abuse and neglect, which appear to be more devastating to the emotional development of children than physical or sexual abuse. We have made advances in problem recognition, in legislation and agency policy development, and in increases in fiscal resources and the required professional preparation of human service providers, but what visible progress have we made in diagnosis and treatment? Until data bases are constructed that provide therapies of choice to the service provider, there will be continuing confusion on which treatment strategy to use for each presenting symptomology. Basically, we have used splintered approaches to problem solving that are dependent on the aspect of the human condition that has our attention at a particular time. It would appear that we tend to view the problem of emotional and social dysfunction in children and youth at the point of the symptom, and the symptom only. Perhaps that is the legacy of the years of looking for criterion cutoff scores from tests as a means of defining, even predicting, the problem. Perhaps it is the legacy of the behavioralists who taught us that the focus is an observable behavior. Human pain may be too overwhelming to observe; therefore we continue to treat the symptoms.

Both of these theoretical positions make sense in some applications with certain forms of disability. If the relative nature of emotional growth and development—and the sensitivity of human emotions to specific environments and human interactions—drives what we see and what we measure, then maybe we need as much soul as we do science. The ability of children with emotional disturbance to develop mechanisms that will promote positive growth is low, which means that they are in a very poor position to even ask for help, know what help they need, or know where to get it. This is one of the critical differentiations between children who are emotionally disturbed and all other disability groups. The disability of a child who is blind, deaf, or mentally retarded is apparent, and the interventions needed also are generally quite obvious. Not so with the emotionally disturbed.

Parents are not always helpful. Children frequently need to justify even cruel mistreatment by parents. Evidence now exists that emotional abuse is more devastating than physical or sexual abuse. Parental rejection and neglect may cause children to dissociate and depersonalize their feeling awareness, relying on limited reality testing structures and other faulty psychological mechanisms that frequently cause them to display their discomfort through inappropriate behaviors. Dysfunctional child and parent relationships are a major contributor to emotional disorders and require both individual and family therapy. Children caught in dysfunctional relationships with parents often transfer their feelings to teachers. School officers may be directly affected as the child resents and acts out, manipulating the teacher before a relationship can be formed. Teachers in turn become defensive and distrusting. In the absence of trust, the child and teacher fail to define a relationship. The child, often angry and frequently alone, has two choices: fight or withdraw.

While behaviors are observable, emotional development, or that which generates the feelings that drive or control behavior, is not so easily observed or measured. Aggressive, antisocial, inappropriate behaviors are quickly observed and just as quickly punished. What if they are an awkward cry for help? Why do we believe that children in emotional pain know how to express their need for care, comfort, and support verbally? In the very manner that we draw attention to unwanted behaviors and punish them, we may have drawn a line in the dirt. The children and youth are on one side of that line and the adult social order is on the other. Do most interactions with adults increase social learning or inhibit it? What does punishment teach? Reason, decision making, and values . . . how are they taught? Are they taught the same way in children whose emotional development has been filled with anger, isolation, and rejection?

These questions represent only a few of the more obvious ones concerning the protective adult role relationships with children. It appears that the social order can only legislate and provide resources that respond after the fact. Perhaps we are more interested in what we teach than whom. It is clear to us that the single most difficult job in parenting, teaching, and interacting with children is to provide a continuous behavioral model of what should be. Few television programs that are of interest to children are free from violence and promote positive social-rule learning. But then we should not dwell only on television; there are many excuses for not being available emotionally to children at home, in the schools, even within the client relationship.

It is our belief that human interaction, especially between children and adults, is the singular most difficult activity we will ever engage in. Parents, teachers, and therapists all describe the emotional interaction with children as difficult, time consuming, very demanding, and draining. It is little wonder that we care to avoid human engagement and simply busy ourselves with the mechanics of living, or teaching, or doing our jobs. Apparently parents of the "Me generation" have found it easier to fill up a child's day with activities than to assist the child in finding the epicenter of his or her feelings. How many of us as adults have assured a child that he or she can trust us with his or her feelings? Perhaps we teach them to model while growing, distrusting their own feelings or even an awareness of their emotions.

For the record, we believe that all human relationship therapy is teaching. We believe that all teaching should therefore be therapeutic, but it is not. We believe that the same children who suffer interpersonal and intrapersonal problems suffer regardless of the environment. School problems go home; home problems go to school. The street is merely a reflection of both. Gang membership is normal; the rules and behaviors of the gang merely reflect the youths' interpretation of the social order and where and how they can rebel and be recognized. That is why schools and youth clubs offering recognition for social responsibility are effective. There is no substitute for self-understanding and self-control. But the social learning principles associated with self-control must be learned, and the initial discipline required to learn social interactive skills is generally learned through adult recognition in the right environment. What did Jaime Escalante provide his students, advanced calculus skills? No, this East Los Angeles Garfield High teacher invested himself and taught the discipline of self-control, which is earned self-respect. He merely used the discipline needed in learning calculus to provide purpose and responsibility to self and others. Long after his students have forgotten calculus, they will remember that self-discipline overcomes tough tasks.

We conclude that the adult interactive-relationship role with children, regardless of what we call that adult—parent, teacher, counselor, coach, friend, or therapist—is the most difficult job on the face of the earth. There will always be a new frontier. It is the task of teaching, among the other developmental processes, to find interharmony at the center of our lives while engaging others and the environment into a world of reason. You may regard that as a deep sense of caring for self, others, and the environment. We call it a developed sense of being, the search to understand the most difficult but most fulfilling of all emotions: love.

The human effort you are about to engage in is also a search for understanding. We hope it brings understanding and enriches your professional being. We thank you for reading it, and we dedicate this effort to those persons whose lives have positively touched so many: the contributing authors of this text.

REFERENCES

Federal Register. (1977, August). Washington, DC: U.S. Government Printing Office.

Forness, S., & Knitzer, J. (1991). *A new proposed definition and terminology to replace serious emotional disturbance in Individuals with Disabilities Education Act.* Alexandria, VA: National Mental Health and Special Education Coalition.

Redl, F., & Wattenberg, W. W. (1959). *Mental hygiene in teaching.* New York: Harcourt, Brace & World.

Introduction

In the course of human interactions, strange and often unplanned and unpredicted courses of events are put into place. Thus it was with the undertaking of this project. The inspiration for this undertaking was begun when Eli M. (Mike) Bower, professor emeritus at the University of California in Berkeley, wrote an article titled "A Brief History of How We Have Helped Emotionally Disturbed Children and Other Fairy Tales" (see Chapter 2).

The article is a personal account of Dr. Bower's beliefs and how they were formed, beginning in 1938 when at age 21 he became a full-time teacher and part-time cottage parent for youths with emotional disturbance at the Hawthorne Cedar-Knolls School in Hawthorne, New York.

It is clear that young Mike Bower spent the rest of his life attempting to unravel the mysteries of how to reach and teach those who seem to live in a world of their own making, hearing no other rules than the ones they conceive in order to justify what they want to do. Bower (1990) wrote of "boys and girls who did not know how to have fun, could not separate play from reality, could not attend to concepts outside of self and were driven by impulses unchecked by reality controls" (p. 12).

What Bower observed and described in the 1940s we know today as early dysfunctional social learning, which teaches the practice of self-deceit. In the absence of self-control there is limited impulse control, and reality is as these kids make it. As self-deceit increases, reality testing decreases. As reality testing decreases, self-doubt increases. As self-doubt increases, self-awareness, including self-worth and self-realization, decreases. It is as though some kids never have a chance to succeed.

Bower drew heavily on the absence of success in children's lives and how early they become dysfunctional in social role relationships. He traced the history of how in the early days adult treatment structures were merely and incorrectly passed down to children, just as a man's suit would be passed down to a child half the size. He reviewed the history of initiating programs for children with emotional disturbance in the public schools with an educational flavor. Bower described his role in the late 1950s in bringing therapeutic education to the schools of California. He agreed with much of what the mental health professionals had to offer, but the goals of education and the therapeutic activities of teaching and learning remained central to his views. He applauded the goals of Project Re-ED (Hobbs, 1974). He promoted the idea (ideal) that children need purpose and must achieve in something, especially schoolwork. He believed in teaching self-control for its own sake. He recognized the importance of the group, peer recognition, and all recognition. He would have us substitute pleasure for hurt and find in each day encouragement and happy events, giving children who are emotionally disturbed a better day to look forward to tomorrow. He believed children who are emotionally disturbed live out their pain-filled lives with "ceremony and ritual," which provide a great deal of comfort and help these kids to interpret their lives meaningfully.

We read and discussed Dr. Bower's beliefs. In our discussion we disagreed as well as agreed with him and, in doing so, clarified some of our own thinking. As the discussion continued, we began to wonder what other leaders in the field would say to the questions we posed, all the while recognizing that the field of emotional disturbance has more unanswered questions than answered ones. As a result of our discussions we formulated 10 questions we thought were timely and important to the future development of the definition, identification, placement, and programming of children who are emotionally disturbed (see p. xix).

The chapters to follow will address these 10 questions from each of the authors' personal, professional perspective developed over years of observations and direct experiences with children with emotional disturbances and behavioral disorders. The contributions they offer were written purposely for this text. This book is not a selection of existing materials taken from other sources. The materials are original; they serve a specific purpose of providing the reader with an orientation to a field that, while young, is highly complex. Many of the complexities reside in the fact that the population places great pressures on all of society for solutions. If for no other reason, it is very expensive for a social order to respond to the aftermath of the havoc that this single population can set into motion.

The contributors to this text represent a select leadership. They have all provided their vision of what is and what can be, putting their beliefs into practice. They have been responsible for program development with children who are emotionally disturbed, principally in the school environment but not exclusively in that setting. Some began and some have continued their professional lives in juvenile correctional facilities, the juvenile justice systems, and some started out in private or state-supported facilities for children and youth who are emotionally disturbed. Some are and have been children's therapists. Some are and have been administrators of state and private facilities. Some have developed model programs in a wide range of settings, while others have worked in consulting as well as in direct service roles. Many have taught in and directed or supervised intervention efforts for children, parents, and citizens, providing preservice professional preparation and in-service continuing education for practitioners. The contributing authors' professional preparation reflects academic training in psychology, social work, behavioral analysis, special and regular education, public policy and educational administration, and an array of other human service and helping professions. They have all made substantial contributions to the identification, education, and treatment of children who are emotionally disturbed. Thus most of them have firsthand knowledge and experience with mental health, the correctional and justice systems, human service agencies, and education. They have worked many sides of the same street, so to speak. And many have spent a lifetime attempting to reconcile and bring coordination and cooperation, beginning with communication, to the various and often varying points of view that abound in this field.

An interesting aspect is that service providers from different agencies can see the same problem from entirely different perspectives. A number of the contributing authors have sought to identify both policy and practices that draw from the strengths of differing viewpoints into one coordinated effort.

One of the obvious but purposeful omissions is our effort to avoid promoting any one definition of emotional disturbance or behavioral disorders. Another is the resistance to use exclusively one of the two major terms, *emotionally disturbed* or *behaviorally disordered*, thus giving more credance to one rather than the other. The purpose for these omissions is that each contributing author will address these issues in the pages to follow. Many will disagree with the current federal definition. Most will disagree with each other. Some will use, and purposely so, the descriptor *emotionally disturbed* to describe these children. Others will use the descriptor *behaviorally disordered*. In some cases the terms will be used interchangeably.

Some of the contributors may in fact offer still another descriptor to discuss the population under study. This points to the very intent of the text: to capture the range of viewpoints, seeing the divergence among the many points of view for what may be the same population or could in fact be a different population. Why does divergent thinking lead to confusion? The overall terminology used to define this population reflects the confusion in identifying and agreeing on the major descriptors or characteristics by which this condition may be classified. There are numerous reasons, both personal and professional, for this disparity of terms.

In the past, disagreement in the field of education regarding treatment of children with emotional disturbance produced another belief, a therapeutic or treatment countermeasure. Having been treated to a personal perspective by Dr. Bower, we wanted the leadership in this field to provide us with similar information. It was our hope that if we could bring such information together in one book, it would be stimulating and informative reading. It might also reduce confusion in the field and perhaps assist readers in clarifying their own thinking. At the very least this volume would identify where and why disagreement exists and where concentrated agreement is occurring as the field matures. Also, understanding how the leaders in this field have advanced their ideas over the past few years and how they came by their ideas brings a personal and professional touch to the reader. After all, there is a possibility that different people are talking about different populations of children, treated and educated in different environments, and therefore requiring different skills to enhance communication and development in forming relationships. Sometimes a novice to the field is overwhelmed with what has occurred and the sheer quantity of information. In this state of being overwhelmed, they fail to take time to find out where the leadership in this field gained its experiences. Twenty years ago this was a very small field, with practically everyone knowing everyone else. We have the advantage that most of the leadership is still living. Therefore, we offer a book written by past, current, and future leaders in the field of emotional disturbance, giving the readers an opportunity to read primary sources under one cover and, in the process, be part of the collective thinking in the education of the emotionally disturbed.

We sincerely hope that these pages are as enlightening and stimulating for you to read as they have been for us to assemble.

REFERENCES

Bower, E. M. (1990). A brief history of how we have helped emotionally disturbed children and other fairy tales. *Preventing School Failure, 35*(1), 11–16.

Hobbs, N. (1974). Nicholas Hobbs. In J. M. Kauffman & C. D. Lewis (Eds.), *Teaching children with behavioral disorders: Personal perspectives* (pp. 142–167). Columbus, OH: Merrill.

QUESTIONS ASKED REGARDING THE FUTURE OF E/BD

1. What is your professional opinion of the current status of the education of children who are emotionally disturbed/behaviorally disordered today (how much good or how much harm are we doing)?
2. What is your working definition of emotional disturbance/behavioral disorders in children and youth?
3. What dimensionalities does your definition provide over the current federal definition?
4. Are emotional disturbance and behavioral disorders one and the same? If not, how are they different?
5. From your own perspective and experiences, what are the most meaningful educational experiences that children who are emotionally disturbed and behaviorally disordered need to have included in their school programs? Describe these experiences in some detail and list in priority order.
6. What are your opinions or philosophy on the inclusion of children who are emotionally disturbed and behaviorally disordered under Regular Education Initiative (REI) and General Education Initiative (GEI) as offered by the proponents of these approaches?
7. Do you have (a) a delivery of services model for children who are emotionally disturbed and behaviorally disordered that (b) should be referenced for further investigation by the reader?
8. In your opinion, is the prevalence/incidence of emotional disturbance and behavioral disorders increasing? If so, what are the major contributors and what should be done to prevent this expansion?
9. Describe, according to the dimension of your working model, the role relationship differential between mental health providers, other human service providers, the juvenile justice system, and educators in the education of children who are emotionally disturbed and behaviorally disordered.
10. Delineate the future, by the year 2000, of the trends, identification process, interagency relationships, and role of the school in educating children who are emotionally disturbed and behaviorally disordered.

About the Editors

BENJAMIN L. BROOKS
Educational Consultant

*B*enjamin Brooks is currently an educational consultant and an adjunct professor of special education in Johnson City, Tennessee. Brooks has taught both special and regular education and has been an administrator of programs in higher education for more than 20 years. In addition to public school and university teaching, he directed an adolescent and children's program in a private psychiatric hospital for 3 years. Brooks has been and continues to be a strong advocate for children with disabilities. He has represented parents in due process hearings in more than 25 different situations and has served as a hearing officer for due process hearings in three different states. Brooks also has authored handbooks and prepared workshops for parents to enlighten them as to their legal status under the Individuals with Disabilities Education Act.

DAVID A. SABATINO
East Tennessee State University

David Sabatino received his PhD from the Ohio State University and has held numerous teaching and administrative roles since he began as a school psychologist in Ohio. Upon entry into Ohio State he was employed at the Columbus Detention Center, a facility for adjudicated youth. That experience dictated the course of his studies and became his primary, overriding professional interest. He has maintained a professional relationship with the juvenile justice system in a number of states and is an active forensic psychologist. His research and direct services include youth in alternative school environments and the carryover into special education programs for children with emotional/behavioral disorders.

PART I
Historical Perspectives

BENJAMIN L. BROOKS
Educational Consultant

DAVID A. SABATINO
East Tennessee
State University

CHAPTER 1

Genesis to a Personal Perspective on Emotional Disturbance

> *It is unconscionable for a nation with such vast resources to allow a substantial number of children to fail in life before they have started.*
>
> Eli M. Bower

In this chapter we will attempt to prepare the reader for the chapters that follow. The immediate pages provide a general overview and orientation to selected historical issues that have plagued the field of emotional disorders in children. Discussion is offered concerning historically relevant issues, prevalence for emotional disturbance and behavioral disorders based on the various definitions being used, and the current status of service providers in identifying that need and meeting it.

The search for solutions brought to the complex issues of when, where, and how to treat the emotionally disturbed are seen in the Jeffrey Dahmer case. Dahmer sodomized, tortured, butchered, and eventually cannibalized his victims in Wisconsin. There is no question that Mr. Dahmer was a serial killer. The question is whether he was emotionally disturbed. If so, should he have been punished or treated? If he was treated, should he have been released, in which case he would have been alive today and not a victim of jailhouse justice? The truth is that the only difference between these questions and those that many teachers and service providers face each day is the gravity. A child who is verbally aggressive and abusive in the classroom has not taken a life, but he or she may be threatening many people. Should the child be referred for possible identification? Should he or she be punished? What if he or she does not respond to punishment? Frequently the school's answer is to suspend or expel the child, which often means the child can have the streets to himself or herself to do as he or she wishes. The question of punishment will be asked every time. How often will a school official ask the question concerning treatment? Have we yet to learn that all behavior is purposeful, even if it is an angry inappropriate request for help?

FINDING THE BEGINNING

The treatment of children with emotional and behavioral problems is not a new phenomenon. The history of past practices, including management from any and all disciplines, merely reflects the broader progression of civilization. Recorded history would indicate that in the evolution of the interaction of humankind and the environment, attention has shifted from a focus on survival with those forces external to ourselves to those that are internal. Physical aggression in its most violent form is first reported in the biblical account of Cain and Abel, two brothers and the sons of Adam and Eve. The nature of problem behaviors and humankind's psychopathology has changed little through the course of history. The changes in social responsiveness and, hopefully, social conscience is the result of purposeful behavior on the parts of persons seeking change.

The human condition of emotional disturbance has always been viewed as a threat to individuals and the social order. While its origin and composition may not be understood, the scope of its deviance has always prompted a social explanation. Most of these explanations were frightening and created negative attitudes and beliefs that guided the very development of traditional wisdom. The threat of what was seen but rarely understood by the larger social order has resulted in four distinct philosophies. These prevailing views are directed to (a) destroy emotional disturbance, (b) segregate or isolate it, (c) reverse it, and (d) prevent it. The four philosophies, either alone or in combination, have generated six distinct eras in the history of the field of emotional disturbance. These eras are (a) the era of extermination, (b) the era of ridicule, (c) the era of asylum, (d) the era of community treatment, (e) the era of education, and, currently, (f) the era of legislation and litigation.

ERA OF EXTERMINATION

In early cultures, mental deviance as evidenced in insanity or mental disorders often was viewed as a life-threatening situation in the struggle for survival. The concept may be reflected in the survival of the fittest. Through much of recorded history, human deviance related to emotional disorders was harshly punished to the point of death.

In ancient Greece a child had to be granted the very right to live. This right was granted by the state or the parent, and if the child was too weak he or she was left to die by exposure. Exposure was sanctioned by law (Despert, 1965).

During ancient Roman times the father had the right of life or death over his children. He could sell them into slavery, banish them from the country, or put them to death. Children, if and when they survived, were treated no differently than adults, and in most cases they were asked to perform actions well beyond their physical and emotional abilities.

These harsh and uncaring practices were justified by beliefs that evil spirits, demons, and other supernatural causes were at work. In the struggle of good against evil, evil thoughts and evil behaviors could be rightfully punished even if it required burning the possessed at the stake. Superstitious beliefs were maintained in place of nonexistent scientific explanations and persisted through many centuries. These beliefs were widely held in the European middle ages. While these practices still dominate a few cultures today, there are more remnants in most societies than the citizens of those social orders may care to admit, including many advanced social orders. Punishment remains a universal principal course of action for many poorly understood or misunderstood behaviors.

ERA OF RIDICULE

While this era is a logical extension of the era of extermination, there appears to be a very thin, fragile line between all of the eras that was often crossed. Indeed, it is not surprising to find considerable overlap between the era of ridicule and the next era to come, that of asylum. The Greek and Roman cultures used persons with deviance as court jesters, fools of the circus, and for the amusement of citizens. Cruel and unusual punishment was still the case in many instances, and much of the treatment of deviance could be traced to the religious beliefs of that time. As Judeo-Christianity took its place in the religions of the world, policies and practices condoning extreme mistreatment began to give way to policies of protection and care for those less fortunate.

A thorough review of the literature on mental illness will reveal that the treatment of children with emotional disorders did not occur until well into the twentieth century. Children have always been the recipients of the prejudice and customs of their times as practiced by their families. The delay in the advent of child labor laws in this country, passed only this century, and not before, is indicative of the American society's regard for children. In the labor force as well as in the helping professions, children frequently were undifferentiated from adults, performing tasks far beyond their physical strength and emotional maturity. Children, then as now, were too frequently viewed as immediate and available sources of cheap and plentiful labor, not valued resources that require time and effort to develop.

ERA OF ASYLUM

This era reflected a transition from cruelty to some care, and later the beginning of scientific inquiry, but carried within it continuing refrains of ridicule. Despert (1965) wrote:

> Another questionable form of entertainment was the accepted custom of

> taking the children to visit the mentally ill at the Bedlam and other asylums. ... As is well known, the mentally ill were chained, starved, beaten and kept in filth and darkness. The visit was a routine holiday program akin to a visit to the zoo in our days. The difference is that strict rules apply to the teasing and tormenting of animals, whereas of the period we speak, teasing was not only legitimate but considered more or less a duty, since the insane were thought to be more or less possessed. (p. 89)

This era had three major thrusts: (a) shelter, (b) scientific inquiry into cause and treatment, and (c) treatment and initial education efforts. The first phase, shelter, can be traced back to the early medieval times when the monasteries were havens for the afflicted individuals, providing food, shelter, and protection and usually treating them with prayer. The intent was to protect and shelter the deviant from society, while at the same time protecting society from the deviant. Following the initial shelter and protection provided by the ministers, came the first and most famous asylum, the hospital of Saint Mary's of Bethlehem, established in 1547 in London. Its most popular name was Bedlam, and thus the current meaning of the term emerged. This era also provided us with the term *lunatic* and *lunacy*, as intermittent insanity was assumed to be related to the phases of the moon.

From the middle of the eighteenth century and carrying over into the middle of the nineteenth century, the scientific inquiry into causation and ultimately treatment was emerging. One of the first attempts was conducted in Paris by the French physician Philippe Pinel when he unleashed the chains of the patients at Labicetre, a hospital for the mentally ill. This was soon followed by the work of one of his students, Jean Marc Itard, who is credited with one of the first systematic attempts to educate an individual who was mentally or emotionally disabled. The boy's name was Victor, the wild boy of Averyon, and he was found roaming the forest in southern France. A prelude to the educational efforts to follow in the United States during this time period was the influential writing of Dr. Benjamin Rush of Philadelphia, considered to be the father of modern American psychiatry. Dr. Rush, who can be considered one of this country's first child advocates, argued the need to discontinue corporal punishment and discipline, substituting public education and public support for problem children.

The initial movement toward treatment and education began in the mid-nineteenth century through the efforts of reformers such as Dorthea Dix and Samuel Gridley Howe. Because of their efforts, training schools and educational programs became established in many of the existing asylums. During the same time period, compulsory school attendance laws were enacted in the northeastern states. In 1805 the city of New York established a special school for poor children, which later was expanded to more than 50 buildings by 1898 and included programs for delinquent and dependent youths. However, most early educational programmatic efforts were delivered in residential or asylum settings. Only gradually was the public sector considered as a potential future site for programming. During this era the professional literature began to focus on etiology, or causes of mental disturbance. At this point a new perspective on children and their role was beginning to develop and emerge. Children's rights were now being discussed, and attitudes toward the emotionally disturbed in particular were starting to turn toward treatment and education and away from the custodial care of the asylum or institution.

ERA OF COMMUNITY TREATMENT

> The longer mental and emotional disorders go without adequate treatment, the greater the possibility they will become more serious. In state after state, child guidance facilities have been established on the theory that if such difficulties are dealt with in youth, many people can be saved from mental illness and blighted lives. (Redl & Wattenberg, 1959, p. 411)

It is not really fair to call this era one of community treatment. We chose to use this descriptor of the period, however, following societal belief in the "out of sight, out of mind" residential placement where countless thousands of persons were warehoused. Many children and adults with emotional disturbance were placed in residential facilities for their lifetimes. Once placed in these human warehouses, they frequently were overmedicated and lost emotional support from immediate and extended family. Employment and independent living skills were reduced or eliminated, denying them the very purpose of being. During this era it became apparent to many that the asylum was really designed to protect society, though in the process affording some protection to the client.

The growth of the treatment era was irregular, and it is difficult to trace a beginning point. Most scholars would place its beginnings in the period following the American Civil War, as this country moved rapidly toward industrialization and urbanization. The initial transition from asylum to treatment can be observed in the zeitgeist, reflecting the prevailing and developing attitudes toward children and youth that began in this period and continue to this day.

The most influential person in this era was the noted Austrian psychiatrist, Sigmund Freud. It was Freud's theories on the development of the mind and the childhood linkages to adult psychopathologies that initiated the concept of mental illness. Other interacting events were happening within and outside of the United States, such as the development of intelligence tests by Binet and his colleagues in France in the late 1890s, as well as the economic and social upheaval following the Civil War that lead to urbanization and industrialization. During this time period more attention would be paid to children and youth than ever before; however, not all the attention focused on children was necessarily positive. The problems associated with the growth of awareness that children had emotional problems were clouded by competing factors, such as the child labor laws and court-related problems associated with in-home, in-school, and street management of chronic disruptive and norm-violating behaviors, introducing what we now call *juvenile delinquency*.

Mass migration from Europe to the United States during this era brought with it further complications. Urbanization and poverty combined to create children of the street. Schools, hospitals, and courts were unsure how to manage these many issues related to home, school, and community management of children. By 1910, the so-called child-saver movement had begun in New York City. This was the beginning of today's human service agencies. By the mid-1920s a number of child guidance clinics, founded on a community outpatient basis, were formed. One of the original ones was the famous Judge Baker Clinic founded in Boston. That clinic served as a model for what would become both child and adult community mental health facilities.

In most areas of the country there were feeble attempts to try to distinguish between and among any of the conditions previously cited and "human warehousing in institutions." The location was changed from the private asylum to the public sector, thus causing the public to become aroused and involved in the problems faced by those who dealt directly with these individuals. Economics would now come into play. The costs were being borne by the average taxpayer, and society in general was affected by the establishment of child welfare agencies and the building of juvenile detention centers and public residential treatment facilities. Not only would the general public become involved, but also professionals from areas other than medicine would now offer opinions concerning the plight of children and adolescents who were being diagnosed under ever-increasing numbers of labels and descriptions.

The transition of services from treatment to education would have its foundation when in 1871 a class for "trouble-making youth" opened in New Haven, Connecticut. The Juvenile Psychopathic Institute in Chicago soon followed, opening in 1909 with William Healy and Augusta Bronner making significant contributions to the study of juvenile delinquents. It was during this era that thinking toward individual mental illness was further expanded and the treatment aspects were brought into a new light by Karl Menninger and his father and brother when they introduced the concept of the total treatment environment of kindness and treatment (milieu therapy).

ERA OF EDUCATION

The twentieth century brought with it significant events and has continued to offer changes that are aimed at improving the welfare of the emotionally disturbed in such areas as definition, identification, and educational programming. During the early 1900s the term *emotionally disturbed* was first introduced into the literature. The term was not originally intended to apply to children, causing professions then and now to debate its utility.

Significant changes in psychology, psychiatry and intellectual measurement, and politics and social reform in education, to mention a few, have been made during this century. Paramount to many of these changes was the founding of several organizations dedicated to the enlightenment of the general public to the condition of emotional disturbance and other disabling conditions. The beginning of the mental health movement and subsequent educational reform can be traced to the founding of the National Committee for Mental Hygiene in 1909 by Clifford Beers and William James. This was a monumental step toward the eventual development of mental health clinics and other treatment programs.

During the first quarter of the twentieth century, the educational movement toward the public school was enhanced when the Council for Exceptional Children and legislative lobbying efforts were expanded. As a direct result of lobbying efforts on the part of parents of children with disabilities in the United States, the White House Conference of Children Health and Protection held in 1930 recognized the need to establish and maintain public school programs for the disabled. Considerable progress was made from the 1930s to the 1960s with the development of model programs for children with emotional disturbance and other disabling conditions. Beginning in the early 1960s more literature became available outlining attempts in the education of the emotionally disturbed.

Such notable individuals as Lauretta Bender, Bruno Bettelheim, Fritz Redl, David Wineman, Carl Fenichel, William Cruickshank, Pearl Berkowitz, Ester Rothman, and Eli M. Bower, to mention a few, provided us with a body of literature for the implementation of programs that led to the development of improved quality in education for the emotionally disturbed. During this time one of the first comprehensive textbooks was edited by Nicholas Long, William Morse, and Ruth Newman. This book, *Conflict in the Classroom* (1965), was the initial attempt at bringing together prominent educators to share their expertise in the effort to identify, assess, manage, program for, and educate the emotionally disturbed. The education movement on behalf of the emotionally disturbed was thus established, and improvements and innovative approaches are continuing.

ERA OF LEGISLATION AND LITIGATION

The 1960s and 1970s found the United States deeply involved with the civil rights movement. This was not only on behalf of ethnic minority groups, but also involved many activist groups that felt they were not afforded an equal opportunity and demanded that their individual rights be recognized in many different arenas. Included in this was the movement toward providing a free appropriate public education for all children with disabilities.

Numerous court cases were decided in favor of the provision of an appropriate education for the disabled, including *Brown v. Board of Education of Topeka* (1954), *PARC v. Commonwealth of Pennsylvania* (1971), *Wyatt v. Stickey* (1971), and *Mills v. Board of Education of District of Columbia* (1971). Each of these landmark cases set in motion a further notation of the establishment of the educational rights of an individual, particularly the disabled, thus leading to state and federal legislation.

Prior to the 1970s most states did not have mandatory legislation for the education of the disabled. Most in fact had a permissive form of legislation that would allow them, if needed or pressured, to fund public school programs for the disabled. With the passage of two major pieces of federal legislation, the states were now forced to comply with the mandate to educate all children with disabilities, including the emotionally disturbed. The two significant federal laws were Public Law 93-112, the Rehabilitation Act of 1973, and Public Law 94-142, the Education of All Handicapped Children Act, later to be retitled Individuals with Disabilities Education Act (IDEA). With the passage of this legislation, the quantity of educational programs and services for the emotionally disturbed increased significantly.

Grosenick, George, and George (1987) reported that 99.4% of all education programs in the public schools were established after the passage of P.L. 94-142. However, even with the advent of new programs for the emotionally disturbed, it has been reported repeatedly that this segment of the population is the most underserved and underidentified.

The passage of the Americans with Disabilities Act (ADA), signed into law on July 26, 1990, promotes continuing progress in the realization of the rights of persons with disabilities. The impact of this legislation will be observed in future litigation. This legislation was designed to protect the civil rights of all persons with disabilities in terms of employment, pay, workplace accommodations, housing, accessibility to public transportation and buildings, and all other constitutional considerations to citizenship. Until the dust settles, the impact of this legislation on persons with a disability remains unknown except for the intent of the law. It clearly marks the current period in which we live as one of legislation and litigation. The precise impact this legislation will have on the emotionally disturbed adults in today's society, a group that comprises the bulk of the homeless since the closing of state-administered psychiatric facilities beginning in 1977 and a population whose dependence on a supply of medically monitored medication is critical, remains unknown. Great strides have been made in public awareness and social consciousness during this era. However, legislation does not always change the human condition, as the human heart cannot be legislated or litigated. There are still many, many more miles to go before we have achieved these legislated, if not common sense, human goals.

EMOTIONAL DISTURBANCE/ BEHAVIORAL DISORDERS

The term *emotional disturbance* first appeared in the literature in the early 1900s. The origin of the term is difficult to pinpoint. Various sources in the literature either avoid identifying the source or relate differing points of origin. With the popular acceptance and use of the term by the public, its meaning became very general and soon was a reference for any person or any behavior that seemed unique, different, unusual. The slang term *crazy* or, as it was used in the early 1900s, *just plain crazy* illustrated what was meant by emotional disturbance. Specificity was lost in a communication practice that was more suggestive of something or, more appropriately, someone who was unwanted, undesirable, different, and unreasonable in defying logic and logical responses. Consequently, what was implied in the use of language relative to emotional disturbance was often confused by those who heard the term and had no idea what the communicator had in mind. This term, unlike *cancer* or *heart attack*, or even *mental retardation* and *learning disabilities*, was for all intents and purposes open to vast interpretation by the listener.

Thirty years ago Kanner wrote,

> I believe that the time has come to acknowledge the heterogeneity of the many conditions comprised under the generic term, "emotional disturbed children." We shall then be in a position to study each of these varieties with true precision. A symposium on the use of the term in scientific publications would, at this juncture, be a major contribution to clarity and mutual understanding. (1962, p. 101)

As if there was not enough confusion, in the 1950s psychiatry began developing definitions for what it termed *mental disorders* that would be precursors to the later *Diagnostic and Statistical Manuals*. Though psychology and psychiatry had standard nomenclature that it used daily, the terminology was not as clear to educators who did not use those terms and perhaps had no clear understanding of their meaning. Educators were left to define childrens' adjustment as they saw it. What they were seeing most frequently were inappropriate antisocial, aggressive, and attention-seeking personal behaviors. It is not surprising that educators were attracted to the term *behavioral disorders* and avoided the more nebulous *emotional disturbance*. While educators did not want the role traditionally occupied by psychologists and psychiatrists, they were willing to promote adjustment and teach appropriate behaviors rather than try to restructure personality. Education per se historically has not been interested in becoming a treatment agency for the emotionally disturbed, nor has it been that involved in the preventive aspects as treatment implies. In fact Redl and Wattenberg (1959) warned, "The fact is that the job of applying mental health knowledge is still at a stage in which the average teacher has to rely on his own ingenuity much of the time" (p. 512).

The dependence over the last few years on behaviors further targeted the more aggressive behaviors, since they were primarily the ones that were inappropriate. Then too, since the primary goal of the schools is to see academic progression, those who displayed reasonable academic achievement were much more likely to be considered normal than those who showed patterns of social and academic failure. The schools seemed to be quick to show intolerance for the combination of social and academic stagnation.

The history of most terminology in the field indicates its growth from and therefore its dependence on medical descriptors. Medicine, since Pasteur, has defined illness in terms of the disease-causing agents, the pathogenesis or etiology that explains the abnormality or pathology in a population. This is called the disease model, or medical model, throughout the literature. Therefore, children displaying behaviors that are inappropriate or draw undue attention to them have been assumed, through the use of the medical model, to have a mental disease. The etiology, or cause of the disease, is thought to have one basic causation and frequently does not account for a number of different disturbances in emotional development that in turn affect social interaction and emotional growth. Drawing from this predominantly medical theory, the behaviors that children with emotional disturbance display are merely symptoms of a deeper emotional disease. The words *disease* and *pathogenesis* are critical to this point of view.

While emotional disturbance and behavior disorders have their roots in medicine and particularly psychiatry, the carryover to the classroom has been limited. Perhaps, as the medical-management advocates assert, this is because most of the recent major treatment breakthroughs have been in psychiatric drug management. The pathogenic approach explains basic brain behavioral differences according to intercellular chemistry and neuronal tissue variations. For example, laboratory data supports neural cellular and biochemical differences in the central nervous systems of schizophrenics, and there is certainly evidence that drug therapy has been the most effective treatment form in treating most mental illnesses.

In sharp contrast are the behavioralists, who focus on the inappropriately displayed observable behavior that draws undue attention to the child. Their position is that faulty learning (conditioning practices) has resulted in children failing to learn to interpret social cues or display socially appropriate behaviors as they attempt to express themselves. Behavioral explanations do not rely on feeling-behavioral associations alone. That obvious omission has been overcome in more recent years by combining behavioral learning and cognitive (social learning) theories.

Behavioral and cognitive psychology in combination provide an explanation for the role relationship between the universal laws of conditioning principles (the outcomes that manipulation of contingencies has on learned responses) and the interaction between given cognitive traits and environmentally specific human behavioral models. Behavioral theories do bring a more precise science to the observations of cause and effect under controlled laboratory conditions with lower animals. The cognitive theories bring the conditions and climate in the immediate environment, the task to be learned or performed (the attitude toward a behavioral response), and contingencies into interaction, adding the dimension of how we will feel about what we do (the emotional feeling-behavioral association).

Cognitive theory and interventions are specific to the interactions between individuals and how children become aware of their role relationships and means of engaging in human interpersonal interactions, recognizing the needs and social orientation of that person. Cognitive theory attempts to explain why we develop certain interactive and social learning characteristics based on previous interactions and experiences. It has applications for the explanation of home and family interactions in a specific home environment and, in the classroom, the interaction between teacher and students as well as peer relationships. It attempts to explain and provide understanding for social learning experiences such as self-concept, the prevailing beliefs toward others or social structures, or sets of social expectations. For example, social learning establishes expectations for behavioral and academic learning and motivational attributes. It provides explanations as to the variance in sibling feeling differences when all were theoretically reared under the same conditioning practices.

The combination of behavioral and cognitive learning helps us understand why selected home and peer-group values are learned under certain conditions and how aspects of various interventions can be selectively applied to thinking (believing) and feeling (emotions) behavioral responses. In children it provides us the capability to factor in changes in human cognitive development (unseen) with observable behavioral change (observed). It explains how cognitive thought drives feelings and why learned behaviors relate in the manner in which they do. That combination provides us a number of treatment options that we did not have in the past.

Feelings are no longer an excuse for behaviors. In cognitive-behavioral therapy, emotions are driven by beliefs (thought) and therefore are under the control of the person. Treatment terminology can be simplified into words that children can understand, i.e., *good* and *bad*. These all-important negative feelings toward self can now be explored for what they are and reshaped cognitively, and new feelings of self-esteem and self-worth can be built into an observable conditioning structure. Children make the cognitive connection between doing well in school and feeling better about themselves. Conditioning is thus structured to reinforce new learning and to decrease old and unwanted behaviors.

This text does not advocate one particular theory or therapy. The contributing authors draw from many. The authors provide a number of theoretical explanations for the treatment methods they propose. Just as most forms of treatment of mental disorders in children are still in their infancy, so are the explanations evolving.

The effort to integrate educational programs for children who are emotionally disturbed/behaviorally disordered in public day institutions is less than 25 years old. With rare exception, such as the 600 schools in New York City, few states had public school programs for the emotionally disturbed as late as 1970. Grosenick, George, and George (1987) reported that 99.4% of all services for emotionally disturbed children developed after P.L. 94-142. The U.S. Department of Education (1990) placed the growth in services and programs for emotionally disturbed children from .54% in 1975 (before the passage of P.L. 94-142) to .99% of the school-age population in 1989. That is the largest single program growth area, a whopping 37%. That growth in programs and services in turn propels a need for trained professionals, accountable interventions, and program delivery models that are also cost-effective.

In the early days, most programs for children who were emotionally disturbed/behavioral disordered were mental health models that were merely transported to the public schools. New theories and therapies are developing and combinations such as the example used with behavioral-cognitive structures are now occurring more rapidly than ever before, pressed by the tremendous needs. This nation needs treatment approaches that are sensitive to human development of children and that are designed to achieve specific results in a given setting, not the hand-me-down therapy or interventions frequently derived from adult practices. Practitioners require approaches that have utility for teachers in the public school settings. Many public school administrators and teachers still do not see the public schools as a therapeutic community for antisocial, acting out students. The absence of clarity regarding goals and interventions facilitates continued resistance.

This text's contributors believe that services and programs for emotionally disturbed children in the public schools are an investment, far less an encumbrance to the taxpayer than wasted adult lives. A recurring theme is that the schools' role is a pivotal one, reaching families and children in a preventative and early treatment effort. Perhaps the overwhelming need has not been stated so that all can understand, and perhaps the economic considerations have not been clearly outlined. If so, greater education of the taxpaying public must be made a very high priority.

With these confusing dimensions in mind, what can we state as facts that will be accepted by most who have used the term *emotional disturbance* and will continue to use it? There are a few assumptions that do appear to have agreement if not acceptance in the professional community.

Those assumptions are:

- The phenomenon of emotional disturbance exists.
- It is experienced by individuals and by communities of individuals as a real phenomenon.
- The problem is a genetic societal problem.
- Emotional disturbance is a distinctive and peculiar human state having multiple manifestations.
- It is not simply something wrong with the organism.
- It is not simply a confrontation between groups of cultural conventions.
- It is a human process involving disability, deviance, and alienation, and mostly it speaks specifically of a human system in distress.

PREVALENCE AND INCIDENCE RATES

This discussion draws us to the point where we must consider the prevalence and incidence of the conditions for which we are seeking clarification. First, however, we must define these two terms so that the reader will have a full understanding as to what we are discussing. *Prevalence* refers to the total number of individuals with a specific disorder in a given population. The prevalence of a disorder is calculated for a given period or for a point in time. Thus, reports of schools typically include the number of students with a disorder counted at a particular time during the school year. It is usually expressed as a percentage. The total number of cases is divided by the total number of individuals in the population.

Incidence refers to the rate of inception, the number of new cases of a specified disorder in a given population. Incidence addresses the question, "How often does this disorder occur?" Prevalence addresses the question, "How many individuals are affected?"

Current prevalence estimates of the number of school-age children having serious emotional disorders that would qualify them for special services vary from 2% to 10% of the total school-age population. As early as 1978 the President's Commission on Mental Health estimated that between 5% and 15% of children and adolescents require some type of mental health service either through traditional mental health services or through the public schools (Kozleski, Cessna, Bechand, & Borock, 1993). Lauritzen and Friedman (1991) drew the conclusion from samples of teachers' opinions that the presence of children with emotional disturbance in the public schools presents today a major challenge to education. Using the current federal definition, the U.S. Department of Education estimated that the current prevalence of emotionally disturbed children within the school-age population is 1.2% to 2% (U.S. Department of Education, 1990). But as mentioned earlier, the current federal definition may be too limited. Forness and Knitzer (1991) reported that a new definition for emotional and behavioral disorders was proposed by the Mental Health and Special Education Coalition, a group comprised of representatives from 11 professional organizations, to replace the present definition of emotional disturbance.

The new definition states:

(i) The term emotional or behavioral disorder means a disability characterized by behavioral and emotional responses in school so different from appropriate age, cultural, or ethnic norms that they adversely affect educational performance. Educational performance includes academic, social, vocational, and personal skills. Such a disability,

(A) is more than a temporary, expected response to stressful events in the environment;

(B) is consistently exhibited in two different settings, at least one of which is school-related; and

(C) is unresponsive to direct intervention in general education or the child's condition is such that general education interventions would be insufficient.

(ii) Emotional and behavioral disorders can co-exist with other disabilities.

(iii) This category may include children or youth with schizophrenic disorders, affective disorders, anxiety disorders or other sustained disorders of conduct or adjustment when they adversely affect educational performance in accordance with section (i). (Forness & Knitzer, 1992, p. 13)

McIntyre (1993) asked the question concerning the profession's readiness to meet the new challenges that this definition places before it, especially those diagnostic practices related to identification of these children, the type of programming, and their placement within the schools.

The new definition would greatly enhance the recognition of those students failing to make intrapersonal adjustments. The current emphasis remains on those having difficulty making interpersonal adjustments. It must be kept in mind that in 1990, according to U.S. Department of Education statistics, of the fewer than 1% of public school students receiving special education or related services less than one half were mainstreamed. The grade point average of this group traditionally is the lowest of any group of students, and their dropout rate is conservatively over 40% (nearly 50% higher than the next highest special education category). Nearly 40% are likely to have a criminal record shortly after leaving school. Moreover, upon graduation these students with emotional disturbance and behavioral disorders have difficulty gaining employment or furthering their education. In the larger community, once out of school, they constitute the majority of those with social ills. They fail to obtain or maintain employment, and they divorce, remarry, then divorce again at an alarming rate. They have continuing struggles with the law, alcoholism, and drug addiction and constitute the bulk of the homeless and the welfare recipients, contributing in an ever-increasing cycle to another generation of youth who are troubled and in trouble with the social system.

Sex and racial distribution also are involved. The ratio of boys to girls is said to be 4 to 1 (Cullinan, Epstein, & Sabornie, 1992). Earlier studies (e.g., Bettleheim, 1955), however, placed it at 8 to 1 and even 12 to 1. Most public school classes would appear to be practically all males, thus having program implications for both sexes. Some of the same racial issues could be raised about inner-city emotional disturbed/behavioral disordered classes that were reviewed negatively by the courts in the 1967 Wright decision (Hobsen v. Hansen, 1967) in Washington, DC. Cullinan et al. (1992) also reported the ratio of white to nonwhite as 3 to 1. However, in class after class of inner-city schools, the composition is predominantly of black children. As one might suspect, the number of students who are emotional disturbed/behavioral disordered who live with both parents is less than one third of those receiving services and 30% less than for the other disability categories.

It would appear that students who are emotional disturbed/behavioral disordered are viewed by most as a breed apart. Therefore, it must be reasoned that they cannot be helped to rejoin society. To society at large, and possibly within the professional communities, it also would appear that they have a greater variety of different problems at a greater level of severity than any other group of children with disabilities. At the same time, these children have the highest risk of failing to receive services. In one study (Grosenick, George, & George, 1987), of the 17,000 children with emotional disturbance surveyed only 1 in every 4 received services. They are the least welcome in regular education. It is as if they are driven to drop out; they are pushed out of school.

This group remains the most underserved, with 20% to 30% of all known children who are emotionally disturbed failing to receive any services. It is now estimated conservatively that nearly 12% of the children in this country are mentally ill, while actual studies report that nearly 22%, or 14 million, are experiencing critical adjustment disorders (Brandenburg, Friedman, & Silver, 1990). It must be kept in mind that the reasons for the wide discrepancy in reported variance on the prevalence statistic of children with emotional disturbance/behavioral disorders are (a) the absence of agreement on the definition and (b) the lack of continuity in diagnostic practices and identification policies at the school district level. The authors once made a comment in a public meeting that in this country if children who were emotionally disturbed were to move from school district to school district within a state, they would need a visa (a legal statement certifying they were eligible for services) if they were to receive services in another district. In response, a director of special education commented that it would require a visa if a child who was emotionally disturbed/behaviorally disordered moved from building to building in his district. There is clearly greater "operational flexibility" in the diagnostic identification process for children who are emotionally disturbed/behaviorally disordered than for all the other categories combined, once again supporting "He who defines, classifies."

THE NEED

On November 27, 1993, a 16-year-old boy killed his mother with a baseball bat. It wasn't even his bat; it was one she purchased at a garage sale for her own protection. He hated the bat that she kept beside the front door for her protection from possible intruders. He does not remember any of the details. He believes that he struck her in the back and that she fell down. He then continued to strike her, taking her to the basement where he continued to hit her. He cleaned up the blood with paper towels and put the towels in the garbage. He went back to his room and watched television, going to bed that night in the same house. The next day, he took $22,000 in cash from her dresser drawer and took a cab 20 blocks to a downtown motor inn across the street from the main shopping mall. He bought some new sweatpants and shirts, as well as several new video games. He stayed in the room for 2 days watching television, leaving only to shop and eat, until the police arrested him.

This boy was described by his teachers and neighbors as quiet, shy, withdrawn. He had but one friend. His school behavior reflected a model student who had never displayed any inappropriate antisocial or aggressive behaviors. He was simply a social isolate who said little and rarely interacted with others. He was physically large, weighing 255 lb on a 5-ft, 5-in. frame the day of his arrest. After he left school the principal called his house only to verify that he had dropped out. His grades in elementary school were As and Bs. His grades in junior high and high school were Bs and Cs. He had never failed a subject, never failed a grade, and he had never had any conduct statements entered into his record. He obtained a full scale IQ of 122 on the *Wechsler Intelligence Scale for Children–Third Edition* (Wechsler, 1991), administered December 28, 1993.

He had been receiving therapy at the local mental health center since 1991. The diagnosis was Axis I = parent–child problem, Axis II = bipolar disorder. One of his many therapists who saw him during the 2 years he was in treatment wrote that he was unaware of his feelings as a result of continuous maternal neglect and abuse. The extent of the emotional abuse goes back to the mother's own abuse as a child. The maternal grandmother was hospitalized for emotional problems most of her life. An uncle on the maternal side had been both an inpatient and an outpatient in a local mental health agency where he was treated for depression. He committed suicide in 1993. The mother had been in treatment for chronic and recurring depression for many years. As a teenager she had married a man 20 years her elder. She divorced him 3 years after this boy, one of two children, was born and married a man younger than herself. The two were chronic alcohol users, and the new husband frequently would run off and be absent from the home for extended periods of time. The biological father continued to live in the home until quite recently, when he moved into an apartment not far from the family. Following an automobile accident, the father died in his apartment and the boy was the one to find him. In the continuing cycle of abuse, the biological father was the boy's only support.

The mother remained a victim and manipulated all the male family members in her continuing need for abuse. In the mother's role she rejected, humiliated, degraded, and in an inconsistent and confusing manner mixed those expressions of abuse with overindulgent control of the boy through money and presents. She continually ridiculed him about his weight and padlocked the refrigerator door. She confused the parental role relationship to the point that he never sought an adolescent break from her and entry into the secondary peer culture.

His view of himself was so limited and negative that he isolated himself from everything and retreated to his room to spend each day, all day, playing video games and watching television. On the night of the incident he went downstairs at 9:00 to get something to eat after staying in his room all day. His mother began ridiculing him for his hunger instead of offering him a prepared meal. The conversation was filled with rejection and demeaning remarks. He left the kitchen and she followed him. He does not remember what was said; he only remembers that he struck her with a bat because that is what the police told him he did.

He was placed in a children's detention center, where the environment is highly structured with an emphasis on simple rules and encouraging behavioral expectations. The staff are very child oriented and have taken a deep personal interest in and liking to this boy. His personal response is that he has never been happier. He is a model resident, engaging in all activities; he has friends and socializes well, even though he remains somewhat withdrawn. When asked why he likes the detention center, he explains that people there treat him well and they are fair about the rules. While his behaviors are appropriate for this environment, he still does not have full awareness for many of his confused feelings. He is very remorseful over his mother, whom he says he loves (he did love the unrealistic ideal he had built of his mother). His personality was defined as one of dissociative depersonalization, with characteristics of psychogenic amnesia and fugue (running away). The only plan he ever had was to run away at age 18, when his mother could no longer bring him back. He had attempted repeatedly to run away in the past, only to be brought back to even greater emotional abuse and neglect. The significance of running away and dropping out was that they were efforts to escape. He had to escape from the abuse. The significance of her death was not that it was murder but that it was an escape from abuse. It was clearly psychological self-defense.

In a 16-year history of abuse, with 12 of those 16 years in school, why was he never referred for any diagnostic services? He was classic in terms of the extent of his social withdrawal, isolation, shyness, and quietness. But he was not aggressive. He never challenged a teacher, became verbally aggressive, or acted out in an antisocial manner. He was one of the many who never are referred to determine why they sit quietly and are in isolation. Ironically, if he had been referred, what would he have been referred to? In most cases it would have been a classroom filled with acting-out, aggressive boys, ones who are probably antisocial. In that milieu what would he have done, retreat even further?

This boy now has been involved in a serious crime. The justice system is attempting to determine if he should be treated as a juvenile or bound over to the adult courts. Judging from his positive response to the environment at the detention center, he should progress well in active treatment. But the reality is that our society is much quicker and more prone to provide punishment than to provide treatment. We are far quicker to punish a behavior than to teach an alternative behavior. Much has been written in the past few years about the abuse cycle. The question is when will society and the schools identify children who are in pain or distress, thereby providing needed treatment to stop the abuse cycle and contributors to other mental disorders? Is there a willingness to identify the need in this country and provide treatment? If not, then many more jail cells will need to be constructed, further reducing the available resources for the education that may prevent or curb at an early stage these complex problems.

The previous vignette did not come from the mind of the authors. It is a true story and is still unfolding even as this is written. The single most striking aspect is the role of the schools and the mental health center. First, the mental health center had a handle on the problem; they recognized it for what it was. They initiated disjointed treatment of the child by not treating the family. If they had treated the family unit beginning in 1991, the boy's mother and uncle might still be alive. As part of the family treatment the school would have been involved. But the service providers in mental health never communicated with school personnel. If they could have created an awareness and sensitized the school to the troubled life this boy had, perhaps he would have remained in school. If he had remained in school, perhaps the incident would not have occurred. The mental health professionals conducted their treatment in their environment. That means he was their client for 1 hour a week; he was in school 30 hours a week.

On the other hand, the schools were so unconcerned that when an intelligent boy dropped out of school, a boy passing all his course work and one who had never failed or engaged in any behavioral trouble, they involved themselves only to confirm for their records that he did drop out. Now the courts may place him in jail for life. The irony is that he has already been isolated from positive social learning for most of his life.

The trouble with a vignette is that it is a single case; hence social recognition of the enormity of the problem may become lost in the reader's response. This case is one situation in a world filled with so many that it is easier not to think about them. In the midwestern floods of the spring and summer of 1993, thousands of people up and down the Mississippi and Missouri river systems would not leave their homes in face of the approaching high waters. It is often easier to overlook or deny the very existence of threat when it is absolutely overwhelming. Maybe the flood of troubled humanity, the mere presence of all those hurting people, is easier to overlook than to be concerned with, given the overwhelming scope and size of this problem. Our ability or inability to accurately define, measure, and assess are inhibiting factors that will become more apparent in the chapter discussions to follow on definition, identification, and program delivery of services for children who are emotionally disturbed.

The following remarks by Morse (1964) would best bring this chapter to a conclusion. Morse stated:

> Well, I would say I think a lot of our business boils down to knowing where the child is hurting. What is bothering him? Have we the sensitivity in our interactions to find it? Those who interact with children are sensitive to their needs and they'll go about doing the things that the child needs in ways that we've never called therapy before, I think. I would suggest we not wait until research proves that wigs on a bald headed little boy are therapeutic but to go ahead with the wig when you see a child needs it. (p. 115)

REFERENCES

Bettleheim, B. (1955). *Truants from life*. New York: The Free Press.

Brandenburg, N. A., Friedman, R. M., & Silver, S. E. (1990). The epidemiology of childhood psychiatric disorders: Recent prevalence findings and methodologic issues. *Journal of the American Academy of Child and Adolescent Psychiatry, 29*, 76–83.

Brown v. Board of Education, 347 U. S. 483 (1954).

Cullinan, D., Epstein, M. H., & Sabornie, E. J. (1992). Selected characteristics of a national sample of seriously emotionally disturbed adolescents. *Behavioral Disorders, 17*(4), 273–280.

Despert, J. L. (1965). *The emotionally disturbed child: Then and now*. New York: Robert Brunner.

Forness, S., & Knitzer, J. (1991). *A new proposed definition and terminology to replace serious emotional disturbance in Individuals with Disabilities Education Act*. Alexandria, VA: National Mental Health and Special Education Coalition.

Forness, S., & Knitzer, J. (1992). A new proposed definition and terminology to replace "serious emotional disturbance" in Individuals with Disabilities Education Act. *School Psychology Review, 21*(1), 12–20.

Grosenick, J. K., George, M. P., & George, N. L. (1987). A profile of school programs for the behaviorally disordered: Twenty years after Morse, Cutler and Fink. *Behavioral Disorders, 12*, 159–168.

Hobsen v. Hansen, 269 F. Supp. 401 (D.D.C. 1967)

Kanner, L. (1962). Emotionally disturbed children: A historical review. *Child Development, 32,* 97–102.

Kozleski, E. B., Cessna, K., Bechand, S., & Borock, J. (1993). Lessons from policy decisions: Politics and services for students with emotional and behavioral disorders. *Behavioral Disorders, 18*(3), 205–217.

Lauritzen, P., & Friedman, S. (1991). Teachers for children with emotional/behavioral disorders: Educator's greatest challenge. *Preventing School Failure, 35*(2), 11–15.

Long, N. J., Morse, W. C., & Newman, R. G. (Eds.). (1965). *Conflict in the classroom: The education of emotionally disturbed children.* Belmont, CA: Wadsworth.

McIntyre, T. (1993). Reflections on the new definition for emotional or behavior disorders: Who still falls through the cracks and why. *Behavioral Disorders, 18*(2), 148–160.

Mills v. Board of Education of the District of Columbia, 384 F. Supp. 866 (D.D.C. 1972)

Morse, W. C. (1964). Summary discussion. In P. Knoblock (Ed.), *Educational programming for emotionally disturbed children: The decade ahead* (pp. 102–115). Syracuse, NY: Syracuse University Press, Printing Division.

PARC (Pennsylvania Association of Retarded Children) v. Commonwealth of Pennsylvania, 434 F. Supp. 279 (E.D. Pa. 1972).

Redl, F., & Wattenberg, W. W. (1959). *Mental hygiene in teaching* (2nd ed.). New York: Harcourt, Brace & World.

U.S. Department of Education. (1990). *Twelfth annual report to Congress on the implementation of the Education of the Handicapped Act.* Washington, DC: U.S. Government Printing Office.

Wechsler, D. (1991). *Wechsler Intelligence Scale for Children* (3rd ed.). San Antonio, TX: Psychological Corp.

Wyatt v. Stickney, 344 F. Supp. 387, 390 (M.D., Ala., N.D. 1972).

ELI M. BOWER

The late Eli M. Bower was a professor emeritus in the special education department at the University of California at Berkeley. This article is reprinted with permission from Celebrating the Past, Preparing for the Future: 40 Years of Serving Students with Emotional and Behavioral Disorders, *edited by Sheldon Braaten, Frank W. Wood, and Gordon Wrobel. Copyright is held by Minnesota Educators of Emotionally/Behaviorally Disordered, Minnesota Council for Children with Behavioral Disorders.*

CHAPTER 2

A Brief History of How We Have Helped Emotionally Disturbed Children and Other Fairy Tales

In all of history the most instructive to a person is his own. As one gets on in years, the years stretch out behind you, and the years ahead shorten. One hastens to look back and ask, "What did it all mean?"

This assignment has given me the excuse to reminisce and reassess the past 50 years of attempting to help emotionally disturbed children and their families. As an observer and participant in the history I give you I am like all historians weighed down by my own biases and distortions. I am aware of some and also aware of others of which I am only dimly aware. Wherever possible, I will share them with you.

The first age of action I encountered might be called the RICE (Resolution of Intrapsychic Conflict Era) age. When I was a lad of one and twenty the nation and the world were in the middle of the great economic depression. This was 1938—50 years ago. I was coming out to this world with a Masters in Botany, a major in proto-zoology. The demand for my services was a trifle below that of metaphysician or tabulator of grains of sand on a beach. A friend concerned with my sad visage and lack of money asked me if I would take a job working with emotionally disturbed children. Considering myself emotionally disturbed at the time, I didn't feel working with such children to be a big deal. I took it.

I had majored in biology and was able to get a teaching credential in biology and general science. I was also asked to serve as a substitute cottage parent when regular parents took a much needed day off. I should explain the place I went to was Hawthorne Cedar-Knolls School in Hawthorne, New York, which housed approximately 100 tigers and 50 tigresses aged 10–16. These tigers and tigresses lived in comfortable cottages, about 20 to a cottage with a couple, usually married, who were called cottage parents. We had a school on grounds that was granted the status of a Union Free School District since the teaching staff were all fully credentialed. In addition to teaching biology, general science and civics I was asked to coach the basketball team and accompany the truant officer on his drives around the State of New York to retrieve runaways. Our runaways were highly accommodating—when they ran they would always go home. The school was well staffed with social workers, psychiatrists, plumbers, carpenters, handymen, teachers, physicians, cooks, household help, one psychologist, and one nutritionist.

I served my time until 1941 when the depression ended and U.S. participation in World War II began. In my free time during the next four years I pondered about the experiences I had with my emotionally disturbed children. Since I had no professional training in any of the mental health fields at that time I was free to think freely without professional blinders. And I did.

At first I decided that our students either had hormonal imbalances or were plain stupid. I was assured by the medical, psychiatric and social work staff of our institution that our boys and girls were in the normal range of physical health and intellectual ability. Yet as I looked at them it became increasingly clear to me that with rare exceptions they would not become effectively functioning human beings. Why not, I asked myself. Among the observations which I and the King of Siam would call a puzzlement were: the boys and girls at Hawthorne had no ability or perhaps capability for having fun. Whatever enthusiasm they could muster for parties, socials and dances they put into hurting oneself and others. At mixed socials and dances the boys and girls would stand around like a bunch of porcupines with contact dermatitis. Or we would find a couple of couples under a stairwell almost ready to begin motherhood and fatherhood.

The streets of New York, Rochester, Buffalo and White Plains had produced an excellent group of large, tall and coordinated hoopsters. As basketball coach, I was pleased by my recruiters—the cops, probation officers, judges and child psychiatrists of the cities. We had been admitted into the league of high schools in our area. But not for long. In our first game three of our better players were disqualified for fighting. In our second game five of our team were thrown out. I sat our group of 15 down before the next game and explained, "Basketball is a game. There are rules in basketball. To play the game we must play by the rules. The rules do not permit fighting. It's OK in boxing but not in basketball." Then in my best truth-in-packaging manner I added, "A game is not real. It is serious, competitive and suspenseful but it is not real. If you fight, the game is over and we lose."

In our next game only two players were disqualified. The following week I received a note from the High School Commissioner of Athletics suggesting we drop out of the league and try again next year. I accepted the suggestion. Back in biology and civics I found students having a difficult time with curricula. To me and to others learning had to do with knowledge assembled and conceptualized in the outer world about significant ideas to human beings. These were matters such as history, literature, physical and biological sciences, mathematics, music and philosophy. These curricula were outside the person. My job as teacher was to get this stuff inside my students. On the other hand my students already had a curriculum inside them and they seemed to have little room for outside, irrelevant junk. Many of the adolescents showed a spark of interest when our biology studies took us to a subject in which they thought they had expertise—human reproduction. Unfortunately they had substituted enthusiasm for knowledge. In civics, a mandatory course for junior high schoolers, I spent a semester with twenty boys and girls trying to develop a discussion group. I had them sitting in a circle (rather I should say that the chairs were in a circle) and explained the theory—one person talks, all listen—another person talks, all listen. Jumping out of chairs, invectives, non-participation, interruptions and fighting were not allowed. The final exam was to conduct a discussion of thirty minutes which did not resemble the running of the bulls at Pamplona. On occasion we came close but never quite made it.

Back in the cottage I tried to interest my children in reading and in Bach, Beethoven, Brahms, Gershwin, and Gilbert and Sullivan. I still had books at home which I had enjoyed as an adolescent and brought them to the cottage to interest potential readers. I would tell them the beginning of some of the stories and ask them to finish it themselves. They couldn't get excited about imaginary beings or times past or unreal (to them) events. Their imagination was chock full of their own fiction. Many had hobbies which kept them busy and a few were apprenticed to some of our skilled maintenance men. Others just sat and daydreamed in their free time.

Some were taken by classical music especially program music. They liked jazz and swing but also such things as "Peter and the Wolf," "Pictures at an Exhibition" and "Carnival of the Animals." We were sitting together on Sunday, December 7, 1941, listening to the New York Philharmonic when the program was interrupted by the unbelievable announcement that the Japanese had attacked Hawaii. I sat stunned. Others weren't quite sure what it meant. "We're at war," I said to the group. An older boy came up. "Good," he said, "maybe now I can get out of this dump and join the army."

So in the period between 1941 and 1945, I thought about students at Hawthorne. For the most part they were a group of 10–16 year old boys and girls who did not know how to have fun, could not separate play from reality, could not attend to concepts outside of self and were driven by impulses unchecked by reality controls. To help them we offered each individual psychotherapy with competent psychotherapists. Each student had a couple of therapy hours during the week which could come at any time. The child was summoned by a monitor with a slip excusing the student from class. In some cases the student would return from therapy hour during class. If educational activity would be going on it would stop so that all could participate in the student's assessment of his or her therapy hour. To the student therapy was doing and saying what would get his or her early release. The therapists were well aware of this kind of "resistance." As teachers and substitute cottage parents we would meet with the psychotherapists to discuss common concerns. One concern I introduced was my interest in the lack of ability to teach some of my students to read. A tall gaunt psychiatrist, Van Ophuisen, who had studied with Freud, sympathized with my concern. "Perhaps," he said, "if we know how to teach them to read, we wouldn't have to resort to psychotherapy. I'm not at all sure that what we do to help adults is really applicable to children and adolescents anyway."

After the war I went to graduate school to find out what might be done about emotionally disturbed children. I searched for answers to two basic questions. What in these children's short existence had produced their marked inability to function as normal children and adolescents? And if we could discover such factors were there levers and fulcra which we might use to reduce or abolish these pathological processes? I was impressed by the speed with which early developmental and interpersonal factors produced human dysfunction. Could such dysfunction be prevented or reversed?

The philosophy of including handicapped children in public education moved along rapidly in the 1950's. Programs were developed and support given for the educable mentally retarded and then for the trainable mentally retarded. In the late 1950's teachers, school administrators and legislators became aware of a group of students who were emotionally and behaviorally retarded. At the time I was an emotionally disturbed consultant for the California State Department of Education. Groups of parents of emotionally disturbed children heartened by the success of parents of retarded children got together and solicited our help in obtaining educational services for their children. One such group in the East Bay headed by Peggy Calder Hayes who was not a parent of an emotionally disturbed child but was the sister of Alexander Calder, the artist who invented the mobile, led a group of parents to Sacramento to meet with the Assembly Education Committee. The proceedings were opened by the testimony of a number of physicians who acknowledged that if the children were indeed emotionally disturbed they were sick and if sick the parents should seek treatment. This was followed by the heartwarming remarks of a committee member who suggested that if these parents who had come to Sacramento for help had been conscientious and loving parents they wouldn't need to come here for help. This provoked sobs and tears from the parents, the spectators and even from a few legislators. In time the State Assembly, Senate and Governor Pat Brown accepted the seriousness of the problem and proposed a three year research study to find out what to do. I was strong armed to conduct the study which was begun in 1958 and completed in 1960.

In the late 1950's other states and communities were beginning to search for ways to help emotionally disturbed children. Many old line mental health professionals saw such children as ill and therefore subjects within their domain. I recall visiting Oregon which had several bills in the hopper to help emotionally disturbed children. These were opposed by the Oregon Medical Association on the grounds that ill children should be in hospitals. In time the RICE Age and Sick Child Age ran out of rationality and were hoisted by their own petard. If such children were sick they should be in hospitals. Some were—the seriously autistic and schizophrenic, but what of the others—the acting out, passive-aggressive, character disorders, personality problems, withdrawn, phobic and depressed children?

The research conducted by a large research staff and myself on behalf of the State Legislature sought answers to two major questions. What are the most effective ways to educate (emphasis on educate) emotionally handicapped children? Of these effective ways which were most administratively and financially feasible for State support? We set up 12 different experimental programs in four different sites in the State. In each we placed randomly selected students from a pool of subjects designated as emotionally handicapped. The programs we tried were special class (elementary); special class (secondary); special placement in reduced size regular class; mental health consultation to teachers (elementary and secondary); Prescott Child Study Program; Social Living Class (secondary); Adolescent Group Counseling; Remedial Reading; Play Activity (elementary); Human Relations Class (elementary and secondary); Parent Group Counseling; and a Child Care-Home Economics program (secondary). All this activity brought a great number of mental health professionals into the school and initiated the problem of teachers being one-upped by insensitive mental health people.

Most of the mental health professionals who came into the school were quite modest and humble about their skills in helping emotionally disturbed children and their parents. In some cases the mental health people and their way of doing things became role models for teachers. Some teachers changed themselves into therapists and ran what might be described as therapy groups. In such groups to make demands and impose discipline on children was seen as unhealthy. Some mental health professionals who came to help from private practice settings had trouble differentiating patients from parents.

For example one intervention we tried out was getting parents of emotionally disturbed adolescents together three times a week with a mental health worker with work experience. After the second week I got a call from two of our research coordinators that all was not well in this program. I talked to several parents in the group who indicated they were not going to continue to attend. "We come and sit. The leader of our group doesn't say much. We don't say much. So we sit and he (she) sits. Nothing happens."

Our leaders had been selected because they were experienced group workers. However the parent groups were not presented to them as "sick" people. The groups were organized as forums for parents who had difficult adolescent children and who wanted to talk about them. Most of the mental health workers had no trouble with this concept. A few, however, did have hardening of the categories and persisted as seeing these parents as in need of "treatment."

Another example of the early difficulties in establishing a collaborative effort between schools and mental health workers took place in a school where teachers had presented a series of questions they wanted the mental health people to address. The school had contracted with the mental health clinic to help the teachers with their problem students. The mental health people reviewed the questions and decided they were not the salient questions which the teachers should be asking. The mental health people then went on to propose questions which they felt the teachers should be asking. The so-called helping relationship between the two groups got off to a rousing start each accusing the other of not listening or understanding. Bloodshed was avoided although there were bruises on both sides. In time a helping relationship was established but it wasn't easy.

In the 1950's and 60's one of the leaders in obtaining services for emotionally disturbed children was SREB, the Southern Regional Education Board which represented 15 southern states in attempting to upgrade mental health services for children. Somewhat appalled by the lack of residential and day programs for emotionally disturbed children, they commissioned Nicholas Hobbs, then at George Peabody College in Nashville, to study the problem and recommend solutions. Hobbs and others had visited France and Canada where programs for emotionally disturbed children had been developed and staffed by educators—trained teacher-counselors who combined the skills of teacher, social worker, psychologist and recreation worker. Hobbs proposed a Re-ED program be established as a demonstration research project and with the help of the States of Tennessee, North Carolina and the National Institute of Mental Health the project was begun in July 1961.

Project Re-ED marked a significant departure from my early experience at Hawthorne Cedar-Knolls. Project Re-ED was concerned with the conflict-free aspects of the ego development as described by Heinz Hartmann (1939), R. W. White (1963) and others. What was not disturbing about disturbed children was their educational and social incompetence (Rae-Grant, Gladwin, & Bower, 1966) or, as White put it, their ineffectance. Hobbs and others (1982) suggested that we approach the treatment of disturbed behavior by attending to the competencies which all children desire as they grow up in a technical-industrialized society. Hobbs proposed a set of principles to guide the Re-ED model:

1. Life is to be lived now not in the past.
2. Children and adolescents should be helped to be good at something meaningful especially at schoolwork.
3. In a period of growth life has a positive and forward thrust.
4. Self-control can be taught without psychodynamic insight. Symptoms can be controlled and managed by direct address.
5. The group is very important to young people; it can be a major source of instruction in growing up.
6. Ceremony and ritual give order to troubled children.
7. In growing up a child should know some joy each day and look forward to some joyous event in the days ahead.

In the evaluation of Project Re-ED, Weinstein (1974) identified improvement in academic competence as the crucial element in the progress of Re-ED children. In addition children in Weinstein's matched control group who also made progress in academic achievement also overcame emotional problems. This finding is also supported by the research of Robbins (1966). There are now Re-ED type schools in Nashville, North Carolina and Virginia (Bower, et al, 1969). The Harrison School here in Minneapolis would also be considered a Re-ED type school.

What better cliche to end this short history than—we have come a long way but we have a long way to go. We have been helped by legislation and lawyers but I'm afraid we have the same difficulties here as we did early on with the mental health professionals. In some cases our efforts are focused on helping children by complying with regulations and rules. Often the best a program can say about its services to emotionally disturbed children is that they obeyed the law.

There is a confusion about concepts and definitions. The definition as used in P.L. 94-142 uses the social context, the school, as the backdrop for evaluating emotional disturbance of behavior disorders. Some insist on using DSM 3 (Dumont, 1987) notions and psychiatric check lists. There is a dearth of trained personnel and funds. Nobody likes emotionally disturbed children. They are costly and unsightly warts on the clean skin of society. Nevertheless they exist in significant numbers and are tragic reminders to the rest of us that they cannot read and will not be ignored.

WHAT ABOUT THE FUTURE?

There is no reason to believe that the future will produce marked changes in our present perils or accelerate our small gains on behalf of emotionally disturbed/behaviorally disordered children. We have come a long way from the "sick child," from office psychotherapy and DSM 3 categorizations. My own look into the crystal ball would produce the following images:

1. There will be a tentative armistice between the proponents of REI or GEI (Regular Education Initiative or General Education Initiative) and advocates of special services to handicapped children. Almost all, in fact let's say all, high minded, right thinking persons subscribe to the theory that *all* children should be educated in regular classes. Almost all high minded, right thinking persons feel that special education services ought to be used for children who are indeed handicapped and not include vast numbers of regular classroom failures. Extreme REIers feel that given the resources, teacher training and size of classes special education would be unnecessary. Less extreme folks accept the need for special services for some children. There are increasing harsh realities in the economics and resources facing the public schools and the capacity of teachers to manage wide ranges of abilities and emotional readiness to learn diverse curricula. Emotionally disturbed children are often unable to manage their own inner curricula sufficiently to attend to material presented to them from the outer world. Unmotivated, withdrawn and highly overwrought children can disrupt the best laid plan of teachers.

To some REI—the wish or desire that all children can indeed be educated in regular classrooms—is tantamount to being in favor of motherhood and against sin. The realities of educating all children in regular classes are on the order of climbing Mt. Everest. Perhaps the future will produce a few more like Sir Edmund Hilary.

2. The need for a new and functional psycho-educational system of classifying and prescribing educational experiences for behaviorally disordered emotionally disturbed children. Such a schema must be related to educational programming and coping competencies in the key integrative social systems related to children. Conceptualizes need to attend to the conflict-free aspects of ego development as presented by Heinz Hartmann, Robert W. White and others. The child will be treated as a functioning organism in an active and responsive system—as a figure related to a ground. The present definition in PL 94-142 attempts to do this. It describes the broad behaviors which to a marked degree over a period of time define the emotionally disturbed/behavior disordered children in the context of the social system which makes the behavior dysfunctional. On the other hand DSM 3-R (Diagnostic and Statistical Manual of Mental

Disorders, 3rd Edition Revised) distinguishes and separates one condition of psychopathology or illness from another with decimal point precision. Dumont in his review of DSM 3-R suggests that the computers of DSM 3-R "want to have the power to define reality while claiming not to be doing so. They consider themselves . . . to be theoretical and purely descriptive as if a kind of brutal empiricism informs these categories and no preconceptions exist to muddy the waters of their crystal clarity. In fact the entire system is an expression of theoretical bias so rigid and pervasive that it renders alternative ways of thinking about mental disorder not just difficult or even impossible, but inconceivable. It has to do with the attention given to the figure rather than the ground, the case rather than the context, the individual rather than the social setting" (Dumont, p. 10).

New systems of psychological and psychoeducational classification of children are on the horizon. Some of the work of Hobbs on an ecologically oriented, service based system for the classification of handicapped children and other ecological psychologists may lead the way.

3. The established professional boundaries and roles between mental health workers and teachers, and mental health workers and parents must be renegotiated and redefined. Mental health workers must seek ways to transmit their knowledge and expertise to other non-mental health professionals as peers in cooperative endeavors. Parents of behaviorally disordered cannot be conceptualized as patients or treated as such. The teacher is the key worker in the school. The mental health worker must find ways of helping the teacher teach more effectively and with greater self satisfaction. Lastly, mental health professionals—psychiatrists, psychologists and social workers—must begin to perceive and conceive positive ego enhancing interventions to assist teachers in their work with troubled and troubling children and their parents. Along with epidemiology equal time must be given to salubriology.

4. School systems need a specifically delineated array of educational services for children with severe handicaps. These must begin with regular classes where teachers are trained to manage and educate mild to moderate problem learners and behavior disordered children. Schools also need access to classrooms for children with severe learning problems and emotionally disturbed behavior. Such an array of services should not be perceived or designated as more or less virtuous, depending on their distance from the regular class. A student who needs the services of a Harrison School in Minneapolis, or other like model, is no more restricted or in a more restricted environment than a student with measles who is hospitalized. The term "restricted" as applied to educational programs offered by public schools to serve children with severe behavior problems adds a touch of "evil" by the school to an already "evil" student. Services

which fit a child's need in a school system are more or less restricted.

5. Special classes or schools for the most severely troubled students should be fully supported with trained personnel who are rewarded professionally and financially by such services. Such programs and schools should include a research component accepted and understood by all staff which can provide valid and reliable data to monitor student progress. Such a research component should be an integral part of the on-going school program but administered independently of the service staff. All students in the program should be monitored at least five years after leaving to ascertain factors making for success or failure in already high risk children.

6. For a society committed to excellence and reason it is clear that the staggering dropout rates among disadvantaged adolescents and some not so disadvantaged exceeds the budget deficit as our prime national problem. In a society where educational skills have become a basic human commodity can we afford to allow one out of two black, Hispanic and poor teenagers to quit school? A recent report by Catterall of UCLA and Cot-Robles of UC Berkeley using Department of Commerce, Census Bureau and U.S. Center for Education statistics is no surprise to anyone. The school dropout problem is a sizzling time bomb with a short fuse. Set aside for a moment the loss of human capacity, dropouts from one single graduating class in a large urban school district will earn 200 billion dollars less than graduates during a lifetime. Each additional year of secondary school reduces the chance of being on welfare by 35 percent. More than 60 percent of jail inmates are dropouts.

This is not a new problem. It is unconscionable for a nation with such vast resources to allow a substantial number of children to fail in life before they have started. As old Will said it, "A little fire is quickly trodden out; which being suffered rivers cannot quench."

REFERENCES

Bower, E., Laurie, R., Strother, C., & Sutherland, R. (1969). *Project Re-ED: New concepts for helping emotionally disturbed children.* John F. Kennedy Center, Peabody College, Nashville, Tenn. (also Chapter 12 in Hobbs book).

Dumont, M. (1987, December). A diagnostic parable (1st edition unrevised). *Readings: A Journal of Reviews and Commentary in Mental Health.*

Hartmann, H. (1939). *Ego Psychology and the Problems of Adaptation.* New York: International University Press.

Hobbs, N. (1982). *The Troubled and Troubling Child.* San Francisco: Jossey-Bass.

Rae-Grant, Q., Gladwin, T., and Bower, E. (1966). Mental health, social competence and the war on poverty. *American Journal of Orthopsychiatry, 36,* 652–664.

Robbins, L. (1966). *Deviant Children Grown Up.* Baltimore: Williams & Wilkins.
Weinstein, L. (1974). *Evaluation of a program for Re-Educating Disturbed Children: A Followup comparison with Untreated Children.* Department of HEW, Washington, DC, Eric ED 141-966.

PART II
Personal Perspectives

DAVID B. CENTER
Georgia State University

David Center was once a high school dropout. To his credit he reentered high school and graduated from Druid Hills High in Decatur, Georgia, and went on to earn a bachelor's degree from the University of Tennessee. He earned his PhD from Georgia State University in the area of behavior disorders. Center has held many positions, from a grocery stock clerk to a professor at Georgia State University. In addition to teaching students with behavioral disorders, he has worked as a diagnostician in a psychoeducational center. Center has researched the areas of social skill development and the area of social reasoning with children who are emotionally disturbed in an attempt to gain insight into the daily problems that confront children who carry the label of E/BD.

CHAPTER 3

Personal Views on the Education of Students Who Are Emotionally and Behaviorally Disordered

CURRENT STATUS OF E/BD EDUCATION

In my opinion, the current state of education of children with emotional and behavioral disorders (E/BD) is deplorable. One need only look at the outcomes for students served in E/BD programs to be convinced of this. In particular, the very high rate of students with E/BD who fail to finish school and who fail to make successful adjustments to adult life demonstrates the failure of E/BD programming. It appears that as a profession we haven't got a clue about what kinds of services these students need. In general, public schools seem to define a successful E/BD program as one that isn't disruptive. Having a program that isn't disruptive is probably necessary, but I doubt that it is an adequate definition of success.

Thus, the job that lies before us is to determine what the true needs of students with E/BD are and how to meet those needs successfully. There are many ideas about what services these students need. One idea that has been at the core of E/BD programming for years is that these students need specialized instruction and remedial services to help them master the standard academic curriculum.

This academic focus is evident to anyone who examines the paper trail left by IEPs over the years. These documents focus almost exclusively on academic concerns. Looking only at the objectives in these documents you often can't distinguish E/BD IEPs from IEPs written for students who are learning disabled or mildly mentally impaired. Academic services certainly need to be addressed if a program is going to turn out a literate student. However, this alone doesn't appear to be sufficient, since so many students with E/BD fail to master basic academic skills and drop out of school.

A second idea that has received attention in the professional literature and some attention in E/BD programs is the inclusion of socioemotional components in the curriculum. In fact, I contributed to this literature through a book I wrote a few years ago (Center, 1989). I advocated programming for both social and emotional domain deficits in students with E/BD. My determination that this was needed was based largely on an examination of the definition of serious emotional disturbance (SED), not on any empirical examination of the actual kind of social or emotional functioning necessary for success in today's society.

Many of the other advocates for this type of programming have based their appraisal on research showing deficits in functioning of children with E/BD in comparison to students without E/BD, particularly in the area of social skills. However, it does not follow that just because one has a deficit in social skills or some other area, the result will be poor adaptation to adult life. There are numerous examples of people who have made quite successful adaptations while deficient, relative to the norm, in one or more areas of functioning.

A third idea is that the proper services exist but what is needed is a coordinated delivery of those services. This idea is roughly that schools can best deliver educational services, family and children service agencies can best deliver social welfare services, hospitals and clinics can best deliver medical services, mental health agencies can best deliver psychological services, vocational rehabilitation agencies can best deliver vocational services, and so on. Unfortunately, each of these service delivery systems have their own problems, and none can be said to be particularly effective. Coordination of flawed service delivery systems will probably not result in exemplary or even adequate services.

A fourth idea that presently is receiving a lot of attention is that of transition services. Unfortunately, this seems to be more of a social policy response to the poor outcomes mentioned above than any actual knowledge about what it takes to make a successful transition from school to adult life. It is, however, satisfying to many educators because it gives the appearance of doing something about an identified problem.

In conclusion, special education for students with E/BD does not appear to be very effective. It remains to be demonstrated whether it can be effective. What is needed, at least in part, is better information about what these students actually need in order to function successfully and how to best meet those needs.

DEFINITION OF E/BD

A student with E/BD is one whose behavior significantly interferes with his or her ability to benefit from educational experiences. The problem can be a deficit in behavior, an excess of behavior, or behavior that in and of itself is neither excessive nor deficit but is under inappropriate stimulus control; that is, it simply doesn't fit the situation. In short, if a student is educationally disabled by his or her behavior, the student is E/BD.

In the above definition, by "educational experiences" I mean experiences designed to teach useful information and skills. By "useful information and skills," I mean information and skills that are relevant to the student. By "relevant," I mean that there are appropriate antecedents and consequences in both the school and community to maintain the information and skills once acquired.

MY DEFINITION AND THE FEDERAL DEFINITION

Rather than contrast my definition with the federal definition, I will address what, in my view, is wrong with both definitions. My personal definition suffers from the same basic problem as the official SED definition, as well as most other definitions. It lacks the level of operationalization needed for reliable application to students. What is needed is an operational definition of E/BD that can be reliably applied by its various users. A good definition also would permit reliable classification of students into at least two subgroups. At minimum, students with E/BD should be classifiable into those who are predominantly internalizers or externalizers. Such classification would make it possible to provide a basis for a minimal level of differential placement and programming.

Reliability alone, however, is not sufficient. The definition needs to be valid for the purpose for which it is being used. Before we can create a valid definition, we need to decide what the purpose of special education for students with E/BD actually is. Is its purpose to facilitate academic achievement, improve personal functioning in nonacademic areas, or both? There appears to be a fairly consistent link between academic achievement and personal functioning, though it isn't universal. What we don't know is in which direction the cause-and-effect relationship runs, or, for that matter, if there *is* a cause-and-effect relationship.

It is certainly possible that problems in both academic and personal functioning are caused by some as-yet-unrecognized third factor. It is unclear whether a focus on one or the other or even both of these problem areas will necessarily correct a student's educational disability. A great deal more empirical data about what kinds of problems result in educational disabilities and what kind of interventions correct those problems are needed.

Since so much of education and special education is driven by social policy rather than facts, it would be useful if we could just reach a social consensus about the nature of E/BD and the purpose of E/BD programs. Having reached such a consensus, it might then be possible to operationalize a definition and get a relatively consistent application. We could then at least conduct research and evaluation studies and know to whom the results apply.

EMOTIONAL DISTURBANCE VERSUS BEHAVIOR DISORDERS

In practice, whether these two labels mean the same thing or something different depends on who is using them. Both terms can be used exclusively or inclusively. When *emotional disturbance* is used exclusively, the intent is to limit its application to disorders of affect. When *behavior disorder* is used exclusively, the intent is to limit its application to disorders of social behavior. When either term is used inclusively, the intent is to apply the term to all disorders of behavior.

From a semantic point of view one might argue that the exclusive interpretation of each label makes the most sense. The term *emotional* certainly implies affect, and the term *behavior* implies, for most people, overt actions that usually occur in a social context. Using this line of thought, some argue that emotional disorders arise from influences within an individual and behavior disorders arise from influences outside an individual.

I would have to say that the term *emotional disturbance*, when used exclusively, is a lot like the term *minimal brain dysfunction*. Both purport to describe something, but both appear to be mostly in the eye of the beholder, rather than an objectively identifiable condition.

E/BD EDUCATIONAL EXPERIENCE

As one might gather from some of my earlier comments, appropriate educational experiences for students with E/BD are difficult to specify with any certainty. Lacking the kind of empirical data upon which to base a curriculum and differentially select the appropriate educational experiences, I will address the issue from a hypothetical perspective. As I mentioned earlier, in a book on E/BD methods I based my recommendations on the current definition. If one looks at the definition that is used to identify students for services, one can infer a number of potential programming needs.

First, I would suggest that, for younger students, instruction and remedial programming in basic academic skills is needed. In older students who have mastered basic skills, I would suggest either extended academic skills for those who are capable of benefiting from such instruction or functional application of basic skills for those who are not suited to extended academic instruction.

Second, I would suggest that all students with E/BD who have deficits in prosocial behavior should receive instruction in both social skills and social reasoning focused on peer relations. In older students this instruction needs to be expanded to include interaction with adults in general and in the workplace in particular. The term *social reasoning* is used broadly to include social perception, reasoning about interpersonal relations, and social values.

Third, all students with E/BD who have deficits in emotional development need programming to facilitate emotional growth. Such programs need to help students better understand and communicate about their feelings and learn how their emotional responses contribute to their behavior. Such programming needs to help students learn to recognize emotional states in both themselves and others. It also should help them learn the language necessary for talking about feelings. Finally, it should help them acquire the necessary skills for examining how their interpretation of events affects their state of emotional arousal and response to those events.

Finally, I think younger students should learn about real life choices they will have to make when they are older. Older students should be assisted in developing decision-making skills. Students who do not have the ability or motivation to pursue postsecondary education should receive training in the work skills they will need in order to function in the adult world. This should include but not be limited to vocational skills and actual work experience.

INCLUSION OF STUDENTS WITH E/BD

The question here is whether the regular classroom program is the most appropriate program for students with E/BD. If you assume that the program outlined above represents the needs of most E/BD students, the answer is no. It is no because regular classroom programs do not provide those kinds of educational experiences. Unfortunately, most special education programs don't provide those kinds of educational experiences either. If you accept the proposition that appropriate experiences will not or cannot be provided, then you could argue that a student with E/BD might as well be poorly served in one setting as another. The simple fact of the matter is, the regular classroom program is not appropriate for most students whether they happen to be E/BD or not. If you don't believe this, ask yourself why so many students vote with their feet (drop out).

Generally speaking, the elementary curriculum is focused on preparing students for high school, and the high school curriculum is focused on preparing students for college. About 25% of public school students drop out of school. Of those that remain in school and graduate, about half go on to college. Of those that go on to college, about half graduate. Thus, less than a quarter of the students who enter school complete college. For the majority of those students who get college degrees, the curriculum is adequate. Even among those for whom it appears to be adequate, I would argue that it doesn't serve the best and the brightest all that well. For the remaining 75% or so, I would argue that the current curriculum is at best inappropriate and at worst a disaster.

If we as a society want to serve all or most students in regular programs, we must change the way we educate most of our students. Inclusion will be successful when and only when there is a significant restructuring of the educational process. This means that schools must become much more flexible and adaptable than they have been in the past. Schools need to be reorganized and teachers trained to deliver a range of curricular options that better meet the needs of their students. When we have a system designed to truly include everyone, we will be able to also include most if not all students with E/BD.

DELIVERY OF SERVICES

As I mentioned earlier, most if not all of the various agencies providing services to children and youth have their own definitive shortcomings. Whether or not coordination of these services would solve any of the existing problems is uncertain. However, one can at least hope coordination of services would produce better results than uncoordinated delivery of those services. Schools are not comprehensive social service agencies. They are best suited to the delivery of educational services. I use the term *education* in a broad sense, intended to include not only academic programs but also those programs designed to facilitate personal development, particularly in the social and emotional domains. However, children with E/BD, like most children with disabilities, have needs far beyond those best provided for by schools. These include but are not necessarily limited to health, mental health, and vocational rehabilitation services.

A comprehensive service delivery model is needed for all children with disabilities, not just children with E/BD. In order to develop a system for the delivery of comprehensive services to children with disabilities, several things need to be done. First, you must have a uniform set of standards that determine eligibility for various services for children, including special education services. Once a student becomes eligible for special education services, he or she should automatically be evaluated for other services in a comprehensive delivery system.

Second, there needs to be a comprehensive budgetary system for funding these services. I would prefer to see this done through some type of privately administered insurance that covers children from birth to adulthood. This could be facilitated through a tax credit to parents for buying and maintaining the insurance or paid for, in whole or part, from public funds for those children whose parents or legal guardians fail a means test. I would have this policy cover not only nonschool services but also excess educational costs as well. My second choice would be to have comprehensive services paid for through a publicly financed insurance program. My last choice would be to have these services paid for through legislative appropriations.

The third and final requirement for a comprehensive service model is a method for coordinating the services needed by a child. In a system funded by insurance, I would place the responsibility for coordinating the delivery of necessary services with the insurer. Under a system funded by legislative appropriations, the coordination of services could be handled by a parent, if he or she chooses to do so, or by a professional case manager who has been trained to fill this role. The case manager should not be an employee of any of the service providers, but rather someone who independently represents the interests of the child.

IS THE INCIDENCE OF E/BD INCREASING?

Until there is a reliable and valid definition, it is difficult to objectively answer this question with any certainty. In my opinion the answer is yes. I believe there are several reasons why the proportion of children with E/BD is increasing and will continue to increase. Most of the increase in incidence of children with E/BD is environmentally determined and is linked to social and family factors. In fact, the resistance to including the so-called socially maladjusted child in E/BD programs strikes me as a recognition of this on the part of some educators and an attempt by them to stem the rising tide of new E/BD cases in the public schools.

We live in an innovative and dynamic society. Whenever there is rapid and continuing change in a society the general level of uncertainty increases. Uncertainty means that there are few, if any, constants that one can depend on and organize one's life around. Perhaps the most important by-product of the state of flux that modern society is experiencing is diminution of our traditional school values. In particular, the values of family, self-reliance, personal responsibility, respect for law (rules), and the work ethic seem to me to be victims of social change. Uncertainty leads to individual stress and conflict. Stress and conflict demand a coping strategy, and coping strategies can be either functional or dysfunctional. Some of the more obvious responses that are dysfunctional include apathy, alcohol and drug use, aggression, and scapegoating. Most behavior disorders, in my opinion, have their origins in the socialization of children. When the adults responsible for that socialization no longer adhere to society's traditional values and have no functional values to replace them, the socialization process reflects this doubt and suffers from inconsistency and disorganization. Inconsistent and disorganized socialization results in disordered behavior.

The deterioration in the value of the family in this society has led to, among other things, a rapid increase in the number of children born to unmarried mothers. The breakdown of the concept of self-reliance has led to a significant increase in the search for security from and dependence upon government. The diminished value of personal responsibility has resulted in an ever-growing victim mentality. The breakdown of respect for law (rules) has resulted in an ever-worsening problem with criminal behavior. The deterioration of the work ethic has led to a demand and expectation for all kinds of entitlements and rights.

Adoption of dysfunctional coping strategies such as apathy leads to decreased involvement in the social process, diminished personal effectiveness, and reduction in productivity. Alcohol and drug dependency often accompanies and enhances the effects of apathy. It also inflicts physiological damage on many children through their exposure during their mothers' pregnancy. Aggression as a coping strategy has led to using violence, rather than law, as a means of resolving conflict and violence against children as a means of discipline. Scapegoating as a strategy has led to the balkanization of society, dependence on so-called leaders of all kinds of cults and organizations, and externalizing of blame for every imaginable problem.

As long as social conditions such as the ones just described prevail and we as a society don't reclaim our traditional values or find new functional values to replace them, the socialization of children will continue to be disorganized. Inconsistent socialization will result and leave many individuals poorly prepared to behave in a manner that contributes to developing and maintaining functional social processes. Thus, I believe that the number of children with E/BD is increasing and will continue to increase.

ROLE OF SERVICE PROVIDERS

Within the context of the comprehensive service delivery model discussed earlier, I will briefly discuss the differential roles of various service providers. Educators should fill a teaching role and should employ an educational model for developing their services. As I mentioned earlier, I use the term *education* in a broad sense to include not only traditional academic programs but also personal development, which can include things within the social, emotional, and occupational domains. Because of their regular and prolonged contact with children with E/BD, schools are also in the best position to make a determination about the need for mental health services. Schools should therefore have a close and formal relationship with mental health service providers.

Mental health should deliver therapeutic services such as formal therapies requiring specialized training and related medical services. In particular, mental health should provide therapeutic services related to substance abuse. They also should provide services to families identified as dysfunctional, not just to their children. These services should include educational services to parents on how to better provide for the proper psychological development of their children. When a family is so dysfunctional that it places a child at significant risk of abuse, mental health should be responsible for initiating involvement by social welfare agencies.

Vocational rehabilitation also should have a close and formal relationship with schools, particularly at the secondary level. Vocational rehabilitation counselors should be assigned to schools for the purpose of coordinating vocation-related evaluations, providing guidance to both students and their parents about a student's potential and opportunities in the occupational domain. Vocational rehabilitation also should play a role in arranging and coordinating vocational and technical education and related services such as postsecondary vocational training, job placements, and job site supervision.

As previously discussed, I think it is critical for a case manager to be designated with the responsibility of coordinating the delivery of services. Simply making services available from various agencies, without an independent party that has the responsibility and the means of integrating those services into a comprehensive and systematic effort, will prove inefficient and ineffective.

Students who become involved in the juvenile justice system, and particularly those who are in correctional facilities, should be eligible for specialized educational, psychological, and vocational services. Juvenile authorities should be responsible for supervision of their charges and should coordinate the delivery of outside services. That is, juvenile corrections should have case management responsibilities for their charges. All services provided to students who are educationally disabled by their behavior outside of the correctional facilities should be available to children and youth in juvenile correctional facilities.

Finally, I don't believe that what has been outlined above is the solution to the problems we see in students with E/BD. At best they are stop-gap measures and at worst they contribute to the further erosion of the cultural values whose displacement is largely responsible for the problems we currently face. As a society we are suffering from cultural instability. Social instability is largely reflected in dysfunctional behavior in institutions, citizens, and their children. The problems we face will not be resolved until the root cause of the problem is corrected.

THE FUTURE OF SERVICE TO STUDENTS WITH E/BD

I have seen little substantive change in the education of students with E/BD during the past 20 years. I see no reason to think that the established trend will deviate significantly from its historic course during the next 5 or 6 years. Once you establish a steady state baseline, you can project it forward in time and make reasonably valid predictions from it. The only time this is not true is when some new and influential variable that has the power to affect the baseline trend is introduced. I don't see any such variables moving into position.

There will no doubt be changes in the way things are done, just as there have been changes in the past 20 years. The problem is that all of the changes amount only to tinkering, when an overhaul is needed. An overhaul is unlikely, however, given the powerful vested interest that exists for maintaining a monopolistic educational bureaucracy. This bureaucracy is out of step with reality and unresponsive to any feedback that could help it make useful changes. I predict that the number of children and youth with educationally dysfunctional behavior will continue to grow. These same children will have an increasingly disruptive effect on schools. Schools, in response, will become increasingly more coercive and intent on exclusion. This will lead to an increase in resistance (disruption) in some students and withdrawal (tuning out or dropping out) by others. It also will lead to a further increase in the number of parents choosing other education options for their children.

When I began my career in special education, I saw the locus of problems as the children and their immediate environments. I now view the locus of problems much more broadly. I still believe that each of us as a teacher can have our greatest impact on children and their immediate environments. I just don't think that is sufficient.

REFERENCES

Center, D. (1989). *Curriculum and teaching strategies for students with behavioral disorders*. Englewood Cliffs, NJ: Prentice-Hall.

MARGARET CECIL COLEMAN
University of Texas at Austin

Margaret ("Maggie") Coleman has experience in corrections, a state hospital, and the public schools. In addition to teaching students who are emotionally/behaviorally disordered, she has served as a consultant to teachers of persons who are emotionally disturbed in a variety of settings. Coleman has a strong background in sociology and counseling with degrees in these areas from Appalachian State University in North Carolina. She earned her PhD from the University of Texas at Austin. Coleman has written a textbook on persons who are emotionally disturbed and is currently researching the areas of identification and assessment of students referred for suspected emotional liability.

CHAPTER 4

Turning the Corner

I would like to be able to say that I knew early on that I wanted to work with children with emotional/behavioral disorders, or that I was inspired by a singular, sensational person or event. However, the truth is that I "backed into" our profession. I did know early on that I wanted to work with people rather than things, and that I was fascinated by human behavior. When I was studying psychology in college, I was affected by books such as *I Never Promised You a Rose Garden* (Greenberg, 1964) and *One Flew Over the Cuckoo's Nest* (Kesey, 1973). I knew then that I wanted to work in a field related to mental health. After working as a school psychologist for a few years, I realized that the children and teachers I most enjoyed working with were those in programs for children with emotional/behavioral disorders (E/BD). So my interests in education and psychology blended nicely into a single interest in special education for children with E/BD.

When asked to write a one-sentence philosophy for educating children with emotional/behavioral disorders, my first reaction was that everything I might say would sound either pedantic or simplistic. I opted for simplistic: We can't educate them if we can't keep them in school. I am pressed to make this statement by the statistic that more than half of our students identified as having emotional/behavioral disorders do not complete high school. According to a report compiled by Wagner (1991), this is by far the largest percentage of any special education category and is over twice the dropout rate of the general population. And it is 23% higher than a general education comparison group with similar demographics. This means that we need to be more creative about finding ways to keep these youth coming to school. We have to make our programs relevant to the skills they need to make it on their own in the world.

CURRENT STATUS OF E/BD EDUCATION

The other day my husband and I were discussing the postoperative health of a favorite uncle, who, my husband remarked, had just turned the corner and was beginning to mend. My 6-year-old overheard the conversation and wanted to know what "turning the corner" meant. I explained that, in this context, it meant that Uncle Bill was feeling much better. He's not fully recuperated, but he's on his way.

"Turning the corner" seems an apt phrase to describe where we are with children with E/BD today. We are not there yet, but we are on our way. Let me explain by describing both where I think we have been and where we should be going. As I see it, education for children with E/BD has gone through a number of phases since the 1960s: the psychoed phase of therapeutic classrooms and life space interviewing (for example, the work of Nick Long, Bill Morse, Fritz Redl, Ruth Newman); the behavioral phase of applied behavior analysis and the "engineered classroom" (the work of Ivar Lovaas, Ogden Lindsley, Frank Hewett, Tom Stephens); and the ecological phase (the work of William Rhodes, Nicholas Hobbs), which was largely philosophical and has contributed to our current emphasis on a systems approach. Each of these phases added something essential to the field. These professionals and many others like them have laid solid foundations for us. That is, we have technologies for teaching and for behavior management that we know will be largely successful if we apply them correctly and persistently in the classroom. And we have given lip service to the idea of ecological programming or a systems approach. This is where we've been.

I think we are turning the corner because we are beginning to recognize that, although we have the tools to improve both academics and behavior in the classroom setting, our ultimate concern is graduating individuals who are socially competent and vocationally prepared to secure and hold jobs. This is where we should be going. Our goal, or destination, is helping individuals to graduate, hold jobs, stay out of trouble, and get along with others to a reasonable degree. We haven't been doing such a great job of that. In fact, we haven't been doing a very good job of even keeping these children in school. Since more than half of the students identified as E/BD drop out of school, we know that much of our energy must be directed toward keeping these children coming to school.

I think we are turning the corner because we are now getting the bigger picture, that we in education can't by ourselves keep children in school and eventually turn out individuals who are socially and vocationally competent. We can't just teach academic and social skills in the classroom and think that we are helping the children make major changes when they step outside the classroom setting. The problems that many of our children and youth bring with them to school today are spawned by major societal problems: poverty, abuse and neglect, gangs, drugs, violence, and inadequate parenting. Therefore, it will take all of our communities' resources working together to make some improvements in our children's lives outside of school as well as inside classrooms.

I think we are turning the corner because, in many communities across the country, we are beginning to act upon the conviction that we need true interagency collaboration to serve these children and their families. I see the mental health system, the juvenile justice system, and the educational system beginning to cooperate as never before. Such partnerships are a theme that I will return to again and again in these pages. Transition programming (between school and work) already has become more of a priority. We have a long way to go, but I believe that we are turning the corner and on our way.

A WORKING DEFINITION OF E/BD

Eli Bower once said, "Along with the hazards of street crime, drunk driving, and Christmas shopping, is that of defining what is meant by 'emotional disturbance.' . . . Emotion is nonrational, nonlinear, and so far has been pretty elusive to being pinned down by precise prose" (1982, pp. 55–56). I agree with Bower and applaud his courage in attempting to write a definition for the field that would be applicable to educational settings. He later commented that he believed that his definition was successful in staying within the conceptual range of school personnel. However, when Bower wrote the definition he didn't know it would later be adopted as the federal definition, and he took issue with the modifications that were made when it was published in the Federal Register (1981). In particular, he took exception to the exclusion of children and youth who are socially maladjusted.

I wanted to begin this discussion by mentioning Bower's work because the federal definition, despite its shortcomings, has given special educators a good beginning from which to work. It has been the target of incessant criticism. Nonetheless, one important point made by the definition is the emphasis on chronicity (over a period of time) and severity (to a marked degree) as factors that differentiate between transient or mild problems and those that persist and are debilitating. Bower saw these dimensions as the defining factors in separating children with emotional problems needing intervention from those without, suggesting that we are talking about a matter of degree rather than of separate, qualitatively different, definable conditions.

My conceptualization of emotional/behavioral disorder is similar, in that I view it along a continuum from mildly disordered/disturbed/disturbing to severely disordered/disturbed/disturbing. At which point along the continuum does the individual's functioning become an emotional or behavioral disorder? At this point in the development of our field, it is still a matter of personal opinion. There are certainly no tests or battery of tests that can answer the question satisfactorily, although I am heartened by the current trend toward using psychometrically sound behavior rating scales from a number of sources and settings in the identification process. The *Diagnostic and Statistical Manual–IV* (American Psychiatric Association, 1994) offers some help by listing observable criteria, including number of symptoms and time lines for diagnosing various disorders. Use of the DSM–IV therefore may aid some professionals in determining at which point along the continuum a problem becomes a disorder. However, most DSM–IV diagnoses have little educational application in that very little information about the student's emotional or social needs accrue from a diagnosis. For this and other reasons, it has been difficult for educators to embrace the DSM system.

There is an exception to the statements I have just made about the continuum of disorders: I believe that schizophrenia (or childhood onset pervasive developmental disorder) is a qualitatively different condition that is organic in origin and can be distinguished from nonschizophrenia and from other disorders. In other words, I believe that we can say with confidence that an individual has a condition called schizophrenia; I have much less confidence in pronouncing that an individual has a condition called emotional disturbance or behavior disorder.

Although we may acknowledge these difficulties in defining what we mean by *emotional/behavioral disorders*, each of us in the field still must come to grips with his or her own personal definition of this population. My own working definition contains many of the same elements as the definition that the Council for Children with Behavioral Disorders is promoting for adoption in place of the federal definition. As of this writing the definition still was being negotiated, so the elements listed below should be considered a working draft. The key elements and my own comments about them follow.

Emotional or behavioral disorder means a disability that is characterized by an emotional or behavioral response that:

Element of Definition	Comment
• is different from age, cultural, or ethnic norms;	• The sociocultural context of behavior is taken into consideration.
• adversely affects educational performance (including academic, social, vocational, and personal skills);	• This recognizes that an educational disability affects more than achievement.
• is not temporary, expected response to stressful events;	• Chronicity, severity, and a degree of abnormality are important.

- is exhibited in more than one setting; and

- can include schizophrenia, affective disorders, anxiety disorders, or other sustained disorders of conduct or adjustment.

- The response cannot be specific to a single situation, setting, or person (i.e., must disturb a lot of people).

- This recognizes internalizing as well as externalizing disorders and specifically includes conduct disorders.

This definition emphasizes that emotional/behavioral disorders are not transitory, situational, or appropriate in certain contexts. These are all clues that help us place emotional and behavioral responses at points on the continuum of severity. It reminds us that some odd or offensive behaviors may be appropriate in certain contexts (e.g., a degree of belligerence or paranoia may be adaptive in some neighborhoods where gangs and street crime are common). It is also important to recognize that educational performance includes more than grades or achievement. High-achieving individuals can be very disturbed, and it should be our business in special education to work with them.

In addition, it is helpful to specify affective and anxiety disorders because children and youth with these difficulties typically have not posed classroom discipline problems and therefore have not been referred for special services as frequently as their acting-out counterparts. We only recently have begun to recognize that children may legitimately become depressed, much as adults do. As depression also coexists with attention-deficit disorder and conduct disorder, it may be increasingly important for us to recognize and treat the depression as well as the more bothersome externalizing behaviors.

As a final commentary, I hope that the term *disorders of conduct or adjustment* makes it to the final draft of this definition. The social maladjustment/conduct disorders controversy has raged for almost 20 years, and except for very specific and limited locations in this country, I believe it is a moot point; despite the federal definition's exclusionary clause, children and youth with conduct disorders do find their way into special education classrooms across this country year in and year out. We may as well admit that we are serving them and commit ourselves to doing a better job of it.

COMPARING THE NEW DEFINITION TO THE FEDERAL DEFINITION

There are four areas in which the federal definition differs from the newer definition that I endorse. First is the sociocultural context of behavior. Whereas the newer definition emphasizes age, cultural, and ethnic norms, the federal definition makes no mention of the appropriateness of behavior relative to normative standards. *Norms* is the key word here: What is considered normal or mildly deviant in one setting can be highly disturbing in another. When I was a school psychologist in rural mountain Appalachia, some local students were caught writing graffiti on the interior walls of the high school. The community was incensed. The students were expelled and the sheriff was called to charge them with misdemeanor vandalism. It was a community scandal that was discussed for weeks. There was talk of not allowing one of the seniors to graduate. A year or so later I moved to an urban area in Texas. I clearly remember a conversation with a friend of mine who was a vice principal at a local high school. She said the majority of her day was taken up with handling drug and weapons violations on the school campus. In her school, graffiti was certainly frowned upon, but there were more pressing problems, such as keeping kids safe. Being caught writing graffiti would exact a penalty, but it would not make the local news.

The second way the definitions differ is in the expansion of the term *educational performance* from the original definition to include academic, social, vocational, and personal skills in the newer definition. It has always bothered me that special education has operated under guidelines to identify and work only with students who have emotional/behavioral disorders and are low achievers. Under such circumstances, even students with obvious disabilities such as schizophrenia or multiple personality disorder could be considered ineligible as long as their grades were good. Adding the term *vocational* is an especially good move because students with emotional/behavioral disorders typically have an extremely difficult time gaining and maintaining employment during the high school years and beyond.

A third point of the newer definition is that the disorder should be manifested in more than one setting. Multiple settings were not specified in the original federal definition, although many states and local school districts included in their identification policies that a student must have exhibited problems in settings other than schools. This component of the new definition means that the offending behavior or emotional response clearly must be pervasive, i.e., it cannot be specific to one setting, person, or situation. Plainly translated, it means that the student must be disturbed or disturbing to a lot of people in a lot of different settings, such as the home, school, neighborhood, and other community settings. For example, Geoff routinely misbehaves in class in an attempt to avoid classwork because he can't read grade-level material. The teacher has tried a variety of tactics but can't seem to get him settled down. Outside of school, he has few problems. He excels at soccer, listens to his coach, and is considered a leader on his team. His parents report problems only when Geoff is compelled to do his homework. Geoff's behavior not only is setting specific but also could be considered an "expected response to a stressful situation."

Fourth is the inclusion of students with "sustained disorders of conduct or adjustment." As I mentioned earlier, even Bower took exception to the exclusion of children who are socially maladjusted in the federal definition. To this day, it is not clear to me exactly who was responsible for adding the exclusionary clause, but I believe it has caused an unnecessary rift in the field. We have spent a lot of time and energy arguing about whose responsibility these children are when, in fact, a number of systems are serving them, including special education. Beginning in 1966, most of the literature has indicated that a substantial percentage of children who are served in E/BD special education classrooms score high on various measures of conduct disorder. These kids may or may not have a DSM–IV label of conduct disorder, but they are in our classrooms.

ARE ED AND BD ONE AND THE SAME?

I'm not sure I have a defensible answer to this one. The problem is that it's easy to discuss this issue in terms of abstract concepts; it's very difficult to discuss this issue in terms of actual disorders and the people who suffer from them. I can make an arbitrary distinction and say that emotions are internal and what one feels, and that behavior is external and what one does. Similarly, it is tempting to oversimplify and say that *emotional disturbance* describes internalizing disorders such as depression and anxiety and that *behavioral disorders* describes externalizing disorders such as oppositional defiant, Attention-Deficit/Hyperactivity Disorder, and conduct disorders.

However, the relationship between emotions and behavior is not so simple. For example, take children with conduct disorders: Are they emotionally disturbed or behaviorally disordered or both? To be so labeled, they must habitually commit any of a number of antisocial acts, such as habitual lying, stealing, or cruelty. In other words, their behavior is in direct conflict with acceptable standards set by society. But what about the emotions of anger, fear, or rage, possibly combined with impulsivity and feelings of inadequacy that may underlie these deliberately offensive behaviors? Can we really successfully treat the behaviors without understanding and addressing the underlying motivation in these cases? Research to date with this group of children would suggest that the answer is no.

I have been reading Cronkite's (1994) *On the Edge of Darkness*, in which an expert on depression discussed whether depression is physiological or psychological. He stated that it is quite simply both, because the brain (physiological) is the organ of the mind (psychological). When one is not functioning correctly it messes up the other. So what we have is a highly interactive relationship between the physiological and the psychological that we do not understand very well. I believe the same characterization applies to emotion and behavior. To accurately describe the population we want to serve in special education, I'm in favor of combining both components, as in the term *emotional/behavioral disorder*. Use of this term suggests a number of possibilities: (a) that we believe all of the disorders to be either emotionally or behaviorally based, (b) that we believe all of the disorders to be both emotionally and behaviorally based, or (c) that we really are unable to distinguish clearly between the two. I can live with option c.

PRIORITY EDUCATIONAL EXPERIENCES FOR STUDENTS WITH E/BD

As I mentioned earlier when discussing the current status of educating students with emotional/behavioral disorders, I believe that we need to keep our sights on the ultimate goal of helping these children graduate into a world in which they can function. To me, this means they should have the interpersonal and vocational skills to secure and hold jobs and to get along with others to a reasonable degree. Our educational programming should be oriented toward this goal. In order of priority, this means (a) acquiring social competence and (b) acquiring literacy/vocational skills.

ACQUIRING SOCIAL COMPETENCE

In my opinion, the ability to get along with others is the most essential ingredient to success on the job, in the home, and in the community. Socially competent individuals take good care of themselves. They are able to communicate well with others and to solve problems. They neither fall apart nor blame others when things do not go as expected. There is a degree of personal responsibility in social competence. My own model of social competence involves three major areas: social skills, affect/emotion, and self-management.

Social Skills

This refers to dozens of personal interaction skills. In schools the skills usually are oriented toward getting along with teachers and with peers, for example, making eye contact, initiating conversation, joining a group, giving and receiving compliments, asking the teacher for help, saying no, resisting peer pressure, finding alternatives to aggression, turning in neat papers, waiting your turn, and so forth. Children often are identified initially as E/BD because of a severe deficit in social skills; however, we sometimes fall into the trap of assuming that all children with emotional/ behavioral disorders need training in all the social skills of a given curriculum. We should assess and individualize for social skills training just as we do for academics. Reinforcement of social skills should permeate the class (and school) setting as much as possible, so that the skills become a part of daily routine rather than be limited to the time set aside for training.

Affect/Emotion

The literature on children with E/BD is replete with the notion that after social skills training, most students can verbalize and role-play numerous skills effectively; however, they may be unable to react skillfully in the real world. Anger, anxiety, depression, and other emotional states may affect these students and their motivation to use the social skills they allegedly have learned. In particular, they may have trouble controlling their impulses and their anger. There are numerous anger-control programs that can be used with these children (e.g., the anger control component of Aggression Replacement Training [Goldstein & Glick, 1987]). Also, a variety of cognitive behavioral techniques can be used to address some of the debilitating thinking patterns that reinforce the symptoms of depression and anxiety.

Self-management

Most students with emotional/behavioral disorders suffer from problems with self-management; they need to learn to rely on internal controls rather than external ones. They need to learn to control their impulses, to plan and execute goals, and to take responsibility for their behavior. All the cognitive behavioral techniques that lend themselves so readily to special education classrooms, including self-assessment, self-instruction, self-monitoring, and self-reinforcement, can be used to accomplish these goals. The research on the effectiveness of these strategies for improving positive classroom behaviors, especially on-task behaviors, is encouraging.

Acquiring Literacy/Vocational Skills

The second major priority area is acquiring literacy/vocational skills. I use the term *literacy* in place of *academics* because I think that acquiring basic literacy skills is a realistic goal for the majority of children with emotional/behavioral disorders. I lump these two major categories together because I think that we should consider literacy and vocational priorities together. If these areas are taught separately and operate independently, we may be either working at cross-purposes or simply wasting our time. For example, consider Angelo.

Angelo is a 14-year-old eighth grader with an E/BD label who has been retained once and reads at about a second-grade level. He has broken virtually every school rule and has been in constant trouble with school personnel since the day he set foot on campus. Quite predictably, he hates school and comes only often enough to stay out of big trouble with his grandmother, with whom he lives. He is on probation for breaking and entering. He lives for the day he can quit school and get a car (and probably a job, too). Angelo's teachers will lose him completely if they work only on academic skills without making some serious plans for figuring out how Angelo's strengths and interests can be parlayed into job skills. Basic literacy skills should not be ignored but should be tied to real-world needs.

Perhaps this is easy to see with adolescents, but even in the primary grades, children need to be exposed to career choices. Very early on, they need to be able to visualize themselves as grown-ups with a job, a career, a way to make it in the world. Children who grow up in the midst of poverty, unemployment, and hopelessness need models with whom they can identify. I am not an expert on vocational programs, so I won't specify what they should entail and whether they should be separate courses or infused into the curriculum. Besides, I think that these issues often are settled by practical matters rather than philosophical ones (i.e., determined by availability of local resources). Instead, I am promoting a philosophy of keeping our eyes on the "big picture" by, first, keeping these kids in school through graduation and, second, helping them to graduate with the social and job-related skills they need to function as adults.

INCLUSION OF STUDENTS WITH E/BD UNDER REI AND GEI

To avoid confusion about terms, I would first like to distinguish between the Regular Education Initiative (REI) and the more recent full inclusion initiative. Fuchs and Fuchs (1994) stated that one major goal of the REI was to merge special education and general education into one inclusive system by restructuring the system with "shared responsibilities" and "inclusive educational arrangements" (p. 297). Such a merger would circumvent the need for the costly, time-consuming, and sometimes arbitrary identification and eligibility procedures. So far, so good. However, the second major REI goal as described by Fuchs and Fuchs was to "increase dramatically the number of children in mainstream classrooms by use of large-scale, full-time mainstreaming . . . as opposed to the more traditional case-by-case approach" (p. 297). Now I have a problem with REI, and it is one of the same problems I have with full inclusion. I am using the term *full inclusion* to mean educating all children with disabilities in the general classroom with support.

To me, the crucial aspects of serving children with disabilities are the following: (a) decisions about services should be made on an individual basis, without preconceived notions of the best place; and (b) good decisions about services for individuals will be facilitated when there is a continuum of services, available in a range from less restrictive settings. If we begin to put children in mainstreamed (general education) classrooms on a large-scale basis rather than on a case-by-case approach, we lose the crucial aspect of individualizing by assuming that the general education classroom is the place where the best education can be offered to all students. On the other hand, a more restrictive setting does not necessarily translate into a smaller teacher–pupil ratio with more individualized instruction, tighter behavior-management controls, and other advantages often needed by students with emotional/behavioral disorders. However, I would argue that classrooms with these advantages are more readily found in the more restrictive settings, and that there is less of a probability that general education classrooms, either now or in the foreseeable future, will be able to offer settings with these advantages.

To date, there is little evidence that general education teachers are equipped or willing to work with children with emotional/behavioral disorders. In fact, studies since the 1960s (e.g., Grosenick, George, & George, 1987) have shown consistently that children with behavioral disorders, along with children with mental retardation, are the most negatively perceived by general education teachers. I hear pro-inclusionists saying that we can change this by restructuring higher education to give regular educators the skills they need, and that we can change attitudes over the long term by forcing the issue now. Attitudinal change will follow legislated action change, they say. And I fear that we may make the same mistake that was made with wholesale deinstitutionalization, when similar opinions were voiced. The thrust of deinstitutionalization was that individuals would be better off in less restrictive settings than institutions and should be placed in their home communities. In response to both this advocacy movement and fiscal pressures, state legislatures opted to shut down many state-supported institutions in the 1970s and 1980s. As a result, some former residents have been appropriately situated in their home communities. Unfortunately, however, in the majority of areas the proposed community-based facilities have not sprung up to take in many of the displaced residents. Local governments have not been willing to fund the alternative facilities or programs, and communities have demonstrated a bias against having such facilities in their backyards. Consequently, and in combination with the massive cuts to federally subsidized housing under the Reagan administration, this well-intentioned movement has contributed to the ever-increasing street population of homeless persons with mental illness.

I mention the impact of deinstitutionalization because I think it has a direct parallel to the push for full inclusion in general education. I fear that if well-intentioned advocates for full inclusion are successful, students with emotional and behavioral disorders will receive fewer and lower quality services than they do now. I am unclear as to what supports might realistically be available in the general classroom and am uncertain about how the attitudes of peers and general education teachers are to be improved. I don't trust that attitudinal change will result automatically as a by-product of closer contact, especially if it is forced.

In an ideal world, special education would never have been created because there would have been no need for it. All children—with and without disabilities—would have been educated well together within the same classrooms. However, here in the real world this was not happening and special education was created to do something about it. Special education was about helping teachers deal with the diversity represented in our classrooms. It seems that somewhere along the way we let ourselves be sidetracked into an "us versus them" mentality, pitting special education against general education, and even the needs of children with disabilities against the needs of children without disabilities. Perhaps we have forgotten the unifying concept of meeting children's educational needs—however diverse they might be.

A DELIVERY OF SERVICES MODEL

To me, this is the most exciting aspect of serving children with emotional/behavioral disorders today. Special educators finally are acting on the belief that we must work with a variety of social systems other than education to deliver services to children with E/BD. Although we have held this belief for years, we have operated in separate systems that were all serving a "piece" of children and adolescents with emotional and behavioral disorders. The best that we could hope for was some kind of integrated case management, in which a number of agencies still adhered to their own eligibility requirements and turf issues but assigned a case manager who was supposed to have the total picture of who was doing what with the child and his or her family. This was considered interagency cooperation. Children were falling through the cracks by the thousands.

In developing a model, I have been influenced by this state of affairs and by the writings of Rhodes and Hobbs, who both eloquently address disturbance as an ecological or systems problem. In addition, I read Apter's (1982) *Troubled Children/Troubled Systems*, which really had an impact on my thinking. From an ecological or systems framework, the child is not viewed as the sole owner of the problem; therefore, interventions stemming from this model target both the child and important individuals in the child's life. Logically, such interventions require the services of a number of agencies outside the education system, which leads to the need for a viable interagency services delivery model. Such a model is promoted by Child and Adolescent Service System Program (CASSP; Coleman, 1992; Stroul & Friedman, 1986), which was developed under the auspices of the National Institute for Mental Health. My own idea of a services delivery model draws heavily on the basic principles of CASSP. Chief among these principles are the following:

- Services are conceptualized as a system of care.
- The system of care is child centered and driven by child and family needs rather than by the traditional configurations of agencies.
- Services are community based, delivered in the school setting whenever possible.
- Agencies cooperate in planning, implementing, and evaluating services.
- A continuum of community-based services are available, including more restrictive and less restrictive settings.
- The children and adolescents who are most severely disturbed are served by the system.
- Services are culturally sensitive.

In addition, the model delineates dozens of services that should be made available to these children and their families by each of the participating systems: mental health, social services, juvenile justice, education, health, and vocational. Services that do not clearly fall under one of the systems also are identified: recreational (e.g., summer camps, mentor programs) and operational services (e.g., case management, advocacy, and legal advice).

Using these principles as a blueprint, many exemplary models for services delivery to children with emotional/behavioral disorders have sprung up across the country. The one I am most familiar with is operating in my own backyard. In the 1992–93 biennium, the Texas legislature appropriated over $22 million to fund the Texas Children's Mental Health Plan (Texas Mental Health Association, 1992). The plan mandated that nine agencies, including school districts, work together in their local communities to come up with a unified plan to serve children with E/BD and their families. These local community management teams were charged with designing plans that are child- and family-centered and designed to fill in existing gaps in a continuum of community-based services. In Austin, the local community management team spends the bulk of its funds on a family-preservation project, round-the-clock emergency psychiatric services, and school-based health and counseling services.

In addition, a community resource coordination group, known locally as CRCG, with representatives from the nine agencies meets on a monthly basis to "staff" some of the cases that used to fall through the cracks due to agency turf issues. During CRCG meetings, people from the various schools and agencies make commitments to provide certain services needed by the child and family being staffed. CRCG develops a plan outlining who will be responsible for what, and the CRCG coordinator ensures that the plan is followed through. For example, David's case was presented to CRCG. A 13-year-old with conduct disorder, David was kicked out of the state hospital for attacking a staff worker. His mother had tried everything she knew with her son but was at her wits' end and did not feel she could maintain him safely in the home. The school district would not agree to pay for residential placement, stating that their day program was sufficient to meet his educational needs. And although he had been in minor scrapes with the law, no assault charges were filed against him for the state hospital incident, so juvenile probation did not have to become involved. There was no place for David to live.

CRCG finally came up with a plan whereby the young man was housed at the local juvenile detention center until a full diagnostic and treatment plan could be developed by the mental health system. The school district offered a half-day, individualized special education program. Juvenile probation picked up the tab for his residency in their facility despite the fact that he was not one of "their kids," i.e., eligible for services according to their agency criteria. Although the plan was a temporary one, it kept David safe and off the streets until the various agencies could make a better long-term plan. At the end of 3 months, two agencies agreed to pay for an out-of-community residential placement until David could be stabilized. Then he was transferred back into his home community to a therapeutic foster group home. Upon his return, the mental health system offered in-home family therapy, respite care, and case management. These solutions were achieved only because the various agencies cut through the bureaucratic red tape and offered needed services, regardless of "whose kid" David was.

One other exciting aspect of this system of care model is its emphasis on the school as the site of social services delivery. This is in keeping with a nationwide trend toward delivering a variety of health and human services through the schools. Support groups, social services, case management, nursing services, and individual, group, and family therapy are examples of services being delivered in schools by external agencies in many locales. This aspect of the model is exciting also because it places the special educator right in the hub of access to all services needed by children with emotional/behavioral disorders.

INTERAGENCY ROLE RELATIONSHIPS

To reiterate, my working model includes all these systems in *real* interagency collaboration that offers community-based and child-centered services. However, a specific model that works in one community will not necessarily work in another because of the tremendous variation in local resources. One of the strengths of the Texas Children's Mental Health Plan described earlier is that the state did not dictate what the programs should look like; rather, the state management team outlined a few priorities and then asked local community management teams to come up with a plan that would work for them, given their own resources and individual sets of circumstances. Similarly, it is difficult to define the role relationships between these systems that would be specific yet work in all communities. I think each community must do that for itself.

For example, let's consider the relationship between the education and mental health systems. In my local community, which is urban, there are a number of private, nonprofit agencies that have established histories of providing quality outpatient mental health services to children, adolescents, and their families in the area. And although it is changing rapidly, our local mental health authority historically has been unable to serve children on an outpatient basis on a large scale due to its funding mandates. So in our community, these private, nonprofit agencies took the lead in developing children's services. In addition to traditional, center-based services (e.g., the 50-minute therapy hour), they developed a variety of school-based programs, including case management, support groups, substance abuse prevention groups, and individual and family therapy. In contrast, in some other communities, especially rural ones, the local mental health center may be the only agency that offers outpatient children's services, and the services may only be offered at the center.

Taking the example a step further, service providers vary greatly even within the local community. In one of the property-rich local districts, there are counselors in the schools specifically to work with children identified through special education. In these schools, children with E/BD may receive a variety of mental health services by their own special education counselor funded by the school district. None of the private nonprofit agencies are offering school-based services in these schools because there is no need. But across town in a property-poor district, the agencies offer school-based services in a large number of the schools. So even within our local community, mental health service providers in the schools vary according to school district funding.

Special education and juvenile justice have had a different relationship over the years. Due to the social maladjustment exclusion clause in the federal definition, special education technically has been "off the hook" for working with juvenile offenders. However, special educators now seem to be recognizing that with no other population is the need greater for involving all systems. We have all been hearing—anecdotally, on the local news, and in published reports—about the increase in crimes, especially violent crimes, being committed by juveniles.

Educators cannot afford to say that this is a problem for the juvenile justice system alone to solve. The relationship between mental health problems, learning problems, and delinquency is well established: Almost one third of incarcerated juvenile offenders are estimated to have a disability. Many juvenile offenders suffer from the "hidden" disabilities, such as Attention-Deficit/Hyperactivity Disorder, learning disabilities, or mild retardation, that can contribute to their propensity for antisocial acts but may go unrecognized and untreated. And the majority of juveniles have serious academic problems, adding to the probability that they will never finish high school if left to their own devices. These are clearly educational problems.

At the very least, special education should get involved with juvenile justice to ensure that offenders with disabilities are being identified. Curry, Posluszny, and Kraska (1993) described a project designed to educate law enforcement, correctional, and probation personnel about offenders with disabilities. In addition to identification training, special educators can offer models for developing appropriate education plans tailored to the needs of individual offenders with disabilities. Based on the resources of the local community, education, mental health, and juvenile justice also should cooperatively develop plans for community-based programs after release.

We often are so pressed to deal with the incarceration/rehabilitation/treatment end of the spectrum that it is easy to forget the prevention end of the spectrum. In many locations, prevention involves yet another system, that of early childhood intervention. Much as Janet Reno has suggested that we need to address the root causes of violence in our society (e.g., poverty, unemployment), early childhood intervention programs are aimed at addressing the root causes of child abuse, neglect, and inadequate care. These programs focus on prenatal and postnatal education for parents who are in their teenage years, single, or of lower socioeconomic status (SES), as well as others whose children may be at risk for neglect, abuse, poor health and nutrition, lack of supervision, and other forms of inadequate care. There is also the Parents as Teachers initiative (Treffeisen, 1989), which is a parent education program operating in several states that hopes to reach *all* parents, regardless of supposed need or SES.

To summarize, I think that each community needs a working interagency group that not only plans cooperative programs but also cuts through the bureaucratic red tape and makes decisions for children on a case-by-case basis. Each community must define for itself what such a group looks like and how it can best function. Prevention should play a role.

THE INCREASE IN E/BD

I believe that the incidence of emotional/behavioral disorders is increasing. Although I have never been one to sit around and talk about how the current generation is going to hell in a handbasket, I have, in the last 2 to 3 years, become very concerned about the children and youth in this country. In fact, I am scared. We have all heard of the teens who have killed other teens for their cars or their tennis shoes. In my community a 15-year-old was arrested for shooting two men who were fishing, killing one and critically wounding the other. He reportedly was incensed at being arrested for the crime because he had a date that night that he wanted to keep.

Pick up a newspaper, read an article in your professional journal, listen to the local news. Here's a cross-section from what I have read in the past 3 or 4 months:

- Three million children (nearly one fourth of all children) live in poverty (Carnegie Foundation, 1994).
- The number of children in foster care rose by 50% in only 4 years (Carnegie Foundation, 1994).

- More than half of women with children under 1 year old are working (Carnegie Foundation, 1994).
- On any given day, 100,000 kids are estimated to be homeless; in addition, there are 1.3 million runaways or throwaways (minors whose parents don't want them) (Carnegie Foundation, 1994).
- More than half of America's children under 18 have spent part of their childhood in a single-parent home (Carnegie Foundation, 1994).
- On an average day, 6 children will be slain and 13 will take their own lives ("Stunted Growth," 1991).
- In a recent poll, 59% of 10- to 19-year-olds said that they could get a gun if they needed one (Harvard School of Public Health, 1993).
- Nine percent of secondary students reported having gone to school drunk in the past year ("Kids Addicted," 1993).
- Forty percent of ninth graders said that most or all of their friends drink alcohol regularly ("Kids Addicted," 1993).
- In a survey of high school seniors, 7.5% admitted to having tried crack cocaine and 31.8% admitted to having used some illegal drug ("Kids Addicted," 1993).
- For juveniles in Texas, there is a violent crime referral every 73 minutes, a property crime referral every 15 minutes, and an "other delinquent" referral every 14 minutes (Texas Juvenile Probation Commission, 1993).

These are all either contributors to or symptoms of the mental health problems that plague our children and youth today. In this context, I am referring to the 12% to 15% of children and youth loosely defined as needing mental health services, rather than the more rigorous designation of youth with emotional/behavioral disorders defined by our education system as the 2% needing special education. I think the lines between these two groups, which were never that distinct, are becoming even more blurred (thus the need for the interagency system of care model). And the recognition of the need to serve these children in schools has contributed to the rise in a variety of mental health services being offered to children who are "at risk," as well as those identified as E/BD.

In studying youth, antisocial behavior, and crime, the American Psychological Association (1993) identified four primary influences on the increase in violence and antisocial behavior: (a) easy access to firearms, (b) involvement with drugs and alcohol, (c) affiliation with gangs and antisocial groups, and (d) exposure to violence in the media. Causal influences include parenting failure and school failure.

In the face of these statistics and reports, it is tempting to say that the whole fabric of our society is unraveling and that its causes are so insidious and so pervasive that we can do nothing to prevent it. The good news is that I don't think this is true. Instead, I think that all professionals who work with these kids and their families must believe that we can make a difference and renew our commitment to do so. Many successful model programs and treatments are available across the country. Almost all of the successful programs not only treat the child or adolescent but also involve families, school personnel, and others in the community when possible. Examples are Walker's work with aggressive, antisocial children in the schools in Oregon (Walker, Colvin, & Ramsey, in press) and Goldstein's work with youth with conduct disorders in residential facilities and in the community (Goldstein & Glick, 1987; Goldstein, Glick, Irwin, Pask-McCartney, & Rubama, 1989). One indisputable fact has arisen from the work with these children and their families: The earlier the intervention, the better. When aggressive or antisocial behavior becomes an ingrained part of the child's repertoire, it is very difficult to change. In fact, some experts believe that intervention should occur by age 8, or else it becomes an issue of "symptom management" rather than of "cure" (Kazdin, 1987; Walker et al., in press). This guideline should influence the thinking of educators, who often want to avoid labeling a child until they are certain he or she is in trouble and needs help. By then, it may be too late.

As a final word, I would like to reemphasize the need not only for early intervention but also for prevention programs. I am convinced that quality home-based programs for parents at risk (teenage, single, lower SES) can begin to nibble away at some of the root causes of the increase in the numbers of children and youth who are mentally troubled.

THE YEAR 2000: WHAT THE FUTURE HOLDS

I can easily remember when the year 2000 evoked futuristic images (e.g., *2001 Space Odyssey, A Clockwork Orange*, the "Jetsons"); now it is merely a few years away. My crystal ball is a bit murky, but it suggests that the trends that will mark education in the year 2000 are the ones that have already begun to gather steam and the ones I have mentioned throughout this discussion. These trends include the following:

1. *Schools will become one-stop centers.* A variety of health and mental health services will be offered by numerous service providers in the schools as one-stop centers for these services become a reality.

2. *Children at risk will receive services.* Service providers will work with all children at risk, including but not limited to children in special education.
3. *Interagency collaborations will work.* For fiscal as well as philosophical reasons, communities will have functional interagency groups that make policy, set up programs, and make decisions that are child centered rather than agency driven.
4. *Conduct disorders will be recognized as E/BD.* Children and youth with conduct disorders will be included formally in the E/BD label of special education.
5. *Emphasis will be on prevention and family preservation.* The current trends toward prevention and family preservation will continue. As a result, more children and youth will be maintained in their homes and home communities.
6. *Out-of-home placements will be reduced.* There will be a reduced need for residential placements for children with E/BD as a result of trend 5. The number of small group homes for temporary placements will increase in communities large enough to fund and maintain them.

I would also hope that special education could escape the categorical restrictions and, along with the many other service providers in the schools, simply serve children who need help. The money (and time and effort) currently put into identification and eligibility procedures could be reallocated to direct services. This change, however, may take place beyond the year 2000, as I see much less progress toward decategorizing than I do toward the trends listed above.

REFERENCES

American Psychiatric Association. (1994). *Diagnostic and statistical manual of mental disorders* (4th ed.). Washington, DC: Author.

American Psychological Association. (1993). *Violence and youth.* Washington, DC: Author.

Apter, S. J. (1982). *Troubled children/troubled systems.* Elmsford, NY: Pergamon.

Bower, E. M. (1982). Defining emotional disturbance: Public policy and research. *Psychology in the Schools, 19,* 55–60.

Carnegie Foundation. (1994). *Starting points: Meeting the needs of our youngest children.* New York: Author.

Coleman, M. C. (1992). *Behavior disorders: Theory and practice.* Needham Heights, MA: Allyn & Bacon.

Cronkite, K. (1994). *On the edge of darkness.* New York: Doubleday.

Curry, K. L., Posluszny, M. P., & Kraska, S. L. (1993). Training criminal justice personnel to recognize offenders with disabilities. *OSERS News in Print, 5*(3), 4–8.

Federal Register. (1981, Jan 16). Washington, DC: U.S. Government Printing Office.

Fuchs, D., & Fuchs, L. S. (1994). Inclusive schools movement and the radicalization of special education reform. *Exceptional Children, 60,* 294–309.

Goldstein, A. P., Glick, B., Irwin, M. J., Pask-McCartney, C., & Rubama, I. (1989). *Reducing delinquency: Intervention in the community.* New York: Pergamon.

Goldstein, A., & Glick, B. (1987). *Aggression replacement training.* Champaign, IL: Research Press.

Greenberg, J. (1964). *I never promised you a rose garden.* New York: Holt, Rinehart, & Winston.

Grosenick, J. K., George, M. P., & George, H. L. (1987). A profile of school programs for the behavioral disordered: Twenty years after Morse, Cutler and Fink. *Behavioral Disorders, 12,* 159–168.

Harvard School of Public Health. (1993). *LH research poll: April 19–May 21.* Boston: Author.

Kazdin, A. (1987). *Conduct disorders in childhood and adolescence.* London: Sage.

Kesey, K. (1973). *One flew over the cuckoo's nest.* New York: Viking Press.

Kids addicted to drugs. (1993, September 19). *Austin American-Statesman,* pp. F1, F12–F13.

Stroul, B. A., & Friedman, R. M. (1986). *A system of care for severely emotionally disturbed children and youth.* Washington, DC: Georgetown University Child Development Center, CASSP Technical Assistance Center.

Stunted growth. (1991, May 25). *Austin American-Statesman,* pp. E1, E7.

Texas Juvenile Probation Commission. (1993). *Eleventh annual report: The second decade.* Austin, TX: Author.

Texas Mental Health Association. (1992). *The Texas children's mental health plan.* Austin, TX: Author.

Treffeisen, S. (1989). *Parents as teachers: Adaptation in child care centers* (Report No. 89-2). St. Louis: University of Missouri, Parents as Teachers National Center.

Wagner, M. (1991, September). *Drop outs with disabilities: What do we know? What can we do?* Menlo Park, CA: SRI International.

Walker, H. M., Colvin, G., & Ramsey, E. (in press). *Antisocial behavior in school: Strategies and best practices.* Pacific Grove, CA: Brooks-Cole.

WILLIAM H. EVANS
University of West Florida

William Evans is a professor of special education at the University of West Florida. He received his PhD from the University of Florida in the area of behavior disorders. In addition to higher education, Evans has taught students with emotional disabilities at the high school level in New Jersey and Florida. He also has served as the director of the diagnostic laboratory at the University of Florida. Evans currently is pursuing his interests in the assessment aspects of the labeling process on children and in the development of ecological interventions for students with emotional/behavioral disorders.

CHAPTER 5

Ethics, Data, and Dignity: Creating a Vision for Special Education

I was introduced to the field of behavioral disorders my first day of teaching. Like most first-year teachers, I was trained to teach social studies content in what now seems the most ridiculous and esoteric of ways. Here I was, armed with a class text and a curriculum guide, planted firmly in front of a group of students who would surely be on the edge of their seats to hear me expound on westward expansion from 1865 to the present. In reading the class roster, I soon discovered that most of the class did not speak English, and they cheerfully volunteered that each of them had failed at least two grades, had been arrested at least twice on felony charges, and had ruined the lives of four teachers the prior year. I had, to put it mildly, a horrible sense that I was about to be launched into a situation for which I was woefully unprepared. The gravity of the situation was driven home when a young man in the rear of the classroom pointed out to me that I had mispronounced his name and that he believed I was involved in an ongoing illicit relationship with my mother.

It was in this context that I began instruction. I was told that I had to use the assigned books and curriculum guide and that I should let my best judgment guide the course of instruction. No one told me how I was supposed to teach students who had huge academic and social deficits. No one provided any advice except "Keep your expectations low and try to survive." In the face of this challenge, I was an eager first-year teacher whose goal was to bring history to life, to make it a subject that was of vital interest to the students, to impart the story of the creation of a great and glorious country from 1865 to the present (which was then 1970). Within 2 months, I was forced to face the reality that I was teaching an irrelevant curriculum to students who could not read and whose behavior was roughly similar to that of professional wrestlers. Using the materials I had been given, I had in 2 short months taught everything I could teach them concerning American history from 1865 through John Kennedy's administration. I realized I had 8 more months left on my contract, and I either had to give up and resign or get a lot smarter real quickly. Fortunately, I chose the latter and learned to listen to my students. My real education was just beginning.

CURRENT STATUS OF E/BD EDUCATION

I have always been fascinated by puzzles, riddles, and things that were broken. Not that I could ever solve or fix them, but they nevertheless presented a challenge that was intriguing. For a somewhat similar reason, I was drawn to the field of behavioral disorders. I'm sure that, like many of my colleagues, my initial attraction to the field of behavioral disorders was driven by a desire to serve as a champion for the underdog and to right the social ills that plague society. These motivations are quickly tempered by social, economic, and institutional realities but, I'm sure, are never completely lost. The outcome in my case has been a growing realization that we are a science in its infancy and that we can in some small way positively change the course of some lives through either what we teach or how we live. I believe that humans are terribly resilient, that we see what we want to see, that behavior is lawful and is the result of complex environmental interactions, and that our interventions produce some effects that can be anticipated and others that are unanticipated.

Recently a neighbor and I roofed a shed that I had built in my backyard. I had a clear plan and pattern in mind, which I implemented on my side of the roof. The first couple of rows of shingles on his side adhered to my expectation of how the job should look. This gave way, however, to what could be described only as a well-intentioned but random pattern. The end result was that the shingles were functional but were applied in a somewhat haphazard manner on part of the roof. In much the same way with children identified as emotionally/behaviorally disordered (E/BD), a significant amount of what we do is well intentioned but is sometimes misguided or not thoroughly thought out.

A friend of mine, who has taken up the crucible of full inclusion for all children identified as E/BD, recently took me to task for the perceived failings of E/BD teachers. He referred to E/BD classrooms as "restrictive and oppressive" and said that the "educational program caused more harm than good." As are most dogmatic and impulsive thoughts, these assertions are, I believe, neither accurate nor fair. I spend a great deal of time in school districts working with administrators, visiting classrooms, and talking with teachers. I firmly believe that the vast majority of these professionals do an outstanding job for all of the right reasons, with resources that are extremely limited. Moreover, they are forced to implement programs in school districts with general education teachers and administrators who are sometimes openly hostile to E/BD and have little knowledge of special education or behavior management. Given this hostile environment, a lack of resources, and burgeoning numbers of students, I believe that most E/BD teachers and administrators do a remarkable job.

I am not suggesting that everything is perfect in E/BD. Quite the contrary, I do have some very real concerns about the programs that are provided to students who are E/BD and their families. Many of the programs that we offer under the title of E/BD suffer from institutional inertia. In other words, we do things a certain way because we have always done them that way. In my visits to schools, I see entirely too many stale educational programs designed solely to control the behavior of the students. These same programs often have little focus or direction to them. Every day teaching becomes little more than crisis management, with very little effort made at building social skills. The fact is that we are in desperate need of a system that will foster and reward creativity and prudent risk taking.

The problem with institutional inertia is made more serious by severe personnel shortages and increasing numbers of students identified as E/BD. The mathematics of this discrepancy between trained personnel and numbers of students in E/BD programs is compelling. We are simply awash in a swelling sea of identified deviance without an adequate supply of qualified professionals. We established a system that puts large numbers of untrained teachers in classrooms in which they are to serve students to whom we have given a potentially stigmatizing label. In this regard, the field is guilty of the worst type of segregation and discrimination. Most of us wouldn't take our cars to untrained mechanics or our pets to unqualified veterinarians, yet we perpetuate a system in which we first label a child as being "emotionally disturbed" and then all too often fail to provide a teacher who is even minimally qualified to meet the identified needs of the student.

I also am troubled by the frequency of use of what could charitably be called "untried and unproven" techniques. I have seen and been presented with far too many interventions that border on the bizarre. When these types of interventions are used, we are making a value statement that we will not use good sense, logic, and data to guide us in our interventions, but rather will rely on emotion, desperation, and ignorance. To do this with our own affairs is one thing, but it is quite another to subject a student to this muddled thinking.

MY WORKING DEFINITION OF E/BD

In answering this, it would perhaps be more useful for me to state that I believe that any definition of E/BD is constantly evolving. Emotional conditions are hypothetical constructs that we define into existence, and behaviors are identified as problems when they violate a standard of acceptability. Given this, it is quite apparent that definitions will change to accommodate changes in values and perceptions of truth. A useful definition must, however, address several factors:

1. The expectations and tolerance of the setting determines whether a behavior is identified as a problem.
2. Problems must be evaluated in terms of their severity, duration, and spread across the ecology of the student.
3. There must be some demonstrable effect of the problem related to school or personal/social performance.

While this list is not meant to be exhaustive, it does embody the salient factors that must be present in any definition. Further, it suggests that any definition must address the ecology of the setting and the interaction of behaviors. We often seem too eager to identify the student as disturbed when the setting, past history, and the behavior of others are really the culprits.

ADVANTAGES OVER THE CURRENT FEDERAL DEFINITION

The current federal definition pleases very few professionals. Identifying things by exclusion makes little sense, and most of us are not very good at determining internalized states. The current definition was a good place to start, but we now need to move the focus toward an ecological perspective in which the effect of environmental variables is carefully addressed and behavior is examined in relation to how closely it matches the demands of the setting.

We are caught in a dilemma in the definition of E/BD. In other areas of special education, tests can be given and performance can be judged in relation to preestablished criteria. We can argue about the reliability and validity of tests or the accuracy of the criteria, but nevertheless we can produce numbers, compare them to a criteria and then determine whether the student qualifies for a program in learning disabilities or mental retardation, for example. I am not suggesting that this is a great system, but it is comforting to professionals and easy to use, albeit mindlessly simplistic.

In E/BD, we have a fundamental problem related to identification. How much of a behavior is too much? How much in excess of the expectations of the setting does a behavior have to be in order to be considered deviant? How pervasive does the behavior problem have to be? In our attempt to deal with this problem, we interestingly have revealed our own limitations by trying to rely on rating scales and assessment instruments that produce comfortable numbers but fail to capture the essence of the student and the setting. The simple fact is that we cannot identify students on the basis of cutoff scores and must identify as we define E/BD by recognizing the need for a complete analysis of the environment of the student. This analysis must allow for a somewhat continuous collection of data over a period of time from multiple data sources and a variety of people in numerous settings.

THE DIFFERENCE BETWEEN ED AND BD

Several years ago I was working with a school district coordinator for emotionally handicapped (EH) programs who told me that she was concerned that we were putting too many students with behavior disorders into EH classrooms. She went on to say that EH programs were really designed for students with emotional problems rather than just behavior problems. When I asked her how she could tell the difference between behavior and emotional problems she indicated that students with emotional problems don't act out and verbalize their problems, whereas students with behavior problems are aggressive and act out. This distinction that the program coordinator tried to make, while grossly inaccurate, is often attempted by professionals.

The difficulty, of course, is in detection: How do you know if someone is experiencing an emotional problem? Since emotions are a hypothetical construct, we can't put our hands in someone's head and feel his or her psyche to determine if a problem exists. The projective tests we use are of unknown validity and meager reliability. Can or should we rely on people who are experiencing emotional problems to accurately and reliably remember and detail their difficulties? Can we tell the difference between behavior that is symptomatic of an internalized condition and that which is merely reflective of past patterns of conduct? We as humans are not very good at detecting our own internalized problems. This may account for the fact that a majority of the American population will seek counseling at some time during adulthood. If we have difficulty detecting our own internalized conditions, how could we realistically expect someone else who has less data and fewer opportunities to be more accurate?

The problem of detection of emotional problems is extraordinarily more difficult than we want to believe. This is not to say that there is not a distinction between BD and ED; there may be. Rather, we have defined both of these terms into existence and they describe an amorphous mass of conditions that are arbitrarily ascribed by convenience and philosophy to either ED or BD.

MEANINGFUL PARTS OF SCHOOL PROGRAMS

For educational programming to be effective, there must be, as Hewett has stated, an "orchestration of success," in which all parts of the educational program act in harmony. I do believe, however, that all E/BD programs should have the following components:

1. a curriculum that emphasizes instruction in social skills;
2. a curriculum that fosters the generalization of social skills in a variety of settings;
3. an academic curriculum that will enable students to gain access to the regular education program;
4. an academic/vocational program that will enable students to prepare adequately for the workplace;
5. a curriculum that will enhance the student's skill in self-mediation; and
6. an instructional program designed to broaden the student's knowledge of people, places, and activities.

Educational programs are not a "one size fits all" sort of experience. I do believe that all students need an educational program with these components, but some students need more of one element than another. Most social skills curricula only attempt to instruct students. While this is a necessary component, more attention needs to be given to the application and generalization of skills.

I also believe that we woefully miss the mark on teaching skills and application in self-mediation. If students with E/BD are to become functioning members of society, they must be given the tools to manage their own behavior separate from the efforts of teachers and therapists.

When visiting schools, I frequently notice that students in E/BD classes often have very limited knowledge of the world around them. They have few hobbies or interests and are rarely engaged in extracurricular activities. This, it seems to me, is tragic. When students' horizons are expanded, there is a greater opportunity for curriculum relevance, life enhancement, and reinforcement by naturally occurring events. If we want school and life to be exciting and not boring, then we need to create a learning environment that fosters excitement and the creation of new and appropriate interests.

INCLUSION

The wonderful thing about inclusion is that no one agrees on what it is, but almost everyone indicates that they support, understand, and practice it. There even seems to be differences of opinion and gradations of "full inclusion." The debate over inclusion is much like a debate about religion, with few facts but strident beliefs. The full inclusion side correctly notes that students with E/BD will be expected to be functioning members of society and, therefore, must have an educational program that reflects the inclusion that is to be expected in adult life. Other voices also note correctly that there are a number of students who need significant assistance with their emotions and behavior. I don't believe this debate would be as dramatic if we as a profession had successfully ameliorated students' emotional/behavioral problems and systematically reintegrated them into the mainstream.

The fact is that we put students into programs, collected the money, and did not have a systematic plan for terminating, reducing, or changing services. In short, students were placed into E/BD programs and never left. This, coupled with increasing numbers of students who were E/BD and at risk, created a situation that simply couldn't continue. Some simple logic needs to be applied to this problem. If students have unique needs, then there must be a variety of settings to meet those needs. We should not expect one curriculum or service delivery model—be it inclusive or restrictive—to be equally applicable to all students. There are times that students manifest behavior problems severe enough to warrant more restrictive settings. When this occurs there should be an earnest attempt to systematically move the student through a service delivery system that leads to inclusion. Such a system must be based on student competence but also must build tolerance and management skills in general education teachers.

We cannot talk about inclusion without addressing the question of teacher retraining. All too often inclusion simply focuses on the behavioral or social skills of the student. It is at least as important to increase the consultation and collaboration skills of E/BD teachers and positively affect tolerance, expectations, and behavior-management skills in general education administrators and teachers. We can train students in social and academic skills, but if we don't alter the things that go on in special and general education settings, inclusion will fail.

SERVICE DELIVERY MODEL

The entire array of service models and how they are conceptualized in a cascade or continuum of services must be rethought. Current models encourage professionals to place students into programs based on the severity of the student's problem. New models must be more ecologically based and consider student behavior as well as a host of other factors, such as environmental variables, expectations, setting demands, and teacher skills. The issue of service delivery and how it is conceptualized in a continuum will be a fundamental issue in the future. Clearly, students cannot and should not continue to be placed into E/BD programs and delivery models as they were in the past. We must develop models that will lead students to develop social competence and move them toward inclusion, while at the same time enhancing educational settings and the skills of teachers and administrators.

INCIDENCE OF E/BD

There are really two questions here: (a) Is there an increasing amount of deviance? and (b) Will the incidence rate of E/BD increase? The answer to both questions is certainly yes. Even a casual observer would have to note the changes that have occurred in acceptable standards of behavior over the past 30 years. Once adolescents were severely chastised if they read certain types of magazines. Now, however, with the flip of an electronic switch adolescents have access to a stream of consciousness that would have been unthinkable in previous years. What once was unacceptable now is accepted or at least tolerated. If you want proof of this insidious decline, watch a few talk shows and then you'll realize how we ended up with cultural icons such as "Beavis and Butthead."

This change in values has been accompanied by an increased awareness and acceptance of mental health services. I am certain that every television station in the nation carries several advertisements daily from hospitals and psychiatric facilities encouraging parents to obtain mental health services for their children who are experiencing behavior problems. In schools, we have successfully convinced teachers and administrators to identify students who have behavior problems and to place these students in programs that will address their behavioral and emotional needs. Schools have built upon this foundation and have thrown the net wider to identify "at-risk" students and create programs that meet their unique needs. Where once we had schools that taught students regardless of label, we now have institutions that have been balkanized to death. This change of values and heightened awareness have combined to unleash the genie from the bottle. It seems quite apparent that for the foreseeable future we will be faced with an ever-increasing number of students with E/BD and an exponentially increasing number of students referred for at-risk or dropout prevention programs.

COMPREHENSIVE SERVICE DELIVERY

The changing nature of service delivery models and declining mental health revenues will necessitate a corresponding change in the level and type of cooperation between agencies. Mental health, social service, education, and juvenile justice professionals have recognized for years that they must cooperate and communicate in providing services. Often this recognition translated into painfully little action and resulted in a wasteful overlapping of services and interagency bickering.

The increasing numbers of individuals needing services and the declining dollars have forced and will force agencies to become creative and expand their interagency efforts. This expanded interagency cooperation will, I believe, foster a level of creativity that has been sorely needed. Clearly, we can't incarcerate all juvenile offenders or put all students with behavior problems into E/BD classes. Therefore, schools and agencies will be forced to deal with problems in a more clever manner and develop alternative service delivery models that use the skills and resources of a variety of agencies. The danger, however, is that there will not be enough money available to fund even the clever projects.

THE FUTURE

Though predictions are often incorrect because of the effect of unanticipated events, I believe several trends will emerge in the coming years:

1. There will be an increasing interest in developing a comprehensive system of program delivery. After flirting with full inclusion as a sole method of program delivery, schools will develop an array of programs with varying degrees of restrictiveness but with a clearly thought-out and articulated system leading to inclusion. In some respects, the move toward full inclusion of students identified as E/BD will be viewed as one more social experiment that didn't quite work. But this experiment fortunately will not leave us as we were before but rather will force us to alter our service delivery options in order to provide more comprehensive services and a clear system that moves students toward inclusion.

2. In-service training models for teacher training in E/BD will become increasingly popular. University training programs will not be able to keep pace with the demand for E/BD teachers. This will necessitate a dramatic change in university programs and also will cause school districts to bond together to form in-service training programs that will certify teachers in E/BD. While this method of teacher training already enjoys some level of popularity, the numbers in such programs will grow dramatically. Ultimately, this new method of training will necessitate a new and closer relationship between universities

and public schools for the purpose of training. If this relationship is not developed, teacher training at all levels will suffer.

3. There will be a major change in the training of general and special education teachers and administrators. Inclusion and the changing nature of the school population will necessitate that general and special education teachers become adequately versed in ESOL (English speakers of other languages), collaboration, behavior management, and assessment. With this training will come a dramatic change in expectations and a growing realization that students identified as E/BD and at risk have a legitimate place in the general classroom.

4. Schools will develop curriculum options that will allow students to pursue a variety of programs while earning a high school degree. Currently, many states have enacted laws mandating that students must earn credits in advanced courses such as higher math, foreign language, and computer applications in order to receive a high school diploma. In these states, students essentially are denied any ability to take vocational courses and are forced into what amounts to a college prep program. When these curricular requirements are combined with minimum competency testing for graduation, a breathtaking dropout rate occurs. States will be forced to either accept extraordinarily high dropout rates or modify their programs to allow curricular options. As a matter of public policy, I believe that they will not accept high dropout rates but that they will move to establish comprehensive educational programs that allow students to earn vocational credits and receive a high school diploma.

5. Assessment practices in E/BD will change dramatically to address a more ecological focus. There is a growing realization that past methods of assessment and identification have been woefully inadequate. Given the changing demographics of the school population, there will be a move away from norm-referenced tests to assessment procedures that comprehensively examine the entire ecology of the student and his or her family.

The real test is not whether any of this or none of this will happen, but rather how we will respond to change. Change is inevitable, and it is clear that we cannot be successful in the future by trying to solve our problems as we have in the past. We have to adapt, be clever, and anticipate change.

STEVEN R. FORNESS
UCLA Neuropsychiatric Hospital

Steve Forness is a professor, chief of outpatient educational psychology, and inpatient school principal at the UCLA Neuropsychiatric Hospital. He is a fellow of both the American Association on Mental Retardation and the International Association for Research in Learning Disabilities, served previously as president of the Council for Children with Behavioral Disorders, and currently is on the DSM–IV committee on learning disorders. Forness also chairs the definition subcommittee of the National Mental Health and Special Education Coalition. He received his EdD from UCLA in 1968, was a Fulbright Scholar in Portugal in 1976, and was the recipient of the Council for Exceptional Children's Wallin Award in 1992.

CHAPTER 6

School Children with Emotional or Behavioral Disorders: Perspectives on Definition, Diagnosis, and Treatment

The field of emotional or behavioral disorders is one that has developed less evenly than other areas of special education, such as learning disabilities or mental retardation. Learning disabilities traditionally have been viewed, although somewhat mistakenly, as a single disorder; thus, programs in that area have been focused more clearly on a limited number of methods and procedures. Mental retardation has been viewed along a single continuum of developmental severity, and, although hundreds of different syndromes may contribute to mental retardation, programs for this disability are likewise limited to a relatively restricted range of curriculum options. Although there is still some disagreement, both of these disorders also have a much greater consensus as to definitional and diagnostic criteria, both within special education and in other related professions such as psychology or pediatrics.

The field of emotional or behavioral disorders, on the other hand, is a specialty that, like the study of mental retardation and learning disabilities, has focused on developmental and academic issues yet, at the same time, must give a certain priority to social or emotional issues as well. Emotional and behavioral disorders are less well understood and enjoy less agreement as to definition, cause, and treatment. There has therefore been an understandable tendency to identify only the children who are the most obviously or seriously disturbed in this category. The outcomes for children in this category are obviously less optimistic than for children in almost every other category of special education (Knitzer, Steinberg, & Fleisch, 1990).

My own introduction to the field of emotional or behavioral disorders emerged gradually from my original training and interests in learning disabilities and mental retardation. I was trained initially as a school psychologist and spent 2 years in classroom teaching that was required in order to become certified as a school psychologist. I gradually came to realize, however, that whatever school psychologists had to offer children in general classrooms with behavioral or learning disorders, it was, at least at that period in time, too little and too late. I therefore decided to enter a special education doctoral program. I focused on learning disabilities, since it was a relatively new and emerging field when I was in graduate school at UCLA in the late 1960s, but I subsequently was offered a position as a special education faculty member in a newly developed interdisciplinary training program in mental retardation. Although this program was located in the Department of Psychiatry at UCLA, it was viewed as relatively separate in most respects from the department's ongoing psychiatric treatment programs.

The overlap among learning disabilities, mental retardation, and emotional or behavioral disorders quickly began to interest me, as children referred to trainees in our mental retardation clinic were often on the IQ borderline between mild mental retardation and learning disabilities. Many also had emotional or behavioral disorders in addition to their learning problems. We subsequently began an educational psychology service in the outpatient psychiatric clinic to assist in diagnosing mild mental retardation or learning disabilities in children with emotional or behavioral disorders. I also was offered a chance to take over duties as principal of the inpatient school in the psychiatric hospital, since many of my special education and school psychology trainees had begun to work in that setting as well.

The inpatient school continues to accept a wide variety of children and adolescents with emotional or behavioral disorders, including many who also have learning disabilities, mental retardation, or other disabilities. This comorbidity with other disorders has always made it difficult to follow traditional special education teaching and placement approaches, because these patients do not fit easily into the usual categories of disability. These children also are admitted now for much briefer periods of hospitalization. Most now remain only 20 to 30 days.

Over the years, I have developed with my staff systematic approaches to organizing and delivering noncategorical special education services for children with emotional or behavioral disorders. These are individualized by readiness for classroom functioning based on each child's developmental or academic levels, type of curriculum materials needed, strategies needed for effective learning, intensity of teacher supervision or management, and type of reinforcers required for effective classroom motivation (Forness, 1977, 1983). This scheme has been used not only to organize and teach children in our own hospital school classrooms but also to gauge readiness for mainstreaming and to develop models for continuation of interventions and services in public schools (Forness, 1979; Forness & Kavale, 1991).

At the time I took over duties as principal of the inpatient school in the psychiatric hospital, Frank Hewett, one of my early mentors in graduate school and one of my closest friends in the field, was developing his "engineered classroom" and his "learning center" in the nearby Santa Monica schools. We collaborated on an introductory text that contained many of these ideas (Hewett & Forness, 1984).

THE DEFINITION PROBLEM

Having worked for more than a quarter century in this setting, I have had countless occasions to confront the problem of eligibility of children with emotional or behavioral disorders (E/BD) for special education, since most of our inpatients or outpatients return to general or special public school classrooms. We have studied not only how they fare in both the long and the short term (Forness & Barnes, 1981; Forness, Barnes, & Mordaunt, 1983; Forness & Caldon, 1980; Forness, Cronin, & Lewis, 1981; Linden & Forness, 1986) but also how their psychiatric disorder affects their eligibility (Barnes & Forness, 1982; Forness & Cantwell, 1982; Forness, Kavale, & Lopez, 1993; McGinnis & Forness, 1988; Sinclair, Forness, & Alexson, 1985).

It seems quite clear that the current definition of serious emotional disturbance (SED) has led to several problems. As I implied at the outset, the term *serious* makes this the only special education category in which only the most impaired will be considered for eligibility. This is comparable to telling parents of children with visual disabilities that only students who are blind and not students who are partially sighted qualify for services, in the hearing disabilities category that students who are deaf but not students who are hard of hearing may receive services, or in the area of mental retardation that only youngsters with severe and profound retardation are eligible but not those with mild or moderate retardation.

The definition (Cline, 1990) has several additional problems. It includes five criteria for eligibility. The first is an "inability to learn," which often confuses the SED definition with the learning disability (LD) definition. The second is an "inability to build or maintain satisfactory relationships with teachers or peers" (i.e., social adjustment problems), but the definition subsequently confuses matters by excluding children whose problems are considered merely "social maladjustment." These and the other three criteria (i.e., "inappropriate types of behavior or feelings," "pervasive mood of unhappiness," and "tendency to develop physical symptoms or fears") also require that a child be classified as a "type" before he or she can be found eligible. These types are based on a single study done more than 30 years ago in the Los Angeles County schools by the late Eli M. Bower and are no longer reflective of more recent educational research or current clinical diagnoses (Cline, 1990).

Many children also are excluded because their problems are considered to be "merely" conduct disorders or discipline problems; their actual underlying emotional disorders, such as depression or anxiety, are not recognized or identified as such, because "social maladjustment" problems become automatic exclusions. Most epidemiologic studies suggest that symptoms of conduct disorders are inextricably woven into symptoms of other psychiatric disorders such that very few children are referred to special education with "pure" conduct disorders (Forness, Kavale, King, & Kassari, in press). In a classic study on SED programs (Knitzer, Steinberg, & Fleisch, 1990), Knitzer found no significant difference in percentage of children served between those states using the term *behaviorally disordered* in their definition (N = 10) and those using only *emotionally disturbed* (N = 13). Some 29 states no longer exclude children with "social maladjustment" as the federal definition requires, presumably because of the impossibility of reliably distinguishing "social" from "emotional" maladjustment.

THE DEFINITION PROCESS

As an early response to these and related issues, the Council for Children with Behavioral Disorders (CCBD), a subdivision of the Council for Exceptional Children (CEC), published position papers on terminology and on identification (CCBD, 1984, 1987). As president of CCBD in 1988, I felt it was time to draft a substitute terminology (*emotional or behavioral disorders*) and an accompanying definition that CCBD reviewed and revised in an ongoing process over the next year. CCBD then approved this revised E/BD draft terminology and definition (CCBD, 1989). This draft was submitted to the National Mental Health and Special Education Coalition, composed at the time of 30 different education, mental health, advocacy, and parent associations (Forness, 1988). In January and June of 1990, the Coalition's task force on definition (composed of 20 members of the coalition) met in Washington, DC, and further reviewed and revised the E/BD draft. This E/BD draft then was submitted to a meeting of the full coalition in October of 1990 and approved more or less in its current form. A full discussion of the new E/BD definition was published (Forness & Knitzer, 1992).

In 1991 and 1992, there were several meetings and phone contacts between members of the Coalition and staff members of the relevant House and Senate subcommittees. There were likewise similar contacts with a wide range of other stakeholders in education and mental health, including members from associations or groups representing ethnically diverse populations such as NAACP and La Raza. Although the terminology and definition change originally was scheduled as an amendment to pending legislation in the summer of 1992 and quick passage was expected, the National Association of State Boards of Education objected at the last minute. This was mainly due to fears that large numbers of children previously unserved in this category would now have to be included in special education at great cost to states and local districts. It was clear, however, that the proposed E/BD terminology and definition had nonetheless been "vetted" in a historically unique process and that it enjoyed widespread support in the special education and mental health communities. It also was clear that families of children with this disorder had both been included in this process and were supportive of its outcome.

For this reason, Congress compromised by directing the U.S. Department of Education to publish a "notice of inquiry" in the *Federal Register* (February 10, 1993) asking for comments on the advisability of changing to the new E/BD definition and terminology in IDEA. Approximately 1,200 responses were received, among the largest number of responses ever received from such a notice of inquiry. As of this writing, the report analyzing these responses has not yet been submitted to Congress for its action.

THE E/BD DEFINITION

The text of the E/BD definition as published in the notice of inquiry is as follows:

> (1) The term "emotional or behavioral disorder" means a disability that is characterized by behavioral or emotional response in school programs so different from appropriate age, cultural, or ethnic norms that the responses adversely affect educational performance, including academic, social, vocational or personal skills; more than a temporary, expected response to stressful events in the environment; consistently exhibited in two different settings, at least one of which is school-related; and unresponsive to direct intervention applied in general education, or the condition of a child is such that general education interventions would be insufficient.
>
> The term includes such a disability that co-exists with other disabilities.
>
> The term includes a schizophrenic disorder, affective disorder, anxiety disorder, or other sustained disorder of conduct or adjustment, affecting a child if the disorder affects educational performance as described in paragraph (1). (*Federal Register*, February 10, 1993, p. 7938)

There are a number of major advantages and improvements in this new terminology and definition. It not only focuses directly on the child's responses in school settings and places this response in the context of appropriate age, ethnic, and cultural norms but also has four qualifying statements that ensure that only children who appropriately qualify will be eligible. The four additional qualifying statements (a) indicate that E/BD is more than a temporary, expected response to stressors and would persist even with individualized (prereferral) interventions; (b) require eligibility to be based on multiple sources of data gathered in more than one school setting; (c) indicate that E/BD can coexist with other disabling conditions; and (d) include a listing of examples of some (but not all) current mental health diagnoses that *could* make a student eligible *if* educational performance is also impaired, thus allowing for greater coordination with other agencies that can provide related services in addition to the school.

The proposed definition has several other advantages over the current SED definition in that the E/BD definition (a) emphasizes a two-step diagnostic process essentially similar to that for the LD and mental retardation (MR) categories; (b) includes ethnic or cultural considerations in identification; (c) stresses the need for multiple sources of case data; (d) enhances the possibility of early identification and intervention; (e) lists examples of clinical diagnoses that *could* create eligibility *if* educational performance is impaired, so as to facilitate referrals to and from mental health, but does not necessarily require such diagnoses; and (f) does not require meaningless distinctions between social and emotional maladjustment, distinctions that often waste diagnostic resources when it is already clear that serious problems exist.

Another potential advantage is that Head Start has already adopted a version of the E/BD definition in its recently revised disability regulations. The Head Start definition is as follows:

> (a) An emotional/behavioral disorder is a condition in which a child's behavioral or emotional responses are so different from those of the generally accepted, age-appropriate norms of children with the same ethnic or cultural background as to result in significant impairment in social relationships, self-care, educational progress or classroom behavior. A child is classified as having an emotional/behavioral disorder who exhibits one or more of the following characteristics with such frequency, intensity, or duration as to require intervention:
>
> (1) Seriously delayed social development including an inability to build or maintain satisfactory (age appropriate) interpersonal relationships with peers or adults (e.g., avoids playing with peers);
>
> (2) Inappropriate behavior (e.g., dangerously aggressive toward others, self-destructive, severely withdrawn, noncommunicative);
>
> (3) A general pervasive mood of unhappiness or depression, or evidence of excessive anxiety or fears (e.g., frequent crying episodes, constant need for reassurance); or
>
> (4) Has a professional diagnosis of serious emotional disturbance.
>
> (b) The eligibility decision must be based on multiple sources of data, including assessment of the child's behavior or emotional functioning in multiple settings.
>
> (c) The evaluation process must include a review of the child's regular Head Start physical examination to eliminate the possibility of misdiagnosis due to an underlying physical condition (*Federal Register*, January 21, 1993, p. 5501).

Since Head Start is perhaps the largest single referral source for children identified for special education in the early years, this represents a significant source of support for the new definition (Forness & Finn, 1993).

SCHOOL PROGRAMS FOR CHILDREN WITH E/BD

There has been valid criticism of the current state of E/BD programs (Knitzer, Steinberg, & Fleisch, 1990). It is clear, however, that this criticism is tempered by the fact that it is *not* that we do not know how to run good and effective programs but that poor funding and lack of knowledge dissemination has led to poorly conceived and poorly run school programs for many children with E/BD (Kauffman et al., 1991). As I discussed at the outset of this chapter, there is a broader mandate not only to teach these children but also to manage and care for their emotional and behavioral well-being that is not present to the same extent in other categories of special education. This means that collaboration with professionals from mental health, social welfare, health, and juvenile justice systems is perhaps even more critical in working with children with E/BD than it is in any other category (Nelson & Pearson, 1991; Wolford, Nelson, Rutherford, & Forness, 1993).

My conception of a model program for children with E/BD is based on a *full* continuum of services but emphasizes delivery of services in a child's local school whenever possible. There will still be a need for acute hospital care for crisis episodes and for residential settings when family or therapeutic foster care is not available or not able to effectively manage or provide care for a child at certain times in his or her life. Whenever possible, however, a range of various service agencies should be able, with careful planning and collaboration, to wrap such care around a troubled child and his or her family.

Within such a system of care, the local school program would focus on systematic early identification (Walker et al., 1988). Once identified, the child with, or at risk for, E/BD would be placed in a noncategorical learning center with children having a range of disabilities. It is clear that emotional or behavioral problems are highly associated with other categories of disability in special education and that E/BD children frequently have learning or developmental disorders as well (Forness & Polloway, 1987; Forness & Sinclair, 1990; San Miguel, Forness, & Kavale, in press). Each local school would have such a learning center or at least a satellite version, and it would be largely dependent on a highly trained special education teacher.

The teacher in this system might have direct or indirect responsibility for perhaps two or more times the number of children ordinarily assigned to a special class teacher, plus at least some responsibility for training and supervising a teacher consultation team, composed of general classroom teachers, as the first line of referral and intervention. In the learning center would be a number of paraprofessionals or assistant teachers, who are given far more responsibility than is ordinarily assigned to classroom aides. They would do most of the hands-on daily teaching, while the master special education teacher makes daily rounds and sees children only for brief sessions, much like a chief of service in a teaching hospital. Children could be included in general classrooms but have the center as a backup.

Within the learning center would be a range of curriculum materials and technologies that might be needed to serve such a disparate special education population, with perhaps separate teaching areas for children with multiple disabling conditions or quite severe behavioral problems that prove to be less than adequately manageable around other children who cannot protect themselves. Although curriculum-based assessment, specialized teaching, and supervision of routine hands-on teaching would be ongoing roles for the master teacher *within* the learning center, periodic outside responsibilities would involve consulting with general class teachers and coordinating services with outside agencies. The learning center concept, with its emphasis on teacher identification and delivery of service, should free school psychologists from current identification and diagnostic preoccupations to provide other, more relevant services more in keeping with the psychological training and tradition, such as ongoing individual or group therapy, family therapy, monitoring of effectiveness of psychotropic medication, and so forth.

As I have noted, most aspects of this learning center model were developed from my experience running such a noncategorical program in a hospital setting and developing it for further use in public school settings (Forness, 1977, 1983; Forness & Kavale, 1991; Hewett & Forness, 1984). Forness and Kavale (1989) and Mattison and Forness (in press) described the relationship and role of other service providers in relation to the school.

CONCLUSION

In most cases, school currently has the bulk of responsibility for children with E/BD because it is the only agency with a continuous mandate to serve children regardless of budget cuts, lack of resources, or problems in training personnel. As the year 2000 approaches, however, there are a variety of possible changes that I foresee. Rather than being the lead agency, as it now seems to be for children in the school years, school increasingly will assume a role as but one of many collaborating agencies. This school-age model will become similar to that of interagency collaboration under Public Law 99-457 for infants, toddlers, and preschoolers. Instead of an individual family service plan for preschool, an individual educational plan for school, an individual treatment plan for mental health, and so forth, there will very likely be a comprehensive individual plan that all involved agencies will sign onto and that will follow the child not just from agency to agency but from one developmental stage to the next. My recent experience in psychopharmacologic research (Forness, Swanson, Cantwell, Guthrie, & Sena, 1992; Forness, Swanson, Cantwell, Youpa, & Hanna, 1992) also has convinced me that psychotropic medication will play an increasingly important if not a primary role in intervention for children with emotional or behavioral disorders. The same might be said for the role that genetic screen will begin to play in early identification (Jensen et al., 1993). The so-called new behavioral disorders associated with prenatal substance abuse, traumatic brain injury, or Fragile X syndrome also will dictate a more significant role for health services as well (Forness & Kavale, in press). As these new developments begin to take hold, it seems clear that school will continue to be an important link in the service system but that other agencies will assume a much greater share in the collaborative network of care for children with emotional or behavioral disorders.

REFERENCES

Barnes, T., & Forness, S. R. (1982). Learning characteristics of children and adolescents with various psychiatric diagnoses. *Monographs in Behavioral Disorders, 5,* 32–41.

Cline, D. H. (1990). A legal analysis of policy initiatives to exclude handicapped/disruptive students from special education. *Behavioral Disorders, 15,* 159–173.

Council for Children with Behavioral Disorders. (1984). *Position paper on substituting "behaviorally disordered" for "seriously emotionally disturbed" as a descriptor term for children and youth handicapped by behavior.* Reston, VA: Author.

Council for Children with Behavioral Disorders. (1987). *Position paper on identification of students with behavioral disorders.* Reston, VA: Author.

Council for Children with Behavioral Disorders. (1989). *A proposed definition and terminology to replace "serious emotional disturbance" in Education of the Handicapped Act.* Reston, VA: Author.

Federal Register. (1993, January 21). Washington, DC: U.S. Government Printing Office.

Federal Register. (1993, February 10). Washington, DC: U.S. Government Printing Office.

Forness, S. R. (1977). A transition model for placement of handicapped children in regular and special classes. *Contemporary Educational Psychology, 2,* 37–49.

Forness, S. R. (1979). Clinical criteria for mainstreaming mildly handicapped children. *Psychology in the Schools, 16,* 508–514.

Forness, S. R. (1983). Diagnostic schooling for children or adolescents with behavior disorders. *Behavioral Disorders, 8,* 176–190.

Forness, S. R. (1988). Planning for the needs of children with serious emotional disturbance: The national special education and mental health coalition. *Behavioral Disorders, 13,* 127–133.

Forness, S. R., & Barnes, T. (1981). School follow-up of adolescents treated in a psychiatric hospital. *Child Psychiatry and Human Development, 11,* 179–185.

Forness, S. R., Barnes, T., & Mordaunt, J. M. (1983). Brief psychiatric hospitalization: A study of its effects on special education placement. *Monographs in Behavioral Disorders, 6,* 66–75.

Forness, S. R., & Caldon, P. (1980). Subsequent school adjustment of children and adolescents discharged from a psychiatric hospital as a function of length of stay. *Journal for Special Educators, 17,* 4–9.

Forness, S. R., & Cantwell, D. P. (1982). DSM III psychiatric diagnoses and special education categories. *Journal of Special Education, 6,* 49–63.

Forness, S. R., Cronin, C., & Lewis, L. (1981). Prediction of post-discharge school adjustment from social and academic gains made during psychiatric hospitalization. *Monographs in Behavioral Disorders, 4,* 70–77.

Forness, S. R., & Finn, D. (1993). Screening children in Head Start for emotional or behavioral disorders. *Monographs in Behavioral Disorders, 16,* 6–14.

Forness, S. R., & Kavale, K. A. (1989). Identification and diagnostic issues in special education: A status report for child psychiatrists. *Child Psychiatry and Human Development, 19,* 279–301.

Forness, S. R., & Kavale, K. A. (1991). School psychologists' roles and functions: Integration into the regular classroom. In G. Stoner, M. Shinn, & H. Walker (Eds.), *Interventions for achievement and behavior problems* (pp. 21–36). Washington, DC: National Association of School Psychologists.

Forness, S. R., & Kavale, K. A. (in press). The balkanization of special education: Proliferation of categories for new behavioral disorders. *Education and Treatment of Children.*

Forness, S. R., Kavale, K. A., King, B. H., & Kassari, C. (in press). Simple versus complex conduct disorders: Identification and phenomenology. *Behavioral Disorders.*

Forness, S. R., Kavale, K. A., & Lopez, M. (1993). Conduct disorders in school: Special education eligibility and co-morbidity. *Journal of Emotional and Behavioral Disorders, 1,* 101–108.

Forness, S. R., & Knitzer, J. (1992). A new proposed definition and terminology to replace "serious emotional disturbance" in Individuals with Disabilities Education Act. *School Psychology Review, 21,* 12–20.

Forness, S. R., & Polloway, E. (1987). Physical and psychiatric diagnoses of pupils with mild mental retardation currently being referred by schools for related services. *Education and Training of the Mentally Retarded, 22,* 221–228.

Forness, S. R., & Sinclair, E. (1990). Learning disabilities in clinical depression. In H. L. Swanson & B. Keogh (Eds.), *Learning disabilities: Theoretical and research issues* (pp. 315–332). Hillsdale, NJ: Lawrence Erlbaum.

Forness, S. R., Swanson, J. M., Cantwell, D. P., Guthrie, D., & Sena, R. (1992). Response to stimulant medication across six measures of school-related performance in children with ADHD and disruptive behavior. *Behavioral Disorders, 18*, 42–53.

Forness, S. R., Swanson, D. M., Cantwell, D. P., Youpa, D., & Hanna, G. (1992). Stimulant medication and reading performance: Follow-up on sustained dose in hyperactive boys with and without conduct disorders. *Journal of Learning Disabilities, 25*, 115–123.

Hewett, F. M., & Forness, S. R. (1984). *Education of exceptional learners* (3rd ed.). Boston: Allyn & Bacon.

Jensen, P. S., Koretz, D., Locke, B. Z., Schneider, S., Radke-Yarrow, M., Richters, J. E., & Rumsey, J. M. (1993). Child and adolescent psychopathology research: Problems and prospects for the 1990s. *Journal of Abnormal Child Psychology, 21*, 551–580.

Kauffman, J. M., Lloyd, J. W., Cooke, L., Cullinan, D., Epstein, M. H., Forness, S. R., Hallahan, D., Nelson, C. M., Polsgrove, L., Strain, P., Sabornie, E. J., & Walker H. M. (1991). Problems and prospects in special education and related services for children with emotional and behavioral disorders. *Behavioral Disorders, 16*, 299–313.

Knitzer, J., Steinberg, A., & Fleisch, B. (1990). *At the schoolhouse door: An examination of programs and policies for children with behavioral and emotional problems.* New York: Bank Street College of Education.

Linden, B., & Forness, S. R. (1986). Post-school adjustment of mentally retarded persons with psychiatric disorders: A ten-year follow-up. *Education and Training of the Mentally Retarded, 21*, 157–164.

Mattison, R. E., & Forness, S. R. (in press). The role of psychiatric and other mental health services in special education placement decisions for children with emotional or behavioral disorders. In J. M. Kauffman, J. W. Lloyd, T. A. Astuto, & D. P. Hallahan (Eds.), *Issues in educational placement of children with emotional or behavioral disorders.* Hillsdale, NJ: Lawrence Erlbaum.

McGinnis, E., & Forness, S. R. (1988). Psychiatric diagnosis: A further test of the special education eligibility hypothesis. *Monographs in Behavioral Disorders, 11*, 3–10.

Nelson, C. M., & Pearson, C. B. (1991). *Integrating services for children and youth with emotional and behavioral disorders.* Reston, VA: The Council for Exceptional Children.

San Miguel, S. K., Forness, S. R., & Kavale, K. A. (in press). Social skills deficits and learning disabilities: The psychiatric comorbidity hypothesis. *Learning Disability Quarterly*.

Sinclair, E., Forness, S. R., & Alexson, J. (1985). Psychiatric diagnosis: A study of its relationship to school needs. *Journal of Special Education, 19*, 333–344.

Walker, H. M., Severson, H., Stiller, B., William, G., Haring, N., Shinn, M., & Todis, B. (1988). Systematic screening of pupils in elementary age range at risk for behavioral disorders: Development and trial testing for a multiple gating model. *Remedial and Special Education, 9*(3), 8–14.

Wolford, B., Nelson, C. M., Rutherford, R., & Forness, S. R. (1993). *Developing collaborative systems for troubled youth: Executive summary.* Richmond, KY: National Coalition for Juvenile Justice System.

ROBERT A. GABLE
Old Dominion University

Robert Gable is eminent professor of special education at Old Dominion University. He began his career as a teacher of students with severe learning and behavior disorders, served as principal of two special education programs, and earned his PhD in special education from George Peabody College of Vanderbilt University. Gable has conducted numerous inservice programs and workshops and serves as consultant to various public and private schools throughout the United States and abroad. Gable has published over 125 journal articles, monographs, book chapters, and books. He also serves as executive editor, associate editor, consulting editor, or reviewer for such professional journals as Behavior Disorders, Education and Treatment of Children, Exceptional Children, Journal of Emotional and Behavioral Disorders, *and* Preventing School Failure.

CHAPTER 7

A Perspective on the Field of Emotional/Behavioral Disorders

In 1966, at the conclusion of a prolonged and otherwise undistinguished undergraduate career, I had the chance to teach children and adolescents diagnosed as "severe emotionally disturbed" in the children's unit of a state mental hospital in Allentown, Pennsylvania. The trouble was that I was not prepared to teach special education, having received a degree in art education from Kutztown University in Pennsylvania. Faced with myriad questions, I was compelled to read extensively, anything related to the education and treatment of children and adolescents who are emotionally disturbed, and to take additional course work in this area. This culminated in a master's degree in special education, with specialization in severe emotional disturbances at Marywood College in Pennsylvania.

At about the same time, I was given the opportunity to establish a special education program within a residential treatment center. In struggling to do so, I relied heavily on a behavioral approach, especially the early work of Richard Whelan, Frank Hewett, Lakin Phillips, and Norris Haring, in an attempt to create a coordinated education and treatment effort. Next, I spent 2 forgettable years in state government, which caused me to pursue a doctorate in special education at George Peabody College of Vanderbilt University. I spent time in the Regional Intervention Program (RIP) and Cumberland House (ReED). I worked closely with Dick Shores, Joe Stowitschek, Jo Hendrickson, Bob Day, Chuck Salzberg, Mary Margaret Kerr, Phil Strain, and Joe Cunningham, among others. It was a remarkable experience, to which I am indebted for much of what I have done on behalf of students with emotional/behavioral disorders (E/BD).

CURRENT STATUS OF E/BD EDUCATION

Public education is in transition. Fueled by a spade of reports critical of American schooling, a succession of reform initiatives now exert powerful influence over virtually every aspect of public education, including special education. Today, there is growing sentiment in some quarters that much of what constitutes special education is fragmented, worthless, and actually detrimental to students with disabilities. Some reform zealots are even calling for the dissolution of special education.

Many of us recognize that some special education practices are flawed and that sometimes there is little that distinguishes programs because of the restrictiveness of the setting. We accept that we must correct this situation. However, policy decisions stemming from various reform movements pose a real danger to students with disabilities, especially students with E/BD. Some reformers seem to assume that students with disabilities make up a homogeneous group that can be transferred unilaterally from more to less restrictive educational settings and served according to the same instructional arrangements. Mounting pressure to conform to the doctrine of "least restrictive environment" has lead to a growing number of students with E/BD receiving at least a portion of their instruction in the general classroom. Unfortunately, many of these students fail to sustain a pattern of acceptable general classroom learning or adjustment. A number of factors contribute to that failure.

The so-called attributional assumptions general educators hold regarding causality and stability of students' emotional or behavioral problems and their views on the severity, contagion, and manageability of the problem separate the E/BD population from other categories of exceptionality. Accordingly, students who evidence maladaptive behavior—especially those who engage in bouts of noncompliance, acting out, and aggression—are among the least acceptable candidates for general classroom reintegration. Most general educators voice strong opposition to their general classroom integration. It may be reassuring to some teachers and administrators to know that attempts to indiscriminately place a student with disabilities in the general classroom may conflict with their federal and civil rights, in that IDEA is clear on the issue of decision making based on individual need, along with the preservation of a continuum of service delivery options.

A WORKING DEFINITION OF E/BD

In *As I Lay Dying*, William Faulkner (1930) wrote that it's not so much what a person does but the way the majority of people are looking at him when he does it that defines who is and who is not crazy. The way we conceptualize individual differences is an outgrowth of social norms, standards, and prohibitions; socially sanctioned decision makers decide what behavior is acceptable and what is not. That some children and adolescents engage in behavior that distinguishes them from the majority of their peers is not in dispute. However, judgments regarding the behavior of individuals—decisions about what constitutes deviance—are, as J. L.

Simmons (1969, p. 4) described, in the "eye of the beholder." These decisions are shaped by ethnic and cultural norms, environment, personal experience, age and gender expectations, and so forth.

At present, I know of no satisfactory definition with which to classify students variously referred to as *seriously emotionally disturbed, emotionally impaired, behavior disordered,* or *emotionally/behaviorally disordered.* Our current definition contains five areas in which problems may be evidenced (e.g., an inability to learn, inappropriate behavior, etc.). Difficulty arises when we attempt to determine exactly what is meant by phrases such as *to a marked degree* or *over a period of time.* The speculative nature of these terms makes any decision subject to wide interpretation and exploitation. Given the fact that there are many legitimate reasons to disagree over what is acceptable versus unacceptable behavior, some degree of subjectivity is inevitable.

There are a lot of reasons why so little unanimity exists regarding a definition of *severe emotional disturbances* (SED), not the least of which is that these students cross paths with many professionals (e.g., educators, physicians, psychologists, lawyers, social workers). Each of these disciplines espouses a different conceptualization of the problem, engages in its own evaluation procedures, and advocates a specific treatment. Still, the absence of an acceptable definition serves only to hinder efforts to better serve this population of students.

During the past several years, a National Mental Health and Special Education Coalition, composed of representatives from various professions, has sought to remedy that situation. Some of the changes in definition under discussion would make clearer the criteria for eligibility, focus greater attention on educational issues, be more reflective of accumulated research and, in turn, facilitate establishment of a coherent body of information and boost our ability to learn from it.

The language of the proposed definition includes concepts such as *sustained disturbances of conduct, attention or adjustment* (Forness & Knitzer, 1992), which has raised philosophical, budgetary, and programmatic concerns among some professionals. Critics insist that these kinds of changes in terminology would open up the floodgates, compelling the public schools to provide services to a substantially larger population of students. While underidentification of students with E/BD is a long-standing issue, I know of no evidence to support the assertion that the number of students would grow as a function of the proposed definition. Even so, because of the strong opposition to the revision of the present definition, a functional definition of E/BD remains more a promise than a reality.

DIMENSIONALITIES OF A DEFINITION OF E/BD

The often contentious debate over definition appears to obscure the fact that eligibility and placement are two separate issues; the former essentially is an administrative function, separate from any subsequent program decisions. The definition of emotional/behavioral disorders should serve as a means of entrance to a system of service delivery options; accordingly, it makes sense to place emphasis on language that relates to the function of education. To be useful, a definition of E/BD should (a) require multiple sources of data on an individual's functioning, gathered within and across settings; (b) differentiate students according to various criteria that are socially valid; and (c) facilitate establishment of a set of pupil-specific treatment options. I suspect that, given the arbitrary nature of decisions about human behavior, it is doubtful that we will arrive at a definition acceptable to everyone.

ED AND BD: ONE AND THE SAME?

The debate over terminology as it relates to distinctions between emotional disorders and behavioral disorders is nothing new. Even so, it is a major point of disagreement among those contesting the revision of our current definition of severe emotional disturbances. One version of the proposed definition supported by the Council for Children with Behavioral Disorders (CCBD; 1984) refers to "behavioral or emotional responses" of an individual. However, it is no surprise that persons from various professional disciplines would view the same types of disorders differently, with regard to both causality and treatment. It is more than a simple matter of semantics; placing importance on observable behavior rather than something that is unobservable enables us to delineate the objectives of instruction and to determine an appropriate intervention. Accumulated research and my own experience suggests that there can be considerable overlap between the internalized (e.g., depression, withdrawal, anxiety) and the externalized behaviors (e.g., noncompliance, verbal/physical aggression) manifested by students with emotional/behavioral disorders. While emotional conflicts and behavior problems are not necessarily synonymous, there is some indication that they can be dealt with through the use of comparable interventions.

MEANINGFUL EDUCATIONAL EXPERIENCES FOR STUDENTS WITH E/BD

Specifying precisely what constitutes a meaningful educational experience for students with emotional/behavioral disorders is always a challenge. We know that there is little justification for simply managing problem behavior while paying scant attention to or ignoring altogether academic instruction. I routinely invite students to find a journal article in which the imposition of some kind of behavioral control spontaneously produced academic gains in students with E/BD. My intent is to underscore the importance of providing a complete program of quality instruction, to decrease the likelihood that improper curricular placement, poor planning and instruction, or inconsistent management will cause a student to "act out" to escape a punishing classroom situation.

Quality programming begins with curriculum-based evaluation and is sustained through sound decision making that flows from a comprehensive system for data collection and evaluation. I find that too few teachers plan systematically for daily instruction; even fewer teachers map out strategies to facilitate maintenance and generalization of that instruction. The relationship between a student's presenting problems and the program of treatment is not always apparent. Further, the criterion against which teachers judge pupil performance may be ill chosen. In short, precious time may be squandered in the pursuit of a misguided program of instruction.

Teaching and learning are reciprocal acts. Teacher and pupil interactions are predisposed to co-vary as a function of the behavior of the other: A teacher loudly reprimands a student and the student shrinks from further interactions. The use of criticism over praise is but one flawed practice. Numerous classroom studies document that there is a discrepancy between what we preach and what we practice, between our knowledge of what constitutes "quality instruction" and our ability to put that knowledge into practice.

We know that it is essential to "engineer" the physical environment (on the basis of the dominant characteristics of the classroom population to arrange the desks and chairs, bookcases, tables, and so on) both to control and to set the stage for various occurrences. For example, the separation of student work areas probably would be advisable in a classroom populated by acting out students, whereas close proximity of student desks might be one way to facilitate appropriate social initiations among withdrawn children. Furthermore, successful teachers establish a routine, communicate it and their expectations to students, restrict noninstructional activities, and are careful to regulate student transitions from one instructional activity or setting to another.

As I suggest in Figure 7.1, a comprehensive management and instructional package should consist of whole group, partial group, and pupil-specific strategies. It should reflect the severity of the presenting problems and the complexity and intrusiveness of their treatment. Finally, it is necessary to assess not only student performance but also teacher behavior, to ensure that we remain faithful to the principles of quality instruction.

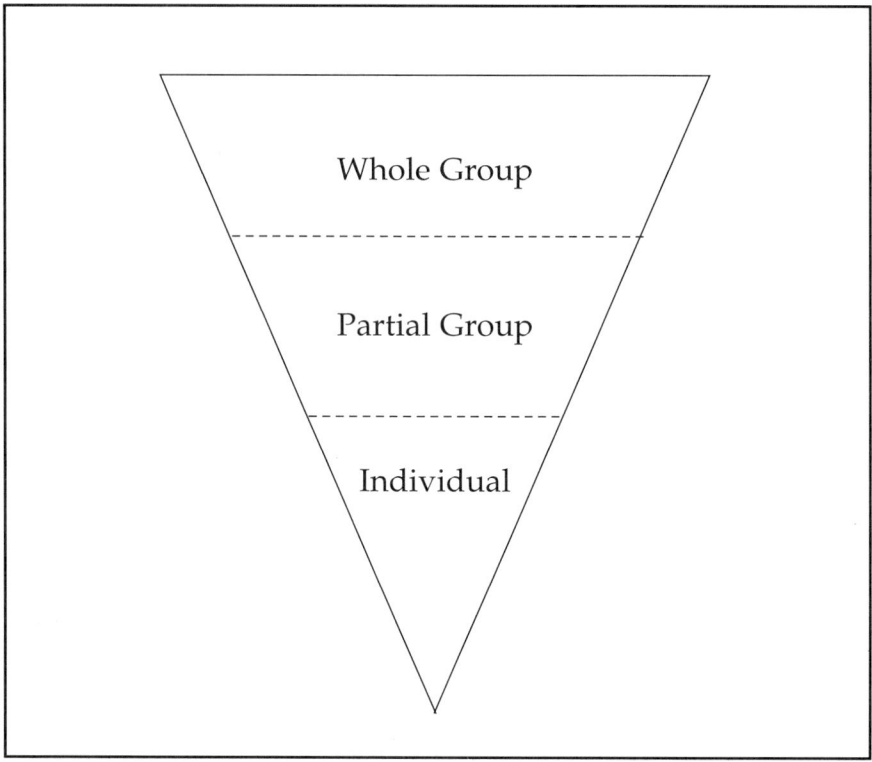

Figure 7.1. Program arrangements.

INCLUSION AND THE REGULAR EDUCATION INITIATIVE

Notwithstanding the assertions of proponents of the Regular Education Initiative (REI), I believe there is ample evidence that there are some students with E/BD who simply cannot be managed and instructed effectively in general classrooms. For some, greater progress occurs in "pull-out" special programs than in "stay-put" general classroom settings. Although promising approaches to serving students in integrated settings are emerging (e.g., cooperative teaching), the very nature of E/BD—maladaptive behavior that often includes physical aggression—necessitates certain considerations apart from other categories of exceptionality.

The literature substantiates the opinion that the construct of a continuum of special education services is conceptually sound. I agree that if placement decisions are not pupil specific or movement to less restrictive settings is not occurring, then these potential abuses warrant concern.

Still, I find insufficient cause to abandon a continuum of service options in support of full inclusion, in which even greater abuses are likely to occur.

Various authorities argue that a "two-box" system of public education, with a box for students with disabilities and another for those without disabilities, is dysfunctional. The relatively short history of public school efforts to educate students with E/BD has been punctuated by a search for programs first to satisfactorily address the needs of these students and, more recently, to support placement in mainstream classrooms. However, Kauffman characterized the bulk of current program development efforts for students with emotional/behavioral disorders as fraught with "confusion, disorder, diversity and inadequacy" (Kauffman & Pullen, 1989, p. 13). I believe we must improve existing programs, not abandon them, and seek to fix practices that are broken, as well as develop innovative service options. In a local elementary school, a current program consists of a "shadowing" strategy in which the special educator accompanies a student with E/BD to the general classroom and is stationed in close proximity to that student to give immediate feedback and support to him or her (and surrounding students). It is working.

Although the subject has sparked widespread debate, not all students with emotional/behavioral disorders are best served in general classroom situations. The enormous effort required makes it doubtful that most general classroom teachers will be able to deal effectively with students with E/BD. The possibility that teachers will adopt proven strategies—especially behavioral interventions—is greater in special education than in general education classrooms.

Like many of my colleagues, I think that any course of action that restricts service options should be plotted with great care. Recently, the Executive Committee of the Council for Children with Behavioral Disorders, with input from its membership, produced a statement on "full inclusion." In crafting that position, my colleagues and I expressed the following sentiments on the full inclusion of students with emotional/behavioral disorders:

> The Executive Committee of the Council for Children with Behavioral Disorders agrees that movement of students with disabilities to "less restrictive environments" should be a major goal. While we support the doctrine of LRE, we question whether students with mild to severe disabilities can be viewed appropriately as a homogeneous group for regular classroom inclusion. Rather, we believe there is ample justification for looking at educational options for students with emotional/behavioral disorders separately from other disability categories. Research and experience suggest to us that an appropriate education of some students with emotional/behavioral disorders is so complex and intrusive that it mitigates against regular classroom implementation. According to the

Council for Exceptional Children, ". . . special education is a means of enlarging the capacity of the system to serve the education needs of all children." The Executive Committee of the Council for Children with Behavioral Disorders maintains that some alternative arrangements are required for those students who are so disruptive or otherwise demanding of the finite amount of time, energy, and resources of general educators that the instructional needs of nondisabled students are significantly impaired. Public Law 94-142—now known as IDEA, preserves a range of alternative service delivery options. Recent court action upholds that an inclusive education does not necessarily mean that all instruction must occur in the regular classroom. We believe it is important to maintain a range of service delivery options that have been shown to benefit students with emotional/behavioral disorders.

For those students with emotional/behavioral disorders who are being integrated into the regular classroom, the committee asserts that consideration must be given to the relationship between the competence level of the student and the expectations of the setting. We hold that special preparation of the student must be coupled with support for the receiving teacher and that the reintegration process itself should be gradual and systematic. Finally, we assume that multiple services (e.g., resource and regular classroom placement) and ongoing technical assistance from qualified personnel will be required, if the student is to sustain a pattern of satisfactory school learning and classroom adjustment.

Within the evolutionary context of "mainstreaming," some authorities believe that special education classes are no longer indispensable. In contrast, we believe that it would be as inappropriate to embrace fully the current doctrine of total inclusion as to ignore it altogether. Arguably, neither action is in the best interests of all E/BD students; we find there is little empirical justification for the elimination of special service options on a pull-out basis for all students with emotional/behavioral disorders. We are convinced that, for some but not all E/BD students, the successful integration into the regular classroom represents a reasonable expectation. Nonetheless, in light of the accumulated evidence, the Executive Committee of the Council for Children with Behavioral Disorders reaffirms the relevance of a continuum of quality service options and our opposition to full inclusion of E/BD students. (Gable, 1994)

The development and validation of standards for determining *when*, *where*, and *how* to integrate students with emotional/behavioral disorders is an extremely worthwhile undertaking. In addition, there are factors that might be incorporated into guidelines for postponing student placement full-time in a general classroom: (a) amount of support and assistance needed in relation to available resources; (b) level of teacher preparation; (c) complexity, intrusiveness, and duration of the required interventions;

and (d) impact on the student or others. Finally, given the weight of negative opinion of general classroom teachers and peers toward students with E/BD, the receptivity of the inhabitants of specific mainstream classrooms also must be realistically assessed. As our counterparts on the National Joint Committee on Learning Disabilities assert, the general classroom is one of many options, not a substitute for the full continuum necessary to assure students the provision of an appropriate education.

As Jim Kauffman and others argue, the lack of a "philosophical consensus" regarding the integration process is a major impediment to successful integration. A standard policy, one that assures careful deliberation over decisions about inclusion of students with E/BD, might encourage more collaboration regarding program options for students and contribute to better reintegration practices.

It may be time to rethink an ecological approach to the education and treatment of students with E/BD, infusing our present knowledge of person–environmental interactions into an "ecobehavioral perspective." We know that single or multiple environmental events, which sometimes are temporally and spatially quite distant, may exert powerful influence over how a person behaves. For example, Johnny engages in a shouting match with another kid while riding on the school bus. That exchange sets the stage for what happens hours later in the classroom, inciting Johnny to strike out physically in response to a relatively meaningless remark by a classmate.

We have made significant progress since Lewin first conceptualized "helping versus hindering" forces. Today, we have the ability to identify and assess "setting events," which are significant, controllable, and unique to an individual student. And we are becoming skilled in the manipulation of those events and in determining a course of treatment that goes beyond simple contingency arrangements. This functional analysis of behavior, combined with interventions that place greater relevance on peer mediation and self-control, seems well suited to treatment across time, conducted in the natural environment.

ARE THE NUMBERS INCREASING NOW AND IN THE FUTURE?

We are witnessing a steady increase in the incidence of emotional/behavioral problems, especially among children and adolescents classified as "conduct disordered." A rise in so-called premorbid predictors (analogous to strikes against a person) contribute—singly and collectively—to the burgeoning number of children classified as conduct disordered. These premorbid predictors relate to negative parental attitudes; deteriorating home and family situations; increased frequency, severity, and chronicity of presenting problems; and early onset and nature of the symptomatology. The subgroup of children labeled conduct disordered constitutes the single largest number of students placed in E/BD classrooms. Since students identified as conduct disordered represent the most prevalent childhood disorder, making up one third to one half or more of all cases, their numbers threaten to reach epidemic proportions. For these reasons, it seems critical that we reexamine our system of service delivery options to find more effective ways to handle the growing variance among students with emotional and behavioral problems.

THE HELPING PROFESSIONS

Forness put it plainly enough: "We simply cannot go it alone" (Federal Register, 1977, p. 474). Throughout the country, school divisions are scrambling to find new ways to deal with students classified as emotionally/behaviorally disordered. The challenge is perhaps greatest for students with a history of violence and aggression. As shown in Figure 7.2, some schools are introducing multiple program options at the building level, programs staffed by general and special educators as well as mental health personnel. In some cases, special educators cooperate with representatives of the juvenile justice system or other community service workers to orchestrate a comprehensive treatment plan.

WHAT DOES THE FUTURE HOLD?

The convergence of social, political, and economic forces and reform initiatives stemming from these forces make it difficult to predict the future of special education for students with emotional/behavioral disorders. Notwithstanding the immense popularity of teacher collaboration in support of stay-put programs for students at risk and with disabilities, we will see a steady stream of students with E/BD referred for special education. The magnitude of the problems evidenced by many of these students makes them especially vulnerable. Once students are identified, teacher resistance poses a formidable barrier to inclusion. It may be possible to lessen that opposition if we bolster the quality of our preparation of both general and special educators.

I do envision increased emphasis on providing students data-based, multidisciplinary service arrangements, services that are multicomponent and longitudinal in nature and that include periodic booster treatment. It

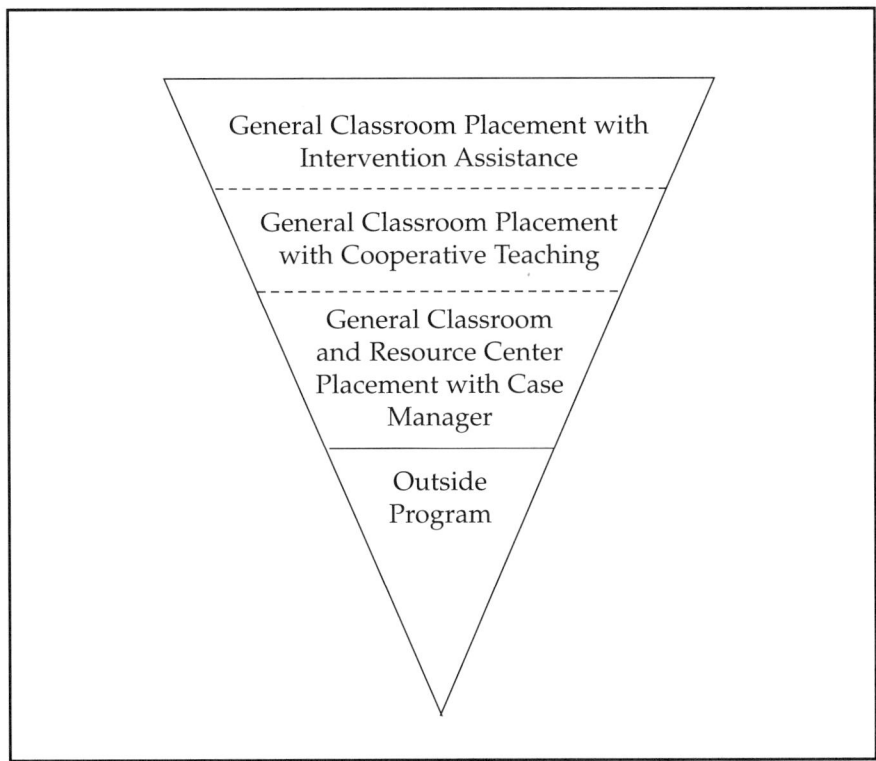

Figure 7.2. Program options for aggressive students.

is feasible that placement will no longer drive services for students. Instead, we may see "clustering," not only of multiple services but also of service providers across settings. Finally, I foresee the service providers across settings dismantling longstanding philosophical and territorial barriers, which will lead to increased professional collaboration and a broadening of the physical boundaries of our service delivery efforts.

REFERENCES

Council for Children with Behavioral Disorders. (1984). *Position paper on substituting "behavioral disordered" for "seriously emotionally disturbed" as a descriptor for children and youth handicapped by behavior.* Reston, VA: Author.

Federal Register. (1977). Vol. 42. Washington, DC: U.S. Government Printing Office.

Forness, S. R., & Knitzer, J. (1992). A new proposed definition and terminology to replace "serious emotional disturbance" in Individuals with Disabilities Education Act. *School Psychology Review, 21,* 12–20.

Gable, R. A. (1994). Spotlight on inclusion. *CCBD Newsletter, 8.*

ELEANOR C. GUETZLOE
University of South Florida
at St. Petersburg

Eleanor Guetzloe received her PhD from the University of Florida in the area of behavior disorders. She has been on the faculty of the University of South Florida since 1968. Guetzloe has served as project director in several key grants in the South Florida area. In addition, she worked as both a general and a special education teacher prior to moving into higher education. Guetzloe has served as president of the International Council for Children with Behavioral Disorders and also as a member of the board of directors for the Institute for Adolescents with Behavior Disorders. In 1991 she served as the site host for the Electronic Town Meeting on Students with Serious Emotional Disturbances, one of eight throughout the United States. Guetzloe's current research interests are in the areas of suicide and depression, aggression, violence, and education and treatment for labeled children.

CHAPTER 8

Where We've Been, Where We Are, and Where We're Going: The Ruminations of a Hard-Core Eclectic

William C. Rhodes once gave me a bit of advice that went something like this: "You have to wear the trappings of civilization until you have established a reputation and people will listen to you. Then you can let your colleagues know how you really think."

Those may not have been his exact words, but the message was clear, and I always share it with a new cohort of university students. For them, this could be translated as (a) "dressing as the natives dress" in the school setting (and coming down on the side of dignity when there's a question), (b) keeping some of their opinions to themselves, and (c) following the directions of their administrators implicitly until their jobs are secure. I remind them that they can't help the children if they're not there.

I must have done all right with the trappings of civilization. Someone has asked me to write what I really think.

My initial interest in special education was piqued by government money. Once upon a time, I was a "normal" person, with a degree in music education; Florida teacher certifications in music, elementary education, and social studies; and 9 years of teaching experience in regular elementary school. I had taken leave to have a child (our second) and then decided to remain at home and have a third. On a sunny summer morning in 1966, my husband and I were drinking coffee on the screened porch, reading the newspaper, and discussing the fact that, after several years of staying at home with young children, I needed to indulge in something more intellectually stimulating than diaper washing.

He called my attention to two announcements in the newspaper, one regarding an opportunity to take flying lessons (which he rated highly, having been a Marine pilot) and the other describing a new master's-level program in special education at the University of South Florida (USF), for which applications were being accepted. This program, which was funded by an Elementary and Secondary Education Act grant, was designed to train teachers in early intervention with children from families that were culturally diverse or of lower socioeconomic status (then called culturally disadvantaged). It would provide (a) 2 full years (including summers) of intensive, full-time study in all categories of special education, (b) weekly seminars led by national experts in special education, and (c) nontaxable

111

(the magic word) fellowships with stipends based on the number of dependent children in the student's family. I applied, took the Graduate Record Examination and the Miller Analogies Test (smelling strongly of laundry bleach), accepted a fellowship, and began my career in special education.

Upon graduation I was invited to become a member of the faculty at USF, to assume responsibility for establishing an on-campus research and demonstration class for emotional/behavioral disorders (E/BD) and to help develop a teacher training program in this area. That commitment led to my completing a doctoral program at another institution while keeping my position at the university. I have been at USF ever since, and my husband often has wished that I had chosen flying lessons.

WHY THE FIELD OF EMOTIONAL/BEHAVIORAL DISORDERS?

Over the years, I have found that my students usually choose this field for one of two reasons: (a) They believe that the omnipresent shortage of teachers in this area will ensure their finding a job (whether or not they'll be willing or able to keep it), or (b) they have a personal "story" (a history of emotional problems in their families, their friends, or themselves). I really had no story. Although my family, students, colleagues, and friends agree that I should qualify for an E/BD label myself, the condition is usually mild and transient.

I settled on this area of special education (as well as teacher training) during my master's program, after some direct experience with children with E/BD in a variety of settings, ranging from regular classes to residential institutions. The most attractive features of this field were (and still are) the following:

1. the children themselves, who were by far the most interesting I have ever met. During my first 3 years at USF, I was director and teacher of the on-campus clinical facility, in which we served children and adolescents with very serious emotional and behavioral problems who also had been excluded from other school programs. Coming to work was challenging, exciting, rewarding, and actually enjoyable.
2. the literature in this field and its related disciplines. In the earliest days of my graduate program, I began what is now an enormous collection of paper, a source of amusement to my friends and despair to my husband. As I began to write this chapter, I got a few of the older texts off of the shelves. They are

like old friends: *The Aggressive Child* (Redl & Wineman, 1957), *On Becoming a Person* (Rogers, 1961), *Educating Emotionally Disturbed Children* (Haring & Phillips, 1962), *Educating Exceptional Children* (Kirk, 1962), *Exceptional Children in the Schools* (Dunn, 1963), *Conflict in the Classroom* (Long, Morse, & Newman, 1965), *The Emotionally Disturbed Child in the Classroom* (Hewett, 1968), *Educating Emotionally Disturbed Children* (Dupont, 1969), *Educating the Emotionally Disturbed* (Harshman, 1969), *Behavior Disorders in School-Aged Children* (Clarizio & McCoy, 1970), and *Psychopathological Disorders of Childhood* (Quay & Werry, 1972), to mention a few. I often have wished that they were all still in print. To attain some sense of the history of this field, our new professionals need a set of their own.

3. the authorities in the field of E/BD (who contributed to that literature)—intelligent, compassionate, and thoughtful individuals, many of whom became friends as well as colleagues. The opportunity to meet and interact with these people resulted from my involvement with the Council for Children with Behavioral Disorders (CCBD), a division of the Council for Exceptional Children (CEC). I also should mention that my involvement with CCBD is the result of the early, continuous, and everlasting nagging of Lyndal Bullock, who became, in chronological order, my doctoral chairperson, valued colleague, and treasured friend.

4. the fact that in this area of special education there is always hope—the possibility of a positive outcome. Although I occasionally find a child that is probably "terminally E/BD," the condition is usually not immutable. We often can document improvement in the behavior of these children, knowing that teachers and schools have helped to effect that change.

Another contributing factor—nothing that could be counted, timed, or saved as a permanent product—was that I discovered some sort of personal affinity for children and youth with E/BD. I always have a healthy respect for individuals who are violent, hostile, and lacking in self-control, but my feelings have never been the negative perception, fear, or abhorrence that others describe. I usually am comfortable with children or adults with E/BD, and they always seem to understand that. My friends often have commented that if there is an individual with an emotional problem in the vicinity, he or she will find me.

Sometimes these individuals are brought to me by others. One of my master's graduates was a supervisor in the probation and parole division of the Florida Health and Rehabilitative Services. During his graduate program, Lewis acquired the distressing habit of becoming very involved with the families he tried to help. I cautioned him that he needed to stop taking the problems home with him.

One fateful day several years ago, Lewis appeared at my door with a 19-year-old male who needed a place to live during his pretrial intervention program, in which I was involved already as a lay counselor. If Lewis could find safe quarters for this young man for a "brief" period, he could keep him out of prison. My husband and I provided housing, food, supervision, and a great deal of parental advice for this individual for almost a year. After his departure, we acted as "house parents" for several other young adult probationers for periods of from 4 to 9 months. (After our last experience, with a "card-carrying sociopath," we gave up this pastime.) At any rate, Lewis had followed my advice: He didn't take them home anymore; he now brought them to me.

All of my direct experiences with both children and adults with E/BD have been of great benefit to me in understanding this complex problem and in determining what might work and how to do it. No professional can learn about these individuals without being in their close company. The students themselves are the most effective teachers in our field.

Finally, the reason that I am still here is that I have achieved some measure of success in this field and in teacher training. I still like my job, my students and graduates, and the children with whom they work.

AN ATTEMPT AT A PERSONAL PHILOSOPHY

If I could limit my personal philosophy about the field of E/BD (or anything) to one sentence, I would claim the promise made by the physician: *Primum non nocere* ("First of all, do no harm"). I have attempted to live by this creed—to help if I can and certainly not to hurt. Beyond that, I am (a) proudly, fiercely, profoundly, and steadfastly categorical; (b) an advocate for a full continuum of educational options (in opposition to full inclusion, "all means all," etc.); and (c) a hard-core eclectic regarding conceptual models.

I also admit to a rather simplistic "If . . . , then . . . ." philosophy. I have never been content simply to study or ponder a problem; I would like to move on, as quickly as possible, to whatever might help to alleviate it. If children are hungry, then we should feed them; if they are homeless, we should find them shelter. Some of these provisions may normally be the responsibility of other public agencies, but if those institutions are not able to provide what our children need, then someone or something else (probably the school) will have to do it. If a child is a social isolate, then we should teach him or her communication and social skills, assign a buddy who can tolerate him or her, and set up situations in which he or she will interact with others—under appropriate supervision—until the skills are mastered. If students have not mastered the basic skills of reading, writing, and mathematics, then we should teach those. If they are too violent and dangerous to come to school, then we should teach them somewhere else—in a store front, church, or jail.

STEADFASTLY CATEGORICAL

One of the most powerful forces contributing to my remaining categorical through the years has been my involvement with CCBD. At the urging of Lyndal Bullock (who has been the driving force behind CCBD regional development ever since), I became membership chair for Florida in 1970. In 1972, I organized the Florida subdivision and then served as its first president for two terms. Since then, I have served as regional coordinator, chairperson of the Standing Committee on Regional Services and Membership, CCBD newsletter editor (for 7 years), CCBD representative to the CEC Board of Governors, and eventually CCBD president. I am currently chairperson of the Standing Committee on Advocacy and Governmental Relations.

CCBD is the largest international organization that has advocated (for more than 30 years) specifically for children and youth with E/BD. It has been, for me, a very positive influence and a source of tremendous professional and personal support. I met many of my friends and colleagues through my work with this organization. A list of these individuals would be far too long to include in this chapter, but they are all delightful, dedicated, and intelligent people: classroom teachers, university faculty, administrators, mental health practitioners, authors, lecturers, and parents of students with E/BD. CCBD has afforded me a categorical identity.

THE NEED FOR A FULL CONTINUUM OF EDUCATIONAL OPTIONS

I have been involved with programs for children and youth with E/BD since I began my graduate program, when there were very few public school programs for these individuals. Over the years, I have observed many children who were labeled as having a serious emotional or behavioral disorder who never should have been moved out of their regular school classes. With appropriate interventions and services made available in the regular school, they could have achieved success in that setting.

I also have observed many children—and the number seems to be growing—whose behavior and affect are such (particularly those who are violent and aggressive) that they *cannot receive an education in the regular school*. For these individuals, more restrictive options are not only desirable but also absolutely necessary. For some, a residential institution (full-time, 24 hours a day, 52 weeks a year, and perhaps for an extended period of time) *is* the least restrictive environment.

A HARD-CORE ECLECTIC

In 1971, I was invited to participate in one of five regional meetings held by the research staff of the Study of Child Variance (Conceptual Project in Emotional Disturbance), then in progress at the University of Michigan. This was an awe-inspiring experience for a new kid on the university block, to be a minuscule part of such an enormous effort to define and explain the theoretical frameworks of E/BD.

Being involved in this workshop was a turning point for me. When William C. Rhodes began the conference by proclaiming that we were there to "celebrate deviance," I was sold on the idea. He, in fact, became my guru (although I didn't tell him until years later), because he publicly expressed so well some of my own perceptions that I did not yet dare to talk about. I was actually inspired to think beyond the "muck and mire" of my everyday tasks. Since then, I have had an opportunity to work closely with him and we have become good friends. He still inspires me to think, and celebrating deviance has become my creed.

The Study of Child Variance also prompted my continuing interest in all of the theories of personality and psychopathology. When I first described myself as an eclectic (a very long time ago), surrounded by colleagues who had made more definitive choices, someone responded with the definition of such an individual as "a person who straddles the fence, with both feet planted firmly in midair." My theoretical preference is probably closer to "integrative" or "interactional," which sounds more acceptable than "eclectic." There is no single theory that can account for all of the complex problems associated with E/BD. Further, on any given day, educators and mental health professionals use strategies and techniques derived from any or all of the major conceptual approaches (e.g., a token system, medication, group therapy, a change of seating, or planning activities that would be meaningful to children from diverse populations). Professionals in the field of E/BD need to know all of the theoretical approaches in order to understand, plan, select, use, or create specific interventions that are appropriate for the situations which with they are confronted. I try to influence my own students toward "informed eclecticism." If that doesn't always work, they still have to memorize the information.

In summary, my personal beliefs are based on (a) observations of a great number of students with E/BD over the past 27 years, (b) countless dialogues with "front-line" practitioners who work with students with E/BD on a daily basis, (c) interactions with my colleagues and students, and (d) the literature in related fields of inquiry as well as in our own.

From all of these sources, I have tried to glean the knowledge and skills that would be of greatest benefit to my students and to the children with whom they work.

CURRENT STATUS OF THE FIELD OF E/BD

There is both good news and bad news. The good news is that there are pockets of excellence across the continent where the student–teacher ratio is manageable, where students with E/BD are accepted in general education classes, where the students have sufficient books and instructional materials, where administrators understand the nature and needs of students with E/BD, where children and teachers alike are safe in the school, and where the outcomes for students are positive.

The other good news is that we know more about E/BD than ever before. We have a considerable amount of data-based information about educational and treatment strategies that result in positive changes in these children. Further, there are many very fine professionals—well-trained, intelligent, and caring individuals—who have the knowledge, skills, and administrative support to implement an effective program.

The bad news is that, for a variety of reasons, we are not always doing what we know would be best for our children. In many programs across the country, our children and the professionals who serve them are not thriving. Although complete and accurate data are hard to come by, we know that many professionals on the front lines are working under conditions that range from less than adequate to downright dangerous. Far too many school programs are marked by overcrowded classes, teachers who are untrained and unmotivated, and administrators who are not only unknowledgeable about E/BD but also much more concerned with the paperwork than they are with the progress of the children. Teachers have been physically attacked by their students and then warned by their administrators not to press charges under threat of losing their jobs.

Many years ago, my mother received word that one of her acquaintances had died, immediately after undergoing an operation that had been deemed successful. This incongruity became part of my mother's standard evaluation of the medical profession: "The operation was a success, but the patient died."

There are distressing similarities between that situation and what is happening now to children and youth with E/BD, their families, and their teachers. Most of us, in this era of accountability, are under mandate to provide school and community programs that result in positive outcomes for children with E/BD and their families. We have proof that we have taught children to read, write, count, practice self-control, communicate with others, balance a checkbook, and fill out a job application, as well as other things that should help them in their future lives. The children achieve their goals and reach their objectives as written in their education and treatment plans. Our programs are successful.

Many children, however, leave our "successful" programs only to find their way first to the street and then to prison, long-term institutionalization, or early death. Their families continually have encountered disappointment and grief, and their teachers are in despair. The operations were successful, but the patients died.

A WORKING DEFINITION OF E/BD

One thing of which I am absolutely sure is that defining E/BD will still be controversial and in progress until the day of my death. It is a bit unsettling but extremely amusing to attempt to explain a condition, problem, or "thing" for which the great authorities in the field cannot agree on a definition. I have accepted these "truths" about E/BD: (a) We know it does exist; (b) teachers recognize it when they see it; (c) psychologists and psychiatrists try to cure it; (d) there is an enormous body of literature about it; (e) we have school programs for it; but (f) we can't agree on how to define it. The inadequacies of the current federal definition have been a topic of discussion in our field ever since the passage of P.L. 94-142. Eli Bower (1969) first wrote the five characteristic patterns of behavior listed in the current definition to describe "socially maladjusted children" in California. He often shook his head in absolute amazement that the children for whom he wrote this description would then be excluded from special education, using these statements as the criteria for that decision. The first definition of E/BD I ever had to memorize was the following:

> A child is emotionally disturbed when his reactions to life situations are so personally unrewarding and so inappropriate as to be unacceptable to his peers and adults. Thus, disturbed children are viewed as having limited patterns of behavior and lacking flexibility to govern and modify their behavior. Their behavior differs considerably from others in their circumstances, not by kind but by degree. They are too excitable or too withdrawn, too brave or too fearful. They are the extremes of any variable of behavior. (Pate, 1963, p. 242)

I still like this one. I often use the comments about the "extremes of any variable of behavior" to explain E/BD to general educators. I once listened to a presentation at a professional meeting years ago when the speaker quoted an earlier work by Reinert (1980) in which he stated that disturbed behaviors are exhibited "in the wrong places, at the wrong time, in the presence of the wrong people, and to an inappropriate degree" (p. 818). I liked that statement for its simplicity and its ecological flavor, so I still use it as well. If I were personally responsible for defining E/BD for educational purposes, I would include elements of both "disturbed" and "disturbing," "troubled" and "troubling," or "aggravating to both self and others." For example, I might try "an emotional or behavioral disorder that is so severe that either (a) the child cannot profit from a regular educational program without special education and related services or (b) his or her presence in that setting is detrimental to the learning of his or her peers."

The National Mental Health and Special Education Coalition, of which CCBD is a member organization, has been working for several years to effect a change in the federal definition that would be acceptable to both major fields (mental health and special education). A 21-member work group developed the definition, with input from all organizations represented in the Coalition as well as many other professionals across the country. CCBD is in support of the terminology and criteria in this definition. I would hope that it will appear in new federal law.

If the definition proposed by the Coalition is accepted, it would provide additional specific criteria for determining the presence of an emotional or behavioral disorder (e.g., developmental, cultural, or ethnic standards) as well as more specific statements about what E/BD is not (e.g., a temporary, expected response to stressful events in the environment). It also includes qualifying statements that the disability is exhibited in two or more settings (one of which is school related) and that the disability is not and would not be responsive to general education intervention. It defines *educational performance* as social, vocational, and personal skills as well as academic achievement. Further, it removes the word *seriously*, which appeared in the definition for emotional disturbance but not in the definition of any other disability.

ED VERSUS BD: ARE THEY THE SAME OR DIFFERENT?

They are the same. Whatever the nomenclature, terminology, or procedures used in the identification process, they are the same. A number of states and provinces refer to their students with E/BD as behaviorally disordered rather than seriously emotionally disturbed, but the same kinds of students are being identified across the continent. In addition, many states have no clause that excludes children who are socially maladjusted, and they fill their E/BD classes with students who are simply mean, nasty juvenile delinquents who are completely in touch with our reality. No matter what term is used to describe the condition, a competent assessment team should be able to determine whether a child should or should not receive special education and related services. The real problem here is that neither general nor special education administrators want the responsibility for serving children who are severely disruptive, delinquent, and dangerous, and they are looking for a quasilegal reason to exclude these children.

What is more interesting to me than the acronyms (ED, BD, or E/BD) is that children with E/BD themselves are the same across time and across geographical boundaries. Several years ago, I participated in a lecture tour to China, during which we visited hospitals, schools, and correctional institutions. I looked at the children and adolescents there with a sense of wonder, because they were the same children that I see at home. The shape of their eyes might have been slightly different, but the expressions were the same. I felt as if I knew these children.

Further, I still see the same kinds of behaviors in children labeled E/BD that were evident in the first group I taught in 1968. There may, in fact, be many more of them now than there were then, they may have greater access to weapons and the weapons may be more sophisticated, but they still exhibit the same kinds of behaviors.

MEANINGFUL EDUCATIONAL EXPERIENCES FOR STUDENTS WITH E/BD

Rather than outlining an entire educational program for E/BD, descriptions of which are readily available in the plethora of texts and articles on the topic, I will speak from the heart and from experience. Our children need every educational experience available to any child who is not disabled and more. They need academics, social skills, thinking skills, computer skills, physical education, moral education, recreation, career exploration, vocational education, job exploration, job placement, and follow-up assistance well into their adult lives. They have missed so much, so many experiences that usually occur naturally in families and communities long before children come to school. They have not eaten in restaurants, learned to swim, or gone camping with their families. They have not been welcomed in neighborhood recreational facilities, community organizations, or even the church. Even when they have been subjected to positive learning situations—in the home, neighborhood, school, and community—their behavior and affect have interfered with their learning.

From October, 1991, through March, 1993, I served as principal investigator and director of an interagency project that was funded by the Office of Special Education Programs (OSEP) Department of Innovation and Development. Assigned to the project for one half of my university load, I had an office in the administration building of a Florida district with a school population of approximately 30,000. The purpose of the project was to form a large interagency coordinating council, which would become the planning body for the establishment of community services for students with E/BD and their families. Our primary target population, for which the council designed pilot programs, were students of middle-school age who were both E/BD and poor.

The school placements of the students with E/BD were not inclusive but were primarily special classes, day treatment centers, and residential programs, so we planned and implemented inclusive recreational and service activities for the hours after school and on weekends. The criteria for selecting activities were that they were (a) "normalizing" experiences, (b) "socially acceptable" to the students with E/BD and their peers without disabilities, (c) reasonable in cost, and (d) expected to continue when the project was no longer funded by OSEP.

One activity in which the students participated was the Coastal Cleanup, a national activity that takes place along the entire coastline of the United States each year. A local environmental group called my office and asked if our children would like to help with this effort. Our assigned area was the intercoastal shoreline of a local island that is also the community beach. We jumped at the chance. Before the big day, the students discussed environmental concerns and studied the forms (furnished by the environmental group) to be used in recording the number, type, and weight of the items they might find in the shallow water and on the shore.

The Cleanup was on a hot Saturday morning. Several teachers, parents, and mental health professionals attended to help with the work and to furnish transportation. I bought food and drink for everybody, begged free baseball caps for everyone from my son (in an effort to avoid any further brain injury), and brought along a first aid kit.

The students with E/BD (including a few who were allowed to leave the psychiatric hospital for this occasion) endured sun, heat, bugs, sandspurs, and each other all day. Standing in the sun, they listened to a lengthy lecture and an explanation of procedures by a junior college professor. They picked up, categorized, and hauled away an enormous amount of trash, competed cheerfully over which group could bring in the largest single piece of debris, and occasionally came back to the car for soft drinks and conversation. After a very hot morning, we found a shady spot on the beach side of the island, had lunch, cooled off in the gulf, packed up, and went home.

That's the whole story. It was a great day. There were no incidents of inappropriate behavior. Everyone, including parents, teachers, and council members, had a good time. When the students were having lunch, one could have mistaken the group for a Sunday school class. They sat together without adults at the tables, conversed, ate a great deal, and looked decidedly undisturbed.

This was not an isolated incident. We found that any activity that was an "ordinary" experience, was away from the classroom, and was aimed at helping others was a winner. Several of the middle school boys, some of whom had never read a book, practiced reading their selections during "group" and then rode with the psychologist (who took driving safety lessons so she would be allowed to furnish their transportation) to an elementary school to read aloud to the very young children with physical disabilities. The boys with E/BD "adopted" the younger group, helped them during play period at school, and took them to see Santa in a local mall during holiday season. The photographs of their efforts brought tears to the eyes of some of the council members.

Another group of students diagnosed as severely emotionally disturbed, accompanied by their teacher, planted poinsettias at important crossroads in their town, not far from their special class in the middle school. They got their picture in the newspaper—for doing something good.

These stories would not surprise any teacher of students with E/BD. Every good teacher I know spends a great deal of time carefully planning activities in which cognitive, affective, and psychomotor skills are taught in an integrated, enjoyable, and normalizing experience. These skills are not used in isolation; they cannot be taught that way.

INCLUSION AND THE REGULAR EDUCATION INITIATIVE

My opinion of the Regular Education Initiative is that it is (a) misnamed and (b) presumptuous. We did not ask the teachers in regular education for their opinions before setting out on this path. This initiative came from special education, not regular education. Further, most initiatives—in business or education—have been accompanied by additional funding. I am afraid, in spite of caveats from those who are knowledgeable about the nature and needs of students with E/BD, that school boards and administrators look to inclusion as a way to spend less, not more. They believe that the general classroom will be the least expensive environment.

Of all students with disabilities, students with E/BD are the least accepted and the least welcome in the general school setting. They disrupt the learning of others as well as their own. They are difficult to manage and to teach and are, in fact, feared by many teachers and administrators in the general school. Placing great numbers of students with E/BD in general education classes without appropriate special education and related services will not work to the advantage of the student, his or her peers without disabilities, the general education teacher, or the special educator.

The general class, however, should be an option for every student with E/BD, provided that he or she can be successful in that environment. *Successful* should be operationally defined as the ability to cope socially as well as academically in that setting.

It should be noted that most of the proponents of full inclusion do not claim E/BD as their primary field of interest (or, if they do, they are either misinformed or stretching the truth). I have engaged in numerous conversations with those who make such statements as "All means all," or who ask, "What part of 'all' do you not understand?" I also have noted that they do not want students with E/BD included in the classrooms with the students for whom they advocate. In fact, their "all" means "all but E/BD" (a statement that I do understand).

Within the past year, I have participated as a speaker or group facilitator in four national forums on the specific topic of inclusion of students with E/BD, two sponsored by CCBD and two by the University of North Texas. The forums were designed to solicit and disseminate information from the field regarding what must be in place in order for students with E/BD to be successful in inclusive programs. The discussants at these gatherings were in agreement that other placement and service options must be available for those students with E/BD who cannot be included successfully in the general school environment. A full continuum of educational services must be retained, as mandated by federal law.

DELIVERY OF SERVICES MODELS

Many school districts have programs of which they are (and should be) inordinately proud, but I have not yet seen all of the necessary components in the same place at the same time. To me, these great programs have been like pieces of a best practices puzzle. I often have wished that I could buy a large part of any state or province and put in place selected programs (and certain people) from all across the continent. I have chosen four to reference here, because I know that each of these is still exemplary, would be happy to share information about their programs, and also would welcome visitors (see the Appendix for contact names and addresses).

1. Westerly, Rhode Island: a well-planned, well-funded, successful, and inclusive districtwide program for E/BD.

2. Education Helps: a middle school special class for E/BD in Bradenton, Florida, that not only is organized around a busi-

ness theme but also actually *is* a corporation and a member of its local chamber of commerce.

3. Floyd I. Marchus School: a special school for students with E/BD in Concord, California. It also is undoubtedly one of the most positive and effective educational programs in the continent.

4. Personal Enrichment Through Mental Health Services (PEMHS): a not-for-profit corporation in Pinellas County, Florida, that provides a wide range of service options to children and adults with E/BD and those at risk of succumbing to mental illness.

There are other desirable components that I have not yet seen (some of which would require some rather extensive changes in law, regulations, and policy). Even when we have a clear understanding of the factors that have contributed to the development of emotional/behavioral disorders in children, we often do not have the resources (or the legal right) to practice appropriate intervention. For example, many children with E/BD are victimized by families with a history of serious problems, including psychiatric illness; substance abuse and alcoholism; and physical, psychological, and sexual abuse. In short, "parentectomies" would be in order, but the school cannot, under present law, provide the needed assistance. We need respite care for children: a shelter to which they could admit themselves (without a court order) when they are in need, which might serve to prevent abuse.

Many of our children have no family or no home. I would like to see a kibbutz-like facility established on or close to the school grounds, staffed by skillful, knowledgeable, and humane professionals.

We need safe, supervised after-school care, where children can receive help with homework, meals, recreation, and rest. Furthermore, it is unrealistic in this day and time to assume that the world runs on a schedule of dawn to dusk. Many loving and caring parents, out of necessity, work at night instead of during the day. There is, therefore, a need for "night care" as well as day care.

Many of the social services that are presently available have not changed with the times. We are in desperate need of some new social institutions, and many of these could be located near, housed in, or directed by the school.

INCIDENCE OF E/BD

In the last several years, a number of authorities have reported an increase in the prevalence of E/BD in the United States. According to the National

Advisory Mental Health Council (1990), at least 12% of America's children (7.5 million children under the age of 18) are mentally ill, and the actual rate may be as high as 22% of that age group. Less than one fifth of the afflicted children receive appropriate mental health treatment.

In the schools as well, the E/BD population is still underserved. If the incidence of E/BD is increasing in any particular school district, it is probably because the school and community have reached the end of their ropes (and their patience) and have decided to provide special programs for the disruptive, mouthy, threatening, and sometimes dangerous students found in the general school program.

It is a common complaint among teachers in both general and special education that students are exhibiting more disruptive and dangerous behaviors than ever before. The number and severity of behavioral problems evidenced by "normal" children in the schools have increased to such an extent that those who once might have been labeled E/BD now fall well within the realm of normality. I believe that we have just moved the scale of E/BD behavior up to a level of greater severity, like the slide on a slide rule.

WHAT ARE THE MAJOR CONTRIBUTORS TO THESE INCREASES?

There is an epidemic of violence among the young that is unparalleled in history. Young people kill for clothes, for love, for respect, for hate, and for no apparent reason at all. Experts lay the major blame on three familiar factors: drugs, easy access to handguns, and the influence of violent youth gangs. The violence is still escalating, and the schools, the last bastion of safety, also are becoming battlegrounds. Reports abound of students with guns holding entire classes hostage; of students assaulting and killing teachers, administrators, and fellow students; and of students killing themselves.

FROM NEUTRALIZATION TO WEAPONS DRILL

In my first few years at USF, I exhorted my students to exercise great care in planning lessons in reading, literature, or social studies so that the content did not "rub salt in a raw wound," subscribing wholeheartedly to "neutralization," as discussed by Jacobson and Faegre (1959). The children in their classes could have been upset by such topics as a happy family going on a picnic (if a student's family was in the process of a divorce) or Jerry teaching Jip to jump (if a student's dog had been killed by an automobile). Now, it is quite possible that if anyone in the family is missing, he or she may be the victim of a homicide (the outcome of domestic violence or a "drug deal gone sour," one of those daily newspaper clichés). If the dog has died, it may have been tortured to death by the student himself or herself.

Over the past 5 years, one of my topics in the behavior-management course is "what to do when the student pulls a weapon." (The question now is not "if" but "when.") Former students often return to my classes to give testimony to the usefulness of this information. They also claim to suffer auditory hallucinations at the critical time. They clearly hear my voice saying, "Do not go for the weapon. If he knows how to use it, which is probably the case, he will be holding the handle. If he has a knife, you are reaching for the pointy part. If it is a gun, you are reaching for the part with the little hole in it." There is more to this lesson, and it has proved to be an important part of the curriculum, but I deplore the conditions that have made it necessary.

MEETING THE INCREASED DEMANDS

We should not, of course, prevent the identification of children with E/BD. Any child who is eligible for special education and related services under the laws, rules, and regulations presently in place should receive those services. The general education program, however, will have to be enhanced and strengthened to meet the needs of the ever-increasing numbers of children who need more help than has traditionally been available. "Ordinary" education must become more "special." Teachers and administrators in general education will have to avail themselves of the knowledge and skills necessary to work successfully with students who are severely disruptive. Training in such areas as (a) the nature and needs of students with E/BD, (b) classroom management of groups as well as individuals, (c) effective instruction, (d) crisis management, and (e) curriculum modification, along with other "special education" knowledge and skills should be made available to all school personnel. "I am not trained to work with these children!" is no longer an acceptable excuse. Special education methods and materials are not classified information, and most of our effective techniques can be implemented in the regular school, with appropriate support systems in place.

INTERAGENCY EFFORTS

In an almost ideal world, any child, whether labeled E/BD or not, could receive any service needed (from either public or private providers), and these services could be made available without delay in either the school or home. Every agency, organization, and institution would provide what it is supposed to provide, eliminating wasteful duplication of effort, and all of these providers would collaborate in the planning and implementation of whatever is needed to enhance the lives of children with E/BD and their families. Decisions regarding the selection and delivery of appropriate services could be made, in cooperation with the family, by a team of professionals from (a) all agencies who might have jurisdiction over the child and his or her family, (b) all service providers, and (c) the school. Further, the agencies involved would agree on an education and treatment plan, so that one provider would not embark on a program that would be in opposition to what another is doing. This is the very essence of the collaboration model.

If I could make the choice, I would like to see the representatives from all of the agencies that serve school-age children (and their families) housed in the schools rather than elsewhere in the community. It is my sincere belief that as long as these agencies operate under separate administrations, with separate budgets and separate offices, they will spend many more hours in planning meetings than they do in providing services to children and families.

I also would like to see the school assume the role of case manager. A school professional (or child study team) is the most logical choice to assume this role for two major reasons: (a) The school has a legal right to interfere in the lives of children and their families, and (b) most children can be found in school for most of their waking hours during most of the week.

FUTURE TRENDS IN THE EDUCATION AND IDENTIFICATION OF STUDENTS WITH E/BD

The most critical issue affecting children and youth with E/BD is historical as well as current. There is still a stigma attached to this disability, whatever the label used to describe the condition. It is still not socially acceptable to be mentally ill. The general public still does not understand this disability, and advocacy for the child with E/BD is a prevailing need. I expect this need to continue.

EXCLUSION WILL STILL BE A PROBLEM

One of the earliest publications by the Council for Children with Behavioral Disorders (Regal, n.d.) was on the topic of exclusion of students with E/BD. This movement has never really died. Like some of the monsters in horror stories, exclusion lives on and resurfaces from time to time, sometimes in a new form. Despite federal mandates to the contrary, and even in school districts that claim to be inclusive, students with E/BD are still being excluded, not only from the general school but also from special education services.

For example, as a result of the "get tough on crime" philosophy, there is a movement toward establishing "boot camps" as a placement option for children who have violated the law (including students previously labeled E/BD). In these settings, children receive an intensive, short-term residential program aimed at teaching obedience and physical fitness, after which they are sent back to the same drug-infested, crime-ridden neighborhoods from which they came. If there is any effect at all, this training probably ruins whatever social "goodness of fit" existed previously. Upon their return home, some of these students are targets of suspicion, ridicule, and even physical violence. Others simply revert to type within days (sometimes hours) of their return and, if they are now stronger and in better physical condition, they are more dangerous than before.

Quitting school may be made easier. One piece of my vast collection of yellowing paper is a newspaper article, now several years old, of a Florida legislator's attempt to lower the age (to 14) at which a child could legally leave school. This was proposed as a solution to both discipline problems in the schools and Florida's high dropout rate (both problems to which students with E/BD contribute). Fortunately, the legislature at that time did not agree with this proposition.

If, for whatever reason and in whatever form, the schools are successful in excluding children with E/BD, we will have a "third world" of troubled children wandering the streets (as is already the case in Brazil, Colombia, some European countries, and even Nogales, Arizona). The children would not be the only people at risk; so would we all.

THE RETURN OF THE MEDICAL MODEL

I believe we will see a trend over the next few years toward increasing medical/psychiatric influence (in both identification and services), particularly if mental health problems are addressed in the national health plan. We will put into place anything for which insurance will pay. Further, there seems to be an increasing interest in research on biophysical influences (e.g., genetic factors, biological insults, poor prenatal care, and chronic physical illness) on the development of E/BD.

REFERRAL AND IDENTIFICATION

Many school professionals are dissatisfied with the identification procedures that are currently in place, primarily because of the enormous time lapse between initial referral and the initiation of special education services and the equally enormous pile of paper necessary to complete the process. There are not, however, enough school professionals to do the job, and the costs are high in terms of both salaries and time. With increasing numbers of children being referred for special education assessment, we will have to move toward a shortened, simplified identification process.

The movements toward inclusion and toward site-based management should facilitate shortening the process. In an inclusive school, individualized instruction and related services could be made available to any child with an emotional or behavioral problem as soon as the problem behavior is observed. In one of the CCBD forums on inclusion, a participant commented, "We should wrap him up *before* he explodes." If we "wrapped him up" before we implemented the lengthy identification process, the child might never need the label. The site-based child-study team of the future should be able to select and procure specific services needed from an array of immediately available options such as (a) a peer "buddy" in the classroom, (b) an adult mentor who comes to the school, (c) individual or group counseling, (d) job counseling for the family, (e) respite care, or (f) full-time psychiatric placement in times of crisis. (This is not an inclusive list.)

INCREASED PRIVATIZATION OF PUBLIC SCHOOL SERVICES

The movement toward hiring corporations, institutes, and private consultants to perform educational functions is already in full swing at the federal, state, and local levels. In special education, private entities are even responsible for promulgating public policy, sometimes with minimal input from the field of E/BD (and particularly from those who work directly with the students).

It is highly likely that school districts will increase the number of contracts with private individuals and agencies instead of hiring more psychologists, psychometrists, and other ancillary personnel (including administrators). In the more inclusive schools, it might even cost less to contract for entire educational programs for children who cannot be successfully included in the regular school than it would to fund separate teachers, classrooms, or buildings. One thing of which we can be assured is that the bottom line will always be prefaced by a dollar sign.

INTERAGENCY COLLABORATION

In 1969, the Joint Commission on the Mental Health of Children recommended the integration of community services for children with E/BD. Since that time, there has been a great deal of professional discussion about interagency collaboration, accompanied by very little change in the actual delivery of services. I believe, however, that collaboration's day has finally dawned, because there will be some "teeth" in the recommendations that were formulated by this group.

The Office of Special Education's (OSEP) *National Agenda for Achieving Better Results for Children and Youth with Serious Emotional Disturbance* (1994, March) contained two target statements related specifically to collaboration. There is little doubt that this document will be used as the basis for planning future funding by the Office of Special Education and Rehabilitative Services. Collaboration (along with the other targets) will become a mandated component of future grant projects and of school programs that receive federal funds. Unless the funding is integrated, real collaboration still will be difficult to achieve. The political war of the almost immediate future will probably be over who controls the money.

Being a teacher and understanding the potential for school intervention, I hope that the school will be in charge. I would like to see the schools become the social institutions of the future, community centers to which all children and their families can turn for help. For many children and youth with E/BD, the school may be the only available intervention.

REFERENCES

Bower, E. M. (1969). *Early identification of emotionally handicapped children in school* (2nd ed.). Springfield, IL: Thomas.

Clarizio, H. F., & McCoy, G. F. (1970). *Behavior disorders in school-aged children.* Scranton, PA: Chandler.

Dunn, L. M. (1963). *Exceptional children in the schools.* New York: Holt, Rinehart, and Winston.

Dupont, H. (1969). *Educating emotionally disturbed children.* New York: Holt, Rinehart, and Winston.

Haring, N. G., & Phillips, E. L. (1962). *Educating emotionally disturbed children.* New York: McGraw-Hill.

Harshman, H. W. (1969). *Educating the emotionally disturbed.* New York: Crowell.

Hewett, F. M. (1968). *The emotionally disturbed child in the classroom.* Boston: Allyn & Bacon.

Jacobson, S., & Faegre, C. (1959). Neutralization: A tool for the teacher of disturbed children. *Exceptional Children, 25,* 243–246.

Kirk, S. A. (1962). *Educating exceptional children.* Boston: Houghton-Mifflin.

Long, N. J., Morse, W. C., & Newman, R. C. (1965). *Conflict in the classroom.* Belmont, CA: Wadsworth.

National Advisory Mental Health Council. (1990). *National plan research on child and adolescent mental disorders.* Rockville, MD: U.S. Department of Health and Human Services.

Office of Special Education. (1994, March). *National agenda for achieving better results for children and youth with serious emotional disturbance.* Washington, DC: Author.

Pate, J. E. (1963). Emotionally disturbed and socially maladjusted children. In L. M. Dunn (Ed.), *Exceptional children in the schools* (pp. 239–283). New York: Holt, Rinehart, and Winston.

Quay, H. C., & Werry, J. S. (1972). *Psychopathological disorders of childhood.* New York: John Wiley & Sons.

Redl, F., & Wineman, D. (1957). The aggressive child. Glencoe, IL: Free Press.

Regal, J. (Ed.). (n.d.). *The exclusion of children from school: The unknown, unidentified and untreated.* Reston, VA: Council for Children with Behavioral Disorders.

Reinert, H. R. (1980). *Children in conflict: Education strategies for emotionally disturbed and behavior disordered* (2nd ed.). St. Louis, MO: CB Mosby.

Rogers, C. R. (1961). *On becoming a person.* Cambridge, MA: Riverside Press.

APPENDIX

Contact Names for Example Programs

1. Sandra Keenan, Director
   Special Education Services
   Westerly School Department
   44 Park Avenue
   Westerly, RI 02891

2. David Jonathan, Teacher
   Education Helps, Inc.
   Middle School
   600 75th Street NW
   Bradenton, FL 34209

3. Michael Grimes, Program Administrator
   Floyd I. Marchus School
   2900 Avon Avenue
   Concord, CA 94520

4. Thomas Wedekind, Executive Director
   Personal Enrichment Through
   Mental Health Services, Inc.
   11254 58th Street North
   Pinellas Park, FL 34666

NORRIS G. HARING
University of Washington

Norris Haring is currently professor emeritus of education/special education at the University of Washington and principal investigator of the Washington Research Organization and Program Development Services funded by the U.S. Department of Education, Office of Special Education and Rehabilitation. Haring received his BA from Kearney State Teachers College, his MA from the University of Nebraska, and his EdD in special education from Syracuse University in 1956.

Haring has been in the university setting for most of his career, but he also served as director of special education for the Arlington County Public Schools in Arlington, Virginia. He served as founding president of the Association for Severely Handicapped (TASH; now the Association for Persons with Severe Handicaps) from 1975 to 1978. He has special interests in research in systematic instruction with children who are mildly or severely disabled.

In May, 1994, Haring was the recipient of the Honored Alumnus Award from Syracuse University.

CHAPTER 9

Some Issues in the Education of Students with Emotional and Behavioral Disorders

Recent trends leading toward full inclusion in the schools have created significant controversy throughout the field of education of students with emotional and behavioral disorders. Aside from the fact that there continues to be an increase in the number of students with severe behavior problems, bringing students who are seriously disruptive into general classrooms without sufficient planning and support tops the list of the most critical issues in educating these students.

PLACEMENT: ALMOST A COMPLETE CYCLE

The issue of responding to the imperative for inclusive education has been formidable, particularly for those students with severe, externalizing behaviors. However, two other issues have endured since educators have assumed responsibility for students with disabilities. These include (a) defining that population to be served as having emotional and behavioral disorders (E/BD) and (b) agreeing on the most effective intervention and management strategies to employ in educational settings.

In this chapter I do not provide solutions to these three issues, but I do present a modest effort to flesh out some considerations that have been reflected from general educators as they proceed to educate these students. As part of a statewide systems change project in the state of Washington, my staff has provided technical assistance and facilitation to support the process of integrating students with severe behavior disorders in their home school and, in many cases, provided support strategies for promoting inclusive education. These experiences have given me an understanding of the dynamics of defining, assessing, discerning eligibility for, placing, educating, and managing these students.

Proper classroom placement and appropriate behavioral management, as mentioned above, are not new issues for educators. Drawing from just one case study in my past, I can state that timely identification and appropriate placement and intervention could have saved at least one student from the institutionalization that was the result of errors in judgment and procedures. From 1951 to 1953 I was a school psychologist in the

Omaha Public School, where I became acquainted with Sally. In the first grade, Sally was referred to a reading specialist for evaluation because of problems she was experiencing in reading. The reading teacher felt that Sally had a "minor" perceptual motor problem but did not recommend any special assistance. Neither Sally's regular teacher nor her reading teacher saw any problem. The teacher's report said, "Sally is a sweet little girl who tried hard at her academic work." Her mother had a different view of Sally. She said she was extremely difficult to manage at home.

During the following months, Sally's behavior at home became even more difficult for her parents to handle. The mother reported temper tantrums that lasted an hour. She had to dress her and force her to go to school. Her academic performance continued to deteriorate, but the teacher didn't feel it merited an evaluation. Although Sally was withdrawn and had no friends at school, the teacher said she had no behavior problems. The teacher added that if there were problems at home they must be due to poor discipline patterns there. At home, Sally's behavior became more aggressive and destructive. She began to break things and punch holes in the walls of her bedroom. Sally's pediatrician recommended a more structured and controlled environment with time schedules for bedtime and definite limits. Sally, at times, would conform to the structure and schedule, but at other times the limits provoked major tantrums.

Finally, Sally's mother felt she had to have more help. She began to feel unsure about her parenting in general. After several attempts to get help from the school and several rejections, the mother took Sally to a private psychologist. The psychological examination resulted in a diagnosis of a below-average IQ. The psychologist brought in a consultant neurologist, and they agreed that Sally was a "multi-problem child" who had signs of organic brain dysfunction and signs of a psychomotor seizure disorder. The educational evaluation revealed that Sally could neither spell nor write any letters past *E*. She was functioning below the first-grade level in reading and math. Apparently, Sally had developed highly refined coping skills and managed to get specific answers from classmates.

Finally, after two additional evaluations from private specialists, the school agreed to an out-of-district private special school. This increased Sally's social isolation, and the tantrums at home continued.

After 1 year in the private special school, tantrums at home continued to increase in both frequency and intensity. Finally, after strong insistence on bringing Sally back to her home school district and seeking special attention to her behavior and academic performance deficits, the school agreed to find a program for children who were emotionally disturbed. The only program in the district was a special school, but the school officials (psychologist and special education director) did not feel Sally's problems were severe enough to be placed in the special school. However, they agreed to the placement. As Sally entered the special school program, her mother began to attend a parent group run by a school social worker. Gradually, the social worker began to agree with Sally's mother about the seriousness of Sally's problem.

The following year Sally was placed in a newly organized special class for students with E/BD, including 19 boys and Sally. The parents became concerned and asked if there were any other placement options; they even contacted the superintendent. The school's response was to search for another girl for the program, but the search was in vain and Sally remained in the special class. After three placements in 1 year—one in an out-of-district special school, another in an in-district special school, and the third in a special class with 19 disruptive, destructive boys—Sally's behavior in school became worse, and at home she begged not to go to school. While at school she began to withdraw from the classroom activities, talked of hearing voices, and practiced self-stimulation. The special teacher referred Sally to the school psychologist and, after another evaluation, a placement meeting was ordered. After the placement meeting, residential placement was recommended.

Looking back, it seems to me now that we made mistakes throughout the first 3 years of Sally's school experiences, beginning with the failure of the school to listen to the parents and provide early attention, to provide a complete evaluation, to develop a comprehensive plan for intervention and management based on the evaluation, and to provide a treatment plan that included an appropriate educational placement.

Special education as a discipline of study, research, and practice has developed largely throughout the last half of the twentieth century, and we have almost come full circle. The special education discipline began with a strategy that involved removing students with physical, behavioral, and learning disabilities from regular education, providing special procedures designed to accommodate or remediate the problem, and providing transition back into society. Now the field has been examining the "pull-out" strategy and has concluded, in large part, that the special services necessary to educate students with disabilities can be achieved in the general class, thus supporting the full inclusion model.

Actual inclusion as a practice for educating students with disabilities has had modest to excellent success in instances that have been reported in recent literature (e.g., DeVault, 1994). Programs with highly successful results are those in which services have been delivered to the students in the general classroom, collaborative teams have provided adequate support to the general teacher, and the student-to-teacher ratio has been considered.

Success in achieving inclusion has been a significant challenge with students who have serious emotional and behavioral disorders. Even with the best practices applied to the inclusion process, the adaptation of these students in the general classroom has been disappointing. Students with serious behavior disorders who have created the most serious concern in general educators include:

- students who assault and attempt to injure another student or adult in school,
- students who self-mutilate or masturbate,
- students who are irrational or incomprehensible,
- students who threaten suicide, and
- students who sexually molest another child.

These behaviors exhibited with any frequency by students in general classrooms create extreme reactions from teachers and students and often result in urgent requests to remove the student (Walker & Fabre, 1987). Clearly, children with these kinds of externalizing behaviors have not, to this point at least, been successfully managed even with collaborative team efforts.

The main concern confronting special education is the challenge of providing adequate services to these children in any placement–general or special classroom. The depressing fact is that students with serious behavior disorders are currently the least adequately served students of all students with disabilities.

> In many states throughout the nation, children with rather severe behavior disorders are having an impact on regular classrooms. This is resulting in serious concerns among regular educators as they are faced with the increased challenge of providing quality education and accelerated academic achievements. Their concerns arise from the challenges of, on the one hand, maintaining high academic standards for the normal students and, on the other, the management of seemingly insurmountable behavior problems in regular classrooms. (Haring, 1987)

It is necessary to make certain discriminations with respect to the students with behavior disorders who do adapt well to the general classroom with the appropriate support systems in place. With few exceptions, students who internalize their emotional disorders, such as students with depression and anxiety, students with obsessive compulsive disorders, and students who hallucinate and have serious reality orientation deficits, often are maintained in general classrooms without adequate or appropriate professional attention to their emotional disorders.

Students with serious social behavior deficits and very poor social relationships represent another category of students often believed to have—and who actually may have—emotional disorders. These students generally do respond well in general classes with the support of collaborative teams and instruction in social skills involving behavior-management packages such as ACCEPTS (Walker et al., 1983) and the PATHS Project (Greenberg & Kusche, 1993).

ESTABLISHING ELIGIBILITY

Students with serious externalizing behaviors (i.e., violently aggressive, destructive, disruptive, and defiant) are the first to be referred for removal from the general classroom. Unless they are removed, they can completely destroy order in the classroom. Generally, the main reason these students are referred is so order can be restored in the classroom.

Establishing eligibility for service has been taken too lightly in many instances, resulting in students who are not actually emotionally disturbed but do have disruptive behaviors being identified and served as emotionally disturbed. Even more disconcerting is the fact that those students with genuine emotional disorders are not being identified (Walker & Fabre, 1987). Determining eligibility of students with E/BD relies on empirically verifiable information, which tends to be identified with greater accuracy than other forms of assessment. A general guide is that in order to be certified as eligible, students must display specific behaviors of concern across school settings and at home, at all levels of intensity and with persistence over time.

The practice that separates our procedures now from those of 50 years ago is that today we screen and identify these children, refer them for complete evaluation, and make a determination of eligibility. Following these procedures we place them into an inclusive education setting by choice and with the full support of the behavior support team. In short, many children with E/BD remain in the general class by our choice.

It is recommended that special educators and members of other disciplines planning for successful inclusion and transition from school to community living consider the behavioral demands in the inclusive setting and the student's behavioral status in relation to the important academic and behavioral demands. Educators should use this information to assist in selecting regular placements, and all of the above information should constitute an integral component of any transition plan.

DEFINITIONS GALORE

While clear, precise definitions of a disability are crucial to accurate classification and ultimate placement and comprehensive intervention, students with E/BD have been defined in many different terms, resulting in conceptual vagueness and disagreement. The lack of agreement about what constitutes emotional disturbance and what should be done about it has led to more confusion in this area of disability than in any other. In addition, special education as an instruction management discipline has made much greater progress with students who have those disabilities that are easier to define and classify. Clearly, the vague definitions we have been working with have made accurate identification more difficult. The basis for the most widely used definition is Bower's (1969) definition, and, with the exception of minor refinements, it is the same definition in use today. While P.L. 94-142 added several caveats to Bower's definition, the additions actually added to the ambiguity. Bower's definition is as follows, with the added federal rules in italics:

(i) The term "seriously emotionally disturbed" means a condition exhibiting *one or more* of the following characteristics over a long period of time and to a marked degree *which adversely affects educational performance*:

(a) An inability to learn which cannot be explained by intellectual, sensory, or health factors;

(b) An inability to build or maintain satisfactory relationships with peers and teachers;

(c) Inappropriate types of behavior or feelings under normal circumstances;

(d) A general pervasive mood of unhappiness or depression;

(e) A tendency to develop physical symptoms or fears associated with personal or school problems.

(ii) *The term includes children who are schizophrenic or autistic. The term does not include children who are socially maladjusted, unless it is determined that they are seriously emotionally disturbed.* (Federal Register, August 23, 1977, p. 42, 478)

After several attempts to improve on Bower's definition, I decided that the definition is as useful as any of my own approximations. It does describe the behavior that gives one concern and, with the frequency and pervasive dimension, gives the evidence that intervention is definitely indicated. As Kauffman (1987) pointed out, however, the federal addenda do not provide further clarification.

I agreed with Kauffman's concern for the redundancy in the federal definition. Is "an inability to learn" the same as educational performance? In addition, if the child exhibits "a general pervasive mood of unhappiness or depression," but happens to be academically advanced, which is very conceivable, then would that student be classified as seriously emotionally disturbed? At any event, we have learned to live with the definition and, anyway, the definition may in fact not be the basis for the problems we are having in the field as we strive for agreement about the most effective intervention strategies.

INSTRUCTIONAL PHILOSOPHY: PROCEDURES AND PRACTICES

Once the student is defined as having an emotional or behavioral disorder, the appropriate placement and instruction must be considered. The first step in the process is the evaluation for instruction. Evaluation involves individualized assessment of the appropriate education requirements of the student. A very comprehensive approach to the assessment is required, including an assessment by the multidisciplinary team (MDT). Generally the MDT consists of the special education representative, the school psychologist, the school social worker, the communication disorder specialist, and a professional representing the medical discipline.

Assessment information from these five disciplines yields data concerning the family interactions and relationship with the students with emotional and behavior disorders: the cognitive assessment from the psychologist, the psychiatric status and drug management from the medical representative, the communication skills from the communication disorder specialist, and the instructional assessment from the special and general educators.

The comprehensive evaluation gathers information from these common available sources (Kauffman, 1993):

- standardized tests of intelligence and achievement
- behavioral ratings
- assessment of peer relations
- interviews designed to obtain information regarding behavior deficits, behavioral excesses, and inappropriate contingencies
- direct observations confirming other sources of information and interview details
- curriculum-based evaluation for planning behavioral intervention and instruction

As instructional and behavioral intervention proceeds, the collaborative instructional team is vitally interested in considering how the student interacts with other students, how the student responds to classroom routines, and other contingencies associated with the student's responses in the school environment. Regardless of severity or intensity of the behaviors of concern, the instructional plan must be based on teaching age-appropriate functional skills that are used regularly by the student to achieve meaningful ends. Instructional guidelines for teachers of students with E/BD must be supported by the parents and the home management plan and include:

1. an individually structured activity plan and schedule providing clearly specified learning objectives, followed by high strength activity and supported by concise instructions;
2. sufficient guidance, demonstration, and prompts for teaching desired behaviors;
3. immediate positive consequences to desired responses; and,
4. opportunities for generalizing acquired responses under other conditions in different settings (Haring, McCormick, & Haring, 1994).

INCLUSIVE VERSUS SECLUSIVE PLACEMENT

All students have the right to be included. This position is starting to become social policy and is supported by such groups as the National Association of State Boards of Education (NASBE, 1992). NASBE also has rejected the notion of a dual system for special education and general education and called for a system that produces better outcomes for all students. Specific goals include training teachers and administrators to work in fully inclusive schools, abandoning labels, and instituting separate funding and separate placements (NASBE, 1992).

As I stated earlier, students with mild to moderate emotional or behavioral disorders and students with emotional disturbances such as depression, anxiety, and obsessive–compulsive disorders have a significantly greater chance of being maintained in inclusive settings. In fact—and this is very unfortunate—it is common to find these students in general classes without being diagnosed or classified as having emotional disorders (Haring, Jewell, Lehning, Williams, & White, 1987). On the other hand, students with serious emotional or behavioral disorders whose behaviors are extremely disruptive create serious concerns about manageability and how, in practice, to provide full inclusive instruction. Certainly, students with severe E/BD are among the most difficult to place and instruct successfully in an inclusive educational program. Endless problems arise in current efforts to achieve full inclusion with these students. The problems seem to center on the nature of inclusive schools, the nature and extent of the services and support systems, the significant planning and preparation of staff members, and the commitment and support of the families toward this goal.

Given the trend toward full inclusion, what special strategies are being devised to educate the most challenging students, those with severe behavior disabilities, including children with autism, in inclusive educational programs? To respond to the critical concern, I will cite an analogy applied by DeVault (1994). Those of us living on the West Coast are particularly aware of earthquakes, and following a quake we often ask, "How far were you from the epicenter?" As would be expected, the closer one lives to the epicenter, the more damage there is. Proximity to the center of the quake is important, but more scientific questions include: What is the cause of the earthquake? Was it horizontal or vertical movement of the tectonic plates? What is the nature of the soil in the affected area? Knowing that we must rebuild our schools, freeways, and other facilities in earthquake-prone areas, we ask more relevant and sophisticated questions about what structural changes and supports are needed to reduce damage, what the relationship is between the subsoil and other geologic variables, and what type of foundation is required to provide a safer structure.

In other words, we ask certain general types of questions when students with severe behavior disabilities are in a neighboring school district. But when you, a teacher, find yourself teaching a student with a severe, out-of-control, behavior problem in your classroom and are asked to add another student with a similar problem, you tend to ask for specific information and support. You need this information and support because, to use our earthquake analogy, you are on the fault line. Your first reaction is to move away from the fault line. Again, it is like rebuilding the buildings after an earthquake measuring 8.1 on the Richter scale. We must start asking the right questions and getting crucial, relevant information. Some quakes are so severe that no measure of contemporary engineering and building technology can result in a structure that can withstand it.

Similarly, there are students who are so violent and unpredictable that management in the regular classroom is virtually impossible even with the full force of the collaborative team effort, consulting teacher services, and the systematic application of positive behavioral support. Those students are rare, and they should not be used as a rationale to exclude other, less disruptive students. The majority of these students, with the application of more advanced strategies and behavior techniques, can be taught quite successfully in the general classroom.

One point of clarification: In general, I have referred to the subject population as students with emotional and behavioral disorders. In this section of the chapter, I am referring to students with severe behavior disorders, including students who have autism or who are disruptive, aggressive, and antisocial. These are the students who, because of extreme externalizing behaviors, are presenting teachers in general education the most challenging problems. These children have tested the best of our strategies and generally have found the weaknesses and gaps in the system. Yet, we have found that well-planned, consistent, comprehensive programs involving collaborative team management can work. Drawing again on the earthquake analogy, with intricate planning, thorough professional preparation, and improved cooperative implementation we can restructure education to include all students in the general education plan.

RESTRUCTURING AND RETRAINING FOR FULL INCLUSION

Through the in-service training of teachers of students with severe behavior disorders, we have come to realize that teachers who are in the schools currently do not have the professional preparation necessary for succeeding with these students. In addition, information and communication across the teaching staff is fragmented and inconsistent. While there usually are adequate staff, administrators, and counseling and psychological services, they do not work together with full consensus and common goals. Often they voice the importance of collaborative team effort, but in actual practice it falls short of being translated to the classroom. As we face the impact of the trend toward including more of these students in general education, we also face the fact that the incidence of emotional and behavior disorders is increasing (U.S. Department of Education, 1992).

In managing student behaviors, finding a way to achieve accurate, efficient communication is crucial. Teachers and administrators are just beginning to use electronic technology (e-mail, Internet) for facilitating their communication across teaching teams. Technology is providing a whole new system of communication that is forming to support all aspects of planning and teaching. Through more efficient communication, collaborative teaming is having a significantly positive effect. Schools are discovering the same truth that has been revealed in industry, which is that communication and organizational structure are intricately related. School structure that supports the creation of closer socioprofessional interactions ultimately leads to closer, more efficient learning.

The most impressive successes we are experiencing in implementing full inclusive education have been gained in situations with a team-based approach to the support of students with severe behavior disorders. The magnitude of management required to support these students exceeds the capability of most general teachers without adequate support. In addition, each member of the behavior support team requires technical skills, administrative authority, and adequate time given to making the team functional (DeVault, 1994).

In establishing behavior support teams, it is prudent to examine the already-existing teams in the school. It is possible to establish support teams within already existing team structures, given, of course, that the team has maintained good communication and is an efficient group. To be effective, behavioral support teams should concentrate their emphasis on students with the most severe behavior problems throughout the school (DeVault, 1994). In addition to the advantage of the collaborative team in providing behavior support in educational programming for students with severe behavior disorders, the systematic application of behavioral principles as a technology has provided the underlying strategy for achieving success with these students.

FROM APPLIED BEHAVIOR ANALYSIS TO POSITIVE BEHAVIORAL SUPPORT

Applied behavior analysis as a conceptual model to manage behavior in educational settings dates back to the late 1950s (Haring & Phillips, 1962). Throughout the past 40 years, this most useful model has developed into a highly refined, comprehensive system of intervention. Early applications of behavior principles combined with ecological structure were carried out in Arlington, Virginia, in the late 1950s and early 1960s (Haring & Phillips, 1962) and at the University of Kansas Medical Center (Haring & Whelan, 1965). Later in the 1970s and 1980s, these principles were applied with students with autism and severe behavior disorders at the University of Washington (Haring & Phillips, 1972) and the University of California at Santa Barbara (Koegel & Koegel, 1982).

Recently, with the emerging influence of the cessation of aversive procedures, a significant refinement known as "positive behavior support" has developed (DeVault & Haring, 1993; Sugar & Horner, 1994). Positive behavior support offers a new way of conceptualizing intervention in an educational setting. While positive behavioral support can be applied in any setting, its most successful applications have been with acquisition, maintenance, and generalization of functional skills; the development of social competence; and the management of severe behavior problems (O'Neill, Horner, Albin, Storey, & Sprague, 1990).

Specifically, positive behavioral support involves implementing the following steps:

- identifying the current function of the behaviors of concern
- changing the outcomes

- applying multiple intervention strategies
- evaluating results of intervention continuously

   Positive behavioral support procedures assume a practical attitude about interaction. They involve determining the conditions in the environment that can be controlled to increase the probability of the desired behaviors. The proactive goals are to teach the desired adaptive behaviors and functional skills; to provide opportunities to perform the skill under conditions different from those in the training settings; to actually perform the skills under conditions different from those in the training settings; and to produce independent, active learners through teaching and self-control, goal setting, self-recording, self-evaluation, and self-reinforcement.
   As part of its philosophy, positive behavioral support applies the "dignity standard," which states that the procedures employed and the way in which they are used do not violate the dignity of the student. To achieve this, the intervention used should be the least intrusive strategy needed to produce the desired behavior change.
   Consistent with the nonaversive philosophy, the positive behavioral support approach includes:

- preventive behavior technology, that is, rearranging the context and conditions associated with the problematic behavior;
- a comprehensive systems approach, using teams of support personnel and peers to strengthen positive behaviors; and
- the establishment of emergency procedures that are distinguished from programming strategies and that are arranged in advance of dealing with difficult-to-predict emergency situations.

   The comprehensive systems component involves a programwide effort, including the arrangement of environmental features such as social interactions with the support of peers, staff, and family. The approach has clear implications for general policy, funding staff training, and collaborative teaming.

FUTURE DEVELOPMENTS AND CONSIDERATIONS

Through the application of the most refined behavioral principle, the field has a technology that will allow for the inclusion of many students with severe behavior disorders who in the past would have been placed in more socially isolated situations. Hopefully, the future will see a widespread application of behavior technology in homes, schools, and communities. As it appears currently, we are facing very critical circumstances in the schools with the inclusive education mandate.

According to statistics reported annually by the U.S. Department of Education, the incidence of students with E/BD has been increasing each year since this category was identified. If the population continues to increase, we are going to have—if indeed we do not already have—a critical problem: Typical interaction programs in the schools and mental health agencies will be unable to keep pace with our growing social problems. (It seems obvious that a paradigm shift is necessary in order to respond effectively to this critical problem.) Why is the population of persons with serious emotional and behavioral disorders increasing? Not only is this population increasing at a geometric rate, but societies also are changing at a rapid rate. With greater population movement, a disintegration of many urban communities occurs, resulting in greater numbers of homeless children, increased substance abuse, and a more complex society. All of these significant changes are reflected in greater numbers of mental health problems in society. The peak in incidence of emotional and behavioral disorders will be reached in the early decades of the twenty-first century. The problem will become so critical that positive social steps will be necessary.

Potential solutions to this problem may include:

- exploring new approaches to building community cohesiveness;
- building comprehensive community-based services coordinated by one community agency, possibly the schools;
- investigating ways of building positive social relationships, social groups based on common goals;
- providing assistance in early intervention, such as Head Start services beginning in the home, including home care and positive child-rearing practices; and
- offering substantial assistance to single-parent families.

PREDICTING THE FUTURE

Predicting the future of research, services, and intervention strategies is an uncertain endeavor. Applying the technology of trend analysis, one technique that yields the most reliable results is to identify the present trends and project those trends and directions into the future.

We have seen increased agreement among professionals in the process of identifying and defining the individuals we are labeling, as the pendulum has swung from *emotional disturbance* to *behavior disorders* and now to *persons with emotional and behavioral disorders*. In general, this label refers to students who can be educated in their neighborhood schools with the assistance and support of the behavioral intervention team. Further, students with serious behavior problems are starting to be broadly defined as students whose behaviors are self-injurious and assaultive, causing personal injury or property damage to the extent that the behavior could require temporary removal from the classroom setting. These and other severe behavior problems are intensively pervasive and maladaptive to the extent that they require systematic and frequent application of a professionally trained team of individuals prepared to provide behavioral support in the school environment.

As we know all too well, teaching students with serious behavior problems is an activity that can, in spite of the most systematically planned program, result in major crises. As the schools have assumed the responsibility for educating these students, and because of national legislative mandates, clearer definitions have had to be defined. Previous practices have been to suspend those students whose maladaptive behaviors are intense and pervasive. Now that P.L. 94-142 has been fully implemented, strict regulations are applied to suspension, and expulsion is practically out of the question as an action for schools to take. This means, of course, that the states have had to develop specific regulations with respect to providing precise definitions and procedures for behavioral interventions. Based on the present legislative mandates, states are including definitions in the code of regulations. It is reasonable to assume that, in the future, and with the application of these definitions, continuous refinements will follow.

State codes of regulation, such as that in the State of Washington, the WACs (Washington Administrative Codes), have had a tremendously influential effect on increasing the uniformity of practices of behavioral intervention. As I mentioned earlier, behavior intervention involves the systematic implementation of procedures that promote positive changes in the students' behavior. Interventions are designed to give students increased access to community settings, social contacts, and public activities. In addition, positive behavioral support provides interventions that do not employ aversion tactics but do protect and respect the students' dignity and privacy. These interventions do promote the students' physical freedom, social interactions, and individual choice.

It must be recognized by society that the schools cannot provide the total solution to the social, emotional, and behavioral problems of youth as they adapt or fail to adapt to our rapidly changing, complex society. So many new, serious problems of society are having an overwhelming effect on today's children and youth. These effects, ranging from parental neglect and abuse to the use of drugs, will continue in the future unless some very major societal intervention can be found. The few projects that have been successful in providing educational environments that support youths in succeeding in school, such as Cities in Schools (Chamberlan, personal communication, April 18, 1993), Youth at Risk (Terrell, 1992), and The Belief Academy (Edgar, personal communication, October, 1994), are magnificent. The principles and procedures implemented by projects like these will need to receive widespread national support, and there has been some talk among members of the present administration to provide legislation that will target this problem.

Children and youth who are at risk for leaving school prematurely and becoming involved in crime or leading a disordered and nonproductive life are not necessarily emotionally disturbed. Their behavior is normal for people of poverty within the context of crowded urban conditions. Among that population, however, are individuals whose aggressive behavior is several times that of normal, even within this context of poverty. When these children and youth are among their peer groups, they often are not identified until they commit a very violent offense. Often they are not diagnosed and given the appropriate professional attention because, within this context, their behavior appears to be more acceptable. This aggressive behavior is likely to increase with aversive responses from parents and teachers, yet punishing responses are tempting, and there seems to be no reasonable positive alternatives.

While these students are the most frustrating to teach and manage in typical classroom settings, the future holds some promise. The strategy of positive behavior support has been successful in the situations in which it has been applied. These students can become engaged in productive activities by using positive environmental support. Their experiencing productive behavior in worthwhile activities provides the best formula for daily management. In general, the order of structuring daily activities has a significant influence on students' productive behavior. Arranging the school day so that highly preferred activities (play) are contingent on (follow) less preferred events (work) improves work performance. After the work progresses and the students experience success in learning, the productive learning becomes the preferred activity.

PSYCHOTIC BEHAVIOR

What does the future hold for students with psychotic behavior? The three common types of psychotic behavior are autistic withdrawal, self-stimulation, and self-injury. The term *psychotic behavior* is defined as seriously deviant behavior of young children, including children with severe mental retardation. The behaviors characteristic of those with psychosis may be present in individuals with a wide range of intelligence, from severely retarded to highly intelligent. It has been suspected for some time that there may be a biological basis for psychotic behavior. Research on the causes of psychoses continues, and perhaps in the future evidence of genetic or biochemical determination will emerge, but at present the cause or causes continue to be elusive.

While these students are difficult to teach because of their unresponsiveness to stimuli, overselective responding, and, in many cases, language deficiency and disorders, some very promising strategies have been applied experimentally, usually under the direction of university-based research projects. Again, positive behavioral support has been a common approach applied in research-based programs and is demonstrating excellent results. Many children with whom early behavioral intervention has been applied appropriately do recover. It is reasonable to hope that as our skill and knowledge become more refined in early diagnosis and behavioral intervention, significant progress will be seen. It is essential that these procedures be adapted in such a way that teachers can apply these procedures in natural educational settings.

Psychopharmacological interventions have provided some relief from the symptoms of psychotic behavior. However, it is essential that the effects of these antipsychotic drugs be monitored regularly because of the idiosyncratic nature of drugs and their interactions. The most optimistic promise for the future combines the use of psychopharmacological intervention with positive behavioral support applied within the context of the home and the school and by the collaborative team.

Finally, drawing from 45 years of experience as a teacher, school psychologist, administrator, and researcher of students with serious emotional and behavioral problems, I have seen a large variety of strategies for intervention come and go, and, in the process, we have developed useful refinements and improvements on behavioral intervention. Unfortunately, our progress has not kept pace with the growing prevalence of the problem. I wish it were clearer to me how we could accelerate our pace. I don't believe that adding incremental refinements to what we have been doing in intervention will offer much promise.

We are dealing with a problem that is involved in a geometric progression with an arithmetic mentality, and it is simply not working. At the same time, at the national level, in areas of the physical and medical sciences, we have seen that, given top priority and commensurate funding, major advances can be demonstrated. We are at a place in history where we need national attention at the highest level in order to gain control of the variables that are responsible for the increased incidence of serious emotional and behavioral problems. Perhaps a national institute could be developed that would bring together scientists from the behavioral sciences dedicated to comprehensive, programmed research designed to investigate thoroughly all aspects of emotional and behavioral disorders.

REFERENCES

Bower, E. M. (1969). *Early identification of emotionally handicapped children in school* (2nd ed.). Springfield, IL: Thomas.

DeVault, G. (1994). *Students with severe problem behavior in inclusive educational systems: When is it a case of NIMBY?* Unpublished manuscript, University of Washington, Seattle.

DeVault, G., & Haring, N. G. (1993). *Positive behavioral support*. Seattle, WA: University of Washington, Project New Share.

Federal Register. (1977, August 23). Washington, DC: U.S. Government Printing Office.

Greenberg, M. T., & Kusche, C. A. (1993). *Promoting social and emotional development in deaf children: The PATHS project*. Seattle: University of Washington Press.

Haring, N. G. (1987). *Assessing and managing behavior disabilities*. Seattle: University of Washington Press.

Haring, N. G., Jewell, J., Lehning, T., Williams, G., & White, O. (1987). Research on severe behavior disorders: A study of statewide identification and service delivery to children and youth. In N. G. Haring (Ed.), *Assessing and managing behavior disabilities* (pp. 39–105). Seattle: University of Washington Press.

Haring, N. G., & Phillips, E. L. (1962). Educating emotionally disturbed children. New York: McGraw-Hill.

Haring, N. G., & Phillips, E. L. (1972). *Analysis and modification of classroom behavior*. Englewood Cliffs, NJ: Prentice-Hall.

Haring, N. G., & Whelan, R. J. (1965). Experimental methods in the education and management of emotionally disturbed children. In N. C. Long, W. C. Morris, & R. G. Newman (Eds.), *Conflict in the classroom: Education of emotionally disturbed children*. Belmont, CA: Wadsworth.

Kauffman, J. M. (1987). Foreword: Social policy issues in special education and related services for emotionally disturbed children and youth. In N. G. Haring (Ed.), *Assessing and managing behavior disabilities*. Seattle: University of Washington Press.

Kauffman, J. M. (1993). *Characteristics of emotional and behavioral disorders of children and youth* (5th ed.). New York: Merrill.

Koegel, R. L., & Koegel, L. K. (1990). Extended reductions in stereotypical behaviors of students with autism through a self-management treatment package. *Journal of Applied Behavioral Analysis, 23*, 119–127.

National Association of State Boards of Education. (1992). *Winners all: A call for inclusive schools*. Alexandria, VA: Author.

O'Neill, R. E., Horner, R. H., Albin, R. U., Storey, K., & Sprague, J. R. (1990). *FAPP: A practical assessment guide*. Sycamore, IL: Sycamore Press.

Sugar, G., & Horner, R. H. (1994). Including students with severe behavior problems in general education settings: Assumptions, challenges, and solutions. In J. Marr, G. Sugar, & G. Tindal (Eds.), *The Oregon conference monograph, 6*, 109–120.

Terrell, C. E. (1993). *Youth at risk follow through program.* San Francisco: Break Through Foundation.

U.S. Department of Education. (1992). *Fourteenth annual report to Congress on the implementation of the Individuals with Disabilities Education Act.* Washington, DC: Author.

Walker, H. M., & Fabre, T. R. (1987). Assessment of behavior disorders in the school setting: Issues, problems and strategies revisited. In N. G. Haring (Ed.), *Assessing and managing behavior disabilities* (pp. 188–243). Seattle: University of Washington Press.

Walker, H. M., McConnell, S., Holmes, D., Todis, B., Walker, J., & Golden, H. (1983). *The Walker social skills curriculum: The ACCEPTS program.* Austin, TX: PRO-ED.

JOHN L. JOHNSON

John Johnson is an educational psychologist trained in clinical work with children and youth who are emotionally disturbed. Johnson received his EdD from Michigan State University in special education and psychology. He has had an extensive career in children's mental health, as a psychoeducational consultant, and as an administrator of urban special education programs. He has taught at the university level since 1962 and has held academic appointments at Syracuse, Michigan State, and Federal City College, in addition to numerous adjunct appointments. Recently Johnson has been working in the field of conflict resolution and in bridging theory and practice on issues of social justice and social action. In 1993 Johnson was honored by the Council for Children with Behavioral Disorders with their prestigious Leadership Award "for a lifetime of service to children with behavior disorders."

CHAPTER 10

The Field of Emotional Disturbance and Behavior Disorders: An Appraisal from a Black Humanistic Perspective

The contemporary field of special education for children and youth classified as seriously emotionally disturbed (SED) is entering an important transition after about 50 years of existence. This field, also known by the term *behavior disorders,* has grown into a movement composed of autonomous segments that are organizationally distinct—mental health, delinquency, school-based SED—but with an overlapping client base thought to "have the problem" and that is "worked with" by a myriad of professionally trained personnel. It is also a field characterized by its polycephalous nature and for its various ideological networks, some of which dominate various aspects of the field, particularly its resources and opportunities for research and development. Over the 40 years of my involvement in this field, there have been a number of major shifts in perspective from the original child guidance–psychiatric programs to school-based psychoeducational programs and recently to the notion of community-based approaches. Throughout this period of development and expansion, residential treatment, outpatient treatment, delinquency programs, and public school programs for delinquency treatment have remained a constant; more recently, addictions treatment and prevention programs have been grafted into the educational behavioral disorders rubric, each supported by federal legislation and dollars.

When I began working in this field in 1956, there were few educational readings. (The major works were psychiatric dynamic or psychoanalytic works by European-trained psychoanalysts and Americans who had been trained in the dominant Eurocentric thinking of the day.) Teachers were adjuncts to the process of therapy, and the classroom was simply a place that was supportive to the work of children in treatment. I began training in Michigan, a pioneer state in the development of a major stream of thinking about how to provide education to children and youth who were diagnosed as emotionally disturbed—in those days with hard DSM–III diagnoses, including psychoses, schizophrenia, and chronic brain syndrome. We also worked with adjudicated delinquents in locked facilities and the other major category: the socially maladjusted. Forty years ago when the Council for Children with Behavioral Disorders (CCBD) became part of the Council for Exceptional Children (CEC), "behavioral disorders" was considered to be a vanguard element—out there on the edge where the action was. This still may be the case because, from everything I see and hear and read, there is considerable action involving these young people in programs that are now required within a myriad of regulations, paperwork, behavioral point systems, administrative concerns, teacher isolation, and staff burnout. Special education for children and youth with SED is now part of the overall educational system and is serving another master, that of trying desperately to justify what it is doing and why it costs so much to do so little. The field has grown remarkably in size but it has not lived up to the expectations placed on it by the regular education system, nor have the theories that have dominated its practice proved helpful in the larger sociocultural setting.

It is my view that the field is experiencing the midlife transition, just as humans do around age 40. However, this crisis is much more serious because the field somewhere in its development became converted to an institutionalized psychology upon which education for SED was grounded. This psychology embodies the very assumptions that have helped to bring about the present unsatisfactory situation. Our current policies and system of intervention for E/BD could be labeled, as Freire (1970) described, anesthetic or aspirin practices. They serve the presupposition that the minds, hearts, and behavior of the children and youth in these programs can be changed while the social structures that made these minds and hearts "sick" can be left intact and unchanged. Most, if not all, of the E/BD practice is dominated by the idea of "individualism" or "individually" prescribed efforts, with faltering lip service given to any understanding of the social system that continues to create E/BDs at a rate that never can be handled by a system organized to deal with each child as an individual.

As a new order of expectations and issues develops nationally, special educators cannot help but encounter the disturbances of the present social field. We are concerned with violence, criminal lifestyle behavior, drug and alcohol addiction at earlier ages, overrepresentation of blacks in certain programs, female involvement in the maladjustment system, stressful staff relations, the breakdown in longstanding ways of doing things, economic troubles, and multicultural maladjustment issues. In the midst of all this turmoil at the level of practice, the academics continue to publish career enhancement research and have formed coalitions to change the definition of SED, as if that will help schools and human service programs find their way in a turbulent society and in the new world order.

We are working in a disturbed field without the slightest clue as to how to proceed. There is a natural phenomena exerting influence on everything and creating a different magnitude of disturbances; both figure and ground are shifting simultaneously. The problems we face are more interrelated than ever. The field of special education for persons who are emotionally disturbed has a serious disturbance. We are faced with a variety of intractable problems—psychological, sociological, moral/ethical, legal, medical, and others yet to be known. We are a field that is being influenced markedly by the breakdown of community, social injustice, the spread of violence and child abuse, urban disintegration, and the general loss of meaning that infects those least able to cope. Need we mention the state of the special education teacher, who daily must find ways to manage what comes into his or her classroom without adequate and competent resources or the proper spiritual foundation to understand what is happening, and how these teachers are now being treated in schools that have made their classes the repository for the failures of their coworkers in the regular education system?

Out in the rest of the world the hidden system of private psychiatric services for children has been brought under the scrutiny of the U.S. House of Representatives. The August, 1992, CCBD newsletter reported a "controversy surrounding the profit orientation of private psychiatric hospitals" (CCBD, 1992, p. 3). The litany of abuses includes billing patients for involuntary stays, transferring patients between settings to hold census, and ordering tests and making diagnoses to get the highest paying benefits. Sociologists long ago discovered that the private inpatient psychiatric hospital is used as a form of adolescent social control, primarily by the middle class, who can afford high-option mental health insurance plans. Some psychiatric treatment is probably genuine, and some special education SED programs may be required, but generally, *I believe that the field, by its practices and failures to fulfill its promises, is itself a disturbed system and in need of some form of political review that could provide the basis for a substantive transformation.*

If anything is to change, we must shift our focus from troubled youth to the troubled system; from the institutionalized psychology of individualism to a psychology of community and group identity; from the Eurocentric theories of behavior that are taught in most training programs to the psychologies of resilience that have helped various cultures and ethnic groups survive and achieve in the American system of racism, sexism, and economic exploitation. The present system of E/BD education is grounded in the American capitalist educational philosophy and is creating its own intentional and unintentional disturbances.

Of course there have been some major positive developments as the field has grown. We remain an energetic and potent part of special education. There is some impressive scholarship, and some important dialogues have developed and are continuing to influence the entire idea of special education. Many of the tools we teach are workable across settings, and there has always been a strong humanistic set of values within the field. We have much to be proud of.

KEY CONCERNS FROM A BLACK HUMANISTIC PERSPECTIVE

I was trained and educated in the dominant Eurocentric education system, including my introduction to the field of emotional disturbance (ED) as an undergraduate and my graduate work through the doctorate. But more importantly, it was through my early schooling in industrialized Detroit, from 1938 through 1950, that the basic foundation of Eurocentric principles was given to me by white teachers. Only in my family and in my college fraternity did I learn anything about myself as a person of African heritage. What I did learn in those schools was to study everything and to read and write critically, and what I learned in my family and fraternity was that there was a separate history and way of doing things of which whites were unaware and unwilling to acknowledge if they became aware.

It was not until 1962 when I went to Michigan State University that I began to become aware that what I was studying and learning had little or no relevance to African-American people. I worked summers at the Lansing Boy's Training School where delinquents were remanded, and I began to see large numbers of young black boys from the industrial cities of Michigan and to observe the overt racism of the program. When I began to talk with the black staff who worked there permanently, I began to understand things better. As I looked back into my own education, I saw that the types of information that I had been given were deficient. I saw clearly that there was something drastically wrong with what was happening to black people in the education system, particularly those young gifted, delinquent boys and their families. I began to read differently and study differently and discovered that there was another way of looking at the world: from a black perspective. I had heard Malcolm X by this time and the civil rights movement was in full force, and I knew then that, as a black scholar in the field of E/BD, I had a unique contribution to make.

In 1966, after moving to Syracuse University, my reeducation continued. There I had opportunity to meet Africans and to learn about African thought and philosophy and, more importantly, African culture and its place in the life cycle of black America. It was at Syracuse that I was radicalized through association with the United Black Brothers of Syracuse and began to integrate my new Black Nationalist direction into the work of personnel training in behavioral disorders. Most of my efforts and thinking were now to be directed toward the inner city—toward my own people and our plight of racial injustice, economic deprivation, educational disadvantage, and social isolation. It was during this period that I came in contact with Freire and his *Pedagogy of the Oppressed* (1970) and with the work of the African-American Teachers in Harlem. There I met

Preston Wilcox. His article, "Education for Black Humanism: A Way of Approaching It," (1969) remains a profound statement of philosophy about how to educate the black youth of America. I came in contact with the writings of Boggs (1969), and I continued to study Malcolm and the schools of the Nation of Islam, the community control of schools movement, the growing literature on the education of the black child, and the development of school programs geared to understanding the roots and learning styles of black children. My consciousness was forever changed.

My own declaration of liberation, based on my reeducation, was issued to special education in 1969 when "Special Education and the Inner City: A Challenge for the Future or Another Means for Cooling the Mark Out?" (Johnson, 1969)[1] was published by the *Journal of Special Education*. It was during this period that I found that *behavior disorder* meant something quite different to the black community than what was being talked about in the CCBD meetings. Finally, it was when I began consultation to the District of Columbia Public Schools Task Force on Special Education and eventually moved there, taking the position of associate superintendent for special educational programming, that I saw the larger scale of the problem of behavioral disorders within a system charged with providing "quality" education for the black masses.

It was here that I began to see that we were dealing with a systemic effect: overlabeling, misdiagnosis, and efforts designed to maintain the very system that was producing the problem. Here were the larger systemic effects of racism, discrimination, economic deprivation, "miseducation" (Woodson, 1933), and an educational process whose main objective was directed toward individuals who deviate from the rules or roles the system deemed appropriate rather than toward the development of self-reliance and self-determination as a people. We were trapped in a system of denial and avoidance, and it was only the advent of legal action on behalf of a misdiagnosed black male (Mills v. Board of Education of the District of Columbia, 1972) that began to loosen the grip of oppression.

Even after the legal action, we were only able to formulate a system that conformed to Eurocentric prescriptions of passive conformity and naive reformist special education for the individual that were predominant at the time. We had not begun to think of how one educates an entire population. How does one liberate an entire race from its disadvantaged

---

[1] This article continues to have a remarkable effect on the contemporary student of special education. Recently, I was introduced to a young professor at a major university who told me that she takes the date off the paper and assigns it for homework. Then she asks for reports in class and students must tell when it was published. She indicated that most think that it is a new paper, published within the past 2 years. The more things change, the more they stay the same!

condition? The narrowly conceived E/BD rubric (now dominated by behavioral theory and methods) was no longer part of my thinking. It was now "education for self-reliance" (Johnson, 1980). A total transformation in my thinking and ideology had taken place, and, in that sense, my work has been as an African-American scholar working for the overall benefit of the black community. I have taken an activist position against the conceptual practices of the field of E/BD that are grounded in the American system of oppression and through which children with problems of adjustment are often labeled as E/BD and sentenced to educational death in E/BD programs and the time-out rooms throughout our present system of education.

THOUGHTS ON DEFINITIONS AND LABELS

Given my position that the structure of the present system of schooling is aimed to tear young black people apart and destroy the naturalness of youth, I believe that part of this effort is the use of labels. There are those who have written that the entire system of education is detrimental to the development of young black minds and to the education of self-reliant, critical-thinking, Afrocentric-minded people. The process of education provided for African-American people is part of the direction of the culture and tends to reinforce that direction. Given the dropout rates, the unemployment rate, the pushout rate, the overrepresentation of blacks in special education, and now the most interesting phenomena, the rate of refusal to learn and the targeting of black boys for failure (Daniels, 1994), one must ask the question: Why should black people be concerned about the E/BD definition in a system that is dedicated to the destruction of black mental health (Harvey, 1984)? P.L. 94-142 reinforced the labeling process through a federal effort that provides funding based on the number of children served. Thus, the more children served, the more money a state can accrue—so the more labels.

Perhaps we need to adjust the present label. I am certain that those leading this effort have developed a rationale for the change, but I don't think that it will make a bit of difference to the black community and to the education of our children. We currently have a system of labeling practiced by black professionals educated in the traditional Eurocentric programs and governed by the regulations of the federal government. The net result in most places is increasing numbers of young black males being shepherded into "alternative" programs because no one really knows how to deal with their aggressive stance toward life.

But if we need a label, I have one that I developed to try to help with the present situation: Reactionary Behavioral Disorder (RBD).[2] It is similar to the DSM–III category of Adjustment Disorder, which is a reaction to an identifiable stressor (or multiple stressors). It gives prominence to events in the educational setting, which over a period of time precipitate, energize, and are immediate antecedents to the emergence of the disorder. Its symptoms are inattention, failure to learn, disruptive behavior, disrespect of teacher and rules, truancy, and other "black" behavior, including defiance of the system itself. Those who seek diagnosis of this disorder should focus on the following: (a) the covert attitudes and ideologies held by the professional staff about the student's socioeconomic status, domicile, skin color, and family structure; (b) the existence of any dehumanizing practices in the organization and management of the school, including the covert attitudes of the principal toward the teachers and cafeteria workers; (c) the salient aspects of the culture of power in the student's classroom; (d) the teacher's system of denial and social defenses against working with black children; and (e) an analysis of the teaching practices that have been used with the student and the target group (videotapes should be available).

The basic assumption underlying this diagnosis is that schools serving black children (whether in the majority or minority) are invested in a process of generating RBD and school failure based on Eurocentric concepts of *behavior management, control, appropriate behavior*, and *motivation*. It is further noted that schools serving black children are involved in a systematic invalidation of the positive family, home, and community experiences that those students bring into the school. These same schools use a capitalist philosophy of education, with full understanding of how the negative features of capitalism manifest themselves in the black community.

So I say, yes, Reactionary Behavior Disorders is my label. The treatment program is much like what Fidel Castro did in Cuba with his Campaign Against Illiteracy (Fagen, 1969). Castro inherited a stagnant educational system, much like ours: one where students were labeled because of their inability to master the symbols of literacy, which then led to exploitation and misery. I recognize that we are not revolutionary Cuba, but what's the difference in terms of the numbers of functionally illiterate young black people our schools are producing now? Changing the SED label or increasing the already overrepresented population won't help. We need to label the system as disturbed and find a way to close the SED programs for at least a year, until we can do a similar piece of work as that done in Cuba in the late 50s and develop a new educational philosophy for dealing with today's generation (O'Neil, 1991). Instead of tinkering

---

[2] Appreciation to Frantz Fanon, *Wretched of the Earth* (1966), section on "Colonial War and Mental Disorder."

around with the Bower definition that was used for political expediency in the first place, perhaps we should find a way to deal with the sociocultural roots of the behavior of the children and youth now in E/BD programs (Eitzen, 1992) or begin to address the major psychosocial epidemics that face us (London, 1987). This would mean turning our attention from labeling students to trying to properly identify and sort through the troubles of our system and work on them first. We need a dynamic social systems perspective in place before dealing with the trite effect of the E/BD definition.

Finally, we need to think about how to address the needs of the young people we serve, not those needs that are listed on the IEP but those that we learn about by direct involvement with them. Many have psychosomatic and relationship problems; mania and depression are present; and most are in "extreme states of consciousness," which is viewed traditionally as mental illness and more recently as spiritual or moral illness. Recent research has shown that these states of consciousness are troublesome not because those who experience them are ill and in need of treatment but because these very states are being repressed and disavowed by society as a whole. Passion, detachment, energy, spirituality, and a sense of the larger context is needed so that these young people can be divested of the projections they carry for the rest of us and so that they can get on with the task of growing up (Mindell, 1988).

INCLUSION: REGULAR EDUCATION INITIATIVE AND OTHER POLITICAL INVASIONS

The first recollection I have about a discussion of the Regular Education Initiative (REI) was during the Reagan years when the Republicans were in charge of the Federal Special Education Policy mechanism and funding priorities. How do partisan politics and, more importantly, partisan ideologies shape the practices of a field that is undergirded by federal dollars? When P.L. 94-142 was being put into place, CEC generated the slogan "Politics is the name of the game." In my view, there followed an unintended and basically unconscious slide into the political side of government from which we have never recovered. The field of E/BD was, of course, involved in this as a matter of association with the powers that be, particularly because the "feds" provided the majority of the money for E/BD training programs and research efforts in the colleges and universities. So, being good "grantsmen," the colleges and universities began to take up the issues that the money brought with it; thus we have the REI debate. It, for me, has Reagan Republicanism written all over it. I have never understood why everyone couldn't see that it was part of a political agenda, put in place as a way of dealing with the way that Republicans wanted to reshape educational policy. I never thought that there was any substance to it, and, if there was, the absence of a discussion of the political agenda of the Reagan administration toward educational programs for disadvantaged people (of which those in special education are a significant number) was always a mystery to me. In fact, the discussion still must occur now that the so-called Centrist Democrats are in a position to set the agenda. Is there any difference between the two?

My opinion and philosophy on the inclusion of E/BD under REI is that there needs to be adequate recognition that REI has nothing to do with providing better programs for troubled children but everything to do with politics and economics of special education, a system that has gotten out of hand and characterizes Reagan's idea that there was too much government. Instead of the current debate involving proponents and opponents, why not set up a debate within CCBD and CEC where Democrats and Republicans set forth their views? After all, politics is the name of the game.

MY DELIVERY OF SERVICES MODEL

I can speak only about what I know. I do not resonate with much of the jargon of present-day work. Terms such as *service delivery systems, continuum of services*, and *case management*, I must admit, I do not really understand. And when I've asked people to explain what they mean by these terms, I have usually come away with the feeling that there is something missing: contact with client groups in a way that offers improvement in their life circumstances or that provides families with a way to carry out their responsibilities and vision for their children, with support from the educational and treatment professional. So I will try to offer some ideas about how to bring what I know to bear on the lives of the groups with whom I have worked intensively.

My working experience has been in a research psychiatric clinic, a training school for delinquents, a children's mental health center, a group foster home for disturbed adolescents, a day treatment program for disturbed adolescents, and a therapeutic community for drug rehabilitation. My experience in public schools is limited to a brief tenure as a central administrator and as a clinical and organizational consultant to various programs for suburban and inner-city populations. I also have consulted to the process of establishing a mandated E/BD program in a large state prison system. I do not limit my thinking to children. A service delivery model, in my view, begins with staff work.

One of the strongest experiences of my career has been my work at City Lights, a day treatment school for adolescents and young adults. There the founders had the vision of establishing a staff process group *before* the first clients were admitted, to begin working with staff on the "person–role dilemma," that is, the many issues of how we bring our person to the role of working with disturbed adolescents in the black community. We conceived a process to deal with occupational health, psychosocial support, and clinical development. All staff as a benefit of employment are provided with an annual staff retreat and the twice monthly staff process group. There we work toward four goals: (a) maintaining and improving occupational health in the agency as a whole; (b) increasing awareness of needs of client groups, psychodynamic processes, and organizational creativity; (c) developing competence in self-managed learning and problem solving; and (d) working in collaboration with colleagues and clients. This group has been ongoing for 12 years, and all new staff are initiated into the group and use what they learn from the group in their work with adolescent and adult students. The process group, the annual staff retreat, and a monthly role-analysis meeting with the senior administrators constitute a service delivery model to support individuals who work with high-risk groups.

I have reported my intensive immersion in a group foster home with inner-city youth who had been abandoned by their families and abused by the individual foster care system (Johnson, 1980). Once again the group model proved effective, and I am convinced that work in the inner-city requires attention to group process and training in group work. The group work model from social work is one I learned and highly recommend (Radian, 1974). It is applicable in the current E/BD program in the inner city, but few people are being trained in these methods. I cannot let the opportunity go by to cite an African proverb from the Akan people of Ghana: "The first step forward is a step back to tradition." I must refer the reader to an early work in the field, *Considerations for Planning Classes for the Emotionally Handicapped* (Hollister & Goldston, 1959). Were this taxonomy in the hands of those responsible for designing service delivery systems, much of the tension that staff members experience could be managed and an atmosphere of competence put into place.

I have always been interested in the therapeutic milieu (in spite of my criticism of my early learning) and I recommend that model as one way of thinking about how to work with some of today's seemingly intractable problems, particularly with alienated, antisocial youth. I have also begun to think less and less of treatment and special education and more and more about healing and the opportunities that a model based on healing might offer to the tough young people with whom I work. We need to look more into holistic studies, based on Buddhist and Yogic practices, body work, and drama therapy. But most of all we should think of developing healing communities as a way of addressing some of the troublesome conditions that children and youth are living with (Almond, 1974).

I also want to recommend the model of the Therapeutic Community for Drug Addiction (Yablonsky, 1989). After I began my involvement in addictions, I found this to be the most powerful way of addressing issues of self-concept, violence, despair, education, and drugs. In the part of the E/BD field where I work and practice, death, dying, and grief is very much a part of the popular culture. We now "treat" young people who know death and violent injury and who have administered it in the course of their chosen lifestyle. AIDS, HIV, STDs, and other types of opportunistic infections have taken lives from us in the midst of our attempts to create a therapeutic place. Yet there is also remarkable talent and giftedness in our population. Any services must offer skills for dealing with despair and grief and, at the same time, offer a revolving door curriculum for talent development and giftedness, particularly leadership development.

ROLE RELATIONSHIPS AND THE ISSUE OF THERAPY

Early on in the formative years of the field, we recognized that there was a stream of behavior taking place and that some of us who had a place on the bank would dip into the stream with our psychiatric-dynamic net, others would dip with their juvenile justice net, and others with their special education net, but the "fish" all came from the same stream. Now the situation is just slightly different, because the fish may be involved in all the systems at the same time. One young adult who came to my behavior-management clinic at the day school told us that she had a public assistance worker, a special education teacher, an art therapist, a case manager, a psychiatrist, a social worker, an addictions counselor, and "God only knows what else," but what she really needed was someone to listen to what she had to say about her life. So, by agreement, one of my class members (an undergraduate student) took on the role of listener whose only task was to listen and not talk. When we agreed to this, the smile that came over this very streetwise 18-year-old problem drinker was a sight to be seen.

As the weeks went by, she eagerly sought out her listener. She confirmed what we already knew, that regardless of the provider, the charge, the diagnosis, the central component seems to be that every part of the youth service system has to begin to listen to the essential message that the clients and their families are conveying. The one place where I have seen this happen is in the addictions work and, particularly, within the various 12-step programs (which in addition to listening have a message to convey, whether we all agree with it or not).[3]

I am also interested in client-governed programs, particularly for youth and family-based programs. I think that each of the subsystems—mental health, special education, delinquency, social services, and child care—are very much part of the problem, but at the same time I think that there are some client populations who can benefit from active participation in whatever system undertakes to listen to them. Meanwhile, new subsystems that specialize in certain "treatments" need to be explored. Work with abused children and youth, sexual offenders, drug sellers, adolescent widows with children, and youthful prostitutes all require differential assessment and people who are sensitive to them and their special direction in life.

Then there is the other very serious problem of parts of the system taking on cases that they are not qualified to treat, such as trying to treat drug addiction within the mental health rubric. There is a lot to be learned from the substance-abuse counseling field. The E/BD worker who attempts to work with drug addicts or users on the basis of an in-service or the staff social worker who provides "therapy" to a drug addict without certification as an addictions counselor is treading the path of unethical behavior. While I mention the issue of ethics, more needs to be said about ethics and the need for ethical practice in a lot of what we do in E/BD, regardless of the place where we work. The human services, and special education as part of it, breaches ethical boundaries quite regularly to the detriment of us all. Somewhere along the path toward building a new working model, ethical decision making must become a part of what we discuss and practice. As an example, no matter what the subsystem, when we "treat" the angry young black male as an E/BD, we are blind to the ethical anger that is part of growing up black in this society. It is unethical for the predominantly white leaders of the field of E/BD to promote programs, policies, and ideas that do not take into account the growing anger among young black males and the growing disturbance that the Hispanic "home boys" are experiencing when they are being sent for treatment, incarceration, or special education.[4]

---

[3] For a strong message about role relationship differential, I refer the reader to Williams (1992), who described a church-based program for working with drug addicts and for empowering the community. This raises the issue of what other resources we can call upon for troublesome populations such as E/BD. What about church-based programs and Africentric educational programs, which seem to be having a modicum of success? The recent book by Dorsey (1993) concerned the power of prayer in the practice of medicine and other mind–body practices, which may prove to be at least as effective as the widespread use of the present religion of the E/BD field: behaviorism.

[4] For an extensive work on young black males and the downward spiral of their lives, see Gibbs (1988) and Way (1993).

Now a brief note about therapy. I believe in therapy and professional counseling. That is, for anyone involved in E/BD, the option of therapy should be available. Simply put, what I have experienced therapy to provide is increased self-understanding, and E/BD programs certainly ought to embrace that idea for everyone involved. There are a number of issues, including the time when therapy was required for parents and children in our early models and schools of course decided that education was their task, not therapy. There is still somewhere in our collective unconscious the discussion of whether teachers of E/BD could be therapists. Perhaps we should resurface that issue and see what is required with today's E/BD situation.

Whatever the finding in relation to students in E/BD programs, I still recommend therapy to teachers and other staff on the basis that we simply cannot ask the children and their families to participate in something so experiential and personal as therapy or counseling and not be willing to engage ourselves around our own affective and relationship issues and problems of behavior that are sometimes obvious to others. Nicotine and caffeine addiction, weight problems, anger management, male/female relationships, divorces, and other problems are evident in many programs, so why not use what we advocate for the children? Therefore, I advocate therapy for self-understanding as a tool in E/BD programs, and, yes, for the behaviorists I advocate cognitive behavioral therapy so that everyone can practice what they preach. Some will recall Jersild's pioneering work in the 1950s and 1960s on self-understanding and education (Jersild, 1955; Jersild & Lazar, 1962).

Given the immense difficulties of teaching and working in E/BD programs, it seems important for E/BD teachers and staff that self-understanding be an open part of the program and not be hidden. I am especially interested in recent work on Jungian counseling (Allen, 1988) and the implications for using the arts as an avenue into the psyche of the younger group and as a way of increasing self-awareness in youth groups. As always, these are tools that must be applicable to the various groups to whom the therapeutic intervention will be used. There is significant literature on the use of psychotherapy in the black community (Paster, 1985), and the Association of Black Psychologists is a resource that should be used by E/BD programs who work with children of African heritage.

There is, as one might imagine, a serious problem of underdiagnosis and undertreatment of African-American children and youth at the same time that there is overrepresentation in public school classes for E/BD. Psychotherapy has a place in the African-American community, and workers in E/BD should become aware of their own biases on this issue, regardless of their working model and service provision system. The development of highly intensive therapies may be required to help programs deal with the violence, depression, and cognitive distortions that are part of delinquency programs. And what about training people to be their own therapists? What about peer counseling programs within E/BD? These are all possibilities if we are to find more potent ways of dealing with the alienation among youth in general and in the field of E/BD.

INTERCEPTING THE FUTURE

Only the Midzimu know what tomorrow brings.
—African Proverb

I would like to see a more differentiated, multicultural system for E/BD sometime in the near future. We must begin to tailor interventions and services to specific populations. I have written here about African-American humanism within E/BD. Who is willing to write about white, middle-class children in the same way? The recent work of Peterson and Ishii-Jordan (1994) is a beginning in this area. We cannot continue to think that what works for one works for all. A more honest and open approach to racism and its effect in E/BD should be part of this effort. Culturally specific programs and culturally competent staff are urgently required.

Most of the present models are grounded in Eurocentric philosophy, and this needs to be changed. Change will require that the behaviorists give up the lock on the methods for determining acceptable proof. Behavioral methods have been successfully promoted and career enhancing for most of the present leadership in E/BD, but they have helped to create a climate that makes experimentation with other antibehavioral models unpopular because they are not, in their view, "theoretical" or "data based." This is a hard wall to climb, especially in academic settings. Intuition, culture, humanism, healing, prayer, chakra counseling, coconstruction and reconstruction of affect and desire, yoga, and holistic studies are being made available to large parts of our society and people are benefiting from them. So why is E/BD limited to what is publishable in the *Journal of Behavioral Disorders*, under the belief that the Eurocentric model of "data" is the only "research" that is available? We need more than that for the future.

We need training that will equip more people to work with extreme states and the shadows of the city as they become conscious to us. This will mean that we will have to study consciousness and develop ways to understand that the present system of "mental health" is the particular belief system that we have adopted. There are other systems of "mental health," and we should not limit ourselves to the present allopathic biomedical ideas that are likely to be ineffective in a multicultural society. And what about studying feminist consciousness? It has much to offer as we go about working with E/BD; after all, many of the "workers" are female. Why aren't we exploring the major ideas of feminism as a way of dealing with the issues of school behavior problems? Mindell's work on altered states of consciousness may have much to offer as we try to develop a psychology of consciousness in the field of E/BD (Mindell, 1988).

What are some of the challenges facing us in a dynamic society? Herr (1991) spelled out his ideas in an article that has had tremendous influence on my thinking. Whenever I use these ideas, others seem impressed. The general themes for the future, as I paraphrase them, are the following:

1. We need to pay more attention to how psychosocial events shape behavior. This will require more study in the behavioral sciences, economics, political science, and religion in addition to our psychoeducational approaches.
2. An understanding of family dynamics and social organization will be essential as we plan programs for E/BD intervention. A shift from the troubled individual to the troubled system will help us understand how and where to intervene effectively.
3. We will need to better understand how public policy affects role behavior for various target populations—the inner city for example.
4. We will need to develop a greater understanding of how macrosystems influence the direction of professional needs.
5. Greater understanding of ethnic, racial, gender, and socioeconomic issues across cultures will become increasingly important.

E/BD programs are part of the psychological ecology of education and have set in place some very important ideas, but they also have provided a set of unintended consequences. Of all the ideas about the future that I can think of, training as futurists may be the most important, so that we can better intercept the future than we have in the past. I cannot be more detailed than this: We must train our people to intercept the future in such a way as to provide programs that serve the E/BD population better than we have until now. If we are to work effectively in the inner city, then we will have to be willing to work with drug abuse, alcohol abuse, teen-age prostitution, suicide, rape, assault, terrorism, ethical anger, abandonment, and despair. How in the world will we do this when we continue to prepare teachers only to teach reading, math, and social studies? We must reconceptualize and rethink. E/BD in the inner city: a challenge for the future or another means for cooling out the mark?

Education for black humanism asserts that:

1. All black children are human and educable.

2. Blacks hold in common African descendancy and victimization by white institutional racism.

3. To subscribe to racism and capitalism is to participate in one's own destruction and that of his own people, the largest oppressed class in America.

4. Education which effectively overlooks the aspirations and technical survival requirements of the black masses is irrelevant.

5. Education for blacks is essentially a retooling process: rehumanization, re-Africanization and decolonization; authentic black men enjoy only one kind of freedom as a conceptual whole: a respect for native cultural differences, a resistance to all kinds of oppression, and recognition of one's right to defend his right to become who he wants to become as long as the expression of that right does not demand the oppression of others.

6. Black men have a right and an obligation to define themselves and the terms by which they will relate to others.

7. Education must become a process that educates for liberation and survival—nothing less. (Wilcox, 1970)

REFERENCES

Allen, J. (1988). *Inscapes of the child's world: Jungian counseling in schools and clinics.* Dallas, TX: Spring Publications.

Almond, R. (1974). *The healing community: Dynamics of the therapeutic milieu.* New York: Jason Aronson.

Boggs, G. L. (1969). *Education to govern: A philosophy and program for learning now!* Detroit, MI: All-African Peoples Union.

Council for Children with Behavioral Disorders. (1992). A national crisis at psychiatric hospitals. *Council for Children with Behavioral Disorders Newsletter, 6,* 3.

Daniels, L. A. (1994). Targeting black boys for failure. *Emerge, 5,* 58–61.

Dorsey, L. (1993). *Healing words: The power of prayer and the practice of medicine.* San Francisco: Harper.

Eitzen, D. S. (1992). Problem students: The sociocultural roots. *Phi Delta Kappan,* April, 584, 586–590.

Fagen, R. R. (1969). *The transformation of political culture in Cuba.* Stanford, CA: Stanford University Press.

Fanon, F. (1966). *Wretched of the Earth*. New York: Grove Press.

Freire, P. (1970). *Pedagogy of the oppressed*. New York: Herder and Herder.

Gibbs, J. T. (Ed.). (1988). *Young, black, and male in America: An endangered species*. Dover, MA: Auburn House Publishing.

Harvey, W. B. (1984). The educational system and black mental health. *Journal of Negro Education, 53*, 444–453.

Herr, E. L. (1991). Challenges to mental health counselors in a dynamic society: Macrostrategies in the profession. *Journal of Mental Health Counseling, 13*, 6–20.

Hollister, W. G., & Goldston, S. E. (1959). *Considerations for planning classes for the emotionally handicapped*. Reston, VA: Council for Exceptional Children.

Jersild, A. T. (1955). *When teachers face themselves*. New York: Columbia University, Teachers College.

Jersild, A. T., & Lazar, E. A. (1962). *The meaning of psychotherapy in the teacher's life and work*. New York: Columbia University, Teachers College.

Johnson, J. L. (1969). Special education and the inner city: A challenge for the future or another means for cooling the mark out? *Journal of Special Education, 3*, 241–251.

Johnson, J. L. (1980). Education for self-reliance. In J. B. Jordan, D. A. Sabatino, R. C. Sarri (Eds.), *Disruptive youth in school*, pp. 35–49. Reston, VA: Council for Exceptional Children.

London, P. (1987). Character education and clinical intervention: A paradigm shift for U.S. schools. *Phi Delta Kappan*, May, 667–673.

Mills v. Board of Education of the District of Columbia, 384 F. Supp. 866 (D.D.C. 1972).

Mindell, A. (1988). *City shadows: Psychological interventions in psychiatry*. New York: Routledge.

O'Neil, J. (1991). A generation adrift. *Education Leadership, 49*, 4–10.

Paster, V. S. (1985). Adapting psychotherapy for the depressed, unacculturated, acting-out, black male adolescent. *Psychotherapy, 22*, 408–417.

Peterson, R. L., & Ishii-Jordan, S. (1994). *Multicultural issues in the education of students with behavioral disorders*. Cambridge, MA: Brookline Books.

Radian, N. (1974). Socioeducation groups. In P. Glasser, R. Sarri, & R. Vinter (Eds.), *Individual change through small groups*. New York: The Free Press.

Way, D. W. (1993). I just have half a heart. *Journal of Emotional and Behavioral Problems, 2*, 4–5.

Wilcox, P. (1970). Education for black humanism: A way of approaching it. In N. Wright, Jr. (Ed.), *What black educators are saying* (pp. 3–17). New York: Hawthorn Books.

Williams, C. (1992). *No hiding place: Empowerment and recovery for our troubled communities*. San Francisco: Harper.

Woodson, C. G. (1933). *The mis-education of the negro*. Washington, DC: Associated Press.

Yablonsky, L. (1989). *The therapeutic community: A successful approach for treating substance abusers*. New York: Gardner Press.

EDWARD J. KELLY
University of Nevada, Las Vegas

Edward ("Jim") Kelly has been involved in higher education personnel preparation, administration, theory development, and research germane to the area of emotional disturbance since 1966. He is author of the Differential Test of Conduct and Emotional Problems (DT/CEP) *and* Conduct Problem/Emotional Problems Interventions: A Holistic Perspective, *as well as a number of topical research and programmatic articles. Philosophical, child raising, and parental involvement topics have also been covered in earlier books. He is currently a professor in special education at the University of Nevada, Las Vegas.*

CHAPTER 11

Emotional Disturbance: A Holistic Reconsideration

Unsparing self-awareness does not encourage facile dichotomies between one's professional and personal selves. I can hardly pretend a wholly detached professional interest in emotional disturbance when the larger truth suggests a career profoundly influenced by the personal legacy of three late-childhood/adolescent disabilities. These included mild neurological impairment, an 11-year history of severe stuttering, and, as I shall subsequently define it, concurrent periods of at least mild emotional disturbance.

While this personal history is a dubious qualification for a professional career in emotional disturbance, it has afforded certain insights that seem to have eluded all too many of my colleagues. If nothing else, it has provided a clearer appreciation of the personal realities of emotional disturbance—what it is and is not, how it relates to other conditions and disabilities, and, most importantly, what kinds of therapeutic strategies appear most appropriate—than what is reflected in much of the current literature and practice of this field.

I have used the specific term *holistic* to describe my view of emotional disturbance only quite recently (Kelly, 1990, 1992, 1993), but even my earliest works reflect many of its essential ideas (Kelly, 1968, 1971). This "perspective on perspective," to use Skrtic's (1986) phrase, is far more an eclectic and pragmatic approach to human study than it is a comprehensive theory with fully elaborated methodologies. Its focus encompasses a variety of human concerns often minimized by more reductionistic viewpoints, but it does not devalue scientific method in their study (Heshusius, 1988, 1991). Rather, it proposes that we expand our empirical inquiries to include those elements—personal, experiential, subjective, qualitative, purposive, and voluntary—that contribute to our better understanding of the totality of the human condition and its problems.

REFLECTIONS ON CURRENT PROFESSIONAL EFFORTS

A holistic rejection of reductionistic thinking and practice necessarily includes behaviorism and its various offspring, among them the behavioral disorders mind-set expressed in the official policy statements of the Council for Children with Behavioral Disorders (CCBD), as well as sanctioned position papers and articles printed in this organization's official journal, *Behavioral Disorders*. My personal opposition to CCBD's position statements is probably notorious by now. Several years ago I challenged CCBD's leadership to an open, "winner-take-all" debate (with each side contributing half of a $2,000 purse) in front of CEC's delegate assembly on the dual topics of Nevada's rather explicit exclusion of students with conduct problems and CCBD's definition of emotional and behavior disorders (E/BD). My invitation has been issued several times and still stands, but CCBD has never accepted. So much for the courage of one's collective beliefs!

Since my formal thoughts about this mind-set and CCBD's efforts on its behalf have been thoroughly covered elsewhere (Kelly, 1992), let me only add here that this doctrinaire viewpoint has dominated disturbance-oriented study entirely too long. It has stifled meaningful theory development and programmatic innovation; produced a succession of ludicrously vague, overinclusive definitions; and promoted various position statements essentially designed to maintain a costly system of segregated, psychologically harmful special education gulags. In so far as the present "system" fails to help meaningfully those who are actually emotionally disturbed—and I fervently believe that it has in every critical respect—this perverse mind-set must assume major responsibility for such failure. Obviously, it is time to consider some radically different ideas about emotional disturbance, ideas that more faithfully reflect its holistic realities than does the present failed system.

EMOTIONAL DISTURBANCE: A HOLISTIC PERSPECTIVE

From a holistic standpoint, emotional disturbance is best understood and effectively addressed when we recognize that its essential realities are personally defined. Such recognition leads us to focus on the role of self-perceptions in promoting affective self-devaluation within the individual. In effect, emotional disturbance can be regarded as a self-defined entity whose relative impacts and severity flow from the affective perceptions of the disturbed person. Because these perceptions are basically affective (i.e., reflecting an emotional sense or feeling about self), the term *emotional disturbance* is quite appropriate.

To consolidate these points into a proper definition, emotional disturbance is a "pervasive affective sense of self-disturbedness within an individual, typically characterized by self-devaluing perceptions in relation to both a hypothesized 'normal' self and significant others, and by concomitant self-destructive actions" (Kelly, 1992). Note first that emotional disturbance is truly "pervasive." It can affect virtually all aspects of a person's life, from internalized thoughts, feelings, and values to whatever actions express them. It also can assume acute or chronic forms, varying from temporary but severe occurrences to persistent, lifetime states.

A "sense of self-disturbedness within an individual" leads one to say, in effect, "I don't feel good about myself because . . . " or further, "I am disturbed because I think or feel as I do." And because emotional disturbance has highly negative aesthetic, social, and even moral connotations in most societies (Pervin, 1989), such a judgment can lead to a further devaluation of one's relative self-worth, which in turn intensifies this sense of self-disturbedness ("I am a worthless person to feel and act as I do, to be as different and dissonant as I am").

"Self-devaluing perceptions in relation to both a hypothesized 'normal' self and significant others" involve two distinctly negative comparisons. First, disturbed individuals often unfavorably contrast their thoughts, feelings, or actions against a personal standard of normalcy (i.e., one's better, well-adjusted, ideal, harmonious self). They perceive, in effect, "If I was really normal I wouldn't think this way," or, conversely, "I can never be a good person since I always have these crazy feelings." Then too they believe other people are typically seen as more normal or emotionally healthy than the disturbed individual ("Because no one else thinks or feels as I do, I must be a really sick person." "Everyone I know is better adjusted and more normal than I am." "Only evil or crazy people act like I do").

While emotional disturbance is primarily internalized, it also can be expressed in actions, including acts of misconduct, that do not obtain positive psychological, social, or other recognizable benefits. Instead, they cause significant others (parents, siblings, peers, teachers, coworkers, employers) to further devalue the disturbed person by their occurrence, to perceive that the actor is emotionally "sick," "inadequate," "weak," "weird," or "crazy." Their negative reactions—overt rejection, shock, disgust, ridicule, bullying—often serve to further confirm or intensify the individual's sense of disturbedness and accompanying self-devaluation.

In sum, individuals who are emotionally disturbed subjectively regard themselves as both different and disturbed. This sense of disturbedness is commonly accompanied by self-devaluing perceptions, as well as less frequent self-destructive actions. Most importantly, such individuals perceive not only that they think, feel, and act in a different or disturbed fashion but also that only "ugly, bad, sick, or crazy people" think, feel, and act as they do. It is this distorted aesthetic/moral judgment that is the generic essence of emotional disturbance as a pathological entity.

RESOLVING CONDUCT PROBLEMS, PSYCHIATRIC DISORDERS, AND ETIOLOGICAL DISTRIBUTIONS

The implications of a holistic view of emotional disturbance are all encompassing. When we regard emotional disturbance as a personally defined sense of disturbedness and self-devaluation within the affected individual, it reshapes our view not only of applicable populations, their characteristics, and needs but also of those assessments, interventions, and programs that best address them (Kelly, 1990, 1992). To clarify this initial focus with respect to specific populations, several necessary distinctions should be noted.

The use of the term *behavioral disorders*, confusing purposive, self-enhancing misconduct with emotional problems, makes no sense from a holistic perspective. Indeed, once both conduct and emotional problems are fully understood as self-defined realities, only their differences predominate.

In contrast to persons who are emotionally disturbed, most students with conduct problem histories do not perceive themselves as disturbed or devalued in any significant sense (Atwood, Gold, & Taylor, 1989; Gottfredson & Gottfredson, 1985; Kelly, 1992; Minor, Karr, & Davis, 1984; Wells, 1988; Wiatrowski & Anderson, 1987). While they may adhere to socially or morally aberrant codes of behavior, their actions typically reflect self-enhancing (as opposed to self-destructive) purposes—for attention, for peer status and respect, to obtain power through intimidation and fear, for money or other material gain, to expose the absurdity of specific rules or the relative powerlessness of their enforcers, for conventional or perverse pleasures—that they justify as psychologically normal and morally appropriate. Further, unlike the individuals with emotional disturbance and other disabilities, they quickly learn not to repeat misconduct that results in consistently applied painful consequences. In sum, whatever else can be said about such individuals, their holistic correspondence with the emotionally disturbed is virtually nil.

I make such distinctions not to deny the possibility of comorbidity in specific cases, although the evidence of its relative occurrence remains largely contaminated by its predominant pursuit in incarcerated settings, settings that we have long known to psychologically damage both conduct-problem (Toch & Adams, 1991) and non–conduct-problem populations (Corrado & Tompkins, 1989; Felsman, Leong, Johnson, & Felsman, 1990; Nagata, 1991; Schmolling, 1984; Ursano & Rundell, 1990) in profound ways. Rather, these distinctions must be stressed to counter those professionals who would foolishly "pathologize" all acts of human misconduct to save children from their necessary moral and disciplinary consequences (Grant, 1982). Such "rescuings" do far more than simply weaken any assumption of personal responsibility for one's actions. Left unchecked, they undermine the central disciplinary purpose of the school to educate students who are capable of functioning as responsible and productive citizens in a constitutional democracy.

For these reasons, I cannot emphasize too strongly that purposive, self-enhancing misconduct reflects nothing but normal psychological motivation. Such actions call for rigorous and consistent discipline if their perpetrators are to assume responsibility for their consequences. This discipline is best effected in normalized school and home contexts, subject to no mitigation for age, gender, ethnic or socioeconomic status, phony designations of pathology or disability, or expedient segregations, expulsions, or other efforts to avoid regular school disciplinary responsibility. In sum, regular school discipline must be for *all* students who engage in purposive misconduct if schools are to function as educational settings in any meaningful sense.

Psychiatric disorders and emotional disturbance are best regarded as essentially independent phenomena, the first being structurally (genetically, neurologically, biochemically) determined conditions with environmental mitigators, reflecting specifically classifiable pathological characteristics, and the second being a self-devaluing sense of internalized self-disturbedness, often in reaction to, but neither caused by nor causing, the psychiatric disorder. This distinction is supported by increasing evidence that most major psychiatric disorders emanate from genetic or biological factors and, further, can be ameliorated by various prescriptive medications (American Psychiatric Association, 1989; Bloom, 1993; Lewin, Schneier, & Liebowitz, 1989; Nasrallah, 1991; Pardes, Kauffman, Pincus, & West, 1989; Reiss, Plomin, & Hetherington, 1991; Searles, 1988; Wakefield, 1992).

To be specific, three types of interaction can occur between psychiatric disorders and emotional disturbance. First, because psychiatric disorders are so negatively perceived in our society, they commonly trigger emotional disturbance reactions related to the specific type of disorder. Here, emotional disturbance can occur as a secondary problem that complicates and intensifies the original psychiatric disorder.

Second, while psychiatric disorders commonly provoke disturbance reactions, emotional disturbance nonetheless stems from the individual's perception of self in relation to such influences, rather than to any specific disorder per se. Individuals can manifest even severe psychiatric disorders and yet not be emotionally disturbed in any sense. Individuals with paranoia, for example, typically do not perceive that they are disturbed even when they act out psychotic delusions of persecution, grandeur, or jealous attachment. Persons with anorexia rarely perceive that they have emotional problems, even as they starve themselves to pursue an "ideal" body. Such individuals should not be regarded as emotionally disturbed in any holistic sense. While drastic interventions may be needed, they are more likely to be effective if we do not assume that such individuals either perceive that they have or want help for any emotional problems.

Third, emotional disturbance can occur independently of any prior or present psychiatric disorder. That is, it can originate in individuals who manifest no evidence of a psychiatric disorder distinct from the disturbance condition itself. Thus, many individuals develop pervasive feelings of disturbedness and corollary self-devaluing reactions to either real or perceived parental and other adult physical, psychological, or sexual abuse; sibling and peer cruelty; social isolation, alienation or rejection; academic and vocational difficulties; and so forth. Their disturbance conditions can be as severe as any that occur in response to a prior psychiatric disorder (Kleinman, 1988).

Collectively, these distinctions lead to equally discrete treatment and therapeutic resolutions. Many psychiatric disorders require prescriptive medications suited to their adverse symptoms. Others, such as phobias, respond well to specific symptomatic desensitization. These approaches are designed to cope with specific disorder characteristics, even though they may do little to change disturbed self-perceptions. In so far as the individual who is psychiatrically disordered is not emotionally disturbed, however, such treatments may be all that are needed to ameliorate the disorder's specifically disabling symptoms.

Emotional disturbance therapy, on the other hand, involves counseling, directive problem solving, parent involvement, and other holistic interventions that focus on the individual's disturbed and devaluing perceptions of self. Such therapy is both thematic and idiosyncratic, i.e., it deals with the major themes of disturbed perception that stem from one's response to a common disorder or social circumstance but that are nonetheless given unique definition by the disturbed person. It is this idiosyncratic reality that hazards uniform prescriptive treatments for individuals who are emotionally disturbed.

Disturbance-relevant therapy should accompany prescriptive treatment when both a psychiatric disorder and disturbed perceptions occur. Here both treatment and therapy are needed to meet the specific needs of each condition. At the same time, individuals who are psychiatrically disordered but not emotionally disturbed in any sense should require only prescriptive treatment, and individuals who are only emotionally disturbed will need therapeutic rather than prescriptive interventions. Such discrete solutions reflect historically sound as well as cost-effective approaches to both conditions.

It has long been assumed that emotional disturbance largely stems from such etiologies as intrafamilial physical, psychological, or sexual abuse (Cryan, 1985); mismanagement of child rearing and parent–child communication processes (O'Connell & Mayo, 1988); sibling and peer social rejection, teasing, bullying, and acts of cruelty (Gottfredson & Gottfredson, 1985; Lane, 1989); pressures to meet school acknowledgment expectations (Larsen, 1975); adolescent-specific stressors; and so forth. As I have defined it, however, none of these circumstances can be regarded as direct "causes" of emotional disturbance in any respect. Because we have mainly studied individuals who are clinically disturbed, we have belatedly discovered that such circumstances are all too common in the developmental histories of normal populations as well (Beck & Rosenberg, 1986; Cheshire & Thomae, 1986; Halverson, 1988; Harter, Alexander, & Neimeyer, 1988; Kelly, 1990; Kleinman, 1988). Many individuals emerge from horrific family and other developmental environments and yet don't become emotionally disturbed in any sense. Equally large numbers become severely disturbed in spite of sound child-rearing practices; excellent, caring parents; and every positive social and educational advantage (Grove & Tellegen, 1991). The presence or absence of disturbance in either case depends on the individual's perceptions of self as normal or disturbed, perceptions that can reflect a chosen rejection as well as acceptance of the best or worst "etiological" circumstances.

CAN WE DESIGN BETTER FEDERAL CRITERIA?

Over the past decade CCBD has proposed a number of "behavioral disorders" substitutions to clarify current federal criteria germane to the "seriously emotionally disturbed." Unfortunately, all of these efforts, including the currently proposed E/BD definition, are fatally overinclusive. In spite of its many revisions, the E/BD definition, for example, could easily qualify more than 20% of most urban school district populations for special education services. Leaving aside its other parameters, the definition's conduct problem–relevant language alone could be used to justify the inclusion of large numbers of socioeconomically disadvantaged or culturally, socially, or morally different students as "disabled" simply by virtue of perceived inappropriate conduct. Obviously, this definition's proponents have never learned (or worse, wish to reinvent) special education's perverse origins in urban settings, origins that essentially reflected society's desire to segregate and control racially, ethnically, religiously, or socially different students rather than any sort of altruistic purpose (Hoffman, 1975; McIntyre, 1993).

Perhaps it may be wiser to redesign the current federal criteria than to effect "solutions" that promise far greater evils than those they might cure. Undeniably, the current criteria lack specificity, especially in their failure to adequately reflect major clinical classifications, including those contained in DSM–III–R (American Psychiatric Association, 1987). However, such vagueness can be corrected simply by providing holistic clarifications of its essential features that incorporate relevant clinical descriptors. These clarifications are covered in the following points:

1. The phrase *over a long period of time and to a marked degree* is covered to some extent by our definitional use of the term *pervasive*. To be more specific, the suggestions of Tibbens, Pike, and Welch (1986) that the phrase *over a long period of time* be regarded as referring to a condition lasting at least 6 months (unless a more severe but acute disturbance episode is indicated) and that *to a marked degree* refer to both the pervasiveness and intensity of the emotional problem should also be considered.

2. The phrase *which adversely affects educational performance* is subsumed in each clarification of the five criteria for serious emotional disturbance cited below:

a) The criterion of "an inability to learn which cannot be explained by intellectual, sensory, or health factors" is most specifically met when the student indicates significantly discrepant achievement performance due to anxiety or reality-distorting conditions characterized by:

(1) disorders in thinking, reasoning, or perception stemming from schizophrenic deterioration.

(2) pervasive depressive symptoms affecting school performance.

(3) obsessive–compulsive neurotic personal achievement standards that negatively influence school performance.

b) The criterion of "an inability to build or maintain satisfactory interpersonal relationships with peers and teachers" is most specifically met when the student engages in action or behavioral patterns that suggest self-devaluation in relation to significant others through:

(1) consistently anxious or fear-driven avoidance of meaningful social or school interactions with others.

(2) withdrawal, isolation, or bizarre interactive patterns suggesting symptom behaviors characteristics of schizophrenia, depression, social phobic reactions, obsessive–compulsive addictive states, etc.

(3) the consistent seeking of excessive approval from others through abusive, self-humiliating, or immature actions.

(4) the seeking of negative attention by being ostracized, punished, humiliated, or hurt by others.

c) The criterion of "inappropriate types of behavior or feelings under normal circumstances" is most specifically met when the student exhibits inappropriate actions or feelings emanating from gross self-devaluation, severe anxiety states, or reality distortion. Such actions or feelings would include:

(1) self-destructive, catastrophic reactions to routine occurrences.

(2) hallucinatory behaviors; student describes hearing, seeing, or experiencing things that do not occur (i.e., cannot be verified as real).

(3) delusions; student believes or acts out grossly unreal self–other perceptions (delusions of persecution, grandeur, grossly exaggerated self-importance in relation to others, jealousy, morbid health or body image preoccupations, etc.).

(4) extreme social withdrawal not attributable to learned family patterns.

(5) excessive preoccupation with fantasy life, including relationships with imaginary others and corollary exclusion of normal peer interactions.

(6) bizarre, nonpurposive emotional responses and actions in common social or academic situations (i.e., consistently inappropriate manic, laughing, crying, rage state behaviors, etc.) without apparent cause or motivation.

d) The criterion of "a general pervasive mood of unhappiness or depression" is most specifically met when the student engages in such behavior as:

(1) chronic rage state behaviors, including aggressive acts, that suggest abnormally nonpurposive (e.g., not seeking attention, power, money, social status among peers, revenge, etc.), self-destructive, or randomly impulsive motivations.

(2) consistently expressed feelings of guilt, moral worthlessness, self-reproach, or gross inadequacy over an extended period.

(3) recurring expressions suggesting obsessions with death, being dead, committing suicide, or similar morbid preoccupations.

(4) observed chronic moods of extreme unhappiness, pro-

longed crying episodes without grief motivation or depression.

(5) depressive concomitants, including inability to make even simple decisions, total loss of interest or pleasure in previously valued activities, unusually slowed thinking and actions, flatness of affect, etc.

e) The criterion of "a tendency to develop physical symptoms, pains, or fears, associated with personal, social or school problems" is most specifically met when the student's physical symptoms, pains, or fears emanate from gross self-devaluation or persistent anxiety states, as evidenced by:

(1) consistent physical symptoms without demonstrable organic cause that suggest an anxiety-state etiology (e.g., chronic stomachaches, migraine headaches, dizzy spells, fainting, etc.) related to school performance.

(2) severe somatic conditions (ulcers, colitis, asthmatic reactions, etc.) demonstrably aggravated by the student's inability to appropriately cope with personal, social, or academic stresses.

(3) persistent, irrational fears or phobic reactions focusing on specific objects, activities, situations, or individuals that result in socially disabling avoidance behaviors.

(4) consistent preoccupations with irrational fears or morbid beliefs (e.g., fear of impending catastrophes affecting self or family, belief that everyone hates them, fear of growing up or of succeeding in school, etc.).

3. The inclusion of "children who are schizophrenic" is specifically cited in the clarifications of characteristics *a*, *b*, and *c* above. The corollary exclusion of students who are "socially maladjusted" is consonant with a presumption that this term is an analogous "conduct problem" referent. In effect, students who are socially maladjusted are regarded as "essentially normal individuals" with conduct problems who demonstrate knowledge of appropriate family, social, or school rules and choose not to conform to them. Such choices/actions do not constitute evidence of a disabling condition in any sense; rather, they illustrate—through attention, power, social status among one's peers, greed, perverse pleasure, the perceived absurdity of specific rules, and so forth—expressions of normal self-interest and purposive intent. Socially maladjusted students do not typically assume responsibility for the personal consequences of their inappropriate actions or their impacts upon others. They perceive themselves as essentially normal and believe that they have a right to behave as they

do (Nevada Department of Education, 1993)[1]. In this context, any determination that such students are also seriously emotionally disturbed mandates satisfaction of the specific descriptions cited in point 2 above, rather than the original, vaguely stated federal criteria.

As these clarifications indicate, a holistic view of emotional disturbance encompasses both legal and clinical perspectives. Thus, it uses clinically recognized descriptors to expand the current federal definition and related criteria, without sacrificing the distinct clinical and educational characteristics of either perspective. Such clarifications illustrate one of the potential values of a holistic view of emotional disturbance conditions.

CLARIFYING THE NUMBERS: THE IMPORTANCE OF HOLISTICALLY APPROPRIATE SCREENING AND DIAGNOSTIC PROCESSES

I am not as moved by the concern over the increasing numbers of students with E/BD served in special education as I am by the restrictive housing that usually accompanies such "service." Obviously, as long as we continue to use ambiguous definitions that confuse conduct and emotional problem characteristics, such numbers are likely to increase in response to demands that we "cure" violent juvenile gangs, drug abuse, poverty, and other intractable societal problems. Unfortunately, one sad constant will remain largely unchanged: Those students who are actually emotionally disturbed will continue to be the most underidentified and inappropriately served of all disability groups. Indeed, this more important concern will never be seriously addressed until we effect holistic screening and diagnostic processes that clearly differentiate between individuals with conduct problems and those who are emotionally disturbed.

A presumption that emotional disturbance is a self-defined entity, clearly distinct from purposive conduct-problem motivations and largely so from the various psychiatric disorders and etiological factors that contribute to it, suggests a fairly complex holistic assessment process. At the

---

[1] Nevada's exclusion of students who are not disabled but have conduct problems was first adopted in 1988 and reaffirmed in 1993. Although most of the state's 17 school districts now identify and place smaller numbers of such students in programs for the "severely emotionally handicapped" (SEH), no forced decertification of previously placed students with conduct problems have occurred since implementation. Some of the state's less populous districts have begun to identify more students with SEH, and a greater emphasis on inclusive programming is seen in most districts. On the whole, however, the relative impacts of this exclusion policy have been much less dramatic than either its proponents or opponents anticipated before implementation.

very least it requires the employment of discrete screening and diagnostic phases and encompasses the use of subjective, qualitative, experiential, and self-perceptual measures as well as "objective" ones. Since such a process can only be summarized here, readers may desire to review earlier work (Kelly, 1990, 1992) for more extensive coverage.

Holistic affective screening is pursued essentially to make clear differentiations among students without significant conduct or emotional problems, students without disabilities who have conduct problems, and those who are emotionally disturbed. These distinctions can be effected through analyses of observed student behavioral patterns; behavior ratings filled out by teachers, other professional personnel, and parents; and interviews conducted with these same individuals and, where appropriate, the affected student. Analysis particularly focuses on behavioral patterns that reveal purposive, self-enhancing versus self-destructive motivations, as well as the relative presence or absence of expressions indicating perceptions of normalcy or self-justification versus those that indicate pervasive disturbance and self-devaluation.

Verification of at least a generic emotional disturbance condition invokes an equally distinct diagnostic process. This latter process focuses on the subjective perceptions of self-disturbedness and devaluation expressed by the individual through the use of various personality, temperament, self-concept, projective, and structured-interview tests and procedures. In so doing, we should make four critical determinations:

1. *type*, which refers to objective determinations of the relative presence or absence of contributing psychiatric disorders, specific disabilities, and other conditions that are contributing to the individual's perceptions of self as disturbed and devalued.
2. *intensity* of the disturbance condition, not only as it may be objectively assessed but also as it is subjectively perceived by the affected person as impairing competent functioning in various personal, social, educational, and adaptive senses. This latter assessment can be a crucial determinant of relative intervention need, for we know that specific individuals may be profoundly disturbed—to the point of imminent self-destruction—and yet objectively appear to function competently in school and other contexts.
3. *antecedents*, which denote "etiological" factors that the affected individual perceives to have contributed to the disturbing condition. Because such factors can include virtually any real or spurious life circumstance, their impact on persons who are disturbed and their families must be identified and resolved to

facilitate the successful outcome of whatever therapy is pursued.

4. *themes*, which refer to consistently occurring expressions of disturbedness and self-devaluation, as well as to related type, intensity, and antecedent perceptions. Themes of self-disturbedness occur in expressed feelings about being psychologically disturbed in relation to others, of being "ugly," "crazy," "sick," or "weird." Self-devaluing themes are reflected in statements of personal inadequacy, of social or moral worthlessness, of being unlovable, or of guilt and shame because of one's thoughts, feelings, or actions. Themes involving type, intensity, or antecedents often are woven into both disturbance and devaluing statements, leading to expressions of worthlessness and despondency over one's depressed state, of being unlovable and irrevocably damaged in response to childhood sexual or psychological abuse, or of feeling alienated and isolated because of one's peculiar thoughts or bizarre actions (Guidano, 1987; Lefcourt, 1986).

In the final analysis, themes constitute the most vital content of whatever diagnostic statements can be made about an individual who is disturbed when assessment is completed. And yet their real value lies more in prescriptive than in diagnostic implications. Assessment of the thematic elements of disturbance should always culminate in appropriate prescriptive interventions, interventions that not only focus on and resolve each important theme expressed by the person who is disturbed but also fulfill his or her personal need for whatever type of therapy is pursued.

HOLISTIC THERAPY: MEETING STUDENT NEEDS IN REGULAR SCHOOL AND CLASSROOM SETTINGS

Holistic therapy emphasizes several points that distinguish its pursuit from much of what is proposed in the professional literature and practice dominated by a "behavioral disorders" perspective. First, a holistic view of emotional disturbance, as a self-defined sense of disturbedness within the affected person accompanied by self-devaluing perceptions, compels a strong focus on such perceptions, using any means that most directly counter and resolve them. For this reason, student-centered counseling and problem-solving interactions, improvements in parent–child and teacher–student communication, and guided student participation in normalcy-enhancing regular school programming and nonrestrictive social functioning are more likely to be pursued than efforts that minimally address or ignore such perceptions.

Second, this valuing of interventions that most directly focus on disturbed perceptions supports the corollary use of problem-solving therapeutic approaches. In this respect, the thematic elements of disturbed perception are best regarded as simple problem statements. As such, they can be identified from prior diagnosis or initial counseling interviews, elaborated and discussed as counseling topics, and resolved through problem-solving and coping skills obtained from directive counseling or related instruction (Kelly, 1992).

This problem-solving therapeutic emphasis also leads us to attend primarily to *currently* perceived emotional problems and their present or future resolutions. While a student's perceptions of disturbance-relevant antecedents can profoundly influence one's present circumstances—and, certainly, their relative impacts should be diagnostically assessed before we begin directive interventions—such perceptions often serve only to deter meaningful problem solving. In this regard, I am inclined to agree with the views of Rogers (1951, 1957) and Glasser and Zunin (1979) that continuing reiterations of past circumstances contribute little to positive therapeutic outcomes. Because one cannot change the past in any sense, it has minimal relevance in holistic counseling interventions.

Third, the self-defined and subjectively perceived nature of emotional disturbance leads me to regard the affected individual as the principal change agent in all therapeutic processes. Notwithstanding its etiological roles or contributions, emotional disturbance is always an intimately personal matter, stemming from the affected person's unique perceptions and choices. I may seek to influence what others say and do to facilitate therapeutic processes, but it is only therapy's subjects who can effect meaningful changes in self-perception and, far more importantly, must live with their impacts.

This emphasis on the individual who is disturbed as the principal therapeutic and etiological agent has two critical implications. In the first instance, it is counterproductive to even imply etiological roles or blame parents for their child's problems, and most particularly in view of my need to involve them as positive therapeutic agents. From a holistic standpoint, parents can only be cooperatively and productively involved if I encourage a "no fault" partnership with them in all therapeutic processes (Kelly, 1993).

In the second place, a holistic presumption of student etiological and therapeutic responsibility is maintained to foster their direct and active participation in therapy. Such participation mandates students' awareness of the realities of emotional disturbance: that it is a self-defined condition of perceived disturbedness and self-devaluation that can be effectively countered within and by the affected person, that one's sense of disturbedness and self-devaluation is not an immutable reality, that every person possesses the potential to change such perceptions in positive ways. Collectively, these values underlay all student participation in whatever holistic therapy is proposed.

Fourth, effective parent–student participation in any therapeutic endeavor requires fully informed and voluntary consent (Corey, Corey, & Callanan, 1984; Ross, 1980). This participation cannot be imposed upon unwilling subjects who deny problem existence or ownership or who reject therapeutic need and involvement. Rather, it assumes that students and their parents perceive that they have problems, actively desire our help to deal with them, and freely participate in whatever interventions are most applicable to their resolution.

Fifth, holistic therapy emphasizes normalization in both placement and programming, irrespective of relatively perceived disturbance characteristics and intensities. This emphasis is best fulfilled in regular school, classroom, and family settings, settings that most naturally and effectively reinforce our efforts at countering perceptions of disturbedness and self-devaluation through the communication of normalcy-enhancing values and the promotion of normalized functioning. And, given our currently dismal reintegration rates from psychologically destructive self-contained placements (Dwyer, 1990; Grosenick, George, George, & Lewis, 1991; Stainback, Stainback, & Forest, 1989; Swan, Brown, & Jacob, 1987), such an emphasis resolves this problem as well by preventing its occurrence in all circumstances.[2]

In sum, holistic therapy is designed to directly counter and resolve perceptions of disturbedness and self-devaluation and to enhance feelings of normalcy, personal competence, and self-worth within the affected student. Such efforts require informed and voluntary parent and student participation to be truly effective. And they are best facilitated when the student is maintained in normalized regular school, neighborhood, home, and other adaptive contexts.

While any number of proposed interventions and programs reflect such attributes to a certain extent, only a few options maximally fulfill

---

[2] Both this and the previous point are further supported by current research indicating strong student preference for the provision of integrated special education services in general school and classroom settings over any kind of restrictively housed alternative (Affleck, Madge, Adams, & Lowenbraun, 1988; Behre, McIntyre, & Rogers, 1993; Blackman, 1989; Coleman, 1983; Jenkins & Heinen, 1989; McIntyre, 1993). Such studies suggest that if we provided for informed and voluntary consent with all students who are emotionally disturbed, special classes would probably become extinct in most school districts.

them. These options, disturbance relevant teacher and parent education and involvement programming, various forms of dire student counseling and related problem-solving/coping skills instruction, and facilitated normalization, are encompassed within the context of holistic "crisis intervention" operations.

THE HOLISTIC CRISIS INTERVENTION SERVICE DELIVERY MODEL

The essential purpose of disturbance-relevant crisis intervention is normalization. That is, it employs whatever personnel and other resources are needed to maintain students who are emotionally disturbed within their milieu, in their neighborhood schools and classrooms, and in all other normalcy-enhancing social contexts. It is best fostered by regular teacher consultation, cooperative parent involvement programming, student counseling and related problem-solving instruction, and facilitated normalization in both home and school.

Public school crisis intervention programs can be implemented either through instructional unit funding (where personnel salaries and other costs are regarded as a fiscal unit) or through student count formulae. If this latter method is used, funding must be adjusted. That would promote serving a greater number of students by crisis intervention (roughly 2 to 4 times more) than are typically housed in self-contained placements.

Crisis intervention roles are best fulfilled by itinerant non–classroom-bound personnel who can serve the relevant needs of one or more schools. Many of these roles can be carried out by school psychologists, social workers, or school counselors, but it is the emotional disturbance program consultants and teacher-counselors who are most likely to fulfill them in the most comprehensive fashion. In this context, the term *teacher-counselor* is most apt, for such individuals will both teach and counsel their students, as well as work with parents, general and special class teachers, and non–school agency personnel. And such personnel will be readily available to assume such roles, given adequate consultive or coordinative mentoring (Kelly, 1992; Newcomer, 1993), whenever school districts effect a wholesale shift from self-contained programs to this more inclusive alternative for their students who are emotionally disturbed.

Crisis interventions call for a number of personnel roles. While these roles vary in scope according to the age and specific needs of individual students, they generally include:

1. participation in Individual Education Program (IEP) meetings to effect a smooth translation of diagnostic/prescriptive infor-

mation into specific interventions involving students who are emotionally disturbed, their general class teachers, parents, and (where appropriate) community agency and other service providers.
2. the management of currently active student caseloads subject to specific direct and indirect crisis interventions. In addition to active cases, monitoring of both potential caseload additions and the subsequent progress of previously served students also must be maintained.
3. the maintenance of students who are emotionally disturbed in general schools and classrooms through:
    a. individual, general-class teacher consultations to promote more positive student-centered communication, instruction, and classroom functioning;
    b. general teacher/administrator in-service education pertinent to a holistic understanding of the discrete treatment and therapeutic needs of individuals who are psychiatrically disordered and those who are emotionally disturbed;
    c. parent training and involvement programming to effect improved child-focused communication, family interaction, and home functioning; and
    d. individual student interventions to effect both positive changes in self-perception and enhanced problem-solving and coping skills.
4. cooperative consultation with community agency and other professional personnel who provide treatment for specific students who are psychiatric disordered or emotionally disturbed.
5. communication and correlation of crisis-intervention operations with those of other specialists, as well as with program-related consultive, coordinative, and administrative personnel. (Suggestions abstracted from Heron & Harris, 1982; Idol, 1993; Idol, Paolucci-Whitcomb, & Nevin, 1986; Kelly & Schacher, 1988; Sandoval, 1987).

Of these roles, individual, general-class teacher consultation is most central to public school normalization. Such consultation has two thrusts. First, all student crisis interventions must be accompanied by teacher communication about the specific disturbance condition, its psychiatric and other contributors, and, most importantly, how their interactions with affected students can promote positive therapeutic change.

Teachers must be trained to counter expressed perceptions of disturbedness and self-devaluation as they occur in their classrooms. Such training focuses on the communication of positive rather than negative themes, the maintenance or improvement of instructional processes that promote the student's normal functioning and relationships within the classroom, and the use of encouragement techniques that enhance feelings of personal competence and self-worth in all school contexts (Neely, 1982).

It should be noted here that general teacher acquisition of such skills does not require formal university-bound training. These skills can be just as effectively obtained through on-site, informal group and individual teacher in-servicing, accompanied by frequent teacher–crisis intervention specialist consultation. Indeed, such case-specific interactions are the best kind of training, for they promote immediate on-site applications of acquired skill.

The general class normalization of students with emotional problems also can be promoted through staff in-services. These in-services can vary from brief, informal presentations on a specific topic to formal courses taken for university or professional growth credit (Kelly, 1992; Neely, 1982). While such in-services may encompass a wide variety of topics, primary attention should be given to those that not only contribute to teacher/administrator understanding of student emotional problems but also enhance their skills in helping to resolve them.

> The effective normalization of students clearly mandates constructive and cooperative involvements with their parents. Such involvements are fostered when parents are trained to act as therapeutic partners in facilitating positive interventions with their own children. This training, carried out in regularly scheduled parent–crisis intervention specialist meetings, is designed to:
>
> a. educate parents about the holistic realities of their child's emotional problems, as well as their need to be cooperatively involved in all home–school amelioration.
>
> b. train them in specific ways to directly counter their child's perceptions of disturbedness and self-devaluation in all situational parent–child interactions.
>
> c. help them improve communication and other positive involvements with their child to enhance his/her feelings of both personal competence and self worth as a valued family member.
>
> d. promote their recognition and mitigation of disturbance-contributing sibling, extended family and neighborhood factors. (Kelly, 1993, pp. 9–16)

School-based student-centered counseling and related instructional interactions are also indispensable holistic crisis interventions. Both require informed and voluntary consent from students and their parents for effective participation. Each acts to directly counter student perceptions of self as disturbed and devalued as well as to promote disturbance-relevant problem-solving and coping skills. Also, they seek the maintenance of the student in all normalcy-enhancing general school and home settings throughout and subsequent to their employment.

Selection of either form of intervention will depend on the relative maturity and insight of the student and the skill of the crisis intervention specialist. Directive counseling emphasizes the identification and practical resolution of student-perceived emotional problem themes in a relatively brief time frame. It is more likely to be effective when students are at least 10 years of age or possess sufficient insight into themselves and their problems to profit from such knowledge (Kelly, 1992; Maher & Springer, 1987). Problem-solving instructional interactions, on the other hand, focus on the amelioration of self-destructive behavioral patterns through student acquisition and use of relevant coping skills in classroom and related social contexts (Gesten, Weissberg, Amish, & Smith, 1987; Glasser & Zunin, 1979; Maher & Zins, 1987; Newcomer, 1993). Such interactions can be effectively pursued with younger students as well as with older ones who evidence minimal potential benefit from directive counseling approaches (Kelly, 1992).

Finally, several liaison and coordinative functions also are vital in crisis-intervention programming. In the first instance, crisis-intervention specialists often need to maintain professional liaisons with public and private agency service providers to:

1. facilitate, in concert with parents and disturbance-relevant coordinative and administrative personnel, appropriate treatment referrals of students with contributing psychiatric disorders to public or private agency service providers.

2. communicate with agency service providers to promote a meaningful coordination of effort between their treatments and the therapeutic and educational aspects of the student's crisis-intervention programming in the public schools.

3. act as a public school coordinator of efforts to reintegrate students previously housed in restrictive, nonpublic school settings into general schools and classrooms. This is an essential function, for general school personnel are far more likely to respond positively to the reintegration efforts of a public school specialist who maintains consistently effective consultive contact with them than to a non–school agency person who may reveal minimal understanding of the general school and its processes (Maher & Zins, 1987; Sandoval, 1987).

Public-school crisis-intervention operations must be coordinated at all levels if they are to be maximally effective. Individual case management, for example, requires that the specialist initially coordinate not only the inputs of diagnostic and other specialists in prescriptive program planning and related IEP development, but also the parameters and scheduling of various participant roles in all subsequent therapeutic interventions. In all of these circumstances, effective communication between the specialist and parents, general classroom teachers, administrators, and other school professionals is an ongoing necessity (Gersten, Darch, Davis, & George, 1991; Grosenick, George, George, & Lewis, 1991).

FUTURE DIRECTIONS AND TRENDS: HOLISTIC RESOLUTIONS AND THEIR ANTITHESIS

Questions about a field's future always evoke a personal dilemma stemming largely from my continuing fascinations with both chess and military and political history. I am not blind to those factors that may shape our futures, but I've always been more certain that significant individuals have far greater power to effect what shall be than do impersonal trends. If I did not wholeheartedly believe this, I might be content to pursue my theoretical speculations and research interests without much regard for their real-world impacts beyond academia.

As a dispassionate academic, I could more comfortably note that the American West's raging tax revolts are spreading eastward. In conjunction with growing public concerns about violent crime and frustration over general education's inability to meaningfully articulate or fulfill its missions, heated "prisons versus schools" debates are beginning to be heard in all too many state legislatures. Special education has not escaped its share of this negative consideration. Its ever-escalating costs and corollary inability to demonstrate the efficacy of much of its programming also has drawn increasingly hostile criticism from frustrated parents, general educators, and the taxpaying public ("Investigative Report," 1993).

None of these trends bode well for a field so dominated by a behavioral disorders mind-set. Nothing about this mind-set—with its intellectually barren "official" literature, its absurdly overinclusive definitions, its promotion of costly and largely ineffective restrictive placements and programs, and its rejection of reasonable inclusive alternatives—warrants any immunity from a wholesale public and professional backlash. Indeed, its foolish pretense that restrictive E/BD programs can effectively resolve individual and collective juvenile crime (Council for Children with Behavioral Disorders, 1990; Nelson, Rutherford, Center, & Walker, 1991), makes it the ideal "poster child" for its worst inevitabilities.

But one must never be content with such academic forecasts, to passively observe and be resigned to such dire possibilities when one's commitments and actions can change them. It has been my personal experience, reflecting involvements with legislative change in New Mexico, with Nevada's explicit conduct-problem exclusion policy, and with current national opposition to the E/BD definition, that convinces me that individuals can move entire social systems when they act from rational convictions and intense personal commitments. And I have gained even from my least successful efforts. As in chess, one's most painful failures are often more instructive than any success; conversely, nothing of merit is ever learned or won through passive resignation.

It is principally for such reasons that this chapter has so strongly emphasized the importance of a holistic view of emotional disturbance. The dismal future that I foresee for this field of study and programming is most likely to occur if we acquiesce to its present course or merely resign ourselves to its inevitabilities. Yet such future "shadows" need not be if we begin to perceive and work with individuals who are emotionally disturbed in more holistically appropriate ways.

To this end, I have noted the ways that a holistic perspective can radically transform our current practices in emotional disturbance. If, for example, we begin to view emotional disturbance as a self-defined condition of disturbance and devaluation within the affected person, we also better appreciate its independence from both the psychiatric disorders and various etiological factors that contribute to its intensity but do not directly cause it. When we regard emotional disturbance as a subjectively perceived qualitative entity, then screening and diagnostic processes must be restructured to assess these attributes. If we view it as a self-caused condition, then all aspects of parental involvement must be changed to reflect no-fault problem-solving partnerships between home and school.

If emotional disturbance is essentially characterized by disturbed perceptions and perverse themes, then therapeutic efforts must focus on the resolution of such elements within the affected person, rather than just the superficial modification of cosmetic external behaviors. And finally, when we see that individuals with emotional problems act from spurious self-devaluing perceptions, then self-contained, segregated placements and programs that reinforce such perceptions must be avoided at all costs in favor of integrated regular placements and normalcy-enhancing crisis-intervention services.

All of these considerations recommend a holistic view of emotional disturbance as a revolutionary perspective that can positively redirect our own professional and personal values as well as our field's future prospects. In professional terms, it tells us that human values must override all other concerns in emotional disturbance programs, that the student's need for normalized education in general classrooms is far more important than any research, methodological or profit motive. Personally, a holistic perspective tells us that we must finally acknowledge our human kinship with persons who are emotionally disturbed—to recognize that we differ affectively only in perceived degree; that all of us are capable of significant disturbance in our lives; that we all share basic personal needs to achieve and succeed, to be accepted, and to be valued in every normal social context—if we are ever to begin to help them in any humanly appropriate fashion.

REFERENCES

Affleck, J. Q., Madge, S., Adams, A., & Lowenbraun, S. (1988). Integrated classroom vs resource room model academic viability and effectiveness. *Exceptional Children, 54*, 339–348.

American Psychiatric Association. (1987). *Diagnostic and statistical manual of mental disorders* (3rd ed. rev.). Washington, DC: Author.

American Psychiatric Association. (1989). *Treatment of psychiatric disorders: A task force report of the American Psychiatric Association. Vol. 1–3.* Washington, DC: Author.

Atwood, R., Gold, M., & Taylor, R. (1989). Two types of delinquents and their institutional adjustment. *Journal of Consulting and Clinical Psychology, 57*, 62–77.

Beck, S., & Rosenberg, R. (1986). Frequency, quality, and impact of life events in self-rated depressed, behavioral problem and normal children. *Journal of Consulting and Clinical Psychology, 54*, 863–864.

Behre, W. J., McIntyre, T., & Rogers, K. (1993). They tell me I'm crazy: Student responses to being labeled behavior disordered. *Perceptions, 27*, 12–13.

Blackman, H. P. (1989). Special education placement: Is it what you know or where you live? *Exceptional Children, 55*, 459–462.

Bloom, F. E. (1993). Advancing a neurodevelopmental origin of schizophrenia. *Archives of General Psychiatry, 50*, 224–227.

Chesire, N., & Thomae, H. (1986). *Self, symptoms, and psychotherapy.* New York: Wiley.

Coleman, J. M. (1983). Handicapped labels and instructional segregation: Influence on children's self-concept vs perceptions of others. *Learning Disabilities Quarterly, 6*, 3.

Corey, G., Corey, M. S., & Callanan, P. (1984). *Issues and ethics in the helping professions* (2nd ed.). Monterey, CA: Brooks/Cole.

Corrado, R. R., & Tompkins, E. (1989). A comparative model of the psychological effects on the victims of state and anti-state terrorism. *International Journal of Law and Psychiatry, 12*, 281–293.

Council for Children with Behavioral Disorders. (1990). Position paper on the provision of services to children with conduct disorders. *Behavioral Disorders, 15*, 180–189.

Cryan, J. R. (1985). Intellectual, emotional and social deficits of abused children: A review. *Childhood Education, 61,* 388–392.
Dwyer, K. P. (1990). Making the least restrictive environment work for children with serious emotional disturbance: Just say no to segregated placements. *Preventing School Failure, 34,* 14–21.
Felsman, J. K., Leong, F. T., Johnson, M. C., & Felsman, I. C. (1990). Estimates of psychological distress among Vietnamese refugees: Adolescents, unaccompanied minors and young adults. *Social Science and Medicine, 31,* 1251–1256.
Gersten, R., Darch, C., Davis, G., & George, N. L. (1991). Apprenticeship and intensive training for consultive teachers. *Exceptional Children, 57,* 226–236.
Gesten, E. I., Weissberg, R. P., Amish, P. L., & Smith, J. K. (1987). Social problem-solving training: A skills-based approach to prevention and treatment. In C. A. Maher & J. E. Zins (Eds.), *Psychoeducational interventions in the classroom* (pp. 26–45). New York: Pergamon Press.
Glasser, W., & Zunin, L. M. (1979). Reality therapy. In R. J. Corsini (Ed.), *Current psychotherapies* (2nd ed.). Itasca, IL: Peacock.
Gottfredson, G. D., & Gottfredson, D. C. (1985). *Victimization in schools.* New York: Plenum Books.
Grant, G. (1982, Fall). Children's rights and adult confusions. *The Public Interest,* 83–89.
Grosenick, J. K., George, N. L., George, M. P., & Lewis, T. J. (1991). Public school services for behaviorally disordered students: Program practices for the 1980's. *Behavioral Disorders, 16,* 87–96.
Grove, W. M., & Tellegen, A. (1991). Problems in the classification of personality disorders. *Journal of Personality Disorders, 5,* 31–41.
Guidano, V. F. (1987). *Complexity of the self: A developmental approach to psychopathology and therapy.* New York: Guilford Press.
Halverson, C. R. (1988). Remembering your parents: Reflections on the retrospective method. *Journal of Personality, 56,* 435–443.
Harter, S., Alexander, P. C., & Neimeyer, R. A. (1988). Longterm effects of incestuous child abuse in college women: Social adjustment, social cognition and family characteristics. *Journal of Consulting and Clinical Psychology, 56,* 5–8.
Heron, T. E., & Harris, K. (1982). *The educational consultant: Helping professionals, parents and mainstreamed students.* Boston: Allyn & Bacon.
Heshusius, L. (1988). The arts, science, and the study of exceptionality. *Exceptional Children, 55,* 60–65.
Heshusius, L. (1991). Curriculum-based assessment and direct instruction: Critical reflections on fundamental assumptions. *Exceptional Children, 57,* 315–328.
Hoffman, E. (1975). The American public school and the deviant child: The origins of their involvement. *Journal of Special Education, 9,* 415–424.
Idol, L. (1993). *Special educator's consultation handbook* (2nd ed.). Austin, TX: PRO-ED.
Idol, L., Paolucci-Whitcomb, P., & Nevin, A. (1986). *Collaborative consultation.* Rockville, MD: Aspen.
Investigative report: Separate and unequal. (1993, December 13). *U.S. News and World Report,* pp. 46–60.

Jenkins, J. R., & Heinen, A. (1989). Students' preferences for service delivery: Pull-out, in class or integrated models. *Exceptional Children, 55,* 516–523.

Kelly, E. J. (1968). Toward a comprehensive paradigm of special educational functions. *Journal of Special Education, 2,* 273–281.

Kelly, E. J. (1971). *Philosophical perspectives in special education.* Columbus, OH: Merrill.

Kelly, E. J. (1990). *The Differential Test of Conduct and Emotional Problems: Manual.* New York: Slosson.

Kelly, E. J. (1992). *Conduct problem/emotional problem interventions: A holistic perspective.* New York: Slosson.

Kelly, E. J. (1993). Building "no-fault" parent–professional relationships to resolve student conduct and emotional problems. *Perceptions, 28,* 9–16.

Kelly, E. J., & Schacher, E. (1988). *The conduct problem/emotional problem handbook.* Las Vegas: Nevada Department of Education.

Kleinman, A. (1988). *Rethinking psychiatry: From cultural category to personal experience.* New York: Free Press.

Lane, D. A. (1989). Bullying in school: The need for an integrated approach. *School Psychology International, 10,* 211–215.

Larsen, S. C. (1975). The influence of teacher expectations on the school performance of handicapped children. *Focus on Exceptional Children, 6,* 1–14.

Lefcourt, H. M. (1986). Perceiving self as an effective agent. In L. M. Hartman & K. R. Blankenstein (Eds.), *Perception of self in emotional disorders and psychotherapy* (pp. 37–49). New York: Plenum Press.

Lewin, A. P., Schneier, F. R., & Liebowitz, M. R. (1989). Social phobia: Biology and pharmacology. *Clinical Psychology Review, 9,* 129–140.

Maher, C. A., & Springer, J. (1987). School-based counseling. In C. A. Maher & J. E. Zins (Eds.), *Psychoeducational interventions in the schools: Methods and procedures for enhancing student competence* (pp. 111–117). New York: Pergamon Press.

Maher, C. A., & Zins, J. E. (1987). *Psychoeducational interventions in the schools: Methods and procedures for enhancing student competence.* New York: Pergamon Press.

McIntyre, T. (1993). Reflections on the new definition for emotional and behavioral disorders: Who still falls through the cracks and why. *Behavioral Disorders, 18,* 148–160.

Minor, K. I., Karr, S. K., & Davis, S. F. (1984). Social and self-perceptions of institutionalized and non-institutionalized juveniles. *Bulletin of the Psychonomic Society, 22,* 557–559.

Nagata, D. K. (1991). Transgenerational impact of the Japanese-American internment: Clinical issues in working with children of former internees. *Psychotherapy, 28,* 121–128.

Nasrallah, H. A. (1991). Neurodevelopmental aspects of bipolar affective disorder. *Biological Psychiatry, 29,* 1–2.

Neely, M. (1982). *Counseling and guidance practices with special education students.* Homewood, IL: Dorsey Press.

Nelson, C. M., Rutherford, R. B., Center, D. B., & Walker, H. M. (1991). Do public schools have an obligation to serve troubled children and youth? *Exceptional Children, 57,* 406–415.

Nevada Department of Education. (1993). *Administration of exceptional pupil education programs*. Carson City, NV: Author.

Newcomer, P. L. (1993). *Understanding and teaching emotionally disturbed children* (2nd ed.). Austin, TX: PRO-ED.

O'Connell, R. A., & Mayo, J. A. (1988). The role of social factors in affective disorders: A review. *Hospital and Community Psychiatry, 39,* 842–851.

Pardes, H., Kauffman, C. A., Pincus, H. A., & West, A. (1989). Genetics and psychiatry: Past discoveries, current dilemmas, and future directions. *American Journal of Psychiatry, 146,* 435–443.

Pervin, L. A. (1989). *Personality: Theory and research*. New York: Wiley.

Reiss, D., Plomin, R., & Hetherington, E. M. (1991). Genetics and psychiatry: An unheralded window on the environment. *American Journal of Psychiatry, 148,* 283–291.

Rogers, C. R. (1951). *Client-centered therapy: Its current practices, implications and theory*. Boston: Houghton-Mifflin.

Rogers, C. R. (1957). The necessary and sufficient conditions of therapeutic personality change. *Journal of Consulting Psychology, 21,* 95–103.

Ross, A. O. (1980). *Psychological disorders of children: A behavioral approach to theory, research and therapy* (2nd ed.). New York: McGraw-Hill.

Sandoval, J. (1987). Crisis intervention. In C. A. Maher & J. C. Zins (Eds.), *Psychoeducational interventions in the schools: Methods and procedures for enhancing student competence* (pp. 177–192). New York: Pergamon Press.

Schmolling, P. (1984). Human reactions to Nazi concentration camps: A summing up. *Journal of Human Stress, 10,* 108–120.

Searles, J. S. (1988). The role of genetics in the pathogenesis of alcoholism. *Journal of Abnormal Psychology, 97,* 153–167.

Skrtic, T. M. (1986). The crisis in special education knowledge: A perspective on perspective. *Focus on Exceptional Children, 18,* 1–16.

Stainback, S., Stainback, W., & Forest, M. (1989). *Educating all students in the mainstream of education*. Baltimore: Brookes.

Swan, W. W., Brown, C. L., & Jacob, R. T. (1987). Types of service delivery models used in the reintegration of severely emotionally disturbed/behaviorally disordered students. *Behavioral Disorders, 12,* 99–103.

Tibbens, T. J., Pike, T. R., & Welch, N. (1986). *Identification and assessment of the seriously emotionally disturbed child*. Sacramento: California State Department of Education.

Toch, H., & Adams, K. (1991). *Coping: Maladaptation in prisons*. New Brunswick, NJ: Transaction.

Ursano, R. J., & Rundell, J. R. (1990). The prisoner of war. *Military Medicine, 155,* 176–180.

Wakefield, J. C. (1992). The concept of mental disorder: On the boundary between biological fact and social values. *American Psychologist, 47,* 373–388.

Wells, R. (1988). A fresh look at the muddy waters of psychopathy. *Psychological Reports, 63,* 843–856.

Wiatrowski, M. D., & Anderson, K. L. (1987). The dimensionality of the social bond. *Psychological Journal of Quantitative Criminology, 3,* 65–81.

NICHOLAS J. LONG
Institute of Psychoeducational Training

Nicholas Long's many contributions include the books Conflict in the Classroom *(with Bill Morse and Ruth Newman) and* Teaching Self Control *(with Stan Fagan). After receiving his master's degree he became a summer camp counselor in a therapeutic camp for children who were emotionally disturbed. It was there that he met and observed Bill Morse, Fritz Redl, and Dave Wineman manage crisis situations. After earning his PhD he became the first principal of the Children's Psychiatric Hospital, which brought him into relationship with Dr. Rabinovitch, a child psychiatrist.*

Other positions include professor at Indiana University (1958–62); executive director of The Hillcrest Children's Psychiatric Center in Washington, DC (1962–70); founder and director of Rose School, a public mental health treatment program for students with severe disturbances (1970–90); and professor of special education at American University (1968–90). He founded and continues to direct the Institute of Psychoeducational Training and currently co-edits The Journal of Emotional and Behavioral Problems *with Dr. Larry Brendtro.*

CHAPTER 12

To Those Who Will Continue the Struggle

I have spent the last 35 years in service to children who are emotionally disturbed, hopefully influencing and preparing others to do so as well. While I have been involved in psychoeducational research and training activities over the years, I believe my ongoing contact with students who are troubled has provided me with a daily reminder of how difficult it is to help these students and how important it is to continue to learn additional intervention skills. In retrospect, I wish I could say that I had more control over my early career, but the truth is that I never planned to be a special educator or to teach students who were emotionally disturbed. I was fortunate to have outstanding mentors and to be at the right place at the right time when a crisis created a career opportunity for me. Perhaps this is why I believe that crises are unique and powerful opportunities for teaching and learning.

I was born in Detroit, Michigan, in 1929. In my career I have served in many different professional roles in various educational and mental health facilities. My experiences have included functioning as the principal of the Children's Psychiatric Hospital in Ann Arbor, Michigan (1955–56); associate professor in education and psychology at Indiana University (1958–62); executive director of The Hillcrest Children's Psychiatric Center in Washington, DC (1962–70); founder and director of Rose School, a public mental health treatment program in Washington, DC, for students who are severely disturbed (1970–90); and professor of special education at American University (1968–90). Upon my retirement from American University and Rose School, I began the Institute of Psychoeducational Training. This institute is dedicated to certifying school and mental health staff in Life Space Crisis Intervention. I currently co-edit *The Journal of Emotional and Behavioral Problems* with Dr. Larry Brendtro.

I began college as a math major, but like many college students of that era I was caught in the crosscurrents of the Korean War and was not sure what I wanted to do professionally. During the summer of my sophomore year, I worked as a camp counselor at the Merrill Palmer Institute in Detroit. This camp was a field placement for graduate students from Cornell University who were studying child development. After this experience, I changed my major, entered Merrill Palmer, and received my BA in early childhood education in 1952. I applied to teach first grade in

197

the Detroit public school system, but I was refused employment because men do not teach young children. My reaction was to apply to graduate school in child development at the University of Michigan.

Like most graduate students, I was strong on dreams and short on cash. The only available part-time teaching position was at the University of Michigan's Hospital School teaching children who were post-polio and confined in living, hence going to schools in iron lungs. This was my first experience with exceptional children, and I hoped that my interest and energy would make up for my lack of skills. Teaching these children who were physically dependent turned out to be a painful and rewarding experience and added a new dimension to my interest in child development. The following summer, I completed my MEd and needed a summer job.

After reading every bulletin board on campus, I was attracted to a flyer describing a summer camp counselor position. The School of Education Fresh Air Camp (FAC) was offering graduate students room, board, and 6 graduate hours if they would work as counselors at this therapeutic camp for children who were emotionally disturbed. I applied, was accepted, and had no warning as to how this experience would change my life.

FAC was a wondrous place. All the counselors were graduate students from psychology, social work, and education, and we all lived and worked together as a team. At FAC we learned about psychopathology from the ground up, meaning that we frequently restrained campers who were out of control. This intensive, hands-on experience in learning was just what I needed after a year of academic course work. More importantly, we had the opportunity to observe Bill Morse and Dave Wineman in crisis situations and marveled at the variety of techniques and skills they possessed. Also, Fritz Redl was a visiting case consultant to the camp. His insights and wit into understanding students who were aggressive created additional excitement and admiration from all of us. I never could have predicted that my contact with Fritz Redl at this camp would cement my career in this field 4 years later.

At the end of that summer, Dr. Morse asked me if I was interested in entering his doctoral program in educational psychology. He had recently received a full-time graduate assistantship that could support my meager needs. I said yes and spent the next 3 years completing my PhD while returning to FAC every summer.

The next turning point in my career occurred in 1955. I was in the final stages of accepting an appointment as an assistant professor in child development at Ohio State University when Dr. Morse called me into his office and asked me if I wanted to be the first principal of the Children's Psychiatric Hospital. Dr. Rabinovitch, a child psychiatrist, and his entire staff decided to leave the university, which created a major crisis within the Department of Psychiatry. The department had a new building but no staff. I remember saying that I was not trained as a principal and didn't know anything about remedial education. Dr. Morse said, "Don't worry, neither does anyone else." With Dr. Morse as my supervisor, I entered the field of troubled children and youth.

Why did I remain in this field? It is difficult to answer that question, since different positive forces emerged at different stages of my career. The three that come to mind are the stimulation of ongoing learning, unusual opportunities, and a belief in the value of helping children and youth who are troubled.

Like life in the depth of ocean faults, there is still little awareness about what exists in the darkness of the human mind. The challenge of this field is the ongoing exploration into the complexity of the human mind. Initially, one learns about one's feelings of vulnerability and helplessness when one reaches out to help others only to experience personal rejection and abuse from them. Next, one learns about one's personal historical luggage, which is carried into every new relationship. Then one discovers the dynamics of the conflict cycle: aggression and counter-aggression and passive-aggressiveness and dependency.

What's exhilirating to acknowledge is that there is no end to self-learning. In fact, once one understands some complex relationship or achieves some insight into one's dynamics, like codependency, the result is a new and deeper list of questions and concerns. Personally, I feel this field promotes the quest for self-actualization.

Another attraction for me was the opportunity to develop psychoeducational programs and intervention strategies. I was motivated to set up a yearlong graduate training program that integrated ongoing academic training in a quality service program. The result was the American University/Rose School Teacher Training Program. I also had the opportunity to pursue my interests in life space interviewing, create video programs on children and youth with emotional disturbance, and publish *Conflict in the Classroom* (1965) with Bill Morse and Ruth Newman and *Teaching Self Control* (1975) with Stan Fagan. Of course, it helped to have a supportive staff and federal money.

The third attraction was a basic belief in the importance of our work. These children did not choose to become emotionally disturbed, and their behavior frequently alienates them from most adults. As a result, they do not have any advocates in the community, even though they frequently have been victimized by their community. Our task is to help these children, who never had a first chance in life, to experience the security of adult psychological protection and caring; the joy of exploring and discovering the satisfaction of learning; and the comfort of sleeping through the night without the pain of demons, devils, and death. This career choice does not provide ample money, power, or fame; however, it does document that individual time, energy, and skills are on the side of goodness, caring, and helping.

What advice or encouragement would I give those new to the field? There is the joke: How many psychologists does it take to change a light bulb? None. The light bulb must want to change. Perhaps this explains why advice is so available and ineffective as a source of brightening up a gloomy world. All I can do is share the advice I have given myself over the years:

1. Before caring for others, care for yourself. Examine your motivation for working with this difficult population. Try not to trick yourself. Accept limitations and appreciate strengths.

2. Focus on living a rich emotional life so that you are not using your students as a source of emotional gratification.

3. Develop outside interests and friends separate from your workplace so that you are not always involved in pathological discussions of students and staff. This means developing clear work and play boundaries.

4. Keep a diary of experiences. It will allow you the chance to reflect on your professional life over the years.

5. Obtain as much training and as many degrees as possible. Whenever you have an opportunity, plan to study with someone who is competent. Also, develop one area of expertise for yourself.

6. Finally, avoid staying in any program that is destructive to your students and your mental health. Crisis work doesn't mean you should accept a sadomasochistic role in which there is little opportunity to build positive relationships and skills with the students. Remember, there are excellent and nurturing programs that are seeking talented and dedicated staff.

I wish I had a more encouraging message for our beloved field, but my senses tell me that the future of reeducating students who are emotionally disturbed in the public schools looks grim, sounds discouraging, feels frightening, smells unhealthy, and tastes bitter.

It is my intent to offer my perceptions of the future and address what can and should be done to alter what I foresee to occur. Before beginning a look into the future, however, I wish to describe briefly those persons and programs that have shaped my perceptions or have influenced and taught me about helping children who face disturbances in their lives.

THE HILLCREST ERA: A NEW PSYCHOEDUCATIONAL MODEL

In the spring of 1962, Dr. Reginald Lourie, a child psychiatrist from Washington, DC, called and asked me to be the executive director of the school and residence program at Hillcrest Children's Mental Health Center, a failing center and clinic for children with emotional disturbance. Once again, the task of directing a treatment program was an uphill struggle. The staff at Hillcrest was demoralized. The place was falling apart physically, and the 30 pupils attending the school and residence was acting out by jumping out of the school windows and running into the woods when they didn't like their schoolwork. In addition, they were breaking windows and taking personal delight in urinating on the hot radiators.

Simultaneously, the school, residence, and clinic staffs also were acting out their own feelings of helplessness by blaming each other for their ineffectiveness. The circle of blame was so active that I called a series of crisis meetings to develop group consensus around appropriate values and principles of reeducating children who are emotionally disturbed. The following list was not meant to be comprehensive, but it represented the underlying assumptions of a newly proposed psychoeducational model. The components of that model are the following:

1. *We are here not to blame but to understand how each pupil perceives, feels, thinks, and believes in this setting.*
2. *We believe that there are no "special" hours or times during the day.* Everything that happens to, for, with, and against the child during the 24 hours of a day is important and can have therapeutic value, including the wake-up routine, therapy sessions, school assignments, food, play, etc.
3. *We believe that children are emotional beings who will behave in immature ways during periods of stress.* They will lie, fight, run away, regress, and deny the most obvious facts of life. If we can expect immature behavior from these immature children, then our hope for change is to expect mature behavior from mature adults.
4. *We believe that children in conflict will create their feelings or behavior in others.* Aggressive children can create counteraggressive behavior in others. Hyperactive children can create impulsive behavior in others. Withdrawn children can get others to ignore them, while passive-aggressive children are amazingly effective in getting others to carry their feelings for days and weeks until they erupt into a rage of anger. If the child is successful in having the adult act out this behavior, he or she suc-

ceeds in perpetuating the self-fulfilling prophecy, which reinforces his or her defenses against the charge.
5. *We believe children who are emotionally disturbed have learned to associate adult intervention with adult rejection.* This frequently is not a distortion but rather an accurate social reality. Our goal as a staff is to interpret adult intervention around inappropriate behavior as an act of protection rather than as an act of hostility. Our task is to tell the child repeatedly that we are here to protect him or her from reality dangers, psychological depreciation, overexcitement, and contagion; to maintain productive activities; and to avoid community problems.
6. *We listen to what the child says but concentrate on what he or she is feeling and thinking.*
7. *We expect and accept a certain amount of hostility and disappointment from others.*
8. *Even with the most ideal, collaborative arrangements, we expect and accept that communication among staff members will always be difficult and never complete.*
9. *We demonstrate that fairness involves treating children differently.* While group rules are necessary for organizational purposes, individualized and different expectations are necessary for growth and change.
10. *We believe crises are excellent times to teach and for children to learn.*
11. *We believe limits are love and that physical restraint can be a therapeutic example of caring for and protecting children.*

With time, staff commitment, and our list of principles, the program began to improve. While there were many valid reasons for this change, one fact that cannot be overlooked was the respect and support I received from the clinical director, Dr. Jean Yacoubian. This point needs to be stressed since it has implications for all programs that are organized around an interdisciplinary model. In most settings, clear rivalry exists between the clinical and educational staffs, and inevitably a power struggle emerges around control and authority that is acted out among the senior staff. In this instance it didn't happen. The personal relationship between Dr. Yacoubian and myself was an example of professional interdependence. Consequently, the school staff could learn about psychodynamic principles without feeling threatened or overwhelmed, while the clinical staff could learn about group management, remedial programs, and life-space interviewing techniques. It was an association of mutual respect. In 1966, Hillcrest moved from its 8-acre estate to a new, $1.5-million center in Washington, DC.

Within a few years the population changed from a majority of middle-class white pupils to a majority of inner-city black students. The medical model, which focused on an individual therapy program, received severe criticism under these circumstances. In addition, I had strong feelings about its effectiveness, its usefulness as a training paradigm, its cost, and the psychological damage of labeling a child as having a psychiatric illness. By late 1968, Hillcrest had been reorganized into two separate institutes: a Clinical Institute and a Psycho-educational Institute, which I directed. This change gave me the opportunity to expand the Conflict Cycle (Long, 1979) as an appropriate model for teachers in understanding and managing inappropriate classroom behavior.

The Conflict Cycle paradigm provided the special educator with the following operational concepts:

1. A student in conflict views the classroom through the eyes of his life history.

2. A student in conflict has to learn to be vulnerable to specific school tasks i.e. completion, separation, etc.

3. Acceptance of positive and negative feelings within and between students is normal, healthy, and necessary to the helping process.

4. Each student has been socialized to process feelings by direct expression, defense mechanisms, or coping techniques.

5. Under severe stress, a student in conflict will regress from coping techniques, to defensive techniques, and to primitive expressions of feelings.

6. The problem behavior of a student in conflict represents his present solution to stress, although it may cause difficulties with adults, peers, learning, rules, and self.

7. A student in conflict creates feelings and behaviors in others (peers and adults) which usually perpetuate this problem.

8. The student's unawareness and recreations to the negative adult environment justifies his conviction that there is no need to change his view of his world or himself. In other words, he has been successful in maintaining his self-fulfilling prophecy of himself and his world. (Long, 1979, pp. 8–10)

During this time, Bill Morse, Ruth Newman, and I published *Conflict in the Classroom* and were actively lecturing on the psychoeducational model. The history of this book illustrates how rapidly this field has changed. In 1965, we had considerable difficulty finding a publisher who was interested in a textbook on the pupil with emotional disturbance. The anticipated market level ranged from poor to terrible. By 1970, the book was adopted by over 150 colleges and universities.

THE AMERICAN UNIVERSITY ERA: A MODEL TRAINING PROGRAM

In 1968, I was awarded a 3-year U.S. Office of Education, Bureau of the Handicapped, Innovation Grant. The idea was to expand the Fresh Air Camp model of training from 8 weeks to 10 months. When American University appointed me to the faculty as a professor of special education, I also joined the staff of the Psychoeducational Institute at Hillcrest program. The then Bureau of Education for the Handicapped (BEH) awarded a grant that provided for eight graduate fellowships but required a full-year commitment from them. The trainees spent the summer on campus but were assigned to our school on a full-time basis for the next 9 months. Each trainee taught with a master teacher each morning and had a remedial case, videotaped sessions, a seminar, collaborative conferences, or independent studies in the afternoon. The program used a saturation approach, integrating practicum and theory in the areas of teaching methods and behavior management. In addition, the trainees spent 1 month teaching in a special class in the greater Washington area and a week in the Hillcrest residential program on a 24-hour basis.

THE ROSE SCHOOL ERA: A MODEL INTERAGENCY PROGRAM

In 1972, The District of Columbia (DC) Commission on Mental Health received a 5-year National Institute of Mental Health (NIMH) grant to develop a community-based, day-treatment program for latency-age children with emotional disturbance. What I proposed was for the city to hire all eight members of my staff. The logic was simple. If the city wanted an innovative program, let them demonstrate it by hiring all of us. We did not think they would accept our offer, but they did and in September of 1972, the Rose School was established. Over the next 3 months we hammered out our missions.

1. *Develop a quality and comprehensive day-treatment program based on community needs and resources.* The plan was to develop an interagency model in which the Mental Health Administration would provide the setting, administrative structure, clinical staff, and supplies. The DC Public School Division of Special Education would provide four teachers, transportation for the pupils, and educational supplies. Finally, the local universities would provide quality trainees, research, and evaluation skills. This proposed arrangement between the Mental Health Administration, the DC public schools, and local universities would result in a quality and

cost-effective program that the Mental Health Administration could not afford by itself. This arrangement prior to P.L. 94-142 benefited the DC public schools by allowing for the placement of 30 of their most difficult, aggressive, and unmanageable pupils at Rose School without any additional costs. The local universities would benefit by having an ideal teaching site for advanced training and research grants, which they could not set up or afford by themselves. To keep the needs of each of these three institutions from conflicting with each other, all service, training, and research activities would function under my administrative responsibility.

2. *Conceptualize the program around community mental health principles of treatment rather than the traditional illness/medical model.* Medical/psychiatric services would be provided, but they would not be the focus of the treatment. The treatment of troubled children was seen as a community problem with community solutions and not solely the problem of the child and his or her family. This program would focus more on helping the child to develop coping skills than on analyzing the origin of his or her psychopathology and defenses. It would provide more time teaching academic and social skills than studying intrapsychic change. The program would extend the parameters of change to include the child's extended family, local school, and neighborhood forces. This ecological approach to treatment was predicated on the assumption that change in any part of a child's environment would create positive change in the child's total ecosystem. For example, it may be as important to the child's mental health for him or her to have his or her father employed again, control his or her grandmother's alcoholic rage, or be involved in weekend activities as it is for him or her to have remedial reading or play therapy. This approach does not neglect the importance of changing the child's behavior; however, it gives equal weight to the importance of changing the behavior of significant adults and peers who interact with this child.

Operationally, this program was patterned after the successful work of Hobbs's (1974) Re-Education Model and Redl's (1959a) concept of a therapeutic milieu for children. The integration of these two models resulted in our nonmedical psychoeducational model of helping children who are emotionally disturbed. The decision to call this program a *school* and not a *day-treatment service of Area A* was determined by our theoretical beliefs about health and illness. School represents a significant part of the lives of latency-age children, and school is the setting in which important cognitive, social, and emotional growth takes place. Therefore, it seemed healthier and less pathological for troubled children to accept the reality of coming to a special school rather than a mental health clinic or center. For this reason, the program was called the Rose School, after Rose Alpher, a creative educator who served as the first principal of this school.

3. *Develop quality and cost-effective training programs with local universities.* The underlying assumption of this mission was that carefully designed yearlong training programs would provide additional staff and services that enhance the quality of the program without costing the city additional expenses. In addition, there was a citywide need for training more mental health professionals who would be skilled and comfortable in working with this high-risk population in the future.

4. *Conduct appropriate research studies and disseminate information about our Psychoeducational Model of Helping Troubled Children, Videotape Project, Self-Control Curriculum, and Stages of Helping.*

Over the past 17 years, the Rose School staff went through much pain, but we were fortunate to have a talented staff and active community support to help us through these difficult times. In many ways, we were like the rubber clowns in our therapy rooms, in that we took some severe blows, but we always managed to bounce back with renewed strength and motivation that kept this program alive and upright. We were dedicated to surviving, and in 1979 Closer Look, a national parent organization, selected Rose School as a "Model Program for Disturbed Children that Works." In 1982, the Children's Defense League also identified Rose School as a "Model Program" for inner-city children. By 1989, Rose School was widely recognized for its contributions in integrating child mental health and special education into a comprehensive psychoeducational service program that successfully helps troubled children and their families.

WHERE DO WE GO FROM HERE: THE FUTURE

In the late 1970s, I believed our well-staffed and comprehensive training and service programs would only get better. Unfortunately, I was wrong. The cycle of improvement plummeted, and the urban school systems, serving students who were emotionally disturbed, assumed the damage. Today, urban schools are overwhelmed by the increasing number of students who are seriously emotionally disturbed (SED), whose needs frequently far exceed the resources of their current placement and the skills of many of the staff who theoretically are there to treat and educate them. This dysfunctional fit between the public schools' programs and their academic and social-emotional needs is not entirely the fault of the public schools. This would suggest a far too simplistic explanation of this very complex personal/societal problem.

The field of educating and treating students with SED and conduct disorders has grown and changed over the last 40 years. This field has many unusual and unique characteristics that have served it well. It grew in its early years as a close-knit professional family. It is the only professional organization in special education in which the founding fathers and their followers never split into rival groups, motivated to depreciate each other. Many of the professional relationships also reflect lifelong friendships based on mutual respect and appreciation of the contributions made to this field by its members. This field has been bound by its belief in the importance of (a) self-understanding, (b) accepting differences in others, (c) advocating and caring for resistant students, and (d) learning teachable concepts and skills. I am delighted to be a part of this written record representing successful communication of these important values and how we have addressed past and present issues and conflicts, which should prepare us for future struggles. Future struggles and conflicts are predictable because the complexities presented by children who are disturbed and disruptive in the educational environment will force society to determine its values. How any society values all of its citizens always determines how it will use its educational resources.

The public schools are a reflection of the pressures, stresses, and other realities that families living in surrounding communities are experiencing. In many urban settings the increasing decay of the family, economic opportunities, and positive community values has spread the seeds that have given rise to current "street values." Self-centered values of violence, gangs, drugs, and immediate pleasure and power have little regard for learning, practicing self-control, and assuming responsibility for self and others. As a result, far too many children enter the public schools already severely damaged by early and prolonged psychological neglect, emotional isolation, and physical abuse. Their life experiences have destroyed their budding beliefs in the values of trust, belongingness, competence, and altruism. Their emotional struggles are not repressed conflicts but rather are socially learned responses that they spontaneously act upon as if their survival depends on feeling isolation and emotional and physical defensiveness. These students come to school burdened with chronic suspicion, anger, and a victim's belief that "nothing works out for them," "life is unfair," and "nothing matters." Within the first school hour, students are roaming the halls, challenging students and staff, or staying in time-out, or they are so depressed that they cannot attend to school tasks, relate to others, or express their sadness. They escape from the brutalities of life by withdrawing from the overwhelming reality of this new social system whose rules are in opposition to all that they know. Thus they create an emotionally defensive wall from which they can passively or aggressively escape.

I don't see anything on the horizon that will reduce the increased incidence of these children coming into our schools and progressing into our society. While there is some talk by our social and political leaders at selected times about stemming the tide of school and street violence, I have heard of no major local, state, or national discussion or planning about how to nurture and develop healthy children and youth. I certainly do not see it occurring in this nation's teacher training programs. This attention and reliance on reactive intervention programs versus primary prevention programs reflects the quick-fix goals of our society. The complexities associated with the psychological development of children into adults includes the development of emotional reason and sense of well-being, decision-making abilities and independent value structure, and responsibility for self, others, and the environment. This development requires many factors, including mature and well-trained teachers who are well grounded in the psychological development of children, non-punitive school environments interconnected with home and community, and support service providers and interagency communication that offers a full range of service provisions to the problem. Within this context, permit me to offer five predictions about our field. It is my desire to see these predictions reversed.

1. There will be vigorous resistance by the general public to spending any additional public money for reeducating students who are emotionally disturbed, unless it is under the administration of the Juvenile Justice Department. The public has grown weary of crime and is more eager to protect society and build additional jails than to alter the courses of children's lives in the developmental stages. Faced with the reality of diminishing funds for needed special education programs, the philosophy of "doing more with less" will become the official banner of special education. Even though P.L. 94-142 is funded at about 40%, the public expects schools to comply 100% with P.L. 94-142. As a result of continuing reductions in funding, many school systems will not be able to meet the minimum staffing conditions for a classroom program for students who are emotionally disturbed as defined by current state board of education regulations.

2. As conditions worsen, fewer students, particularly males and minorities, will choose majors in the education of children with serious emotional/behavioral disorders. Males can supply needed role models, and minorities can relate to and have personally experienced the issues at hand. The consequence of this trend is obvious. Local, state, and federal efforts are needed to reverse this trend and make the education and treatment of children who are emotionally disturbed an attractive field to

men and minorities, especially the all-important male who is a minority.

3. Given the number of special education teachers needed, and less financial resources to employ the better professionally prepared persons, the general trend will be to reduce training levels. I believe teacher training programs in education of children who are behaviorally disordered or emotionally disturbed will move from a graduate to an undergraduate level. These undergraduate training programs will be based on a single conceptual model of deviancy and intervention that will not adequately prepare teachers to manage and teach many of the students assigned to their classrooms.

4. The concept of collaborative services between mental health and special education for students who are emotionally disturbed will continue to erode. Even when mental health services are available, they have proven to be of marginal use with the majority of the students who have chronic life crises. There appears to be a growing territorial boundary between treatment and education. The education, in the education of children who are emotionally disturbed, is the environment, and the task to be learned is one principle tool in the intervention. The major tool in the intervention is the teacher. The gains we have made over the last 20 years have been to elevate the role of the educator in the treatment team and increase fluidity in interagency relationships and communications.

For example, expansion of Redl's (1959b) life space crisis interviewing (LSCI) to include cognitive, behavioral, and prosocial skills into this therapeutic strategy offers psychologists, counselors, crisis teachers, and social workers a powerful set of interventions and hope for even the most demanding students. LSCI, as first developed by Redl and Wineman, taught by Morse, and revised in 1990 by Wood and myself, is an innovative psychodynamic concept. As a result, LSCI is a comprehensive and multidimensional strategy for managing students presenting a severe discipline problem in school or during personal crises. LSCI not only identifies the student's chronic self-defeating pattern of behavior but also uses the student's crises as opportunities to teach the student insight and responsibility for themselves. For students who are experiencing ongoing abusive life experiences, LSCI is an effective and realistic source of help. Outside of a total school and community milieu, LSCI reduces its effectiveness as an intervention.

5. The proposed inclusion plan, which returns students who are emotionally disturbed to the regular classroom, is based on the theoretical belief that this plan will be an educational improvement for these students, their peers, and their classroom teachers. Unless there is massive, ongoing, and realistic training for the classroom teacher, I predict it will turn out to be an illusion that David Copperfield would be proud to accomplish.

Public school programs for students who are emotionally disturbed have had limited success because they generally have been unidimensional and poorly funded, administrated, and staffed. There are excellent public school programs that demonstrate that money, skills, and comprehensive resources make a difference. The outcome measures and success rates of these school programs are impressive. The modern-day inclusion efforts, however, offer teachers and the public an appealing way to deny the complexity of helping students who are emotionally disturbed by lulling them into acceptance by their caring rhetoric and soothing promises.

The proposal to solve the difficult problems of reeducating children with SED by reorganizing the resources and personnel of special education will be as successful as the 1960 education revolution called the Open Classroom. The Open Classroom was a philosophically appealing idea based on the concept of breaking down the walls of rigidity and communication between teachers and classrooms by having learning stations, team teaching, differential groups, and independent studies. The time was right for an educational change, and this was a new idea imported from England; however, except for a few outstanding schools that had stable and effective programs and staff prior to their Open Classroom reorganization, this creative plan resulted in organized chaos. For the majority of schools looking for a quick educational fix, the Open Classroom experiment caused them to slip to a new educational low.

Are there any similarities between the inclusion efforts in today's schools and the open classroom plans developed in the 1960s across the country? Yes. They are both theoretically convincing. No one can argue against the merit of having students who are emotionally disturbed return to the general classroom when it is appropriate. If I remember correctly, however, the approved educational concept of returning students who are emotionally disturbed from a more restrictive environment to a less restricted environment was called mainstreaming. This was a logical plan. What went wrong? Why did mainstreaming for children with SED have such limited success? In my experience over a 10-year period, the basic problem with mainstreaming students was not the reluctance of our special education teachers but the lack of receptiveness by the general classroom teachers. There were many exceptions, but even with ongoing consultation the central attitude was unwillingness to add one more disruptive student to the classroom. As one classroom teacher said to me, "If I am forced to take Tyrone, this will be a process of mainscreaming and not mainstreaming!"

General classroom teachers are already weighed down by new responsibilities and increasing levels of academic achievement expectations. Their number one concern, as reported by National Education Association's (NEA) yearly survey of teachers, continues to be classroom discipline or disruptive behavior. This finding has been true for the past 10 years. Classroom teachers in urban schools are telling anyone who will listen that they are having difficulty finding the time and the energy to meet the social-emotional needs of their students without disabilities in a crisis, not to mention the demanding needs of their "high-risk students" and the few unidentified but active students with SED in their classrooms.

The proposed solution to this complex social and educational problem is to add additional students with diagnosed emotional problems into the general classroom. Let's be realistic. If a new student who has asthma is assigned to a classroom, we would expect this student to wheeze and cough. If a new student who has cerebral palsy is included, we would expect this student to lose his or her balance and perhaps fall (and continue to fail academically and socially) under certain conditions. It is as if a chain reaction occurs, and all of it is out of control and unstoppable.

Thus, if we include a student with SED in the general classroom, we can predict that (a) the student will bring stressful home and community problems to the classroom; (b) he or she will come to inclusion conditioned to being academically and socially unsuccessful and noncompetitive; (c) in the educational setting, the student will be prone to overreact to disappointment and frustration; (d) he or she will misperceive teacher behavior during times of stress and may respond to failure with self-abusive behaviors; (e) he or she will have immature social skills and consequently will manipulate peers and teachers (having the skill to limit-test people and situations) and will create a chaotic and disruptive environment; and (f) in the chaotic and disruptive environment, there will be less attention on the student, thus less attention focused on his or her failure to find success (display appropriate behaviors) in a rule-regulated environment.

These are only some of the typical and expected disruptive behaviors commonly displayed by students with SED or conduct disorders. Are we really expecting general classroom teachers, who are not trained to have the therapeutic understanding and the advanced skills to be the best adult models for these students, to take over this problem? If special education teachers, who are certified to work with these students, are having difficulty with these students, will classroom teachers who have 30 students and who are academically oriented be more effective?

The advocates of the inclusion plan might say I am not representing the level of support that is proposed. For example, advocates say the classroom teachers will not be alone, but rather they will be assigned additional resources and personnel. They will be a part of a collaborative support team and feel more empowered and less helpless, and when life gets rough in the classroom, a crisis team will be available immediately via a beeper or other system. It sounds wonderful. It sounds innovative. It sounds very democratic, but without massive training and resources, I believe it is a formula for failure. I think it is a clever way of saving public money without having to feel guilty if inclusion fails. I don't believe the proposed training and support conditions for this plan will be implemented or completed before the students arrive. Remember, it's an imperfect world and screw-ups drop out, and dropping kids out of school has been a traditional intervention for those whose personal/social problems overload the schools. Also, remember that programs and services for students who are seriously emotionally disturbed or conduct disordered have had the least amount of public and administrative support of all the special education services.

I suggest a visit to any urban school and a long talk with the staff about their plans for inclusion. Then convince me the plan will work. If it does not work in our urban schools, then it is not a viable plan but rather another failure experience for our rejected and alienated students.

As special educators of students who are emotionally disturbed, we have been taught to face the pain of reality squarely and not to be intimidated by the multiple and complex problems of our students or schools. This does not insulate us from wondering if our professional efforts are worthwhile, whether our staff is making a difference in the lives of their students, or whether our collective work is enough to turn these students around. When I have these thoughts, I think of the story about the young boy walking along the beach after the tide went out. He noticed the stranded starfish and started throwing them back into the ocean. An older gentleman observing his action said, "Sonny, there are hundreds of stranded starfish on the beach. You realize your efforts will not make a difference?" The boy stopped and pondered his words and said, "It did to the last one I threw in!"

Likewise, we cannot change society or stop abuse and neglect, but if we can do one thing, improve one concept, help one teacher or parent feel more competent, and find one humpty dumpty kid and put him back together again, we can make a difference. This is how we make a contribution. This is how we create hope, and with hope, there is always a better future. Early in my career I realized that the standard educational programs and methods of teaching students without disabilities were useless when applied to children who were troubled and disruptive. The psychological needs and emotional limitations of these students succeeded in stripping away my enthusiasm and exposing in me a profound sense of inadequacy as a special teacher. I remember feeling helpless and hating the feeling. It was during this period that I learned the first principle of special education, which was to find ways of reinforcing a student's strengths before attempting any remedial program. This concept gave me the structure I needed and the direction that enabled me to appreciate the importance to these students of learning new skills in their helpless state of forced dependency.

REFERENCES

Fagen, S. A., Long, N. J., & Stevens, D. J. (1975). *Teaching children self-control: Preventing emotional and learning problems in the elementary school.* Columbus, OH: Merrill.

Hobbs, N. (1974). Nicholas Hobbs. In J. M. Kauffman & C. D. Lewis (Eds.), *Teaching children with behavioral disorders: Personal perspectives* (pp. 142–167). Columbus, OH: Merrill.

Long, N. J., Morse, W. C., & Newman, R. C. (Eds.). (1965). *Conflict in the classroom: The education of emotionally disturbed children.* Belmont, CA: Wadsworth.

Long, N. J. (1979). The conflict cycle. *Pointer, 23,* 6–11.

Redl, F. (1959a). The concept of a therapeutic milieu. *American Journal of Orthopsychiatry, 29,* 721–734.

Redl, F. (1959b). The concept of the life space interview. *American Journal of Orthopsychiatry, 29,* 1–18.

RICHARD L. McDOWELL
University of New Mexico

Richard McDowell is a professor of special education at the University of New Mexico and the coordinator of teacher training programs in the area of emotional/ behavioral disorders. McDowell received his EdD from the University of Kansas in 1969. He has been a general classroom teacher as well as a special education teacher in the public school system of Kansas. In addition to being a classroom teacher, he has served as a director of special education and school psychology, a psychologist, and an educational consultant at various points during his career. McDowell has been very active as an author and as a member of the Council for Children with Behavioral Disorders (CCBD), of which he was president from 1981 to 1982.

CHAPTER 13

Emotional and Behavioral Disorders: A Personal Perspective

One September morning during my seventh-grade science class, the school principal opened my door and asked me to step into the hall for a minute. He asked me to lend a helping hand "if things got out of control" in the new special education classroom located close to my room. He explained that they had hired a first-year teacher for this position and that the class was for students who had been diagnosed as emotionally disturbed. I didn't know a thing about teaching students who were disturbed, but I agreed to help. After I met the new teacher, I learned that she had been trained as a special education teacher with an emphasis in emotional disturbance. I later discovered that her approach was very permissive when it came to dealing with disruptive behavior. That year she was plagued with behavioral episodes that tended to "get out of control." I got to know her students pretty well, and I often thought to myself, "There has to be a better way." (Years later when I remembered her class, I thought that it was too bad that she had forgotten the statement made by Berkowitz and Rothman (1960) that students who are emotionally disturbed need limits.)

The very next year I found myself teaching special education—not by choice but as a result of the opening of a new junior high school. When I interviewed with the superintendent of schools for one of the new positions, he discovered that I had 12 hours of graduate-level training in special education. He gave me the opportunity to teach the only special education class in the new school and even offered me a $300-a-year raise. Now how could I turn that down? I was given a beautiful, large room and whatever funds I needed to equip it in any way I wanted, which I did. Then the students arrived! I had 16 students; two were mentally retarded, seven were emotionally disturbed, and seven had severe learning disabilities. That first semester was probably the most difficult 4 months of my life. I could hardly wait for school to end each day so I could go home and take a nap. Matters improved significantly late in January, when I finally figured out how to manage this type of class. I know I learned more than the students did that year.

When I completed my master's degree in psychology, I left the classroom to become a school psychologist. I found myself trying to assist classroom teachers in finding effective ways of managing disordered behavior in the classroom. Later when I became a director of special education, we set up the first two classes for students who were emotionally disturbed in the district. The year prior to this I had approached Dr. Richard Whelan of the University of Kansas for information on how to go about this process. With his help and a summer stipend from the State Special Education Department of Kansas, I went through the summer training program for teachers of the emotionally disturbed. That next year, the two classes were in place and serving students. I remember requesting that the Board of Education approve the use of carpeting in those two rooms to reduce noise levels. The president of the Board refused my request and told me that tile floors were plenty good enough for classrooms. The superintendent later told me my request was denied because the president of the Board didn't have carpeting in his home. So, the next year I asked for acoustical flooring and got it!

Later that year, Dr. Whelan approached me about entering the doctoral program in special education with an emphasis in the area of emotional disturbance. Because of my experiences with students with emotional/behavioral disorders (E/BD) and the size of the stipend, I felt that this was a golden opportunity. So I accepted and here I am.

GENERATING A PHILOSOPHIC POSITION CONCERNING CHILDREN WITH E/BD

All students have a strength in something, and eventually they will demonstrate it in the appropriate setting at the right time. When they do, reinforce it! I believe that, given order, structure, consistency, and support, the student with E/BD can learn the strategies necessary to function successfully both in school and in the community. The student with E/BD has extreme difficulty recognizing the relationship between his or her behavior and the resulting consequences. The two major factors that contribute to the distress that students with E/BD feel are (a) a loss of the feeling that they have some control over the events that directly affect them and (b) an inability to predict what will happen as a result of their behavior. Loss of control is a loss of the ability to recognize alternatives. The student with E/BD struggles when he or she must identify the expectations of others at a time when he or she seems to have a loss of control and difficulty predicting outcomes. The introduction of order, structure, and consistency by a trained, caring teacher into the student's life provides the framework for teaching the student to overcome such problems. They can learn to recognize and choose alternative ways of behaving that will benefit them in more positive ways.

CURRENT STATUS OF THE EDUCATION OF CHILDREN WITH E/BD

There are many fine teachers working with the student with E/BD today. They are committed to assisting the student in learning academic skills, social skills, problem-solving skills, self-discipline, and self-control, all of which are necessary if the student with E/BD is to be able to function successfully in the school setting and within the community.

Unfortunately, not all teachers of students with E/BD have made such a commitment to helping these students. Studies such as the National Needs Analysis (Grosenick & Huntze, 1979) have shown us that we are not even providing services to the 2% of students that the federal government has allowed as the prevalence figure for individuals with E/BD. Even with the E/BD programs that presently exist, there is enough turnover in qualified teachers each year that the training programs cannot turn out graduates fast enough. As a result, many school districts across the country cannot hire certified special education teachers in adequate numbers. To remain in compliance with federal regulations, these districts hire teachers with training outside special education and seek a waiver for that teacher from the state education agency. The motive of these waivered teachers may be less than a concern for the student with E/BD. In granting such a teaching waiver, many states require the waivered teacher to complete a set number of semester hours of university course work in special education for each year they are waivered until they complete a certification program. The quality of service provided the student with E/BD by a teacher on a waiver may suffer drastically as a result of (a) little or no training on how to manage and work with the student with E/BD, (b) limited or no experience with students who exhibit emotional or behavioral disorders, and (c) the possible lack of a genuine concern for the welfare of students who are experiencing emotional or behavioral problems. We have to admit that this is not the most desirable method for selecting and hiring teachers who will have the responsibility for working directly with students who have been labeled as emotionally or behaviorally disordered.

The effectiveness of programs for the student with E/BD correlates directly with the motivation of the teacher, foundational training for understanding and working with student behavior, concern for the welfare of the student with E/BD, the ability to establish realistic goals and objectives for the student, an awareness of the necessity for an organized and consistent program, and the amount of administrative support given the teacher of students with E/BD. There are many very effective teachers who operate very effective programs serving the student with E/BD.

However, there are two additional problems that hamper the field in general with regard to program effectiveness.

1. *The idea that E/BD is a homogeneous grouping, which ignores the problem that there is tremendous behavior variance within this category.* Whether it is human nature or some other variable, once we label children and place them in a category, we behave as if all those placed within that category have the same characteristics. For example, we all use some definition to help us identify and place the student with E/BD. Many of our definitions are rather limited in the characteristics or behaviors they include for identification purposes. We know that behavior variance exceeds the limited characteristics suggested by definitions. We also know that no single intervention strategy will be effective with all students with E/BD. Much of our early writing was directed toward influencing the field as to the importance of a particular conceptual model. The arguments of the 1970s left us with the knowledge that a single conceptual model cannot effectively address all of the issues that arise from trying to successfully intervene in such a wide range of behavior variance. Some of these models have had more to offer the classroom teacher of students with E/BD than others. Each of the major conceptual models has something to contribute to the effectiveness of programs serving the student with E/BD.

   I do not suggest here that, to be effective, teachers need to be eclectic in their approach to working with students with E/BD. What I am suggesting is that teachers should build themselves a foundation for understanding human behavior in a particular conceptual model and that they learn to use relevant factors or strategies from the other models for working with the student with E/BD. Such a foundation allows the teacher the consistency necessary to operate an effective program and gives them a familiar information base from which to approach problem solving. The behavior variance among students with E/BD requires that the teacher have a solid foundation and an information base of relevant intervention strategies to allow for the planning and implementation of a program that addresses the unique needs of the individual students within that program.

2. *Length of stay in the E/BD program.* Once, when listening to a presentation being made by a public school administrator, I heard him refer to students with E/BD as "lifers." The term was familiar to me in connection to the justice or correctional

system but seemed out of context, since we were discussing the student with E/BD in the public school system. As I listened more closely, the presenter pointed out that a majority of children who are labeled as E/BD and are placed in public school special education programs remain in those programs until they either drop out of school or complete the necessary requirements to exit the program. If our programs are successful, why are we keeping these students in the special program so long? As far as the student's school life is concerned, he or she has become a lifer.

The work of Haring and Phillips (1962) suggested to the field that if a special education program serving the student who was emotionally disturbed was going to be successful it would be so within 2 to 3 years. After that, very little positive change would occur as a result of the special education program. This window for effective change sets a standard or set of criteria for the school program that stresses the importance of always keeping in mind that the student will return to the general program. The special education classroom is not a warehouse for storing children but is an integral program for helping the student gain the self-control necessary to function as a part of the regular program. Special class placement implies that a difficult problem exists but it is a problem that can be managed and corrected. Thus, the expectation is for short-term intervention. Recent information tells us that the longer we hold on to a student in the E/BD program the less likely the student will be to function successfully in the community once out of the school program. Emery (1989) in her research discovered an extremely high incidence of students with E/BD losing their jobs within 1 year of leaving the school program and that an inordinate number of these students were living with their parents 5 years after completing the school program.

Again, when we ask why the student with E/BD remains in special education classes for such a long time, we must look to existing practices and beliefs. Part of the answer lies in the way in which classes for the student with E/BD evolved and the expectations we allowed to be made. We borrowed heavily from elementary classes for children with mental retardation, particularly in the way they were segregated from general classrooms. The model was that these students would remain in the special program throughout their school career. With this model came the same expectations by other teachers that not only were the students to be placed in a segregated program but they would remain there. After all, wasn't all special education the same? In reality or in just plain and simple words, the general program did not want these students back even when they were pronounced "cured." We didn't emphasize strongly enough or in a clear enough manner that the intention was to provide short-term intervention and return the students with E/BD to the general program so that this would become the expectation of the general teachers. Obviously, this has been an error that has created many problems and that greatly interferes with the effectiveness of E/BD programs. The student with E/BD should not be a lifer in the special education program. The segregation of the student with E/BD may be a necessary part of the intervention process but not segregation to the point of total exclusion from the general program for long periods of time.

A WORKING DEFINITION OF E/BD

My working definition for the student with E/BD is rather short and to the point. The student with E/BD is one (a) who has difficulty establishing and maintaining positive, supportive, and lasting relationships with others and (b) whose behavior either fails to meet or exceeds the expectations of those around him or her. It is important to consider the intensity of the disorder, the frequency of the disorder, and the length of time the disorder has been present when applying these two criteria.

RELATIONSHIP TO THE FEDERAL DEFINITION

I believe that my working definition includes the major aspects of the federal definition. I believe it helps the diagnostician to more clearly identify the major factors to be evaluated. When a student is having difficulty getting along with other people (peers, teachers, others) it becomes rather simple to assess that student's relationships or interactions with others. Personal observations, behavior checklists or rating scales, and interviews with the student and others provide direct information about how the student is doing and what is not working well.

The second part of my working definition moves away from the set characteristics of the federal definition and places the emphasis on expectations for behavior. Today there are a variety of factors commonly accepted by the field that are determined by community, cultural background, and linguistic background as well as developmental factors that directly influence and contribute to expectations or standards for behavior. Most of these expectations are relevant only when considered within the context of the individual school or community. Students who fail to meet expectations are those students who don't measure up to the school or community standards in specific areas. Students who exceed expectations may have gone beyond the accepted standard for behavior. It makes more sense to me that these expectations or standards should be established at the local level rather than at the federal level. Granted there are standards for behavior that are somewhat universal, but criteria for placing a student in a special education program should be more in line with the local or community expectations for acceptable behavior.

As a case in point, for many years in the southwestern part of the United States, it was quite common for students who did not speak English or did not speak English well to be evaluated for special education placement. Because the expectation was for all students to be proficient in English, many Hispanic students were penalized severely for not meeting this expectation. Once we recognized that this national expectation was simply an inappropriate criterion for the concerned local community, revisions were made to the criterion for placement in special education. A non–English-speaking student could no longer be placed in special education programs solely for having difficulty speaking the English language. California (*Diana v. State Board of Education*, 1973) was the first state to require that a student be tested in his or her primary language. This type of modification is commonplace today.

IS IT ED OR BD?

Neither ED (emotionally disturbed) nor BD (behaviorally disordered) is a diagnostic category or label in the field of mental health. Rather, both are political categories or labels that are used for the purpose of acquiring funds to provide programs for students with a variety of problems. The federal legislation (P.L. 94-142, IDEA) uses the term *seriously emotionally disturbed* to represent students with mental health problems. Individual states may use the federal label or any of a variety that they have developed for themselves. For example, some use labels like *emotionally disturbed, behavior disorders, emotionally handicapped, emotionally impaired, personal social adjustment problems*, and *emotionally and behaviorally disturbed*. Again, these labels have little meaning within the mental health system. These are labels used by governing and law-making bodies to represent a specific group of students who are impaired in their mental health skills to the point that they require some type of special intervention within the public school system that has been mandated by federal or state law and that will allow the system to receive special funding to establish and maintain classroom programs.

Within the field, the terms *ED* and *BD* typically have been used to identify the philosophic stance or conceptual model that the user represents. The term *emotionally disturbed* was first applied to children in the early 1930s at about the same time the movement to establish child guidance centers was taking place in this country. The first public school program for the child with ED was established in 1946. From the first use of the term *ED* until the late 1950s, the primary conceptual model used for these children was the psychodynamic model (Morse, Cutler, & Fink, 1964). As a result, the ED label has been associated with the psychodynamic model and, more recently, with the psychoeducational model (Life Space Interviewing) (Long, Morse, & Newman, 1971). Even when the behavioral model (e.g., Hewitt, 1968) was introduced in the late 1950s, the ED label continued to be used.

It wasn't until the early to mid-1970s, when a considerable amount of work was done to clarify the specific elements of a variety of conceptual models, that the BD label (behaviorally disordered) was used consistently. Those professionals representing the behavioral model were concerned that behavior was something that could be observed and measured as well as something that was capable of being repeated. To the behaviorist, emotions were something that did not meet those criteria. It was believed that BD was a more functional label in that it implied that the disordered behavior could be observed and measured. Thus, BD came to represent the behaviorist approach for understanding and explaining behavior change.

For those who did not accept any model as gospel, the labels of ED and BD took on different meanings. These labels began to represent the degree of severity of the disorder. ED represented the more severe and debilitating disorders such as Pervasive Developmental Disorder NOS (childhood type schizophrenia). BD, on the other hand, was seen to include those disorders considered to be of a milder variety, such as conduct disorders and anxiety disorders. Kelly (1988) suggested that one of the differences between the two was that in ED the individual might not understand the concept of right or wrong and have very few internal controls over his or her own behavior, whereas in BD (more specifically conduct disorders) the individual is able to make a volitional choice of how to behave. That is, the individual has enough internal control to choose how he or she will behave or respond in any given situation. For a majority of the field today, the two terms (*ED* and *BD*) are used interchangeably.

NEEDED SCHOOL EXPERIENCES FOR STUDENTS WITH E/BD

One of the more meaningful experiences a student with E/BD can have is to have the support of a good teacher who cares for the student when he or she is at his or her worst, someone the student can rely on whatever the situation, someone who is consistent, follows through, and provides good feedback. These characteristics, as well as the existence of a clear, understandable management system that allows the students to know where they stand at all times and that reinforces desired behavior choices, will provide students with the foundation from which to overcome most of the issues that resulted in their being placed in a program for students with E/BD.

The overall goal of the E/BD program is to produce a student with reasonable academic skills who is able to demonstrate appropriate self-control and who has good feelings about himself or herself and his or her abilities. To accomplish this, the teacher must provide an atmosphere conducive to growth in each of these areas. The foundation of any E/BD program is its management system. This system includes considerations for academic management, behavior management, and crisis management.

ACADEMIC MANAGEMENT

Academic management consists of identifying and preparing all task activities, scheduling those activities, keeping accurate records, identifying and preparing possible reinforcing consequences, helping the student with E/BD learn time management, introducing a reliable routine, developing a social skills curriculum, and helping the student with E/BD acquire learning strategies. The teacher promotes the success by carefully evaluating the student with E/BD as to his or her strengths and weaknesses and by designing learning materials and activities that will build on his or her strengths and help him or her to overcome his or her weaknesses.

The concept I like to think of here is to stack the cards in the students' favor. In other words, initially guarantee the students' success. Most of these students have experienced considerable failure before they entered the E/BD program. For many, it takes a great deal of effort to try again when they have failed so many times before. By carefully selecting work on which the students can be successful and reinforcing those efforts, the teacher helps the students gain some self-confidence and eventually some self-worth. Academic success and the opportunity to demonstrate that success as well as the skills involved is one of the strongest intervention strategies available for helping the student with E/BD.

BEHAVIOR MANAGEMENT

Behavior management consists of identifying desired personal behavior, providing opportunities to learn and demonstrate those desired behaviors, identifying a system for applying reinforcement, identifying and preparing possible reinforcing consequences, identifying punishing consequences, helping the student with E/BD learn strategies to manage feelings of frustration and aggression, increasing verbal skills so that the student can resolve conflict with words rather than actions, teaching problem-solving techniques, providing the opportunity to learn and practice social skills, offering activities directed toward motor development, and providing guides for developing positive and supportive relationships.

The behavior-management system must be geared toward recognizing and using the principles of reinforcement with desired student behavior. The teacher, in using this system, cannot take for granted that the student with E/BD knows the appropriate behavior but is choosing not to use it. In fact, in most cases it is necessary to actually teach the behavior, whether it is as simple as standing in line or as difficult as resolving a conflict in a class meeting. The student with E/BD needs to know the rules, that is, how the system works, at the earliest possible time. When the system becomes the foundation for how things happen and the student understands it, the system will do most of the work in providing guidelines and identifying consequences. I like what Hewett (1968) had to say about his system (the "engineered classroom"). In a case where a student misbehaved, the teacher applied the consequence and the student began complaining how unfair it was. The teacher's response to the student went something like this: "I just work here, and, according to the program, this is what is supposed to happen." It's amazing how often such a statement resolves the issue right at that point.

I think one of the better systems available to teachers today is the Crane/Reynolds Levels System (Crane & Reynolds, 1988). This management system encompasses all three areas of management (academic, behavior, and crisis). It uses a point system to reinforce various student behaviors. The points are used to provide immediate feedback to the student, can be exchanged for activities, and are used to determine whether or not a student is ready to be advanced to a higher level. Each level has its own set of privileges. The lower the level, the fewer the privileges; the higher the level, the more privileges that become available to the student. At the lowest level, the student has no privileges and must be escorted everywhere in the school by the teacher or teacher aide. The highest level has the most privileges; in fact, the student is mostly self-directed and is able to move about freely in the classroom and to activities outside the classroom. Reaching the highest level is the first step in returning the student with E/BD to the general classroom. It is a very effective system.

Long (personal communication, November 20, 1986) once suggested that you could determine the effectiveness of a behavior-management program by asking a student how things worked in the class. If the student can clearly explain points, levels, punishers, etc., then the program is working well. I have yet to enter a classroom where the Crane/Reynolds system is being used that the students can't explain how it works. It provides the structure that students with E/BD need.

Crisis Management

Crisis management is a strategy used by the teacher when a student with E/BD has lost self-control and is in danger of doing injury to himself or herself or to others. The strategy involves staying calm, talking quietly to the student, using directive statements, knowing when to move the other students in the class, knowing when to get assistance from outside the class, using reflective statements to help the student identify the anger, and giving the student a way of "saving face" in front of his or her peers.[1] Every teacher of students with E/BD needs these strategies. Experience has shown that when such strategies are not part of the teacher's repertoire, the teacher has a tendency either to withdraw from the situation without resolution or to counteraggress toward the student. Neither of these two reactions help the student to resolve the issue or give relief to the student or the teacher.

Another meaningful experience for the student with E/BD is to participate in a general class group or class meeting. This is a regularly scheduled activity that gives the students in a class the opportunity to verbally interact with each other and function as a group. Many issues can be subjects for discussion in class meetings, such as some academic topic or question for problem solving. Generally, the chairs are arranged in a circle so that each student has equal access to the group. The teacher is a part of the group and sits as part of the circle. Rules for interaction are discussed before the first class meeting with reminders before each meeting if needed. Rules pertain to raising a hand before speaking, not interrupting someone who is already speaking, talking to the group when speaking, paying attention and listening when someone else is speaking, being courteous, and so forth.

One of my most embarrassing moments came after I had been expounding the virtues of class meetings to my graduate students in one of my classes. After class, one of my students who was teaching in a middle-school E/BD program came up and said she was interested in using this procedure with her students. She asked if I would come to her class and conduct a class meeting with her students to demonstrate how it worked. Since I had been doing some work in her class and knew her students, I agreed to do so. When the day came, I arrived early to do some other work with the class. When it was time for the class meeting, she

---

[1]The process is too detailed to go into it here. Instead I refer the reader to the work of Gilliam (1981). He has published on this topic and has some fine handout materials that he uses when presenting workshops on the topic.

turned the class over to me and stepped back to observe. The students and I got the chairs arranged in a circle and sat down to begin the meeting. We talked briefly about the rules, and everyone seemed to have the idea. Our topic was an impending school party. We began to discuss what kind of party it was going to be, but from this point on the process began to break down. The harder I tried to get them back on task, the further away they got from the topic and the rules. I can still see the teacher laughing at my loss of class control in the meeting. All I could say afterward was that everyone has a bad day some time. In spite of my poor showing, she continued the class meetings. The class became pretty good at using the time to solve classroom problems, and the teacher became a very good group leader. It is a very effective technique, and I highly recommend it to all teachers of students with E/BD.

INCLUSION OF CHILDREN WITH E/BD?

Personally, I believe that full inclusion of the student with E/BD in the general school program is detrimental to the student. In a vast majority of the general school classrooms in this country, teachers simply do not have the management skills necessary nor the management system in place that will allow the student with E/BD to function to the best of their ability. Those who set the guidelines for full inclusion prior to the writings on the Regular Education Initiative (REI) and the General Education Initiative (GEI) did not have the student with E/BD in mind when it was suggested that there were a number of students in special education programs who could probably benefit from placement in general classrooms. The self-contained classroom had become the standard for special education classrooms, with little regard for the characteristics of the populations being placed there. Students with physical problems, health problems, and mild learning disabilities were being segregated under the guise that the regular classroom teacher could not provide the optimum learning experiences for them because of their disabilities.

The concept of the least restrictive environment had been misdefined for many of these students. REI and GEI suggested strongly that all special education students should be removed from special education and returned to the general classroom. Many school districts took this as a serious recommendation, particularly since it would reduce the cost of educating students with disabilities. Essentially, the actions that have been taken have illustrated the complete swing of the pendulum from one extreme to the other. Rational thinking should prevail regarding this issue if we can get past the economic attractiveness of such a concept and consider the overall impact on students. The student with E/BD requires a great deal of structure in order to manage and function successfully within the school setting. I don't believe that the general classroom teacher can provide this structure and at the same time teach large groups of students. Remember, it was their inability to function well either academically or behaviorally in the general classroom that resulted in students with E/BD being placed in the special education classroom.

SUGGESTED SERVICE MODEL

I still prefer the continuum of services model. I particularly like a variation of the Fail Save model developed by Adamson and Van Etten (1972). It is an appropriate way to identify the most correct level of service required by a student. Its continuum consists of five service levels ranging from least restrictive to most restrictive. Each level suggests a teacher–student ratio as well as a configuration for the class (e.g., consulting teacher, itinerant teacher, resource room, self-contained classroom, self-contained with teacher aide, or residential). The self-contained classroom with a teacher aide was designated as a Level 4 program. Class size is limited to eight students. I believe that this is a reasonable class size when working with students with E/BD, particularly when they are supported by a teacher and a teacher aide. This program is strengthened when assisted by various support services such as speech and language therapy, occupational therapy, physical therapy, counseling, and so forth.

INCIDENCE OF E/BD

It appears that the incidence of E/BD is increasing. One factor I have trouble reconciling is the 2% incidence figure that the federal government operates with versus the figures reported in various studies (Grosenick & Huntze, 1979; Wunsch-Hitzig, Gould, & Dohrenwend, 1980). First, these studies indicated that we are not even providing services for the 2% figure, and second, they report that a more realistic figure is closer to 10% or 15%.

I don't believe that there has been much of an increase in the incidence of those disorders that have a known biogenic origin, such as Pervasive Developmental Disorder NOS. However, there has been an increase in conduct disorders. Attention Deficit Disorder (ADD) and Attention-Deficit/Hyperactivity Disorder (ADHD) both are "popular" diagnoses and seem to be increasing significantly. However, there is little doubt that there has been an increase in violent behavior in our society, particularly by adolescents. Whether it be gang behavior or individual acts of violence, we are seeing a higher frequency of these acts, including more serious acts such as murder. The effect of viewing violence on television and its results have been well documented. Family violence is also a contributor. The problem of violent behavior in children and adolescents is a complex issue. We know that what a child is exposed to will influence what he or she does.

One major issue is the lack of consequences that can or will be used when a child or adolescent commits a violent act. Society today is not sure how to respond. Do we punish the offender, do we write it off as child behavior, do we try to rehabilitate the offender, or is the violence a product of a disordered mental process for which the child is not responsible? I hate to point the finger at families, but families have got to take responsibility for their children. The disintegration of the family unit is a major player in this dilemma. Children learn values from their families and they learn how to treat and interact with others through the models available to them in the family unit. The reestablishment of a sense of community by all involved will help considerably. Teaching values such as the worth of the individual, respect for self and others, right and wrong with appropriate consequences, self-discipline or control, and taking responsibility for one's own actions will help to prevent the expansion of these problems.

RELATIONSHIPS WITH OTHER SERVICE AGENCIES

The primary contact point with the student with E/BD is the teacher. Students are expected to attend school a certain number of hours per day, days per year, and years. The principal occupation of children is school and learning. Other services such as mental health, human service providers, and the juvenile justice system only become involved when specific incidents occur or when these services are affordable. I believe that it is important for each of these services to learn to work together as a team, each contributing their expertise to ensure the well-being of the child. When they work together as a team, they are able to coordinate their efforts and reduce areas where they overlap, as well as problem-solve the unique issues to each case. It is possible that a student with E/BD could be involved with each of the services mentioned above. A student may require regular counseling services from mental health providers, speech and language training or therapy, and occupational therapy, and he or she may be involved with a probation officer of the juvenile justice system. Although each has a different role to play with the student, it is their combined effort that makes the most significant impact on the student.

WHAT IS IN THE FUTURE FOR CHILDREN WITH E/BD?

I believe that there will be a number of changes in programs for the student with E/BD. These trends, as I see them, represent the refinement and implementation of a variety of strategies we struggle with today. First, we will recognize that many of our programs for the student with E/BD have become holding places, rather than an environment used to deliver intensive intervention. In the past we have verbalized this goal but have gotten rather sloppy with our ability or intent to follow through. We will begin to attempt to determine at the time of placement what specific behavior changes must be accomplished for the student to exit the E/BD program. Second, more emphasis will be placed on using the wide array of learning strategies developed in the area of learning disabilities with students with E/BD. Third, we will continue our efforts in the refinement of the social skills curriculum as a standard part of the daily curriculum. Social skills training will become a planned, scheduled, and formal activity as a daily component in classroom routine.

Fourth, the field will recognize that "transition" is not a single process, moving from one setting to another. Rather, it consists of a number of levels of transition, each of which must be addressed when preparing for and facilitating the transition process. Transition is an ongoing process from the student's first day at school until he or she leaves school. Fifth, less emphasis will be placed on full inclusion for the student with E/BD in the general education program. More effort will be made to use partial inclusion when such a process can be done in a way that will benefit the student more directly and efficiently. Sixth, there will be an expansion in the alternatives available to the student with E/BD for career/vocational experiences. We will expand our present methods of providing training prior to employment and will continue to refine how to best use job coaches and community liaison personnel in the evaluation and support of those students placed in the community. And seventh, as a field we will continue to develop and refine strategies to assist teachers to teach anger management to students and to resolve crisis situations involving students.

The very nature of today's society requires that we review and modify our present identification and assessment procedures. Wood, Smith, and Grimes (1985) suggested in *The Iowa Assessment Model in Behavioral Disorders* that we should seriously look into and consider a number of additional factors when evaluating a student for placement in an E/BD program. These factors include ethnicity, cultural background, linguistic background, socioeconomic background, developmental pattern, situational factors, and any possible medical contributor.

Interagency relationships should become more amenable. Meaningful cooperation will become the standard so that we all may become better advocates for the student with E/BD. New agreements will be established to involve those concerned with the daily operation of the school program. This should move us to a true team approach for working with the student with E/BD. Each agency will understand its role and what it has to offer to benefit the welfare of the student. In addition, each agency will recognize the expertise the other agencies bring to the team.

The basic role of school will remain the same, that is, to provide the students the opportunity to achieve to the best of their ability in academic skills, social skills, cognitive skills, vocational skills, and motor skills. There will be a revision of competencies to be acquired at school that the community believes will help the student become a productive member of the community. I believe that the schools will expand their interaction with the community. Schools and communities will find ways to teach a variety of skills or competencies in the community, thus helping the student with E/BD with the problem of generalization of behavior to settings outside the school environment.

REFERENCES

Adamson, G., & Van Etten, G. (1972). Zero reject model revisited: A workable alternative. *Exceptional Children, 38,* 131–137.

Berkowitz, P., & Rothman, E. (1960). *The disturbed child: Recognition and psychoeducational theory in the classroom.* New York: New York University Press.

Crane, C., & Reynolds, J. (1988). *Behavior management levels systems.* Houston, TX: Crane/Reynolds.

Diana v. State Board of Education, C.A.N. C-70-37 R.F.P. (N.D. Cal. Feb 3, 1970).

Emery, M. (1989). *Current status of young adults identified as behaviorally disordered during elementary or secondary school.* Unpublished doctoral dissertation, University of New Mexico, Albuquerque.

Gilliam, J. (1981). *Crisis intervention: Project SED. Teacher training module.* Austin, TX: Education Service Center, Region XIII.

Grosenick, J., & Huntze, S. (1979). *The national needs analysis in behavioral disorders.* Columbia: University of Missouri.

Haring, N., & Phillips, E. L. (1962). *Educating emotionally disturbed children.* New York: McGraw-Hill.

Hewett, F. (1968). *The emotionally disturbed child in the classroom.* Boston: Allyn & Bacon.

Kelly, E. (1988). *The differential problem sorter: Manual.* Las Vegas: University of Nevada.

Long, N. J., Morse, W. C., & Newman, R. G. (Eds.). (1971). *Conflict in the classroom.* Belmont, CA: Wadsworth.

Morse, W., Cutler, R. L., & Fink, A. H. (1964). *Public school classes for the emotionally handicapped: A research analysis.* Washington, DC: Council for Exceptional Children.

Wood, F., Smith, C., & Grimes, J. (1985). *The Iowa assessment model in behavioral disorders.* Des Moines, IA: State Department of Public Instruction.

Wunsch-Hitzig, R., Gould, M., & Dohrenwend, B. (1980). Hypotheses about the prevalence of clinical maladjustment in children in the United States. In S. Salzinger, J. Antrobus, & J. Glick (Eds.), *The ecosystem of the sick child* (pp. 27–35). New York: Academic Press.

THOMAS McINTYRE
Hunter College

Thomas McIntyre is a professor of special education at Hunter College of the City University of New York. A former teacher of culturally diverse students with emotional and behavioral disorders (E/BD), McIntyre has written and presented widely regarding students with E/BD and how culture affects their learning, behavior, and education. He has advocated for their rights and needs in many capacities for the National and New York State Councils for Children with Behavioral Disorders (CCBD). Tom is past president of the Teacher Educators of Children with Behavior Disorders and the New York Council for Children with Behavioral Disorders.

CHAPTER 14

Entering Uncharted Waters with Tattered Sails and a Broken Compass

The teacher sees one student sitting in a group give a backhand slap to the chest of another, who then becomes sullen.

"All right, my brilliant scholars, show me that you've mastered this material by creating a project related to it. You know your team roles, so let's get to it."

The teacher walks back to the table where the incident occurred and rubs the head of the victimized student before placing a hand on his shoulder and leaning over to the attacker. "Casey, please join me in the hallway for a moment."

The teacher and the offender walk to a nearby corner of the hallway. The teacher gently and respectfully opens the conversation. "You seem upset with your man Derrick."

"F— off."

"Thanks. I hope I get some lovin' tonight too. But first let's talk about what happened in there."

"F— you."

"No. I'm not available tonight."

The student quickly lifts his head and casts a shocked look at the teacher.

"Hey, seriously, why the anger? Then tell me why I'm the target of it. I don't see where I fit into all of this. What's up?"

"You don't give a sh-t."

"You're right. I don't give that, but I do care about you. What's up?"

"Man, don't no one care."

The teacher makes a game-show buzzer sound indicating a wrong answer. This sound has been used by the teacher in humorous ways throughout the year. The student tries to hide his emerging smile.

"Don't say no one, Casey, 'cause you're looking at someone who does. We've teamed up to beat problems before. Let's do it again."

"Why you punishin' me then?"

"We haven't decided on anything yet. But even if we do decide on consequences, don't you *ever* forget that *everything* I do is done because I believe in you. You've got a whole lot of potential, and I'm not quitting 'til you've reached it."

"Man, Mr. Mac, Derrick had it comin'. He got smacked 'cause he ranked my momma." The student tells his story, venting his emotions before becoming more reflective and open to teacher input.

"Casey, your feelings are justified. You've got a right to be angry, sad, upset, whatever. But your behavior was out of line. We've got to be sure that when these emotions crop up again, you handle the situation in a way that makes things better instead of worse. What could you do the next time someone starts playin' the dozens?"

The discussion continues. Strategies for restitution and handling similar future events are considered.

This story illustrates the point in my career when I became confident in my ability to deal with tough street kids. I realized that personal attacks toward me were a reflection of a student's emotional turmoil or street-corner training, and that if we could negotiate the shallow water hazards of foul language and other attempts to distract me from helping, we could go out to troll where the big fish swam in the deeper waters of the mind. There we could hook onto the real issues. Once we hauled in "the big one," we would then go back to deal with the inappropriate actions and language.

In reaching a phase where I could turn a confrontation into a "care-frontation," I had passed through the earlier stages of teaching children with emotional and behavioral disorders (Foster, 1986; McIntyre & Stephanides, 1993). When I first entered the field, I was anxious but optimistic. I believed that if I just revealed my concern for my students' welfare, they would view me as being different from those other, "mean" teachers. They would realize how much I cared for them, and they would care for me in return. We would have a congenial classroom atmosphere, unlike the coercive and punitive environments of other classrooms I had observed. If my kids misbehaved (which was unlikely with a nurturing teacher such as myself), I would conduct a "classroom conference" (McIntyre, 1987). After our informal counseling session, they would see the error of their ways and say, "Gosh, Mr. Mac. I'm really sorry. I'll change my behavior right now."

Within days of starting teaching, I entered a second phase: disillusionment. My students liked me, but they didn't respect me. They misbehaved more and more. Out of embarrassment, I taped wrapping paper over the door window so that my administrators and colleagues wouldn't discover the rampant disorganization inside.

Seeking respite, I went to the teachers' lounge during my planning period. There, I was given advice such as "Get tough with them," "Don't smile 'til Christmas (Hanukkah, Kwanza)," and "Keep 'em under your thumb." The angel on my shoulder was now drowned out by the stronger voice of the disciplinary devil yelling into my other ear. My child-centered views evaporated, revealing a voice from my manly, factory-town upbringing: "These kids are making you look like a fool. You're a man, dammit. Show them who's the boss here."

I "got tough." I berated, punished, and even physically coerced my pupils. And you know what? I did get more frequent (if begrudging) compliance. But now my students disliked me, and I still hated getting up in the morning after a fitful night's sleep of seeing my students' faces in my dreams.

After a particularly distasteful incident, brought on by the contrast of my coercive demands for compliance to a student's attempt to salvage his dignity and self-respect, I called my director to resign. I was not the teacher I had hoped to be. I was hurting not helping children.

I'm still here today because my boss recommended that I enroll in a behavior-management course. Things started to change quickly. I entered a fourth stage of teaching. I became progressively more effective at managing behavior in positive ways. Teaching became more rewarding. I regained my optimism and finally created that nurturing (yet structured) classroom environment I had envisioned as a novice teacher.

I came to love my profession so much that I sought a doctorate in the area of teaching students with emotional and behavioral disorders. Today, I try to instill in teachers the professional values I came to hold: Always treat students with respect; provide positive and attainable challenges; encourage and recognize a student's efforts; don't view behavior directed at you as a personal affront (it's part of their disability); try positive, neutral, or "tricky" interventions before coercive ones; defuse escalating conflicts by finding ways for both parties to exit with their dignity intact; always do what is in the student's long-term best interests; and use humor and have a good time in class. Last and most importantly, *never* give up on a student. Believe in his or her ability to change for the better even though he or she is more resistant than others.

HALF FULL? HALF EMPTY? A LOOK AT THE CURRENT STATUS OF OUR FIELD

These are tremendously exciting times for those involved in the education of children who possess emotional and behavioral disorders (not that our field has ever been boring). For our profession, this is the best of times and the worst of times. In practice and in the literature, there is a hotbed of controversy in areas such as assessment, identification, terminology, and treatment. The state of flux, change, and conflict that has existed for the 20 years or so since I decided to enter teaching continues today. Now, as yesterday, some professionals hold up certain views or practices as truths and advocate for their cookie-cutter approaches to teaching or disciplining all students. Our field needs to evolve beyond the "group think" of ideologic zealots who try to proselytize others to their simplistic views. Given the diversity of our student population, we need diversity in our interventions.

Many of the field's popular instructional and behavior-management techniques, while fairly effective with the majority of our students, are often ineffective or even counterproductive for many others, especially those students who are conduct disordered or come from culturally different households (McIntyre, 1993). Good people often have been taught, via poor role models or teacher trainers, to do bad (or at least ineffective) things. While their caring and concern is evident, many professionals are using disrespectful techniques that increase alienation and resistance in our pupils. These will be addressed later in the chapter.

A ROSE BY ANY OTHER NAME: LOOKING FOR A LABEL

At the time of this writing, the federal identification term for our children is *seriously emotionally disturbed*. A great deal of disagreement exists regarding whether students whose behavior *does not* reflect a disturbed psyche should receive special education services under the present definition. Fewer argue whether society would actually be better served if those who have learned their aberrant ways changed for the better. However, many professionals advocate against what is necessary to accomplish this prosocial change in behavior: intensive programmatic intervention. To guarantee this programming, a change in label and definition must occur. The term *emotional and/or behavioral disorder* (E/BD) is a better descriptor in that it would guarantee necessary services to *all* students who need to develop prosocial skills.

Whether children act in inappropriate ways due to emotional turmoil, child-rearing practices, or modeling of intimidating and manipulative actions displayed by elders or peers on the street corner, their behavior needs to be addressed. If we truly want to help this world, we must teach our antisocial students how to live in it.

PROGNOSTICATIONS

When we put an ear to the professional rail, we can tell that a train is approaching but not from which direction or what distance. We don't yet know the power of the engine or what it is pulling. Certainly I am no Nostradamus, and foretelling the future is an inexact science at best, but I'll hazard a few educated guesses based on the rumblings of trends apparent or emerging today. I fear that the light at the end of the tunnel could be an oncoming locomotive.

Despite pressure by concerned groups for legislation mandating that schools be required to serve any and all students whose behavior impairs success in academics or socialization (regardless of etiology), this probably will not come about. Powerful groups representing school administrators and school boards are exerting their influence to assure that students who are socially maladjusted are excluded from services. In order to obtain some improvements over the present definition and terminology, child advocacy groups probably will sacrifice these youth.

Federal legislation probably will make service provision optional at the state level. While various progressive states will legislate services to these youth, the metamorphosis to the goal probably will be slow in developing. There are those who will try to circumvent the letter and intent of these regional laws for philosophical, financial, or personal power reasons. Newtonian law also applies to education. The negative parts of the system will continue in motion until stopped by the positive friction of overseers and concerned advocates.

The expected change in the federal definition will also reflect the emerging concern regarding cultural background and its influence on behavior (McIntyre, 1993). On one hand, students who are culturally different are overrepresented in E/BD enrollments. On the other hand, children of undocumented immigrant families and children from war-torn and politically repressive countries are especially vulnerable to emotional and behavioral disorders yet are unlikely to have their needs recognized (Coburn, 1992). The new definition will likely require that identification procedures and disciplinary interventions respect the values and behaviors of the students' homes.

The determination of whether behavior is "normal" becomes problematic when students from culturally different homes are involved. The new definition will require evaluators to assess the extent to which apparent misbehavior is the result of one's cultural heritage. Unfortunately, most teachers (and their professors and supervisors) are unable to identify the cultural traits of any group (including their own). Fortunately, an instrument has been devised that assesses the effect of culture on behavior and learning and helps to differentiate between a cultural difference and a true behavioral or learning disorder. *The McIntyre Assessment of Culture* (McIntyre, 1994), developed by this author, is the first instrument designed to help in determining whether cultural background is a factor in the behaviors that have been identified by teachers as being of concern.

Schools can then recommend culturally sensitive placements and interventions.

However, what if culturally determined behaviors are in opposition to "reasonable" school decorum? Perhaps schools will need to provide services to students who are not E/BD but are culturally different to assist them in becoming "cultural chameleons," capable of displaying school behavior if their culturally based actions (e.g., a more flexible view of promptness, adolescent male rejection of female authority figures, reacting aggressively to commentary on one's female family members, ritual testing of an adult's authority, etc.) interfere with educational achievement, prosocial interaction, or safety and order within the school building.

For our children with E/BD, the learning of appropriate behavior typically is accomplished via social skills training. However, these curricula tend to promote middle-class, European-American values and behaviors to the exclusion of others (McIntyre, 1992). Educators must determine if this training is appropriate for pupils from cultural minority groups. What is needed are social skills training kits that are based on, or include, other life-view models (e.g., Afrocentric, Arab convergent, Asian focused, Hispanic centered, Native American oriented). Either way, teachers must assure that pride in one's original culture and its values and behaviors is promoted while teaching new behavioral patterns. However, it is not just the students who should be taught to be "cultural chameleons"; teachers also should familiarize themselves with the cultures of their students.

In an interesting twist of logic, the forthcoming definition's increased emphasis on respecting cultural heritage would actually nullify any requirement to serve students who are socially maladjusted. If the street-corner culture (Foster, 1986; McIntyre, 1991) with its manipulative, antisocial, and aggressive actions were deemed a valid culture with its own situationally useful social behaviors, we wouldn't be able to identify and serve streetwise, socially maladjusted youth (McIntyre, 1993).

This would occur because individuals wishing to deny services to these youth would claim, appropriately so, that the behaviors of children who are socially maladjusted have been taught to them by a longstanding subculture common to low-income areas. They would argue that these learned behaviors, which are contrary to those promoted in the typical North American school setting, are "cultural" and therefore fall outside the domain of special education. This rather odd manner of reasoning would mean that "streetwise" students would still be ineligible for special education services even though another part of the upcoming definition required that they be served.

Another part of the proposed definition also would work against services to students who are socially maladjusted. The new legislation would require that the presence of aberrant behavior be demonstrated in at least two settings, at least one of which is in the schools. If these students are cutting classes or truant from school, they would not be served. Additionally, their behavior could be viewed as valuable and appropriate social skills and survival strategies in the tough neighborhoods outside of the school building.

Some advocates claim that we could still obtain services for these students under the *Diagnostic and Statistical Manual of Mental Disorders–Fourth Edition* (DSM–IV) criteria of the American Psychiatric Association (1994) or Section 504 criteria. This is unlikely. Under DSM–IV (which is not used as identification criteria in public schools anyway), socially maladjusted behavior would be addressed on an axis for mental disorders. However, socially maladjusted behavior does not have an emotional basis. It is learned. Section 504 would cover conditions generally perceived to be disabling. However, few people view antisocial street-corner youth as being disabled.

Behavior-management approaches can be expected to come under closer scrutiny, as many are disrespectful or inappropriate with some students who come from culturally different homes (McIntyre, 1992). Modifications will need to be made to many popular approaches to behavior management. For example, Canter's Assertive Discipline approach (Canter & Canter, 1992) recommends practices that could be culturally insensitive, such as gaining eye contact from students when disciplining them. This technique fails to respect the many African American, Asian American, and Hispanic American pupils who have been taught to look down when being disciplined out of respect for the authority figure. Canter also recommends a technique that involves warning a student about misbehavior by writing his or her name on the board. Further breaches of rules and regulations result in check marks following the scribed nomer, each indicating a more severe punishment than the previous one. While it is expected that all students would dislike this procedure, it can be especially distressing for students from traditional Asian and Arab households, for whom being publicly chastised can result in a loss of "face," bringing dishonor upon their families (McIntyre, 1992).

Losing face also can occur when one uses Glasser's (1986) Power of Choice program or Hobbs's (1966) Pow Wow, both of which require public commentary on one's actions during the class session. Having to publicly admit to or be chastised by peers for less-than-perfect behavioral or academic performance can bring forth a traumatizing sense of having dishonored one's parents, relatives, and ancestors.

The future also will bring recognition of behaviorist techniques as being racist, although unknowingly and unintentionally so. The analytic, sequential, mechanical, and observable nature of behavior-modification procedures reflects the European American life orientation. This is at odds with the life-view of many other cultural groups. For example, a common Native American metacognition style is one of paradox and mystery, not cause and effect (Tafoya, 1982). Life is based on a circular rather than linear view of time and events. Behaviorist principles also conflict with the traditional African American view of the world (Anderson, 1988). Most psychological models, constructs, and practices also reflect the Euro-American outlook on life and alienate or confuse many pupils who are culturally different during counseling and guidance sessions.

Much further down the road, another change to the federal definition is likely to occur that considers gender issues in behavior and its management. This amendment would likely address commonly found differences between the sexes in cognition, communication, and interaction styles (Gray, 1992; Tannen, 1990). First, however, this area will need to be investigated and discussed further in the professional literature.

On another legal front, the courts, we can expect to see a new litigative approach to cultural issues. Currently, activists are seeking simple solutions to complex problems. Given the superficial cultural understanding of most individuals (including legal activists), court cases focus on desegregation efforts, financial redeployment, and hiring of "better" teachers (i.e., those with greater experience or more extensive preservice training). However, these changes have little impact and produce minimal change in achievement at best. Because of this increasing awareness of cultural influences on learning and behavior, lawsuits probably will emerge to claim that placement in E/BD (and learning disability) classes is discriminatory and that typical practices within those classrooms comprise educational malpractice.

This new generation of lawsuits will address deeper levels of culture and its influence on behavior, learning, and education in general. They will look beyond the "what" to the "why" of the lessened academic performance of students who are culturally different and their overidentification for E/BD. These future court cases will not concern themselves with simply addressing overrepresentation figures, realizing that they are not automatically indicative of discrimination, as presently understood. Rather, they will base their cases on emerging research and writings that indicate that traditional instructional and disciplinary practices do not match students' culturally based learning and behavioral styles and thereby penalize students who are culturally different.

Child-oriented legal advocates will argue that failing to modify practices to match a cultural style is discriminatory in that it forces students who are culturally different to learn in an alien, European American manner and adhere to a middle-class, Euro-American value and behavior code. These activities will litigate to ensure that home/cultural values, behaviors, and learning styles are identified, considered, and taught.

PREPARING FOR THE FUTURE TODAY

While 80% of students with E/BD are males (Lauritzen, 1990) and certain minority cultures are overrepresented (Chinn & Hughes, 1987; Viadero, 1992), approximately 80% to 85% of their teachers are European American females (Lauritzen, 1990). This percentage is increasing as fewer males and individuals who are culturally different enter the profession (Nicholas, 1990). Thus, an increasing number of teachers will have a different gender and cultural and socioeconomic background than their charges. Indeed, there exists the possibility that some of the overrepresentation of males and minorities is due to middle-class European American women viewing behavior different from their own style as being misbehavior.

However, the system will not automatically balance itself with the recruitment of more teachers who are culturally different or male. It is not just European American female teachers who must critique their present practices. Nearly all educators who are male or culturally different have been successful as children in this Euro-American, female-oriented setting. This process of natural selection is then combined with teacher training that promotes strategies found effective with middle-class European American students who speak standard American English. Because nearly all teacher trainers are unaware of the effect of culture on behavior and learning (McIntyre, 1992; McIntyre, 1993; Yates, 1988), this results in the molding of culturally unaware instructors.

Essentially, many of our often-used interventions will need to be discontinued or modified for certain students. Many of our techniques (even beyond the interventions discussed earlier) are outdated and inappropriate. I would be especially happy to see the technique of providing choices meet its demise. When a teacher tells a student that he or she can do either A or B with regard to actions (e.g., "You can do your math sheet or go to the office. Which one do you choose?"), we all know that the student is offered no real choice. It should be recognized for what it is: a teacher-imposed restriction on free choice. The technique also may be biased against many low-income, Hispanic, and African American children who are not exposed to this practice during their child rearing (Banks & Banks, 1993; Chilman, 1988; Strom, 1965; Vasquez-Nuttall & Romero-Garcia, 1989).

Additionally, while positive and respectful ways of gaining compliance are preferred, even supposedly good advice such as "praise their efforts" may be inappropriate for some students at some times. I have had members of minority cultures remind me that the emphasis that I place on validating students' concerns, involving learners in their own behavior change, using nonjudgmental listening, and "catching 'em being good" (as opposed to focusing solely on the punishment of misbehavior) is reflective of middle-class European American practices. They remind me that not everyone admires and wants to emulate the majority culture and that their ways have thousands of years of proud heritage behind them. For example, in the traditional Asian cultures, children are not praised. Rather, a child behaves well in order to avoid criticism.

The use of negative reinforcement is also present in many African American homes, where the traditional black style of child rearing ("Why Are We," 1993; "Endangered Family," 1993) expects children to behave appropriately. If they do not, verbal chastisement or physical punishment is administered.

While I am cognizant and respectful of traditional cultural practices, *all* cultures (including my own) could benefit by incorporating less punitive methods into their child-rearing repertoires. Positive procedures increase self-esteem while promoting prosocial behavior. Cultural values and behaviors can be inculcated even more efficiently this way than by negative ways.

In my behavior-management classes, I ask all students to engage in homework assignments that require the use of positive behavior-management practices. Many report that due to the child rearing they have seen modeled, it was initially quite difficult for them to address behavior in this manner. They still wanted to wait for misbehavior to occur and then punish it. However, the vast majority discover that, with these new procedures, they can actually enjoy teaching while building internal motivation in their pupils. When they notice the smiles on their students' faces (and their own), the prosocial changes in behavior, and the emergence of a pleasant classroom climate, they then decide to include positive techniques in their behavior-management repertoire.

PROGRAMMING: WHO, WHAT, WHEN, WHERE, WHY, AND HOW

Our students with E/BD are square pegs that don't fit well into society's round holes. Our role is to help them metamorphose to a more congruent interface with society. Problems with some of our attempts (e.g., social skills training, behavior management) have been addressed earlier in this chapter. Given those cautions, what else must be undertaken?

If our students with E/BD are to function productively within society and develop positive perceptions of themselves, they must be able to "do." They must acquire adequate vocational and career skills. Optimally, vocational training would be supplemented with training in conflict resolution and aggression replacement. Emphasis would also be placed on imparting social and work skills needed as adults so that they contribute to, rather than detract from, the social climate in the workplace. By learning interaction skills and how to pursue their wants and needs in a socially acceptable manner, they will be better prepared to relate to a future spouse, coworker, employer, and person on the street.

While most of our students with E/BD are better prepared for riding life's merry-go-round than when they first entered our programs, many fall short of grasping the brass ring of positive self-esteem and adequate interpersonal skills. For them, vocational preparation in high school should focus on occupations (e.g., cook/chef, auto body repair, building and grounds maintenance) that don't demand the supervisory and peer interaction that would reveal their lessened frustration tolerance and inadequate social skills.

Still, the ultimate goal of our programs should be to help our students feel good about themselves and develop in them the qualities of respect and empathy for others. To accomplish this, we will need to find better ways of breaking through the diamond-hard antisocial exterior of our students who are socially maladjusted or delinquent. Without a prosocial internal value code and an optimistic view on their future, these angry and misdirected children will grow into adults who hurt and take. Therefore discipline should not focus solely on behavioral compliance in specific settings. Instead, we must promote a positive sense of self and be sure that an internal sense of right and wrong is fostered. We must reach our youth at the level of the heart to convince them that prosocial actions are preferable to antisocial outbursts. Otherwise, if just taught to subdue their impulses because punishment will ensue if caught doing otherwise, when coercion is not present (or can be avoided), they will display antisocial actions.

For adolescents, time also will need to be spent on instruction in child-rearing techniques (including positive disciplinary practices) so that, upon having children of their own, they raise emotionally healthy and behaviorally appropriate children. It is important that the passing on of antisocial behavior to future generations be stopped.

EXCLUDE TOTAL INCLUSIONISTS (TOTALLY)

In the 1990s, we have seen the continuum of services recommended a quarter century ago by Deno (1970) come to fruition. Now, some would dismantle this well-reasoned structure. After 25 years of seeking multiple placements toward the differing needs of our students, it is now in vogue to advocate for the total inclusion of all students into one instructional setting, the general education classroom. Advocates of this one-size-fits-all model of service provision tend to hail from one of two very disparate camps. They see a common vision from very different perspectives.

One cohort contains callous professionals who are heartless in their efforts to deny special services to students who are emotionally or behaviorally disordered. This group has been around for centuries. The most recent generation, in their shortsighted attempts to save money and "teach these kids a lesson," regard detention, suspension, and expulsion as the interventions of choice. With full inclusion, they can more easily circumvent restrictions on suspending and expelling disruptive students.

Other inclusionists lead with their (bleeding) hearts, failing to engage their minds. These sad-hearted rubes have bought the ploy of the latest snake oil salesman, who promises a quick cure for all ailments. These caring yet misguided advocates believe that all children with E/BD will develop appropriate behavior and positive self-concepts in the presence of appropriate behavioral models. They are unable to explain why this did not occur the last time these students were in that setting.

Inclusionists frequently try to justify general education placement by citing statistics showing that students with E/BD, once placed in special education settings, rarely return to the general education classroom. They insist that special educators are consciously creating a need for themselves and their services. They fail to consider another explanation for the settling of these pupils in alternative programs: Perhaps we've accurately identified the students who are most in need of special services. Perhaps we have found the least restrictive environment for some of our students.

While we might admire advocates of total inclusion for their optimistic view of human nature, we must condemn them for their failure to recognize that being treated equally does not mean being treated the same. These naive inclusionists fail to truly understand the disturbed thought processes and severity of behavior found in many of our children with E/BD.

Some inclusion advocates would suggest the assignment of a personal aide to our more involved students with E/BD. However, few paraprofessionals have the talent or training to manage these active, manipulative, and intimidating students. We also must ask, "What general education classroom is appropriate for the 17-year-old 'gangbanger' with a first-grade reading level?" and "What teacher of 25 students is prepared to work with the hyperactive child with a defiant personality who seeks immediate gratification of his or her needs?"

Additionally, the goal of full inclusion is impossible due to the presence of another group of our adolescents: those who are incarcerated in prison settings. We certainly won't see them (and their corrections officers) being bussed to local schools. It is difficult to write while wearing handcuffs or participate in physical education while in leg irons.

If inclusion is going to be a viable option for more of our students with E/BD, general educators will first need more training in instructional modification, respectful and effective discipline, and cultural influences on behavior. At present, they are not adequately prepared, professionally or psychologically, for the majority of our students. Most still hold negative views of our children and their potential. Without the extensive teacher training that is required, pupils with E/BD will be set up for failure and continue to present the behavior that resulted in their initial referral to special education.

TAKING A HEAD COUNT

An increasing percentage of children are arriving at the schoolhouse door with emotional or behavioral problems (Knitzer, Steinberg, & Fleisch, 1990). The numbers are increasing for a variety of reasons: the decline of social standards during complex and changing times; the preoccupation with one's rights, while failing to observe one's responsibilities; the pampering of the children of the baby boomers while the harsh and inconsistent child-rearing practices most common among low–socioeconomic-status families produce large numbers of children who act out unless continual external pressure to behave is applied; and the media promotion of a youth culture that is immune to societal regulations and mature enough to make decisions devoid of input from elders. It is difficult to teach prosocial values in a narcissistic, "spend and use" society.

Lastly, as odd as it seems, educators often create or increase misbehavior in their pupils. As a result of the frequently found mismatch between instructional practices and culturally based learning styles, teachers oftentimes create emotional distress and much of the misbehavior about which they complain (McIntyre, 1992). This happens in a number of ways. For example, an active learning style, common among African American learners, might be misinterpreted as lack of self-control or a display of defiance. Second, the teacher's disciplinary response to these culturally determined behaviors can result in these pupils rebelling against what they view to be unjustified chastisement. Third, academic failure caused by culturally incompatible instructional style and discipline can affect a student's self-esteem. Finally, in an attempt to prevent the continued lowering of self-esteem, or due to frustration in their attempts to learn in a manner that does not suit their culturally based style of acquiring information, students may exhibit defensive behaviors (e.g., truancy, refusal to work, destroying products).

In the above situations, teacher and student, each battling for respect from the other, are at risk of falling into a destructive interactional whirlpool, dragging each other deeper into its educationally deadly depths. Rather than viewing an escalating confrontation as solely attributable to the student, teachers must evaluate their own role in the conflict.

Our reaction determines whether a bad situation escalates or de-escalates. When we seek "payback," conflict is inevitable. Power-based coercive strategies create resistance in many students. We should always be looking for ways to escape the swirl so that both parties leave the situation with their dignity intact. Consider the Chinese symbol for *crisis*, which is a combination of the characters for *danger* and *opportunity*. When we find ourselves in conflict with a student, we should seize the opportunity for a positive outcome.

Unfortunately for future educators of children with E/BD, there is a shortage of professors who can offer them effective positive strategies for reorienting a student's misaligned behavioral compass. Only 11% of university-level vacancies are filled by personnel specifically trained in the education of students with E/BD (Center & Kauffman, 1993). To adequately and appropriately equip our prospective instructors for their chosen profession, there is a need for university-level trainers who come from the classroom, not the clinic. While clinically oriented trainers have much to offer, they are inadequately prepared to offer real-life, effective, and respectful interventions to their special education majors.

Additionally, those who hail from the clinic often promote the categorization system of the American Psychiatric Association, which has little application to the identification and treatment of youth with E/BD in school settings. DSM–IV should remain in the hospital clinic.

As for those with a behaviorist orientation, most of these professors, having been exposed only to this perspective, need to engage in the study of other intervention models to escape their cold, calculating, and dehumanizing recommendations. Indeed, too often discipline is viewed as something we do *to* someone rather than *for* them. We often attempt to teach polite and respectful behavior via impolite and disrespectful means.

Evidence of behaviorists' failure to promote long-lasting behavioral patterns is provided by their own data analysis of their machine-like interventions. You have no doubt seen graphs in behaviorist journals drawn to show the effectiveness of the intervention on the rate of behavior. The "ABAB" research design "proves" the effectiveness of the intervention if, upon its removal, the behavior returns to its previous level. I ask you then: Of what use are interventions that fail to produce long-term change? Would we continue to use a certain approach to reading instruction if the students returned to previous levels upon its termination?

We also must consider other issues in behavioral change. Prosocial behavior should be enticed, not coerced. All children deserve to be treated with respect. Additionally, we must act without vengeful rancor. When we react in a knee-jerk way in order to teach them a lesson, we don't. Acting in anger removes the honor from what we do. Discipline should be a noble act, not a shameful one.

ENDNOTES

I trust that my frequent naysaying does not disguise the excitement and optimism I feel regarding the future of our field. It is my fervent hope that the coming years will bring more effective child-oriented strategies to replace the present emphasis on impersonal and detached behavior-modification procedures. Before this occurs, however, teacher trainers will need to familiarize themselves with culturally competent, respectful behavior-management interventions and the true nature of the classroom realities faced by teachers of students with E/BD. If they do not acquire and distribute this material, they give many of our future instructors the professional kiss of death.

While finding clarity in issues and foci in practices will no doubt be difficult to achieve, hopefully the ensuing years will provide us with a better understanding of the emotional workings of the mind and how to repair damaged psyches. That would then enable us to develop more effective procedures to build self-respect and empathy in children who easily hurt and victimize others.

To my fellow teacher trainers: Keep in mind that we still influence the lives of children. In fact, our influence is even greater now than previously. Additionally, we train the teachers of those children who are the most difficult to reach and teach. The frequency and intensity of classroom behavioral episodes take their psychic toll on our teacher trainees. Compared to teachers working with other categories of students, our trainees experience greater emotional exhaustion, job dissatisfaction, and negative feelings toward their students. These reactions to stress result in the largest attrition rates of any group of teachers. If we are to help them survive and succeed in their classrooms, we must avoid becoming removed and isolated in ivory towers.

To our teachers, the heroes and heroines in the effort to redirect youth with E/BD: Don't let an often impersonal and nonsupportive system break you down. Seek out information on better practices and implement them. If need be, work your miracles in isolation while supporting and influencing others (especially new teachers who arrive in your building). If possible, create a support group of colleagues who also care about children. Welcome those who have "burned out" but keep the focus a positive one. Avoid an emphasis on commiseration and helplessness. Once you earn tenure, work to change the system to better serve our children.

To everyone in the professions that serve children with emotional and behavioral disorders: Keep in mind that we're all in it for the children. Remember that helping students with E/BD is a sweat-equity profession: The more effort you put into it, the more you get out of it.

REFERENCES

American Psychiatric Association. (1994). *Diagnostic and statistical manual of mental disorders* (4th ed.). Washington, DC: Author.

Anderson, J. A. (1988, Jan/Feb). Cognitive styles and multicultural populations. *Journal of Teacher Education, 39*, 2–9.

Banks, J. A., & Banks, C. A. M. (1993). *Multicultural education: Issues and perspectives* (3rd ed.). Boston: Allyn & Bacon.

Canter, L., & Canter, M. (1992). *Assertive discipline: Positive behavior management for today's classroom*. Los Angeles: Canter and Associates.

Center, D. B., & Kauffman, M. E. (1993). Present and future needs for personnel to prepare teachers of the behaviorally disordered. *Behavioral Disorders, 18*(2), 87–91.

Chilman, C. (1988). Child rearing and family relationship patterns of the very poor. *Welfare in Review, 3*, 10.

Chinn, P., & Hughes, S. (1987). Representation of minority students in special education classes. *Remedial and Special Education, 8*(4), 41–46.

Coburn, C. (1992). Stress and trauma compound school problem for immigrants. *New Voices, 2*(3), 1–2.

Deno, E. (1970). Special education as developmental capital. *Exceptional Children, 37*, 229–237.

Endangered family. (1993, August 30). *Newsweek*, 17–27.

Foster, H. (1986). *Ribbin', jivin', and playin' the dozens*. Amherst, NY: Foster and Associates.

Glasser, W. (1986). *Control theory in the classroom*. New York: Harper & Row.

Gray, J. (1992). *Men are from Mars, women are from Venus*. New York: Harper Collins.

Hobbs, N. (1966). Helping disturbed children: Psychological and ecological strategies. *American Psychologist, 21*, 1106–1115.

Knitzer, J., Steinberg, Z., & Fleisch, B. (1990). *At the schoolhouse door: An examination of programs and policies for children with behavioral and emotional problems*. New York: Author and Bank Street College of Education.

Lauritzen, P. (1990). *Comprehensive assessment of service needs for special education in Wisconsin, 1990*. Madison: Wisconsin Department of Public Instruction.

McIntyre, T. (1987). Classroom conferencing: Providing support and guidance for misbehaving youth. *Teaching Behaviorally Disordered Youth, 3*, 33–35.

McIntyre, T. (1991). Understanding and defusing the streetcorner behavior of urban black socially maladjusted youth. *Severe Behavior Disorders of Children and Youth, 14*, 85–97.

McIntyre, T. (1992). The culturally sensitive disciplinarian. *Severe Behavior Disorders of Children and Youth, 15*, 107–115.

McIntyre, T. (1993). Reflections on the new definition for emotional and behavioral disorders: Who still falls through the cracks and why. *Behavioral Disorders, 18*(2), 148–160.

McIntyre, T. (1994). *The McIntyre Assessment of Culture: An instrument for evaluating the influence of culture on behavior and learning.* Columbia, MO: Hawthorne Educational Services.

McIntyre, T., & Stephanides, M. (1993). Do I really want to teach these kids? *Beyond Behavior, 5*(1), 16–23.

Nicholas, G. (1990). *ASCUS research report: Teacher supply and demand in the United States, 1990.* Evanston, IL: Association for School, College, and University Staffing.

Strom, R. (1965). *Teaching in the slum school.* Columbus, OH: Merrill.

Tafoya, T. (1982). Coyote's eyes: Native cognition styles. *Journal of American Indian Education, 21*(2), 21–33.

Tannen, D. (1990). *You just don't understand: Women and men in conversation.* New York: Ballantine.

Vasquez-Nuttall, E., & Romero-Garcia, I. (1989). From home to school: Puerto Rican girls learn to be students in the United States. In C. Garcia-Coll & M. Mattei (Eds.), *The psychological development of Puerto Rican women* (pp. 60–83). New York: Praeger.

Viadero, D. (1992, April 29). New definition of 'emotionally disturbed' sought. *Education Week,* 24.

Why are we beating our children? (1993, March). *Ebony,* 80–129.

Yates, J. (1988). Demography as it affects special education. In A. Ortiz & B. Ramirez (Eds.), *Schools and culturally diverse exceptional students* (pp. 1–5). Reston, VA: ERIC/Council for Exceptional Children.

WILLIAM C. MORSE
University of Michigan

William C. Morse, professor emeritus of psychology and education at the University of Michigan, held a distinguished professorship and was chairman of the combined program in psychology and education. Morse is past director of the University Fresh Air Camp, a milieu therapy program for adolescents who are disturbed and a graduate multidiscipline training facility of the university. He is currently a visiting research professor of special education at the University of South Florida and educational consultant to the Hawthorn Center, a psychiatric inpatient unit for children, and public school programs for special pupils. Morse's primary research interests include the training of special teachers, educational and mental health programming for children who are disturbed, and the self-perceptions of children with and without disabilities. Morse has presented at national conferences and has authored books and articles in these areas.

CHAPTER 15

Involvement in the E/BD Field

You could say that I backed into or, more accurately, was pushed into the field of emotional/behavioral disorders (E/BD). In the early 1940s I was a budding educational psychologist involved in ophthalmograph research to discover how children read difficult material. There was no E/BD specialty back then, though of course there were students with E/BD. Schools excluded them or referred them to child guidance clinics and, sometimes, when there was one, to inpatient hospitals for mental health treatment. Thus, I came in on the initiation of our specialty, and colleagues tell me that if I last a few years I will be in on the demise of the field as we have known it, since all students will be sent back to the general classroom from whence they came. I am certain of one thing: Whatever the schools do, there will still be children with E/BD somewhere and in even greater numbers.

As Bandura (1965) said, so much of our so-called planned life is really fortuitous. One spring day, my dean asked me to ride with him through the hamlet of Hell, Michigan, to the University of Michigan Fresh Air Camp to check out some things. After we inspected the camp, he told me that my summer assignment would be to teach in the multidiscipline training program that the graduate school operated in this summer camp for boys who were disturbed. The boys were sent by social agencies where they were in treatment. The counselors were graduate students getting a type of education impossible on the campus. So it came about that I began to work with children who were disturbed. After the first year I was hooked! Here psychology had to do with very real, live, and challenging children 24 hours a day, with days that often seemed twice that long.

Over the years, after becoming director, I changed the seminars from academic courses about children to the clinical study of how to survive with and help these disturbed children who were given to shouting unseemly epithets in our classroom window. I would invite them in, and sometimes they would come and join us for a while and inform us about the world as they perceived it. The exciting challenge of E/BD work is found not in books but in collegial clinical work. Today when I see a distraught child, the quest is still the same: How does the child see his or her life dilemma and how can an adult help this child toward a more successful journey? Parenthetically, when I see former students from camp days, now professionals, they still have vivid recall of the camp experience as imprinting their professional stance. The ride through Hell with the dean set my professional course. I still believe strongly that only intensive, supervised actual experience is the way to learn the craft of teaching special children.

It was my good fortune to have had many excellent career tutors over the years. I mention only the early and pervasive mentors. Fritz Redl taught the importance of helping through mediating the everyday milieu where children do their living. He saw working through crises as a corollary to formalized therapy. I have come to the conclusion that crisis exploitation is actually a better way to work with most children than ritualized therapy. Another mentor was Ralph Rabinovitch, a child psychiatrist, who demonstrated how to share the inner life of children and to use the discoveries in helpful ways. Eli Bower, a realist without illusions about the fragility of mental health and educational programs for these children, reminded me to focus on the essentials of helping and to keep the faith regardless of the fad of the month. Currently, both Bill Rhodes and Jim Paul prevent mental atrophy. But mostly, my continuing education credits are provided by interactions with children with E/BD, who continue to surprise and inform, and with their teachers, who do not stop trying, even against great odds.[1]

STATE OF THE FIELD

There have been a number of "state-of-the-field" studies following our original analysis (Morse, Cutler, & Fink, 1964). Since then the number of programs has greatly increased, though it is still far short of meeting the need indicated by epidemiological studies. Also, there is still a wide range of quality observed in the programs, with overall quality being rated as low. Singular use of behavior-modification and point systems is now the program mode. The most recent studies use outcome evaluation, and our special education graduates do the poorest of any students in percent finishing school, finding postschool employment, and in the quality of their young adult lives. Before getting out the crying towel, is it not appropriate to ask, "Does mental health do any better?" Will the proposed shotgun marriage of E/BD education and mental health provide the solution to successful programs? I think not, unless both establishments drastically change their ways (Morse, 1992).

---

[1]Should anyone be interested in details of a professional saga, it is recorded in the Council for Exceptional Children's *Oral History Project* that is now being developed in concert with Columbia University. It will be available sometime in 1995.

It is enlightening to visit classrooms where children with E/BD and teachers are struggling if one wants to see what is actually taking place. In the past several years I have seen miracle teachers who have won the trust of these difficult children and made a mutually supportive group out of 10 entrepreneurs in obstruction. Usually these teachers have administrative and cohort support, but sometimes they succeed almost alone and in spite of the bureaucracy with its rules and paper storm. Such teachers love their students, students who have generally been despised and rejected. For the first time children who have been abused and neglected have found an authentic educational experience administered with care. As the students tell it, caring is the essential ingredient. These teachers reach far enough into the life of the child to make a difference. This is despite the fact that most of these students remain vulnerable to a degree and require above-average support in transitions and even in adult life. These adult teachers see not an IEP but an LP, life plan. The quality teaching I see is highly individualistic in the methods employed. The class is a therapeutic place with exciting projects going on.

When former students come back to visit such teachers, they show that they were well aware of what was going on even when they gave the teacher a hard time. It is not uncommon to hear, "How did you stand me?" Often the teacher was the first consistently caring person in the student's life. Such teachers function as facilitators and collaborators with children, far removed from the old-style authority consumed by the need to be powerful and to control the children in the most expedient way. Recently I was talking to three teachers I had known in their training who were now in their second year out. The first year they described as literal hell under impossible conditions. In the second year, two found jobs with somewhat appropriate support and felt they were doing well. One moved from E/BD to LD, which he described as a piece of cake. All still wanted to continue teaching because the children were so interesting and they felt they were now able to reach many of their students.

But I must say that, more often than not, another story line is frequently being enacted, with exhausted teachers, a punitive no-win atmosphere, boring lessons, and classrooms serving as a virtual holding tank for the school hours. Most classes represent minimal, perfunctory efforts, and there are a few that can only be called destructive, providing no hope and no reason to hope. There are a certain number of teachers, aides, and administrators who appear to scorn these children. Much more common than hate for these students, however, is frustration in being unable to produce expected cures. Frustration easily can turn into anger. Often such teachers are inadequately trained, but even those who are well prepared can be dumped into a classroom with no aid and inadequate support.

Teachers do not fail. Systems fail. No one has researched how much of the aggressive behavior put out by children with E/BD is reasonable reaction to provocation of bureaucratic systems and arbitrary adults. As one child said to me, "I'm put here because I got problems. Every time one shows up I get punished. What's the deal?" The children tell me that certain teachers should not be teaching because they don't like children and don't know how to teach or help children. A few are described as burned out or mean. A special education service can leave a child with less hope, lower self-esteem, and reinforced worthlessness.

I see a wide range in the quality of E/BD classrooms. But I remember a central fact. If even only one child in the class is redirected from a life of failure, that teacher has paid back to society the cost of the whole operation, so expensive is malfunction in our society. There is the added dividend of improved quality of a life. If we conducted individualized followup, we would know that we are decisive in redirecting the lives of some children. We know better than we practice partly because of cost and partly because of outmoded ideology. There are families, and even children, where the haphazard community services tab is a million dollars, with little to show for it. There are more effective procedures for helping children with E/BD, as we shall see subsequently. Workers today are ideologically opposed to any institutional placement, opposed, that is, until there is a criminal act, and then there is a cry for putting the child away. Our too-little-too-late-and-too-wrong approach is not working. Education is imitating mental health in the reduction of the intensity of services provided, much to the detriment of the clients. We have seen how poorly mental health localized care has worked. Yet special education is in haste to do the same.

In my opinion, the reason for limited success of even well-staffed programs is obvious. The task of significantly altering personal behavior and bringing well-being to a hurt child is a monumental expectation to be foisted on a school. In many cases the task is whole-family rehabilitation, a complex task even when the family is willing, to say nothing of recalcitrant ones. In P.L. 94-142, parents have rights but no obligation to carry out responsibilities with their children, though most parents want the best for their children and do the best they are able to do. The fact is, many of the families are beset with overwhelming problems in addition to those of the offspring with E/BD. When we say families, we often really mean working mothers. Many of the family problems are related to poverty status, which the school recognizes by giving free lunches, good until dinnertime hunger. We complain about the lack of family cooperation, but we neglect many things schools could do to increase family collaboration, such as providing transportation and child care. It is an uphill battle for many parents to do more than respond to school crises. For most parents, having a sympathetic school program for their child is a considerable boon and much appreciated. For once they have a caring ally.

While some of our programs are seriously inadequate, the true reason for our modest success lies in the nature of the task. Even with the best of interventions and effort, it is difficult to change attitudes and mitigate those conditions in children's lives that exacerbate unacceptable behavior. Children often continue to live in the same conditions that brought on their problems. Undoing the effects of poor or disastrous parenting is even more sophisticated than first parenting. And there are other sources of negative input from peers, neighborhood conditions, and, yes, even from schools. The ecological factors are even less available to us than the child factors, but together they comprise one whole (Morse, 1993). At the same time the teacher provides schooling, the teacher as parent surrogate must erase the impact of the past as well as create the new. Accomplishing this restructuring of a self requires not only deep human relationships but also astute management of the ecological influences to prevent the week's progress being lost over the weekend. Monday mornings are notorious for the discharge of weekend accumulations.

Everyone agrees that we should restore the family as the primary child raiser, and sometimes we can, but often this is a dream. Whether the family becomes functional or not, we do recognize that the child's primary emotional attachment to the generic family runs deep. While the attachment is strong, qualitatively the attachment may be positive or negative and sometimes both. Families, regardless of their composition, often are overwhelmed by adversity. Changing the condition of destitute families has not been accomplished by any of the policies from the Great Society on. The fact is, we are not willing to invest in these children enough to compensate for social injustice. We even shortchange the educational programs, write platitudinal IEPs (being careful to leave out the hard parts), and call whatever program we have on tap the right program, regardless of goodness of fit.

Speaking overall about programs, it would be well to intervene earlier and stronger when the problems first are evident, and we have the literature on reclaiming those at risk to guide us. The increased difficulties of working with middle-school early adolescents and high school adolescents are reason enough not to wait. The ecology of the older child provides many invitations to career lines of malfunction that are very difficult to monitor, much less counter. We are still largely in a janitorial business, trying to mop up the spills of poverty, uneven access to health care, and family life in transition in a culture addicted to aggression and hedonistic pursuits. The child products of our society all come to school for a while at least, and there stands the icon of the Statue of Liberty, special education with its dream.

DEFINITIONS OF E/BD

I have never seen a definition of E/BD that I considered satisfactory, given the range of individual cases included in this broad category. Usually, after trying to set inclusive boundaries, the definition adds an additional note that also included are children with schizophrenia or some other recognized group that doesn't fit in well. Part of the problem is that we do not know how to deal with the various contributions of biological and sociological etiology. Certainly, I cannot do better than the recent Forness and Knitzer (1992) report. In a recent conversation, Forness said that there were forces lined up on both sides and it was about a 50/50 chance that the new definition would be accepted by the Individuals with Disabilities Act (IDEA). Then, one wonders if the definition will mean service for the 7% to 10% who need treatment. This could mean a vast expansion over the less than 1% now in school programs. P.L. 94-142 is not mental health based, since it is directed to those children with a disability that impacts negatively on academic learning.

As to the campaign to exclude children who are behaviorally disordered, Bower (1969), who provided the substance that was written into the law, never intended that these children be left out. Of course they are not left out in practice. Since they are the school's biggest problem, they do get in somehow. Definitions are designed to serve different masters, some with little relationship to the actual children in need of help. A major factor is political, to control intake through classification. This in turn is driven by budgets and the high cost of including all children who need a given service. Clinicians want definitions that fit their theoretical biases. Both special education definitions and the *Diagnostic and Statistical Manual of Mental Disorders–Third Edition: Revised* (DSM–III–R; American Psychiatric Association, 1987) play into reimbursement formulas. Nothing is said about how information would enable the defined person to get more appropriate help or even assist the teacher in providing individualized interventions. A proposal that the term *seriously* be dropped from the present definition to make our definition similar to the other special education rubrics is cosmetic but does reduce one of the barriers.

The Forness and Knitzer rethinking parallels new efforts by the American Association for Mental Retardation (AAMR) to move the definition of mental retardation to a new understanding. From status aspects, they now focus on systems of needed support. This moves from an individual to an interactive definition of person and environment assessment. Specific necessary adaptive skill areas are listed. It reduces the emphasis on classification and increases the emphasis on the individual profile. Forness and Knitzer, though still school oriented, based their definition on inadequate school adaptation in academic, social, vocational, and personal domains. I would add failure in intrapersonal resilience (anxiety, depression, low self-esteem). I also would add failure to adapt to appropriate school demands, inability to relate to peers and authorities in the school or home, and inability to achieve reasonable self-esteem except by behavior that violates the rights of others. I say *appropriate* school demands because so many demands belong in the theater of the absurd where the actors practice noncommunication and irrational expectations. The essential caveats incorporated in the Forness and Knitzer proposal include cultural norms and developmental age expectations. Children reacting to situational trauma such as abuse and divorce are to be helped by mental health intervention until the wounds heal. I wonder if they do not need the same intensity of help as students with E/BD are supposed to get. Thus, "normal" reactions to abnormal stress and crisis situations are not included. Dual certifications are included under comorbidity since E/BD often is linked with other difficulties. I think these new guidelines are a significant step ahead, opening up E/BD services to more children in need. Because it is expansion, I am not surprised that many local directors, who would have to find the money, are opposed.

Part of the definitional problem lies in trying to cover etiology, status, interventions, and prognosis. Frankly, I don't find that teachers see the current diagnostic information as being that useful since it is collected to decide whether or not a child fits a category. Teachers' questions revolve around what interventions are appropriate and what prognosis can be expected. My own interests are not in categorical definitions but in individualization. Even young children are complicated human beings, hard to comprehend. What does one know from a definition about the within-category variance? To say I am a WASP is hardly enough to define my individual nature.

We are a clinical profession, which is to say we individualize not categorize. At the Fresh Air Camp, we used to read the voluminous records on the children coming to the camp to prepare us for a brief initial interview just to doublecheck the appropriateness of placements we had made. In these interviews we usually saw a child so hidden in the records as to be invisible. We saw the whole child in a lump as he interacted with us. Sometimes record monsters turned out to be scared waifs, and sometimes "really nice little fellows" turned out to be skillful operators casing the place for exploitation as soon as they were off the bus. The contrast of the records with our interview impressions is not really strange. We saw different children because of different settings. The sending case worker wrote with an objective of getting the boy into camp. Our interview sifted out critical elements of how the child was going to be to live with.

This brings me to the essential point. What we need in order to work effectively with a child is not the category, especially those fantasy splits in DSM–III–R. We are not about an understanding of children who are disturbed as a generic condition but about a comprehensive understanding of each individual child. Usually the diagnostic information is so inadequate that the teacher has to start all over again from point zero, turning on the teacher radar, which, with an experienced E/BD teacher, is a keen instrument penetrating the obtuse verbiage in the file. The initial interview (which should precede a student being placed in a class) not only provides information but also allows for shared information and begins the relationship. Records cannot accomplish that. Only the human exchange when talking together can. It is opening the door to trust through teacher authenticity.

What we need is differential diagnosis on several important dimensions, such as attributions and moral development. I want to know where the child is in values. What does he or she consider right or wrong? It makes a great difference whether I find values I can use or whether I have to try to inculcate a serviceable value system. What about the future? Any hope for the next year? Five years? One student told me, "It's fifty/fifty, Bill. I will be in Jackson Prison or the University of Michigan." When I asked what would make the difference, he explained his attribution theory: "It all depends on the breaks you get. You can't do nothing about it. What's going to happen will happen." His percentages may have been wrong, but he had potential for both possibilities. At least I now know what we must work with, for I do want to change the odds. The child is the critical source of what we come to understand, with test data secondary. We begin to build the possibility of bonds through sharing.

In our work we put a great deal of emphasis on the initial interview a teacher has with a student. This is where the social contract on both sides is initiated. We also use a time line, where the child goes back to early memories and traces the significant events in his or her life (with the help of record data) and projects to the future, even to adulthood (where he or she would like to be and thinks he or she will be). Suppose the student has lived in 12 different home settings. What have these settings meant to the child? A teacher can open up what these "rejections" might mean in feelings. There is nothing to be gained by playing footsy with life realities. A list of personal assets and things the child would like to change is compiled, along with what will help to bring change. The discussion also can open up discipline options. We usually end with a stress/support chart on which the child lists the people present in contemporary living who produce stress and those who give support. Sometimes there is a contract drawn up as a task agenda. All of this material goes into the student personal portfolio, which can be consulted by the student and added to over time. When crisis events occur, the child does a writing assignment describing the way he or she views the event, and the teacher does the same. Disparate views as well as progress notes become the focus for dialogue.

All teachers are applied psychologists, sophisticated or naive. I see the teacher becoming a psychologist of individuals, which is a respected emphasis in psychological theory with a long history, temporarily covered over by behaviorism. This individual psychological approach meshes with the IEP. Individual psychology is a process rather than a set of dicta and does not preclude the use of various approaches, including behavior modification, when a process is appropriate to the nature of and goals for an individual child. The teacher psychologist knows students both from their behavior and from their inner lives. Such information is considered in conjunction with the ecology of home and neighborhood. A while back teachers did shadow studies, following the student for the school day. This proved to be an enlightening experience. We ask the child to do this for us by depicting the day and what goes on before school, on the bus, after school, and on the weekends. Given the vicissitudes of their lives, many are doing much better than might be expected. Knowing about their lives generates empathy and caring in most professional adults. We need these qualities to carry us over the tough times that are inevitable in E/BD teaching.

THE ED–BD DEBATE

In addition to the political and legal aspects, the ED–BD argument is confounded by several issues. First is the pervasive question concerning categories discussed previously. Are two students with schizophrenia one and the same? Are two children who are depressed alike? Are two special education teachers identifiable as peas from the same pod? Special education is dedicated to the concept of individuality, so its motto should be "To each his own." But education is a classifying bureaucracy, and no more than 2% are permitted in the E/BD category, though we know conservatively there are at least four times that number. There are political overtones to the ED–BD argument. Students who are behavior disordered (BD) usually are identified as acting out in a delinquent or predelinquent manner, and special education has never been hospitable to serving delinquents. No one has proposed a special education category of delinquency, and God forbid we do.

The prognosis for students with very serious BD is anything but encouraging. These students present very difficult management problems, usually reject our fine curricula, and are recalcitrant in general. Their pleasures do not please us. Since they represent the most disruptive group for the traditional school, they have always more or less found their way into the ranks of students with E/BD, in spite of efforts to keep them out. And since when is the lack of empathy not an emotional problem in the first place? The germane question concerning them is the same as that for any special child: Can we provide the resources to respond hygienically to the behavior the child is expected to produce? It will not be a quick fix.

In multidimensional assessment for individualizing, a pattern rather than a category is the outcome. One dimension, as said before, should be the degree to which a child has internalized the essential societal values for his or her age. While there is a tendency to make assumptions about values and socioeconomic class, that is an error. Value defects can be found in children with wealthy, indulging, upper-class backgrounds. In fact, one profile called *super ego lacuna* includes children who have a Swiss cheese conscience, a conscience with significant open spaces. They may have a generally adequate code except for specific areas. Often the transmission track is from parental unconscious to child unconscious, where tacit permission for certain immoral behavior is inferred through parental innuendo. The parents often appear shocked when the child acts out a hidden parent pathology, such as a deep rejection to all authority. The trip wire for BD is deficient conscience or morality. There is a lack of empathic feeling for others.

Such children are regulated by their perception of expediency: What you can get away with is the code, rather than what is accepted as morally right by the community. They lack remorse, although I have found they soon learn to say "I'm sorry" (until the next time). Expedient anxiety in fear of getting caught substitutes for guilt over doing wrong and seeking atonement. We make two major mistakes in working with value-deficient children. One is to think their misdeeds are a cognitive matter of not knowing any better. The second is to persist in appealing to a conscience that is nonexistent. Since we try to live by moral codes, we assume they do too. They have a code, but it is not what we would classify as moral. And the erosion of weakly held values that takes place in response to group forces is another aspect. One child's explanation in place of contriteness was "We wuz all doin' it." Ergo no responsibility. When we ignore the reality of BD pathology, we get taken and then we get angry at the betrayal, often exploding in a tirade of moralizing.

While there are those extreme cases given to violence, many students with BD can be helped by a program of caring and control, with lavish gratifications to be earned. The teacher models moral behavior rather than verbalizes a list of "you shoulds."

I maintain that most of us have some little streaks of sociopathology, especially when opportunities arise to cheat institutions or retaliate on people we have decided "deserve it." We drive over the speed limit when we think there are no cops to catch us. Morality is sometimes a matter of degree and location. We can tell early who are the children at high risk for sociopathy if we have the courage to look. Of particular concern are those who have substituted a peer-culture gang code for one we can live with.

Education and special education are enterprises resting on values of what is right to do for students. We make an ethical decision when we select curricula and teaching methods. Should the purpose of school for children with E/BD be to prepare them to enhance the gross national product, transmit the cultural heritage, or focus on child development relevance? Perhaps our goal is to cultivate the characteristics necessary for a democratic society. What is schooling for? Does it include not wearing a hat in school? Being motivated by our curriculum? We select what we think is right to impose and then hope our processes are adequate to the task. Be prepared that children who are sociopathic will challenge whatever our values impose because they are on a different track.

Programs are supposed to be individualized on the basis of the IEP for each child, although we know from studies that this most important condition of special education is also the least observed. There are, of course, some children who say they don't give a damn but who really do share legitimate concerns. Their negative verbalization is a defense against any involvement in change. Very few care about absolutely nothing except protecting their essential narcissism. Some of the toughest of these children also are depressed. Their future hope index is zero. Since their lives have demonstrated that they can't make it, there is no reason to trust or try, only to fail again. There are degrees of value defects, as mentioned. Not all are going to engage in random, remorseless drive-by shootings.

On the other hand, there are those easily given to violence, so damaged and maltreated from infancy that the prognosis, even with extended, benign institutional treatment, is for very little change. Our diagnostic processes should be shared with a child not to place blame but to get a level playing field. The goal of getting all such children back in the regular education mainstream is nonsense. Some will respond to alternative education where the return is immediate and preferably monetary, though they will con a work placement if not monitored just as readily as they would be in a school placement. Being system savvy, they soon can manipulate any program we establish, especially programs with punitive and behavior-modification rigidity. Once in a typical institution for delinquents, they solve that code and join the corruption. As I see it, when it comes to child raising, this society is doing an effective job of producing value-defective offspring. Many children have been cheated so long that it is next to impossible to provide the caring required for socialization. We have to start very early with intensive programs.

MEANINGFUL EDUCATIONAL EXPERIENCES FOR STUDENTS WITH E/BD

There are two facets to the educational experiences conundrum. First, what is the substance of the program? Second, how is the substance delivered? The aim is a potent IEP-driven program in a group class setting.

Then, what are the elements that should be available and activated in patterns as needed for individual students? To list these components by importance is not possible. Some students need all, some only a few. Many of our pupils have or should have dual certifications, especially those with learning disabilities (LD) and mental retardation (MR). They may major in one and minor in the other or have two majors. Needs from the list should be stipulated in an honest IEP based on a thorough assessment of the individual and his or her personal and ecological situation. What supports will the student need in school, home, and community to survive and hopefully to improve? What are the risks and what are the appropriate interventions? Incidentally, these supports are just as essential whether the pupil is "included" or in a special classroom. You might say these comprise an E/BD Bill of Rights.

1. *The first right is a well-trained, warm, and caring teacher, since the interactions between student and teacher comprise the core of the program.* That teacher should have adequate support: aides, materials, collaborative consultation, etc. What these children with E/BD have missed most growing up is continuity of caring, mature caring with incorporated implicit standards (Morse, in press). As Bronfenbrenner (1979) said, every child needs a sustaining adult who is irrationally committed to his or her welfare. It is very hard to provide this in a strong enough prescription to counteract the past (which often is also the present) but this is what good teachers do, serving as parent surrogates.

There has been a transformation in the conceptualization of *helping*, which is a more useful term than *therapy*, with all of its ritualistic constriction. Children restore themselves through action-oriented therapies such as the arts, game playing, and dramatic portrayal and through helping others, learning new things about their world and how to cope, receiving supportive peer and adult experiences, writing about their lives, and being in a meaningful school experience where they learn new skills. It is therapeutic to mastering fears and overcoming failures and can supplement or replace formal therapy. This is what we mean by therapeutic education, and there is no question that our good teachers are therapists. It will be a sad day when we expect restitution to come only in formal talk therapy or behavior management.

It is not just the classroom that must be trustworthy and caring. Recently teachers have told me their biggest problem is systems that are noncaring and even corrupt in the way they respond to all students, especially those with E/BD. While no one expects all adults to be identical, every staff member, including the cafeteria workers, bus drivers, and administrators must sign on to respect all students, listen to get their perceptions, and provide reasons behind rules. Student respect has to be universal. When someone held one of our summer campers too tight or yelled like a fishwife, we all heard about it ("You said you didn't yell or hurt kids here but . . . ."). To maintain a trustworthy milieu, any such violations have to be worked out thoroughly, with all parties and adult mistakes admitted. Otherwise our sins become their reason for rejecting our efforts. There are times we lose our cool, but we should not put the blame on the children.

2. *A second essential element of an E/BD program is a maximum involvement with parents or caretakers on a continual basis.* It is still too common to blame and write off parents on one hand or to consider them mental health clients on the other. The first obligation we have is to ensure that they know their rights. Parent support groups, counseling, and education should be made available. Many parents have been treated as harshly in their school contacts as their offspring. One important thing to talk over with the parent is what identification figures the child seems to be emulating. Is there need for a Big Brother or Big Sister relationship? Children are tied deeply to their families and what goes on in the home, whether the family is dysfunctional or not.

3. *A student should be assured a curriculum that is seen as relevant.* This does not always mean replicating the mainstream offering. Many students with E/BD have struggled with numbers, reading, writing, and spelling to the point of giving up, and they need study skills, social skills, the arts, and vocational education as appropriate. The essential point is that the curriculum should be presented in innovative ways and as much as possible emerge from their experiences rather than workbooks. One bright spot in specialized curriculum is an advance over past affective education or social skills training. This is Rhodes's new personal empowerment curriculum, called the Life-Impact Curriculum (1992). Cooperative learning, peer tutoring, and new methods of evaluation through portfolios are examples of new methodology.

4. *While students with E/BD are described as laden with personal problems, some programs offer no direct formal provision for working on personal problems, despite the fact that having personal problems is an entrance requirement.* Programs should include one-to-one counseling as well as class group meetings or powwows as Hobbs (1974) advocated for ReEd. There are times when even the recovering student with E/BD cannot handle the presenting situations and crisis support is required to prevent escalation. This is an action-oriented therapy using crisis for understanding. Crisis intervention will become more and more essential as inclusion marches over us.

5. *There is much talk about related services, though they often are not available.* Children fall through the cracks between services. Most of the children and families need the support of multiple agencies, such as mental

health, health, social service, and juvenile justice, recreation programs, and religious activities. The families often need more in terms of economic, housing, and job opportunities. I see the Full Service School as the coming model.

6. *A most often neglected program service is transition and follow-up support.* We certainly cancel much of the gain made in an effective program when we cut these students loose as they leave our door. It is not uncommon for our students to act out more as the day of freedom from a special class approaches. Some actually delay their departure by regressing to prove they are not yet ready. Behind this is usually the reenactment of the fear of failure from past experience. Will they be able to do the work without getting upset? Will the kids be friendly? Will the teacher help enough? They have been in the nurturing greenhouse and now are about to experience a traumatic transplanting.

Those going out to the work world are leaving the only occupation they have ever known, going to school. The E/BD employment histories are not good out there when there is no support crew. Many will need protected employment just as they need protected living, at least for a while. Every E/BD program should have a transition component to help maintain any gains the child has made. While there are a few children who do not wish to be contacted after they leave, most of them are glad to come back to tell students about their experiences. A phone call is one way to keep in touch.

It is even more important for the program to study what happens to their specific graduates, successes and failures. Only in this way can we become more astute at our individualizations. In one predictive follow-up we did, the predictive success was about chance. It turned out that the relevant factors appeared to be more in the ecology than the child.

To say the curriculum is the child may be overdoing it, but it is as much the child as it is a teacher's lesson plan. Because they are academically behind, we are driven to fix this at all costs, putting last things first with a stream of work sheets. What is needed is emergent teaching from the child's life experience. They can write, type, or tape-record what is going on in their lives, what went on last night at home, what they think of their life right now. When they trust the teacher, they can share the journal. When they trust a peer or the group, they can share the significant life events. Some prefer drawing to writing their story. This brief excursion into program elements provides only a glimpse (Morse, 1985).

PHILOSOPHY ON INCLUSION OF CHILDREN WITH E/BD

Inclusion, déjà vu! I remember the days before we had E/BD programs, when it was the mainstream or exclusion. The central reason students come to be special is that they fail to thrive in that all-nourishing mainstream. Now they are to go back, even though the evidence shows the intensive special education services do not follow them. The essential question is, what is equity for these pupils, and where are they most likely to get that equity (Morse, 1994a)?

There are obvious ethical issues involved, conflicting beliefs about what is most important. The courts are much involved, with cases suggesting that sitting with peers without disabilities takes precedence over other values. The question should be, where is the best potential for recovery? To say that there is no student with E/BD who would do well in the right general classroom is absurd. But they tell us all means all. It is just as absurd to say that all will flourish back from whence they became special because they couldn't make it. What miracle has taken place to purify the mainstream? Most general classes already have enough illegitimate (that is to say unclassified) students with E/BD to keep teachers entertained. And it is these teachers who will have to pay the price for what the academics have advocated. As we know, in many places all does not mean all anyway. In practice it means all but the children with E/BD.

There are many false issues confusing the real concerns we should be addressing about inclusion. First, does not this class action that puts all special education children, regardless of degree or nature of disability, into one clump violate the individual basis of special education? The decision should be an individual one, not a class action. The ecology of the specific mainstream fit with support for a particular child should be examined for fit with the IEP. Most integration literature is based on a fantasy mainstream, not the one that is there and in need of considerable renewal. Being with so-called normal peers can enhance positive growth or provide more failure, as anyone who has studied peer culture should know. Will there be efforts to create a supportive social classroom culture for all students (which is not the case now)? There is nothing automatic about socialization gains in the typical classroom, and students with serious emotional disturbances (SED) are known to be low on the sociometric choice list.

We ask, can the needs as defined by a true IEP be provided in the general classroom? If so, why was this not done before removal? How many of the available resources listed in the prior section will be delivered in the mainstream, where there is a reluctance to adapt the curriculum to individual needs of even the so-called normal learner. Will there be in-depth crisis support? The simplistic practice of the current behavior specialists who try to solve complicated problems with an automatic point penalty will not suffice. The overgroup persons, who will have both the general and the special education groups in the same classroom, need to be trained in both education and mental health practices using Life Space Interviewing and remedial tutoring (Morse, 1979). When students with

E/BD cannot make reasonable use of the group learning situation, they need such services.

While we are familiar with the burnout and high turnover of E/BD teachers, we sometimes ignore the number of general teachers who regress to zombies or quit. I have had teachers express willingness to take a student with E/BD after good salesmanship, but only if special education would take one or two unclassified students already in the class. One district that closed its E/BD day school and did maintain the same degree of services for the included students found it necessary to add more staff to operate in the decentralized format. There is no cheap migratory assistance unless one reduces the intensity of service, which is the main move now taking place.

The best thing educators could do would be to take the heat now generated by the idle inclusion argument and fuel prevention through early and continual screening and intervention, starting with preschool. Special education co-opted what were the school mental health personnel for special education certification, further diagnosis, and reevaluation. Perhaps it is time to give some personnel back to the cause of prevention. What ever happened to Deno's (1973) cascade of services, which was supposed to eliminate a single in or out choice of placement?

There is no doubt that we sinned by extruding some children who could have remained included with crisis support. And we sent children afar to institutions rather than provide local mental health programs or mental health–oriented day schools. The current inclusion debate is a complex of financial issues, diverse value issues, legal matters, presumed human rights, and the current ground swell of criticism of all education. One of the saddest points of extrusion, especially for adolescents, is the bureaucratic way it is done. As one boy put it, "That man gave me them tests see. I guess I failed again. My mom went to a meeting, and I got to ride a different bus from the other kids and go to this different school. We don't have many kids in this class, but they are all funny type kids." Special classes are not automatically useful or destructive in and of themselves. Much depends on how we can help the student see the purpose. A special class can be a rescue mission or the pits. We have to sift out the meaning to the student. It can take a teacher a year to counter the psychological abuse inflicted in placement processes.

IS THE INCIDENCE OF E/BD INCREASING?

Except for one esteemed colleague, teachers who have taught for some years and administrators I talk to hold that the incidence of E/BD is increasing. Not only are the numbers higher, the severity of the problems has increased. My own position is that the society is producing more children with BD who are value deficient. Less frequent are the old-style naive, relating, but confused neurotics referred for special education, again unless there is also acting out. More children, like adults, lack hope and, seeing no way to solve their dilemmas, are depressed. But depression is often overlooked unless the despair is acted out.

It is interesting that adolescent suicides are seldom on the special education rolls. How did we miss them? Does anyone see less aggressive behavior? Fisticuffs have been replaced with gun battles. The behavior of children mirrors the behavior of the society that produced them. Reading cases, talking to our children, and working with teachers convinces me the millennium has not yet arrived. Life stories contain more abuse and more neglect. Drug babies are now of school age. No doubt some of the increase is due to recent awareness and willingness to report rather than to increased incidence. It is hard to find an E/BD file that does not contain a series of past and present traumatic events, enough sometimes to make one wonder how the child survived. I believe we are not born civilized beings but come to be human through the investment of the societal caretakers, which I admit leads to linear reasoning. There is increased poverty, which is the bedrock deleterious condition, since it closes the door to so many needed services for safe growth. All the while, services to the child and family have been curtailed, creating a monumental mental health debt that may overtake us before the economic deficit does.

Support is scarce and fragmented, since agencies have not changed their ways to meet the crises. The school, being the only socializing institution in place for all children, is caught between equity and excellence, between what teachers or school boards think the schools should be doing and what students really need to manage their lives in our partially democratic, though power-based, social order. The school restructuring now going on across the country is largely tinkering with artifacts, neglecting special education and other children at risk. For many children school is their only hope, and yet schooling remains for so many part of the problem rather than part of the solution.

ROLE RELATIONSHIPS: SPECIAL EDUCATION, MENTAL HEALTH, JUSTICE

We have become a crew of specialist professional helpers, each attending to a part of the child and doing our work in virtual isolation from each other. No one is responding to the child as a whole, though teachers have the best opportunity. We have meetings to put the individual child pieces together, making a composite image that is often as distorted as in a carnival house of mirrors. Each profession has its own liturgy or variety of liturgies for helping owned by the guilds that certify the various child helpers. The guild rituals often end up with each seeing a different child, yet there is just one real child. Meanwhile, that child is trying to figure a way out of his or her situation and seeks out his or her own helper, usually a peer or sometimes a trusted adult, who may not be a professional.

At this writing, coalescing education and mental health is advocated as the solution to providing adequate E/BD programs, with juvenile justice sometimes added to make the new Holy Trinity. Having had considerable experience with the mental health education merger, I have written in detail on these shotgun marriages (Morse, 1992). Some of these marriages turn out to be a marvelous synthesis of two helping modes. Others turn out to be disasters and end up in divorce.

It is not just two disciplines getting together. It is two groups of workers who represent different ideologies coming together. When the workers develop trust and collaboration, the student and family are more effectively served. When there is no common child perceived and put in the center of the effort, little is accomplished. I have seen the examples of mental health workers joining in classroom activities and co-leading group sessions with the teacher. The two make an on-the-line service team. But frankly, unless both disciplines undergo a metamorphosis in how they practice, I see little advantage in joining forces. Therapy is every bit drowning in outmoded models as is E/BD special education. The topic of collaboration goes beyond even the agencies of special education, mental health, and justice.

WHAT OF THE FUTURE: YEAR 2000 AND E/BD

What of the future of E/BD special education? Pick your prediction. In this chaotic period in educational change, one assesses the power blocks that seem to be in a state of constant flux as they debate excellence and equity matters with no agreement in sight. I do not expect there to be a single E/BD service pattern in the near future. Just as now many schools do not practice inclusion of students with E/BD (also excluding their scores from the achievement statistics), I expect there will continue to be special classes. I think there will be much more pressure to do whatever mainstreaming that can be arranged to reduce the isolation of these students. In some places the classes will begin to offer more complete services as outline above, but many will stay at the warehouse level. There are rumblings of making teacher training more realistic and experience bound, and one hopes that the internships and later jobs will follow best practice. The idea that a required course in exceptional children for all teachers will cure the system is too absurd to discuss.

On the other hand, the rush to total inclusion may dominate even this field unless parents advocate for comprehensive IEPs. When special programs are reduced does anyone doubt that resources will dry up? A generation of students with E/BD will be sacrificed and then some newfound wisdom will restore classes. I would like to see the inclusion experiments combined with intensive crisis intervention as described before, along with group work when needed. We used to maintain a lot of children with E/BD in the mainstream this way and I think we could do it again. We certainly need Deno's cascade of opportunities, not any single approach. In one location I know well, the day school has been sized down to only the most serious cases with very poor prognoses, a repository for the unredeemable. We may all end up with a few classes for children who should be candidates for institutional treatment.

When I speak frankly on these matters, I often am asked by students, how do you keep going? Well, on odd days of the week I get depressed, not just about our field but the state of the country. Then on even days, hope regenerates, especially when I visit teachers who are doing great things for children. I know all is not being lost. But beyond this awareness, I sense an ideological shift that is taking place in the whole matter of service to children and parents. Parents have become families. The goal is now family preservation through a new delivery system. I am speaking of the Full Service School (FSS; Morse, 1994b) concept, which is the pattern for the future already operating in many communities. If combined with early screening and preventive interventions through the school, this could be a way to stem the tide. The community must unite its service enterprise.

The Full Service School requires multiple agency collaboration with service representatives housed on the school campus. It ends up as a one-stop neighborhood service center for the many needs of children and their families. Teachers have immediate access not only to mental health and juvenile protection but also to health services. Referral of families is simplified. Further, as housing, welfare, and employment services join the collaboration, there is a chance of doing more than putting a surface bandage on symptoms. Family preservation is the goal; if not that, then multiple support services.

Getting agency collaboration and change is not at all easy. To manage the help-giving process, case managers are assigned to work with the family, engage the necessary services, and monitor progress. Money follows the child in need rather than programs. While the services are wrapped around the child and family, let us also see that they are more caring services. The FSS projects are idiosyncratic, matched to fit local community needs. While no one sees this as easily accomplished, there is progress being made. Most of all, those engaged in the work realize they are on the right track in bringing these changes. One major goal is to provide integrated local services to prevent unnecessary institutionalization of students with E/BD, which can cost over a thousand dollars a day. There is soon to be a full report of the FSS endeavor as it now stands in Florida. To me it is the single most promising development for students with E/BD we have seen yet.

So, in the midst of chaos, there are some positive things happening. We are beginning to realize how complex it is to provide free appropriate public education (FAPE) for students with E/BD and why the effort wears out so many devoted teachers. There is new recognition that this work is a total community enterprise. We may even begin to screen for mental health problems as well as academic achievement. With the new laws, P.L. 98-199 and P.L. 99-457, we are able to activate early intervention at a time in the child's life when the odds of success are higher. There is a reality that shapes our ends, even though we gyrate in our responses. The truth is, there are many children with E/BD who need our help. If we ignore them, the social fabric will be further eroded as they become adults. When we realize it is our own salvation that is involved, I suspect we will embrace new concepts more vigorously. Perhaps even by the year 2000.

REFERENCES

American Psychiatric Association. (1987). *Diagnostic and statistical manual of mental disorders* (3rd ed., rev.). Washington, DC: Author.

Bandura, A. (1965). *Principles of behavior modification*. New York: Holt, Rinehart, & Winston.

Bower, E. M. (1969). *Early identification of emotionally handicapped children in school* (2nd ed.). Springfield, IL: Thomas.

Bronfenbenner, V. (1979). *The ecology of human development: Experiments by nature and design*. Cambridge, MA: Harvard University Press.

Deno, E. (1973). *Instructional alternatives for exceptional children*. Arlington, VA: Council for Exceptional Children.

Forness, S. R., & Knitzer, J. (1992). A new proposed definition and terminology to replace "Serious Emotional Disturbance" in the Individuals with Disabilities Act. *School Psychology Review, 21*, 1, 12–20.

Hobbs, N. (1974). Nicholas Hobbs. In J. M. Kauffman & C. D. Lewis (Eds.), *Teaching children with behavioral disorders: Personal perspectives* (pp. 142–167). Columbus, OH: Merrill.

Morse, W. C. (1979). The helping teacher/crisis teacher concept. In E. Meyer, G. A. Vergason, & R. J. Whalen (Eds.), *Instructional planning for exceptional children* (pp. 308–325). Denver, CO: Love Publishing.

Morse, W. C. (1985). *The education and treatment of socioemotionally impaired children and youth*. Syracuse, NY: Syracuse University Press.

Morse, W. C. (1992). Mental health professionals and teachers: How do the twain meet? *Beyond Behavior, 2*, 12–20.

Morse, W. C. (1993). Ecological approaches. In T. R. Kratochwill & R. J. Morris (Eds.), *Handbook of psychotherapy with children and adolescents* (pp. 320–356). Boston: Allyn & Bacon.

Morse, W. C. (1994a). Comments from a biased viewpoint. *Journal of Special Education, 24*(4), 531–542.

Morse, W. C. (1994b). *Full service school concept.* Unpublished manuscript, University of South Florida, Tampa.

Morse, W. C. (in press). The role of caring in teaching children with behavior problems. *Contemporary Education.*

Morse, W. C., Cutler, R., & Fink, A. (1964). *Public school classes for the emotionally handicapped: A research analysis.* Washington, DC: Council for Exceptional Children.

Rhodes, W. (1992). Life-impact curriculum. *The Journal of Emotional and Behavioral Problems, 2*, 10–28.

MARY BETH NOLL **BARBARA A. BRAATEN**
St. Cloud State University Minneapolis Public Schools

Mary Beth Noll has had extensive teaching experience with students with emotional disturbance both in public schools and in the hospital setting. Noll received her PhD from the University of Kansas in the area of emotional disturbance. In addition to her university teaching responsibilities, she has research interests in the areas of integrated teacher training and educational programming issues for students with E/BD.

Barbara Braaten is currently a program coordinator for a self-contained, special site, collaborative special education program in a middle school in the Minneapolis public school system. She has more than 15 years of experience working with students with emotional and behavioral disorders in both suburban and urban schools. Braaten received her MS degree from Mankato State University (Minnesota).

CHAPTER 16

Successful Educational Outcomes for Students with Emotional or Behavioral Disorders: A Dream Deferred

> *What happens to a dream deferred? Does it dry up like a raisin in the sun . . . . Or does it explode?*
>
> Langston Hughes

When we embarked on our paths as special educators 20 years ago, we dared to dream that we could make a difference in the lives of students with emotional or behavioral disorders. We dared to dream that by providing an atmosphere of caring and optimism for our students we would enable them to believe in themselves and their abilities. We dared to dream that by providing appropriate educational services for our students we would enable them to lead productive lives as adults.

Unfortunately, good teaching in nurturing classrooms is not all that is needed to transform the lives of students with emotional or behavioral disorders (E/BD). Our dreams did not consider the staggering political, economic, and social realities of today's society. In a world increasingly beset by poverty, homelessness, drugs, violence, and the brutal inequities of class and race, our students' struggle to survive has spilled over into the classroom and created new challenges for us as educators.

CURRENT STATUS OF THE EDUCATION OF CHILDREN AND YOUTH WITH E/BD

As we try to assess the current status of children and youth with E/BD, we cannot help thinking back to when we began our teaching careers. We were then encouraged to create "therapeutic" classrooms, classrooms that fostered comfort and trust, that provided less stress and viewed academic success as the first intervention to bringing balance to what was often an otherwise chaotic life beyond a young person's control. Something happened along the way, however. Most educators agree that it has become more difficult to create classroom environments that are successful for our students. The magnitude of children's needs and the severity of their problems are greater than ever. For example, students are difficult to keep in school, and regardless of how effective our teaching skills, if students do not show up, we cannot teach them. Students with emotional or behavioral disorders are transient, moving in and out of relationships, schools, and neighborhoods. As a result, they also are often adrift in a sea of educational and social service systems.

The widespread use of crack and other "new" drugs has brought about alarming changes in our students and our schools. Drugs (and their correlates: gangs, guns, and violence) and the economics that drive them have taken our children's honor away. Drugs have robbed them of their will and self-control. The loyalties have switched from families and neighborhoods to associates and "colors." In our early days of teaching, we were seldom afraid for our physical safety. If a teacher was injured while interacting with students, the incident was considered accidental, or the students were usually viewed as not being cognizant of the injury they inflicted because of their intense emotional state. Now, however, we are negligent—or stupid—if we do not watch our backs at all times due to the unpredictability of students' behavior and the increased potential for physical harm. Many of our colleagues work in environments that include metal detectors and security personnel. While the times may require these precautions, the impact on a comforting and trustful classroom has been profound. The realization that violent conflict is a recognized way of solving problems and competing for status in many of our students' lives does little to calm our nerves (or those of our students) when we are placed in physically threatening situations.

Much has been written about the desperate needs of children and families in our country and the failure of societal systems to adequately address their problems. Students are disconnected from families, families are disconnected from communities, and schools are disconnected from the realities our children and families face in their homes and communities. We work with students whose values reflect those of their families and communities, values that may conflict with what we feel will benefit them as they enter mainstream society. While we have always been advocates for our students, we find that we must now advocate for services and resources that speak to the health, safety, and economic needs beyond school. A new role for teachers is to work with social service personnel to address the needs of the entire family. If, as Edgar (1990) maintained, persons in the United States achieve a lifestyle based much more on their family status than on skill level, addressing the realities faced by our students in their homes and communities becomes a priority task for any special educator.

It is ironic that while families and communities have continued to deteriorate, political and economic resources for mental health services are less available now than they were 20 years ago when families and communities were more intact. Community mental health agencies have been forced to take care of only the most serious or more desperate needs. Others in need of services have not vanished; many of the people who were once served in clinics or hospitals are now on the streets. Children and youth who are identified and placed in special education programs for students with E/BD are also in need of mental health services. In one state, for example, only 16% of identified students with E/BD received mental health services (Rhys, 1993). Dumont, a pioneer of the early community mental health movement in Massachusetts, was quoted as saying that community mental health services in his state were "returning to the era before Dorothea Dix" (Wylie, 1992, p. 13).

The schools are currently on the front lines of dealing with both students and parents who have been lost in the system. This is particularly true of teachers of students with E/BD. The families with whom we work frequently do not have telephones, transportation, employment, child care, or access to health services. Most teachers rely on these resources to support the educational process for students with E/BD. We typically are not able to plan a curriculum that requires home reading materials, media resources, field-trip monies, or a foundation of basic general knowledge on which to build. Therefore, while we are charged with the responsibility of working with the "whole child," we have not been given the resources or access to channels that permit that to happen. E/BD teachers are groping to plan effective educational programs while circumventing the unmet basic needs of children and families.

At a time when mental health services for our students and families are limited and fragmented, a similar situation is occurring in education. Students once placed in self-contained classrooms with extensive special education intervention are now being served in general education settings with minimal or no support. Students previously served in residential settings are now being served in resource or self-contained classrooms in public schools or at home by means of homebound instruction. Rather than providing specially designed instruction and doing "whatever it takes," we have adopted a minimalist approach that opts for simpler and less expensive interventions. Rather than expanding the continuum of services, our efforts often are focused on fitting the child into the mainstream educational program. Perhaps the special education equivalent of the Dumont quote might be "The state of services is returning to the era before P.L. 94-142."

We would not be as concerned about this if we could see changes forthcoming that support its implementation. However, training for general education teachers does not seem to be keeping abreast of mainstreaming demands and inclusive education models. Lerner (1987) indicated that training programs now are no different than they were when people fought so hard for special education for students with disabilities. General education teachers are no better prepared to deal with students with special needs than they were 20 years ago. In our teaching experiences, even when teachers are adequately prepared, they are not likely to welcome our students with E/BD into their classrooms when their class sizes are becoming larger and students' needs more significant and diverse. Teachers are required to assume the roles of parent, counselor, friend, and even police as part of a normal day (prompting one detective who worked with violent offenders in an urban gang suppression unit to comment, "Teaching is a job I wouldn't want"). Again, if we believe that classrooms for students with behavioral problems must provide comfort, security, and academic success, the general education environment must undergo significant changes before successfully accommodating the needs of our students.

INCIDENCE OF E/BD

Given the bleak picture of the status of children and families in our country today and the increased number of factors that precipitate and aggravate their problems, one would expect to see drastic increases in the numbers of students identified as having emotional or behavioral disorders. However, the data continue to indicate that, on the average, less than 1% of school-age children are identified and served in E/BD programs (Kauffman, 1993). This is in stark contrast to estimates suggesting that, at any given time, a minimum of 10% of our school-age children are experiencing mental health problems (Kazdin, 1987).

There is no question that significant numbers of children are mildly to moderately impaired by numerous social risk factors and manifest their difficulties in different ways in different school and community domains. Although only a small percentage of students receives specially designed individual instruction in special settings due to the severity of behaviors, a large percentage of children with significant emotional and behavioral needs receives minimal or no services (Smith, Wood, & Grimes, 1988). The general education teacher often is caught in the dilemma of whether to refer or not to refer. Unfortunately, many general education teachers seem to be getting the message that it is a negative to be referred for special education services. As special educators, we believe that we have something positive to offer children with special needs. The debate about labels, overrepresentation of males and persons of color, the inability to "cure" the disability, and the enormous burden of proof (and paperwork) create pressure on special educators to apologize for our profession. We believe that all students with emotional or behavioral needs, identified or not, should have access to the support services they need in the school and community.

A WORKING DEFINITION OF E/BD

To a teacher who works with students with E/BD, a definition is unimportant other than to meet the requirement of the federal law. The important work is with the child. However, we also recognize the need for a definition that will guide program development and, hopefully, ensure quality services for students who meet the definition.

We feel that the definition proposed by Forness and Knitzer (1992) through the National Mental Health and Special Education Coalition is a positive step toward resolving the problem of underidentification while also safeguarding the rights of the child regarding unnecessary categorization. The proposed E/BD definition focuses on the degree to which a child's behaviors differ from age-appropriate, ethnic, or cultural norms. In addition, it avoids meaningless distinctions between behavioral, social, or emotional conditions that have been the subject of so much controversy (Forness, 1991). We support this proposed definition not only because it is workable for a teacher but also because it represents the collaborative efforts of both the mental health and educational fields. As mentioned previously, we welcome collaboration of all service providers in the education of children with E/BD.

EMOTIONAL DISORDERS AND CONDUCT DISORDERS

The exclusionary social-maladjustment clause in the current definition of serious emotional disturbance (SED) has been used by school districts to deny services to students with conduct disorders, based on the justification that conduct problems and social maladjustment are one and the same. According to this interpretation, therefore, students with conduct disorders are not eligible for services.

We have found that it is usually difficult to discriminate between a child with emotional disturbance and one with conduct disorders as defined by DSM–III–R. In fact, the vast majority of children served in our programs have either a primary or a secondary diagnosis of conduct disorder. Regardless of diagnosis, their behavior is difficult to manage in the typical classroom and school setting. Both students with SED and students with conduct disorders are a challenge to educate; we feel just as exhausted from working with either group. Both groups require long-term, intensive intervention, although students may manifest their anxiety, stress, and inner conflicts differently. Children with SED and children with conduct disorders are relationship resistant, making it difficult to establish the bond necessary for emotional development. Further, both groups are rejected by peers because of their antisocial behavior. The bottom line, teachers tell us, is that "It doesn't matter what you call it, it's tough to deal with."

Children who are aggressive are particularly difficult, as their behavior presents substantial management and safety issues in most settings. These are the children who often find social interaction only at school because school cannot remove them. A conversation with a mother of a child with SED reveals the anxiety and anguish experienced by parents as a result of their children's antisocial behavior. Mrs. Doe expressed fear and concern about her son's ability to learn appropriate social interactions. Her fears were founded in the fact that he had never been permitted to be a member of a sports team. Every coach had asked him to leave the team because of his low frustration tolerance and violent behavior. He had been sent home from overnight camp, excluded from Sunday school classes, and told he could not participate in Scouts, and he had never completed a series of sports training lessons (skiing, tennis, or swimming). His disability affected every aspect of his life and was so pervasive that he was excluded from extended family events because the family could not tolerate his behavior.

Walker (1993) presented some interesting findings regarding the status of antisocial children and youth. For example, he noted that "antisocial children display a singular disinclination to be cooperative; their level of participation in group activities is often low as a result" (p. 21). He reported negative outcomes for this group that are similar to the negative outcomes reported for students identified as E/BD (e.g., school failure and dropout, relationship difficulties, vocational adjustment problems, higher rates of adult psychiatric referral). Further, he observed that children's early aggressive patterns are very likely to continue throughout their school careers and beyond, and that an intergenerational cycle of antisocial behaviors can be observed in families. In fact, he and others have pointed to this stability of aggressive, antisocial behavior over time and the difficulties in successfully changing these behavior patterns, emphasizing the importance of intervening early before this pattern becomes intractable.

Walker echoed the sentiments of Caplan, a psychiatrist and pioneer in the field of mental health. Caplan argued that the first line of defense against mental illness was to eliminate its causes, the second was to discover incipient cases early enough to prevent them from becoming chronic, and the third was to rehabilitate those who had already become seriously ill (Wylie, 1992). We agree with these sentiments. Why must children's problems persist for so long and become so severe before they receive special attention? The importance of prevention and early intervention cannot be overemphasized.

An analogy discovered in the special education literature (source unknown) aptly described our current system's approach to early intervention. The author described a scenario in which children are playing at the top of a cliff and delineated what could be done to address the situation. Two options are available: (a) Put a fence at the top of the cliff to keep the children from falling off, or (b) put an ambulance at the bottom to collect the children if they do fall, and then argue endlessly about what type of ambulance it should be, who will drive the ambulance, where the children will be treated, who will pay for it, and so on. In the case of students with E/BD, we wonder if another argument might involve deciding who will receive treatment and who will be left at the foot of the cliff.

THE INCLUSION MOVEMENT

Inclusion has been the center of protracted debate for a number of years now. Although the primary focus of this debate has been on children with cognitive and sensory disabilities, the issue has been extended to all students with disabilities, including students with E/BD. We feel that many of the issues regarding inclusion have not seriously considered the complex and challenging needs of children with E/BD. We contend that our students are different from students with physical, learning, or cognitive disabilities and, therefore, require different intervention and treatment approaches.

The inclusion movement has isolated one component of the federal law: the *least restrictive environment* component. We believe that an equally important component is being overlooked: the *most appropriate environment* component. We believe that the inclusion movement fails to recognize the incredible diversity among children with E/BD and the many different types of support services they require, particularly at the secondary level. We are concerned that our students not be placed in situations that emphasize their disabilities. Our students frequently are accused of willful behaviors when they are unable to control aggressive tendencies or when they demonstrate poor judgment and impulsivity. In our view, this not only erodes any progress made to help these children socialize but also undermines their self-esteem. We have discussed already the importance of establishing an environment of trust, where students' individuality and privacy are respected. The multitude and intensity of interventions required to address their problems may be beyond the scope of the typical classroom. As we know all too well, the task is a difficult one even with sufficient resources and adequate teacher preparation, neither of which is usually the case in most general education settings.

Further, in our experiences, few general education teachers are eager to include our students with E/BD in their classrooms. As one teacher said, "I would prefer that the special ed kids I have be academically needy. I don't want the behavior problems." Even when teachers feel capable of managing difficult behaviors, class sizes and setting demands limit intervention choices.

And what about the students? How do they feel? In the name of inclusion and least restrictive environment, we have failed to acknowledge the stress and anxiety our students may experience in general education settings. For example, one of the authors recently was involved in the case of a sixth-grade student who was making the transition to middle school from elementary school. Both the student and her mother had expressed a desire for the girl to attend a "more restrictive" special school setting. The student was terrified of crowds and noise. She was adamantly opposed to attending a mainstream middle school, and her past history indicated that she was extremely resistant to mainstream experiences. Her mother and her teacher were supportive of the special school option. However, a team that had never worked with the student but that does a "paper check" of all special school placements to assure that no student be denied the opportunity of a less restrictive environment had to be convinced that the student should not attend the large school for a minimum of 6 weeks to evaluate her potential for success. This review required extra work on the part of the teacher and had the potential to negate the recommendations of the team that worked with the student.

Are such reviews of team decisions designed to safeguard the rights of the student or the inclusion philosophy? Even though some contend that neither special education nor general education is doing a good job with students with E/BD, we fail to see the logic in educating these students in programs that have even less ability or potential to provide the necessary network of academic and social support they require to be successful. Rather, the continuum of alternative placements should be broadened, and the array of service options should be expanded. In fact, we would argue that not enough students have access to services that address their physical, emotional, social, and educational needs.

MEANINGFUL EDUCATIONAL EXPERIENCES FOR CHILDREN WITH E/BD

Most professionals who work with students with emotional or behavioral needs agree that programs must provide opportunities for academic success as well as for students to value themselves. It is important to address both academic and affective curricula. Creating a learning environment that connects students' lives at home and in the community to their lives in school is a logical means of addressing both the affective and academic domains. We feel strongly that community service should be a focus in our classrooms. Such opportunities help students feel that they are valuable and valued in our society. Students who share ownership in a community tend to strengthen both the community and themselves. Community service and a strong service curriculum help students gain skills and the ability to reflect on their actions, both of which are vital for students who have emotional or behavioral problems.

We have learned over the years in the classroom that the relationship between theory and practice is crucial. Sometimes it feels as if the research does not reflect equity between the theoretical approaches and the needs of the student. Practice and practicality go hand in hand. The researchers who have actually taught and who have maintained direct ties with classroom teachers provide the most meaningful information to us. Teachers do not work with "subjects," and the children are not "ns." Every action we take has a direct (and long-lasting) effect on students. The voices of the students are loud and clear. We would like the grant reviewers and researchers to listen. Please help the classroom teachers implement the theory; stress the philosophy but be realistic about the resources we have. Tell us how to conduct life-space interviews while supervising eight children eating lunch. Examine techniques for dealing with crises that happen 3 minutes before bus time. Help us understand insurance clauses. Help us improve parent communication when the parent arrives at 10:30 a.m. for an 8:00 a.m. conference and teacher prep time is over.

THE STUDENT

In 1991, Pittman conducted a series of interviews with inner-city youth in Washington, DC, who were in every sense considered to be high risk because of their economic and social status. During these interviews that focused on youth development, not one youth asked for a prevention or treatment program, nor did anybody even suggest the need to be "fixed." Rather, they discussed the need for opportunities to "learn, observe, and contribute to the well-being of their neighborhoods" (Pittman, 1991, p. 5).

Similar results were obtained by one of the authors during interviews conducted with youth participating in a diversion program in another eastern United States metropolitan area. During the interviews, teens expressed the importance of teachers getting to know them as individuals and relating to them "as more than teachers." While expressing strong feelings of both anger and despair at their plight, these students overwhelmingly urged parents and schools to "step into their world." Specifically, they expressed their frustration that school had little to do with their "real life" and that teachers did not care to learn about their lives. They emphasized that their boredom with school and their preferences for "doing real stuff" were not typically considered.

Another example of how students feel alienated from school is evident in a story shared by the director of a community center in an urban housing project. She reported that 30 individuals had been arrested in a drug bust in the project. Although as many as 30 families might have been directly affected by this event, none of the middle-school teachers she randomly surveyed had discussed the incident in any of their classes in the 2 days subsequent to the event (Willard, personal communication, April, 1993). Furthermore, she expressed concern that few of the teachers had contacts with the families in their community, even though the middle school was located in the center of the community.

These interviews point to the urgent need to deal with the discouragement felt by a major portion of our troubled and disenfranchised youth. Brendtro, Brokenleg, and Van Bockern (1990) addressed the importance of fostering children's self-esteem in "reclaiming environments." They discussed the four bases of self-esteem and how self-esteem is related to children's basic needs of belonging, mastery, independence, and generosity—all qualities and values that are embraced by traditional Native American philosophy. The practices of several well-known educational pioneers (e.g., Glasser, Montessori) are closely aligned with this Native American philosophy, which promotes education and empowerment of children as life's central purpose. Thus, these theories emphasize the importance of children's roles in decision making and working together in cooperative groups to achieve mutually agreed-upon outcomes.

Allowing students' interests and experiences to drive the curriculum is one powerful means of meeting the basic needs listed above. The curriculum must be flexible and responsive to students' interests. We will use one of our identified students with E/BD as an example of the need to be flexible in creating curricula.

Jimmy, who lived with his single mother, was in the 10th grade and experiencing tremendous conduct problems. He was more than 3 years behind in academic performance, was frequently truant or late, and was an abuser of multiple substances. He also had a long history in the child welfare system. Yet he worked hard for people in his neighborhood and skipped school to shovel snow or mow lawns. His teacher proposed to the school administration that, instead of meeting the traditional Carnegie requirements, Jimmy be allowed to meet graduation requirements by means of a modified curriculum that incorporated (a) an apprenticeship with a landscaping firm and (b) completion of IEP goals and objectives. This proposal was rejected by the school administration. To make a long story short, he eventually dropped out of school. He still lives with his mother and shovels snow and mows yards, but the majority of his time is spent "unengaged."

Given what students are telling us, we are negligent if we do not incorporate methods that allow students to take ownership of their own learning. They must have a say about what they are studying and how they can best do it. The Foxfire approach is one approach in which students relate the learning of a skill to something meaningful in their lives, thereby assuming control and responsibility over their learning. For example, students together negotiate the topic of study, select a project related to the topic, plan the steps, identify the learning objectives, and document progress toward attainment of the objectives (Ensminger & Dangel, 1992). When students feel that they have some mastery over their learning, it is natural that the focus will shift from correcting student deficits to enhancing their abilities.

INSTRUCTIONAL PROGRAM

To meet children's basic needs, teachers must provide a learning environment that is safe and predictable. Schools and classrooms must provide structure and build effective routines that promote academic achievement. Although the literature is replete with strategies for effective teaching, we subscribe to a philosophy adopted many years ago by an uncle of one of our colleagues, Jerry Wellik.

Uncle Frank raised horses, adhering to a specific set of training procedures that have particular relevance for special educators (Wellik, personal communication, February, 1994):

1. Make sure you and the horse are going in the same direction.
2. Reward small steps.
3. Be consistent.
4. Manage your own emotional state.

GOING IN THE SAME DIRECTION

We have a sense that most teachers and schools do not have a clear vision of where they are going. Obviously, if we do not know where we are going, any road will take us there. One way to ensure that we are all going in the same direction is to use clear and effective communication between teachers and students and among students.

Effective communication is fundamental to effective problem solving and conflict resolution and, therefore, integral to any classroom for students with E/BD. Effective communication also enables us to obtain more relevant assessment information about students' physical, emotional, social, and educational status. With this information, we can work with students to create a curriculum that is more interactive and meaningful. For example, a teacher will need to understand the type of negotiation skills used by students in different communities and cultures to be successful in teaching conflict resolution. Skills that incorporate middle-class approaches to conflict resolution may be inappropriate and ineffective. The Re-ED model (Hobbs, 1974) and other psychoeducational approaches with multiple strategies of intervention have provided guiding principles that will help keep educators going in the same direction.

REWARDING SMALL STEPS

Effective communication continues to be critical as we establish a means of collecting performance data to recognize the steps students are making toward attaining their goals. Typically, data are required in the areas of social behavior and academic behavior. Systems that promote student self-evaluation and monitoring are most beneficial, though a student's age and developmental level *must* be considered when implementing any type of feedback system. Academic and behavioral monitoring systems allow students to see their own progress, thereby empowering them.

BEING CONSISTENT

Another important element in a successful learning environment is consistency, which is enhanced by the use of rules and routines. Students with E/BD respond to rules that are concrete and unambiguous, and perform better when rules are frequently reviewed and reinforced. Rules and routines provide predictability and help to create a more harmonious environment.

MANAGING OUR OWN EMOTIONAL STATE

Educators of children with emotional and behavioral disorders are in an emotionally exhausting profession. We must extend ourselves every day to meet the demands of teaching our students. Although our profession becomes very much a part of us, we must guard against allowing the demands to become burdensome. We must prevent burnout by incorporating positive methods of relieving stress.

THE SCHOOL

The size and scale of many of our nation's schools exacerbate students' feelings of alienation and lack of connectedness. Hence, rates of absenteeism, classroom misconduct, and dropout are higher in larger, more impersonal schools (Grant, 1994). The importance of community in the lives of children and families has been widely acknowledged, and schools and classrooms are potentially powerful models for community. Some schools have implemented various strategies to develop a sense of community and continuity, including multiage grouping and other arrangements that allow students to stay with the same teachers for more than 1 year. Some secondary schools have established advisory groups, where teachers are responsible for 15 students who meet twice a day, both within and outside of the school setting. Other schools implement extensive cross-age peer tutoring programs. In schools that attempt to foster more personal, positive relationships and create more effective learning climates, the principal plays a key role by using creative strategies that reach out and connect with all students.

THE FAMILY

As special educators, we like to believe that we have a clear understanding of what parents of children and youth with E/BD experience. Our role is to work with parents as an integral part of a team that is "helping the child get better." However, rather than parents feeling that they are part of the team, they often feel they are treated as if they are part of the problem. When a child fails to make progress, parents sometimes feel that professionals judge their behaviors (e.g., not consistent enough, need to be more accepting or less angry). While most of our parents acknowledge that their reactions may be a part of the problem, this is true for almost everyone who has contact with these troubled children. A parent cautions that "Professionals must view their role and power with humility . . . " (Smith, 1992, p. 293).

Creating a partnership with families requires that we talk with parents to be able to determine how we can best support them. Sometimes we may appear to be judgmental when we ask the questions we must ask to determine what types of services and supports families need. The process of seeking help for their children requires parents to open their personal lives to numerous professionals, thereby intruding on their privacy and creating additional stress. We must be sensitive to this problem and improve our communication with parents so that they do not feel that we are questioning their values and family dynamics. We need to communicate that we understand how challenging the demands of parenting a child with emotional or behavioral needs can be.

Sometimes an adversarial relationship with parents is created as a result of school policies that dictate that children be disciplined in ways that may not seem supportive to the family. Suspension is one example of a policy that can create adversarial relationships. Suspension can result in both parents and teachers feeling betrayed by programs that were put in place to help our students. We find more truth than humor in a note from a parent whose child was returning from suspension, "Mikela has been home for 5 days now. I think I've been punished enough."

THE YEAR 2000

Like our society, the educational system is being overwhelmed by the complex needs of children and families. The American dream of equal opportunity for all has been subverted by the injustices in our society that produce despair and helplessness in our children and families. In the past, the school has been viewed as the vehicle that could provide individuals a means to a better life. Unfortunately, this is not the case for many of our students, as indicated by the dropout and expulsion statistics.

This is not to be interpreted as a gloom-and-doom perspective. We are encouraged by what we see as a shift from blaming parents and families for their children's problems to a broader ecological perspective that considers the effect of the way our children are living, the social distress that contributes to their problems, and the economic circumstances that keep them from fully developing themselves. We see a trend toward developing classrooms and schools that attempt to meet the needs of children and families, rather than simply managing or controlling behaviors. We are hopeful that the trend toward collaborative and wraparound services will lead to changes in both political and educational arenas and will result in improved services for our children and their families.

In spite of these positive trends, we are not optimistic that marked changes in our educational system will occur during the next 5 years. Although school reform and restructuring efforts have produced an abundance of rhetoric addressing positive outcomes for all students, the solutions to these problems have thus far been conservative and driven by economics. Because of these conservative practices, the students with whom we work often have fewer options available to them in the educational system than in the juvenile justice system. Arguments over definition and classification do not create more options for our students. The role of the special educator and the schools must be reconceptualized as being part of a systems approach, one that will require a profound commitment to change and a massive infusion of resources. Such a total support system would enable educators to work in communities where children and families have access to an array of mental health services and residential treatment/respite programs, vocational training and job placement programs, social and recreation programs, self-help and family programs, and after-school and weekend programs. These programs must go beyond advocacy and therapy to provide a network of support that is driven by the collective efforts of the community. For these community programs to succeed, primary care givers (child care workers, day care providers, personal care attendants, etc.) must be valued and respected. Unfortunately, these are positions that provide few professional or financial rewards and minimal education or training. We concur with Whelan (personal communication, May, 1994) when he lamented that those who spend the most time with children and do the most healing are paid the least.

As a society, we are paying the price for ignoring the needs of our children and their families. The dream for our students and their families has been deferred far too long. We are witnessing the results of deferring this dream: the explosion of anger and violence in our youth. Nonetheless, we continue to dream about what might be and keep striving to be the best teachers we can be, motivated by those students for whom we have made a difference.

REFERENCES

Brendtro, L. K., Brokenleg, M., & Van Bockern, S. (1990). *Reclaiming youth at risk: Our hope for the future*. Bloomington, IN: National Educational Service.

Edgar, G. (1990). Is it time to change our view of the world? *Beyond Behavior, 1*, 9–13.

Ensminger, E. E., & Dangel, H. L. (1992). The Foxfire pedagogy: A confluence of best practices for special education. *Focus on Exceptional Children, 24*, 1–26.

Forness, S. R. (1991). Resolving the definitional and diagnostic issue of serious emotional disturbance in the schools. In S. Braaten & G. Wrobel (Eds.), *Perspectives on the diagnosis and treatment of students with emotional/behavioral disorders* (pp. 1–16). Minneapolis, MN: Minnesota Educators of the Emotionally Disturbed/Minnesota Council for Children with Behavioral Disorders.

Forness, S. R., & Knitzer, J. (1992). A new proposed definition and terminology to replace "serious emotional disturbance" in the Individuals with Disabilities Education Act. *School Psychology Review, 21*, 1, 12–20.

Grant, G. (1994). Schools where kids are known. *American Educator, 18*, 38–43.

Hobbs, N. (1974). Nicholas Hobbs. In J. M. Kauffman & C. D. Lewis (Eds.), *Teaching children with behavioral disorders: Personal perspectives* (pp. 142–167). Columbus, OH: Merrill.

Kauffman, J. M. (1993). *Characteristics of emotional and behavioral disorders of children and youth* (5th ed.). New York: Merrill.

Kazdin, A. E. (1987). *Conduct disorders in childhood and adolescence.* Newbury Park, CA: Sage.

Lerner, J. W. (1987). The regular education initiative: Some unanswered questions. *Learning Disabilities Focus, 3,* 3–7.

Pittman, K. J. (1991, September). *A new vision: Promoting youth development.* Testimony presented before the United States House of Representatives Select Committee on Children, Youth, and Families, Washington, DC.

Rhys, H. J. (1993). Personal reflections: Prevalence. In J. M. Kauffman (Ed.), *Characteristics of emotional and behavioral disorders of children and youth* (5th ed., pp. 59–62). New York: Macmillan.

Smith, C. R., Wood, F. H., & Grimes, J. (1988). Issues in the identification and placement of behaviorally disordered students. In M. C. Wang, M. C. Reynolds, & H. J. Walberg (Eds.), *Handbook of special education: Research and practice* (Vol. 2, pp. 95–123). Oxford, England: Pergamon.

Smith, J. C. (1992). Parenting seriously disturbed children. *Social Work, 37,* 293–294.

Walker, H. M. (1993). Anti-social behavior in school. *Journal of Emotional and Behavioral Problems, 2,* 20–24.

Wylie, M. S. (1992). Community mental health? Revising the dream. *The Family Therapy Networker, 16,* 11–23.

JAMES L. PAUL
University of South Florida

James Paul is a professor and chairman of the Department of Special Education at the University of South Florida. Prior to assuming his present position, he was a professor of special education at the university of North Carolina in Chapel Hill for 21 years. Paul received his PhD at Syracuse University. He studied at Duke University and served as a visiting scholar at Harvard University Graduate School of Education and a clinical fellow at the Erickson Center in the Harvard Medical School. Paul's research and writings have focused on emotional disturbance, learning disabilities, mainstreaming, advocacy, teacher education, public policy, and ethics. His most recent work focuses on inclusion, university–school partnerships, the changing view of knowledge, school-based policy development, and ethics. Paul has written or edited 17 books, in addition to numerous articles and chapters.

CHAPTER 17

Educating Children with Emotional and Behavioral Disorders: Reflections on Our History and Mine

A CASE FOR BEGINNING AT THE END

Most writers start at the beginning of their argument and proceed in some logical way to their conclusions. I will begin at the end with some conclusions and then share some experiences that helped me arrive where I am in my thinking.

It would not have occurred to me to share these ideas in this form except that I was asked to write about my own "personal" view of emotional disturbance. Having devoted the better part of my career to thinking, studying, writing, and teaching about it, reflecting on my own beliefs took me to the roots of personal experiences with children, parents, colleagues, and pioneers in the field, as well as my own research and readings.

My professional education came at the beginning of the field of educating emotionally disturbed children, as they were called then. I had an opportunity to study with and be mentored by several of the pioneers who created the field. Many of my own views took early form in my experiences with those leaders and my experience of the times, the beginning of the civil rights movement that changed the social and economic topography and shaped the political and moral ideology of the last half of the twentieth century.

The following are ideas that I regard as tentative conclusions about the nature of emotional disturbance as thought about, spoken about, and acted upon by professional special educators. These ideas cohere quite dissimilar fragments of experiences and understandings for me. I find them useful as I attempt to know and understand more about the field of emotional disturbance and the educational meaning such a label connotes. They have more the status of a compass in guiding my thinking about my work than a map of the choppy and complex social, psychological, and educational terrain of emotional disturbance.

I did not reach my own understandings in a classroom listening to lectures, in a study, in reading the research and philosophical literature, or even in a decade of thought. Rather, my views reflect 35 years of puzzlement about and reflection on all of my personal, professional, and academic experience. After stating my conclusions, I will describe my own journey as a student of the condition and a card-carrying member of the guild that works on it, now indirectly, through the education of teachers and doctoral students.

Some of the views are common in some circles, and some would, I imagine, be unfamiliar or unacceptable to many if not most in our field. I am not aware of any school of thought that would find all of the views acceptable. Space limitations require me to select issues that I consider to be of particular significance to the field of educating children with emotional and behavioral disorders (E/BD) in the future. I have decided to focus on the nature of emotional disturbance and the problematics of the knowledge and moral perspectives that have shaped the working understandings that have grounded our research and our instructional practices. My arguments are not, however, uniquely addressed to the issues associated with emotional disturbance. With these disclaimers, the following are some of my own conclusions, accompanied by brief rationales. They are ideas I have come to value and take seriously in my understanding of emotional disturbance.

1. We have been better psychologists and special educators than we have been philosophers. Now we must rethink the knowledge base of our work and risk very different understandings of emotional disturbance and the educational meaning we make of the label when we assign it to children.

Rationale: A fundamental difference between modernity and postmodernity is the search for certainty. Certainty is an absolute state in the positivist tradition. Wittgenstein said, "Wovon man nicht sprechen kann daruber muss man schweigen" (What we cannot speak about we must consign to silence) (Ayer, 1982, p. 112). In the logical empiricist tradition, things were true if and only if they were either empirically verifiable or if they were true in the statements themselves, i.e., logical. A quite different world appeared with the work of Einstein, Bohr, Bohm, and other physicists whose work pointed out the objectivist fallacy. Since the end of the first third of this century, the work of physicists and, later, the work of philosophers and historians of science has challenged the assumption of objectivity and the certainty principle so central to the modern project. This challenge to modernity has formal epistemological meaning in terms of how we conduct research, ontological meaning in terms of our attributions about the states of disturbance we study, and ethical meaning in terms of our own presumptions as observers and reporters.

Positions in the debate are well stated by Smith and Gergen in separate articles in the May, 1994, issue of the *American Psychologist*. Smith (1994, p. 407) argued that "the direction the postmodern school of thought leads is not one that is good for science. The pursuit of truth, goodness, and beauty remains possible if psychology can formulate a constructive stance toward the postmodern challenges to the Self and to Science." Gergen (1994, p. 414) countered that "the problematics of truth and ethics as transcendent ideals do not mean we must abandon empirical research or deliberations on the good. Postmodernist thought does not operate as another totalitarian discourse; rather, it invites consideration of the limitations of the local language."

We are in a deep transition that is shifting the foundations of thought and the imaginative rhetoric of the field. Connolly (1993) described our lingering attraction to modernity as our "homesickness," which leads to a feeling of homelessness. Most of us were trained to be objective and systematic and to employ a particular algorithm in analyzing, drawing conclusions, and using data. The postmodern world that challenges our values and the foundations of our work leaves us without the comforts we had in reporting the validity and reliability of our instruments and the confidence we had in our probability estimates. We don't give up this reality easily. I, for one, do not think we should. I feel more comfortable with critiques of confidence than with the abandonment of any way of talking about certainty. Rorty (1979) claims philosophy is dead, and deconstructionists argue that there is no life beyond text or, as Derrida (1981) argued, that textuality and reality are coextensive. This is difficult for those of us in a field born in phenomenology and warmed by the fires of psychoanalytic thought.

It is equally hard for those trained in behavioral theory who, consistent with their positivist roots, believe that the mysteries of metaphysics had been solved in the laboratories of behavioral scientists. Since the 1920s and 1930s the behaviorists have tried to extract us from this morass of mystery, but they offered, as it turns out, an epistemological vehicle whose shine was better than its wheels. We were, or so it would seem, better psychologists than we were philosophers, or we would have paid more attention to Kantian arguments that had rejected the view of an empirical world independent of reason 150 years earlier. The literature in special education is beginning to address policy and clinical issues from more informed philosophical perspectives. This is well illustrated by the excellent deconstructive analysis of the field by Skrtic (1991).

2. *Emotional disturbance is a sociocultural construction, not an objective reality partially understood by limited data interpreted with inadequate theories.*

Rationale: Divisions between and among the sciences and humanities are blurring, and interdisciplinary understandings of children are in reality clinical and sociopolitical constructions. In my opinion, the soft science/hard science distinction in some of our literature is, like the old nature/nurture debate, no longer useful. Understanding children labeled emotionally disturbed is a metaconstruction of the understandings from different disciplines. The metaconstruction is a creation of those who study the child for the purpose of fitting him or her to an agreed-upon system of classification. We have made too much of the science, the acknowledged problems with reliability of diagnosis notwithstanding, and not enough of the artistic task of creating a narrative, our narrative, from the fragments of the lives of children we analyze. The artistry of interdisciplinary teams using technical data about children to construct a story dramatically illustrates what Geertz (1983) has called the blurring of the genres of the sciences and the humanities.

The clinical diagnosis of children is a cultural act and a social statement by those who make it. Diagnosis is a well-developed process of concensus building aimed at a common discernment, a picture of the child that tells a story ostensibly revealing the mystery of the child's predicament (i.e., difficulty with himself, with others, or both). This is not to disparage the clinical and psychometric tools used in diagnosis or the philosophy of measurement used by sensitive clinicians. Neither is it intended to discount the utility of diagnosis and treatment in many instances. Rather it is to acknowledge the artistry as well as the science used by professionals in the interdisciplinary task of diagnosing children, and to emphasize the discontinuity between the child and the clinical tale that is ultimately told, however useful it may be. This has profound implications for racist, sexist, and classist constructions of the problem.

Much of the language of behavioral science is propositional (e.g., children's acquisition of knowledge about arithmetic facts will be positively correlated with their time on task in studying those facts) or attributional (e.g., the child's learning disability results from an inability to refrain from responding to extraneous stimuli that is caused by a lesion). We need more language of wonderment that considers the possibilities for understanding in imaginative ways. Here the part of ourselves that is engaged corresponds most to the part of the child we are seeking to understand. The language of life—*hurt, broken, wounded, lost, confused,* and other metaphors with common existential and spiritual meaning—is more authentic and demands more of us than the technical or formal language of behavioral science, such as *reactive disorder, compulsive disorder, behavior disorder.*

Eisner (1991) commented,

> What is ironic is that in the professional socialization of educational researchers, the use of metaphor is regarded as a sign of imprecision; yet, for making public the ineffable, nothing is more precise than the artistic use of language. Metaphoric precision is the central vehicle for revealing the qualitative aspects of life. (p. 227)

The important issue, from my point of view, is not the particular vocabulary used but the hermeneutic cost of technical language in our attempts to communicate human pain. We have a moral as well as professional obligation to understand the politics of language and the effects of the words we use. Formal language is not wrong; indeed, it has specific uses. It also can distance us from those we purport to help, limit our ability to speak about experience that extends beyond the taxonomic system being employed, objectify phenomena that are fundamentally personal and implicate our selves and our values, and pretentiously imply more science than the words represent. It is interesting to see the scope of behavioral science expanding and the language being challenged as reflected by the appearance of the concept of "spiritual problems" in the *Diagnostic and Statistical Manual of Mental Disorders* (DSM–IV; American Psychiatric Association, 1994). Social and behavioral theories and the language systems associated with them are useful in guiding practice if they are self-consciously developed and applied rather than offered as arrogant claims, ignorant of their political roots and consequences.

3. *As a social construction, emotional disturbance can be understood by examining the lived experiences of those so labeled. We need to understand the lived experiences of children and the stories that live them.*

Rationale: The clinical and educational literature on emotional and behavioral disorders contains spiritually and culturally disembodied accounts of children. Our theories have led us to seek understanding of particular aspects of a child's world while leaving others unacknowledged and unexamined. Interpretive researchers are beginning to focus on broader and deeper aspects of experience and to refine methods for investigation.

Qualitative methods have been available for decades, but they have not had a valued place in the behavioral sciences. Gendlin (1962) studied the "experiencing" of schizophrenic patients and their creation of meaning. Coles (1990), a psychiatrist using oral history method, made significant contributions to our understanding of the spiritual lives of children. Erikson, a psychoanalyst using the methods of psychobiography, contributed to our understanding of lives lived productively and well by studying the lives of Luther (Erikson, 1969) and Ghandi (Erikson, 1962). Katz used ethnography, a well-developed anthropological field research method, to study the !Kung (Katz, 1982) and the Fiji Islanders (Katz, 1993) and added to our understanding of healing and connectedness.

The basic sciences, e.g., neurochemistry and genetics, do not substitute for, or provide a model for studying, lived experience. There are important and powerful new genres of research beginning to penetrate the modernist frameworks of special educators, perhaps especially those whose work focuses on children with emotional disturbance. Webb-Mitchell (1993), a special educator using methods similar to those of Coles, added to our understanding of the spiritual lives of children with disabilities. Danforth (1994), a special educator using oral history, added to our understanding of the construction of emotional disturbance in the life of an individual.

Fine (1994) discussed the need for self-conscious qualitative researchers to unpack "notions of scientific neutrality, universal truths, and researcher dispassion" (p. 71). Fine invited qualitative researchers to "imagine how we can braid critical and contextual struggle back into our texts" (p. 71). She sought to "rupture the textual laminations within which others have been sealed by social scientists, to review the complicity of researchers in the construction and distancing of others, and to identify transgressive possibilities inside qualitative texts" (p. 71).

We pay a heavy price when we ignore realities that don't fit our models. There is too much there. What we counted as error variance in studies that paved the path of mainstream doctoral education in special education in all likelihood usually contained a relevant story, or perhaps the crucial story. By predetermining the reality we could apprehend with the design of our studies and the statistical models employed in analyzing our data, we constrained ourselves to see only that portion of reality illuminated by our tools. Much of the rest of the story is told by the methods of the humanities, left on an island from which philosophy of science departed more than a century ago. We left eyes for seeing, ears for hearing, intuitive capacities for sensing, and, most of all, the modesty of self-consciously reflecting on the manner in which we apprehend the world, i.e., the paradigm guiding our work.

Our preoccupation with particular methods of inquiry has not been balanced by concern with the epistemological assumptions of our methods or what they are designed to reveal. Rigor has been more a concern of the research community than relevance. Janesick (1994) used the term *methodolatry* to describe "a preoccupation with selecting and defending methods to the exclusion of the actual substance of the story being told" (p. 215). It is the "slavish attachment and devotion to method that so often overtakes the discourse in the education and human services fields" (p. 215). In being so obsessed with the "trinity"—validity, reliability, and generalizability—it is always tempting "to become overinvolved with method and, in so doing, separate experience from knowing" (p. 215).

Methodolatry moves us away from understanding the actual experience of participants. This is part of the problem with educational research employed to support or argue against inclusion. In some research, inclusion has been treated as a dependent variable leaving us with limited information about the experiences of all the children involved in inclusive classrooms: How do they see themselves? How do they feel about their experience in an inclusion classroom? How do they experience and construct the social life of the classroom? Stories about the actual experiences of children are left out of analyses that use norm-referenced test scores as dependent variables.

   4. *The professional practices of defining and teaching children with emotional and behavioral disorders are not amoral activities. What passes as theory is, in many instances, a particular social and moral stance about an issue of importance to us. If we are to take seriously the moral and political foundations of our work, we need to accord a greater role to ethics and criticism in the formulation of our research, our clinical practices, and the theories that guide them.*

   Rationale: It has come to me with time that the likelihood of doing the good we want to do and hope we are doing is reduced because we were not educated to reason ethically and to be self-critical of the moral perspectives embedded in our work. We were socialized into the methods and taught the rules of the social sciences. We have spent more time with engineering, design, and analysis of technical issues than with the moral force and pretense of our decisions and actions. Most of us were not introduced to the study of ethics or the epistemological foundations of knowledge. This has tended to leave us with hammers, nails, and materials for building without understanding the culture and changing technologies of construction, architecture, or aesthetics.

   Emotional disturbance is a drama of individuals (children, families, teachers) and systems (schools, home, community, and churches, synagogues, and temples). Our values are much more central to the construction of emotional disturbance than we had earlier thought. We do not think of ourselves as racists, sexists, or classists. We are generally hopeful that our laws and the due process provisions now so embedded in the delivery of public services, including education, will ultimately assure reasonably equitable and fair policies. The canon of objectivity that has governed our research and the procedural safeguards of the human subjects review provision now in place will, we believe, reduce the likelihood of harm or unfairness to those we study.

   We have labored over (and under) the theories that guide research and practice, and the technologies of interventions, while working under the misguided assumption that, since we believe we are good people with good intentions, our work was inherently of value and, at a minimum, harmless. It turns out that the good we wish to do is extraordinarily more complex in the doing.

   Part of the complexity lies in the foundations of the policy-making process. Our policies continue to drive research, rather than knowledge guiding policy development. The ethical principles guiding policy development, then, become very important. Whether thinking about the policy of inclusion at a national level, or the policy process affecting students with severe emotional disturbance at a local school, decisions regarding competing interests account for more of the substance of policy than any particular public knowledge base. The ethics of the policies, then, rely heavily on the ethics of the policymakers. The social and spiritual welfare of students is ultimately placed in the hands of adults whose authority is predicated on the premise that good people make good decisions. Both the argument that not all people are good and the argument that doing good, or the right thing, is sufficiently complex that error from ignorance occurs emphasize the importance of understanding the substance and form of ethical process in all aspects of our work.

One of the important paradigms of inquiry now affecting our work is critical theory, which focuses on the ethical and moral principles in all aspects of inquiry and practice. Critical theory has become a scalpel for scraping the veneer of science off of institutionalized racism, for example. It is a rhetorical tool to remove the cloak of science and "best practice" from institutionalized racism, sexism, and classism.

One of the charges leveled in the courts, the clinics, and the classroom is racism in special education. The behavioral science we employ and the presumed color blindness of our knowledge belie our continued insensitivity to the color of our values as reflected in our institutionalized practices. Johnson (1969) and a few others in the Council for Children with Behavioral Disorders in 1968 attempted to make this argument with the International Council for Exceptional Children. It is difficult. In all aspects of our work, we continue to cloak racism, sexism, and classism in a shroud of science.

5. *The theories teachers use in their work with children with emotional and behavioral disorders are much more personal and complex than the theories we teach them in teacher education programs.*

Rationale: There is, of course, an extensive literature on "theories in use" (Argyrus, 1972, 1990) and the nature and role of personal constructs in behavior (Kelley, 1963). We have focused a great deal on the psychological theories we teach teachers and hope they use in understanding and teaching children in their classes. However, the nature and complexity of the process of educating children with emotional and behavioral disorders requires us to look more carefully at the nature of personal theory construction.

Our boldest convictions, those things about which we have the greatest passion, emerge from our experience. It may be an intellectual experience of facts resonating to a framework or way of reasoning with which we are working, such as is the case in various forms of science. If we trust our framework, the data we generate with judicious use of that framework are believable to us and we hold them with varying degrees of certainty. Sometimes (some argue always) our experience is the datum, and our framework or way of thinking is transformed by it. The framework itself then becomes an object of our passionate commitment.

Psychoanalytic theory is an example. Freud and those who followed in the psychoanalytic tradition were deeply invested in a view of personality development that emerged from experience with patients in analysis. The view that emerged from listening, observing and understanding, or making a particular meaning of those data, ultimately became the organizing framework, or theory, for the analysis of the mind or, as Bettleheim (1983) argued, the soul.

In this sense the application of theory takes on the form of a treatment or roughly of an independent variable. Since the rules for falsification are not specified, the development and verification of the theory are seriously problematic. Hence, Freud was never honored as a scientist by the scientific community—one of the disappointments of his life. Rather, he has been honored for his contribution to literature, philosophy of history, and biography. His creative work was brilliant in form and in providing a structure for a particular understanding of persons. His story of human development resonates with experience and has offered a way of thinking about interpersonal conflicts, feelings, unexpectable behavior, dreams, and so forth. He did not, however, create a reliable knowledge base, notwithstanding the rather substantial clinical treatment guild that used the theory, or more accurately, the philosophy.

This kind of iterative and interactive relationship between data (experience) and organizing framework (theory) is not uncommon in the behavioral and social sciences. It is, in part, this process that makes behavioral science a political activity and the scientist—or therapist in the case of one using the science—that makes the values of the scientist a major concern in the ethics of science and clinical practice. The Victorian values reflected in Freud's work are a good example, as clearly described in the work of Miller (1983).

Some would separate personal (private) experience and ways of thinking from replicable (public) data and frameworks that follow known and shared canons and have the support of academies and professional guilds. Within the last 10 to 15 years, that distinction has become more problematic. The public/private distinction serves as a general means for partitioning experience, and we accord the reality of this distinction a special ontological meaning, e.g., self-interest and public interest, or objectivity and subjectivity. So long have these been embedded in our language and way of thinking that they now have a priori status. A similarly problematic distinction has divided the sciences and the humanities. Fields like anthropology and history illustrate the dilemma by studying both the empirical world and contextualized reasoning and, at the same time, investigating the symbolic systems and narrative/textual accounts of cultures.

6. A teacher's biography is important not just because of the clinical perspectives that have led us to be concerned about their personality and character but because their relationships with children are shaped by the images of teaching, civility, and humane care in the classroom that saturate their memories.

Rationale: In special education, the premise of a postmodern understanding of the phenomenon of emotional disturbance as co-constructed by children and others leads to the necessity of understanding the values and views of the teacher as well as the characteristics of the children. While our research at various times has focused on different characteristics of teachers (e.g., personality, teaching competencies, etc.), we have always known and generally believed that it was important to have a "good" person as well as a well-trained and educated teacher in the classroom. Some argue that this is especially true for teachers of children who are emotionally disturbed, who demand more and who leave less space for teacher error in the classroom. Hobbs (1966), for example, talked about needing "decent adults" who are able to know joy in their lives and share it with children, people who are able to renew their psychic energies in healthy ways.

There is a vast literature on teachers bordering on a heroic myth in some writings. We believe good teachers are good people who do good things for children. Analytic frameworks and behavioral frameworks have been used to describe the same teacher, each view bringing a compelling argument about why the person is a "good" teacher and how he or she does what he or she does. There are now several eloquent essays on care and the caring pedagogy in the classroom. Noddings (1984), Gilligan (1982), and other feminists have added to our understandings of the nature of care and how it works. Noblit's (1993) research helped dislodge caring in teaching from the common assumptions of liberal perspectives about structure and discipline.

If the teacher is a co-constructor of emotional disturbance with the child, a caretaker of the institutionalized bond that labels the child and provides the social form and structure for the child's deviant career in school, then it is important to understand more about the teacher and the issues that form and maintain that bond. One of the important aspects of the teacher's life I think we need to know more about in this regard has to do with the teacher's understandings about school and his or her experience in it. Most of us have had teachers who loved us and made our lives better. Some of us may have been protected from labels or even rescued from deviant careers by such a caring and competent teacher. Most of us also have been hurt and even damaged by thoughtless and, perhaps, less caring teachers. We spend a long time in school under the care and watchful eyes of teachers. Not all of those eyes see the same things. Yet our sense of place and our value of ourselves as competent and worthy, rather than inept and unworthy, come from these experiences. These experiences help shape career choices to become teachers and for some to become teachers of children who are disturbed and hurt. We need to understand more about the mental constructions of those experiences. The affective memories and imagination of teachers are the raw materials with which teachers construct emotional disturbance in their classroom. Self-conscious construction, then, is essential in sensitive teachers. This understanding should impact our selection decisions for those who enter our teacher education programs, the curriculum we offer, and our work with teachers in the classroom.

THE CONSTRUCTION OF ARGUMENTS: HOW I ARRIVED AT THESE AND OTHER CONCLUSIONS

So how did someone trained by Nicholas Hobbs, a clinical psychologist, and William Cruickshank, a neuropsychologist, and supervised in my clinical work with children who are emotionally disturbed by a child analyst, a clinical child psychologist, and a psychiatric social worker in the early 1960s end up with beliefs like those just described? Perhaps it had something to do with the fact that Hobbs was an existential psychologist who, along with his humanistic colleagues in psychology such as Rogers and Maslow, had a deep confidence in human potential and the predisposition of individuals to act wisely given the psychological opportunity to do so. Perhaps I was influenced by the fact that he was more interested in my knowledge of Kant than my reading in dynamic psychology. Perhaps it relates to the fact that Cruickshank was as supportive of my interest in George Herbert Mead as he was of my reading of Werner and Strauss. Perhaps it grew in part from my appreciation for the fact that the analyst's work was more a cultural art form with a rich body of myth used to interpret human development and personality than a behavioral science.

There is no straight line of intellectual development that led me from my early study of the psychological understandings of children to the textual and constructive views that now guide my work. It has been, rather, an interesting and, as is the case with all our lives, complex journey. In many ways, my own development of ideas parallels aspects of the ideological history of the field of educating children with E/BD. My own experience and my understanding of what was occurring in the field are interwoven in the chronological narrative that follows.

I had the opportunity to study in an interesting intellectual climate and to receive a good liberal arts education in the late 1950s and the early 1960s. In my studies at Vanderbilt I read Nietzsche, Kierkegaard, Sartre, Jaspers, Marcel, Ayer, Wittgenstein, Moore, and other existentialists and logical positivists. At Scarritt I read Tillich, Barth, both Niebuhrs, and other theologians and historians, while reading Redlich, Benedict, Mead, and other cultural anthropologists. At Peabody I read in the arts and in the social sciences.

In the spring of 1961, I finished my second degree in the humanities, with a focus primarily on philosophy and religion. During my master's program I had served as a graduate assistant for a cultural anthropologist who had received her education at the University of Chicago and had a strong interdisciplinary orientation. Her analysis of the ways people lived their lives and the regard they had for one another focused on the history of settings, mores, and beliefs. She emphasized the complexity of social life and the power culture in particular settings as determinants of behavior. She told endless stories of behavior that was valued in one culture and considered deviant in another. I assisted her with her library research while she was writing her book on understanding other cultures. I read ethnographies and was fascinated by the detailed accounts of people's lives. One of her favorite expressions was "as far as we now know." It was a simple way of communicating modesty about knowledge and knowing, not a comment on the nature of knowledge.

Having grown up in rural and conservative middle Tennessee in the 1940s and 1950s, I was especially struck by the variability of patterns of culture and the relativity of values that had seemed so absolute in my own socialization. Deviance was understood as a departure from custom, a violation of something valued by others who lived similar lives and believed similar things. Learning that my own behavior, as appropriate and even valued as it was in my own culture, would be considered deviant in some other cultures was a significant revelation.

My studies were in an international community, a small college with approximately half the students being from other countries. There I learned about lifestyles and values that were truly "foreign" to me. Also, since I had grown up in a segregated, racist, sexist, and homophobic culture, some of my own values and deeply socialized prejudices collided with the reality of cultural pluralism. It was a time of deep learning and change.

My thesis research, an empirical study of cooperative planning and problem-solving group skills, was supervised by an educator who was interested in psychological and social variables. He was committed to experimental and quasi-experimental research as a way of learning about and understanding behavior. For him, as for others working out of the positivist tradition, the individual, like the universe, is governed by basic laws, and those laws are ultimately knowable through the judicious application of and allegiance to the methods of science. By carefully following the rules of science in the investigation of naturally occurring variability, one can understand those laws and, ultimately, predict events, including human events. It was not enough to describe the world, and there was no place for aesthetics. The important research task was to develop and test theories of individual and group behavior and to advance the science of behavior. I decided to study psychology and education and to work within this epistemological tradition.

In the fall of 1961, I entered an experimental program aimed at testing a radical social hypothesis: that teachers, with the support of mental health professionals, could work with children who were emotionally disturbed. Mental health manpower studies, as they were called then, had indicated that it was not likely that adequate numbers of psychiatrists, psychologists, and social workers could ever be trained to treat persons with mental illness. Children with emotional problems who could not succeed in regular classrooms, or whose behavior was sufficiently deviant to precipitate their suspension or expulsion from school, were left on their own in the community where many of them got into trouble with the police. There were mental health clinics in some communities where some children received treatment, but there were not sufficient services available to support a public health policy aimed at comprehensive care. Children who could not "make it" in their community ended up in correctional facilities or in psychiatric hospitals on adult wards. Further, the limited efficacy data on psychotherapy was unimpressive.

Serious social class bias was evident in the delivery of mental health services. One's socioeconomic position accounted for more of the variance in the kind of treatment provided than the person's needs. Poor people were more likely to receive shock treatment and hospitalization in a public psychiatric hospital. People from the middle class were more likely to have outpatient treatment with drugs. Individuals from the upper class were more likely to be in long-term psychoanalytic treatment and in private psychiatric hospitals, and to receive some drug treatment. Treatment facilities were racially segregated. If you were poor and black, the likelihood of receiving appropriate mental health care was very low. If you were also a child, your chances for appropriate treatment were even less.

Mental health services—they could only loosely be referred to as a system—were nested in an ecology of human services that included public health, social welfare, and corrections. There were also human services sponsored by religious institutions. Again, all of these services became involved in some way in providing care for the mentally ill. The social welfare system provided financial support and some counseling services for poor families. The correctional system provided counseling, monitoring, and, in some instances, detention for children who got into difficulty with the law. It was generally understood that if a person were mentally ill—a condition with only general and vague definition—his or her behavior could best be understood in the context of psychoanalytic thought, and persons were certified to understand, classify, and treat the illness. This was the ideological and institutional context in which I began my studies of children with E/BD. I was privileged to work with some of the first teachers of children with emotional disturbance early in the day of what Hobbs (1964) later called mental health's third revolution. I had the opportunity to study with leaders in the field of psychology who were creating a new field and crafting a different language and conceptual foundation for public policy. My experience during this early period in the 1960s and the understandings I later came to advocate can serve as a marker for some of the work going on at that time. Changes in philosophy, science, and politics during the late 1950s and the early 1960s have had lasting effects on the work we now do in special education for children with emotional disturbance and behavioral disorders. The perspective of this history is useful to help us resist trivializing the foundations of the perspectives that guide our work and decontextualizing our practices.

In 1961 I entered the reeducation program to learn to teach children who are emotionally disturbed. The program was conceived by Hobbs and funded by the National Institute of Mental Health. At that time, education had no responsibility for children once they acquired a label of emotionally disturbed. Adapting the educateur model from France and the School Psychology model from Scotland to fit into the policy environment of this country, Hobbs set out to test two major hypotheses. First, teachers could work successfully with children with emotional and behavioral disorders. Second, emotional disturbance could be understood and treated as a systems problem. In order to test these hypotheses, he developed 12 core beliefs about the nature of emotional disturbance and its treatment (Hobbs, 1966). These included the following:

- Life is to be lived now.
- Time is an ally.
- Trust is essential.
- Competence makes a difference.
- Symptoms can and should be controlled.
- Cognitive control can be taught.
- Feelings should be nurtured.
- The group is important to children.
- Ceremony and ritual give order.
- Stability and confidence are necessary.
- The body is the armature of the self.
- Communities are important.
- A child should know joy.

These beliefs reflect the depth of Hobbs's understanding of psychology and philosophy and his humanistic values. He was a well-trained psychologist who contributed to the development of the client-centered perspective. He believed in and valued the scientific method, and he recognized and focused on the intrapsychic life, but he also aligned himself with Rogers, Maslow, and others in advocating a humanistic perspective. His philosophy of behavior was hopeful and respectful of the power of the individual to make the best decisions for his or her life. He was not impressed with insight as a necessary condition for healthy functioning.

He was one of the leaders in the choir of psychologists attacking the medical or disease model of mental illness. He joined other leading psychologists in challenging the assumption that mental illness was a condition manifesting symptoms that should be understood and treated by medical specialists. He was more impressed by behavioral and systems perspectives of human and institutional adaptation. He found more useful and parsimonious concepts of behavioral functioning in ecological psychology, especially the work of Barker (1968) and others, than in traditional psychoanalytic thought. Hobbs was also a philosopher, interested in epistemological and ethical issues. He was especially interested in Kant and his critique of pure reason that challenged the partitioning of logical and empirical realities. His commitment to articulating the ethical foundations for mental health policy in general and the practice of psychology in particular resulted in his providing substantial leadership in developing and advancing the American Psychological Association's (APA; 1981) Code of Ethics.

Hobbs was able to obtain funding from the National Institute of Mental Health (NIMH) to establish two experimental schools in order to test his basic hypotheses. The strategies of these schools were to remove the child from his or her home and school on a short-term basis in order to: (a) improve the behavior and performance of the child, (b) improve the coping skills of the parents, (c) increase the understanding and ability of the child's teacher to teach the child, and (d) improve the community support systems for the child. The goal was to increase the tolerance threshold and support capacity of the school, home, and community while improving the child's behavior and academic performance in order to increase the likelihood of success.

Hobbs recruited Bill Rhodes to help conceptualize the program's philosophy and methods and to head the curriculum and research aspects of the program. The two of them created a rhetoric about emotional disturbance that was to help change public policy and the ways of thinking about the nature of the problem. Their work was buoyed by the person power dilemma in mental health, the efficacy data on mental health practice, and the emerging social consciousness about institutional abuse and an advocacy ethic that focused on individual rights. Also, in the early 1960s an ethos of doubt emerged that took many forms, including questioning the ideological authority of established traditions. The moral force of customs that had the effect of public policies and that kept schools desegregated, African Americans in the back of the bus, and minorities disadvantaged in the workplace was being challenged in a wide and deep cultural upheaval that reached into the racist and classist systems of care for persons with mental illness. The political authority of psychiatry became one of the many ideological and policy targets embedded in the civil rights movement. In psychology and education, the voices of Hobbs and Rhodes, making radical claims that teachers could work with children who were emotionally disturbed, were joined by Szasz (1961) in psychiatry who argued that mental illness is a myth that should be replaced by a view of human adaptation. Goffman (1961), a sociologist, added power to the arguments with his work on stigma and institutions.

Hobbs and Rhodes recruited 12 teachers into the first reeducation class with the idea they could be taught basic mental health understandings, clinical skills, and the ability to use professionals from the traditional mental health disciplines as consultants in teaching children with emotional and behavioral disorders. Some of the teachers were trained to be liaison staff in the experimental schools. Their responsibility was to link the family, school, community, and the re-ed school.

This was a radical program in the early 1960s. One faculty member in child psychiatry at a major medical center raised a question of whether we were practicing medicine without a license.

The curriculum for the training program, developed by Hobbs, Rhodes, and Trippe, all three of them clinical psychologists, focused on systems and ecological understandings, a major departure from traditional clinical psychology. Trippe headed the training program and worked with the group on an intensive basis. It was a young, open, experienced, coffee-drinking, and cigarette-smoking (mostly) group of young teachers. We read Redl, Aichorn, Bettelheim, Kanner, Rubin, and others who wrote about children with emotional problems. These cases, or clinical tales, were rich and colorful in their depictions of children's lives. They were not as clear about the nature of the interventions and what was helpful.

There was an emphasis in the program on how to be with children with emotional disorders, how to listen and pay attention to affect. We were trained as observers and desensitized to the language one often encounters with troubled children. There was attention to the importance of self-renewal and play to balance the emotional demands of teaching these children. We studied counseling with Hobbs, developmental psychology with Gray, and special education with Dunn. We went to visit clinical facilities, primarily psychiatric hospitals and a center for persons with mental retardation where, I still recall so clearly, persons with profound mental retardation were in cages. There were no public school programs for children with emotional disturbance in Nashville. When we were ready to do our internships, we had to search for appropriate places in this country and abroad. Most of us did our internships in children's units in psychiatric hospitals or in private schools.

We did not learn a particular approach for managing behavior. There was an existential premise to the clinical part of our work, but existentialism lacks a methodology. In my own internship at a psychiatric hospital, I was given a paper on Hullian theory and told to implement it in the children's unit, where there were children who were autistic and psychotic. It was a medically managed interdisciplinary unit. It was an interesting period in the history of educating children with E/BD, and the unit reflected some of the early signs of ideological discontinuities among therapists and educators that was to deepen in the years that followed. I was supervised by Pappanikou and learned a great deal about children and even more institutional dynamics and the politics of care.

Several things were clear in the early 1960s. The political and ideological hegemony of psychiatry in the field of mental health, euphemistically called the medical model, was being challenged. Public school policies that failed, expelled, or ignored children with emotional problems were beginning to wane as a psychoeducational model was being developed and federal funding for the preparation of teachers of children with emotional and behavioral disorders was made available in 1963. Leadership for pursuing educational models was coming primarily from psychologists. There was a great deal of talk about coordination of disciplines and service delivery systems, although in reality little was occurring. There was no systematic science of behavior, theory of learning, or well-developed philosophy of education that was guiding the changes. Rather, changes were propelled by national policies anchored in humanistic values of care and the right to dignity.

The rhetorics of wise and caring psychologists like Hobbs, Rhodes, Morse, Bower, and a few others helped build conceptual bridges from psychiatric to psychoeducational perspectives for working with children with E/BD. They helped legitimize the emotional problems of children as a responsibility of educators as well as traditional mental health specialists. They were social engineers, designing systemic interventions such as reeducation schools, liaison teachers, crisis teachers, school consultants, and so forth. They were integrators and leaned heavily on the humanities as well as the social and behavioral sciences, especially developmental, ecological, and clinical psychology. They emphasized personal virtues, the quality of persons, their ethics, and their ability to sustain themselves in emotionally healthy ways as having at least as much importance as the professional skills they might develop. The result was a new field of practice and more options for children.

An important definition of emotional handicap in children was advanced in the late 1950s by Bower and Lambert (1962) in California that was based on a factor analytic study of teachers' perceptions of the difficulties children have in school. This definition, which enabled epidemiologists and policymakers to estimate the size of the population, was to have a profound and lasting impact on the legal and policy construction of emotional disturbance in children.

While there was very limited funding for research and there were philosophical differences among researchers, no one was seriously questioning the nature of the research needed. Rigorous, objective, well-controlled experimental and longitudinal research was needed. We needed more knowledge of how children develop emotional disorders, how those disorders are manifested, how they can be measured, how they can be treated, and how they can be prevented. Developmental research had limited financial support, and intervention research focusing on the education of these children was practically nonexistent. The first major funding of psychoeducational interventions came out of NIMH, not out of the Office of Education.

No one in the new field of "special education of emotionally disturbed children," neither the leaders nor the newly trained professional corp, was paying much attention to the work going on in the philosophy of science. No one took note of Kuhn's significant publication on scientific paradigms in 1962. The historic paradigm shift that had occurred in physics was not a part of the analysis of emotional disturbance as a phenomenon. No one claimed that a solid science underpinned the new field. Neither did anyone seem to doubt the eventual development of a science and technologies to define and treat the emotional problems of children. Substantial strides in this direction emerged in the mid-1960s.

The field of experimental psychology had not figured heavily in the emergence of the field of educating children who were emotionally disturbed. The laboratory work of learning and behavioral theorists had limited clinical human applications. The work of Ferster (1961) and others guided by the operant conditioning model developed by Skinner had provided a more systematic way of understanding the behavior of children with emotional disturbance. The behavioral science that emerged from this tradition was much more precise, making it possible to more accurately define the troubling or disturbing behaviors of children and to specify interventions for modifying those behaviors.

The power of the behavioral technologies was impressive to educators who, beginning to assume responsibility for these children in the mid-1960s, had no clear way of understanding their problems and no powerful interventions for changing the behavior that was most troubling in the classroom. Behavior-modification technologies freed teachers from concern about the subjective state of the child. It gave them precise ways of teaching and controlling behavior and a clear data-based accountability for their work.

Behaviorism and all of the technologies for teaching and modifying behavior became a powerful and encompassing movement in the field of educating children with emotional disturbance from the late 1960s until the mid-1980s. The name changed from *emotional disturbance* to *behavior disorder* in most special education publications. The preparation of teachers to work with these children became training programs focusing on learning and applying the technologies. The humanities foundation that had substantially grounded the early development of the field was replaced by a more technical and empirical foundation. Interest in the phenomenology of disturbance and the clinical tales that contextualized the social lives of children and support for theories that focused on experience waned. History and philosophy, including ethics, were relegated to minor status, if they were kept at all, in the teacher training curricula.

My doctoral studies at Syracuse University were supervised by William Cruickshank, who had strong views about brain-based behavior and the essential role of an interdisciplinary team in diagnosing and treating children's disorders. He also had strong views about the role of the curriculum structure and administrative environment in schools in providing an appropriate education for children and the necessary support for teachers. Believing that the role of the principal is so important as a leader in setting the tone and providing the support for teachers, he included principals in the training of teachers. He, Junkala, and I (Cruickshank, Junkala, & Paul, 1968) wrote a book on the philosophy and curriculum of the teacher training program he had developed and a second book (Cruickshank, Junkala, & Paul, 1969) on principals who were defeating the efforts of able teachers to work with students with learning and behavioral disorders.

I continued my study of philosophy at Syracuse with Tom Green. Being interested in the history of the mental health movement and the changing philosophies of care since my studies at Duke, I had the opportunity for some interaction with Thomas Szasz, who had just written *The Myth of Mental Illness* (1961). Knoblock, Kulen, Weatherford, and others were important in my continued study of psychology and the characteristics of children with emotional disturbance.

If the 1960s were characterized by attacks on the psychoanalytic model and the political hegemony of psychiatry in mental health, the 1970s were characterized by a broader debate of different competing theoretical perspectives and interventions. In the early to mid-1970s, Rhodes and Tracy (1972a) and their colleagues provided an intellectual inventory of the conceptual systems that had been employed in the 1960s when school services were developed for children with emotional disturbance. The primary purposes of the project were to classify and clarify the foundations of the field and to provide content for teacher training programs. Psychodynamic, behavioral, ecological, sociological, psychoneurological, and countertheoretical positions were described. Interventions associated with these theoretical orientations were described in a second volume (Rhodes & Tracy, 1972b) and delivery systems in a third (Rhodes & Head, 1974). Teacher trainers debated the relative merits of training in one theoretical orientation or providing an eclectic foundation for practice. There was general acceptance that the theory/practice analysis was appropriate for developing a science of practice.

During the late 1960s and early 1970s, I had a joint appointment as the children's consultant in the State Department of Mental Health in North Carolina and a faculty member at the University of North Carolina in Chapel Hill responsible for developing and teaching in a program to train teachers of children with E/BD. The special education department and the program to train teachers in special education was, like most at that time, separate and apart from the general teacher education program. I developed a federally funded program to train teachers of children with E/BD. It was based on an interdisciplinary model and had participants from social work, child and community psychiatry, and clinical child psychology, as well as from different programs in the school of education.

In the mental health system I saw limited educational programs for children with E/BD. In psychiatric hospitals some of these children were on adult wards. Programs were psychoanalytically oriented, and education was a paramedical service. Mental health clinics were providing individual psychotherapy for children and, in some instances, providing consultation to schools. The deinstitutionalization movement, driven in part by the civil rights movement, was gaining force. A great deal of my work during this period focused on advocacy. Several of my colleagues and I developed an advocacy program in the North Carolina mental health system. There were many who felt that the within-systems advocacy would not work. Two of my colleagues and I (Paul, Neufeld, & Pelosi, 1977) wrote a book on our experiences in attempting to define it and make it work. I continue to be ambivalent about whether or not advocates can function effectively in a system that employs them.

The State Department of Mental Health was staffed primarily by a small group of psychiatrists, one psychologist, and a social worker, accurately reflecting the mental health philosophy of that day. However, in addition to myself, there was another person on the staff who had a different history. He was a sociologist whose work centered primarily on systems theory. He conducted seminars with the staff over a period of several years, taking us through basic readings in systems science including Berrien, Bertylanffy, and others, for the purpose of helping us develop a systems focus in the delivery and evaluation of mental health services. This work had a major impact on my way of thinking about human variability and social context.

The passage of the Education for the Handicapped Act in 1975 (P.L. 94-142), with its provisions for the participation of parents, culture-fair assessment, Individual Education Plans, and so forth, had an important impact on the education of children with E/BD, as well as other children with disabilities. Because P.L. 94-142 emphasized the right of all children to an education and provided accountability measures for decisions that would remove children from school, these children who had earlier been expelled because of their behavior problems gained a more secure place in school. It was difficult for schools to expel a child because of his or her disability, such as a behavior disorder.

One of the most challenging provisions of the law, however, was the so-called mainstreaming provision. All children were to be educated in the least restrictive educational environment. A primary strategy for serving these children had been to put them in special classes. Now they not only had a right to be in school but also had a right to be in the least restrictive setting. There were different pullout strategies, such as providing resource rooms in which individual and small groups of children could be provided special instructional support. The goals for children with E/BD removed from general classrooms and placed in special classes in the 1960s had been for them to learn how to adapt to the general classroom without any special curriculum modifications. Special educators were armed with behavioral strategies for working with these children. General classroom teachers, with more students and untrained in special education methods, were not prepared to mainstream these children, who had been removed in the first place because they were not manageable.

I learned a great deal about the challenges of mainstreaming children with emotional disturbance in my work with A. J. Pappanikou and John Cawley in the Philadelphia public schools. Implications for teacher education and program planning and policy development in schools are discussed in a book based on our work (Pappanikou & Paul, 1977).

With the passage of P.L. 94-142 there were attempts to better coordinate if not integrate the parallel systems of general and special education. Success with children with emotional and behavioral disorders was modest by the most generous appraisal. Teacher education programs in special education proliferated, as did services in schools, most of them adopting behavioral perspectives.

I spent the 1970s teaching doctoral students and teachers preparing to teach children with E/BD and, during the last half, chairing the special education division of the School of Education at the University of North Carolina. I had worked with Rhodes over time, consulting on the child variance project, and in 1978 we co-authored *Emotionally Disturbed and Deviant Children: New Views and Approaches* (Rhodes & Paul, 1978). It reflected our belief in a pluralistic and interdisciplinary view. I never felt there was one best view, although 10 years earlier Rhodes and others working with Southern Regional Education Board (SREB) had discussed with me the idea of directing a major research project they had submitted for funding aimed at evaluating the various conceptions of emotional disturbance. I probably would have done it if it had been funded. In retrospect, it would not have been a wise investment of time and resources. Comparative theory, I now believe, is more a philosophical issue than an empirical one and considering the relative efficacy of theories would present enormous research challenges.

My work with Betty Epanchin as a valued colleague began in the late 1970s and has continued. We wrote a book on teaching children with E/BD (Paul & Epanchin, 1982), a book of case studies (Epanchin & Paul, 1982), and a third book on the characteristics of these children (Epanchin & Paul, 1987). Like most books written between 1972 and the mid-1980s, our work was located, conceptually, in the context of the theories classified and described by Rhodes in the child variance project. We went further, however, in the first and second editions of our book on teaching by addressing specific instructional implications of the theories.

In the 1980s several things began to change. Developmental perspectives on behavior began to broaden and provide alternatives to the prevailing behavioral models. For me, one of the most fortuitous events was having the opportunity in 1984 to spend a year at Harvard as a visiting scholar. There were extraordinary changes in perspectives in the social sciences and in the culture that were underway at that time. I had the opportunity to study with Gilligan, who had just written her important book, *In a Different Voice* (1982), which challenged the gender bias of moral development theory developed by Lawrence Kohlberg, her former mentor. I studied with Richard Katz, who was interested in multicultural healing practices and had just published *Boiling Energy* (1982), an ethnography of the !Kung. Also important in my experience there were my studies with Israel Scheffler, an analytic philosopher of education, and Henri Nouwen, a Danish theologian. It was a good time to rethink my earlier roots in philosophy and religion, from which I had become separated in my work in special education.

During the past 10 years my own work has focused on two areas: educational reform and the changing perspective on knowledge. My interest in reform has guided much of my work for the past 5 years. In 1989 I accepted responsibility as the chair of the Department of Special Education at the University of South Florida. My purpose in moving from Chapel Hill to Tampa was that I saw an opportunity to participate in a rather bold experiment in changing the relationship between a university special education department and public schools. My colleagues and I, with the support of William Katzenmeyer, a visionary dean, have had an extraordinary experience trying to understand and do things differently. We think we are having some success in focusing on inclusion and restructuring in partnership with schools. We define our work in terms of an opportunity to create school-based contexts in which we work as colleagues with teachers and other school leaders in transforming the educational services and support systems for children with disabilities and their families. It is an enriching experience for those of us working with doctoral students and teachers in these schools. Our research program is being driven by our commitments to these partnerships, to school-based teacher education, and to inclusion. Our specific research interests include, among other things, the moral perspectives guiding school-based policy development, diversity in policy development and teacher education, alternative systems for educating teachers, teaching case methodology for integrating general and special education teacher education, and research on young children and families.

One of the most rewarding experiences for me at the University of South Florida has been having the opportunity to work in this setting with leaders in the field who have been my mentors over the past 3 decades. William Rhodes, William Morse, and William Cruickshank have all served as visiting research professors here in the Department of Special Education and have had a profound impact on me and others who are participating in this experiment on the west central coast of Florida.

My interest in the changing view of knowledge has been reflected in my teaching and studies. At the University of North Carolina in the mid to late 1980s, I developed a doctoral seminar on the work and knowledge base for special education practice in the context of the physical sciences and another on the work and knowledge base for special education practice in the context of the humanities. Currently, I am working with other faculty in developing two required doctoral seminars. One is on ethics in special education, and the other is on the nature of knowledge. In the knowledge course, we are examining the history of science; the politics of knowledge; Eastern, African, and Western views of knowledge; paradigm issues; and research ethics. The course on knowledge will provide a basic literacy about knowledge as a foundation for the study of quantitative and qualitative research methods. My doctoral students, my work with colleagues, and my own studies in the sciences and the humanities are continuing to shape my own understanding of the special education project at the end of this century.

CONCLUDING RETROSPECTIVE GLANCE: THE LESSONS I HAVE LEARNED

In the l960s the assumption of educational responsibility for children with emotional disturbance created the necessity of new technologies and spawned new alternatives. The 1970s were a time for developing the legal protections for children and the authority for schools to provide an appropriate education for children with disabilities in the least restrictive educational alternative. The 1980s were a time for rethinking the philosophy of special education and the policies that implement that philosophy. The mainstreaming or least restrictive provision of P.L. 94-142 was modified by the regular education initiative that later became a more radical commitment to inclusion. The concept of least restriction was rethought by many, with the resulting advocacy for no restriction in educational placement. The debate has centered on geography of placement with, in my opinion, inadequate attention to the quality of care and education.

The commitment to inclusion as an approach to reform special education in the mid to late 1980s occurred in the context of school restructuring, or the reform of general education. The policy shifts triggered by the school reform movement had profound implications for educating children with E/BD. The site-based management philosophy meant that local schools would be responsible for developing and implementing school policies that would support the inclusion of all children. The outcomes-based approach to assessment and curriculum-based assessment challenged the traditional normative testing of children, including those with E/BD. The children who had, uniquely, been removed from general classrooms in the 1960s and expected to change and adapt to an unchanged curriculum in the general classroom were now being returned to the general classroom with the view that both they and the general classroom would change. Unfortunately, the needed changes in in-service and pre-service training of both special and general classroom teachers to accommodate this policy have not occurred. Also, the technical support needed for general classroom teachers to help them absorb this new responsibility has not been put in place.

The national commitment to reforming education in the 1980s and the 1990s was accompanied by substantial changes in thought. The cognitive revolution changed the environment that had been so dominated by behaviorism. The concept of multiple intelligence focused attention on an important dimension of diversity and the narrowness of the philosophy of measurement and tools for assessment. The paradigm upheaval and the dialogue that resulted changed the landscape of educational discourse. Driven by changes in philosophy of science that had occurred several decades before, the challenge to the traditional paradigm of logical positivism focused attention on the problematic assumptions of the knowledge base for practice and the epistemology guiding research. This had profound implications for the field of educating children with emotional and behavioral disorders, which had been so guided in its practices by a behavioral perspective.

My journey through this history has been influenced by what I brought to my studies when I entered the field in the early 1960s—my own personal history in a small southern community and a good liberal arts education—and several primary forces, mostly my friends and teachers, who have shaped my philosophy of special education in general and the education of children with E/BD in particular. I will list 10 that come clearly to mind as I reflect on the sources of my current beliefs.

First was the impact of the clear, humanistic, and dynamic philosophy of behavior and human development represented in the work of Nicholas Hobbs. He helped me understand that it was as much the poetry and art of psychology as its science that makes it a valued human project. Second was the change of my own mindset in my early study of systems theory that led me beyond the intellectual habit of associating problems with people. Third was the civil rights ethos of the 1960s that brought social and moral philosophy, especially the ethics of care, into focus. Fourth was the influence of two anthropologists, Ina C. Brown and Jean Cleveland, who helped me see the cultural embeddedness of behavior and taught me the meaning of ethnocentrism. Fifth was an appreciation for the complexity of learning and learners that I learned from William Cruickshank.

Sixth was the responsibility to doubt the prevailing views, which I learned from Leo Rippy, theologian and educator, and from the massive challenge to public policy and mainstream institutions during the 1960s and 1970s. Seventh was an appreciation for epistemological, ethical, and ontological questions that has grown in my continuing conversations with William Rhodes for more than 30 years. These conversations built on my early study of logical positivism and existentialism. Eighth were my lessons on patience and looking for the high road taught to me by one of the most gentle and wise leaders in our field, William Morse. Ninth was my learning about diversity from good and patient teachers. I followed a dimly lighted path from my early living and learning experience in an international community through the 1960s, with occasional markers such as those provided by John Johnson and others at a CCBD meeting 25 years ago, until one of my doctoral students in the 1980s, Daphne Thomas, helped me see more clearly the subtleties, persistence, and profound power of racism in our society and in special education. I learned from her and other thoughtful and insightful students, colleagues, and friends that the errors of scholars and researchers, no less than politicians and priests, can originate in the heart and, unchecked, can exact a moral and spiritual toll on the human community. I now believe that coming to terms with the moral implications of ethnic, racial, gender, ideological, and ability diversity in our society is perhaps the most central challenge we face in a field that has, at more times and in more places than we imagine, been used, however unwittingly, as an instrument of social injustice. Tenth was the deep ontological lesson my own two children taught me. It was with them, over time, that I came to understand that our theories of human development leave out the central story of joy and wonder in learning and joining the human community. (The voice of science is mostly silent on matters of the heart, the substance of experience.) It is that story of "becoming a person," as Rogers liked to say, of joining as valued participants in the diverse affairs of humankind that is somehow altered in children and families when we speak, often with far less sensitivity than we should, about emotional disturbance.

REFERENCES

American Psychiatric Association. (1994). *Diagnostic and statistical manual of mental disorders* (4th ed.). Washington, DC: Author.
American Psychological Association. (1981). *Ethical principles of psychologists*. Washington, DC: Author.
Argyrus, C. (1972). *The applicability of organizational sociology*. Cambridge, England: University Press.
Argyrus, C. (1990). *Integrating the individual and the organization*. New Brunswick, NJ: Transaction Publishers.
Ayer, A. (1982). *Philosophy in the twentieth century*. New York: Vintage Books.
Barker, R. (1968). *Ecological psychology: Concepts and methods for studying the environment of human behavior*. Stanford, CA: Stanford University Press.
Bettelheim, B. (1983). *Freud and man's soul*. New York: Alfred A. Knopf.
Bower, E., & Lambert, N. (1962). *A process for in-school screening of children with emotional handicaps*. Princeton, NJ: Educational Testing Service.
Coles, R. (1990). *The spiritual lives of children*. Boston: Houghton-Mifflin.
Connolly, M. (1993). *Political theory and modernity*. Ithaca, NY: Cornell University Press.
Cruickshank, W., Junkala, J., & Paul, J. (1968). *The preparation of teachers of brain-injured children*. Syracuse, NY: Syracuse University Press.
Cruickshank, W., Paul, J., & Junkala, J. (1969). *Misfits in the public schools*. Syracuse, NY: Syracuse University Press.
Danforth, S. (1994). *A life history of a child considered emotionally disturbed: Critical interpretations from research and child*. Unpublished doctoral dissertation, University of South Florida, Tampa.
Derrida, J. (1981). *Positions* (A. Bass, Trans.). Chicago: University of Chicago Press.
Eisner, E. (1991). *The enlightened eye: Qualitative inquiry and the enhancement of educational practices*. New York: Macmillan.

Epanchin, B., & Paul, J. (1982). *Casebook for educating the emotionally disturbed.* Columbus, OH: Merrill.

Epanchin, B., & Paul, J. (1987). *Emotional problems of childhood and adolescence: A multidisciplinary perspective.* Columbus, OH: Merrill.

Erikson, E. (1962). *Young Man Luther: A study in psychoanalysis and history.* New York: Norton.

Erikson, E. (1969). *Gandhi's truth on the origins of militant nonviolence.* New York: Norton.

Ferster, C. (1961). Positive reinforcement and behavior deficits of autistic children. *Child Development, 32,* 437–456.

Fine, M. (1994). Working the hyphens: Reinventing self and other in qualitative research. In N. Denzin & Y. Lincoln (Eds.), *Handbook of qualitative research* (pp. 70–83). Thousand Oaks, CA: Sage Publications.

Geertz, C. (1983). *Local knowledge: Further essays in interpretive anthropology.* New York: Basic Books.

Gendlin, E. (1962). *Experiencing and the creation of meaning: A philosophical and psychological approach to the subject.* New York: Free Press of Glencoe.

Gergen, K. (1994). Exploring the postmodern: Perils or potentials. *American Psychologist, 49,* 412–417.

Gilligan, C. (1982). *In a different voice: Psychological theory and women's development.* Cambridge, MA: Harvard University Press.

Goffman, E. (1961). *Asylums.* New York: Doubleday.

Hobbs, N. (1964). Mental health's third revolution. *The American Journal of Orthopsychiatry, 34,* 822–833.

Hobbs, N. (1966). Helping the disturbed child: Psychological and ecological strategies. *American Psychologist, 21,* 1105–1115.

Janesick, V. (1994). The dance of qualitative research design: Metaphor, methodolatry, and meaning. In N. Denzin & Y. Lincoln (Eds.), *Handbook of qualitative research* (pp. 209–220). Thousand Oaks, CA: Sage Publications.

Johnson, J. (1969). Special education in the inner city: A challenge for the future or another means of cooling the mark out? *Journal of Special Education, 3,* 242–251.

Katz, R. (1982). *Boiling energy: Community healing among the Kalahari !Kung.* Cambridge, MA: Harvard University Press.

Katz, R. (1993). *The straight path: A story of healing and transformation in Fiji.* New York: Addison-Wesley.

Kelley, G. (1963). *A theory of personality: The psychology of personal constructs.* New York: Norton.

Kuhn, T. (1962). *The structure of scientific revolutions.* Chicago: University of Chicago Press.

Miller, A. (1983). *For your own good.* New York: Farrar, Straus, Giroux.

Noblit, G. (1993). Power and caring. *American Educational Research Journal, 30,* 23–38.

Noddings, N. (1984). *Caring: A feminine approach to ethics and moral education.* Berkeley, CA: University of California Press.

Pappanikou, A., & Paul, J. (1977). *Mainstreaming emotionally disturbed children.* Syracuse, NY: Syracuse University Press.

Paul, J. (1985). Behavior disorders in the 1980s: Ethical and ideological issues. *Behavior Disorders, 11*, 67–71.

Paul, J., & Epanchin, B. (1982). *Emotional disturbance in children.* Columbus, OH: Merrill.

Paul, J., Neufeld, R., & Pelosi, J. (1977). *Advocacy within the system.* Syracuse, NY: Syracuse University Press.

Rhodes, W., & Head, S. (Eds.). (1974). *A study of child variance: Vol. 3. Service delivery systems.* Ann Arbor: University of Michigan Press.

Rhodes, W., & Paul, J. (1978). *Emotionally disturbed and deviant children: New views and approaches.* Englewood Cliffs, NJ: Prentice-Hall.

Rhodes, W., & Tracy, M. (Eds.). (1972a). *A study of child variance: Vol. 1. Theories.* Ann Arbor: University of Michigan Press.

Rhodes, W., & Tracy, M. (Eds.). (1972b). *A study of child variance: Vol. 2. Interventions.* Ann Arbor: University of Michigan Press.

Rorty, R. (1979). *Philosophy and the mirror of nature.* Princeton, NJ: University Press.

Skrtic, T. (1991). *Behind special education: A critical analysis of professional culture and school organization.* Denver, CO: Love Publishing.

Smith, B. (1994). Selfhood at risk: Postmodern perils and the perils of postmodernism. *American Psychologist, 49*, 405–412.

Szasz, T. (1961). *The myth of mental illness.* New York: Harper & Row.

Webb-Mitchell, B. (1993). *God plays piano too.* New York: Crossroads.

WILLIAM C. RHODES
University of Michigan

William Rhodes completed a PhD in child clinical psychology in 1954 while serving as acting director of the Georgia Mental Health Program. In 1957, he joined the faculty at Peabody College where he directed the Child Study Center and was codirector of the project on Re-education of Emotionally Disturbed Children (Re-Ed). Rhodes also served as associate director of children's programs in the community health branch of the National Institute of Mental Health. He joined the faculty at the University of Michigan where, among other things, he was the principal investigator of the project Studies in Child Variance, *producing five volumes related to children with emotional disturbance. Rhodes retired in 1981 and in 1984 became a visiting professor at the University of South Florida.*

CHAPTER 18

Postmodernism and Disturbance/Disorder

With the sincere desire to invite dialogue, I would like to quote a response from one of the editors of this text to the initial version of this chapter:

> We feel this material will be foreign enough to many of our readers that it may need more small vignettes to make it concrete. As we read it there are three major themes: all reality is relative, the nature of emotional behavioral adjustment is relative to the now socio-cultural frame of reference. Why then do we have juvenile gangs, violence, etc? What are the perceptions of these adolescents—what are the perceptions of society—why do they bump into one another? It seems that the social relative point of view pushes that aspect of behavioralism that likes to count and make baselines into oblivion? It also has much to say about us guys who depend on the MMPI-A [Minnesota Multiphasic Personality Inventory–Adolescent] and BASC [Behavior Assessment System for Children]. It clearly places the practice of differential diagnosis into diagnosis dependent upon the environment, role-relationships, and task. This chapter says we need multiple interventions to habilitate in many cases and rehabilitate in others, life skills. It would argue for a functional model to "teach" those skills necessary to survive in the immediate local society in which they find themselves. (Sabatino, personal communication, May, 1994)

I would ask the reader to keep this editorial response to my chapter in mind as they read the text itself. In doing this, they will have both my text and an interpretation by the editor. Their own personal rejoinder will comprise their own interpretation or construction of the text, the meanings they make for themselves. This interpretation will be a creative act, an attempt to give personal meaning to both the text and the editor's response. The meaning comes out of their own apperceptive mass, the body of culturally conditioned and personally developed understandings and experiences through which they read the text and its editorial interpretations. In a sense, this is how we make knowledge, make reality.

My own experience spans a period of 40 years in the field. My own thinking has traveled through an interesting streambed, wending its way through the familiar waters of learning theory (behavioral theory), ecological theory, and systems theory. I see these theories as nothing more than useful tools to use or discard as it suits our purpose in making sense of our world and our field. Then, in the late 1970s, my stream of thought took a strange leap into the audacious new scientific paradigm, a consequence of the physics revolt of relativity and quantum mechanics. What helped me take this leap was the prior constructivist work of Kelly (1955) and Piaget (1986). Kelly was one of my professors in my PhD program and Piaget, my ideal research model. Mechanistic, formula-type research made no sense to me for our field.

However, up to the time that my mind took this strange leap into the new scientific paradigm, I had forced the flow of my thoughts to view the reality we called *emotional disturbance/behavioral disorders* (E/BD) as though it was a thing, or something separate from me and the way I construed or constructed it. I really believed I was separate from what I saw. I believed I was a spectator, an objective observer of E/BD, that I was not participating in making it real.

I then encountered that huge, quirky, oceanic flow of thought called the New Science, a looking-glass science in which the world becomes a mirror of the mind, a subject–object flow, moving out and back simultaneously. Without theories of what the world is, we can see nothing. In a sense, what we believe is what we see. Piaget showed us how this works in children as they learn to see objects, space, time, and causality. He thought of the process as assimilation/accommodation.

The New Physics of relativity and quantum mechanics has used Piaget's work to explain the fundamental quantum phenomena that occurs below the threshold of awareness. All reality (and this includes E/BD) is only a potential, only a lurking possibility, until we engage it with our current level of perception and bring it into existence. Apparently, perception is necessary for inception. If we can't think of it, it isn't there. If we can't see it, it doesn't exist. We cannot pretend to be objective about E/BD (or anything else in the world) without, at the same time, making it what it is.

Ever since education, by law, took on responsibility for this field, we have been deconstructing its medical meanings. We are in the process of making it something else. In the process, it is becoming something else within our educational context. But we are not fully aware of the implications. It is still a pathological reality within the medical context. Before that, it was, and still is to an extent, a religious reality—a possession. Thus, side by side, we have three existing realities, multiple realities. The medical reality has been given a privileged position by the larger society. However, if we trace the history of emotional disturbance and behavioral disorders, we find deep roots in Western thought. As the context of history has changed, our construction of emotional disturbance has changed. *Behavioral disorders* is the most recent one. Unfortunately, it is tied to an eroding worldview, the prerevolutionary view of "positivism." Positivism is a way of thinking that affects what we see and how we see it. It says that what is actual, what *is* or what may be directly affirmed, depends on the "facts" of physical science or the senses. Since the first quarter of the nineteenth century, the work of the physical sciences has recanted that position. Nothing *is* or *can be* until we can think about and notice it. What we think about or how we attend to it brings what is lurking there into actuality.

Interestingly enough, at about the same time, social philosophy and social science rejected positivism and adopted a radical new worldview called *postmodernism*. Both of these revolutions say that we "make" knowledge, that we construct rather than discover knowledge. Education is rapidly moving toward that worldview. The area of E/BD has not, and positivists still control publication sources in our field and train our teachers and university faculty.

Therefore, I find myself, like our labeled children, on the outside of the field, not quite understandable. However, I believe the oceanic view of the new scientific paradigm and postmodernism is reaching flood tide and beginning to seep into the thinning mainstream. You can hear it in all the recent American Educational Research Association (AERA) conferences. I find it in the thinking of many of my students and some of the teachers in the field. It is being expressed in the diverse disciplines and practices in this country and throughout the world. I find it in the work of special educators like Popline, Heshusius, Skrtic, and Sailor.

A POSTMODERN DEFINITION

Emotional disturbance/behavioral disorders, from my point of view as a postmodern constructivist, is a constructed linguistic category whose meaning is historically rooted deep within Western culture (Foucault, 1973). From this postmodern perspective, a frame of awareness can be constructed that takes its meaning from local perceptual contexts. Therefore, from the view of postmodern constructivism, E/BD is context bound, locally embedded, historically developed, and perceptually constructed. Like a chameleon, it takes much of its color from its surroundings. It depends on the particular local context and the historically developed perceptual system constituting it. A particular school is a context, a particular dominant culture is a context, a particular state or locality is a context. The perceptual system dominating a particular school, state, or locality, in turn, grows from the larger prevailing context in which its relative meaning and interpretations are derived.

There is no essence of E/BD. Therefore, there is no quintessential feature. There is no "God's eye view" of E/BD. There is no *reality* of E/BD apart from its contextualized frame of reference in a particular locale. It occurs in the eye of the beholder embedded in a particular context.

Ethnographers such as Benedict caught a glimpse of this wholistic, variable, fluid-matrix perspective on emotional disturbance very early in the social sciences, although Benedict did not fully realize its New Physics implications. She saw psychosis as tied to sociocultural interpretations of its observer/participator. She clearly demonstrated that what can be interpreted and made real as psychotic irrationality in one cultural-perceptual context is real shamanistic wisdom in another. She envisioned the postrevolutionary, postmodern view of "multiple realities." Borrowing from the updated postmodern social philosophy of Gertz (1983), we might think of knowledge vis-à-vis emotional disturbance/behavioral disorders as "local frames of thought" applied or realized fully in a particular local context.

Local frames of thought, like the children and teachers embedded in them, can be said to be potentially malleable. Since each of these (children/teachers and thought frames) can be seen as embedded in each other, a shift in one effects a shift in the other. A change in thought frames—in professional development, for instance—can change teachers or children and vice versa. The job of special education, from this postmodern perspective, is to bring about reciprocal changes in the thought frames at all levels: communities, systems, teachers, children, etc. What this amounts to is a change in the reality context, a change in reality as lived in the immediate context. We can get an idea of such reality shifts by looking at an Escher painting and its amazing figure-ground reversals. Or, better still, we can grasp it by reading Kuhn's (1970) discussion of scientific revolutions that have literally changed reality periodically throughout history, just as the physics revolution has done most recently.

From this postmodern perspective, in spite of special education's efforts to extract an independent "self" of the child from the composite contextual matrix in which that self is embedded, the child remains an integral part of that context. It's like saying, "You can take the individual out of the country, but you cannot take the country out of the individual." So special education is working with a matrix, a mosaic that includes the individual. Like a hologram, the whole is greater than the sum of its parts, but each part contains or reflects the whole.

THE WORLDVIEW

From this view of a constructed reality that is localized and contextualized, a radical general shift in a frame of thought about emotional disturbance can bring about a radical shift in the whole text of E/BD at various levels. We find that the reality we have been looking at and working in all these years is, in fact, some *other* reality. A good example of such a radical mosaic or matrix shift is women's studies, which is constructing a new women's-eye view of the yin/yang, or men's/women's reality, that had existed across the centuries.

In my own opinion, the dominant thought frames about E/BD existing in our various local contexts have failed us and are in a period of collapse. We need to totally reframe the dialogue about E/BD. And that is what I am trying to do here.

Let us take an example. At the present time, one of our struggles is over whether *emotional disturbance* and *behavioral disorders* are the same thing or two different things. We should take a leaf from the equanimity of the New Physics in accepting the wave-particle duality as "complimentary" realities. We should discard our outworn mode of thinking, requiring an either/or logic, and adopt the new both/and logic of physics: both emotional disturbances *and* behavioral disorders and, perhaps, more.

This brings us back to my postmodern interpretation of E/BD as contextually bound, and locally originating frames of thought. The meaning and interpretation of the historically rooted reality of the linguistic category, *emotionally disturbed/behaviorally disordered*, is constructed in the frames of awareness in the same local context in which it occurs. It can, of course, be enlightened or informed by a legislative text originating at a state or national level. Ultimately, however, the legislation is enacted into existence in the frames of thought embedded in the local context, or colored by the sociocultural matrix and frames of thought in which that context is embedded. Hence, for instance, some states use *emotional disturbance* in their legislative and administrative regulations, and some use *behavioral disorders*. The construction of E/BD cannot exist "out there," suspended free of the context and perceptually created frames of thought that activate it.

THE HERMENEUTIC ANCHOR

In the beginning of this chapter, I asked you to read the text through your own accumulated mental mass, or what I called your apperceptive mass, with which you interpret and make sense of it. That process of creating your own knowledge through your own translations is called *hermeneutics* in postmodernism. That is your reality. Through dialogue, that reality can reach a consensus, so that most of us "see" alike. However, as applied to texts, the "hermeneutic circle" is the process of entering the text from your own point of view and then going back to reflect on your point of view and any changes brought in it by the text. Your point of view has been shaped by your own past experiences and past knowledge. Hermeneutic readings of the text are, therefore, necessarily diverse, refluent, and interpretative, depending how local knowledge, values, understandings, experience, and frames of thought shape it. Reading my chapter depends on what you already "know" about E/BD, and if you stick with it, you will transform it closer to what you already know than to what I am trying to say. The same is true of any legislative text. The reading moves into the legislation and back again to your own locally embedded apperceptive or perceptual context. Legislation does not *make* reality. It provides a flexible screen against which you project your own reality and transform it into action.

FLAWED SCIENTIFIC PARADIGM

In my own reality, our present thinking about E/BD fits a flawed, prerevolutionary scientific paradigm. In this flawed modernist or classic paradigm, we sought predetermined, free-standing, absolute, objective, mechanical "truths." These "truths" or "facts" were considered to be independent of the observer. They had nothing to do with the individual's participation with them, with his or her perceptual constructions of them, his or her "head frames," or his or her personal theories about them. That was the now embattled modernist worldview.

In the postmodernist worldview we do not stand free of what we see. We are participants, not observers. Reality is like projections on a screen: In and of itself, it has only a potential to exist until engaged, as is now held in the "new" science of relativity and quantum mechanics. In this changed perspective, things and thinking cannot be separated. They are embedded in each other. In postmodern awareness, a whole mode of seeing things in a new light, buttressed by the science underpinnings of the New Physics, reality is only a potential. This potential is waiting for perceptually guided registration of phenomena to help actualize it. It is this registration that makes it real.

This is very different from the mystic system of positivism that now guides our field. We take the theories of our field for a reality that has nothing to do with what our minds have been set to see. It is not a matter of our interpretations making what we see visible to us. We are very concrete, practical people. We just, by God, *know* what is there because we have experienced it. And experience doesn't have anything to do with our interpretation of it, our construction of it.

For the postmodernist, we live in a different world, one that is, to a significant extent, of our own making. We do not *know* what E/BD is. If you ask me, "What is emotional disturbance?" I have to say, "From what contextualized frame of thought?" Such frames are very persistent even though potentially malleable. They are also very resistant to change, repelling other competing frames of awareness attempting to enter their context. Awakening to their growing obsolescence over time requires the capacity for self-reflection. If the thinker cannot introspect, the firmly held frames of awareness become to him or her, over the same period of time, absolute, predetermined, objective truths possessing a mystic existence of their own, somewhere "out there," free of the thinker's self and his or her thinking about them. In the postmodern worldview and in postrevolutionary science, such absolutes are no longer believable. Indeterminacy or uncertainty, participatory reality, has won out over determinacy, certainty, and uninterpreted observer reality.

Therefore, the postmodernist would say that we should stop asking, "What is emotional disturbance *really*?" Furthermore, to ask "Is the prevalence/incidence of emotional disturbance and behavioral disorders increasing?" makes E/BD a determinable *thing* free of its contextualized frame of thought. With a postmodern shift in perspective, this is an unanswerable question. As a question, it has no context, no anchor.

In the same vein, to ask "How much good or how much harm are we doing in the education of emotionally disturbed children?" is meaningless without specifying the anchoring framework to which and in which it is grounded. Bower's (1969) personal-social perspective of emotional disturbance was compatible with the educational thinking at the time it was encased in the 1975 legislation. At least, this prospectus took it out of the medical frame of reference, that is, the disease or pathogenic model in which it was contextualized at that time. The medical construction or interpretation, dominant and privileged, actually dictated that children were not educable until "cured" of the disturbance. The 1975 politically constructed definition, embedded in federal law, at least opened the way for such medically diagnosed children to attend school and be educated like other children.

However, even now, we are still insisting that there must be a final, right, or real definition awaiting to be discovered, like a natural diamond in South African sand. This is in spite of our accumulated experience, grounded in the great diversity of interpretations, meanings, belief systems, and practices vis-à-vis the Bower-influenced legislative definition that now guides our work. Here we see the hermeneutic circle in operation, providing variable historically embedded, locally contextualized readings of the legislative text. The text becomes open to interpretation.

This is not to suggest that a new awareness dynamism cannot shake up or deconstruct and reconstruct national and local knowledge about disturbance disorder. In fact, that is the central argument being made here. We need a conceptual earthquake, or worldview shift of major dimensions, in order to rearrange our current frames of thought about emotional disturbance. It is further argued that the postmodern worldview provides such an earthquake.

With the multiplying number of school children from increasingly diverse backgrounds who are disturbing us, it seems evident that we must redo our thinking about E/BD. Too many locally dominant frames of reference are being shaken up. Instead of asking, "What are the most meaningful educational experiences that emotionally disturbed or behaviorally disordered children must have included in their school programs?" we must now revise the question: "What shifts in frames of thought and experiences, of a reciprocal or complimentary nature, do we educators and the large proportion of *disturbing* children and their teachers need to change the context of our lives?" In order to be meaningful, the shift has to be reciprocal.

Furthermore, we have to stop thinking about our *selves* and their *selves* as disembodied from the local thought frames or cultural-perceptual contexts in which we are embedded. In postmodernism, the processes of our *selves* are continuous with, or refluent with, the processes of the matrix in which they are embedded—as in the Möbius strip, with its lines constructed to flow back into itself. The Möbius strip is like a figure eight lying on its side but in which the crossing lines of the eight do not touch. Most dictionaries have instructions teachers can use to have their students construct a Möbius strip. The Möbius strip gives us a concrete way of understanding the new looking-glass science way of seeing our connection to nature, our inclusion in nature. It shows how the objective and the subjective are inseparable, or reciprocal and refluent.

AN EXEMPLAR PROGRAM

To give a fleshed-out example, let us tell a story featuring a relatively young doctoral student who is part of a professional development team sent into a local school from a nearby university. Experienced teachers reading this story may see it as a typical story of power politics in the school building, but it is intended to be much more than that. It is intended to illustrate what I mean when I say that in postmodern thinking E/BD can be constructed as context bound, locally embedded, historically derived, and perceptually constructed.

The members of the professional development team in our example consist of a faculty professor and three doctoral students from the student's department. Our young doctoral student is one of them. In view of the idea of a collaborative effort, each team member has a specific assignment in a particular part of the school. This is because it is the intent of the university not only to provide lectures but also to include "hands-on" demonstrations. All except the university professor have assignments related to E/BD. Two are reimbursed by the school system in sharing a position listed as "behavior specialists." The third functions as a liaison with parents and agencies.

Our exemplar team member is a highly experienced special educator of such children. However, she has never worked in the context of a very rural, homogeneous, overwhelmingly uniform, locally dominant culture. Her primary previous successful experience with individuals who were disturbed/disordered had been in a very large metropolitan locale where schools drew their students from one of the most diversified population centers in the United States.

In this experience, her worldview over the years had become predominantly postmodern. Most recently, she had been inspired by the views of a professor in California who had been very successful in developing a university training program and staffing schools in the surrounding area, all built on the constructivist point of view, similar to the one being expressed here.

Our university team member intended to attempt to translate this constructivist awareness into her teaching and practice in the school to which she had been assigned.

CONFLICTING THEORIES AND CONTEXTS

However, not only was the assigned school into which her team was sent located in the matrix of a very rural, very southern, ultraconservative context, but the principal and vice principal seemed to have assimilated and accommodated to the most anachronistic of the local thought frames. In the larger county context, on the other hand, the higher-level administration reflected the fluid, rapidly changing thought frames of that particular county. Although this school was reflective of the most isolationist frames of thought, in a local context where there was very little movement of population, the rest of the county was experiencing an explosion of population that was more highly educated, relatively sophisticated, and coming from all parts of the nation. In keeping with this transformation, the district-level personnel were eager for the university professional development team to help them with their countywide school restructuring by establishing a professional development school in the county.

Alas, the local school principal and vice principal scheduled to collaborate with this incoming team, who, in line with their success in other very rural schools, were much more in tune with where the county had been than where it was going. This led to a great deal of confusion and misunderstanding. To compound this situation, the vice principal had, until recently, been responsible for administering a program for children with behavior disorders in another setting, and she saw herself as the in-house expert. Not only did her mind-set reflect the most conservative, rural South, but her frame of reference with regard to such children accentuated most of the caricatured assumptions of prerevolutionary scientific positivism. She brought into the school the most rigid thought frames and interpretations of prerevolutionary scientific positivism, stressing strict mechanistic absolutism, determinism, and the most slavish ideology of subject–object separation, along with a profound belief in her ability to predict and control. As a punishment–reward purist, she had the total trust, acceptance, and respect of the principal, who was, herself, cut from the same mold. This principal, highly hierarchically oriented, also saw her vice principal as *the* authority on children with behavioral disorders.

Thus, the stage was set for an imbroglio of one of the most disturbing, chaotic, turbulent years either representative group had ever experienced. Except for those to whom it happened, it is a story that is very hard to believe. This excludes, of course, those who have already developed an allergy to systems. Each representative body, steeped in its own awareness and frames of thought, lived out distinct, separated realities within the same context and locale in the same period of time.

It is hard to say whether this story is a comedy or a tragedy, but as its main interpreter, I feel that it was a tragedy for many of the targeted children and families caught between clashing frames of thought. One frame, in my view, was determinedly and unabashedly aligned with the local struggle to stem the rising tide of changing frames of thought engulfing the county. The other was flowing with and leading the rising tide of change in the county but finding it difficult to penetrate the two congealed islands of reference frames firmly set against the tide surge.

The principal/vice principal duo apparently had, from my postmodern perspective, little appreciation for, or understanding of, a collaborative model of administration. For them, it now seems, the educational system was a hierarchical, politicized, dominance-oriented, fixed structure. When the university team arrived, they apparently had mixed feelings. On one hand, they were pleased to be selected as the site of the professional development effort. On the other hand, they unconsciously viewed the incoming team as a foreign transplant, threatening the organizational integrity of their existing system. To principal and vice principal, apparently, the school was a thing, an absolute, deterministic structure more or less carved in stone. To them, reality must have been something totally "out there," unalloyed by the way they saw or thought about it. The idea that reality might be a construction of their minds must have been both foreign and threatening to them. Even the idea that their local frames of thought should be changed to meet the changing conditions of the county must have been anathema to them.

It was clear from the stance of the vice principal, the reigning expert on the reality of "behavioral disorders"—her favorite term—that there was only one true educational avenue to preparing children for life. That avenue, I would judge from her actions, was pure, unadulterated, immediate punishment of "wrong" behaviors, both in academics and demeanor. From my point of view, although she must have thought of herself as applying the principles of Skinnerian behavior modification, she was not aware that Skinner said rewards were better than punishment in modifying behavior. Her processes were much more like Pavlovian behavior modification, but most of Pavlov's work had to do with conditioning neuroses in laboratory animals through punishment techniques.

Although this interpretation may seem harsh, it grows out of her frequent direct orders to our exemplar team member and to the other doctoral-level team members not to introduce any dialogue into group meetings of the behavior disorders staff that was contrary to her own view. Since she had served as sometimes chair of such meetings, this had been her standard way of operating before the team arrived. She wanted it to continue that way. When she meted out punishment to the children with behavior disorders, which she frequently did, she wanted no discussion of her decisions. In one meeting she ordered our exemplar team member to be quiet. At another time she ordered another team member responsible for liaison with the parents of the children who were behaviorally disordered not to have any contact with any of the children. When the two team members who were nominally behavioral specialists did not suspend children for bad behavior or bad language, she took the action herself.

PERCEPTIONS OF LEADERSHIP

In all fairness to the principal and vice principal, they were hired for this demonstration school with the understanding that their leadership would spearhead professional development in the county to accompany restructuring. From the principal and vice principal's perspective, this mantle of expertise laid upon them could simply have confirmed their own self-appraisal and frame of awareness. One could imagine that, from their perspective, a group of university theorists, unacquainted with the locally contextualized frames of thought and awareness, had strayed outside their own boundaries of knowledge. Such a foreign team had to learn the given reality of the locale. Furthermore, their previous experience of authority had probably taught them that, within *their* system, these university people were outside the power structure of the school. They had no right to share any of the power granted by educational tradition to the administrators of the school. Within the school lexicon, these outsiders had no place in the given table of organization, other than specific structured roles assigned to any one of them. In their mind, if a member was paid to occupy a table-of-organization position, he or she was bound to carry out the precise job description written for that role. Since the university cooperative process was new, there was confusion in everyone's minds about the dual roles. However, because two members of the team were assigned to the role of "behavior specialist" for the purpose of reimbursement of their time by the school system, the principal and vice principal arbitrarily insisted that they must fulfill the job description of that role under their control and that their authority over these team members was absolute. As far as the principal and vice principal were concerned, there was no ambiguity at all about the fact that these two members were under their control. It seems as though this included their ad hoc role as university professional developers. The principal and vice principal must have felt that no matter what the agreement at the district level had been, the "state" had given decision-making authority to the school base, and they were the traditional, legitimate decision makers at the school base.

THE LOGIC OF ILLOGIC

Our exemplar team member wrote a very well-reasoned, interpretative, system's-research paper on the school at the time of the team's entry. It portrayed the school as a rigidly structured, highly hierarchical system, with each level of the hierarchy fearful and angry at all the others.

The principal and vice principal had both welcomed the team, saying that the children with behavior disorders had been running wild in the school. It was going to be good to get the professional development help of the two members called behavior specialists and the one called parent and agency liaison. At the same time, although there was some uncertainty in everybody's minds, the principal and vice principal resolved the ambiguity very simply. Within their own perceptual framework, it must have been very clear to them that they would dictate the terms of any "professional development" that would follow.

My own interpretation of the flow of the thinking of the principal and vice principal, perceptually contextualized as it was, makes sense in the following way: It seems, as often happens in school systems from my own experience, that the behavior disorders program had become the lightening rod for all the disordered dynamics existing in the chosen school. Apparently, the convenient, organizationally dissociated population of the behavior disorders program continued to be the principal's and vice principal's projected source of all school system disturbance. It seems as though, after the team's arrival, they continued to project all of the dysfunctions of the system upon that labeled population. When the team members did not concentrate on teaching appropriate punishing techniques and tried to retain children rather than suspend them, the vice principal and principal probably saw the team as joining forces with the children and their families. However, since no dialogue was allowed, there was no way for the team to check this perception. Whenever one of the team members went into the vice principal's office to discuss something, the vice principal would get very busy on the phone and continue interrupting the team member to take care of front-office business. This got worse as the year went along. If parents came in to discuss something about their children or to attend a staffing meeting, they were ignored; only professional discussants, other than team members, were listened to.

My own interpretation of the school administration was that it seemed to be acting toward the professional development team as the demeanor of a nation does toward inside and connected outside scapegoats. The children became the resident scapegoats and the team the outside scapegoats. Just as a demagogue tries to distract a nation away from its internal disorders by focusing anger and fear toward the danger of these scapegoats, the leadership of the school seemed to be trying to portray the team as outside agitators, joining forces with the inside children with behavior disorders and their parents. Thus, the stage was set for inordinate obstacles and misunderstandings vis-à-vis professional development within the behavioral disorders program of the school.

When the team initially arrived, principal and vice principal were, from all appearances, delighted to have it. They probably felt at that time, judging from their comments, that the behavior disorders program was out of control and the team would help bring it back into control. They probably thought that the team members would teach and demonstrate to their behavior disorders staff how to control these offensive children through a single dimensional behavioral frame. As for the parent liaison program instituted by the member of the team responsible for it, they were dismayed. Initially, they had expressed their attitude toward the parents when they said that the parents only reinforced the student's disordered behavior.

The principal and vice principal were, obviously, very upset when the team began deescalating suspension and punishment of these students. Instead of getting rid of them for 10 days at a time, allowable by the state, the team was trying to keep the children in school. The ad hoc nature of the school's conflicting use of suspension was indicated very early in the team's experience. In the case of one child in school whose parents were on the verge of prosecution for the child's constant truanting, the vice principal heard him using bad language to one of the teachers and suspended him on the spot for a 10-day period. The vice principal continued to suspend him every 10 days for various infractions.

She was particularly angry with our exemplar team member whose previous successful experience had been with a large metropolitan, highly diverse population, because she failed to notice and punish the bad language of children. The fact that this team member equated such language with the constant, everyday expressions of a much more diverse population, or that the teachers in that school constantly used the same language in the teacher's lounge, was considered of no consequence.

Suspension, used very liberally by the vice principal, was considered the most strategic punishment technique. The fact that many parents dreaded it because of how it interfered with their work schedule made it even more desirable. You punished both student and parent at the same time. The vice principal even stepped up the frequency and length of suspension (within the 10-day limit) when she saw that the team was trying to limit it. Whether it was to show who was boss or to try to compensate for what she saw as the "laxness" of the team members, suspension was exercised to the point that many of the children were out of school much more than they were in. When they did return, it was frequently only for 1 day every 10 days. By this point, principal and vice principal began to act as though the university team was trying to undermine their authority and control of *their* teachers and *their* children with behavior disorders. The interlopers were not teaching punishment and control techniques, and, therefore, the administration seemed to have to counteract this example by stepping up the modeling of these appropriate teacher behaviors.

At times, when the vice principal was chairing group meetings of the staff of the program for behavior disorders, if the university members would try to bring up alternative points of views or procedures, she conveyed the impression that these were "unrealistic." When they would try to talk about the use of student–teacher relationships in education, she would brush it off as irrelevant. If they would talk about or demonstrate the use of whole language techniques for literacy skills, learning about the student, or the student learning about himself or herself, she would consider it beside the point of trying to establish decorum in the school.

MEANINGS AND INTERPRETATIONS

What meanings and interpretations can we draw from this imbroglio vis-à-vis E/BD? Does it give us further insights into the relationship between behavior disorders and emotional disturbance? Does it say anything about the current federal definition? Does it give us clues to additional dimensionalities revealed through the local perceptual context and the two realities existing side by side within that context?

We know that both the university and school bodies were informed of the national definition. We see, however, how differently each read and interpreted it. My own interpretation reaffirms for me the broader and deeper dimensionalities of emotional disturbance, which includes the layered contexts of local thought frames. I am convinced that we cannot confine our perspective to the child's inner life or outside behavior. It confirms for me that all knowledge regarding disturbance/disorder, just as knowledge in general, is filtered through many levels of contextualized thought frames, including one's own experiential-perceptual matrix. All of this colors our hermeneutic reading of texts. Furthermore, specific knowledge of E/BD rooted in a Western historical context shifts from time to time. Burke's (1985) book, *The Day the Universe Changed*, showed the numerous radical shifts in the very "ground-level" meaning of knowledge across history as the greater world context shifts. If we read Foucault (1973), we can see that the same thing has occurred across history in the area of E/BD. Kuhn (1970) showed us the hermeneutics of science revolutions and the important part that scholarly professional politics plays in those revolutions. We can see, from our own experience, that the dialogue around disturbance/disorder is not purely a scholarly or scientific one. There are many voices in the dialogue, including public policy constructors, parent groups, religious leaders, spokespersons on "political correctness," ethnic spokespersons, and representatives of agencies or human delivery systems. The ensuing constructions are embedded in the times, and the times are always "achanging."

From the postmodern worldview, which focuses on connectedness rather than disconnectedness, inclusion rather than exclusion, I can only applaud inclusive approaches. The prevalence/incidence constructs no longer have any meaning to me. They talk about absolutes where, for postmodernists, there are no absolutes. They talk about "outside reality" where, in my postmodern view, particularly in regard to science, there is not outside reality independent of the participants in the construction of, or realization of, reality. There is no subject–object split as in the positivist, mechanistic, classic era. Thus, my frames of thought, although fitting a community of postmodern constructivists, may be totally incommensurable to many disturbance/disorders specialists. Yet, both of our frames of thought are built around the same children.

RETURN TO THE STORY

But what about the three doctoral students who spent a full year on the team? Wasn't this a failure experience? Not by any means. To them, as to me, it was a profound learning experience.

Although the voice of this exemplar team member was somewhat muffled by the vice principal in the school context, it was very vociferous in other contexts: in long, nightly telephone conversations with team members; in all her doctoral program classes; in a flood of papers and research reports in these classes; in frequent conversations with her mentor (me); and with other faculty members in the doctoral program. She reported to me frequently during that year that she had taken long, rambling walks in the woods around her house to sort out her postmodern constructivist frame of reference. Stimulated by the vice principal's antithetical frames of awareness, she tested out her own views in her class in which she was a graduate teaching assistant. She seems to have had enough political sense, sharpened by her study of critical pedagogy or emancipatory pedagogy not to make a public display of the political–ideological conflict going on in her school placement.

Toward the end of the year, she was one of the people in the university team who called for a meeting with particular members of the university to sum up the events of the year and their implications for professional development collaboration within schools.

Following this meeting, the faculty leader of the team arranged a meeting between a few "power figures" from the college of education and the receptive district-level school authorities for a similar discussion and summation. The outcome is not yet clear.

FURTHER IMPLICATIONS

The moral of this story could be interpreted as power politics, and certainly that would be appropriate. However, the major point of the story from the postmodern constructivist perspective is that more than one reality can exist side by side. Ultimately, knowledge about disorder/disturbance is context bound, locally and personally embedded, historically developed (within the individual and her or his locally embedded context), and mentally constructed.

The story I have told is not about good guys and bad guys, even though I have slanted it that way from my own perspective. It is about radically different ways of constructing reality. I gave mine privilege over the vice principal's. However, in a greater sense, I have argued within the genre of Burke, Foucault, Kuhn, and all the postmodern social philosophers. Their message is that basic ground-level meanings of *knowledge, reality, observer, disorder/disability* are not fixed and absolute. Historically, they have, and will, change from time to time. They are like, and related to, the science "revolutions" that Kuhn talked about. At the present time we are in the midst of such a worldview revolution. In our own field of disturbance/disorder, all our settled notions are being unsettled.

In my version of the above story, the vice principal, embedded in her context, represents a local, extremely reductionist edition of the positivist worldview that is fading, and the university team represents a wholistic, constructivist worldview that is rising on the horizon.

My own interpretation, which I made clear in my story, is one that favors the postmodern constructivist view. However, I have buttressed it with the postrevolutionary science prospectus (Bohm & Peat, 1987), which follows the New Physics. This view is that perception takes place through the mind and our "inward" intention and locally contextualized general disposition, and this most strongly affects what is seen. Thus "local knowledge" literally constructs reality.

From this point of view, incoming information is apprehended by our mind and, in turn, produces an outgoing activity in which further scanning and information gathering takes place in order to confirm, explain, and reinforce what has been seen. This new activity then gathers further information, which is again apprehended by the shifting contours in the map of the mind, leading to further ongoing activity.

Knowledge of reality, therefore, is a construction that does not lie either in the subject or in the object but in the dynamic flow between them.

Although the disorder/disturbance dialogue in the professional development program of my story was silenced by the vice principal, I contend that the clash of realities was, nevertheless, very productive. It has already borne fruit in the thinking of the doctoral students and in related professional-development programs in other cooperative schools. In spite of the vice principal's attempt to control the reality dialogue and reduce it to the local, contextual frames of thought (which, by the way, are local "theories"), the incursion of the university team clashed with that reality and forced it open.

Both groups began with the "official" interpretations of disorders/disturbance, but how differently the reality they encountered turned out to be. Thus, my story was told to exemplify both the paradigm of the new science and the worldview shift to postmodernism, which overturns modes of thinking that held sway for more than 300 years. It challenges our current perspective on E/BD and says that we are the constructors of that reality. It has no existence apart from the way we think about it.

REFERENCES

Bohm, D., & Peat, D. (1987). *Science, order and creativity*. New York: Bantum Books.

Bower, E. M. (1969). *Early identification of emotionally handicapped children in school* (2nd ed.). Springfield, IL: Thomas.

Burke, J. (1985). *The day the universe changed*. London: London Writers, Ltd.

Foucault, M. (1973). *Madness and civilization: A history of insanity in the age of reason*. New York: Vintage Books/Random House.

Gertz, C. (1983). *Local knowledge: Further essays in interpretive anthropology*. New York: Basic Books.

Kelly, G. (1955). *The psychology of personal constructs* (Vols. 1–2). New York: W. W. Norton.

Kuhn, T. (1970). *The structure of scientific revolutions*. Chicago: University of Chicago Press.

Piaget, J. (1986). *The construction of reality in the child*. New York: International Universities Press.

RICHARD L. SIMPSON
University of Kansas

Richard L. Simpson is a professor of special education and school psychology at the University of Kansas. He also is co–project director of several programs in the department as well as editor of Focus on Autistic Behavior. *Simpson has been a teacher of children who are emotionally disturbed at the Western Missouri Mental Health Center as well as a school psychologist in the Olathe, Kansas, public schools. Simpson received the 1992 Outstanding Scholarship Award from the University of Kansas School of Education.*

CHAPTER 19

Humbling Experiences and Significant Challenges: A Personal Perspective on Students with Emotional and Behavioral Disorders

An interesting and common activity among professionals who work with children and youth with emotional and behavioral disorders (E/BD) involves describing how each person came to commit their professional life to a group of children whom most individuals invest considerable effort in avoiding. When confronted with this soul-searching issue, some individuals note with pride that it was their "calling." Thus, in an almost religious sense, these individuals speak of their summons to work with troubled children. Others have described that they entered the field because they themselves (or a sibling) experienced emotional or behavioral difficulties as a child and thus may have a unique capacity or motivation to understand and work with problem children. Still others describe their migration to work with students with E/BD with trepidation, almost as if their journey were an admission of some type of character flaw. In my own case, special education as a career choice was a function of a variety of factors.

First, while I have never had a particularly deviant, disorderly, or troubled history, I have always found myself fascinated by individuals who did. I did not "run around" with the students with emotional and behavioral problems while I was a public school student. However, I routinely found myself watching them with great curiosity and informally interacting with these students. I spent considerable time trying to figure out why they did the things they did, and on more than one occasion I discussed with them various school issues, especially those related to their problems with faculty and school staff. Second, I had a sibling with emotional problems. While I might be cavalier and state that the family experiences associated with this situation are independent of my career choice, in all honesty I don't believe that to be the case. Finally, I attribute my work in special education partially to chance. As an undergraduate psychology major and as a master's student in psychology, I had limited contact with students in the special education department. Thus, it wasn't until I was working as a psychologist that I had the opportunity to interact and work with several talented special educators whose work seemed to be directly associated with my primary professional interests. These individuals, including Dick Whelan of the University of Kansas and Roger Kroth of the University of New Mexico, were the original models and impetus for my pursuing a career in special education.

My personal philosophy in working with children and youth with E/BD is based on a preference for pragmatic, empirically based models. While I generally prefer behavioral approaches, I consider myself to be eclectic. That is, I use and have used a number of instructional, curricular, and intervention alternatives that have an empirical, scientific base or that appear to have clinical or educational utility. This preference is associated with my belief that education and treatment of children and youth with E/BD should be based primarily on scientifically proven, best practices methods, as opposed to non–scientifically based legislative and policy enactments, value-driven advocacy programs, and attempts to "do the right thing," independent of a foundation for what the "right thing" is.

CURRENT STATUS OF E/BD EDUCATION

Knitzer, Steinberg, and Fleisch (1990) suggested that identification of children and youth with E/BD may depend on local tolerance levels and resources and on the student's race, class, or socioeconomic status, rather than individual needs. They also suggested that students are often identified because they are "mad, bad, sad and can't add" (p. 9) and because their teachers are unable to tolerate them, rather than because there were diagnoses based on valid clinical assessments. Moreover, recent attacks on the integrity and efficacy of special education (e.g., Shapiro, Loeb, & Bowermaster, 1993) suggest that little of value comes from the work of special educators. While these sobering indictments may (arguably) contain some degree of truth, they generally fail to recognize the overall worth and effectiveness of special education services for children and youth with disabilities, including those with E/BD. Thus, while there are numerous challenges facing the discipline, I am of the opinion that the profession has reason to be proud and to rightfully believe that progress is being made.

There are myriad issues and factors that might be considered relative to the current state of education of students with E/BD. One current trend that I think deserves discussion relates to attempts to radically reform education in this country and, specifically, the impact such reform and restructuring may have on students with E/BD.

That general and special education are currently under tremendous pressure to more effectively address the needs of students and society is very clear. Indeed, educational programs for all students, including those identified as E/BD, are undergoing significant changes in the manner in which they are structured and designed. However, school reform efforts have focused almost exclusively on students with disabilities, with little regard for children and youth with disabilities. The much proclaimed *America 2000: An Education Strategy* (U.S. Department of Education, 1991), for example, virtually ignored the needs of students with special needs. As further evidence of the lack of attention being given special education students in this era of school reform, Ysseldyke, Algozzine, and Thurlow (1992) observed that "in a summary of the 'education reform decade' (ETS Policy Information Center, 1990), there was not a single mention of students with disabilities or even special education" (p. 140). The National Council on Disability (1989) observed that "for the most part school reform efforts have not been directed toward addressing the special challenges that students with disabilities face" (p. 2), leading the Council to recommend that a national commission on excellence in the education of students with disabilities be established. Support for increased involvement by special education personnel in school reform has been voiced by a number of individuals and groups (Ysseldyke, Algozzine, & Thurlow, 1992).

Neglect of students with disabilities in school reform and restructuring enterprises has been a particular problem for students with E/BD (Leone, McLaughlin, & Meisel, 1992). Indeed, the potential impact of school reform initiatives on children and youth with E/BD is, in my opinion, one of the most pressing current issues in the education of students with E/BD. In this regard, identifying methods of facilitating successful education of students with E/BD in restructured and reformed schools—especially as related to increased inclusion and integration, merging general and special education, partnership formation (i.e., between schools and businesses, schools and parents), making curricular and instructional modifications, school choice initiatives, and assessment and evaluation modifications—will be a significant challenge now and well into the future.

WORKING DEFINITION OF E/BD

There is general agreement that the criteria and procedures used to identify students as E/BD are problematic. Central to this problem is the current educational definition of *seriously emotionally disturbed*, which has been characterized as vague and confusing (Forness, 1988; Wood, 1990). Because there exists a lack of agreement among professionals on the interpretation and application of the current definition and because of the belief that the current definition excludes students who need services (e.g., those with conduct disorders and those who are socially maladjusted), a new definition has been proposed by special education and mental health organizations, one that includes cultural and ethnic norms, expansion of the number of environments in which student problems are manifest, and use of multiple data sources (Council for Children with Behavioral Disorders, 1989). Advantages of the proposed definition include elimination of the current definition's exclusion of students with social maladjustment from special education services and diminution of students with conduct disorders being denied service opportunities. In my opinion these and other advantages of the proposed definition change would directly facilitate a more accurate diagnosis and appropriate services for students with E/BD; thus I am in favor of its adoption.

I am also of the opinion that any functional definition of children and youth with E/BD must consider a range of disability factors. Accordingly, I personally adhere to the notion that children with behavioral disorders are those with characteristics falling into three major categories: (a) feelings of personal discomfort and distress, as revealed through overt behavior, self-disclosure, physical symptoms (e.g., illness), and anxiety; (b) inefficiency in educational performance, as revealed through poor academic performance, avoidance behaviors (e.g., truancy, failure to do assigned work, frequent use of escape strategies during difficult or disliked subjects), and restricted functioning (e.g., behavioral rigidity, lack of sustained effort for academic exercises); and (c) poor interpersonal relationships (e.g., impulsiveness, inability to abide by rules and group customs, lack of acceptance by others, and withdrawal). I also include a fourth component in my personal working definition of E/BD: bizarre behavior, for those children and youth who demonstrate patterns such as delusions and hallucinations, loss of contact with reality, emotional blunting, shallow affect, and so forth. Admittedly, my personal working definition of E/BD lacks precision and probably would be difficult for others to reliably use. Nonetheless, I have found this working definition to serve my own needs quite well.

DIMENSIONS OF DEFINITION OVER THE CURRENT FEDERAL DEFINITION

I favor the adoption of the Mental Health and Special Education Coalition's definition proposal for a number of reasons, most of which have been thoroughly discussed by others (Coleman, 1992). These reasons include the following: (a) The proposed definition facilitates more reliable identification of children and youth with E/BD by clarifying definitional and diagnostic guidelines and sensitizing diagnosticians to environmental, age, cultural, and ethnic variables; (b) it broadens and clarifies the clinical categories associated with emotional and behavioral problems of children and youth; (c) it expands the notion of what constitutes a problem of school performance to include more than academic difficulties; (d) it eliminates the automatic exclusion of students with social maladjustment (and conduct disorders) from E/BD eligibility; and (e) it narrows the gap between clinical and educational perceptions of what constitutes an emotional/behavioral problem. There is a question, however, of whether the proposed definition will actually be adopted to replace the current definition of *seriously emotionally disturbed* under the Individuals with Disabilities Education Act. In my opinion, criticisms of the proposed definition have been based on political and financial considerations rather than conceptual and logical issues. Thus, if the definition fails to be adopted, it will be for reasons other than what it offers the profession.

My own personal conceptualization of E/BD (i.e., feelings of personal discomfort and distress, inefficiency in educational performance, poor interpersonal relationships, and bizarre behavior) reveals my preference for a pragmatic model that allows me to conceptualize salient elements of emotional and behavioral disorders unencumbered by policy-oriented definitions. Thus, while I recognize the need for agreed-upon generic definitions and conceptualizations, I also think it is important for professionals to develop their own working definitions of E/BD.

RELATIONSHIP OF EMOTIONAL DISTURBANCE AND BEHAVIORAL DISORDER

I am of the strong opinion that it is fruitless to attempt to discriminate between emotional disturbance and behavioral disorders. There are, of course, those who contend that such distinctions can and should be made, and that special education should be reserved for students who exhibit internally perceived disturbedness (Kelly, 1992) or who otherwise display symptoms of psychopathology that transcend behavioral problems (Slenkovich, 1983). Proponents of making such distinctions contend that children and youth with conduct disorders and other types of behavior problems are in control of their behavior, perceive themselves to be normal, operate in a purposeful manner relative to their behavior, and are frequently reinforced for their aggressive and aberrant behavior.

Accordingly, those who argue for discriminating between emotional and behavioral problems contend that students with behavior problems can best be served by disciplinary measures and other procedures commonly available within general education classrooms and thus should not qualify for special education services. Of course, many school administrators are in favor of such distinctions because it allows them greater flexibility in using suspension and expulsion alternatives, and making distinctions between "true emotional disturbance" and behavior disorders allows administrators the luxury of avoiding potential due-process conflicts. In spite of all the attention given this topic, there are some basic truths that I think negate making reliable distinctions between children and youth with emotional problems and those with behavior disorders. First, there is overwhelming evidence that making reliable distinctions among students with conduct disorders and other externalizing problems and those with emotional disorders is virtually impossible (Kavale, Forness, & Alper, 1986). Neither the measurement tools nor the theoretical models currently exist to allow such distinctions to be made reliably. Second, there is strong evidence that students with E/BD have a variety of problems, rather than a disorder that falls neatly into either a behavioral disorder or emotional disturbance category. Many of the students with whom I work present with a variety of excesses and deficits, including conduct problems, depression, anxiety, and so forth. Finally, it is irresponsible for students with certain types of behavior problems to be denied appropriate services.

MEANINGFUL EDUCATIONAL EXPERIENCES FOR STUDENTS WITH E/BD

In spite of the progress we have made in meeting the needs of children with E/BD, there are obviously a number of things we need to do better. Knitzer et al. (1990) noted that only about 10% of students placed in E/BD programs return to full-time regular education, that only about 30% of these children and youth perform at or above grade level in their academic subjects, and that only one third are able to pass minimum competency tests. Moreover, there is an alarming dropout rate for students with E/BD (U.S. Department of Education, 1992, 1993). Transition issues are also evident, as revealed by findings from a study conducted by Neel, Meadows, Levine, and Edgar (1988), who reported that only 60% of the youths with disabilities in their study who had graduated or "aged out" were employed.

Counseling and support services are also lacking, as revealed by findings of Knitzer et al. (1990). These researchers reported that more than 50% of the districts they surveyed indicated that they did not provide counseling services and that when services were provided, they were on a short-term basis and generally were paid for by parents. Community mental health programs, therapy, and crisis intervention services were also found to be lacking, as were parent and family involvement programs. Finally, there is overwhelming evidence that students with E/BD who return to public school programs from institutional, hospital, and other restrictive placements are provided limited support, and that phase-in and transfer services are inadequate or nonexistent.

While these factors bode poorly for children and youth with E/BD, they do point to programs and experiences that these students require. That is, we need to do a better job of keeping children with E/BD in school and giving them the skills and knowledge to obtain and keep jobs subsequent to their graduation. We also need to make sure that these students and their families have opportunities for counseling and therapy services at school. Finally, there is an obvious need to do a better job of working with community mental health programs and other services that are involved in providing services for children and youth with E/BD and their families.

INCLUSION OF STUDENTS WITH E/BD IN GENERAL EDUCATION

General education inclusion of students with E/BD dominates other issues in the field, and there is every indication that it will remain the preeminent issue for at least the next few years. Justification for and decisions regarding inclusion have been value oriented rather than scientifically based. That is, inclusion is justified by references to "the moral and just thing to do" rather than by scientifically established benefits (Sailor, 1991; Stainback & Stainback, 1990, 1992). In this regard, I agree with Lieberman's (1992) analysis of full inclusion:

> There seem to be two different camps of full integration advocates. One group does not attempt to justify its position in logical, pragmatic, or curricular terms. When asked what has to be done in order to make full integration work successfully, they generally reply that nothing has to be done. Just do it. Just doing it will make it happen. (p. 22)

Because of educators' reluctance to use scientific methodology to validate value-driven decisions related to inclusion, the profession has had few reliable guidelines to assist it in making prudent judgments related to including students with E/BD in general education classrooms.

In my opinion there are several significant logical flaws related to full inclusion of students with E/BD. First and foremost, full inclusion has been advocated for *every* student. Thus, the individual needs of students with behavioral disorders become secondary to exposing students to general classroom expectations and their peers without disabilities, regardless of their ability to profit from these experiences and to be satisfactorily integrated in general classrooms. Second, variables related to functional life skills development (e.g., social skill, vocational, community living) are supplanted by the purported benefits of integrated school experiences. Finally, advocates of full inclusion of students with E/BD appear to have ignored empirically validated procedures in favor of a model that reflects not what we know to be true but instead how some individuals would prefer things to be.

I also think it is important for educators to challenge the moral imperative of full inclusion, i.e., that full inclusion is somehow the moral highroad or always the right thing to do. Kauffman (1992) poignantly makes the point that doing the "right thing" has various interpretations when he relates an incident involving himself and several students watching a video called *Regular Lives* (Goodwin & Wurzburg, 1987). In this incident, Kauffman noted that he was particularly struck by the closing commentary on the practice of including all students with disabilities in ordinary schools and classrooms:

> "It really doesn't matter whether or not it works. It does work, and that's great. But even if it didn't work it would still be the thing to do, because it's right. It's treating people with dignity. It's caring about people and letting people know that they're worthwhile humans."

> At the moment we punched the VCR's rewind button, actor Wilford Brimley appeared on a regular commercial channel, hawking instant oatmeal. 'It's the right thing to do,' he advised with great sincerity. The humor of this entirely fortuitous event was not lost on us, but our burst of laughter was followed by the saddening realization that much of the advocacy in our field is painfully close to advertising 'hype', unsettlingly like the deceptive 'sound bite' that makes a politician's chicanery attractive to voters. We understood that 'right' has clear ethical connotations as used by the speaker in *Regular Lives*; its ethical meaning as used by Wilford Brimley is, at best, obscure. Nevertheless, this juxtaposition of statements about "rightness" prompted us to think more about what is 'right' about inclusion. (p. 3)

The full inclusion debate too often has been reduced to superficial arguments over who is right, who is ethical and moral, and who is a true advocate for students with behavioral and emotional problems. Much of this shallow and baseless rhetoric obscures the real issue of what is best for students with E/BD through claims of moral and ethical high ground and denouncements of nonbelievers as not caring about students with emotional problems.

I am of the opinion that full inclusion of children and youth with E/BD is the right thing to do only if it benefits them or their normally developing peers, or if it is beneficial for both groups. That is, "the right thing to do," in my estimation, is that which provides the most educational and social benefits, not something that someone or some group considers appropriate because it is congruent with their value system, is a fashionable movement, or is an alternative that is touted as the preferred option but in reality is an unsupported action of misguided people. I am in agreement with Kauffman's (1993) assessment that "empirical evidence does not indicate that we currently have effective and reliable strategies for improving and sustaining outcomes for all students in regular classrooms" (p. 8).

PREFERENCES FOR DELIVERY OF SERVICES

I am of the opinion that service delivery models have come to be used synonymously with the location in which a student receives his or her education. That is, rather than critically examining what it is we should be doing with children and youth with E/BD, we have become spellbound with the location of a student's education. In this regard, I am of the opinion that preoccupation with placement of students with E/BD and other disabilities in full-time general education programs has confused and diminished the real task of effectively addressing the needs of children and youth, which I think is the real test of effective service delivery. Thus, I am of the opinion that a range of service options (e.g., collaborative, resource room, self-contained) should be available to best meet the needs of students with E/BD, and that each option must focus primarily on effectively addressing students' needs. Thus, the true test of service delivery is translating a range of effective curriculum and intervention options to meet the individual needs of unique students. In this regard, I agree with Ensminger and Dangel (1992) in their assessment that "best practices" for curriculum content and instructional format should include holistic/cognitive learning approaches, human motivational learning, and cooperative learning.

These elements may be implemented with students with E/BD via thematic curriculum content generated from student-chosen, high-interest, self-directed learning materials; opportunities for a variety of learning activities, coordinated by a teacher who serves as facilitator (e.g., Knitzer et al. [1990] suggested integrating social skill training into authentic social situations through athletics and extracurricular school clubs); limited penalties for formative academic mistakes; teacher and staff respect for children and youth as individuals and as learners; frequent active learning opportunities (e.g., group class discussions, hypotheses testing, hands-on activities, and problem solving); and cooperative peer learning experiences. Service delivery for students with behavior disorders also must address issues of behavior management, and these elements should be linked directly to the curriculum.

Service delivery, curricular considerations, and instruction also should be designed to address postschool transition. In this sense I advocate for comprehensive, secondary-education transitional models initiated in elementary and middle-school programs, such as those described by Frank, Sitlington, and Carson (1991), which allow for community-based career instruction and experiences and use of adult community personnel who are trained to work collaboratively with schools to support students with E/BD as they move to postsecondary settings. Finally, service delivery systems must be coordinated with community service programs in order to provide social support, facilitate skill generalization, and assist with employment opportunities.

Community service programs also should focus on assisting students and their families to identify and use recreational resources, respite care programs, parent and family support groups, and so forth. Moreover, effective service delivery requires that an effective link be formed between institutional settings, social service settings (e.g., juvenile justice), and other community-based agencies.

INCIDENCE ISSUES

There is absolutely no doubt that the needs of children and youth with E/BD are largely unserved and underserved (e.g., U.S. Department of Education, 1993). However, in my opinion, the prevalence of emotional and behavioral disorders has not significantly increased. Nonetheless, there appear to be current trends that make it appear that the prevalence is accelerating: (a) an increased incidence of students at risk of school failure and other problems; (b) increased aggression and violence in schools and communities; (c) limited availability of restrictive options for students with E/BD; and (d) increased awareness of mental health problems of children and youth and improved identification and recognition capabilities.

Morrison (1990) noted, "Every eight seconds of the school day, an American student drops out, according to the Children's Defense Fund. Every 67 seconds, a teenager has a baby. Every seven minutes a child is arrested for drugs. Every year the U.S. school system graduates 700,000 young people who cannot read their diplomas" (p. 8). These data clearly point to the fact that numerous factors and circumstances put many children and youth at risk for educational failure and other problems, and that students are experiencing increased levels of stress and emotional anguish. While the majority of students "at risk" are not E/BD, they do present with a variety of problems associated with these variables (e.g., behavioral problems secondary to stress and family problems) (Frisby et al., 1991).

A second element associated with issues of E/BD prevalence and incidence relates to increased school and community aggression and violence. That educators are facing more aggression and violence is undeniable

(Simpson, Myles, Walker, Ormsbee, & Downing, 1991). For instance, the Office of Juvenile Justice and Delinquency Prevention (1989) reported that 76,000 aggravated assaults and 3 million attempted or completed assaults, rapes, robberies, or thefts occurred within school buildings or on school property. A recent national survey, conducted by Harris (1993) for the Harvard University School of Public Health, indicated that 39% of youths in the United States reported knowing someone who had been killed or wounded by gunfire; more than one third of the students perceived that the easy availability of guns made it unlikely that they would live to an old age. Children and youth with E/BD often are prone to violent episodes; however, it is also abundantly clear that, statistically, violence and aggression is primarily a problem of students who are not disabled. Yet, it is easy to understand why many individuals would confuse these problems with an increased incidence of emotional and behavioral disorders.

A third issue associated with perceived increases in E/BD prevalence and incidence relates to fewer restrictive options for students with severe emotional and behavioral problems. That is, deinstitutionalization, preference for programs in least restrictive settings, and a general decrease in restrictive treatment and educational options related to various social and health care movements (e.g., limited health insurance support for residential program treatment) have resulted in students with E/BD becoming more prominent in general education classrooms and public school settings. Thus, while the incidence of E/BD among school-age children has not increased, these students are more evident, making it appear that there are currently more of these individuals than in previous years. This situation is exacerbated by limited or poor-quality transition services when students with E/BD return from hospital and residential placements to less restrictive settings, and when transition from acute care hospitals to public schools occurs without support of community mental health services.

Finally, increased awareness of mental health problems of children and youth and improved identification and recognition capabilities appear to have sensitized professionals and the public to the emotional and behavioral problems of children and youth. Thus, while these problems have always existed, they currently are much more recognized and discussed.

ROLE RELATIONSHIP DIFFERENCES AMONG VARIOUS AGENCIES AND PROVIDERS WHO SERVE STUDENTS WITH E/BD

Virtually every professional and organization in support of students with E/BD has recognized that these children and youth and their parents and families have multiple needs that require attention by appropriate organizations and agencies. Accordingly, comprehensive and convenient services must be available. It is my opinion that public schools are in the best position to orchestrate such services.

Taking the necessary steps to position schools to effectively coordinate comprehensive and convenient services will not be particularly easy. However, there are initial efforts that I think will produce desired outcomes. First, I think it is important that schools and communities work to create and train teams of school and community professionals and parents empowered to provide a range of services for students with E/BD and their parents and families. As recommended by Comer (1980) and Lauffer (1978), teams consisting of school administrators, related services personnel, teachers, professionals representing community organizations (e.g., mental health), and parents should regularly meet to discuss and offer solutions to various student and family problems and issues. These teams also may coordinate support programs between and across agencies and organizations and act as liaisons between professionals.

A second basic step in coordinating and improving services would be to train professionals to more effectively interact and work with students with E/BD and to become more effective in working with these students' parents and families. Improved preservice and in-service education on collaboration and team functioning with parents and families is an initial step in improving services. In this regard, staff training and development may include understanding and responding to parent and family needs, accommodating family diversity (e.g., cultural), working with single-parent and reconstituted families, developing rapport in family–professional relationships, and so forth.

Similarly, training also should focus on facilitating parent and family involvement in children's treatment and educational programs. A third important step in improving service coordination involves training school professionals to more effectively work and collaborate with other professionals. Thus, teachers and other school personnel must expand and strengthen school–community partnerships and work to establish and maintain effective communication systems between educators and community and state mental health, social service, and other agencies (juvenile corrections). In my opinion, resources must also be invested to train parents and families of students with E/BD to interact and work effectively with educators and other professionals. That is, parents and families of children and youth with E/BD should be assisted in learning how to understand community agencies and how to work with professionals and advocate for their children.

YEAR 2000 TRENDS

I have never been particularly good at predicting the future. Nonetheless, I think there are several trends that are underway that will continue into the twenty-first century. First, I think it is beneficial and inevitable that efforts to serve the needs of students with E/BD and their families will involve increased cooperative efforts among public schools, community service programs, private entities, and colleges and universities. This is particularly likely to occur on an expanded basis in cooperative programs between schools and private businesses and organizations. Indeed, these collaborative relationships are increasingly evident. While these relationships up until now have been indirect and limited (e.g., material and equipment contributions), they will likely expand and become more functional in the future. Interagency collaboration will also hopefully increase and improve in the twenty-first century. Thus, I expect to see public and private agencies and services joining force with the public schools in support of students with E/BD. The impetus for agencies to pursue such collaborative relationships stems from legal initiatives, limited financial resources, and public concern over fiscal responsibility of service providers who work with individuals with disabilities.

I am also of the opinion that the twenty-first century will see increased attention for children and youth at risk for school failure and other problems. I think there will be increases in resources allocated to address the needs of students who are not E/BD but who have significant emotional and behavioral problems, which if not dealt with will become more serious. In terms of staff preparation for meeting the needs of at-risk students, I am in agreement with Frisby et al. (1991) in their assessment that teachers need basic skills related to risk issues, including awareness of factors that create risk for children and youth, awareness of cultural and linguistic diversity and at-risk variables, and training in collaborating with others in support of at-risk students.

I expect that students with E/BD will continue to receive their education in general education classrooms and integrated programs. While I am of the opinion that a range of service options will continue to be the accepted model and that the full inclusion movement will become far less of an issue, children and youth with E/BD most likely will continue to be instructed primarily in integrated schools and general education classrooms. However, I am hopeful that far greater attention will be paid to supporting students with E/BD in integrated settings. Provisions such as support services and modifications needed to effectively accommodate students with E/BD and development of supportive attitudes toward students with E/BD will hopefully be common in the twenty-first century. Integrated placement of students with E/BD in the twenty-first century obviously will require much better preparation of general educators to teach students with diverse needs. Accordingly, a single course about disabling conditions that emphasizes categorical characteristics will no longer be sufficient. Rather, understandings and skills related to educating students with emotional and behavioral problems must be infused throughout the preservice curriculum and reinforced and updated through regular in-service training.

Another trend that is predictable is the continuation of service delivery models based on collaborative consultation. The prevailing "two-box" system of separate general and special education delivery systems is more and more being supplanted by collaborative team strategies, and this trend will continue into the twenty-first century. Thus, special education consultants will need to be able to work cooperatively with general classroom teachers to develop interventions for specific educational problems, and special educators working with and coordinating a variety of resources will increase. Moreover, it is likely that these collaborative efforts will be expanded to include more nonschool systems such as medicine, mental health, corrections, social welfare, and so forth.

I am also of the opinion that recognition of the importance of attracting and retaining competent general and special educators for students with E/BD will increase in the twenty-first century. Thus, I am optimistic that significant investments will be made to attract and retain talented educators to serve children and youth with E/BD, including individuals from diverse groups who may be uniquely qualified to understand and respond to the needs of underrepresented populations.

Finally, it is evident that use of technology with students with E/BD will continue to increase into the twenty-first century. While the rapid development of technology such as fiber optics, compressed video, and satellite communications makes it difficult to reliably speculate on the total extent of its future uses, it is abundantly clear that technology will play a significant role. For instance, use of virtual reality technology to improve social skill training curriculum and procedures, enhanced computer programming to support cognitive and academic skill training programs, and videotaped practice of academic and social skills by students with teacher feedback and self-evaluation are only a few of the potential uses of technology with children and youth with E/BD.

REFERENCES

Coleman, M. (1992). *Behavior disorders: Theory and practice.* Boston: Allyn & Bacon.

Comer, J. P. (1980). *School power: Implications of an intervention project.* New Haven, CT: Yale University Press.

Council for Children with Behavioral Disorders. (1989). *A new proposed definition and terminology to replace "serious emotional disturbance" in the Education of the Handicapped Act.* Reston, VA: Author.

Ensminger, E., & Dangel, H. (1992). The foxfire pedagogy: A confluence of best practices for special education. *Focus on Exceptional Children, 24*(7), 1–15.

ETS Policy Information Center. (1990). *The education reform decade*. Princeton, NJ: Educational Testing Service.

Forness, S. (1988). Planning for the needs of children with serious emotional disturbance: The National Special Education and Mental Health Coalition. *Behavioral Disorders, 13*(2), 127–139.

Frank, A., Sitlington, P., & Carson, R. (1991). Transition of adolescents with behavior disorders: Is it successful? *Behavioral Disorders, 16*(3), 180–191.

Frisby, C. L., Heflin, L. J., Altman, R., Shaw, S. F., Collier, C., Elliott, R., Ochsner, G. J., & Fleischner, J. (1991). Innovative practices for meeting the needs of students who are at-risk. In L. Bullock & R. Simpson (Eds.), *Emerging trends in special education and implications for training personnel* (pp. 111–123). Denton: University of North Texas.

Goodwin, T., & Wurzburg, G. (1987). *Regular lives* [Videotape]. Syracuse, NY: Syracuse University Press.

Harris, L. (1993). *Harvard University School of Public Health survey on child and youth violence*. Cambridge, MA: Harvard University School of Public Health.

Kauffman, J. (1992). Preface. In K. R. Howe & O. B. Miramontes (Eds.), *The ethics of special education* (pp. 1–5). New York: Teachers College Press.

Kauffman, J. (1993). How we might achieve the radical reform of special education. *Exceptional Children, 60*(1), 6–16.

Kavale, K., Forness, S., & Alper, A. (1986). Research in behavioral disorders/emotional disturbance: A survey of subject identification criteria. *Behavioral Disorders, 11*(3), 159–167.

Kelly, E. J. (1992). *Conduct problem-emotional problem interventions: A holistic perspective*. East Aurora, NY: Slosson.

Knitzer, J., Steinberg, Z., & Fleisch, B. (1990). *At the schoolhouse door: An examination of programs and policies for children with behavior and emotional problems*. New York: Bank Street College of Education.

Lauffer, A. (1978). *Social planning at the community level*. Englewood Cliffs, NJ: Prentice-Hall.

Leone, P. E., McLaughlin, M. J., & Meisel, S. M. (1992). School reform and adolescents with behavior disorders. *Focus on Exceptional Children, 25*(1), 1–15.

Lieberman, L. M. (1992). Preserving special education . . . For those who need it. In W. Stainback & S. Stainback (Eds.), *Controversial issues confronting special education* (pp. 13–25). Boston: Allyn & Bacon.

Morrison, A. (1990). Saving our schools. *Fortune, 121*, 8–10.

National Council on Disability. (1989). *The education of students with disabilities: Where do we stand?* Washington, DC: Author.

Neel, R., Meadows, N., Levine, P., & Edgar, E. (1988). What happens after special education: A statewide follow-up study of secondary students who have behavioral disorders. *Behavioral Disorders, 13*(3), 209–216.

Office of Juvenile Justice and Delinquency Prevention. (1989). *Report of acts of aggression and violence*. Washington, DC: Author.

Sailor, W. (1991). Special education in the restructured school. *Remedial and Special Education, 12*(6), 8–22.

Shapiro, J., Loeb, P., & Bowermaster, D. (1993, December). Separate and unequal. *U.S. News and World Report, 115* (23), 46–60.

Simpson, R. L., Myles, B. S., Walker, B. L., Ormsbee, C. K., & Downing, J. A. (1991). *Programming for aggressive and violent students*. Reston, VA: Council for Exceptional Children.

Slenkovich, J. E. (1983). *PL 94-142 as applied to DSM III diagnoses*. Cupertino, CA: Kinghorn Press.

Stainback, S., & Stainback, W. (1992). Schools as inclusive communities. In W. Stainback & S. Stainback (Eds.), *Controversial issues confronting special education* (pp. 29–43). Boston: Allyn & Bacon.

Stainback, W., & Stainback, S. (1990). *Support networks for inclusive schooling: Interdependent integrated education*. Baltimore: Brookes.

U.S. Department of Education. (1991). *America 2000: An education strategy*. Washington, DC: Author.

U.S. Department of Education. (1992). *Fourteenth annual report to Congress on the implementation of the Individuals with Disabilities Education Act*. Washington, DC: Author.

U.S. Department of Education. (1993). *Fifteenth annual report to Congress on the implementation of the Individuals with Disabilities Education Act*. Washington, DC: Author.

Wood, F. H. (1990). Issues in the education of behaviorally disordered students. In M. C. Wang, M. C. Reynolds, & H. J. Walberg (Eds.), *Special education research and practice: Synthesis of findings* (pp. 101–118). New York: Pergamon.

Ysseldyke, J. E., Algozzine, B., & Thurlow, M. L. (1992). *Critical issues in special education* (2nd ed.). Boston: Houghton Mifflin.

JAMES R. TOMPKINS
Appalachian State University

James Tompkins received his PhD in educational psychology from the Catholic University of America in 1971. He was coordinator at the Unit of Education of Emotionally Disturbed Children, Division of Training Programs, Bureau of Education for the Handicapped in Washington, DC, from 1965 to 1971. He has served as director of the Governor's Child Advocacy Council in North Carolina and as an adjunct professor at the University of North Carolina, Chapel Hill. Tompkins also has worked as a consultant in public and parochial elementary schools and in residential treatment of children who are emotionally disturbed. He currently is a professor of special education in the area of emotionally disturbed at Appalachian State University. Tompkins recently co-authored a text on the use of milieu therapy entitled Surviving in Schools in the 1990s: Strategic Management of School Environments.

CHAPTER 20

Special Education Movement in the Education of Students Who Are Seriously Emotionally Disturbed
Motto: *Move as Slowly as You Can*

The gift of nature to man responsible for his rise from the oozing sludge by the edge of the sea in the Middle East to the dust laden waste of the moon by the Sea of Tranquility, is his unprogrammed brain. The task of education for each era is to use the accomplishments of the past as a guide to the kind of programming necessary for the next state and not, as much of education is today—to use the brain as an information retrieval system for information better stored on tape or microfilm. Today we must, as that education, concern ourselves with the programming needs of kids presently in school, in order to serve them best for a life of living in a tomorrow that is beyond our capacity to anticipate or predict. I have suggested that both for individual and species survival in the spirit of individualism, such programming must be guided by concern for the accomplishment of three goals: (1) Individuals must love life—fun, joy, aesthetics, literature, the arts, etc.; (2) They must love truth, i.e., the solution of problems through rational inquiry—scholarship, discipline, curiosity, etc.; and finally, (3) They must love Man—i.e., we all must possess compassionate concern for the welfare of others. (Trippe, 1970, p. 1)

One of the more troubling paradoxes of our time is the apparent positive correlation between human misery and the accumulation of knowledge and skills for the alleviation of that misery. Our increasing knowledge about man and his institutions is not accompanied by reduction in his failure to have meaningful social participation. Inner-city violence, violence in schools, and fundamental breakdown in family life suggest the extent of the failure of some of our most basic institutions.

At the same time, there is increased "participation" in those institutions such as correctional facilities, psychiatric hospitals, and special education classes whose social function is to contain and remedy. School dropout rates, populations of juvenile correctional facilities, numbers of children seen in mental health clinics, increases in special education populations, and rising admissions of children to psychiatric hospitals have been documented and serve as a reminder that all is not well. Both public and professional concern calls for reexamination of the knowledge we have accumulated. We need to reexamine the following: (a) the relevance and utility of our formulations of the issues, (b) the institutions that represent our formulations, (c) the logistics of deployment of the professional cadre who dispense the services based on our knowledge, and (d) the extent to which our professional practices with people are actually consistent with our best understanding. We must seek to expand our knowledge of problems experienced by our children. To do less is to become increasingly irrelevant as professionals and to reinforce those phenomena that are destructive to our children.

SERIOUSLY EMOTIONALLY DISTURBED: THE ADOPTION OF A DEFINITION

The now-accepted definition of *seriously emotionally disturbed* (SED), authored by Eli Bower (Bower & Kaczynski, 1968), emerged with the establishment of the Bureau of Education for the Handicapped (BEH). In 1968, James Gallagher, appointed the first associate commissioner for the newly established BEH, was requested by congressional directive to establish definitions and prevalence figures for all disabled or special education categories. The two special education areas that were most controversial were the areas of seriously emotionally disturbed (SED) and learning disabilities (LD). The National Advisory Committee for BEH developed the LD definition under the leadership of Sam Kirk. The other categorical definitions were recommended by the various expert specialists in BEH.

In 1968, Gallagher directed me, then coordinator of the Unit on the Education of Emotional Disturbance, to recommend a SED definition. These times were hectic in our first year in the Bureau. A doctoral-level general educator from the Bureau of Elementary and Secondary Education (BESE) was "detailed" (assigned temporarily to assist BEH personnel) for all definition development. I persuaded him and others to give me time to reach out to the experts in the field in this special education area to construe a definition that reflected wide consensus. All agreed! However, a week or so after this meeting with the BESE person, his program assistant, also detailed to BEH, walked into my office and announced that she was going to develop the SED definition unilaterally, independently of my efforts. With this new and strange development, I sent a memo (see Appendix 20.1) to the leadership in BEH. This memo recommended immediate action but *only* as a temporary position until the experts throughout the country had time to consider the question. This memo clearly stated a request for the National Advisory Committee to include in their meeting the problem of providing an acceptable definition of children with serious emotional disturbance. At the same time, for expedience and for an interim period, Bower's definition was offered until the committee held their deliberations.

The National Advisory Council of BEH met but did not review or study this problem, and, as a direct result, the BEH adopted the Bower definition. However, following this adoption, special education experts in the area of emotional disturbance did convene in Washington and endorsed the SED definition as authored by Bower.

Since 1968, this definition has been the official position of Congress, as expressed in P.L. 94-142, as well as the Department of Education and by most state education agencies. Neither I nor the conference participants submitted any exclusionary or qualifying amendments on the Bower definition that was offered in my memo to BEH personnel. Therefore, the section in the Council for Children with Behavioral Disorders (CCBD; 1969, p. 2) position paper, "Historical and Legal Precedent . . . ," is unequivocally aligned with BEH, Congress, and experts in this special education area from onset of the definition adoption and use for 1968.

During a November, 1968, BEH-sponsored conference on the seriously emotionally disturbed, Eli Bower, Lawrence Peter, Grace Kaczynski, Don Mahler, and others who were in attendance at the conference recommended criteria to delineate what should be included in the definition if another or any definition is to be adopted. Any adopted definition:

1. should lead to effective remedial programs in and out of the school setting.
2. should be understandable to the layperson, especially legislative laypersons.
3. should not have unnecessary connotations.
4. would be appropriate to school and to present conditions.
5. should be stated in terms of general educational objectives and student–teacher roles.
6. would be related to social objectives.
7. should center in observable behavior.
8. should include the degree and deviation of the problem.
9. should reflect multiple causation.[1]

---

[1] It should be noted here that these criteria were never published or disseminated for discussion by the practitioners in the field. This is the first time that they have been placed into publication for the field's edification at large.

To summarize these nine criteria, the definition should be school based; clearly understood; as positive as possible; appropriate to present conditions; related to teacher–child relationships; and relevant to important skills in the student's role, such as impulse control and attention, and to important skills in the teacher's role (Bower & Kaczynski, 1968).

Recently, Tompkins-McGill and I published a textbook, *Surviving in Schools in the 1990s: Strategic Management of School Environments* (1993), on the education of disturbed children and refer to a definition that we have proposed. Several characteristics were outlined, with cautions that the following indicators should be reflected in children to a marked or serious extent and should be chronic or of high frequency:

- They are at the average or above average level of intellectual functioning.
- They are failing most academic subjects, usually failing two or more years behind in academic achievement.
- They are socially alienated. They have few social skills and enjoy few or no meaningful interpersonal relationships.
- Their behavior is so seriously inappropriate that it interferes with their own and often other children's learning progress.
- Their behavior may get them in trouble with the law or other authorities in their lives and contribute to their isolation from their peers and adult support systems.
- They are often depressed, but their depression may be expressed as angry, hostile, acting-out behavior as well as the typical withdrawn behavior usually associated with depression.
- Their self esteem is low.
- They may have psycho-somatic complaints. (Tompkins & Tompkins-McGill, 1993, pp. 6–7).

The similarities of our position with the current federal SED definition is clear. I concur with the Executive Committee of the CCBD that conduct disorder is one of the several behavioral patterns subsumed under the behavioral disorder/emotional disturbance label. We simply have no diagnostic or definitional criteria to make valid discriminations between social maladjustment, conduct disorder, and emotional disturbance. When I presented the Bower definition to BEH, I assumed that Bower held this position and I continue this belief (Bower, 1982, 1989). If in the future a new definition is adopted, it should include three important characteristics: (a) references to educational consequences, (b) provision for different levels or degrees of consequences, and (c) recognition that these conditions and consequences can exist in conjunction with other disabilities.

A basic problem with an educational diagnosis of emotional disturbance is that we are asking a social–educational system to undertake a serious task in which school teachers and administrators are chastised for not supporting programs when they have not been given the problem in terms they can understand. It seems that special educators are resistant to restating the problem of definition in educational terms. Too often the new definitions and descriptions look much like the old. Almost without exception, the definition of the children to be served is based on pathology, and admission requires a clinical judgment that is largely subjective in reality (Mahler, personal communication, October 31, 1968).

CONTEMPORARY STATUS OF TROUBLED CHILDREN

> Behavior and discipline problems in schools have become epidemic, spreading far beyond those children who have already been labeled or are in special education. Concerns in schools about children's behavior have moved from gum chewing and noise making to drug and alcohol abuse, assault, arson, pregnancy, suicide, and robbery. Children who are not considered as having special needs also may exhibit unacceptable behavior and social and effective difficulties requiring management in micro-settings across the entire school environment. So-called "normal" students have notable though episodic behaviors that appear like temporary disabilities, such as regression to younger developmental behaviors or acting-out fears and conflicts through aggression or other unacceptable behavior. Regular teachers must deal with a wide spectrum of student problems in their classroom, but they lack the training or support that would aid them in this endeavor. Rather than improvise, these teachers need to be able to individualize significant program approaches that meet the needs of their special clientele. (Tompkins & Tompkins-McGill, 1993, p. 8)

The scope of the problem in the education of children who are emotionally disturbed is complicated. The numbers of children who are troubled have increased 33.2% over the past 20 years. Very few troubled children are placed in general classes. They are usually separated in special classes or are pushed out or drop out of school. These children are the least served, have the fewest programs, and have the least number of in-force teachers, yet they are the most inexpensive children to serve in public schools in comparison with other children with disabilities. No one really knows how many disturbed children there are in the United States. Due to the confusion and disagreement on the definition of troubled children, the reported numbers of these children vary depending on the definition. However, it has been reported that teachers can predict up to 69.3% of a given population as disturbed (Tompkins & Tompkins-McGill, 1993).

Adolescents go virtually unserved, and children in other age ranges go unreported. Government and private estimates range from 2% to 15% of the school-age population. Children and youth age 10 to 17 commit more than half of all serious crimes in the United States, and during the past decade almost 2 million children under age 18 were arrested and adjudicated. Millions of children are involved in violence in schools, drug abuse, teenage pregnancy, and child physical and sexual abuse. There are more than 300 cases reported of children killing their parents, and 90% of these children have been abused. Statistics indicate that in the United States about 500,000 children and youth live without parents in detention centers, hospitals, foster homes, and mental health centers; it is predicted by 1995 that the number may reach 840,000. On any given night, 100,000 of these children are homeless (Tompkins & Tompkins-McGill, 1993).

The Institute of Medicine Committee (1989) suggested that 12% to 22% of American children, or 14 million children, under the age of 18 are mentally ill. On the average, approximately 25% of this estimate get medical assistance and another 25% receive special education assistance (Tompkins & McGill, 1988). The number of juveniles arrested for murder and manslaughter climbed 93% from 1982 to 1991 (Children's Defense Fund, 1994); arrests of persons 15 years of age and younger for violent crimes increased 100%. In Grades 9 through 12, 20% of students reported that they carried a weapon to school at least once, including knives, clubs, and firearms (Ferrell, 1994).

According to Ayers (1994), the number of children with disabilities between the ages of 6 to 17 receiving services was 4,272,101 in the 1991–1992 school year. Of this total, 0.89% of these children receiving services were seriously emotionally disturbed (at a drop of 0.01 percent from the 1990–1991 school year). The total number of children with SED getting services was 392,559 for 1991–1992 school year (at the 2% estimate of total school population). Only 45.2% of 392,559 children with SED completed school. About 30% of the children receiving services are minorities (Ayers, 1994; Tompkins & McGill, 1988). In addition, of all the special education areas, the area of SED is one of three categories that have the highest need and the most considerable shortage of programs and teachers. Teacher attrition rates in some states go as high as 50% to 60% of teachers in the SED area.

Imponderable federal accounting of students with SED from the U.S. Department of Education (1992) indicated that about 400,000 students in the United States, or approximately 0.1 percent of the school-age population, are identified as children with SED. The National Institute for Mental Health, Joint Commission on the Mental Health of Children, and recently the Institute of Medicine predict 10% of school-age population as behavioral disordered (Tompkins & McGill, 1989; Institute of Medicine, 1989; Center & Kaufman, 1993).

Finally, federal and other reporting sources indicate that approximately 0.80% of identified children with SED are served in regular schools but in isolated specialized programs, 10% in regular classes, and the remainder in specialized other settings (Steinberg & Knitzer, 1992).

Given these statistics by recent documentation, it is ironic that in 1968 the BEH leadership elected the 2% estimate of the school-age population as SED on the basis of political expediency. Their position was that a credibility gap would be generated between BEH and Congress (during hearings) if the estimate figure was proposed higher and would jeopardize the funding of other special education categories.

Without a national parent advocacy group and with conflicting and confusing professional muddling in this special education area, I believe that the growth and progress of better and more services for children who are disturbed has hardly progressed in the last 25 years. In the late 1960s, a small group of educational leadership in the CCBD during the Council for Exceptional Children's (CEC) convention in Denver issued a proclamation that charged that special educators had allowed themselves to perpetuate the means of harming children through practices that shield American education from its failures. The leaders in the area of emotional disturbance then called on CEC to:

1. Seek a definition of exceptionality that is educational in its origin and conception, and in its diagnostic and remedial implications, and
2. Strongly affirm the inadequacy of the traditional education model of remediation, and actively affirm the need for the development of new models that involve the total system and all children. (CCBD, 1969, p. 1)

As was the recommendation for definition clarification, this resolution was also ignored by the leadership in the field of exceptionality.

HISTORY AND ISSUES ON TEACHER PREPARATION

The early and mid-1930s provided little understanding about the problems of teacher training for children with SED. In October of 1938, U.S. Office of Education Commissioner John W. Studebaker convened a conference on clinical adjustment of behavior problems. The conferees from various disciplines were mainly concerned with the treatment of problem children and how general class teachers should treat such children. There was no mention of specialized training for teachers of disturbed children. This is surprising since Martens (1937) reported that 13 colleges and universities had preparation programs for SED children. Kirk (1962) in a later report found that only 10 colleges and universities in the nation provided a sequence of courses, and only nine states certified teachers in the special education area of emotional disturbance. He further stated that many of the services provided to disturbed children in the public schools were administered by guidance personnel, counselors, school psychologists, and noneducational personnel. Kirk further concluded that so little progress in the development of concepts and programs concerned with training teachers in this area was due to the "tenuous and theoretical nature of our knowledge of causative factors and remedial processes, and to the fact that, until recently, teacher training institutions have steered clear of involvement in this area, relying rather on psychiatrists, psychologists, and social workers to handle the problem" (p. 384).

Cotter (1960) indicated that only 27 state departments of education had not set policy, requirements, or other provisions for requiring the preparation of special teachers for children who were emotionally disturbed. Only 8 states had established specific requirements for teacher certification, and only 4 other states had specific guidelines for "approval" teacher status.

The BEH (1970) estimated that in 1968 through 1969 in the area of seriously emotionally disturbed, there were 1,207,200 children between the ages of 5 to 19 and 180,800 between the ages of birth to 4, a total of 1,388,000 children. Only 99,400 children with SED were served by 11,400 special education teachers, with an additional 175,800 special education teachers needed in the SED area. (The 2% estimated level of total number of children with SED in the school-age population was used.) The estimate of the number of teachers and specialists needed and employed was based on the state education agencies' state plans submitted to BEH via legislative mandates (BEH, 1970).

Tompkins (1969) estimated that by the academic year 1968–69 approximately 132 colleges and universities would be training or preparing to train teachers for children who are emotionally disturbed. It should be pointed out that prior to the mid-1960s, and up to the establishment of BEH, there were only about 12 ongoing and 13 developing teacher preparation programs in the nation for children with SED. Center and Kaufman's (1993) review of sources indicated that there were approximately 256 BD teacher training programs in the United States and a minimum of 256 BD teacher educators employed by colleges and universities, with a yearly attrition rate of 10%.

Teacher preparation and services for children with SED is all the more difficult since we are not dealing with a single class of behaviors but rather with whatever the school rejects. Until we can talk about what kinds of programs are needed for what kinds of children and be more clear about the interaction of a particular child with a particular school's organizational structure, this will continue to be a most frustrating area in which to work. We are often called upon to rescue the school failures without a chance to alter the organizational basis of the school contributing to a particular child's adjustment. Because of our commitment to both service for children with SED and sound teacher preparation, much can be done to facilitate the translation of what we now know into responsible service programs and to create research necessary for improved programs to reduce the waste of human potential (Tompkins, 1968, 1969; Tompkins & Tompkins-McGill, 1993; Trippe, 1964).

I contend that teacher preparation and services should include therapeutic milieu principles and practices. The classroom is the place where affection, approval, and acceptance can be part of and structured in the remedial program for children with SED. I feel that teachers must understand the processes of affective education and the influence of a positive learning milieu. Affective education must be a full partner along with cognitive development. It is not an "extra" that can be deflected when things get tough and money is short. Too often, affective education is boxed up in a kit to be used for 1 hour a week. This will not work. Affective education requires an understanding of one's self and others and how feelings, interest, attitudes, and appreciations influence a troubled child's learning milieu and life space. It is likely that the teacher's role in affective education will receive more attention in the near future because it is as critical as the three *R*s.

DEBATE ON FULL INCLUSION OR REGULAR EDUCATION INITIATIVE

Changes in federal laws for special education students are placing increased demands on schools. The least restrictive environment provision of P.L. 94-142 favors educating children with disabilities in regular environments, and the Regular Education Initiative (REI) advocates maintain that there is no student who cannot be served in a general classroom if necessary supports are provided. The REI proponents want the general education system to assume unequivocal primary responsibility for all students in our public schools, including those with identified disabilities as well as those who, while not "labeled," have special needs of some type (Tucker, 1989; Will, 1986). The REI debate reflects a basic issue: How can schools better assist students who require special attention, intervention, and support to enjoy a better quality of life? These quality-of-life issues are based on human needs and should be much more significant than political or legal considerations (Davis, 1989; York, Vandercook, MacDonald, Heise-Meff, & Caughy, 1992).

More and more teachers find themselves facing students who need assistance beyond traditional curricula if they are to thrive in schools. As implied in REI proposals, general classrooms must begin to adopt more sophisticated treatment and educational interventions for more divergent students and tap the potential of classrooms for the development of healthy environments and influences in schools (Vergason & Anderegg, 1991). All teachers confront behaviors that reflect children's development, home influences, situational and social pressures, and fears and anxieties about new learning tasks and requirements. All children, disabled or not, react differently to these influences and circumstances. Troubled children, with their adjustment problems, find it all the more difficult to function in the life space of the school and classroom. They have greater needs for more sophisticated programs (Lawrence, 1988; Myles & Whelan, 1991). In this regard, I feel the REI and the full inclusion movement may dilute the educators' full recognition of human differences and dilute or neglect appropriate services for children's diversities. This will unwittingly place undue responsibility on regular education's capacity to educate our widely diverse children with disabilities, especially without reference to changing teacher preparation programs in regular or general education.

DELIVERY OF SERVICES MODEL: BOARDS FOR CHILDREN IN TROUBLE

In spite of judicial and legislative efforts, children with emotional disturbance are neglected or rejected by the American public school system. These children and their parents continue to have a right to legal consultation and, if need be, to advocate to obtain civil rights and liberties in their pursuit of gaining the full benefits of American education. Since the 1970s, change has not really taken place in the American system of public education for children and youth who are troubled, disturbed, or disaffected. All the so-called revitalizing in American public education to assure the proper implementation of appropriate educational and mental health programs to produce an adjusted, educated citizenry will fail unless the power structure of local, state, or federal/national groups that are organized and educationally oriented have a structured role and function in creating the best education and socialization programs in the nation's schools for troubled children.

We must begin early interventions by reaching the child who is disturbed or troubled in his or her own home long before the beginning of formal schooling. In this approach, the school may succeed in intervening early enough to influence the learning climate in the home, where the most influential behavior patterning takes place. Instruction outside the school building may be necessary to help some children who are disturbed or troubled to maintain pace with their peers. The school-sponsored programs could reach these children through such channels as community school agencies, neighborhood services, church programs, job training, pediatric services, and mental health centers. As the schools find ways to make their programs less institution bound and communicate something of value to children who are disturbed regardless of time and place, they will come closer to a position of centrality in community life.

In this context, I suggest the establishment of parent and child centers to service communities in the earliest interventions; provide elaborate school readiness services and school orientation for parents, pressing for achievement in the home; and finally establish the position of child development specialists and services in the school.

The chief vehicle to achieve this reorientation is the creation of Boards for Children in Trouble. The Boards could then reach aggressively into the community: sending workers out to children's homes, recreational facilities, and schools; developing new services; contracting for others; and modifying existing agencies so that the range of needs discovered is matched by the range of services available. They should assume full responsibility for all education in the community that is peripheral to schooling, including preprimary education, parent education, and community education. They should take steps to ensure parity in planning and decision making on the part of all relevant publics.

These Boards for Children in Trouble should be organized around individual schools. The schools would then become, under the auspices of these Boards, wide-ranging developmental centers bringing to bear agency and community resources and using professionals from a variety of disciplines and professional systems in a total developmental program for children in trouble.

Special education personnel should be responsible for assuring that all children benefit from highly specialized and general education programs. In the schools, the mental health needs of the organization and the training needs of teachers and the school staff become a primary focus. The test here, however, relates to the children in trouble and their teachers and not to the needs of the school. Teachers should not seek out special educational services to help them end up with the students they wish they had, rather than the ones who are there for them to teach.

Too often, children in trouble are the losers because the necessary services are nonexistent or overcrowded if available, adding to the problems children must overcome. An effective Board for Children in Trouble would clarify the problems on the basis of child needs, and our sophisticated research and development can then be brought to bear—uncomplicated by a myriad of social variables and failures—on questions related to the developmental needs of highly divergent children (Tompkins & McGill, 1989).

CHALLENGE TO THE FUTURE

The profession of working with children who are troubled as it now exists has several needs. Basic among these is the need for planning and programming. The nature of children's needs must be identified. Necessary and appropriate resources must be determined. Ongoing children's programs can be used, and cooperation among them must be developed. New services are not proposed immediately, but there must be better planning of existing services. There is the need for development of new ideas, improvements of present arrangements, inventions of methods of intervention, and ways of coordinating services and agencies.

Another need is for continuing evaluation of children's services. This means not only studying the effectiveness of programs and services but also developing the capability to know the resources of the community, the way they work together, and the degree they utilize the best in current practices and knowledge about children's services.

Finally, there is the need to assure the legal rights of children. Children have a right to adequate living arrangements, food, clothing, education, medical attention, and the like. In light of these concerns, we should view and define advocacy as the process of constructing programs connecting children to appropriate programs. More specifically, the interagency effort should include the support of all community child-serving systems and formats that would endeavor to:

1. increase sensitivity to the "why" and "how" children are isolated from their normal and natural environments;
2. increase assessment of programs that isolate children from their normal and natural environments;
3. reduce the isolation of children from their normal and natural environments;
4. develop more successful plans in returning isolated children to their normal and natural environments;
5. determine how children are placed out of normal and natural environments and sensitize the environments to maintain children; and
6. increase community, family, and school support in maintaining children in their normal and natural environments.

CONCLUDING REMARKS

In general, programs for troubled children and youth need to be developed that will:

1. ensure that all children in designated areas have access to whatever human services they need that are now available in the community;
2. identify required preventive and direct services that are not available and mobilize resources to initiate those services; and
3. evaluate and improve the effectiveness of children's services, both by formal research techniques and by participation of parents and other interested community members in decisions affecting new programs or modification of old ones.

The implications are (a) provision of adequate services for children; (b) development of community responsiveness, responsibility, and accountability to and for children; (c) involvement of both public and private resources to assist children; and (d) development of program standards.

The challenge is that it is more difficult to find a solution to fit the child than to fit the child to the solution. The challenge is to create engineering capacities to help child-serving agencies to reassess policies, standards, procedures, and practices and to hold ourselves and them accountable for sustaining appropriate goals and programs on the basis of children's needs.

The challenge is to attract individual and groups of parents, citizens, and professionals at all levels to pick up the gauntlet on behalf of children and to dispel and correct the recurring responses to the needs of children, among which are:

- Things are going well for children.
- There is no money available.
- There is no resource available.
- There is no expertise available.
- We are doing our best.
- What can you do for them anyway?
- They are hopeless and stupid.
- They are delinquent and handicapped.

Perhaps the best way to begin is to accept what is being said at face value and add, "Yes, but . . . ."

REFERENCES

Ayers, G. E. (1994). Statistical profile of special education in the United States, 1994. *Teaching Exceptional Children, 26* (Suppl.), 1–4.

Bower, E. M. (1982). Defining emotional disturbance: Public policy and research. *Psychology in the Schools, 19,* 55–60.

Bower, E. M. (1989). A brief history of how we have helped emotionally disturbed children and other fairy tales. In S. Braaten, F. H. Wood, & G. Wrobel (Eds.), *Celebrating the past, preparing for the future: 40 years of serving students with emotional and behavioral disorders* (pp. 18–20). Minneapolis: Minnesota Council for Children with Behavioral Disorders and Minnesota Educators of Emotionally/Behaviorally Disordered.

Bower, E. M., & Kaczynski, G. (1968). *Report on conference in the definition and incidence of emotional disturbance.* Paper presented at the Bureau of Education for the Handicapped/USOE-sponsored conference, Washington, DC.

Bureau of Education for the Handicapped. (1970). *Handicapped children in the United States and special education personnel required 1968-1969.* Washington, DC: U.S. Department of Health, Education, and Welfare, Office of Education.

Center, D. B., & Kaufman, M. E. (1993). Present and future needs for personnel to prepare teachers of the behaviorally disordered. *Behavior Disorders, 18,* 87–91.

Children's Defense Fund. (1994). *State of America's children yearbook.* Washington, DC: Author.

Cotter, K. C. (1960). Emotionally disturbed children and teacher preparation. *The Catholic Education Review, XLIV,* 457–469.

Council on Children with Behavioral Disorders. (1969, April). Position paper presented at the meeting of the Council for Exceptional Children. Denver, CO.

Davis, W. E. (1989). The regular education initiative debate: Its promises and problems. *Exceptional Children, 55,* 440–446.

Ferrell, M. (1994). *Juvenile delinquency.* Unpublished memorandum, Appalachian State University, College of Education, Boone, NC.

Institute of Medicine. (1989). *Research on children and adolescents with mental, behavioral, and developmental disorders.* Washington, DC: National Academy Press.

Kirk, S. A. (1962). *Educating exceptional children.* Boston: Miffin Company.

Lawrence, P. A. (1988). Basic strategies for mainstream integration. *Academic Therapy, 23,* 349–355.

Martens, E. N. (1937). Present status of opportunities for the preparation of teachers for exceptional children. *Exceptional Children, II,* 141.

Myles, B. S., & Whelan, R. J. (1991). The regular education initiative without waivers. *Focus on Exceptional Children, 23,* 8–10.

Steinberg, Z., & Knitzer, J. (1992). Classrooms for emotionally and behaviorally disturbed students: Facing the challenge. *Behavioral Disorders, 17,* 145–156.

Tompkins, J. R. (1968). Program development concept. *Exceptional Children, 35,* 547–549.

Tompkins, J. R. (1969). An analysis: Needs progress and issue in the preparation of personnel in the education of emotionally disturbed children. *The Journal of Special Education, 1,* 101–111.

Tompkins, J. R., & Tompkins-McGill, P. L. (1993). *Surviving in schools in the 1990s: Strategic management of school environments.* Lanham, MD: University Press of America.

Tompkins, J. R., & McGill, P. L. (1988). *Report: Needed educational and treatment services for children in trouble.* Unpublished paper, Appalachian State University, Boone, NC.

Tompkins, J. R., & McGill, P. L. (1989). Lack of educational and treatment services for students in trouble: A new proposal for help. *Pointer, 33,* 41–42.

Trippe, M. J. (1964). *Preparation of teachers of seriously emotionally disturbed child: Under P.L. 85-926 as amended by P.L. 88-164.* Unpublished paper, HEW, Washington, DC.

Tucker, J. A. (1989). Less required energy: A response to Danielson and Bellamy. *Exceptional Children, 55,* 456–458.

U.S. Department of Education. (1992). *Fourteenth annual report to Congress on the implementation of the Individuals with Disabilities Education Act.* Washington, DC: Author.

Vergason, G. A., & Anderegg, M. L. (1991). Beyond the regular education initiative and the resource room controversy. *Focus on Exceptional Children, 23,* 5–6.

Will, M. C. (1986). Educating children with learning problems: A shared responsibility. *Exceptional Children, 52,* 411–415.

York, J., Vandercook, T., MacDonald, C., Heise-Meff, C., & Caughey, E. (1992). Feedback about integrating middle school students with severe disabilities in general education classes. *Exceptional Children, 58,* 244–257.

Appendix 20.A

MEMORANDUM

To: Dr. Gallagher, Dr. Martin, Dr. Marge, Dr. Lucito, Dr. Withrow, Dr. Moss, Dr. Lawrence

From: James R. Tompkins, Coordinator, Unit on Education of the Emotionally Disturbed

Subject: Guidelines for the identification of children with serious emotional disturbance

Date: May 1, 1968

This represents a formal protest and deep sense of chagrin that I harbor over the issue of providing a definition of children with serious emotional disturbance. It is with this personal reaction that I formally request the leadership of the Bureau of Education for the Handicapped to recommend to the National Advisory Committee at their next official meeting to include in their agenda the problem of providing an acceptable definition of children with serious emotional disturbance. I am providing guidelines in the interim period for use of administrators of federal legislation dealing with programs for the education of emotionally disturbed children. This is only a tentative alternative at providing guidelines and it is my guess that a more acceptable meaningful definition will be forthcoming as a result of the deliberations of the National Advisory Committee. In this frame of reference, I recommend the following guidelines in the identification of disturbed children: Bower, E. M. "Early identification of emotionally handicapped children in school." *Children,* 1957, 4, 143-147. Bower defines emotionally handicapped children as those who demonstrate one or more of the following characteristics: (to a marked extent and over a period of time)

1. Inability to learn which cannot be explained by intellectual, sensory, or health factors
2. Inability to build or maintain satisfactory interpersonal relationships with peers and teachers
3. Inappropriate types of behavior or feelings under normal conditions
4. A general pervasive mood of unhappiness or depression

5. A tendency to develop physical symptoms, pains, or fears associated with personal or school problems.

A widely accepted definition of children with serious emotional disturbance is not available presently. However, there are many and various attempts to define the emotional disturbed child provided by professional educators and mental health specialists. According to Dr. Matthew J. Trippe of the University of Michigan in his recent contribution to Volume I of *Educational Therapy:* "when we ask questions, 'How do we identify emotionally disturbed children?' 'what are their characteristics,' we assume that they possess a "thing" which is out there and can be correctly identified through proper definition. In a sense, this puts the cart before the horse since an educational definition of disturbance as much as any other definition, has to be evaluated on the basis of its *clarity* and *usefulness* and not on whether it leads to the correct selection of the children who are "really" disturbed. Current practices suggest that there are two definitions of disturbance which are used at different levels for different purposes. The first definition disclaims participation by educators in formulating the definition. By this definition, an emotionally disturbed child is one so diagnosed by an appropriate mental health specialist. Most legislation for disturbed children is tied to such an [sic] definition. This is not surprising since citizens intent on obtaining school services for disturbed children have looked to and worked in association with psychiatrists and other mental health professionals for support, guidance and even assistance in drawing up legislation.

Educators should resist such a definition and consequent eligibility for service on two counts. The first is that such a classification might not be the most useful for providing educational services. The second is that the definition is not clearly communicated. The diagnosis of emotional disturbance has been shown to be extremely unreliable and, therefore, much depends on who sees the child under what circumstances and in what context. Surveys of the extent of serious emotional disturbance in the population of school children range from less than one percent to fifteen percent and more. Even though the rates differ by age and sex, which may account for some of the differences, these finding make it clear that the diagnosis of emotional disturbance is vague and unreliable.

The other prevalent definition is organizationally based, and as suggested earlier, involves the classification of the child as disturbed if he violates classroom norms and no other customary way of explaining this violation is readily available. If children who show disturbed behavior in school have no other readily detectable disability and particularly if they may be seen as disturbed. Many view this situation with alarm, correctly observing that it amounts to a definition by default and urge that it be guarded against. Unfortunately, the most often stated alternative is to recommend diagnosis by a mental health specialist and the difficulties with this resolution have been pointed out. The task for education is to concentrate on developing relatively clear definitions that relate to provisions that can be made for children through the pattern of education."

One attempt at an operational definition for purposes of early detection and screening of disturbed children in school was proposed by Bower (1961) and subjected to research in an extensive study in California. Bower suggested that the term disturbed be replaced by the term "emotionally handicapped." An emotionally handicapped child is defined as one whose behavior over a long period of time shows one or more of the following: (1) an otherwise unexplained learning disability, (2) poor relationships with other children or adults, (3) immaturity, (4) pervasive unhappiness or depression, and (5) a tendency to develop physical symptoms in the face of stress. The concept is measured by a combination of teacher's judgments, peer ratings and self rating. A major difficulty is that the measuring instruments do not directly measure the aspects of behavior cited in the definition. Apart from this, however, it does represent an attempt to define the condition from the point of view of the school. It is appropriate to ask at this point, if these are school related behaviors or problems, what is to be gained by choosing to view the behavior as caused by emotional disturbances. In this sense, by suggesting a procedure which results in identifying from five to ten per cent of the general school population as being emotionally handicapped, Bower is engaged as much in social reform as he is in scientific discovery."

BRENDA L. TOWNSEND
University of South Florida

Brenda L. Townsend received her PhD from the University of Kansas and is currently at the University of South Florida. She co-authored a constructive classroom management book and is actively engaged in facilitating numerous presentations and workshops for school personnel and families. Her focus is on strategies for culturally affirming children and youth as they develop academically and socially. Townsend's current research interests are in school restructuring initiatives as they impact all children, but particularly ethnic minority children who have been less successful in school settings. She is also investigating family- and peer-mediated social and leadership instruction with African American males in preventing juvenile gang affiliation. As the recipient of a McKnight Fellowship, Townsend is developing and facilitating site-based and community-based teacher and family reeducation to identify educational and child-rearing practices for children and youth at risk for school failure.

CHAPTER 21

"Sankofa" in the Field of Emotional/Behavioral Disorders: Returning to the Past in Order To Move Forward

MY ENTREE TO THE FIELD OF BEHAVIOR DISORDERS

In West Africa, *Sankofa* means simply returning to the past in order to move forward. As I revisit my past, I realize that I have a long-standing interest in behaviors that pose problems for children and youth in school settings. Attending school with three brothers was a case study in and of itself. There was a dramatic difference between my in-school behaviors and theirs. School personnel constantly granted and denied privileges, and sometimes not so judiciously. I was very conscious of what I needed to do to be privileged in the educational enterprise. I thought it was pretty simple. You had to comply with teacher directives and refrain from any behavior that could even remotely be construed as rebellious or disrespectful. If you did what was asked when it was asked, you usually reaped many academic and social benefits. That was fine, if you valued the reward systems offered by schools.

My preoccupation with conforming to school norms was the only way I could ensure my enfranchisement within those settings. My brothers, however, behaved in ways that schools not only don't reward but penalize. As a result, they were denied many educational opportunities. That was troublesome for me, but not nearly as much as knowing that they didn't care that they weren't among the "privileged."

As an example, most of the boys in our neighborhood had a certain walk that was considered cool. It took a great deal of practice to perfect it. When my youngest brother was in the fourth grade, he entered his classroom leaning slightly to the right in a slow stride. His teacher repeatedly told him to come in the room "appropriately." Each time, he refused to change his walk. He was sent to the office and suspended because of the "arrogant" way he entered the classroom.

We all thought that was pretty ridiculous, as my mother had to miss work to get him back in school. I was upset with the school and with him. The school enforced a ludicrous request based on a behavior that was hurting no one. And I was upset with him for not doing what the teacher wanted in school and realizing that he could walk any way he wanted outside of school.

I initially wanted to be a child psychologist (maybe because of the conflicts I experienced as an African American child constantly negotiating among the worlds of school, community, and home). It wasn't until I had an experience teaching adults that I decided that teaching was indeed rewarding and would be even more so with children. Having reached that conclusion, I naturally wanted to teach children with emotional or behavioral disorders (E/BD). In particular, I wanted to teach them strategies for reducing conflicts with school personnel when student attitudes, values, expectations, communication styles, or behaviors differed from school expectations.

My first teaching job, however, was with children with learning disabilities. Most of the children were seemingly referred for academic deficiencies, yet their behaviors were probably more at odds with the referring teachers' standards than their academic problems. When I did begin teaching students with behavioral disorders, I noticed that my classes, along with many others, were predominantly composed of African American males. While neither of my brothers was identified as having a behavior disorder, I couldn't help but wonder if their early schooling experiences, as I observed them, were predictors of an impending crisis that would affect African American males in particular. It seems that African American males who do not conform to school demands create the most dissonance and discomfort for school systems. As a result, these students are readily suspected of having behavioral difficulties.

Suspicions of potential behavior problems, even if they don't lead to identification for E/BD classes, pose threats to students' educational processes. Even when children are not labeled and remain in the general education setting, school personnel may perceive them negatively and lower expectations regarding those students' academic and social skills.

While many caring and nurturing teachers work daily with children with behavioral disorders, there are those among the ranks who are not as caring and nurturing. Much has been said about the soaring dropout rates among children with behavioral disorders, members of ethnic minority groups, or those from impoverished backgrounds. Students drop out of school in more ways than physically removing themselves. As I talk to African American students, I attempt to get a sense of how they perceive their schooling processes. Consistent themes running across their conversations have everything to do with those students' relationships with school personnel. They relate incident after incident indicative of poor teacher/administrator–student relationships. With frightening regularity, students voice concerns that school personnel desire to gain respect from students yet hold little or no respect for the students.

In my experiences, it's not uncommon for students to also express their disappointment concerning school personnel who appear to know very little, and care even less, about student lives and experiences. I frequently wonder if educators are fully aware that many of these students who have poor relationships with teachers and administrators occupy seats in their classes daily but have "checked out" long ago. Problematic relationships with these students are not limited to dominant school personnel. Students also report negative relationships with ethnic minority teachers and administrators. I staunchly believe that the quality of teacher–student relationships and interactions can powerfully influence school success for many learners who typically are on the fringes of educational experiences and activities in school settings.

Ironically, my motivation for entering the field of behavioral disorders was to be a gatekeeper of sorts. I wanted desperately to facilitate the exodus of certain children and youth from our programs, those considered deviant for the wrong reasons. Without question, there are students who truly have deviant behaviors and will have a host of negative outcomes if no one intervenes. But there are increasing numbers of others who could be successful in general education settings where their diversity is enthusiastically welcomed and affirmed. Most importantly, their differences would not be perceived as problematic. I am very concerned with the inherent miseducation of students for whom schools are unable, for whatever reason, to winnow cultural differences from deviance.

I believed then, as I do now, that too much emphasis is placed on getting children to comply with irrelevant school norms. Genuine relationships created when teachers demonstrate care and high regard for children's welfare in school and other settings are all too often forsaken to exercise power and control over students. Traditional behavioral expectations exist that have little to do with improving the quality of life for children in public schools today. To illustrate, the standards and expectations traditionally held for dominant-culture children are used with increasingly diverse student populations. When held to yesterday's behavioral norms, many of today's children and youth will continue to appear deviant.

THE STATE OF E/BD EDUCATION

Since its inception, the field of behavior disorders has been enigmatic. The identification and education of children and youth with E/BD have posed myriad challenges to practitioners and researchers. For instance, the field has been plagued by its definition, terminology, identification procedures, ethical dilemmas, and intervention choices. Perplexing questions have been posed repeatedly, and, in most cases, consensus has yet to be reached. Some debatable questions immediately come to mind.

How Should Emotional or Behavioral Disorders Be Defined?

Based on the federal definition, which is frequently incorporated in state guidelines, deciding who should be included and who should be excluded from receiving services has been a quintessential exercise in illogical thinking. The federal definition, much of which originated from Eli Bower's (1960) work, excludes children and youth who have social maladjustment. Bower himself (1982) noted his intent for the inclusion of those students in the classification of emotional disturbance.

Any child suspected of having an emotional or behavioral disorder risks being misdiagnosed and miseducated due to the complexities involved when characterizing human behavior. Determining whether ethnic minority children have behavior disorders is an even more formidable task. Every facet of the placement decision-making process for these children has been suspect for biases: the prereferral, referral, evaluation, and placement stages.

One shortcoming of the federal definition is that it narrowly contextualizes behaviors. For example, student behaviors need only violate school norms to be considered deviant. Students can be emotionally, behaviorally, and socially competent in their home and community settings yet to be identified as having emotional or behavioral disorders if they appear deviant in the school setting. Hoping to remedy some of the inadequacies of that definition, the National Mental Health Coalition (Forness & Knitzer, 1992) proposed a new definition to broadly examine student behaviors relative to age, ethnic, and cultural norms and across more than one setting.

The intent is laudable. However, the waters of identifying ethnic minority children will grow even murkier. It will be more difficult to operationalize the condition of E/BD, as identification procedures will be rife with ambiguity and vagueness. Daunting variations in prevalence rates will persist, if not exacerbate. The new definition calls for making determinations that the "Emotional or Behavioral disorder must be exhibited in at least two different settings, at least one of which is educational" (Forness & Knitzer, 1992). Assuming the other settings would include home, community, or workplace, school personnel would have to obtain accurate information from individuals in those nonschool settings. Doing so requires schools to develop positive, genuine relationships with various people, many of whom historically have had unfavorable experiences within school settings. Most schools have not yet forged authentic partnerships with ethnic minority families and business and community leaders that would facilitate reciprocal information exchanges on customs, mores, values, and belief and reward systems that are culturally appropriate and age-appropriate in the various settings in which children interact.

How and Where Should Children and Youth with E/BD Be Educated?

More recently, the setting in which children and youth with E/BD are taught has evoked considerable (and sometimes rather heated) conversations and debates. Advocates of inclusion believe that these students should be taught in general education settings. Those who are cautious about including students with E/BD are concerned that, particularly with this population of students, their needs will not be met by merely including them in the general education classroom.

The primary reason for educators maintaining a cautious posture regarding the full inclusion of students with E/BD is that general education teacher preparation rarely includes the implementation of effective behavior management and affective strategies. Teacher preparation programs minimally include techniques for assessing and implementing behavioral, social, or therapeutic interventions. Another concern is that the protection granted these students in more traditional service delivery options will no longer be available. That is, as a result of their offending behaviors, they will be subjected to disciplinary practices that don't consider the effect of their disability on the offense. More attention should be paid to what occurs in the settings in which our students are educated, as opposed to focusing solely on the setting. Considerable time and energy is spent casting the general education classroom as the optimal learning environment for all students with behavior disorders. Determining the components or elements that enhance students' social, behavioral, and emotional competencies might be a wiser investment of resources.

How Should We Effectively Program for Children and Youth with E/BD?

Educating students with identified behavioral disorders is no easy task. Whenever I reflect on the field of behavioral disorders, I'm immediately reminded of the classic writings of Dunn (1968) and Johnson (1969), who leveled serious criticisms against the special education system. The field of E/BD was not spared. Dunn admonished special education for its segregated classes and overrepresentation of ethnic minority students. Johnson accused school systems of using special education programs as a means of "cooling the mark" when dealing with black, inner-city youth. He contended that special education programs conveniently allowed schools to blame their inner-city charges for failing to effectively educate the students.

I use those treatises as benchmarks by which to determine our progress. Since the 1960s, the field's movement reminds me of the childhood game, Mother, May I? In that game, a designated "mother" stands with her or his back to the other players (to appear objective and impartial to all players), while each requests permission to move forward. Players usually ask permission to take giant steps forward. At the discretion of the mother, the players are granted either the number of giant steps for which they asked or a negotiated smaller number. Or the player is granted a number of baby steps forward. If the player takes the steps granted by the mother without again asking, "Mother, may I?" she or he has seriously violated the rule and must return to the starting mark, thereby neutralizing any previous progress.

Unfortunately, that scenario resembles the field's movement in educating all children and youth with behavioral disorders. Many efforts are made to make giant strides forward, and, on occasion, that happens. But more often than not, baby steps are granted instead. For children from ethnic minority or poverty backgrounds, the field is sent begrudgingly back to the starting line.

Educators of children and youth with E/BD are presented with many challenges. Societal conditions are dramatically different from the past. Increasing numbers of children and youth come to school as victims or observers of sexual abuse, substance abuse, neglect, and violent and aggressive acts. In addition, more students are perpetrators of these acts on others. To this end, school settings have become fertile grounds for sexual and physical assaults, shootings, and drug trafficking. Consequently, many school environments are equipped with various safeguards against such acts of terrorism that were once unique to airports.

Due to this rising tide of violence in schools and communities, many children and their families are living in fear. To compound matters, there are vast generational differences in children's experiences. Contemporary youth experience many events that are anxiety producing and drastically different from those experienced by youth in the past. For example, in some communities, common experiences for youth include witnessing violent deaths of family members or friends, reconstituted families as a result of increased crack cocaine abuse that renders parents unable to provide their children with even the most basic needs, and a constant fear of being victimized by random or intentional acts of violence. These youth must contend with vastly different experiences than those characterizing our generation and others. Similarly, manifestations of E/BD may be markedly different than in the past.

Acknowledging the societal forces contributing to E/BD is only part of the solution. We also must recognize the limitations inherent in continuing to use traditional means to serve students with E/BD and their families. Moreover, innovative interventions that are multifaceted are needed to promote student socialization and moral development. Additionally, their academic, emotional, behavioral, and social success is dependent on the implementation of individually and culturally sensitive teaching and communication strategies and other services that are well coordinated to meet and provide follow-up on the needs of children and their families.

I believe that, for many students who truly have E/BD (whatever that is), the services provided in school settings are unintentionally harmful, if for no other reason than that they neglect to address the myriad needs of children and their families in a comprehensive manner. In essence, much of the programming for those students is isolated and does not consider their lives in settings other than the school. Rarely are their family members and community leaders maximally involved in the interventions designed to teach alternative behaviors or social skills, or in strategies that will provide insight for students into their own behaviors. If a student has a behavioral disorder, there is considerable impact on the family. Family members may contribute to the child's maladaptive behavior or may be frustrated by repeated reports of these behaviors. Nevertheless, they should be involved in school interventions on a variety of levels.

Educators must be mindful that families are constituted much differently than in the past. Thus, our notion of family must be broadened to include members of the community, fictive kin, and extended family members. Schools should make every effort to forge partnerships with those individuals holding the most influence over the lives of children and youth in nonschool settings.

WORKING DEFINITION OF E/BD

My definition of E/BD is by no means entirely original, as it includes some elements of others. I present it knowing full well that it, too, is imperfect. I question whether any definition can describe a condition so precisely that all cases would be included. At best, this exercise is my way of addressing my own concerns with the federal definition of *serious emotional disturbance*. I must caution, though, that my definition is intended for use when schools have developed reciprocal, respectful, and cooperative partnerships with families and communities:

> Emotional/behavioral disorders (E/BD) can exist at any time in an individual's life and can coexist with other conditions. E/BD is evident when school personnel and family or community members determine that:

(a) a pattern has been established in which the individual's behaviors differ from school, work, cultural, ethnic, or societal norms to the extent that their academic, social, mental, or physical health is in jeopardy;

(b) suspect behaviors are not accounted for by individual or cultural differences; and

(c) the behaviors are problematic in school or work and at least one other setting.

The condition of E/BD should be determined only after strategies addressing environmental factors have been planned, implemented, and evaluated by a team that actively includes and involves a family member or community leader. E/BD can be the result of deliberate or uncontrollable acts.

In comparing my definition to the federal definition, the term *serious emotional disturbance* is replaced with *emotional/behavioral disorders* to avoid use of the word *serious*. The term *serious emotional disturbance*, in and of itself, gives rise to negative connotations of E/BD, and many have proposed that it not be used in reference to students with behavioral disorders (Huntze, 1985).

The federal definition contains vague terms to describe the condition. My definition also includes broad and somewhat vague terms. It is virtually impossible to write a definition that will both narrowly define a condition and remain broad enough to avoid excluding children who stand to benefit from such programs. Due to the variability within and among individuals and ethnic groups, I deliberately don't delineate how long a behavior must be exhibited before a pattern is established. Nor do I specify how academic, social, mental, or physical health can be jeopardized to qualify one for these services. These determinations should be made with the assistance of members of the child's family and community.

To reduce the risks of students being identified as having E/BD on the basis of individual and cultural differences, I believe that the condition should not be suspected unless it can be shown that it persists in spite of interventions targeting the environment, as opposed to the child. My definition also attempts to facilitate the parent and family involvement upon which P.L. 94-142 was predicated. To guard against the idiosyncratic nature in which some students are identified for E/BD programs, family and community involvement in educational decisions are even more critical than in the past. Thus, these adults are needed to more actively participate in the identification process to ensure that the behaviors that pose problems for children in school settings are also problematic in home or community settings.

The federal definition has incited considerable discussion concerning the eligibility of children with social maladjustment or conduct disorders in E/BD programs. The crux of the debate has centered on whether students choose to engage in aberrant behavior. If students make deliberate choices to violate norms, it is proposed that they be excluded from services for students with E/BD. Knowing why or how a student exhibits disordered behavior does little to teach alternatives to the behaviors that are inappropriate in various settings. Thus, my definition emphasizes the behaviors, instead of the etiology or motivation for those behaviors.

ED AND BD: CAN WE DIFFERENTIATE?

Yet another problem that has confronted the field is terminology. There has been a standing debate regarding the preferred lexicon for the condition of E/BD. There is a difference between emotional disturbance and behavioral disorders. I believe that maladaptive behavior can be caused by a number of factors, one of which is emotional disturbance. Behavior that is maladaptive, albeit subjective, is usually observable, even withdrawn behaviors. Emotional disturbance, on the other hand, is more inferred. While I do believe that there is a difference between the two, as educators it is difficult to differentiate. Therefore, the focus should be on the behaviors demonstrated by students, not underlying feelings or causes. By and large, school personnel are not trained to detect and treat emotional disturbance. Therefore, regardless of suspected etiology, I prefer using the term *behavior disorders*. It is less clinical and more applicable to educational practice.

INCLUSIVE EDUCATION FOR CHILDREN WITH E/BD

Several educators are calling for the inclusion of children and youth with E/BD in general education settings (i.e., Stainback & Stainback, 1990; Thousand & Villa, 1989). Various definitions exist regarding what it means to be inclusive of children with disabilities. Primarily, those individuals are advocating that students with disabilities receive educational services in general education settings with their peers without disabilities. All too often, it appears that the principle of the least restrictive environment has become synonymous with the general education setting for all students.

I find this problematic because the individuality that is supposed to be the cornerstone of special education is not acknowledged. We sometimes lose sight of the relativity of the concept of the least restrictive environment. The general education classroom is not universally the least restrictive environment for all students. In fact, for students with observable behavioral disorders, that environment may be more restrictive when all factors are considered.

I am not in favor of the full inclusion of all students with E/BD in general education settings for several reasons. Granted, proponents of the Regular or General Education Initiative have set forth cogent arguments on the need for special and general education reform. I must say I was almost swayed by the insistence that special and general educators jointly provide more efficient and effective educational services to all children, not just those with identified disabilities. When the movement for inclusion was characterized as a moral imperative, I struggled to remain unfazed. When the initiative was analogized to the need for racial and ethnic integration during the Civil Rights era, I could barely resist hopping aboard the inclusion train.

After much thought and temptation, however, I believe that, of all students with disabilities, children with E/BD stand to be most harmed by wholesale inclusive education. Students with behavioral disorders are perceived differently than students with academic disorders. Teachers and students often shape their perceptions of students on their behaviors. In a current research project on school restructuring for the inclusion of children with disabilities, I and several colleagues have been interviewing various school personnel from five school counties and family and community leaders on their perceptions of their schools' restructuring efforts. When they were asked which students are more accepted and more likely to be included in the general education classrooms, their independent responses, as a rule, were identical. They repeatedly noted that students with learning disabilities and students with educable mental retardation were most likely to be included in general education settings. The students least accepted were those with behavioral disorders or serious emotional disturbance.

Teachers themselves have noted limitations in their teacher preparation programs and feel ill-prepared to effectively manage those students' behaviors. While I truly understand the impetus for including students with E/BD in the general education setting, I'm also well aware of the reality. Several actions must be taken to ensure student success before promoting full inclusion. Preparation is critical for students, teachers, and families. Teachers in their general education training must be prepared to work with students with wide-ranging abilities and characteristics in terms of academics, behaviors, and social skills. In addition, because of the intersection of ethnicity and social class in creating disabilities among school-age students, teachers must be more knowledgeable about individual and cultural differences and proficient in methods for affirming those differences throughout the curricula.

Students with E/BD also must be prepared to enter or reenter general education classrooms. Their curricula in their self-contained settings often do not parallel those used in general education classrooms.

Consequently, they fall farther and farther behind their peers academically. As part of the preparation process, their learning in the general education and in the E/BD classrooms must be similar.

Students with behavior disorders and their general education peers must be prepared to work and play cooperatively with students who may differ along lines of ability, class, gender, and ethnicity. In doing so, they must be taught techniques for resolving conflicts, negotiating, and problem solving.

Family members also must be prepared for inclusion if it is to be successful for students with E/BD. Many families do not wish their children with E/BD to be included in the general education setting. They often prefer the smaller class size, the paraprofessionals that are often in those classes, and the sense of security that comes from having the same teachers over time. In order for families to promote inclusion, they must believe that it will produce results greater than the benefits they attribute to self-contained or resource room service delivery options.

As well intended as the movement is toward the full inclusion of children and youth with E/BD, its success will be minimal if certain actions are not taken. Inclusion involves both presence and participation. Returning those students to general education classrooms would certainly increase their presence but would do little to increase their participation in the educational process with their peers without disabilities. As long as the old conditions are in place, those students will continue to be denied equal educational opportunities.

Inhibiting conditions include negative perceptions held by school personnel toward behaviors that are different, and rigid, uniform standards and policies (i.e., grading, disciplinary, assessment) for all students regardless of individual characteristics.

I, too, wish for total acceptance of students with E/BD and their inclusion in all aspects of the schooling process. However, I also know that many conditions in schools diametrically oppose the full inclusion of students with E/BD. Unfortunately, you cannot automatically mandate the acceptability of students with histories of posing behavioral problems for school personnel. At best, one can hope that optimal conditions are in place prior to returning those students to the very settings where their behaviors were considered inappropriate.

Like the proponents of full inclusion, I question when the time is right for full inclusion and understand the urgency. In comparison, proponents of full inclusion have noted that Rosa Parks didn't wait for the "right time" to remain seated on the bus and thereby launched the civil rights era. As with full inclusion, conditions then were anything but optimal and facilitative of integration. There are similarities between racial integration and the integration of children with disabilities. It is those similarities that strengthen the argument that full inclusion will victimize the very students it proposes to benefit.

The landmark case *Brown v. Board of Education* (1954) prompted racial integration to provide quality education for black children. No one was prepared for integration. Specifically, teachers were not educated on methods for effectively teaching culturally different learners, and students were not prepared to accept each other's differences. Hence, 40 years following Brown, issues involving lack of access to, and inequitable, educational opportunities continue to give rise to African American children faring poorly in schools. Students with E/BD require proactive teaching, behavior management, and communication strategies. At times, these students elicit behaviors that require teachers to provide them with insights into their behaviors. To respond effectively, individuals must be reeducated.

As long as present conditions remain, I believe that students with E/BD will not benefit from full inclusion in the general education classroom. Instead, a broader concept of inclusion must be embraced for students whether or not they are in general education settings. For them, inclusion must entail their maximal involvement in their own educational experiences. Regardless of setting, students with E/BD, who are often turned off to what's going on in the classroom, must be included in every facet of their learning. Teachers must use constructive approaches when interacting with these students.

According to Poplin (1988), student experiences must become the foundation upon which new learning is hung to enhance relevancy of learning. Inclusive education for these students would mean building community in that setting and encouraging students to make meaningful decisions regarding academic and social activities. It also means ensuring that all students believe that they have roles to play in the life of the classroom or school. For some students, it is a matter of getting them involved in a school club or organization. For others, it could mean assisting others in the school community in their areas of strength or interest.

SERVICE DELIVERY MODEL

Deno's (1970) Cascade of Services has been used for years to depict the continuum of service options for students with behavioral disorders. As the needs of children and their families change and educational trends become evident, the service delivery continuum must be altered to reflect those changes. A more recent service delivery model should first emphasize the prevention of disabilities. That is, it should present proactive strategies that will be used to prevent children from developing aberrant behaviors. Thus, service delivery should start with prevention among students and families. Prevention could take many forms, one of which is referrals by schools that allow families to take advantage of services offered by other agencies. School personnel could provide a nexus among other agencies, themselves, community, and home environments to reduce children's risk of developing behavioral disorders.

At each point along the continuum, a dimension of services provided to family members should be included. For example, accompanying the option of self-contained settings for students with E/BD should be family services (which could take the form of family counseling, community agency service coordination, etc.). Another proposed modification to Deno's Cascade of Services would be to differentiate the components of the various general education settings in which students with E/BD may be placed.

Within general education settings, there are differences in the ways students are educated. Various strategies are being touted as facilitative of the inclusion of students with disabilities. In some settings, special and general educators coteach, or they may team teach. Key elements of settings should be identified to improve research and practice. I envision a service delivery model in the 1990s to present even more options for providing educational and other services to children and their families at all phases of their schooling. As needs differ greatly from family to family, the model must allow individualized service delivery to the greatest extent possible.

INCIDENCE OF E/BD

A commonly heard criticism of the field's vague identification procedures has been that they have led to underserving the population of students who have emotional or behavioral disorders. Comparisons of the conservative estimates of students with this condition show that there is a discrepancy between prevalence estimates and the number of students who receive services in this category. Among some children there appears to be an increase in those identified as having emotional or behavioral disorders. Many school districts are identifying students at early ages for these programs. In my recent conversations with public school teachers, they often lament their schools' seemingly overzealous identification of kindergarten and first-grade students for E/BD programs.

I believe that large numbers of students who may truly have emotional or behavioral disorders continue to be overlooked for E/BD services for various reasons, while others are quickly identified. Schools must exercise extreme caution when employing early intervention/identification practices that result in placement in classes for students with E/BD.

I am not arguing against early identification. I do think that educators must ensure that they are acting in the student's best interest when making those decisions. I understand the aim for early identification of students with behavioral disorders. However, I'm concerned that those identification and placement practices may appear to be well intended and driven by the desire to intervene early but actually may be the result of schools' early intolerance and misinterpretation of behaviors that don't fit their commonly held notions of "appropriate behaviors." For many students, once they are placed in E/BD programs, their chances of returning to general education are nil. The dilemma involves determining the extent to which placement in E/BD programs will be more advantageous than the services provided in general education. The benefits for many of those students who are identified so readily may not be sufficient enough to counteract the harm.

While there appears to be a rise in certain populations of students served in classes for students with E/BD, other students aren't so readily identified. Forces other than student characteristics serve to delimit the numbers of students identified for programs for students with E/BD. Schools also must exercise caution in the disciplinary actions used with students with E/BD; namely, these students have the right to due process when schools suspend or expel them. Therefore, some students are not identified in order to withhold those protections. Another reason some students are not identified is because of the political climate. As Tucker (1980) found with students with learning disabilities, when schools are sensitive to the overrepresentation of ethnic minority groups in one category, those students are frequently identified as being eligible for services in other disability categories.

Again, I believe that students with behavioral difficulties continue to be underserved in public school classes, while members of certain groups are overidentified. In some districts, overidentification may affect young children more. Certain ethnic groups also might be more at risk for identification. African American males or students living in poverty might be in jeopardy of overrepresentation in classes for children with E/BD. Nevertheless, our field's prevalence rates continue to vary dramatically from state to state and even among school districts in a given state.

A disproportionate increase apparent among any group of children in classes for students with E/BD is cause for concern. The likelihood that some of those children may be placed inappropriately increases. Schools could take actions to reduce the number of children who are placed in these classes. School personnel should receive specific instruction and practice in understanding cultural and individual differences. Education is needed to provide information on alternative responses to diversity. Another measure is to provide school personnel with proactive behavior-management strategies that will increase teacher skill in effectively teaching students to positively manage their own behaviors. In addition, school, agency, and community must focus their efforts with families to prevent behavioral disorders from occurring among children and youth.

Many of the interventions used with students with E/BD in the past have served us well. In my own work, I have been most influenced by Rhodes's (1967) work on ecological interventions and child variance, Hewitt's (1968) engineered classroom, and Long's crisis-exploitation techniques (Long & Newman, 1961). I found Ellis's Rational Emotive Education and Rational Emotive Therapy (Ellis & Grieger, 1977) beneficial for students with behavioral disorders and their teachers in providing insight to irrational thinking. More recently, I have been influenced by the social skill instructional approaches of Walker, McConnell, McGinnis, and others.

I have the utmost respect for many interventions that have been used over time with children with E/BD. While the traditional techniques have changed little, the children with whom they are used have changed much. For example, children vary on communication styles, motivational levels, value systems, behavioral codes, and so forth. If we intend to respond to the field's wake-up call, we must recognize the monolithic communication and teaching practices often embedded in those traditional interventions and techniques.

Many children and youth alluded to in this chapter will not respond to the sole use of those techniques. Imagine using a social skill instructional approach in standard English with Hispanic students, or with African American students who do not speak standard English regularly. Practitioners and researchers must solicit the assistance of family and community partners to modify existing social, behavioral, and emotional intervention components to be more responsive. For example, who is better positioned to authentically guide school personnel on the use of techniques and language that are relevant to students than family and community members who play significant roles in nonschool settings?

As a result of the many challenges that face today's children and youth, coupled with the diversity among them, I believe that school personnel must be proficient in implementing multiple interventions with children and their families. In addition, when planning and implementing interventions, educators must consider sociocultural differences. Educational programs for children and youth with E/BD should have several components in place to effectively meet the needs of these youth.

First, children and youth with behavioral difficulties frequently come in contact with many systems. It is not uncommon for them to encounter social service, juvenile justice, mental health, public health, and various other agencies. More and more, the responsibility befalls school personnel to coordinate these services to better meet the needs of children and their families. Many of these students will not lead productive lives if interagency collaboration of fiscal and human resources does not exist.

The education of students with behavioral disorders should look much differently than it did for students in previous decades. If we sincerely expect to provide relevant educational experiences, we must first be serious about recognizing, understanding, and affirming individual and cultural differences. That must be the message that resonates in all interactions with these children and their families. Regardless of setting, the programming options must be broadened to appeal to those differences. All educational programs for students with behavioral disorders should be guided by the following principles:

- *Caring relationships.* School personnel must demonstrate their acceptance of, and concern for, students in school, home, workplace, and community settings.
- *Commitment to affirming diversity.* The angst and fear often associated with student populations increasing in diversity must be replaced with attitudes of welcoming and affirming individual and cultural diversity.
- *Advocacy.* Professionals, parents, families, and community members must advocate for students with emotional or behavioral disorders. School personnel can work with family and community members on strategies that ensure that their rights are protected in school and community settings.
- *Ethical decision making.* When decisions are made to intervene with students suspected of E/BD, conscious efforts must be made to address the ethical and moral quandaries common to altering student behavior. Frequently used interventions often lack empirical data that will allow confident comparisons of anticipated benefits for students with predicted harm of not intervening (Kauffman, 1984).

While those principles should guide programmatic efforts, the following options should be available to children with behavioral disorders based on their needs:

- *Mental health component.* As a sign of the times, children and their family members are frequently in need of long-term mental health or therapeutic services. Teachers of children with behavioral disorders frequently complain about the lack of consistent counseling services received concurrently by their students and their families. When these services are provided, the duration is often too short to effect long-lasting changes.

- *Family and community partnerships.* School personnel must acknowledge their limitations in solely meeting the needs of all students. They also must enlist the support of family and community members in educating children and youth with behavioral disorders. Educational experiences should include the involvement of these individuals in a number of ways. It becomes even more critical for children of color. Fewer ethnic minority students are aspiring to become teachers. In fact, minority teachers will comprise less than 5% of all teachers by the turn of the century (King, 1993). Therefore, caring, same-ethnicity adults must be recruited from students' communities to serve as support systems or mentors. Such community involvement will ensure that the educational experiences that children receive are relevant.
- *Social and leadership skill enhancement.* Students must be taught prosocial skills that will improve their quality of life in the settings in which they interact. Strategies must be used that are culturally sensitive and relevant to student experiences (Epanchin, Townsend, & Stoddard, 1994; Franklin, 1992; Gilbert & Gay, 1985).
- *Academic component.* To the greatest extent possible, students should participate in the academic curriculum that parallels that of their peers without behavioral disorders.

CONCLUSIONS

I approached this chapter with ambivalent feelings. I was most excited about sharing my personal perspectives on the field of behavioral disorders but somewhat daunted by the status of the company I would be keeping (the other chapter authors). Unlike many of the authors of this book, I cannot relate firsthand accounts of events that have shaped the field. What I have done, however, is offered my reflections on the field through various lenses: as an educator, as an early career researcher, and as an African American woman.

I realize that our field has inherited many of its complexities. It is difficult to discuss emotional or behavioral disorders without first noting what is occurring within general education. More specifically, the intolerance of and insensitivity toward individual and cultural differences in general education have created some of our ethical and moral dilemmas relative to identification and service delivery. I also believe that many of our issues are not unique to the category of E/BD, as the fields of learning disabilities and mental retardation are similarly vexed. I say that not to commiserate but to contextualize what appear to be phenomena.

The field of behavioral disorders can, and should, take the lead in moving beyond the rhetoric on issues that keep coming back to haunt us. We must change the way we respond to identified educational, social, and ethical concerns. This is a time when innovation and comprehensiveness must be the order of the day. There are increased demands for practitioners, teacher trainers, researchers, and other related professionals to meet the challenges head on. Alternative prevention, identification, service delivery, and follow-up practices must be explored that affirm individual and cultural differences. After writing this chapter, *Sankofa* takes on a new meaning for me. When I reflect on the past, I realize why I am compelled to champion the cause of ethnic minority and poor children. They are positioned much differently in schools and society than their dominant-culture peers. I am even more convinced that when educational practices are defensible for these disenfranchised students, they undoubtedly will be defensible for all.

REFERENCES

Bower, E. M. (1960). *Early identification of emotionally disturbed children in school*. Springfield, IL: Charles C. Thomas.

Bower, E. M. (1982). Defining emotional disturbance: Public policy and research. *Psychology in the Schools, 19*, 55–60.

Brown v. Board of Education, 347 U.S. 483 (1954).

Deno, E. (1970). Special education as developmental capital. *Exceptional Children, 37*, 229–237.

Dunn, L. (1968). Special education for the mildly retarded: Is much of it justifiable? *Exceptional Children, 7*, 5–24.

Ellis, A., & Grieger, R. (1977). *Handbook of rational emotive therapy*. New York: Springer.

Epanchin, B. C., Townsend, B., & Stoddard, K. (1994). *Constructive classroom management: Strategies for creating positive learning environments*. Pacific Grove, CA: Brooks/Cole.

Forness, S. R., & Knitzer, J. (1992). A new proposed definition and terminology to replace "serious emotional disturbance" in Individuals with Disabilities Education Act. *School Psychology Review, 21*, 12–20.

Franklin, M. E. (1992). Culturally sensitive instructional practices for African American learners with disabilities. *Exceptional Children, 59*, 115–122.

Gilbert, S. E., & Gay, G. (1985). Improving the success in school of poor black children. *Phi Delta Kappan, 67*, 133–137.

Hewitt, F. M. (1968). *The emotionally disturbed child in the classroom*. Boston: Allyn & Bacon.

Huntze, S. L. (1985). Statement to support replacing the term seriously emotionally disturbed with the term behaviorally disordered as a descriptor for children and youth who are handicapped by their behavior. *Behavioral Disorders, 10*, 167–174.

Johnson, J. J. (1969). Special education in the inner city: A challenge for the future or another means of cooling the mark out? *Journal of Special Education, 3,* 242–251.

Kauffman, J. M. (1984). Saving children in the age of big brother: Moral and ethical issues in the identification of deviance. *Behavioral Disorders, 9,* 60–70.

King, S. H. (1993). The limited presence of African-American teachers. *Review of Educational Research, 63,* 115–149.

Long, N. J., & Newman, R. G. (1961). The teacher and his mental health: The teacher's handling of children in conflict. *Bulletin of School of Education, Indiana University,* 5–26.

Poplin, M. (1988). Holistic/constructivist principles of the teaching/learning process: Implications for the field of learning disabilities. *Journal of Learning Disabilities, 1,* 401–416.

Rhodes, W. C. (1967). The disturbed child: A problem in ecological management. *Exceptional Children, 33,* 449–455.

Stainback, W., & Stainback, S. (Eds.). (1990). *Support networks for inclusive schooling: Interdependent interrelated education.* Baltimore: Brookes.

Thousand, J. S., & Villa, R. A. (1989). Enhancing success in heterogeneous schools. In S. Stainback, W. Stainback, & M. Forest (Eds.), *Educating all students in the mainstream of regular education* (pp. 89–104). Baltimore: Brookes.

Tucker, J. (1980). Ethnic proportions in classes for the learning disabled: Issues in unbiased assessment. *Journal of Special Education, 14,* 93–105.

JO WEBBER
Southwest Texas State University

Jo Webber is an associate professor in the Department of Curriculum and Instruction at Southwest Texas State University. Most of Webber's experience has been with students with emotional disturbance who were residentially placed. She also has worked with children who have carried the diagnosis of autistic and severely emotionally disturbed. In addition to her teaching experiences, she has served as an administrator and director of programs for students with disabilities. Webber is immediate past president of the Council for Children with Behavioral Disorders and has published in the areas of emotional disturbance, autism, and behavior management. Her current research interests include cognitive psychology applications for students with emotional disturbance and all aspects of educating students with autism.

CHAPTER 22

The Field of Emotional and Behavioral Disorders: Past, Present, and Prescriptions

I was first attracted to the field of emotional and behavioral disorders (E/BD) because I wanted to impact the lives of children and youth who needed help and were not getting it. I knew I wanted to teach, but I had a feeling that most students would learn in spite of their teachers. I wanted to work with students who would not advance or, worse, might regress without a good teacher. I had a conversation one day with a teacher who told me about her students, who were the "behavioral problem kids" in the school. The other teachers in her school refused to teach these students, and she was chosen to teach them under some special circumstances. Something clicked. That was the type of challenge I was seeking. So I sought the best avenue for becoming certified to teach "tough" students. This path took me through elementary education to special education, specifically, a master's degree and, ultimately, a doctorate in the area of emotional disturbance. In my first graduate course I read *Conflict in the Classroom* (Long, Morse, & Newman, 1971), and I knew I had found my niche.

My philosophy has been twofold. First, I have attempted to stay focused on the ever-growing number of children and youth with E/BD in our society, who desperately need help and who generally have been neglected; second, I work to help these young people by teaching them, establishing programs for them, training others to teach them, and advocating on their behalf. This philosophy was developed through my religious bent to "feed the hungry and let the oppressed go free," and through a continuous fascination with human development. I grew up reading books such as *Pollyanna, Little Women, Death Be Not Proud*, and *Exodus* and wondered what made some people strong in the face of adversity while others became overwhelmed by everyday activities. This question still intrigues me. My choice to focus on needy children has been reinforced through the psychoeducational literature of Hobbs and Rhodes and through a particularly rewarding friendship with Nick Long. My teaching has been greatly influenced by the works of Skinner and other behavior-

399

ists, and by many humanistic educators who wrote in the late 1960s and early 1970s (e.g., Kozol, Gordon, Greenberg, Kohl, Ginot, Maustakas, and Silberman). I recently have become interested in the application of cognitive psychology with students with E/BD and have enjoyed the works of Ellis and Seligman. My list of colleagues in this field who continue to support me philosophically would be quite lengthy. In order to test my own commitment to my philosophical perspective, I daily assess the correlation between its premise and my professional activities as I regularly dialog with others who also are interested in the welfare of these young people.

PAST AND PRESENT

Since I'm generally an optimist, I think this is a great time to be in education. General education is undergoing major reform, and special education has joined them in many respects. Specifically, in the field of E/BD, the general public and many service agencies have developed a growing interest in the treatment of children and youth who cause others pain if they are left untreated. The general public is still not at the point of full "ownership" of young people with E/BD, but the mass media is beginning to highlight fragile young people and pinpoint the social factors that seem to put them at risk. Content analysis of newspapers and television programming is often a good indicator of social change, so the fact that many TV programs and newspaper articles have addressed child abuse, mental disorders, depression, substance abuse, gangs, youth violence, teen sexual behavior, and other such issues is reason for hope.

The field of E/BD is receiving a lot of attention. It's now up to those of us who care about these young people to assure that this attention results in productive policies. Despite this positive trend, school programming for students with E/BD generally has deteriorated in the past 20 years. My view of the current status of school programs contains both good and bad news.

WHO'S BEING SERVED AS E/BD?

Students served in special education as E/BD in the public schools tend to display one of three types of disorders: (a) conduct disorders (e.g., antisocial, acting-out juvenile delinquents), (b) anxiety and personality disorders (e.g., immature, fearful, thought disorders), or (c) neurological impairments (e.g., identified brain dysfunction, functional retardation, psychotic, autistic). Most of the students served in special education as E/BD are those with conduct disorders. In fact, current statistics show that most young people in general who need mental health services are violent and manifest disorders of conduct. Gangs, guns, murders, and drugs have become a way of life for many. Further bad news is the fact that students who are violent are most often not identified for special education services; thus, many students with disorders of conduct are left basically neglected by public education. This is despite the fact that a disproportionate number of individuals in the criminal justice system have learning disabilities and emotional disorders and a majority are school dropouts.

Because of the reluctance to serve aggressive students in special education, we have identified only approximately 1% of the school population as E/BD (National Mental Health Association [NMHA], 1993). According to Hewett and Forness (1984), in 1975 the federal government estimated (very conservatively) that 2% of the school population would meet the P.L. 94-142 definition criteria for seriously emotionally disturbed (SED). The mental health field currently (and conservatively) estimates 10% to 12% of all children and youth are in need of mental health services (e.g., Office of Technology Assessment, 1986; Institute of Medicine, 1989). So it appears that we are not qualifying the numerous students suffering from emotional and psychological disorders who might need special education services. This is cause for alarm because, left untreated, these students cause the most problems for their schools and for their community.

Most of the students served as E/BD are male, nonwhite, and poor and tend to come from single-parent homes (Knitzer, Steinberg, & Fleisch, 1990). For me, these facts raise many questions. What is it about our society that perpetuates the tendency for nonwhite children to be poor and to suffer physically and psychologically because of it? What is it about our societal value systems that might be contributing to the higher prevalence of deviance in youth? Why aren't more resources invested in addressing the predisposing conditions early, thus preventing mental disorders? How do we go about impacting a society that says on the one hand that drugs, sex, and violence are not things to value and, on the other hand, supports (through corporate sponsorship) those very things in hours and hours of TV programming? The United States seems to be entwined in a mass neurosis and manifests its values confusion in its disorganized public school policy and ultimately in the behavior of many of its young people.

Academically, students labeled E/BD do not fare well. Most have a below-average IQ, and only about 35% function at or above grade level (Kauffman, 1989). Additionally, about 46% will drop out before completing their education (NMHA, 1993). Whether IQ and achievement were adversely affected by existing emotional conditions or whether failure in school precipitated unhealthy emotional responses and behavioral difficulties is an interesting dilemma. In any case, the factors are interrelated and make for a challenging combination in the classroom. Not only do teachers have to manage aggressive, defiant, noncompliant, withdrawn, immature, and often bizarre behavior, but they also must teach subject matter to students who are neither motivated to learn it nor likely to learn it easily. Add to this the need for psychological intervention due to depression, anxiety, personality disorders, or psychosis and it becomes apparent that effective treatment is complicated and expensive.

Who's Teaching Them?

It is interesting to note that most of the school personnel who are labeling students as "deviant" and providing special education services are white, middle-class females who tend to be undertrained and undersupported (NMHA, 1993). Teacher turnover is high. The average classroom stay for teachers in E/BD classrooms is approximately 3 years. Because of the high turnover, many states have responded to the resulting teacher shortage by reducing their certification requirements. Alternative certification, fewer required university courses, fewer field-based options, and emergency certificates have caused many classrooms to be staffed with teachers who simply do not know how to effectively instruct students with E/BD. Master teachers are difficult to find, and field-based mentors are few.

Additionally, many university programs have moved to a generic certification program, so there are fewer categorical specialists. Most of these university programs also have adopted a predominantly behavioral philosophy. Where once the field was dominated with psychoanalytic treatment strategies (e.g., life space interview, group process, reality therapy, therapeutic milieus), it now appears to be dominated by the behavioral perspective (e.g., reinforcers, time-outs, and level systems). Instead of functioning as teacher-counselors (Hobbs, 1982), teachers today are trained to "control" behavior through contingency manipulation (Morgan & Jensen, 1992). Less time is spent on facilitating the student's psychological coping strategies, and more time is spent on teaching behavioral skills (such as social skills).

Because teacher training is often generic to match certification standards, teacher education is watered down and little is presented that is specific to students with E/BD. Secondary teachers, who are expected to teach in all content areas in Grades 7 through 12, and elementary teachers, who are expected to teach the "tool subjects" (i.e., reading, writing, and arithmetic), often are offered the same special education training program. Thus, one of the most basic requirements of teaching (knowledge of the curriculum) is not mastered by most first-year special education teachers. Teachers working with students with E/BD historically have struggled to provide adequate academic instruction. That is still the case today.

Public school evaluations of teachers of students with E/BD are usually completed by principals and supervisors who usually do not know more than the teacher about effective treatment for students with E/BD. This means that in many cases teachers who are ineffective are often rewarded. This is particularly true at the secondary level, where the teacher either demands nothing or punishes harshly, thus minimizing acting-out behaviors. These teachers are often evaluated highly because acting-out behavior is not visible. Whether the students are being taught something useful, whether they have learned to generalize appropriate behavior, or whether their disturbance has been alleviated seems to be irrelevant. Because advocacy for these students is minimal, few people insist on effective instruction. So the cycle continues: undertrained and ineffective teachers, high turnover, undertrained teachers, ineffective instruction, high turnover.

Inaccurate teacher evaluations also result in many good teachers not being recognized and "burning out" from lack of status and support. Well-trained teachers usually are found in states where certification is contingent on completion of a full general education program and training (usually categorical) consists of a combination of psychoeducational techniques (Hobbs, 1982) and sound behavioral techniques (Morgan & Jensen, 1992). These are states where the state education department provides leadership in the field of E/BD and where school administrators often come out of the special education ranks. Segregated facilities actually possess the best circumstances for training teachers well and retaining good teachers because there is more opportunity for close supervision and because the administrators are usually specialists in the field. Additionally, most segregated facilities adopt a uniform educational philosophy. In effective segregated programs, master teachers may be developed and may be used to train new personnel. Unfortunately, the same opportunities are not as readily available in the public schools.

WHAT'S IN A DEFINITION?

Since the inception of P.L. 94-142, the SED definition has caused controversy. Even Bower, its author, referred to it as the defective definition. The issue of eligibility determination does not hold much interest for me. I prefer to assign my energy to the larger issues mentioned in this chapter. However, I can appreciate the fact that, in most instances, general educators and the general public will not, of their own accord, plan and program for students with E/BD. If the federal law were not in existence, most of these students would receive little or no educational services. The presence of the federal law has not succeeded in promoting a positive view of these students; thus, we are still dependent on the top-down mandate for educational programming. As long as this situation remains unchanged, eligibility determination will be a major portion of special education.

It is obvious from our low and variable prevalence rates that the current federal definition of SED is too restrictive and too easily manipulated. It would be better to use a less restrictive and more reliable definition. The proposed definition for E/BD put forth by the Special Education and Mental Health Coalition (*Federal Register*, February 10, 1993, p. 7938) seems a viable alternative. This definition is preferable for several reasons. It acknowledges the characteristics of most of the students now served as SED (i.e., students with disorders of conduct), it provides for cultural- and age-appropriate comparisons in order to determine deviance, and it describes educational performance as more than academic achievement. Finally, use of this definition would allow more of the children and youth who need mental health services to obtain them under the auspices of the federal law.

I would like to think that we would identify all students who are socially or emotionally fragile and in need of mental health services, self-control training, and social skills training, and that we would provide them with quality services. Trying to differentiate emotional disturbance from social maladjustment or from behavioral disorders seems like a useless exercise. Rather, we need to decide what to do about all the students who need help and who have heretofore been neglected.

Presently, special education seems best designed (because of the federal mandate) to help these students. Instead of restricting placement into special education, educators should allow more students to receive special education. Many disagree with my views (usually because of the cost involved), and many make the case that general education (and, even better, juvenile justice) should be serving students with conduct disorders. But general education is currently struggling to meet its own mandate and to prevent any further detrimental effects caused by society's negligence of its children; juvenile justice is still primarily a reactive system unable to provide adequate treatment. Special educators, with the support of various community agency personnel, should educate students who manifest significant problems. That would mean adopting a better and broader definition of this needy population.

CURRENT ISSUES AND TRENDS

It's hazardous being a kid in the United States. It is a well-known fact that more and more of our children and youth have mental health needs and fewer of them are receiving any services. It has been estimated that 12% to 15% of the 63 million children and youth in the United States are in need of mental health treatment but up to 80% of these children and youth are not receiving any (National Mental Health Association, 1989). During the 1980s we became less generous with services for families and children. Since then, the general health and well-being of our young people has deteriorated. It appears that the need for special education for the nation's fragile children (particularly those with E/BD) is more crucial now than ever before.

The U.S. Department of Health and Human Services (1989) estimated that 25% of the youth (ages 10 to 17) are at high risk for multiple problem behaviors, including drug abuse, school failure, delinquency, and unwanted pregnancy. Many other factors contribute to the risk for emotional and behavioral problems. Approximately 20% of our children live in poverty, and more than that live in single-parent households (Reed & Sautter, 1990). Twelve million children in the United States go to bed hungry each night, approximately 1 million children will be without a home for some period of time this year, and 1.3 million teenagers will run away or be living on the streets due to parent rejection (Harris, 1991). Our country is increasingly characterized by massive family disruption that adversely affects child development and poses serious health hazards for our children and youth.

Additionally, some experts estimate that an extra 10% of students entering school will need special education due to their mothers using crack cocaine during pregnancy (Jones, 1990). One in six children tests positively for lead toxicity, which negatively impacts their educational performance (National Health/Educational Consortium, 1991). It is important to note the interaction of socioeconomic status, health, family integrity, and emotional well-being if we are to prevent children's psychological problems. Rates of E/BD are approximately 3 times less for middle- and upper-socioeconomic groups than in lower-socioeconomic groups (U.S. Department of Health and Human Services, 1989).

Other horrifying statistics regarding the emotional well-being of children and youth in the United States are publicized regularly. It has been estimated that 90,000 juveniles are incarcerated and more than 625,000 pass through those facilities yearly (Price & Vitolo, 1988). There is a rising trend of suicide among young people age 15 to 19 (approximately 10 in 100,000), and depression, personality disorders, and alcohol or drug abuse are major contributing risk factors (U.S. Department of Health and Human Services, 1989). One report stated that 39% of high school seniors reported getting drunk regularly, and more than 3.5 million 12- to 17-year-olds have tried marijuana, one third being regular users (National Commission, 1990). This same report stated that 1 in every 10 adolescents gets pregnant every year and that we have an epidemic of sexually transmitted diseases (including AIDS) among our youth. Furthermore, each day, 135,000 students in the United States bring guns to school, and 9 out of 10 young murder victims in the industrialized world are from the United States. The national high school dropout rate is estimated to be 15% overall and as high as 50% in some large cities (Hahn, 1987). This very bad news points to the fact that much needs to be done to promote prevention efforts and to treat those who are already suffering.

SERVICES HAVE BEEN INADEQUATE

The dirth of services to needy students continues because few advocates intervene on behalf of these young people. Funding, not the needs of children, seems to be the primary determinant of who receives treatment and training. A catch-22 exists in that it is difficult to obtain funding if the prevalence figures do not warrant it, but the current limited funds (particularly in special education) put pressure on policy developers and legislators to restrict the eligibility criteria for services; thus, prevalence figures stay low. For example, because most states require that a certified psychologist or psychiatrist supervise the eligibility assessment for E/BD, small school districts with limited resources tend to choose an alternative (cheaper to assess) label or to deal with the student solely through exclusionary techniques.

Additionally, school administrator groups (e.g., National Association of School Boards) that are strenuously objecting to the more inclusive proposed definition of E/BD are acting out of fear that schools will be obligated to educate (at some cost) aggressive and defiant students who currently tend to be punished, expelled, ignored, or referred to the criminal justice authorities at little cost to the schools. Even for students who do qualify for special education services, placement into classrooms where the student–teacher ratio is unmanageable, where mental health or counseling support is unavailable, where the curriculum is often irrelevant, and where interagency coordination is only mentioned in jest is commonplace. Special educators are struggling to adequately serve students currently identified as E/BD, and many are probably thankful for the more restrictive definition.

The lack of interagency coordination is more bad news in the field of E/BD. Mental health, human services, juvenile justice, and special education have, in most cases, continued to act separately and keep separate records due to separate funding, separate mandates, and separate training. This means that many students fall through the cracks, and, if they are receiving multiple services, these services seem to be disconnected. For example, in our urban district in which I consulted, a student was adjudicated and ordered by the judge to attend school. The judgment stated that his mother would be fined $50 a day for each day that he was not in school. This was a single, poor mother. The next day in school, the student cursed at a teacher and school administrators kicked him out for 3 days! Case management is very rare for students with E/BD, and instances of miscommunication or contradictory programming abound.

Although most state education departments and local school districts attempt to provide a range of services for students with E/BD, these services are often differentially applied. For instance, psychiatric inpatient care often is only available for those who have insurance coverage. Thus, white, middle-class students with E/BD may get inpatient care while poor minority students get "served" by the juvenile justice system or get no treatment at all. Private psychiatric inpatient providers have recently been under fire for unethical practices such as "paying bounty" to school personnel for referrals, refusing to release children at their parents' request, not providing purchased services, releasing patients before they are ready because their insurance runs out, and falsifying documents (Council for Children with Behavioral Disorders [CCBD], 1992). Although many psychiatric inpatient providers are ethical and provide appropriate treatment, there is rarely an adequate transition for students returning to the public schools or an accountability system for documenting treatment effects.

In rural school districts, necessary services often are sorely inadequate or lacking altogether. Additionally, these districts have few or no teachers trained to educate students with E/BD. Thus, there is an overreliance on consultants to provide assessment and technical assistance. This type of assistance is often inadequate for the ongoing needs of the students, and most teachers (because they do not know better) rely too heavily on controlling the students with punishment. The good news is that in rural districts there is more often a desire by school personnel to "take care of their own." They are generally reluctant to ship students off to other geographical areas for treatment.

On the other hand, urban school districts, while having more available resources, find that agencies operate in isolation. That fact and the challenge of trying to serve massive numbers of students with complex social problems often result in a lower tolerance for serving students with E/BD in the schools. Many urban school districts have the least amount of funding per pupil and the highest teacher turnover. The predicament of students with E/BD in poor urban school districts is very disheartening.

GENERAL EDUCATION IS STRUGGLING

The public schools have not fared well over the last 15 years. Because we still fund public education with property taxes and some tax bases have dwindled, the schools are trying to do more with less. Students are coming to schools with a myriad of problems (e.g., undernourished, abused, neglected, unsupervised, undersocialized), but the charge to public education has been and still is to create literate students who excel in math and science and who can function well in a global economy (see Education Goals 2000 [Bush, 1991]). Since many students are not ready to learn, educators are caught in the bind of trying to meet the academic achievement charge while temporarily alleviating students' social and emotional problems.

The result has been a poor job of both—thus the public's harsh judgment of the education system. Additionally, inconsistent educational philosophies, untrained school boards, overwhelmed school administrators, high dropout rates, high failure rates, chaotic instructional environments (especially in inner-city secondary schools), and an overdependence on punishment to keep order prevail. Unfortunately, humanistic education has been condemned consistently by conservative factions that believe that values and beliefs should be addressed only at home. Any curriculum designed to provide students with thinking skills, social skills, assertiveness skills, and coping strategies has been soundly criticized.

Recently, however, the educational reform movement has set a new course. At least school personnel, if not the general public, have recognized that students need more than academic instruction. Some school boards across the country are considering alternative strategies for dealing with students' social and emotional problems. Evidence of this new perspective is seen in school-based health clinics, drug intervention programs, dropout-prevention programs, coordination with mental health agency personnel for services, day care for students' children, an emphasis on problem-solving curriculum and team decision making, and a move toward most personalized education for all students. However, these things are not happening in most schools. There is much disagreement about the best way to educate our youth so, in too many instances, curriculum is compromised and educational methodology is subject to fad. Curiously, there are now private entrepreneurs seeking to run public schools more effectively at less cost. Can this be done? Will various types of students be included in the experiment? For all practical purposes we must be content that the jury is still out.

REASON FOR HOPE

Even though the picture seems bleak, some very positive changes have started to take shape pertaining to the field of E/BD, particularly in the realm of prevention. The Individuals with Disabilities Act (IDEA) now includes guidelines and incentive funding for programming for infants and toddlers. This preventative model has been extended by the U.S. Attorney General, who also has targeted early intervention as a priority for crime prevention. Head Start funding continues to be increased—more evidence that prevention is becoming a federal priority.

Obviously, childhood in this country has fundamentally changed, for it seems to be more uncertain, more dangerous, and more confusing. It is also obvious that we need to support and assist with the healthy development of our children. It seems better to plug up the hole in a leaky boat than to continue to bail out the water (Knitzer et al., 1990). Some school programs, following the prevention initiatives, have initiated efforts to identify children and families who are at risk for developing psychological disorders and through community education or multiagency programs provide them with education regarding child-rearing practices, vocational skills, access to resources, and strategies for coping with economic and personal crises.

The current health care reform also includes positive implications for services to children and youth with E/BD. President Clinton's original bill to Congress in 1993 included mental health benefits such as coverage for inpatient and residential care (e.g., therapeutic family homes, therapeutic group homes, crisis residential facilities, residential detoxification centers, or residential treatment centers) (Stroul & Pires, 1994). This bill also included coverage for intensive nonresidential services such as day treatment, partial hospitalization, psychiatric rehabilitation, home-based services, and behavioral aides. Finally, outpatient care such as assessment, crisis services, psychotherapy, substance-abuse counseling, medical management, and case management would be covered. This move toward the universal availability of less expensive, less intrusive, and least restrictive service delivery is heartening. However, it appears that this intended legislation has a long haul prior to its acceptance by our nation's lawmakers.

Most hopeful has been the initiation of mental health reform, specifically the Children and Adolescent Social System Program (CASSP) in 1984 (Stroul & Friedman, 1986). This movement set the stage for the development of comprehensive systems of care for children and youth with SED across the country. The primary tasks for the CAASP were to (a) delineate the components of an ideal service system for children and youth with SED and improve access to these services, (b) increase the priority for budget allocation for child and adolescent mental health services, (c) improve agency coordination and include family participation in services, (d) ensure culturally competent services, and (e) evaluate the progress of states and communities. To date, 35 states have received CASSP development grants, and the National Institute of Mental Health has added a major research component, the National Plan for Research on Child and Adolescent Mental Disorders (Hoagwood & Hohmann, 1993), to address critical gaps in our knowledge of mental disorders in children and adolescents.

Inspired by the momentum of the CASSP initiative, the Mental Health Association spearheaded an effort in 1987 to gather several organizations representing parents, mental health, and special education and formed the Mental Health and Special Education Coalition. This coalition was to reach agreement on the extent and nature of the problems facing children and youth with E/BD and further attempt to address these problems (National Mental Health and Special Education Coalition, 1987). The coalition identified problem areas such as parent advocacy, identification and assessment, delivery of appropriate services, ethnic and culturally diverse children with SED, coordination of multiple service agencies, training, and research.

The coalition was, in turn, instrumental in the passage of the IDEA authorization for federal special education initiatives, one of which was Programs for Children and Youth with Serious Emotional Disturbance. The Office of Special Education Programs (OSEP) in the Department of Education subsequently developed a national agenda for the purpose of focusing the "attention of educators, parents, advocates, and professionals from a variety of disciplines on what needs to be done to encourage, assist, and support our nation's schools in their efforts to achieve better outcomes for children and youth with serious emotional disturbance" (Osher, 1993, p. 8). This agenda is well coordinated with the CAASP efforts.

As mentioned previously, more good news lies in general education school reform. General educators seem to be attempting to change how schools do business by providing "special" education for all students. The general education literature is repleat with information regarding "personalized" education, criterion-referenced assessment, side-by-side learning, multimodal strategies, thinking strategy curriculum, integrated classrooms, team decision making, self-paced instruction, cooperative learning, innovative motivational techniques, and functional curriculum. Additionally, school reform has forced an inspection of public school organization in general, and many school personnel have developed a more humanistic attitude toward students with problems. These attitudes seem to be resulting in a more responsive system.

There's also hope in the current special education literature. There is more interest in targeting functional life skills for students with E/BD, instead of persisting with a nonfunctional academic curriculum. Various social skill, problem-solving, and self-management curricula have been developed and are being researched. Emphasis also has been placed on teaching students to generalize those skills. Behavior-management techniques have improved with the mass training of applied behavioral analysis. The use of functional analysis of behavior to discover the relationship of a behavior to its context has improved behavior planning. Manipulating antecedent variables (e.g., instructional strategies, scheduling, classroom arrangement, prompts, self-monitoring) and differential reinforcement of alternate behavior has switched the teacher's emphasis from simply reacting to students' behavior to that of a proactive training philosophy. The Regular Education Initiative movement in the late 1980s and the recent full inclusion movement out of The Association for Severe Handicaps (TASH), while seeming to threaten the well-being of many students with E/BD, have at least provoked an inspection of resource room programming and encouraged a move toward more serious integration efforts. Finally, there seems to be more emphasis on advocacy and applied research in the literature.

Particularly hopeful is the fact that federal agency initiatives and the E/BD literature seem to agree. We appear to be flying in formation. Federal agendas and policies are targeting what we know in special education to be best practices (e.g., prevention, a full range of services, child/family-driven programs, appropriate assessment, multiagency collaboration, quality treatment, well-trained personnel, and applied research) and this unified view of treatment for children and youth who are at risk for E/BD is trickling down to state and local levels. Thus, we are beginning to see more community services and many "model" public school programs for students with E/BD develop nationally.

PRESCRIPTIONS

What should be done for students with E/BD? Promising practices abound. In my opinion, however, programs for students with E/BD need to contain several key components:

- a good teacher
- academic instruction
- behavior management
- affective education
- social skills instruction
- generalization training
- case management and community services
- individualized programming for integration

These components work best if they are interrelated so they are not necessarily listed in priority order. These components might be pertinent to any type of educational setting but were developed with public school programming in mind.

A Good Teacher

Students with E/BD will fare best with a teacher who uses effective instructional techniques, who communicates so that students will listen, and who listens so that students will disclose their feelings and thoughts. A good teacher should have knowledge of pertinent content and have the ability to develop age-appropriate relevant curricula in a variety of areas (e.g., academic areas for various grade levels K through 12, tool subjects, social skills, prevocational and vocational skills, self-control strategies, learning strategies, affective education). This teacher should be able to deliver instruction in innovative ways to make it interesting, challenging, and fun. She or he should be able to use various lesson delivery systems such as learning centers, computer-assisted instruction, well-paced direct instruction, visual media, group discussion, cooperative learning, and discovery lessons. A good teacher also needs to manage and alter the challenging behavior of each student using appropriate applied behavior-analysis techniques while protecting each student from psychological and physical harm.

In addition to effective instructional strategies, a good teacher would do well to have some applied knowledge in psychology, preferably cognitive psychology. Facilitating a student's social/emotional development is of primary importance, and a good teacher will understand the difference between training skills and facilitating this development. Teachers need to regularly enhance students' self-esteem, teach self-control strategies, facilitate optimistic mind-sets, and promote accurate perceptions of the world.

Good teachers remain psychologically sound themselves and behave in appropriate and healthy ways. Hobbs (1982) suggested that teachers who are successful with students with E/BD must "have the qualities of personality that make [each day] . . . rewarding and . . . must have the resilience to keep at it week after week." This person must "be able to do things with competence and assurance" (p. 89), and, further, is a person who is

> able to give and receive affection, to live relaxed, and to be firm; a person with private resources for the nourishment and refreshment of his own life; not an itinerant worker but a professional through and through; a person with a sense of the significance of time, of the usefulness of today and the promise of tomorrow, a person of hope, quiet confidence, and joy; one who has committed himself to children and to the proposition that children who are disturbed can be helped. (p. 82)

Additionally, a good teacher will be a creative problem solver, will be sensitive to the plight of his or her students, will possess a good sense of humor, and will be able to act appropriately in crises.

ACADEMIC INSTRUCTION

The second component for a model E/BD program is good academic instruction. For elementary-age students this means quality instruction in the tool subjects (reading, written expression, spelling, handwriting, oral language) and in common content areas (i.e., math, social studies, health, science, physical education, art, music). For secondary students, instruction in academic content areas (i.e., social studies, math, science, language arts, computer literacy) and vocational preparation is preferable. Instruction should incorporate motivating activities and materials such as high-interest, low-level reading materials; building projects; learning centers; instructional games; and stimulating computer software. Instructional content would best be task analyzed and presented in small chunks with frequent opportunities to practice. Correct responses need to be reinforced frequently until behavioral maintenance is targeted. It's best for students to be engaged in successful learning activities for at least 80% to 85% of the school day. Downtime should be avoided. Sponge activities (fun activities, such as Hangman, that provide practice for old learning) might take the place of free time. Even if free time is offered as a reinforcer, it should be structured and include activities that result in functional learning.

Routines and schedules are important and should change infrequently. Procedures for things such as obtaining materials, entering and exiting the classroom, asking questions, and asking for help should be taught and reinforced. Each student should be working at his or her instructional level, which may require individual folders, special instructions on audiotapes, small-group instruction, and side-by-side learning. Multimodal strategies often are effective. The rule of thumb is to have the students See-Say-Do for each learning objective presented. Mastering learning strategies is an important companion to academic instruction. Most students with E/BD need to learn to organize their materials, study, attend to auditory stimuli for longer periods of time, read for understanding, take notes, manage their time wisely, listen for understanding, incorporate various methods for remembering, solve problems, and ask for help. Acquiring learning strategies and school survival skills can allow more opportunities for success in school.

BEHAVIOR MANAGEMENT

If a strong academic component is in place, then the behavior management component is more easily developed. Usually effective instruction alone is not enough to alleviate aggressive and noncompliant behavior resulting from things such as low frustration tolerance, anger, fear, and confusion. It is best to establish a structured contingency-management system, including functional assessment, several methods of differential reinforcement, and a continuum of reductive techniques to be used as necessary. Some of the best behavior-management systems rely on token systems and provide various powerful backup reinforcers. Students may be awarded points for periods of time without inappropriate behavior or points for alternate behaviors such as readily following directions, task completion, on-task behavior, conflict avoidance, conflict resolution, appropriate social skills, and task accuracy. When the management of behavior is turned over to the students themselves in the form of self-monitoring and self-evaluation, the entire system becomes stronger. Students might be required to keep track of their own behaviors (particularly positive ones) or rate themselves as to how well they matched the classroom standards and individual behavior goals. (See Young, West, Smith, & Morgan, 1991, for additional information regarding the application of self-management strategies.)

Many classrooms for students with E/BD now incorporate level systems whereby the reinforcers, points, and required behavior are arranged into levels, with movement to the general education classroom at the highest level. I do not usually recommend level systems because of misuse (see Scheuermann, Webber, Partin, & Knies, 1994) and because a well-developed token system can promote similar results and can allow for the easier application of individualized programming. A strong behavior-management system might best include a response-cost (fining) system built into the token economy for further reducing inappropriate behavior. Overcorrection is another effective reductive technique. Students are required to perform restitution or engage in positive practice to an exaggerated level as a consequence of inappropriate behavior. For example, the student who throws food in the cafeteria must wash all the tables and mop the entire floor in the cafeteria, or a student who makes a rude comment must shake hands and apologize 20 times that day.

In some cases it might be necessary to have a series of time-out options for aggressive students. This is usually recommended when there is a history of violent or dangerous behavior. One obvious drawback to time-out is that it is very difficult to teach interpersonal skills and prosocial behavior when a student spends a great deal of time in isolation. Also, time-out, particularly seclusionary time-out, tends to be overused, because teachers are reinforced when a student is removed from the classroom. If time-out is incorporated, staff should be well-trained in the technique and behavioral data should be inspected regularly to assure its proper use. Positive reductive techniques (e.g., effective instruction, differential reinforcement, counseling) are preferred and should occur in conjunction with any reductive techniques.

An ideal program for students with E/BD includes a crisis-intervention component as part of the behavior-management system. Since students with this disability often display violent, aggressive, and destructive behavior, it is prudent to have a plan for dealing with individuals in crisis. The plan should include staff training in crisis prevention and intervention, steps for dealing with various crises, procedures for including the local police and other emergency personnel, and crisis follow-up strategies. It also might be wise to practice the procedures regularly.

The goal of a strong behavior-management system is to eventually fade external reinforcers and punishers and to bring students under more naturally occurring antecedent control. In order to have students internalize the management of their own behavior, they should be taught self-management strategies (e.g., self-monitoring, self-evaluation) and social problem-solving, rational thinking, and relaxation techniques. Students can be better motivated to use these self-management strategies and to internalize behavioral control if their social and emotional needs are adequately addressed.

AFFECTIVE INSTRUCTION

An effective educational program for students with emotional and behavioral disorders should contain a component for regularly addressing the students' social/emotional development. Students with E/BD, by definition, exhibit an inability to express feelings appropriately and to relate well to others. One method of addressing affective development is through a group process. Many students could benefit from participation in a group where they are encouraged to discuss individual problems and feelings, set goals for the day or week, analyze individual performance, and practice social skills. In order for this group process to be effective, the teacher needs group facilitation skills, the students need to be trained and reinforced for "group" behavior, and everyone needs to feel safe psychologically and physically. Group process time can be used to facilitate the development of generosity, honesty, altruism, and tolerance. Self-concept enhancement exercises can be incorporated into groups. Groups can also be a forum for facilitating coping strategies, rational thinking, optimism, self-efficacy, moral development, and social problem solving.

In effective school programs, adults should work hard to establish a trust relationship with the students. By communicating respect and interest, by choosing words deliberately, by asking good questions, and by listening carefully, teachers can encourage students to disclose their feelings and thoughts and to explore new ways of thinking and acting. The safety, belongingness, and esteem needs of each student are important considerations in effective school programs, and addressing these needs should be a regular part of the school day.

SOCIAL SKILLS INSTRUCTION

Closely related to behavior management and affective development is the training of social skills. When students are directly taught skills to enhance interpersonal relationships, reduce stress, handle anger, and make friends, they can learn to behave better and may, subsequently, feel better. In the past 10 years, many social skills curricula have been developed and researched (e.g., Mastropieri & Scruggs, 1994).

Direct instruction is usually recommended for social skills training, and the published curricula often contain suggestions for modeling, role-playing, homework, and review activities. Most social skills programs include a screening instrument and curriculum-based assessment. Effective E/BD programs should include daily instruction in social skills, regular assessment of student performance, reinforcement for demonstrating the skills, and generalization training. The emergence of social skills training in E/BD programs has added a very important and effective component. Rather than assuming that students won't act right, it is now assumed that students do not know how to act right and need to be taught. This is an essential concept.

GENERALIZATION TRAINING

Once students master academic and social behaviors, the instructional emphasis switches to that of teaching them to perform under different conditions. The issue of generalization has historically been of concern in our field because so many students with E/BD are not able to "make it" in the real world. Even when students show academic and social progress in special education, many never succeed in general education, and rates of criminal behavior, dropping out, and unemployment are extremely high. Success in special education means that students are able to function well without us. We have not finished our job until this is so.

Behavioral literature has delineated several methods of training generalization (e.g., Morgan & Jensen, 1992). By targeting generalization in every aspect of the program, teachers might find many opportunities to encourage and reward independence. The following strategies might assist with this endeavor:

1. Choose strategies and reinforcers that are easy to fade and that can easily transfer to other pertinent settings (e.g., bus, general education, home, work.

2. Develop a curriculum for each student that will provide him or her with essential competencies for the targeted setting and that might mask some of his or her deviances (e.g., academic curriculum matched to general education, school survival skills, social skills [especially compliance], or vocational skills matched to available jobs).

3. Try techniques such as "sequential modification" that are discussed in the behavioral literature.

4. Train self-management techniques, particularly self-monitoring and self-evaluation (see Rhode, Morgan, & Young, 1983).
5. Assure that learning goals and objectives are socially valid (i.e., significant people in the child's life agree they are important).
6. Teach behaviors that will likely receive natural reinforcement.

The motivation for people to incorporate learned skills into their daily activities often has to do with whether they believe they can successfully perform the behavior and whether they perceive the outcomes to be desirable. Thus, generalization training and affective education are interrelated. Teachers need to work to promote self-efficacy, optimism, and persistence, for, ultimately, externally applied motivators must be faded. In order for generalization to occur, students must have mastered appropriate skills, understand how to apply the skills under different conditions, and be motivated to use them. Training generalization may be one of the greatest challenges for educators.

CASE MANAGEMENT AND COMMUNITY SERVICES

In addition to effective instruction in the classroom, good practice requires the coordination of various aspects of a student's life. In 1966, Project Re-Ed (Hobbs, 1974) promoted the notion of case management as an essential part of a student's educational program. Based in ecological theory, the thinking was that, in order to educate a student with E/BD, school personnel needed to also target the operation of a student's entire social system. Liaison teachers were trained as case managers and were assigned the task of assessing and intervening in the student's social system in such a way as to compliment and enhance what the teacher was trying to accomplish in the classroom. Because of the expense, most public schools today do not have such a case management function, and, subsequently, students often remain in dysfunctional family units, continue to fail at school and work, receive few effective services, and often are "mainlined" into the most restrictive (and expensive) settings. Fortunately, the concept of case management for students with E/BD has been renewed through the Children and Adolescent Social System Program (CASSP).

The CASSP model provides case management and recommends a massive interagency effort to provide family and child-driven services. Many CASSP programs include a team of agency personnel (education, mental health, social services, juvenile justice, vocational rehabilitation, health, recreation) that reviews cases and develops a comprehensive service system for a particular student and his family. The student is assigned a case manager (usually from mental health or social work) who oversees the program and who coordinates all its aspects. This person can become a regular advocate and provide the type of coordination that might greatly augment the likelihood of skill generalization. In CASSP programs, special education teachers are often included on the planning teams, and their students might receive mental health, social, and other services in the school.

In the CASSP comprehensive service system, mental health workers take the role of counselor and case manager. Often they are involved in family preservation efforts to facilitate the family's ability to operate productively and to cope with the target child. Social service agency personnel (e.g., child protective workers, food stamp specialists, social workers) also serve in these capacities. Juvenile justice authorities work with the team to prevent students from committing crimes, to obtain judgments that are educational and constructive, and to return young people from the legal system to the schools. The key is that various professionals work together to plan and deliver the multiple support services that a student with E/BD needs in order to remain at home and in the community.

Best practices in school programs for students with E/BD should include many community services in and around the school for families and students who need them. This concept is known as "one-stop shopping." With this ecological model of planning and service delivery, the special education teacher's job is greatly enhanced and prevention/intervention efforts for students with E/BD are usually quite successful.

INDIVIDUALIZED PROGRAMMING FOR INTEGRATION

The integration of students with E/BD into the mainstream of society is a primary goal in good educational programs. Good programs provide many options for students in terms of curricula, methodologies, and placements so that individual students can receive what they need at any given time. Current literature is repleat with professional opinions regarding the integration of special education students. I personally think we would do well to follow the current legal mandate (i.e., IDEA), which stipulates that a student should be removed from general education only to the extent necessary for his or her appropriate education. This mandate implies that services would best be delivered in general education classrooms but that removal to other settings is always an option. We currently have case law (e.g., *Daniel R. R. v. State Board of Education*, 1989) that provides guidelines for determining when a student should be included in general education and when more restrictive options would be better. An important premise of IDEA is that this decision should be determined individually and should be based on the assessed needs of a particular student.

Special education programs resulting from the 1975 law (P.L. 94-142) have been criticized for many years because parallel education systems were established, pullout programs have not always been effective, and special education costs too much. When the Regular Education Initiative (REI) emerged as the second special education effort to integrate students with disabilities, proponents (mostly representing students with learning disabilities) wrote that students with mild to moderate disabilities would achieve better academically in the general education classroom with adaptations. The REI proponents recommended cooperative learning, team teaching, teacher assistant teams, and professional development for general educators. This movement was criticized by advocates for students with E/BD because it ignored the research that some students fared better in pullout programs, and because general educators had already failed with our students.

A third special education integration movement is now upon us: the full inclusion movement. This reform movement was initiated within advocacy groups representing students with mental retardation (e.g., TASH, ARC). The premise of this movement is that segregation is bad and that integration is good. The reformers believe that placement of students with disabilities into general education will afford them an opportunity to make friends and to progress socially. Full inclusionists write that *all* special education students would fare best in general education classrooms, that special education should be deconstructed, that individualized approaches should give way to community building, and that anyone who disagrees with them is a bigot and an all-around bad person. This movement has been criticized by advocates for students with E/BD as insular, radical, unrealistic, illegal, and not in the best interest of most special education students, particularly those with emotional and behavioral disorders. Critics also have reiterated support for a full continuum of educational options (CCBD, 1994) and have appealed to the radical reformers to become more responsive to general education and more reasonable in their reform efforts.

Now that general education is reforming, it is a perfect time to join them. This general education "inclusive" schools movement is based on a premise of ownership of all students and on an effort to provide personalized education for each student. It seems that general education is finally ready to consider more integrative strategies, something special education has been attempting since 1975. That means special educators need to consider the general education perspective and promote the integration agenda in a responsible and deliberate fashion. A merger of the two systems could mean an expansion of the continuum of services for more students who need them.

Inclusion could benefit students with E/BD, but only if advocates resist the zealots and assure that these students are not dumped into general education with no support and without generalization training. There is reason to be hopeful if advocates assure individualized programming, prevent harsher punishers and a tendency to push the students out of school altogether, and work to obtain ideal program components for all students. Some students would best be served in general education classrooms, and support services such as "class-within-a-class" models, self-monitoring, crisis centers, and comprehensive wraparound services have worked to make this a reality. However, some students with E/BD would not fare best in general education classrooms, and they have a right to the placement best suited to their needs.

CONCLUSION

My prescription for students with E/BD includes myriad interrelated best practice components, competent adults, and child-driven treatment. Striving for more effective educational programs will demand our unwavering persistence and our focused energy. The time is now right for positive change in regard to students with E/BD. It's time to move toward providing more students with more and better services while they are in school; to move toward more coordination and co-funding of services; to move toward better trained special educators and more effective school programs; to move toward sharing special education expertise with general education and becoming involved in educational reform; to move toward educating people about how to care for their children; and to move toward advocating, not abdicating. We can and should shape the future for students with E/BD. The ball is in our court. "There is no single answer or quick fix to the problems now facing these children. But as we stand at the schoolhouse door, we can see many windows of opportunity . . . ." (Knitzer et al., 1990, p. ix). It is up to us to seize them.

REFERENCES

Bush, G. (1991). *America 2000: An education strategy*. Washington, DC: U.S. Department of Education. (ERIC Document Reproduction Service No. ED 327 009).

Council for Children with Behavioral Disorders. (August, 1992). A national crisis at psychiatric hospitals. *CCBD Newsletter,* 1.

Council for Children with Behavioral Disorders. (1994). *Council for Children with Behavioral Disorders Newsletter, 8,* 1.

Daniel R. R. v. State Board of Education, 874 F.2d. 1036 (5th Cir. 1989).

Federal Register. (1993, February). Washington, DC: U.S. Government Printing Office.

Hahn, A. (1987). Reaching out to America's dropouts: What to do? *Phi Delta Kappan, 69,* 256–263.

Harris, R. (1991, May 26). Stunted growth. *Austin American-Statesman*, p. E1, E7.

Hewett, F. M., & Forness, S. R. (1984). *Education of exceptional learners* (3rd ed.). Boston: Allyn & Bacon.

Hoagwood, K., & Hohmann, A. A. (1993). Child and adolescent services research at the National Institute of Mental Health: Research opportunities in an emerging field. *Journal of Child and Family Studies, 2*(3), 259–268.

Hobbs, N. (1974). Nicholas Hobbs. In J. M. Kauffman & C. D. Lewis (Eds.), *Teaching children with behavioral disorders: Personal perspectives* (pp. 142–167). Columbus, OH: Merrill.

Hobbs, N. (1982). *The troubled and troubling child*. San Francisco: Jossey-Bass.

Institute of Medicine. (1989). *Report of a study: Research on children and adolescents with mental, behavior, and developmental disorders*. Washington, DC: National Academy Press.

Jones, R. (1990, January 28). Experts say crack babies will flood school system. *The Houston Post*, p. A16.

Kauffman, J. M. (1989). *Characteristics of behavior disorders of children and youth*. Columbus, OH: Merrill.

Knitzer, J., Steinberg, Z., & Fleisch, B. (1990). *At the schoolhouse door*. New York: Bank Street College of Education.

Long, N. J., Morse, W. C., & Newman, R. G. (1971). *Conflict in the classroom*. Belmont, CA: Wadsworth.

Mastropieri, M. A., & Scruggs, T. E. (1994). *Effective instruction for special education*. Austin, TX: PRO-ED.

Morgan, D., & Jensen, W. R. (1992). *Teaching students with behavioral disorders*. Columbus, OH: Merrill.

National Commission on the Role of the School and the Community in Improving Adolescent Health. (1990). *Code blue: Uniting for healthier youth*. Washington, DC: Author.

National Health/Educational Consortium. (1991, January). *Healthy brain development: Precursor to learning*. Washington, DC: National Commission to Prevent Infant Mortality and Institute for Educational Leadership.

National Mental Health Association. (1989). *Invisible children project: Final report and recommendations of the invisible children project*. Alexandria, VA: Author.

National Mental Health Association. (1993). *All systems failure: An examination of the results of neglecting the needs of children with serious emotional disturbance*. Alexandria, VA: Author.

National Mental Health and Special Education Coalition. (1987, October). *Meeting the needs of children with serious emotional disturbance through Education for All Handicapped Children Act (P.L. 94-142): Recommended goals for action* (Draft). Reston, VA: NMH/SPED Coalition.

Office of Technology Assessment. (1986, December). *Children's mental health. Problems and services: Background paper* (OTA-BP-H-33). Washington, DC: U.S. Government Printing Office.

Osher, D. (1993). *Building a national agenda to achieve better outcomes for children and youth with serious emotional disturbance: The historical context* (Draft). Washington, DC: Chesapeake Institute.

Price, T., & Vitolo, R. (1988, December). The schooling of incarcerated young people. *Education Week,* 30.

Reed, S., & Sautter, R. C. (1990, June). Children in poverty: The status of 12 million young Americans: Kappan special report. *Phi Delta Kappan,* K1–K12.

Rhode, G., Morgan, D. P., & Young, K. R. (1983). Generalization and maintenance of treatment gains for behaviorally handicapped students from resource rooms to regular classrooms using self-evaluation procedures. *Journal of Applied Behavior Analysis, 16,* 171–188.

Scheuermann, B., Webber, J., Partin, M., & Knies, W. C. (1994). Level systems and the law: Are they compatible? *Behavioral Disorders, 19,* 205–220.

Stroul, B. A., & Friedman, R. M. (1986). *A system of care for severely emotionally disturbed children and youth.* Washington, DC: CASSP Technical Assistance Center.

Stroul, B. A., & Pires, S. (1994). Health care reform and mental health. *Focal Point: The Bulletin of the Research and Training Center on Family Support and Children's Mental Health, 8,* 4–6.

U.S. Department of Health and Human Services. (1989). *Year 2000 national health objectives.* Washington, DC: Author.

Young, K. R., West, R. P., Smith, D. J., & Morgan, D. P. (1991). *Teaching self-management strategies to adolescents.* Longmont, CO: Sopris West.

FRANK W. WOOD
University of Minnesota

Frank W. Wood graduated from Harvard College in 1951. He did graduate work at Haverford College and completed his doctorate at the University of Minnesota in 1965. Wood taught secondary school in Connecticut, taught Seminole Indians in Florida, and has taught and coordinated programs for students with emotional and behavioral disorders in the Minnesota public schools. He has been on the faculty at the University of Minnesota since 1965, currently serving as professor of educational psychology and special education. Wood has been an active member of the Council for Children with Behavioral Disorders (CCBD) at the state and national levels, serving as president and representative to the Board of Governors for the National CCBD. He edited Behavioral Disorders from 1987 to 1993 and received the Council for Exceptional Children's Wallin Award in 1984 and the CCBD Leadership Award in 1989.

CHAPTER 23

Dodging the Bandwagon on Our Way to the Future

A PERSONAL PERSPECTIVE

"Special" education exists because none of the efforts to individualize instruction through manipulations of the ways in which students are grouped or materials are organized and presented have enabled general class teachers to meet the needs of all learners. For many years, parents and educators with a concern to develop the potential present in all children have pointed out that, at best, the educational reach of the general classroom teacher only touches the 70% of the students within one standard deviation of the average. Students at the high end of the normal distribution are more able to take over direction of their own education to compensate for deficiencies in instruction than their peers with disabilities. Low-achieving or disruptive students struggle and fail or are neglected as "uneducable." Special education is the name given the pedagogy for the outliers. Special educators have accepted the challenge of developing instructional approaches that will better facilitate the learning and development of students failing to benefit from the educational programs that meet the needs of the typical student, a formidable challenge by any measure.

I began my teaching career as a general classroom teacher. I knew little about special education, which in my experience at the time meant the education of students with mental, physical, or sensory disabilities. Each year, I had students in my class who needed much more than I could give. I was especially concerned about the students whose lack of motivation or time-wasting acting-out behavior seemed to arise from deep-seated fear or anger. My instruction fell far short of meeting them in the place where their disordered emotional and behavioral patterns held them. When in 1958 the Minneapolis public schools announced plans to form a class for students with "emotional disturbance or social maladjustment," I called for more information in hopes of finding a spot in the program for one of my needy students. I found that the new program was in the earliest stage of development.

To make a long story short, the following fall I found myself working with Evelyn Deno to organize the state's first elementary-level class for students with emotional and behavioral disorders (E/BD) located in a nonhospital setting. I had no real understanding of what I was undertaking. My little group of 10 students shared only one feature: one or more years of total exclusion from school. In search of help, I sought out Bruce Balow, Maynard Reynolds, and Frank Wilderson at the University of Minnesota. I can only acknowledge my debt to the many, many others who have helped me along the way in a general reference without mentioning their names. In pursuit of individualization, I had become a special educator, and almost 40 years later I am still advocating for individualized programs for students with special needs and seeking better ways to achieve them.

CURRENT STATUS OF CHILDREN WITH E/BD

Several years ago, Smith, Wood, and Grimes (1988) attempted to summarize what we know about the status of students with E/BD as part of a project with the ambitious goal of synthesizing the knowledge base for special education (Wang, Reynolds, & Walberg, 1988). More recently, Wood, Bloomquist, and Chalmers (1992) reviewed the recent literature on this topic. The comments I will be making throughout this chapter reflect what I learned through undertaking those reviews and through my more personal experiences with parents, students, teachers, and colleagues in teacher education and research.

Almost any comments offered will sound commonplace. There are at least as many persons suffering and inflicting suffering on others because of emotional and behavioral disorders as there were when I began working in this field. We can estimate prevalence in society as a whole and predict incidence, but if we are truly honest with ourselves, we have to admit that we still understand little about the reasons for any single individual's disorder. We want to believe that with wiser public policies and more resources to implement them we would make dramatic improvements in the mental health of our citizens, but we do not really know that this is true. We are in about the same spot that Durkheim was 100 years ago when he sought to understand why persons committed suicide in the France of his day. We know a lot, but what we do not yet know is vast.

My view of "current status" is that there are a lot of young people out there who need support in working through their problems. I will do my best to help. There is more than enough to do. In her unfinished novel, *Leaving Cold Sassy*, Olive Ann Burns planned for Sanna to say to Miss Love, "I read some psychology books in college. Everything that's supposed to warp a child happened to me." Miss Love, who had been raped as a child, would reply, "Everything that could warp a child happened to me, too. But understanding that doesn't help. I figure that what you do with your life now is all that counts. I try not to look back" (Burns, 1992, p. 164 with additions).

I do not think we are very successful with the Sannas in our programs, those who are preoccupied with their pain, but we cannot predict the moment when a Sanna will transform herself into a Miss Love, pick herself up, wipe her tears, and get on with her life. Not captured in the latest gloomy statistics on mental disorder is the prevalence of the seeds that will produce Miss Loves with the small amount of help we can provide them. Their current status is not so good, but their future status looks better.

A PERSONAL WORKING DEFINITION OF E/BD

Along with many others, I have spent much time working on issues related to terminology and definition. Any anxiety I felt about whether this was time well spent disappeared when policymakers and educators in some states began to use ambiguous wording in the current federal definition to deny service to students with "conduct disorders." A little reflection suggests that most of the cruelty of people to each other is based on exclusionary terminology and definitions.

The terminology used in Minnesota for this disability is *emotional or behavioral disorders*. The same term has been chosen by the coalition task force representing parents, mental health, and educational organizations currently leading the efforts for change in the federal terminology and definition. I am comfortable with it, although my personal preference would be *emotional and/or behavioral disorders*. While the slash mark is somewhat awkward, this usage matches my own clinical impression that externalized disorders (behavioral) can be and often are present with internalized disorders (emotional). Restricting the label to either term alone, *emotional disturbance* or *behavioral disorders*, seems to stimulate debate that cannot be resolved by appeal to a generally accepted set of facts. Combining both terms is a small price to pay for fuller collaboration among service providers.

THE MINNESOTA DEFINITION

The Minnesota definition identifies three major clusters of disordered behavior: (a) severely aggressive or impulsive, (b) severely withdrawn or anxious, and (c) severely disordered thought processes and distorted interpersonal relationships (Minnesota Education Rule 3525.1329 [Minnesota Department of Education, 1991]). For a student to be eligible for special education services, the disorder must prevent the student from benefiting from education through disrupting interpersonal relations and educational or developmental progress. A link to mental health terminology is provided by stating that the eligible group "may include children and youths with schizophrenic disorders, affective disorders, anxiety disorders, and sustained disorders of conduct or adjustment when they adversely affect educational performance" (Minnesota Education Rule 3525.1329).

THE CURRENT FEDERAL DEFINITION

According to Cline (1990), the current federal definition for *seriously emotionally disturbed* was first used during congressional hearings in the early 1970s, becoming fixed in the regulations implementing P.L. 94-142 in 1977. The core of that definition had been written by Bower (1957, 1960) 20 years earlier for use in a survey of the incidence of emotional disturbance among students in California schools.

At the time Bower wrote his definition, emotional disturbance and social maladjustment were considered to be closely related, as they are now in all major classifications of mental disorders, such as in the *Diagnostic and Statistical Manual of Mental Disorders–Third Edition: Revised* (DSM–III–R), which is published and periodically updated by the American Psychiatric Association (1987). More recently, Bower (1982) wrote that he was puzzled by the clause added to his definition excluding students who were socially maladjusted unless they were also seriously emotionally disturbed, since he had always considered social maladjustment to be an aspect of emotional disturbance and thought that was made clear in his definition. At the time the regulations with the exclusionary clause were adopted, I wished that the drafters had used the word *delinquent* instead of *socially maladjusted*, since I assumed that this was the intended meaning.

Unfortunately, as the costs of providing full special educational service to students with disabilities climbed, interest in restricting the class of students eligible for such services grew among some educators and school board members. Students showing aggressive, acting-out behavior were singled out for exclusion from the definition and from school. Their antisocial behavior invites punishment.

There are many theoretical reasons to explain their behavior. Frequently they are members of dysfunctional family systems and lack the support of parents and community advocates who speak out for students whose disabilities stimulate a more sympathetic response from the public. Behavior changes achieved with these students by special education interventions in special settings seldom generalize to general classrooms or the community. Providing a textbook example of scapegoating, angry policymakers and educators charge that these students do not deserve special education because, unlike "truly disturbed" children and youth, they are responsible for their behavior. They *choose* to be behavior problems. During the 1980s, several states adopted rules permitting school districts to provide alternative programs for students who were socially maladjusted without certifying them as eligible for special education. Students placed in these programs can be disciplined using the standard school procedures for suspension and expulsion from school, which lead to penalties that are more harsh than those the courts have allowed to be applied to students certified as eligible for special education because of disabilities.

Often the DSM–III–R (American Psychiatric Association, 1987) classification of *conduct disordered* has been substituted for the original label, *socially maladjusted*. The use of the new label ignores the research evidence showing substantial comorbidity of conduct disorders and other DSM–III–R classifications (McConaughy & Skiba, 1993).

These punitive exclusionary policies are tragically shortsighted. Students with conduct disorders appear to learn little from punishing experiences for many reasons. Years ago, Bandura and Walters (1959) made a compelling presentation of a social learning theory explanation of externalizing behavior based on modeling and differential reinforcement. About the same time, Redl and Wineman (1957) offered a more dynamic explanation, ego of a deviant in the service of the child's impulsivity, which aptly describes the way these students appear to think about their behavior. Shapiro and Hynd (1993) reviewed some recent research suggesting a psychobiological basis. The truth may lie in some combination of these explanations. While we are searching for reasons, the federal definition should be changed to protect the right of this at-risk group of students with E/BD to appropriate special education.

THE COALITION DEFINITION

The troubling ambiguities of the current federal definition became obvious as soon as it was applied. Efforts at revision culminated in the development of a proposal (Forness & Knitzer, 1990) to change the language in legislation and regulation by a coalition of parents, special educators, and representatives of mental health organizations. The coalition proposes to change the terminology from *seriously emotionally disturbed* to *emotional or behavioral disordered*. The language of the definition reflects new patterns of interagency cooperation and the desire of professionals to make their definitions interchangeable even when every word is not identical.

INCIDENCE OF EMOTIONAL AND BEHAVIORAL DISORDERS

Differences between definitions and procedures for identification account in part for the variability in reported incidence of students with E/BD (Smith, Wood, & Grimes, 1988; Wood, Bloomquist, & Chalmers, 1992). The percentage of the child population that is regarded by teachers at any one time as "being a behavior problem" was found by Rubin and Balow (1978) to be as high as 25% to 30%, although the group of individuals so labeled changed from year to year. The percentage of all students whose emotional and behavioral disorders interfere with their educational programs to such an extent that special education is required is usually much lower, about 2% of the total school population. Since this is an average figure, applying it to individual school districts may yield an overestimate or underestimate of how many students need services. The actual number of children served has remained close to 1% nationally, with a range from a fraction of a percent (see Crowell, 1993, for a discussion of Mississippi) to as many as 4% receiving services under that label in different states. Estimates of the number of students who might benefit from mental health intervention because of emotional and behavioral disorders that do not seriously interfere with their educational progress run as high as 10%.

In the absence of compelling data on prevalence or incidence, some scholars assert that the data on students receiving service indicate that large numbers of students go unserved (Beare & Lynch, 1986; Center & Obringer, 1987; Kauffman, 1984). On the other hand, Long (1983) presented data that she interpreted as demonstrating that "the severity label placed on any given child's condition by districts in [her] sample was related to the level of specialized service available" (p. 52). Districts with large service programs identified enough students to fill their programs; districts with small service programs identified enough students to fill their programs. Long suggested that the relative allotment of resources to service programs may be as much a factor in the number of students identified as the actual prevalence of students with behavioral disorders. Because of federal and state penalties for failure to serve identified students, districts have an incentive to have the number classified as eligible for services match the capacity of the existing service programs. Long's analysis is plausible but difficult to prove conclusively.

My personal view is that there are a small number of students, perhaps as much as 2% to 3% of the student body in some schools, who have chronic emotional and behavioral disorders that will have a lifelong negative impact on their adjustment. Many of these students will need mental health, medical, and welfare services as well as special education. Needed individualization of their programs can sometimes be met by providing supportive services while the students remain in general classrooms. Those who are highly aggressive or disruptive will need to receive some of their education and supportive services in special settings.

The areas where other students are distributed along the mental health continuum will vary from year to year, and their needs for more individualized educational programming will vary accordingly. Generalizing from the Rubin and Balow (1978) findings, it appears that most children and youth are viewed by concerned adults as experiencing transient periods of E/BD as they cope with the stresses of growing up in our society. They make it through to adequate adult adjustment because of spontaneous self-adjustment or the support they received from others.

CRITICAL ELEMENTS IN EDUCATIONAL PROGRAMMING

Functional Assessment

I am very interested in the current discussion of "functional assessment," which seems to combine strengths of both the behavioral and psychodynamic approaches to supporting behavior change. Psychologists guided by dynamic models of behavior have always placed emphasis on the value of using information obtained by asking "why" questions when generating hypotheses about the functional value of disordered behavior. Behaviorally oriented psychologists also have found it useful to gather data to support hypotheses about "the motivational properties of behavior disorders" (Iwata, Vollmer, & Zarcone, 1990, p. 301; Sasso & Reimers, 1988, p. 9; Sasso et al., 1992). Research conducted by investigators such as those mentioned has demonstrated that interventions selected with attention to the function the disordered behavior serves for students produce desired changes more quickly and support the learning of behavior that students will apply in a variety of settings.

When we widen the focus of assessment to include the function as well as characteristics of behavior, we document that "the same behavior exhibited by two individuals can be maintained through different mechanisms [of reinforcement]" (Iwata et al., 1990, p. 303). For one student, hitting may be a means to obtain positive reinforcement; for another, it may be a negatively reinforced means to escape from an unpleasant classroom situation to the relative peace and quiet of time-out. Although the problem behavior is the same, our choice of an alternative behavior to teach or suggest to the student would be quite different. One of the procedures that can be applied as part of a functional assessment is an oral "life space" interview (Wood, 1993; Wood & Long, 1991).

Four Basic Components of Programs for Students with E/BD

Regardless of level of student development and degree of E/BD, an effective teacher's management style should include four components: communication, support for appropriate behavior, teaching of new behavior, and control of inappropriate behavior. Skill in communicating with students is listed first because it is basic. Supporting appropriate behavior so that it is maintained and generalizes to new situations and teaching new behavior patterns in areas of current maladjustment are somewhat arbitrarily ranked second and third. Control of inappropriate behavior, which many teachers see as their major task, is clearly last on my list. When we implement control procedures—and at times each of us must do so—it is because our efforts to communicate, support, and teach have not prevented a breakdown in the teaching/learning process. Likewise, control procedures are not successful as instructional interventions if their only result is suppression of inappropriate behavior. Full success results only when the teaching/learning process is restored.

Communication Interventions

Communication from the teacher or classroom leader establishes the tasks and boundaries for group members. Communication from group members helps the teacher plan appropriate tasks and adjust boundaries so that desirable behavior can be maintained and student needs are satisfied. Good communication builds trust. Good communication strengthens bonds among group members. Communication interventions include the structuring of time and space, the structuring of expectations and rewards, and the structuring of rules and sanctions, as well as counseling and feedback of information. The time, energy, training, and other resources required to implement communication and other interventions vary greatly, an aspect of program planning sometimes forgotten when planning for the inclusion of students with severe emotional and behavioral disorders in general education settings.[1]

Support Interventions

This group of interventions includes those that maintain behavior and contribute to students' sense of well-being. Attention, praise, tokens or points, and other forms of reward support the work of the group. Grouping for instruction and the organization of cooperative groups or peer tutoring help reduce the frustration some students experience when working alone on difficult tasks and provide the setting for positive group experiences. Some support interventions, such as full individualization of

---

[1] For further discussion of this issue and a more extensive list of interventions, see Wood, 1991.

instruction for students, are extremely difficult and time consuming, requiring ongoing assessment, lesson construction, individualized instruction, and immediate evaluation. As in the case of communication interventions, attention must be given to these cost factors in planning the use of support interventions.

Providing support to students is closely related to maintaining communication with them. For this reason, there is inevitably some overlap between the interventions classified under these two headings. The important point is to recognize the important group functions played by communication and support and to help teachers incorporate interventions that foster both in their overall classroom leadership style.

Teaching of Social Behavior

Sometimes students' failure to meet teacher expectations results from lack of the required social skills. Teaching the missing behavior is relatively costly in terms of teacher time. So as not to waste instructional time, it is important that a careful functional assessment be completed to determine whether the student lacks the skill needed or simply fails to apply it because it does not lead to satisfaction of a high-priority need. The new or alternative skill taught must help the student meet an important need. Time for assessment and evaluation as well as teaching must be considered in tallying up the cost of teaching interventions.

Control Interventions

Control interventions are used when undesirable behavior occurs in spite of skillful use of communication, teaching, and support procedures. Successful control procedures manage or stop the problem behavior that is occurring and, in addition, bring the student back to the teaching/learning interaction with the teacher. Control procedures tend to have a high cost because their application disrupts this interaction. Many heightened student and teacher levels of physiological arousal must be provided the opportunity to calm down.

A Total Program

A total program including these four elements must be flexible so as to meet the basic purpose of special education for students with E/BD: better individualization of instruction. There is no single recipe that will be appropriate for meeting the educational needs of students with disabilities whose characteristics place them at the tail of the normal distribution. The task of individualization is made more difficult by the absence of assessment procedures that will infallibly match students with best methods. Finally, and most importantly, there is no method for assessment, program planning, or instruction that is person-proof, i.e., the most important variable in effective individualization is the individual teacher. Except in closely controlled situations where fragments of knowledge or skill are being taught, teacher effects are almost always stronger than method effects. Individual teacher effects become even more potent in our case because of the strongly idiosyncratic likes and dislikes of students with E/BD.

THE POWER OF THE "TEACHER EFFECT"

In the early 1930s, a group of researchers studied the effects of various changes in working conditions on worker productivity at Western Electric's Hawthorne plant. They found that productivity continued to increase even when the innovations were discontinued and the original conditions restored. Based on interviews with the workers and their own informal observations, the researchers concluded that the increases continued because the workers' efforts were reinforced by the attention they received as participants in an experiment (Roethlisberger & Dickson, 1939).

Borg and Gall (1983) described two associated effects. One, the "John Henry effect," is observed when teachers assigned to a control group condition pour so much effort into their teaching that the performance of their students matches that of the groups whose teachers are applying the experimental method. The "Pygmalion effect" was named by Rosenthal (Rosenthal & Jacobson, 1968), a researcher whose somewhat controversial findings demonstrated that teacher expectations had a major effect on student achievement. If a teacher expected a student to do well, the student excelled. While a serious threat to the validity of research, these "teacher effects" are generated by gifted teachers of students with emotional and behavioral disorders and must be regarded as invaluable assets. While as difficult to define as any other manifestation of "quality" (Pirsig, 1974), positive teacher effects must be recognized and cultivated by administrators of programs for students with disorders.

I like to call the teacher effect the "Shimshock effect," in honor of one of the finest teachers of reading I have ever known. The school system and desperate parents sent their most disabled readers to Cyrilla Shimshock, and in an extraordinary number of cases she succeeded where others had failed. She found ways to allow students with perceptual disabilities so serious that they were obvious to a casual observer to read and write at levels that brought them a sense of accomplishment and satisfaction. She taught teenagers with histories of school failure associated with severe conduct disorders to read the magazines and song lyrics they wanted to read, even when it was material she required them to lock in a cupboard so the younger students would not see. She had "the gift," and it had little to do with method. She used the method and materials that seemed to her the best match for the individual student's needs. Every effort was reinforced. Every success received individual and group recognition. She regarded a student's failure to make progress as her responsibility. On the rare occasions when she felt she could not help a student, she said so and tried to find a better place for him or her. Her students, even the "bad actors," respected and loved Cyrilla Shimshock. Teachers like her, whose students show us they are responding to a powerful teacher effect, should be cherished.

We all know that a teacher effect exists, and additional research might be cited in support of my contention that it is more powerful than method. The challenge is to explain and, ideally, to be able to create and manage positive teacher effect. Behavioral psychologists explain teacher effect in terms of modeling and reinforcement. Hobbs (1981) provided an interesting dynamic explanation in terms of "an interpreter of the belief system" in his analysis of sources of gain in psychotherapy. But the source of the effect seems too subtle for easy detection. To date, the best I have been able to do is to watch for Cyrilla Shimschocks and give them my support whenever I find them.

A DELIVERY OF SERVICES MODEL

The need for an interagency full service, or wraparound, model, in which all human services agencies (health, mental health, legal, correctional, welfare, vocational, and recreational, as well as educational) collaborate with parents and each other to provide children and youth with special needs whatever support the community can provide, has long been recognized. Unfortunately, such collaboration has been a long time in developing as the result of conflicting mandates and mistrust among professions. Only education had a mandate to serve all children and youth. The other agencies either set their own criteria to a large extent (mental health), conformed to criteria set by law or noneducation agencies (welfare), or served clients referred by other agencies (juvenile courts).

Recently this had begun to change. Legislation at the state and federal level has provided grants to support a variety of experimental programs (Pearson & Nelson, 1993). Minnesota adopted a modified version of the Child and Adolescent Special Services Plan (CASSP) model (Stroul & Friedman, 1986) to guide local planners. I served as a member of a task force involving parents and representatives from most of the agencies mentioned who collaborated to develop a plan to provide coordinated intake and services as needed to children and youth with E/BD in Hennepin County. The task force members focused on finding out how collaboration could take place rather than on barriers that made it difficult. The implementation of the resulting plan is only beginning, but the prospect is exciting.

AN AGENDA FOR THE NEXT FIVE YEARS

THE GREATEST CHALLENGE WE FACE

Racism, the negative side of the American preoccupation with the racial diversity of our population, exerts a corroding effect on the mental health of every individual in our society. There has not been space here to discuss this issue and how it manifests itself in special education, but to fail to acknowledge its presence among us would be inexcusable. Racism is not a problem of others. Can I deal with its insidious effects on my behavior? Can you deal with it in yourself? Love is on our side, but it will not be easy.

EDUCATIONAL REFORM

In the year that I decided to make teaching my profession, I read Albert Schweitzer's *Out of My Life and Thought* (1949). At his jungle hospital in Lambarene, Schweitzer wrote, "To the question whether I am a pessimist or an optimist, I answer that my knowledge is pessimistic, but my willing and hoping are optimistic" (p. 240). This statement provides the basis for my thinking about the prospects for students with E/BD in our society. I know enough to realize how short we have fallen of the mark to date, suffering from lack of resources as well as lack of knowledge and skill, and that knowledge informs me that our task will not suddenly become easier. But my knowledge does not immobilize me. I believe that by applying ourselves we can do better than we are doing at present. Change is a constant. Change will come, and you and I can do our best to see that change carries us forward rather than backward.

Special educators of students with E/BD have come under strong attack from some quarters for failing to accomplish the objective of providing an appropriately individualized education for all students with disabilities. Criticism should always be heeded, but its *usefulness*, the extent to which it guides constructive change, can be debated. There is only limited empirical data to which either side can appeal, and both critics and defenders cite it selectively. Two fine articles in *Exceptional Children* (Fuchs & Fuchs, 1994; Kauffman, 1993) helped place the debate in proper perspective.

The major criticisms advanced against special education appear to be the following:

1. Special educators damage the social status and self-concepts of students by applying disability labels to them and segregating

them in special programs away from the normal school environment. To this criticism is sometimes added the charge that the labels themselves lack empirical validity.
2. The negative social effects of labeling and isolation are not adequately compensated for by increased learning by special students.

Some critics stop at this point. Others suggest that they have plans that will be effective in overcoming these problems.

In my opinion, much depends on whether we judge special education primarily by its outcomes, without attending carefully to the difficulty of the task undertaken and the resources that have been committed to completing the projects undertaken. Special educators have often succeeded in individualizing instruction for students with E/BD. They have been much less successful in normalizing outcomes. Is this a partial success, or a partial failure?

The task we have undertaken is complex and intractable. We certainly have not met all of our hopes and expectations. This certainly should be no surprise to anyone. Facetiously, I would suggest that when special educators do fully attain the goals we have set for our programs, we will have developed the skills and knowledge needed to bring in the messianic age. Certainly, it is easier to criticize than to suggest credible alternatives. But, to be honest, our successes have been spotty and lack a clear pattern. The social and academic skills of students we identify and label sometimes develop positively and sometimes deteriorate, and, in my experience, we cannot reliably predict the course of individual changes. Our hopeful promises typically run far ahead of our accomplishments. The challenge is how best to improve our outcomes.

Some critics oversimplify the complexity of the task, offering solutions that have little likelihood of bettering the situation. Usually the models they criticize have never been fully implemented, one example being the collaborative service model mentioned earlier. In my view, while critics have every right to compete for the limited research funds available to support trials of alternative models, I cannot support their suggestions that we divert some of the limited funds available for special education to fund experimental programs. The traditional continuum of services or cascade model (Deno, 1970), for all its faults, was developed over many years through trial and error. It has served many individual students well. It includes but is not contained in the so-called inclusion initiative. It fits well into the expanded full services model. The major problems in both models are associated with the cost of implementation. I think we should be particularly suspicious of claims that a proposed reform will accomplish our goals in a way that is both better *and* cheaper.

There is another reason for responding to criticism with caution. Criticism is popular in contemporary American society. Ours is an age preoccupied with the limitations of every institution and every individual. The flattering attention that critics receive is not conditional on their developing solutions to the problems they identify. As a result, some of the statements made by critics without appropriate qualification demean and threaten the partial successes we have achieved for students with special needs. Feature articles like the "investigative report" entitled "Separate and Unequal: How Special Education Programs Are Cheating Our Children and Costing Taxpayers Billions Each Year," which appeared in the December 13, 1993, issue of *U.S. News and World Report* pick up the extreme statements of critics and exploit them more for their sensational impact than from a concern for the best interests of students with disabilities. I think we must bear some responsibility when our ideas, however well meant, lend themselves to misuse or abuse.

Is the appropriate response to special education's partial successes to dump traditional programs and implement completely different approaches? Or is the appropriate response to continue our efforts to develop special procedures for special students slowly and pragmatically, recognizing that most often what succeeds with one student will not be as effective with the next? If our knowledge and theory of human behavior was sound and reasonably complete, I would favor the first approach. But, in my judgment, our knowledge and theory are too weak to support a fully developed master plan. The weakness of my knowledge and theory allows me to continue to work in a hopeful spirit. Knowledge and theory in their present state can provide only suggestions. While working toward our goal of individualizing instruction for all students pragmatically, step by step, is a plodder's strategy and is less dramatic than announcing that we have discovered a bold, new reform plan that will solve the problems that have baffled generations of earnest educators, it appears to me to be the best strategy we have. I find lots of good company as I continue to plod along, dodging the latest bandwagon, on our way to the future.

REFERENCES

American Psychiatric Association. (1987). *Diagnostic and statistical manual of mental disorders* (3rd ed., rev.). Washington, DC: Author.

Bandura, A., & Walters, R. H. (1959). *Adolescent aggression*. New York: Ronald.

Beare, P. L., & Lynch, E. C. (1986). Underidentification of preschool children at risk for behavioral disorders. *Behavioral Disorders, 11*, 177–183.

Borg, W. R., & Gall, M. D. (1983). *Educational research: An introduction* (4th ed.). New York: Longman.

Bower, E. M. (1957). A process for identifying disturbed children. *Children, 4,* 143–147.
Bower, E. M. (1960). *Early identification of emotionally handicapped children in school.* Springfield, IL: Charles C. Thomas.
Bower, E. M. (1982). Defining emotional disturbance: Public policy and research. *Psychology in the Schools, 19,* 55–60.
Burns, O. A. (1992). *Leaving Cold Sassy.* New York: Delta.
Center, D. B., & Obringer, J. (1987). A search for variables affecting underidentification of behaviorally disordered students. *Behavioral Disorders, 12,* 169–174.
Cline, D. H. (1990). A legal analysis of policy initiatives to exclude handicapped/disruptive students from special education. *Behavioral Disorders, 15,* 159–173.
Crowell, A. R., Jr. (1993). Contrasting perspectives on programming for students with emotional disturbance and emotional disorders in Mississippi. *Exceptional Children, 18,* 228–230.
Deno, E. (1970). Special education as developmental capital. *Exceptional Children, 37,* 229–237.
Forness, S. R., & Knitzer, J. (1990, December). *A new proposed definition and terminology to replace "serious emotional disturbance" in Education of the Handicapped Act.* Alexandria, VA: National Mental Health Association.
Fuchs, D., & Fuchs, L. S. (1994). Inclusive schools movement and the radicalization of special education reform. *Exceptional Children, 60,* 294–309.
Hobbs, N. (1981). The role of insight in behavior change: A commentary. *American Journal of Orthopsychiatry, 51,* 632–635.
Iwata, B. A., Vollmer, T. R., & Zarcone, J. R. (1990). The experimental (functional) analysis of behavior disorders: Methodology, applications, and limitations. In A. C. Repp & N. N. Singh (Eds.), *Perspectives on the use of nonaversive and aversive interventions for persons with developmental disabilities* (pp. 301–330). Sycamore, IL: Sycamore Publishing.
Kauffman, J. M. (1984). Saving children in the age of big brother: Moral and ethical issues in the underidentification of deviance. *Behavioral Disorders, 10,* 60–70.
Kauffman, J. M. (1993). How we might achieve the radical reform special education. *Exceptional Children, 60,* 6–16.
Long, K. A. (1983). Emotionally disturbed children as an underdetected and underserved public school population: Reasons and recommendations. *Behavioral Disorders, 9,* 46–54.
McConaughy, S. H., & Skiba, R. J. (1993). Comorbidity of externalizing and internalizing problems. *School Psychology Review, 22,* 421–436.
Minnesota Department of Education. (1991). *Minnesota's identification and eligibility for children and youth experiencing emotional and behavioral disorders.* St. Paul, MN: Author.
Pearson, C. A., & Nelson, C. M. (1993). Interagency community-based services for children and youth with emotional and behavioral disabilities. In R. B. Rutherford, Jr., & S. R. Mathur (Eds.), *Severe behavior disorders of children and youth* (Vol. 16, pp. 81–89). Reston, VA: Council for Children with Behavioral Disorders.

Pirsig, R. M. (1974). *Zen and the art of motorcycle maintenance.* New York: Morrow.
Redl, F., & Wineman, D. (1957). *The aggressive child.* New York: Free Press.
Roethlisberger, F., & Dickson, W. (1939). *Management and the worker.* Cambridge, MA: Harvard University Press.
Rosenthal, R., & Jacobson, L. (1968). *Pygmalion in the classroom.* New York: Holt, Rinehart, & Winston.
Rubin, R. A., & Balow, B. E. (1978). Prevalence of teacher identified behavior problems: A longitudinal study. *Exceptional Children, 45,* 102–111.
Sasso, G. M., & Reimers, T. M. (1988). Assessing the functional properties of behavior: Implications and applications for the classroom. *Focus on Autistic Behavior, 3*(5), 1–15.
Sasso, G. M., Reimers, T. M., Cooper, L. J., Wacker, D., Berg, W., Steege, M., Kelly, L., & Allaire, A. (1992). Use of descriptive and experimental analyses to identify the functional properties of aberrant behavior in school settings. *Journal of Applied Behavior Analysis, 25,* 809–821.
Schweitzer, A. (1949). Out of my life and thought. New York: Henry Holt.
Shapiro, S. K., & Hynd, G. W. (1993). Psychobiological basis of conduct disorder. *School Psychology Review, 22,* 386–402.
Smith, C. R., Wood, F. H., & Grimes, J. (1988). Issues in the identification and placement of behaviorally disordered students. In M. C. Wang, M. C. Reynolds, & H. J. Walberg (Eds.), *Handbook of special education: Research and practice* (Vol. 2, pp. 95–123). Oxford, England: Pergamon.
Stroul, B. A., & Friedman, R. M. (1986). *A system of care for severely emotionally disturbed children and youth.* Washington, DC: CASSP Technical Assistance Center, Georgetown University, Child Development Center.
Wang, M. C., Reynolds, M. C., & Walberg, H. J. (Eds.). (1988). *Handbook of special education: Research and practice. Volume 2: Mildly handicapped conditions.* Oxford, England: Pergamon.
Wood, F. H. (1991). Cost/benefit considerations in managing the behavior of students with emotional/behavioral disorders. *Preventing School Failure, 35,* 17–23.
Wood, F. H. (1993). *May I ask you why you are hitting yourself?: Using oral and self-reports in the functional assessment of adolescents' behavior disorders.* Manuscript submitted for publication.
Wood, F. H., Bloomquist, J., & Chalmers, J. (1992). Research issues in behavioral disorders. In R. Gaylord-Ross (Ed.), *Issues and research in special education* (Vol. 2, pp. 43–124). New York: Teachers College Press, Columbia University.
Wood, M. M., & Long, N. J. (1991). *Life space intervention.* Austin, TX: PRO-ED.

MITCHELL L. YELL
University of South Carolina

Mitchell L. Yell is currently a faculty member at the University of South Carolina. He studied under Frank Wood at the University of Minnesota and received his PhD in 1992. Yell has taught children and youth with emotional and behavioral disorders and learning disabilities for 15 years in Anoka, Minnesota. During this time he worked with elementary and secondary students in both resource rooms and self-contained settings. He also has served as a consultant to a number of school districts. Yell has published widely and is currently finishing a textbook on special education law. His primary areas of interest lie in the preparation of teachers to work with students with emotional and behavioral disorders and legal issues in special education.

CHAPTER 24

Having to Believe

My behavior management paraprofessional, Terry Giesen, and I had just begun our second year of working together in a self-contained program for elementary students with emotional and behavioral disorders (E/BD). She and I had started the students on their morning routine of what they referred to as "brain warm-ups" (e.g., acrostics, crosswords, puzzles, secret codes to be broken). I glanced out the window and noticed the parents of John, a third-grade student in the room, walking briskly toward the school with determined looks on their faces. This was John's second year in my class. Soon they were standing at the classroom door, which was always open. John's father asked if I would accompany them to the principal's office immediately. We were joined in the office by the school social worker, Dennis Cleveland. When we were seated the principal, Elaine Burgess, asked what we could do for them. John's father said that the last year had been a difficult one, and that as much as we had tried to help John there was nothing we or they could do; it was out of our hands. He and his wife knew the source of John's problems. I asked them what that might be. "Mr. Yell, Mr. Cleveland, Mrs. Burgess," John's father said slowly, "we can do nothing for our son. He is demonically possessed."

When I tell this story in my introductory course on the education of students with E/BD, the first reaction is usually one of laughter. However, after the class discusses the incident, the mood quickly turns to one of silence and reflection. John's parents were not kooks or zealots, they were parents who were so totally overwhelmed by the situation they found themselves in that they desperately sought answers outside of the harsh reality they were experiencing to explain John's incredibly violent episodes of rage and anger.

While this instance is obviously extreme, the conditions that led to it are not. John had been adopted when he was a toddler. Even at that young age he displayed temper tantrums that would last for hours. Because of John's behavior, his parents became more and more socially isolated. Neighborhood parents would not allow their children to associate with John, nor would they associate with the parents. John's parents could not find a baby-sitter so that they could spend time by themselves, and they feared for the older daughter's safety when she was alone with him. Being socially isolated, they did not have the experiences of other parents to draw upon. Therefore, their only source of comparison was their daughter, who was precocious and well behaved. They concluded that John's behavior must be typical of an overactive boy and that he would outgrow it. However, when John was kicked out of three preschools at 4 years of age, they began to accept the seriousness of his problem. In kindergarten, John spent the majority of the year on indefinite suspension. First grade consisted of a number of early suspensions followed by a lengthy period of homebound instruction. In second grade he was put in my self-contained special education classroom.

John was a good-looking, bright boy. He had an infectious smile, pleasant personality, and serious attitude about doing well with his schoolwork. During the summer I supervised a day camp for students in special education. One summer John attended the camp. I especially remember his love of fishing.

John also had very serious problems. He could quickly turn from a pleasant boy to a screaming child so violent and vicious that it would literally take your breath away. Two years of a structured, behaviorally oriented program with counseling had lessened the problem in school. The violence, however, continued and actually intensified at home. The principal, social worker, and I had numerous meetings with John's parents. Their frustration was palpable. It eventually was revealed that in his frustration John's father had begun to physically abuse him. After third grade John's parents moved out of my school district. I heard from his new school once. I was invited to an IEP meeting, which the parents canceled. That was the last I heard of John.

A few years ago I ran into John's mother in the parking lot of a shopping center. What started out to be a pleasant exchange soon became painful. She apologized for the demonic possession episode (12 years after the incident) and recounted to me what had happened to John and the family. John was in and out of psychiatric hospitals in his early teen years. She told me that he was "sent away" following an attack on their daughter. He lived in a series of foster homes and dropped out of school when he was 16. The last she had heard, John had been put in a state correctional institution following a fight in which he had severely injured someone.

There was little left to say so we went our separate ways. Driving home I thought of the John I knew in second and third grade. Despite my best efforts, and the best efforts of many other concerned professionals, life had not gone well for John. Unfortunately, long-term outcomes for many of the students served in special education classes for children with

E/BD, especially those with conduct disorders, are not good. Longitudinal research with children who display aggressive, antisocial, and noncompliant behavior tells us that this behavior is a good predictor of adverse adult outcomes. Such outcomes include criminality, substance abuse, low occupational achievement, and antisocial behavior. However, while studies have shown that problem behaviors in childhood almost always precede problem behaviors in adulthood, not all children with behavior problems continue this behavior into adulthood. Clearly, some children are able to recover from their behavior problems prior to becoming adults.

Studies of twins and adopted children indicate that many human behaviors and mental traits are influenced by genes. Antisocial behavior, aggressiveness, and conduct problems are characteristics that have strong genetic influences. However, environmental influences are extremely important in the development of human behavior. In fact, many behavior problems probably require both a genetic liability and an environmental trigger (Robins & Rutter, 1990). As educators we have no control over genetic influence; however, we can influence the environment in which the child learns and potentially the environment in which the child otherwise lives and grows.

If we are truly to have a positive effect on the lives of the children with whom we work, rather than merely serving as a rest stop on the path toward adult pathology, we must be willing to critically examine our profession and the effects we are having on the students we teach. Additionally, we have to believe that we can be a positive influence in the lives of our students. The students we teach are challenging and the energy we must commit to our work can be exhausting. There will be times, as was the case with John, when, even though we give our best efforts, the eventual outcomes are not encouraging. However, we must be committed and persevere in our efforts to give our best.

A colleague at the University of South Carolina, David Smith, said that teaching is a journey of the heart and mind and an opportunity to touch lives in a profound way. If we believe that we can make a contribution and touch the lives of our students, then we will make a difference.

Special education for students with E/BD has come a long way since I first started teaching in 1975. That was the year the Individuals with Disabilities Education Act (then the Education of All Handicapped Children Act) was passed. As was the case with many special education teachers in earlier days of special education, my first classroom was a janitor's storage closet. We have come far in 20 years. But we have much further to go. If we are to continue our impressive advancement, we all must be able to answer the basic existential questions of our profession: Who are we? Why are we here? Where are we going?

WHO ARE WE?

Defining the Population

Kauffman (1993) described the population of students we work with very aptly when he referred to them as

> children and youth who arouse negative feelings and induce negative behavior in others. They are often not popular or leaders among their peers. Typically, they experience academic failure in addition to social rejection or alienation. Most adults choose to avoid them as much as possible. Their behavior is so persistently irritating to authority figures that they seem to be asking for punishment or rebuke. Even in their own eyes, these children and youth are usually failures; they obtain little gratification from life and repeatedly fall short of their aspirations. They are disabled; compared to nondisabled individuals, their options in important aspects of daily living are highly restricted. Their disabilities are the result of their behavior, which is discordant with their social-interpersonal environments; their behavior costs them many opportunities for gratifying social interaction and self-fulfillment. (p. 7)

Additionally, these children's problems often persist beyond school. Nearly 55% of youth labeled as E/BD drop out of school prior to graduation. That percentage is much higher than dropout figures for youths labeled as learning disabled, which is 36%, or youths in the general population, which is 24%. Many of them will become adults living on the margins of society, becoming involved in antisocial activities, crime, and substance abuse.

The above statement by Kauffman is an excellent description, but it is not a definition. According to Kauffman (1993), a definition is a set of guidelines that help us to reliably and validly discern who is and who is not E/BD. Different definitions of children with E/BD exist for different purposes. In addition to the federal definition, many states have their own definitions that are essential for administrative purposes. Researchers and authors of textbooks frequently have their own definitions. As can be seen by the many different state definitions and the recent controversies over the federal definition, it is easier to describe than define the student with E/BD. To paraphrase a familiar cliché, we may not be able to define it, but we know it when we see it.

Perhaps the most salient reason for definitional difficulties is that ultimately all definitions are subjective. Labeling someone's behavior as deviant or disturbed can only be accomplished within a social context. The behaviors of students with E/BD are not different in kind from the behaviors exhibited by all children at one time or another but are different in intensity, frequency, duration, or the settings in which they occur. To borrow from legal terminology, there is no "bright line formula," no clear and objective way, to determine when a behavior is deviant rather than normal. A further problem in determining a definition that professionals from different disciplines who work with students with E/BD (e.g., psychiatrists, psychologists, social workers, teachers) could agree upon is satisfying their need for a definition suited to their own particular needs and purposes.

To further complicate matters, many believe that it is important to distinguish between emotional disorders (ED) and behavioral disorders (BD). The distinction is often seen as a difference in how behaviors are manifested. The student with ED manifests internalizing disorders (also called personality disorders); that is, the student may be depressed, overanxious, or withdrawn. The student with BD manifests externalizing disorders (also called conduct disorders). The BD student is seen as aggressive, disruptive, and noncompliant. However, it is often very difficult to separate BD and ED. Forness (1993) referred to the problem of comorbidity of ED and BD in the same child. An example of comorbidity might be a clinically depressed child who manifests his or her depression through aggression and acting out. Forness further stated that these distinctions are not useful and that it usually is not even possible to distinguish between the two. There are currently no assessment devices that are both technically adequate and specifically validated for the purpose of distinguishing emotional and behavioral disorders. The presence of the two dimensions of behavioral disorders, internalizing behaviors and externalizing disorders, often equated with emotional and behavioral disorders, has been widely accepted. However, not even instruments based on these dimensions have been validated for discriminating between the disorders. Therefore, the lack of diagnostic validity, as well as comorbidity, makes differential diagnosis extremely problematic.

However, it is important for a number of reasons that we be able to define what emotional and behavioral disorders are, so as to appropriately serve students that manifest them. The field of special education for students who are emotionally and behaviorally disordered would probably best be served by the adoption of a single definition. To this end, I believe the definition proposed by the National Mental Health and Special Education Coalition is the best currently available (Forness & Knitzer, 1990).

> (i) The term emotional or behavioral disorder means a disability characterized by behavioral or emotional responses in school programs so different from appropriate age, cultural, or ethnic norms that they adversely affect educational performance, including academic, social, vocational, or personal skills, and which

(A) is more than a temporary, expected response to stressful events in the environment;

(B) is consistently exhibited in two different settings, at least one of which is school related; and

(C) persists despite individualized interventions within the educational program, unless, in the judgment of the team, the child's or youth's history indicates that such intervention would not be effective.

(ii) Emotional or behavioral disorders can co-exist with other disabilities.

(iii) This category may include children or youth with schizophrenic disorders, anxiety disorders, or other sustained disorders of conduct or adjustment when they adversely affect educational performance. (p. 2)

Attributions of the Effective Teacher

In examining who we are it is important that we address those attributes that make for an effective teacher of students with E/BD. There are many potential attributes that could be listed. These are seven that in my experiences I have found to be crucial:

1. *Strong leadership abilities.* In 1907 one of the first books on classroom management was published. The book suggested that teachers be leaders and authority figures in their classrooms. Teachers were instructed that above all they must get order in their classrooms. In 1991 F. M. Wood wrote that "no one can teach effectively unless they can establish themselves in a leadership role in their classrooms" (p. 62). We teach in a different world now, but the important ingredients of the successful teacher remain the same. The teacher must be the dominant figure in the classroom. This is of paramount importance in classrooms for students with E/BD.

Wood further stated that as teachers of students with E/BD we can expect to have our authority tested every day. Testing limits is a way students try to assert control. It is important that we assert these limits in order to maintain control. If teachers assert their authority inconsistently, weakly, or apologetically, their leadership will not be as strong as when they assert their authority consistently and confidently. It is only as leaders that we can teach our students effectively and help them to learn to control their behavior.

To be a leader does not mean that our classrooms are to be run in humorless and oppressive ways. Rather, strong leaders earn the respect of their students by respecting and caring for them and by being fair.

2. *Ability to structure and manage a classroom.* When Benjamin Franklin wrote in *Poor Richard's Almanac* that "an ounce of prevention is worth a

pound of cure," little did he know he was writing about classroom management! The research of Kounin and others strongly supports the importance of organizational and management skills in preventing misbehavior.

Almost a quarter of century ago, Kounin (1970) found that teachers who effectively managed student behavior could be distinguished from ineffective managers by the classroom-management strategies they used to prevent behavior problems. According to Kounin, effective managers are constantly aware of everything happening in their classrooms, maintain student involvement in lessons, anticipate student needs, and effectively hold student attention. According to Jones and Jones (1990), instructional management skills that facilitate on-task behavior and academic achievement include giving clear instructions, maintaining attention, pacing, using seatwork effectively, providing useful feedback and evaluation, and making smooth transitions. Emmer, Evertson, and Anderson (1980) found that good classroom managers have their classroom planned and organized within the first few weeks of school. This confirms the widely held notion that a highly structured classroom can be successfully relaxed a bit over time, but it is difficult, if not impossible, to tighten the structure of a classroom from a disorganized and permissive atmosphere.

Only programs that run in a disciplined manner can teach self-discipline. And as we all know, self-discipline may be our students' greatest need. For the students' benefit and the teacher's ability to teach, rules must be clearly stated and consistently enforced. The teacher must determine what behaviors will be rewarded and what behaviors will be punished. If rewards and punishments are to be successful they must be applied with consistency.

If a child finds that a teacher sometimes ignores an inappropriate behavior, sometimes punishes it, and sometimes reinforces it, the child cannot possibly learn the rule the caregiver is attempting to teach. Wilson (1993) equated inconsistency with a lottery. If the teacher has a rule concerning behavior that he or she wants the child to learn, he or she must be very consistent in using reinforcement and punishment. If a child behaves inappropriately and the caregiver is inconsistent—sometimes punishing, sometimes inadvertently reinforcing, but usually ignoring—the child will not learn the rule. To the child, behaving inappropriately is much like entering a lottery: Sometimes he wins big (is reinforced), sometimes he loses (is punished), but most of the time he is ignored. The best strategy for the child in playing the behavior lottery is to enter as often as possible hoping for the win. Therefore, the inconsistency of the teacher will result in an increase of the inappropriate behavior.

Effective classroom managers clearly communicate behavioral expectations and rules to students, monitor classroom behavior, and consistently reinforce behavior and consequate inappropriate behavior.

3. *Ability to collect and react to formative evaluation data. Formative evaluation* refers to evaluation data that is collected during the course of instruction or when skills are being developed, while *summative evaluation* refers to evaluation data collected at the end of a lesson or program (Kerr & Nelson, 1989).

Perhaps the most significant advance in educating students with academic problems has been the development by Deno and colleagues of curriculum-based measurement. The purpose of curriculum-based measurement (CBM) is to improve student performance through the collection of data to allow the teacher to formatively evaluate the effectiveness of an individual student's instruction (Deno, 1992). CBM reading data is collected by having students read aloud from teacher-selected reading passages. Words read correctly are graphed and compared to the results of previous sessions. CBM measures are collected frequently so as to create a data base for making instructional decisions. The rate of change exhibited by the student in the repeated CBM measures is the relevant student performance measure. The graphed data, which is an indication of a student's growth in reading, enables teachers to improve student performance by making instructional changes when the data indicates that it is necessary.

The technology by which we can collect formative data of behavior is well established. By systematically monitoring student behavior through collecting data, in both the academic and the social realm, we will be able to make better decisions about how to work with our students. Careful monitoring is a critical element in our educational programs (Kerr & Nelson, 1989).

Deno (1992) stated that two major problems in special education are the lack of clarity about essential student outcomes and a need for vital signs of student growth. When we are unsure about essential student outcomes for our students or we do not measure students' progress toward these outcomes, we lack a clear focus in designing our instructional programs. The result of this lack of focus, Deno further argued, is that we are like "pilots flying by the seat of their pants" (1992, p. 6). This familiar saying refers to pilots who rely exclusively on pressure sensations from the buttocks as a basis for determining the orientation of the airplane. When the weather is clear and the horizon is easily seen, flying by the seat of their pants is satisfactory. However, if the weather is not clear and the horizon difficult to see, flying by the seat of their pants can prove fatal. For most students in our schools teachers can fly by the seat of their pants. However, for students in special education, lack of clarity and sensitivity about our programs can lead to academic and behavioral casualties. Flying safety has been greatly improved through the use of instrumentation. Clarity and sensitivity concerning essential student outcomes can be greatly improved through the use of formative evaluation procedures.

4. *Ability to function as a role model.* In the *Nicomachaen Ethics,* Aristotle (trans. 1959) wrote that "the habits we form in children make no small difference, but rather they make all the difference" (pp. 125–126). He went on to draw a distinction between the intellect, which is developed through instruction and learning, and moral behavior, which is developed through observation and practice. If we are to follow the advice of Aristotle, we will teach our students not only through instruction but also through the example of our own behavior.

Children learn behavior by watching others. As teachers we are constantly modeling behavior to our students. The behaviors we model must reflect the values we hold and are trying to inculcate in our students. We cannot teach students to behave in a particular way if we do not behave in that manner ourselves. Putting students in the presence of a mature, responsible adult who exhibits self-discipline and deals with students in a respectful and honest manner is the best means by which we can foster growth in our students.

5. *Ability to relate to and effectively communicate with students.* Ralph Waldo Emerson (1883) reminded us in his essays that the heart of education lies in respecting the pupil. Teachers must behave toward students in a respectful manner. The two great mistakes I have observed in beginning teachers is that often they feel that they will earn the respect of students by being their friends, and, at the other extreme, some feel they will earn respect by being harsh with students. If the mistake is of the first variety, I tell the teacher that the student does not need a friend; he or she needs someone to be a teacher and role model. In the second case, the teacher must understand that respect is not earned by being harsh and punitive but by fair and consistent treatment.

Teachers must listen to students. They must talk and act toward them in respectful and caring ways. We must be willing to be honest and open with students. When students behave in ways that are appropriate and show self-control, we must acknowledge this and communicate approval. When students behave inappropriately, we must communicate disapproval, but this should not be done by belittling or humiliating them.

Research indicates that high expectations for students is an important component in student success. The expectations we hold for students must be based on realistic appraisals of ability. We should, nevertheless, expect good behavior and academic success from our students and communicate this expectation.

6. *Ability to be a good consumer of information.* In 1932 a tugboat by the name of the *TJ Hooper* was guiding a ship in from the Atlantic Ocean. A sudden storm blew up. Because the tug did not have information warning of the storm, it was not able to pull the ship to safety. The storm damaged

the ship, causing injury and property loss. The company that owned the ship sued the tug company. In the early 1930s the common practice of tugboats was to get weather information via hand signals from the shore. However, radio had been invented, and its ability to relay weather signals to tugboats had been demonstrated. Because the common practice was the use of hand signals, the *TJ Hooper* did not use the radio. If the tug had been equipped with a radio the tugmaster would have known of the dangerous storm and would have been able to take the ship to a safe port, thus avoiding damage to the ship, its cargo, and its operators. The case turned on the question of the *TJ Hooper's* responsibility. Was adherence to common practice among tug operators sufficient or did the situation demand the use of state of the art knowledge? The court ruled that when important matters are at stake, the legal obligation is to use the state of the art.

When important matters are at stake for children in our classrooms, the legal obligation is also to use the state of the art. Gilhool (1991) stated that the Individuals with Disabilities Education Act (IDEA) directs educators to draw on state-of-the-art educational practices. The only way teachers can ensure that their classrooms reflect state-of-the-art educational practices is to be good consumers of information concerning new and proven practices. Teachers need to be apprised of new, innovative practices through reading research, taking classes, and attending in-service training. Teachers, like lawyers, doctors, and engineers, need to adopt lifelong learning perspectives. Because of the rapid production of information through research, structural mechanisms must be created whereby teachers can access this information and become good consumers of new information. Only then can we be assured that our classrooms will reflect the state of the art.

By being good consumers of information we also can avoid falling into the trap of adopting educational fads before hard evidence exists as to their effectiveness. Slavin (1989) referred to the fad fetish of education as the pendulum. He argued that educational innovations tend to follow a cycle of early enthusiasm, widespread dissemination, subsequent disappointment, and eventual decline. A major reason for the continual swinging of the pendulum is that educators rarely wait for reliable data before adopting the newest practices. Often programs will be adopted based only on publications of promising preliminary evidence in a small number of locations. The results of the swinging of the educational pendulum are particularly damaging in special education. This is because the use of unproven practices tends not to have as deleterious consequences for the average or above-average student as for students who are disabled or disadvantaged. Unfortunately, the disappointment and decline phase of the fad often occurs after the damage has already been done. The movement toward full inclusion through the elimination of the continuum of services seems to meet Slavin's criteria of an educational fad. While students with E/BD clearly have a right to be educated in general classrooms, to argue for the dismantling of the continuum of services based on the feeling that it is the right thing to do may do irreparable harm to the students we serve. Decisions to adopt new practices must be based on hard data, especially for students who cannot afford the time lost to the latest fad.

7. Attention to our mental health needs. A friend of mine, diagnosed with bipolar affective disorder, once described his life to me prior to his successful treatment as being somewhat like a roller coaster ride. He was either very very high or very very low; things were very good or very bad, with little in between. Sounds somewhat like teaching children with E/BD! Sometimes it's very good, sometimes it's very bad, and often it seems like there are not many times when things seem mundane or prosaic.

Teachers of students with E/BD meet four challenges that must be overcome if we are to succeed in our profession. The first is exhaustion, the second is unrealistic expectations, the third is overinvolvement, and the fourth is the feeling that we are inconsequential.

F. M. Wood (1989), in detailing the fears of E/BD teachers that he had interviewed, stated that many were afraid that they would eventually become so tired out from dealing with students who seem to be living with all systems at full throttle that they would no longer be able to gather the needed energy. Working with students with E/BD can be exciting, but it also can be very exhausting.

The second challenge is overcoming unrealistic expectations. When I started teaching I believed I could make a positive difference in the lives of all my students. However, I found the real world of the classroom to challenge my idealism. Despite my best efforts, some students didn't succeed. This will always be the case. Although idealism and commitment are essential, the reality is that we will face situations that will challenge both.

Overinvolvement is the third major challenge. I have known numerous teachers of students with E/BD who have become too involved in the lives of their students. Our students frequently lead lives fulfilled with many problems. Too often we see young children whose lives consist of neglect, abuse, familial problems, crime, and drugs. In an attempt to deal with myriad problems, we can become so involved that we become emotionally exhausted.

The final challenge is the feeling that we are inconsequential. This problem is related to the problem of overidentification. The prognosis for many of the children, especially those with conduct disorders, is not good. We have all experienced the feeling of doing our best with a student and his or her family and later finding out that the outcome was not positive. The story I related about John at the beginning of the chapter was such an instance. It is easy under circumstances such as these to feel that, although we've done our best, it wasn't enough and that, regardless of what we do, the results will be the same. As a reaction to the feeling of being inconsequential in the lives of students, some teachers stop trying.

There are no answers or proven methods for overcoming these problems. What we do know is that if we face them and develop a realistic understanding of our profession we will be more likely to succeed. We can only do so much. To ensure that we don't become exhausted, it is important to balance our efforts in teaching with our own emotional and physical needs. Developing realistic expectations concerning the limits of what we can do will help to maintain our equilibrium. The answer is not to give up or distance ourselves from the problems we face but rather to maintain perspective in both our personal and professional lives. Developing support systems among fellow teachers can be very helpful in this regard.

WHY ARE WE HERE?

During the 15 years I taught students with E/BD in public schools, when I first met with the parents of my students I always asked what they wanted for their child from the school. Almost invariably I heard the following or some variation: (a) Teach my child to read, write, do math, etc.; (b) teach my child to control his or her behavior; and (c) help my child to develop standards of right and wrong.

Teaching Academic Skills

My first year of summer school teaching was my initial exposure to a method of teaching academics to students with E/BD that I was later to find out was, unfortunately, very common. This method of teaching basic skills to students was the "no teaching" method. Rather than directly instructing students, the teachers in the program assembled baskets of between 20 and 30 worksheets prior to class and placed them under the student's assigned desk every morning. When the students entered the room they were to quietly proceed to their desks, take out their baskets, and begin working on worksheet number one. Except for two short breaks and lunch, that was the sum total of their school day. The students' task was to behave and complete the worksheets. Teachers would answer questions, but for the most part they hovered over the students with point sheets attached to clipboards to record behaviors. When I asked the supervising teacher if the students were directly taught anything, I was informed that "we cannot teach academics until we get the behaviors under control." End of discussion.

Research as well as personal experience tells me that one of the greatest failings in the education of students with E/BD is that we are far less concerned with the academic behaviors of our students than with their social behaviors. So much energy and attention is devoted to managing behaviors and emotional crises that questions of what students need to learn and how they should be taught are relegated to secondary status (Knitzer, Steinberg, & Fleisch, 1990; Paine & Anderson-Inman, 1988). However, poor academic achievement is a defining characteristic of students with E/BD. Additionally, we know that improvement of academic skills also can have positive social and emotional results (Cranston-Gingras, 1991).

A major focus of programs for students with E/BD must be the improvement of academic skills. Fortunately, we have extensive research on what makes an effective teacher and what makes an effective school. We know what works, and we must scorn educational fads and concentrate on the principles derived from experience and the research in teaching academic skills to students. Students with E/BD do not learn differently from other students, and the teaching/learning process and the principles of effective instruction are the same.

Effective teachers develop clear, measurable instructional objectives, provide for direct instruction, and continuously monitor student progress toward meeting goals and objectives.

I have found the teaching of reading in many E/BD classrooms to be especially problematic. Children do not learn to read by doing phonics worksheets; children learn to read by reading. Yet in many of the classrooms in which I have observed the teaching of reading, one would think that the end goal is a child who can pronounce isolated sounds, fill in the most words in a cloze passage correctly, or read words in isolation, rather than a child who can read fluently and derive meaning from text.

Books should occupy a central place in our classrooms. When I taught reading, I read to my students for at least 30 minutes each day. I found the oral reading time was one of the most enjoyable activities of the day for both my students and myself. I always felt the books I read should be interesting and well written, books like *Winnie the Pooh, Where the Red Fern Grows, The Hobbit, The Chronicles of Narnia, Charlotte's Web, Treasure Island, Kidnapped, Swiss Family Robinson, Tom Sawyer,* and *Huckleberry Finn.*

TEACHING SELF-CONTROL

Lack of self-control is one of our students' greatest areas of failures. One of the most important skills we can help students to develop is self-control, the ability to manage one's own behavior. Kaplan (1991) argued that so many students with behavior problems have been conditioned to rely on external controls, such as token economies and medication, that as a result they have an external locus of control. They view their behavior as being controlled by an external force, such as the teacher. Therefore, they believe they have little to do with what happens to them. We want students to take responsibility for their own behavior. We want them to see themselves as being able to control what happens to them by controlling the way they behave. Students that take responsibility for their own behavior are said to have an internal locus of control. When students can manage their behavior they are moving toward gaining an internal locus of control (Workman, 1982).

Direct instruction in self-management (e.g., self-monitoring, self-instruction, self-evaluation, and anger-control training) is an important component of programs for students with E/BD. Advantages of teaching students to manage their behavior include the following: Teaching self-management is a proactive rather than reactive approach to behavior management; students with self-management skills can learn and behave more appropriately even without the supervision of the teacher; self-management may be an effective method of promoting generalization; and behavior change established through self-management may be more resistant to extinction (Yell, 1993). In addition to teaching self-management through direct instruction, cognitive–affective interventions such as life space intervention (Wood & Long, 1991) and rational-emotive therapy (Zionts, 1985) can be very useful.

The teacher of students with E/BD should be a model of self-control. We cannot realistically expect students to learn self-control if we do not exhibit it ourselves. I once had a student tell me that his teacher was really great because he would jump across chairs and push over desks to get at students with whom he was angry, and that he could pick students up over his head! The student found this behavior admirable. It would be an understatement to say that this teacher was not modeling or teaching self-control. His actions spoke much louder than his words to this particular student. As Kauffman (1993) stated, "Teachers whose own behavior is not exemplary may corrupt rather than help students, regardless of their fitness with other teaching strategies. Imitating the teacher should lead to behavioral improvement, not to maladaptive conduct" (p. 498).

HELPING STUDENTS TO DEVELOP STANDARDS OF RIGHT AND WRONG

To many parents of children with behavior disorders, the primary problem is that they seem to have no moral compass, no sense of right or wrong. They seem to be governed by impulses and self-interests.

Wilson, in his thought-provoking book, *The Moral Sense* (1993), stated that many people have persuaded themselves that children will be harmed if they are told right from wrong. They believe that children should be encouraged to discuss the merits of moral alternatives and that educators should be neutral toward questions of what is right and what is wrong. These views, Wilson argued, are mistaken and can only lead to confusion.

When I ask preservice teachers why they entered the field of teaching students with E/BD, they often answer something to the effect that they believe they can make a positive contribution to the lives of their students and that they want to help them to succeed in life. To accomplish these goals teachers must articulate standards of right and wrong to their students. We must be willing to speak honestly with students about ethical behavior. Students in our programs must learn what behaviors are irresponsible and then behave in a more responsible manner. To assist students to become responsible for their actions we must be willing to be directive. By being nonjudgmental or unconditionally accepting of all behavior, we may be encouraging dependence and excusing misbehavior. In addition to speaking honestly and candidly, we must be examples of ethical and responsible adults.

WHERE ARE WE GOING?

The incidence of E/BD is increasing. The 1990s may see the pell-mell expansion of the E/BD category just as the 1980s saw a similar expansion of the LD category. This will be due in large part to societal problems and the concomitant difficulties of children entering schools without preparation for the academic and behavioral expectations required of them.

Society is beset with problems. According to the United States Department of Commerce Bureau of the Census (1993), in the last 30 years we have witnessed the following with respect to our nation's youth:

- The number of children living in poverty has increased 40%.
- There has been a three-fold increase in the percentage of children living in single-parent homes. In approximately 90% of these homes there is no father. According to Wilson (1993) more than half of these fathers never see their children, and the majority of these pay no child support.
- There has been a doubling of the divorce rate, and more than 1 million children each year see their parents divorce or separate. It is estimated that close to 50% of children entering schools will live in single-parent homes for some period of time in their school careers.
- The number of births to unwed teenage mothers has increased 300%. Teenage mothers are much more likely not to complete high school and to live with their children in poverty.

- The rate of teen runaways, suicide, and violent crime has tripled. The fastest growing segment of the criminal population is our nation's youths.

In a speech to the graduating class at Howard University in 1965, President Lyndon Johnson said, "The family is the cornerstone of our society. More than any other force it shapes the attitudes, the hopes, the ambitions, and the values of the child. And when the family collapses, it is the children that are damaged. When it happens on a massive scale the community itself is crippled." These statistics are a grim portrait of the accuracy of this contention. In congressional testimony, Lee Rainwater, a Harvard University sociologist, predicted that if current trends continue, by the year 2000, 40% of all births in the United States will be to unwed mothers. If this prediction is realized, the functional family may become the exception rather than the rule. What does this data portend for the field of emotional and behavioral disorders?

At a conference in Minneapolis in 1988, M. M. Wood (1989) stated that the family in this country was on the verge of no longer being functional. Nonfunctional families are certainly less capable of raising, educating, nurturing, and protecting children. The National Center for Health Statistics, in their annual *Survey on Child Health* (1988), stated that children from disrupted, single-parent families are two to three times more likely than children from intact, two-parent families to have emotional and behavioral problems, drop out of school, become pregnant as teenagers, abuse drugs, and become entangled with the law. William Galston, the deputy assistant to President Clinton for domestic policy, and Elaine Kamarck, senior policy advisor to Vice President Gore, have written eloquently of the shattering emotional and developmental effects of divorce and disrupted families on children (Galston & Kamarck, 1993). The lack of a stable family structure creates emotional stress in children; they are more likely to have inadequate personal skills and will be less able to cope with the academic and social demands of the school setting (Jones & Jones, 1990). The dissolution of the family has adverse affects on the biological and psychological health of our children, and of these children, boys are affected more adversely than girls (Hoffman, 1981).

Well-meaning people can have disagreements concerning solutions to these problems. What we can agree on is that the dissolution of the family is having and will continue to have an impact on the educational system. If these trends continue, the incidence of children in E/BD programs may increase rapidly.

Given the increase in the E/BD population and the severity of problems that are entering our schools, the role of schools may have to undergo an alteration. Increased emphasis will be placed on prevention, interagency collaboration, and an alliance of home, family, and school.

PREVENTION

Special education teachers trained in appropriate behavioral procedures will be able to maintain students with E/BD in the controlled environments of their classrooms. However, in order to have an impact on the lives of our students, we will have to turn increasingly toward preventive procedures. The elementary school years may be the most crucial time in the lives of students. This is the time when they can most readily be taught the basic academic skills and when we can work to develop the characteristics of self-control and a sense of right and wrong. If we fail in elementary school years and inappropriate characteristics develop, they will be much more difficult to ameliorate as the child grows older.

INTERAGENCY COOPERATION

With the breadth of the problems we see today it is apparent that no single agency has all the expertise needed to serve our children and their families. We must move to models of interagency collaboration and develop comprehensive, integrated systems of care for children with E/BD and their families. Although frequently given lip service, the future will require true collaboration among educators, mental health workers, social services, health agencies, vocational services, and the family. None of these agencies by themselves can adequately serve the needs of children at risk and their families. However, by acting in concert we may.

THE ALLIANCE OF HOME, FAMILY, AND SCHOOL

Educators cannot replace a family, but we can provide expert help and advice. We must develop strategies and procedures to involve parents in the education of their children. Effective teacher–parent communication is essential if we are to improve the success of our programs. We must reach out to parents, and we must involve them in our educational programs. Many parents of the children in E/BD programs are worn out by the constant negative calls home and the complaints from school about their children. It is important that we share the good things with them. Rather than focusing totally on failures with parents, we should attempt to focus on the successes.

We also must be honest with parents and let them know what expectations we have of them. Recalcitrant parents must be told that the school by itself can do much but not nearly as much as when the parents and schools work together. Attempting to involve parents in the educational process in a meaningful way can be a frustrating experience. However, when parents do become involved with their child's education, the possibilities of success are greatly increased.

HAVING TO BELIEVE

Some believe that the students we teach will become part of a permanent underclass. These are children, it is argued, who will fail to learn much and will not be helped by our efforts. We must categorically reject this notion. It is true that many of our students come to us from backgrounds that do not foster a belief in the importance of education, and we cannot control the conditions in which children are raised. The belief that there must be a fundamental transformation of the conditions in which the children come from before we can expect them to succeed is, however, wrong. Research indicates that as teachers we can have profound effects on students. Through our influence we have control over variables that can significantly influence their academic achievement and behaviors.

There are many schools where students, despite disadvantaged backgrounds and severe behavior problems, succeed beyond expectations. Examples include Eastside High School in Patterson, New Jersey; Artesia High School in Lakewood, California; Clara Westropp Middle School in Cleveland, Ohio; and Eastern High School of Washington, DC. These schools are all inner-city schools serving low-income students. At one time, these schools were characterized by violence against students and teachers, vandalism, extortion, excessive absenteeism, and open drug abuse and drug dealing. The prosecutor's office of Patterson once referred to Eastside High as a cauldron of violence and terror and recommended that it be shut down. Reputations of the other schools were very similar. Something happened in these schools that turned them around to such an extent that all received the United States Department of Education's prestigious Secondary School Recognition Award. Changes occurred in all these schools that resulted in increased enrollment and attendance figures, increased graduation rates and number of graduates going to college, higher SAT scores, and the elimination of violence and drugs. From being examples of failed schools they became model schools. Educators can learn from the successes of these schools. Among other things, we can learn what kinds of environments were created in these schools and what traits and skills were encouraged in these schools to foster success.

In commenting on basic values that he thinks should guide teachers of students with E/BD, F. H. Wood (1993) wrote of two principles. The first, the professional's commitment to serve, he defined as giving a higher priority to the needs of our students than is expected in human relationships in general. We can make a difference, and we must do our best to help our students. However, this commitment cannot be so great as to exhaust us.

Wood's second principle is that we must understand the limits of the service we provide. We need to develop realistic expectations. Idealism and commitment are extremely important, but they must be tempered with reality.

We will find no cure for students with E/BD; there will never be a magic bullet or program that is successful with all. There will never be an easy answer. What will work in the future is what has worked in the past: good teachers, effective programs, involved parents, and hard work. A successful educational experience is possible for our children. We can make a positive contribution to the lives of the students we teach. We have to believe that we can make a difference and that every child can learn and succeed. When we believe and act as if we can make a difference, we will.

REFERENCES

Aristotle (trans. 1959). *The Nicomachaen ethics of Aristotle.* London: Oxford University Press.

Cranston-Gingras, A. M. (1991). Teaching emotionally disturbed children. In J. L. Paul & B. C. Epanchin, *Educating emotionally disturbed children and youth: Theories and practices for teachers* (2nd ed.). New York: Merrill.

Deno, S. L. (1992). The nature and development of curriculum-based measurement. *Preventing School Failure, 36,* 5–10.

Emerson, R. W. (1883). Education. In R. W. Emerson (Ed.), *Lectures and biographical sketches* (pp. 124–138). New York: Riverside.

Emmer, E., Evertson, C., & Anderson, L. (1980). Effective management at the beginning of the school year. *Elementary School Journal, 80,* 219–231.

Forness, S. R. (1993). Personal reflections: Definition. In J. M. Kauffman (Ed.), *Characteristics of emotional and behavioral disorders of children and youth* (5th ed., pp. 34–37). New York: Merrill/Macmillan.

Forness, S. R., & Knitzer, J. (1990). *A new proposed definition and terminology to replace "serious emotional disturbance" in Education of the Handicapped Act.* Alexandria, VA: National Mental Health Association.

Galston, W., & Kamarck, E. (1993). *Mandate for change.* New York: Berkeley Books.

Gilhool, T. K. (1991). Eight powerful national strategies designed to evoke powerful teaching and learning: The uses of law in the schools. *Quality Outcomes-Driven Education, 1,* 35–55.

Hoffman, M. L. (1981). The role of the father in moral internalization. In M. E. Lamb (Ed.), *The role of the father in child development* (2nd ed., pp. 359–378). New York: Wiley.

Jones, V. F., & Jones, L. S. (1990). *Comprehensive classroom management: Motivating and managing students* (3rd ed.). Boston: Allyn & Bacon.

Kaplan, J. S. (1991). *Beyond behavior modification: A cognitive-behavioral approach to behavior management in the school* (2nd ed.). Austin, TX: PRO-ED.

Kauffman, J. M. (1993). *Characteristics of emotional and behavioral disorders of children and youth* (5th ed.). New York: Merrill/Macmillan.

Kerr, M. M., & Nelson, C. M. (1989). *Strategies for managing behavior problems in the classroom* (2nd ed.). Columbus, OH: Merrill.

Knitzer, J., Steinberg, Z., & Fleisch, E. (1990). *At the schoolhouse door: An examination of programs and policies for children with behavioral and emotional problems*. New York: Bank Street College of Education.

Kounin, J. (1970). *Discipline and group management in classrooms*. New York: Holt, Rinehart, & Winston.

National Center for Health Statistics. (1988). *Survey on child health*. Washington, DC: U.S. Government Printing Office.

Paine, S. C., & Anderson-Inman, L. (1988). Teaching academic skills to behaviorally disordered students. In D. P. Morgan & W. R. Jenson (Eds.), *Teaching behaviorally disordered students: Preferred practices* (pp. 195–241). Columbus, OH: Merrill.

Robins, L., & Rutter, M. (Eds.). (1990). *Straight and devious pathways from childhood to adulthood*. Cambridge, NY: Cambridge University Press.

Slavin, R. E. (1989). Riding the pendulum of educational change. *Phi Delta Kappan, 70*, 752–758.

United States Department of Commerce Bureau of the Census. (1993). *Statistical abstract of the United States*. Washington, DC: U.S. Government Printing Office.

Wilson, J. Q. (1993). *The moral sense*. New York: The Free Press/Macmillan.

Wood, F. H. (1989). Learning and teaching: The special teacher of emotionally disturbed and behaviorally disordered students. In S. Braaten, G. Wrobel, & F. Wood (Eds.), *Celebrating the past, preparing for the future* (pp. 1–10). Minneapolis: Minnesota Council for Children with Behavioral Disorders.

Wood, F. H. (1991). Cost/benefit considerations in managing the behavior of students with emotional/behavioral disorders. In S. Braaten & G. Wrobel (Eds.), *Perspectives on the diagnosis and treatment of students with emotional/behavioral disorders* (pp. 61–73). Minneapolis: Minnesota Council for Children with Behavioral Disorders.

Wood, F. H. (1993). Personal reflections: Conceptual models. In J. M. Kauffman (Ed.), *Characteristics of emotional and behavioral disorders of children and youth* (5th ed., pp. 34–37). New York: Merrill/Macmillan.

Wood, M. M. (1989). Lesson learned and insights garnered. In S. Braaten, F. H. Wood, & G. Wrobel (Eds.), *Celebrating the past, preparing for the future* (pp. 59–75). Minneapolis: Minnesota Council for Children with Behavioral Disorders and Minnesota Educators of Emotionally/Behaviorally Disordered.

Wood, M. M., & Long, N. J. (1991). *Life space intervention*. Austin, TX: PRO-ED.

Workman, E. A. (1982). *Teaching behavioral self-control to students*. Austin, TX: PRO-ED.

Yell, M. L. (1993). Cognitive behavior modification. In T. J. Zirpoli & K. R. Melloy (Eds.,) *Behavior management* (pp. 199–241). Columbus, OH: Merrill/Macmillan.

Zionts, P. (1985). *Teaching disturbed and disturbing students: An integrative approach*. Austin, TX: PRO-ED.

ROBERT H. ZABEL
Kansas State University

Robert Zabel is a professor of special education at Kansas State University, where he coordinates training of teachers for students with emotional/behavioral disorders (E/BD). Zabel has been a general classroom teacher as well as a special education teacher of students with E/BD and has been a house parent in a residential treatment center. Zabel's research interests are in the preparation of E/BD teachers, teacher stress and burnout, and behavior management. He serves on several editorial boards and is currently co-authoring a new text on classroom management for general classroom teachers.

CHAPTER 25

Perspectives on Education of Students with Emotional/Behavioral Disorders

CURRENT STATUS OF E/BD PROGRAMS

Commenting on the current status of the education of students with emotional/behavioral disorders (E/BD) is akin to generalizing about the status of American education. It's difficult to determine the frame of reference for evaluating the status quo. The question is: How we are doing compared to what, to when, and to whom? At least three considerations influence my judgments of the current state of affairs: (a) the changing status of special education generally, (b) the diversity of E/BD programs, and (c) the context of the life experiences of students with E/BD.

THE CHANGING STATUS OF SPECIAL EDUCATION

Special education is experiencing a phenomenon found in second-generation reforms: institutionalizing reform. First-generation enthusiasm and optimism, stimulated by landmark litigation and legislation and the start-up of new, "special" programs for previously unserved children, has faded. In the second generation, attention has shifted to outcomes, to evaluating how well we are doing.

Advocacy is no longer sufficient. The prevailing perception, both within and outside of special education, is that, despite good intentions, despite legal mandates, and despite infusion of resources, special education is not doing a very good job. After all, there are more identified students, more programs, and much bigger budgets, alongside challenges seemingly as great as a generation ago.

In the first generation, special educators were viewed by others and by themselves as self-sacrificing missionaries trying to save children who were drowning in the educational mainstream or who had been left along the shore. Special educators took on the children no one else wanted (often in little rooms next to the boiler in the school basement). In the second generation, special educators are more likely viewed as pirates kidnapping children from the mainstream, assigning them to the hold and demanding an ever-increasing bounty for their care.

No longer are special educators viewed as benign masochists; we apparently have sadistic tendencies as well. We are no longer the "good guys" trying to save children abandoned by others; we are self-serving professionals who assign stigmatizing labels, segregate, and offer costly, substandard programs. Much of the criticism of special education is self-inflicted as we question our motives and practices and scurry to return our exceptional "boat people" to the mainstream.

DIVERSITY OF E/BD PROGRAMS

Education of students with E/BD must be considered within this evolving context of special education. We have more identified students with E/BD, more programs, and more resources than a generation ago, but are we doing a good job? The Knitzer, Steinberg, and Fleisch (1990) study of E/BD programs gave mostly failing marks. In most programs they examined, students appeared to be making little progress in unstimulating, segregated classrooms dominated by a curriculum of control. Still, Knitzer et al. (1990) found islands of innovation and effectiveness. Others (e.g., The Peacock Hill Working Group, 1991) responded to this dismal portrayal by identifying effective interventions and exemplary programs (mostly using behavioral approaches) for E/BD students and recommending steps for improving practice.

There is a tremendous variety and range in the quality of programs for students with E/BD. As I read Knitzer et al. (1990) and Steinberg and Knitzer (1992), my reaction was, "It's not all that bad." Certainly, there are incompetent, uncaring teachers and unstimulating, control-oriented programs, but they are the exception rather than the rule. Most teachers I know are well-prepared, follow sound educational approaches, and attempt to nurture their students in therapeutic environments.

Students with E/BD can be characterized as undercontrolled (acting out, externalizing, conduct disordered) or, less often, as overcontrolled (acting in, internalizing, personality disordered). There are many good reasons why control is a central issue (Nichols, 1992). A greater degree of control is necessary for these students to successfully interact with others and feel better about themselves. Without control, there is chaos, in which no growth can occur. External control should not be the goal but a means to other ends.

Control and suppression of behavior are sometimes confused. Control need not be aversive and should never be abusive. In an E/BD classroom where I often place practicum students, the overriding structure is provided by a token economy, that ubiquitous feature of E/BD programs found by Knitzer and her colleagues. However, there is nothing mechanistic and impersonal in this program. The atmosphere is pleasant, and students work hard and productively in challenging, engaging activities and generally treat their teacher and classmates with respect. The students, the teacher, and the paraprofessional like being there. Any visitor senses a relaxed, happy environment.

This program cannot be described adequately in a few paragraphs, because it is too complex. There are too many dimensions. The atmosphere is one of safety, organization, motivation, and success—elements usually missing in the lives of the students. Every feature of the classroom environment, every activity, has been carefully planned to build students' competence and self-esteem. Space is efficiently and deliberately arranged to minimize problems and to facilitate educational purposes. The token economy goes far beyond some system of mechanistically doling out points for isolated behavior. It resembles a giant board game with an annual theme where individual and group behavioral and academic goals are embedded and progress is recognized and rewarded.

This program is far more than a creative use of a token economy. Individual and group counseling and social and affective skills development are integral features. Ongoing and varied records of academic and social behavior performance are maintained and summarized for students and parents and used as a basis for team decisions about student progress within and outside the program. Parent communication and involvement is encouraged with daily and periodic report cards, weekly class newsletters, videotape tours of the classroom, group and individual parent meetings, and telephone communication aided by an answering machine. Students and parents are even asked to provide evaluations of the program and teacher, with results compiled and disseminated to them and others.

Is this an effective program? Without a doubt. The students progress behaviorally and academically, and their progress is documented. Is this program representative of all special programs for students with E/BD? Perhaps not, although I know many other teachers and programs for students with E/BD that are equally good, even though their delivery models, intervention approaches, and atmospheres are different.

What makes this an exemplary program? First, there is an exemplary teacher: intelligent, creative, nurturing, and skilled. There is no single template for "good" teachers of students with E/BD. Each one is unique, although the necessary or important traits and competencies of successful teachers include a combination of identified personal traits and professional understandings and skills (Bullock, Ellis, & Wilson, 1994; Zabel, 1988).

The teacher in the program I have been describing has degrees in elementary education and psychology and switched from a successful business career to a more personally rewarding career. After completing a graduate program in special education, he began creating a program that has evolved over 10 years. He has worked with many of the same colleagues and with the same paraprofessional during that time.

The teacher has a high energy level and works hard every day, arriving an hour before the students and continuing to work for 2 or 3 hours after they leave. He reads professional journals, attends conferences, and participates in workshops. Every summer, and part-time during the school year, he takes university courses related to his work. He frequently guest "lectures" in special education classes. He continually introduces innovative approaches to the program.

Teaching students with E/BD is one of the most challenging jobs in education. There are perennial shortages of trained personnel and high levels of occupational distress, burnout, and attrition (Zabel & Zabel, 1982). Some of our educational policies and practices have actually contributed to more than they have obviated this situation. For example, to address teacher shortages, in some places virtually anyone who is willing to take a job teaching students with E/BD can be granted an "emergency" license. A widely adopted approach for recruiting teachers is lowering licensure (and thus preparation) requirements. In some places, no specialized training or demonstration of competence is required. Even persons who have no general teaching preparation are allowed to teach these most challenging students. These unprepared and underprepared persons are also the most likely to provide inadequate programs and to rely on coercive control techniques, since they know of no alternatives and the control techniques seem to have an initial effect.

When the standards for admission to the profession, as well as the status and rewards, are raised, we will find enough teachers. Attrition and burnout will decrease. Until that happens, we will have some persons and programs that are exemplary, some that are good, some that are barely adequate, and others that do damage to children.

CONTEXT OF THE LIVES OF STUDENTS WITH E/BD

Education for students with E/BD cannot be considered in isolation from other influences in their lives. Less than 20% of a child's waking life between birth and age 18 is spent in school. Most students with E/BD spend only a relatively small proportion of their educational careers in special programs. Clearly, there are other powerful factors within their school, family, and community ecosystems that place them at risk. What is surprising is that some of these children have survived as intact as they are. Often, they have adopted the kinds of defensive strategies described years ago by Redl and Wineman (1951) that enable them to survive but also make them especially difficult to reach.

It is naive to think that educational programs that comprise only 10%, or 5%, or less of a child's life experience, beneficial as they may be, will be an effective antidote to their other experiences. An analogy could be made with the plight of millions of people in Somalia, or Sudan, or Yugoslavia, or the dozens of other war-ravaged locations where people are dying of starvation, disease, and violence. Relief efforts may deliver medical personnel and supplies to treat injured people, yet despite the quality of this medical care, can we say this relief effort "works"? A cynic might say that the medical relief simply gives some people a chance to survive.

Special education for students with E/BD can work. Competent teachers and exemplary programs are necessary for healing some wounds but not sufficient for curing the disease. Truly effective services require more ecologically oriented approaches that address the other 90%, 95%, or 99% of our students' lives. The last two sections of this chapter include some thoughts about promising approaches.

A WORKING DEFINITION OF EMOTIONAL/BEHAVIORAL DISORDERS

The definition developed by Eli Bower and his associates nearly 40 years ago (Bower, 1981) and adopted in the federal legislation has served pretty well, although some of the revisions have made it less helpful. The primary shortcoming of the Bower/federal definition is its reliance on a medical model that ignores contextual considerations and implies the child is the problem. The addition of the term *seriously* and the exclusion of *social maladjustment* are additional weaknesses. Of course we are concerned with *serious* emotional/behavioral disorders. I have yet to find identified students whose problems were mild or transient when they were identified. The exclusion of social maladjustment is implicitly contradictory and confusing since, as Bower himself pointed out, the definition was intended for children with emotional and social maladjustment (1988).

I empathize with anyone charged with writing a definition that can be operationalized, since it must be sufficiently general to apply to a variety of characteristics and situations yet sufficiently specific to generate eligibility criteria. The following definition may offer a starting point:

> Behaviorally disordered youth typically exhibit deficits of those behaviors considered desirable and/or excesses of those behaviors considered undesirable by teachers, parents, peers, and society in general. In other words, they engage in too many inappropriate, disruptive, disagreeable behaviors and too few appropriate, cooperative, agreeable behaviors. (Zabel, 1981)

This definition identifies patterns of excessive and deficient behavior and points to the significance of how others view that behavior.

Graubard (1973) went a step further, stating that behavior disorders are "a variety of excessive, chronic, deviant behaviors ranging from impulsive and aggressive to depressive and withdrawal acts which 1) violate the perceiver's expectations of appropriateness and 2) the perceiver wishes to see stopped" (p. 246).

Not only are the troubling behaviors excessive, chronic, and deviant and considered inappropriate, but those judging the behavior want to stop or change it.

The definition proposed by the National Mental Health and Special Education Coalition (Forness, 1988) represents multiple perspectives of several disciplines about emotional and behavioral disorders. The proposed definition keeps the focus where it should be: on agreement about the nature and the severity of the problems. Also, instead of excluding problem behavior that is presumed to reflect social maladjustment, it requires that the behavior be evaluated in its sociocultural context.

IMPORTANT DIMENSIONS OF THE PROPOSED DEFINITION

The proposed E/BD definition is an improvement over the serious emotional disturbance (SED) definition because it "contextualizes" problem behavior. Rather than listing the types of disorders that may make a child eligible, it refers more generally to "behavioral and emotional responses in school programs *so different from appropriate age, cultural, or ethnic norms* that they adversely affect educational performance" (Forness & Knitzer, 1992, p. 13; italics added). Emphasis is placed on determining the discrepancies between the behavioral or emotional responses and expected, appropriate norms within the context where they occur.

Another desirable feature of the proposed definition is the statement that the behavioral or emotional responses must be "*unresponsive to direct intervention applied in general education,* or the condition of a child is such that general education interventions would not be sufficient" (Forness & Knitzer, 1992, p. 13; italics added). This statement requires us to acknowledge that the maladjustment is extreme and that efforts have been made to change the behavior but have been unsuccessful. These two clauses should guide development of identification procedures that include comparisons of referred students to relevant norms and documentation of prior intervention efforts.

OVERLAP OF EMOTIONAL DISTURBANCE AND BEHAVIORAL DISORDER

It is fruitless to distinguish between emotional disturbance (ED) and behavioral disorders (BD). How can we say a child's problems are emotional or behavioral when emotions are manifest in behavior and behavior is a reflection of emotions? The characterization of disturbances as "externalizing," or conduct disorders, or "internalizing," or personality disorders (Achenbach, 1966), makes a distinction largely on the basis of how others respond to the child. In the current SED definition, the exclusion of the term *social maladjustment* (unless the child is also emotionally disturbed) is reminiscent of "double speak" in *1984* (Orwell, 1947). When a child's emotions and behavior create environmental dissonance sufficient that significant others concur that they exceed toleration, there are problems that must be addressed.

The effort to equate social maladjustment and conduct disorders makes even less sense, since it assumes that the behavior is simply the result of social conditions and not a reflection of "true" disturbance. I believe this search for a distinction is motivated primarily by an interest in finding ways to exclude troublesome children from eligibility for identification and services because they are difficult to treat.

MEANINGFUL EDUCATIONAL EXPERIENCES FOR STUDENTS WITH E/BD

It is impossible for schools to address all the needs of every student with E/BD. The core problem for most students with E/BD is their low self-esteem. They are what Dreikurs called "discouraged" children (1968). Their life experiences lead them to believe that they are unloved and worthless. There usually are associated problems (inadequate control, difficulty getting along with others, academic failure) as well. Consequently, our efforts should be directed at building students' belief that they can be loved and worthwhile. This is no easy task, because there is so much to be done. I think the most meaningful educational experiences include three elements: structure, deliberate social and emotional education, and encouragement.

STRUCTURE

Knitzer et al. (1990) struck a responsive chord when they criticized many programs for relying on a "curriculum of control." It is probably true that too much emphasis has been placed on establishing and maintaining external control. Still, students identified as E/BD exceed the boundaries of acceptable behavior, distracting, disturbing, and even hurting others. Some control is necessary to ensure their (and our) physical and emotional safety and security, but our efforts at external control by manipulating contingencies are shortsighted if that is all we do.

Our emphasis needs to be on raising self-esteem and promoting self-control. We need to help students understand how their feelings and behavior are related. They need opportunities to learn social behavior that will enable them to more effectively interact with others while meeting their own needs. Most of all, students need to become more motivated to change feelings and behaviors that are destructive to themselves and others.

There are many ways students can be helped to acquire new beliefs and behaviors. We can work from the inside (helping students understand how they feel and think), and we can work from the outside (directly teaching new communication and social skills). I think both the cognitive/affective and behavioral approaches are essential. Used in sensitive and creative ways, contingency management, in token economies and other forms, can be an integral part of meaningful programs. There must be sufficient structure, consistency, and predictability in the classroom environment to ensure safety and security for students and teachers alike. Contracting is another application of contingency management that can be used in a variety of situations and behaviors, provides a motivation system, and places the student in key decision-making and management roles.

Deliberate Social and Emotional Education

Deliberate teaching of affective and social skills is a critical ingredient of E/BD programs because it can help develop communication skills. Better communication skills offer alternatives to "fight or flight" responses to distress. Teachers can use approaches they are most comfortable with and that seem to fit the needs of their students. Group meetings for discussing topics of interest and concern in structured formats, affective education activities, life space interviews, cooperative learning, peer tutoring, and social skills training offer opportunities to learn and practice communication skills.

Encouraging Atmosphere

A third element of meaningful educational experiences is an atmosphere of encouragement. To use the psychoeducators' term, we must create a "therapeutic milieu." The physical and psychological climate must communicate safety, structure, caring, and valuing of the individual. It should include activities that engage students' interest and at which they can succeed. Obviously, this is no small order, but there are many ways a therapeutic milieu can be developed.

In addition to an empathetic teacher who objectively cares about students and who routinely shows and tells students that they are likable and competent, the environment must be comfortable and appealing. Too often we have eliminated fun from our programs because we don't think our students can handle it (Morse, 1971). We have denied them experiences that can make school attractive. There are so many ways to make school more appealing. Drama, music, art, puppetry, dance, cooking, and sports are some arenas where we can find the hooks to catch our students and opportunities for them to explore and develop competence and confidence.

It should go without saying that effective educators of students with E/BD need a well-developed sense of humor. Teachers need to be able to laugh with their students and sometimes at themselves. Humor communicates security to students and can provide a release from the stress of working with emotionally challenging behavior.

INCLUSION OF STUDENTS WITH E/BD

Integration of students into the educational mainstream is a goal to be pursued, but like some other advocates for students with E/BD, I am skeptical of *full* inclusion. Of course, students should not be removed from general programs if their individual educational needs can be met there and if sufficient accommodations and support are provided in regular programs. Many classroom teachers already have, or can learn, necessary skills and can utilize support services for students with E/BD. For some students, general classrooms provide more appropriate, acceptable peer models absent in special programs. But inclusion does not happen simply by placing students with E/BD in general programs.

Philosophical, legal, pedagogical, and financial arguments are used by inclusion advocates. Some say it is stigmatizing to segregate any subgroup from the mainstream, some claim that segregation denies the right to an equal education, some believe that special education is not so special and that instruction and support can be provided equally well in general classrooms, and some are primarily concerned with the financial costs of special programming.

For students with E/BD there are equally compelling arguments against inclusion: It is no less stigmatizing to be considered "bad" or "crazy" than to be labeled E/BD; equal rights are not guaranteed by equal treatment (some children need more than equal treatment); teaching students with E/BD requires special understandings and skills that general classroom teachers generally do not have; and providing appropriate inclusive programs will be more costly than special programs.

In this debate over inclusion, we often lose sight of the mandates for appropriate education and least restrictive environment. The way to determine an appropriate education is to examine individual student characteristics and needs and then determine how those needs can be met.

Location of programs is not the only, or even the most important, concern. Least restrictive environment should guide delivery of services, but a general classroom is not necessarily the least restrictive environment for a student with E/BD.

I am concerned when advocates of REI, and more recently of inclusion, lump students with learning disabilities, educable mental retardation, and E/BD together as "mildly" or "judgmentally" disabled. Students with E/BD pose different kinds of challenges in general classrooms than other students who are "mildly" disabled. Directly, and often adversely, their behavior affects their classmates and teachers. They are disruptive, threatening, and sometimes even dangerous to others. They demand a disproportionate amount of teacher time and energy and can diminish the quality of education for other students. Students with E/BD experience significant dissonance in general classrooms. I do not believe there has been a "bounty hunt" mentality (Reynolds, Zetlin, & Wang, 1994) for them. Nobody wants these children in their programs, regardless of the categorical dollars that may follow.

It is fine rhetoric to assert that students with E/BD will develop prosocial skills through association with their typical classmates, and that that will lead to greater understanding and acceptance of deviance. If these benefits exist, why have prior social interactions in general programs not been self-healing?

Students with E/BD can and should be educated in general classrooms, but only if those programs are prepared to deal with them. Classroom teachers will need substantial preparation in understanding and effectively dealing with challenging behavior. They often will need smaller classes and support from skilled personnel to modify expectations, manage behavior, and teach new ways of thinking and behaving. To use the support, they will need training in collaboration. These are no small tasks, as they require time, energy, and financial resources. Costs and benefits of special interventions for students with E/BD must be evaluated (Wood, 1991).

General classrooms could become more accommodating for students with E/BD and other disabilities *if* there were not other reform initiatives confronting educators. The major school reform agendas of the past 10 years have virtually ignored the educational needs of students with disabilities generally and those of students with E/BD specifically. Over the past 10 years, educational reform has emphasized raising standards and improving academic outcomes. The "effective schools" movement, for example, emphasizes high academic expectations. *A Nation at Risk* (National Commission on Excellence in Education, 1983) called for higher standards, more homework, more time on task, longer school years, and longer days. The "back to the basics" movement calls for a common core curriculum, while the "back to the classics" movement stresses studying the classics of the EuroAmerican tradition. The Reagan and Bush administrations pushed for "school choice," using voucher systems to create an educational marketplace where consumers could choose schools they found satisfactory. The goals of America 2000 pushed by the Clinton administration also emphasize academic achievement.

As appealing as these reform proposals may seem, there are many unanswered, and even unasked, questions. How many magnet schools are devoted to providing exemplary programs for students with E/BD? How many private schools say they will accept any student? How can we balance the needs to deal with distraction and disruption with demands for more time on task? How do we balance accommodating behavioral diversity with higher achievement? How do we incorporate the social and affective skills development with the stress on academic outcomes?

In fact, these major educational reform proposals seem antithetical to full inclusion. America in the mid-1990s is ambivalent about which direction to follow in dealing with society's rule breakers. On the one hand we talk about universal health care, deinstitutionalization, and community-based programs, while on the other we lock up a larger proportion of our population in prison than in any other nation, we enact sentences of "three strikes and you're out" for violent crimes, and we reintroduce capital punishment.

In schools, we push for full inclusion at the same time we establish intensive special programs for students whose behavior is too disturbed to be contained even in self-contained classrooms. Wood (1982) summarized that we have countervailing impulses to punish and to heal students with behavior problems. Successful inclusion of students with E/BD will require changes in attitudes about disordered behavior, improvements in the skills of educators to deal with them, and greater support.

A DELIVERY OF SERVICES MODEL

It is not a new idea, but we need to provide a continuum of special education services. There seems to be an assumption that the continuum of services has been tried, has not worked, and should be discarded in favor of inclusion. The truth is that schools rarely offer a true continuum (Peterson, Zabel, Smith, & White, 1983). Where elements of a continuum have existed, there is seldom sequential, planned provision of services up or down the continuum. A continuum should not be a description of places but of levels of programming from less to more intensive that could be provided in a variety of different places.

IS THE INCIDENCE OF E/BD INCREASING?

It is hard to judge whether (or how much) the incidence of E/BD is increasing. Our individual and cultural judgments of normal, abnormal, and deviant behavior continually change. When I began teaching in a general classroom 25 years ago, some of my colleagues commented on how much worse students behaved than earlier in their careers. And, indeed, some of my students seemed more challenging than I recalled being when I was a sixth-grade student. We have a tendency to view the past through spectacles that screen out memories of unpleasantness while focusing on the harsh realities of the present.

Also, it is hard to select a base rate of E/BD to compare the present to the past, as the context changes to reflect evolving cultural values and beliefs. Not so long ago, the American Psychiatric Association classified homosexuality as a mental disorder. It no longer does. Until recently, syndromes like autism and hyperactivity were subsumed under the category of serious emotional disturbance. Now they are viewed as distinct classifications.

The annual reports of the implementation of IDEA show steady increases in the number of identified students with SED over the past 20 years, yet we still think we are underidentifying "qualified" students. These statistics do not necessarily indicate that there are more children with E/BD, just that we are identifying more than in the past. In 1969, my school district had no special programs for these students, although three students from my sixth-grade class would likely qualify for services today. Our beliefs about emotional/behavioral deviance and the role of schools for dealing with it have changed. They will continue to change in the future.

Despite this "relativity" issue, I would not minimize the serious problems of our children today. We are witnessing and participating in dramatic societal changes. Although many of the societal changes seem to expand individual rights and opportunities, they are not without some cost. The principal downside of these changes, as they influence child growth and development, is apparent in family structures.

It would be naive to assert that in some past golden age all nuclear families provided nurturing, healthy environments for their children; that the only healthy family is of the traditional, two-parent variety; or that family is the sole determinant of children's emotional and behavioral adjustment. There have always been unhappy, dysfunctional, abusing, and neglectful families, and many different family constellations can offer environments that contribute to children's healthy development. Still, the number of children who experience stable, nurturing families has dramatically decreased over a relatively short period (Children's Defense

Fund, 1992). Approximately one half of all American children will live in a nontraditional family by the time they are 18. This trend is not just a moral issue. These are direct and indirect risks for children (Whitehead, 1993).

At minimum, at least two ingredients are necessary for healthy emotional and social development: Children need to experience safe environments where their basic needs are met in fairly predictable ways, and children need to have models of caring and nurturing adults. Children need to know that adults are monitoring their behavior. Young children whose homes are not safe places where they can expect to be cared for are at high risk for emotional and behavioral problems. These conditions are missing in the lives of many children. Many children are not cared for, not cared about, and not supervised.

We see large numbers of disaffected students in conflict with teachers, schools, and others. Senator Daniel Patrick Moynihan provided a relevant analysis of the cultural relativity of deviance in an article entitled "Defining Deviance Down" (1993). Drawing upon the work of the sociologist Kai Erikson, Moynihan proposed that a culture can tolerate only a certain level of deviance. When deviance exceeds that level, the culture redefines it as normal. Compared to 30 years ago, Moynihan wrote, the United States today is much more violent. However, we have locked up and punished about as many violators as we can afford to. Consequently, we are redefining our standards and accepting more violence as normal. In the 1920s, the "Saint Valentine's Day Massacre" made national headlines; today, gang killings of similar scope are not always front-page news stories. In a sense, Moynihan asserted, we have come to expect, and even accept, more violence in our society.

The reason for dramatic increases in crime, Moynihan asserted, can be traced to a dramatic increase in single-parent families. Citing an article he wrote in 1965, he stated that "there is one unmistakable lesson in American history: a community that allows a large number of young men to grow up in broken families, dominated by women never acquiring any stable relationship to male authority, never acquiring any set of rational expectations about the future—that community asks for and gets chaos. Crime, violence, unrest, unrestrained lashing out at the whole social structure—that is not only to be expected; it is very near to inevitable" (Moynihan, 1993, p. 26).

Clearly, if we are going to address these tremendous social problems, our efforts must be aimed at causes of deviance. More prisons, harsher punishments, and more special education programs are not solutions. We have tried this approach; it has cost a lot, but it has not worked. Our resources must be directed up front, in programs and support systems for children and families that will help prevent the emergence of problems.

ROLE RELATIONSHIPS BETWEEN MENTAL HEALTH PROVIDERS, JUVENILE JUSTICE SYSTEM, AND EDUCATION

Better supported and coordinated multidisciplinary approaches must be part of the prevention and early intervention effort. We have a long way to go to effectively and efficiently use the expertise and resources of the various service providers that may be involved with children who have E/BD. Some of the roadblocks are bureaucratic hurdles to sharing personnel, resources, facilities, and budgets. More challenging impediments are the role perceptions in the different systems and disciplines that result in suspicion, mistrust, and mental health turf battles.

Recently, our local director of special education tried to respond to concerns expressed by school personnel about their inability to effectively serve several students with severe behavior disorders. The students of concern were being taught in self-contained classrooms or on homebound instruction due to extremely disruptive and violent behavior. Most had earlier placements in institutional and hospital settings and represented part of a state- and nationwide trend to provide more community-based services. Even in self-contained programs, these students' behavior could not be effectively managed or even contained. Other students, teachers, and support personnel in special and general education were threatened and sometimes even physically attacked.

After discussions among school and public mental health agency personnel, the director presented a plan for an intensive therapeutic program, physically separate from the middle school. The central feature of the program was a team consisting of an E/BD teacher, a counselor/therapist, and a paraprofessional. The facility and educators would be provided by the school district, the counselor/therapist by the local mental health clinic. This effort in transdisciplinary collaboration offered a unique pooling of professional skills and funding. The proposal seemed promising; however, when the plan was presented to the school board, some therapists in private practice objected to being left out of the planning process and not allowed to bid on providing the therapy services. They asserted that the proposed program put the school district in the business of providing mental health care—a service, they believed, it had no business engaging in. One stated, "There needs to be a clear distinction of who provides mental health." The school board concurred and shelved the proposal.

Who provides services ultimately comes down to who pays for the services. Most of our students do not have access to private mental health services. They simply cannot afford it. Even if the services were available, many of our students might not benefit much from the kinds of in-office talk therapies offered by some therapists. More ecologically oriented programs, such as those proposed in the above plan, where therapy would be provided in the context of the environments where students are living, would be more promising.

FUTURE TRENDS IN IDENTIFICATION, INTERAGENCY RELATIONSHIPS, AND THE ROLE OF SCHOOLS

If Erikson and Moynihan are correct in stating that a society will recognize and treat a fairly stable amount of deviance, the prevalence rate of E/BD should remain fairly constant, even though the severity may actually increase. I think the proposed definition of E/BD, perhaps in a somewhat more restrictive form, eventually will be accepted.

The future of educational programs for students with E/BD will not be all onward and upward, if the past is a good predictor. Due to the collision course of the school reform agenda and inclusion and the countervailing impulses "to treat or to heal," there will be clashes ahead.

Despite the roadblocks to transdisciplinary collaboration, or even cooperation, identified earlier, we will make progress toward more coordinated, interdisciplinary delivery of services within and outside of schools. At least we are all beginning to recognize that balkanization of services is ineffective and inefficient.

Within schools, more teachers will function in the role of consultants. There will be more collaboration among general and special education teachers. These consulting and collaborative delivery models will require highly trained special educators who are skilled not only in working with students with E/BD and other disabilities but also in operating in collaborative relationships with colleagues. Likewise, general educators will need greater understanding and skills to function collaboratively. None of this coordination, cooperation, and collaboration will come easily. There are role and status barriers among the various disciplines, different kinds of professional training and skills, and logistical hurdles (e.g., finding time for teams to meet), as well as individual personal differences that influence the course of education–mental health liaisons (Morse, 1992).

Teacher training will become longer and more interdisciplinary for both general and special educators. Classroom teachers will need higher entry-level skills to work with diverse learners and behaviors than they can obtain from the single introductory course that is now required. Special educators need the skills of general educators. We will see more movement toward more integrated training of special and general educators (Simpson, Whelan, & Zabel, 1993).

However, it is unrealistic to expect that inclusive programs can offer appropriate programs for all students even when all reasonable accommodations and adaptations are made. There will continue to be a need for special education programs for some students with E/BD separate from the mainstream.

More ecologically oriented, coordinated human resources, or wraparound programs, involving the various systems that serve children and their families—education, mental health, medical, recreation, social services, corrections—will move toward better coordination of services. Although there will be no single design (Morse, 1992), the regional interagency councils established for coordinating early childhood special education programs may serve as a model. Some form of the individual family service plans prepared by representatives of the various service agencies and care providers who are involved with a child will be the vehicle for coordinating services. For this to occur, funding formulas that more readily allow for coordination and delivery of services will be necessary. Because education will be the common service for students with E/BD, responsibility for coordination will likely fall on the shoulders of teachers, who will serve as case managers, coordinating services within and outside of schools (Forness, Sinclair, & Russell, 1984).

REFERENCES

Achenbach, T. M. (1966). The classification of children's psychiatric symptoms: A factor-analytic study. *Psychological Monographs, 80* (Whole No. 615).

Bullock, L. M., Ellis, L. L., & Wilson, M. J. (1994). Knowledge/skills needed by teachers who work with students with severe emotional/behavioral disorders: A revisitation. *Behavioral Disorders, 19*, 108–125.

Bower, E. (1981). *The early identification of emotionally handicapped children in school* (3rd ed.). Springfield, IL: Charles C. Thomas.

Bower, E. M. (1988, December). Ten reflections on behavior disordered children. *Behavior in Our Schools, 3*, 2–6.

Children's Defense Fund. (1992). *The state of America's children, 1992.* Washington, DC: Author.

Dreikurs, R. (1968). *Psychology in the classroom* (2nd ed.). New York: Harper & Row.

Forness, S. R. (1988). Planning for the needs of children with serious emotional disturbance: The national special education and mental health coalition. *Behavioral Disorders, 13*, 127–133.

Forness, S. R., & Knitzer, J. (1992). A new proposed definition and terminology to replace "serious emotional disturbance" in Individuals with Disabilities Education Act. *School Psychology Review, 21*, 12–20.

Forness, S. R., Sinclair, E., & Russell, A. T. (1984). Serving children with emotional or behavioral disorders: Implications for educational policy. *American Journal of Orthopsychiatry, 54*, 22–32.

Graubard, P. S. (1973). Children with behavioral disabilities. In L. M. Dunn (Ed.), *Exceptional children in the schools: Special education in transition* (2nd ed., pp. 245–285). New York: Holt, Rinehart, & Winston.

Knitzer, J., Steinberg, Z., & Fleisch, B. (1990). *At the schoolhouse door: An examination of the programs and policies for children with behavioral and emotional problems.* New York: Bank Street College of Education.

Morse, W. C. (1971). Education of maladjusted and disturbed children. In N. J. Long, W. C. Morse, & R. G. Newman (Eds.), *Conflict in the classroom: The education of children with problems* (2nd ed., pp. 330–336). Belmont, CA: Wadsworth.

Morse, W. C. (1992, Winter). Mental health professionals and teachers: How do the twain meet? *Beyond Behavior, 4,* 12–20.

Moynihan, D. P. (1993). Defining deviance down. *American Scholar, 62,* 1, 7–30.

National Commission on Excellence in Education. (1983). *A nation at risk: The imperative for national reform.* Washington, DC: U.S. Government Printing Office.

Nichols, P. (1992, Winter). The curriculum of control: Twelve reasons for it, some arguments against it. *Beyond Behavior, 4,* 5–11.

Orwell, G. (1947). *1984.* New York: Harcourt, Brace, Jovanovich.

The Peacock Hill Working Group. (1991). Problems and promises in special education and related services for children and youth with emotional or behavioral disorders. *Behavioral Disorders, 16,* 299–313.

Peterson, R. L., Zabel, R. H., Smith, C. R., & White, M. A. (1983). Cascade of services model and emotionally disabled students. *Exceptional Children, 49,* 404–408.

Redl, F., & Wineman, D. (1951). *Children who hate.* Toronto, Ontario: The Free Press.

Reynolds, M. C., Zetlin, A. G., & Wang, M. C. (1994). 20/20 analysis: Taking a close look at the margins. *Exceptional Children, 59,* 294–300.

Simpson, R. L., Whelan, R. J., & Zabel, R. H. (1993). Special education personnel preparation in the 21st century: Issues and strategies. *Remedial and Special Education, 14,* 7–22.

Steinberg, Z., & Knitzer, J. (1992). Classrooms for emotionally and behaviorally disturbed students: Facing the challenge. *Behavioral Disorders, 17,* 145–156.

Whitehead, B. D. (1993, April). Dan Quayle was right. *The Atlantic Monthly,* 47–84.

Wood, F. H. (1982). Defining disturbing, disordered, and disturbed behavior. In F. H. Wood & K. C. Lakin (Eds.), *Disturbing, disordered or disturbed? Perspective on the definition of problem behavior in educational settings.* Minneapolis: University of Minnesota, Department of Psychoeducational Studies.

Wood, F. H. (1991). Cost/benefit considerations in managing the behavior of students with emotional/behavioral disorders. *Preventing School Failure, 35,* 17–23.

Zabel, R. H. (1981). Behavioral approaches to behavioral management. In G. Brown, R. L. McDowell, & J. Smith (Eds.), *Educating adolescents with behavior disorders* (pp. 192–212). Columbus, OH: Charles E. Merrill.

Zabel, R. H. (1988). Preparation of new teachers for behaviorally disordered students: A review of literature. In M. C. Wang, M. C. Reynolds, & H. C. Walberg (Eds.), *Handbook of special education: Research and practice* (Vol. 2, pp. 171–194). New York: Pergamon Press.

Zabel, R. H., & Zabel, M. K. (1982). Factors involved in burnout among teachers of exceptional children. *Exceptional Children, 49,* 261–263.

CHAPTER 26

Where Do We Go From Here?

The preceding chapters presented statistical and demographic evidence on a very pressing condition that appears to be increasing dramatically in modern society. Children with emotional disturbance and behavioral disorders (E/BD), unlike other disability groups, represent and reflect societal changes. In fact, in many ways these children mirror society. The reflection seen in the behaviors and lives of these children is not always an easy one for established institutions and policymakers to recognize.

The chapters in this text offer the views of several of the senior contributors, whose thinking has shaped this developing field during its infancy. The treatment and education of children with E/BD are recent occurrences in the history of humankind. Therefore, the "history" in this text represents the immediate past; the concerns and issues raised are reflections on immediate needs. The future in most cases is now.

All of the contributing authors agree that the incidence of children failing to adjust to various social environments is increasing more rapidly than any other modern-day school-age disability group. It is a national concern that should not be overlooked, and yet it is painfully ignored by many in our society, disregarded, to some degree, by one of the very professions to which the education of all children has been entrusted: the public schools. Children with E/BD are the most underidentified and underserved disability group covered by the Individuals with Disabilities Education Act (IDEA).

Beginning with Bower's observations, we are struck by the fact that we have not been able to keep pace with the growing numbers and intensity, as well as the changing complexity, of these populations. It is clear that the populations being described are complex behavioral mosaics, tapestries of multifaceted sociological, personalogical, biological, and psychological threads that must be woven together. Childhood, a period of social learning, is a time when balance among and strength from the contributing systems should be learned, or confusion begins and deviance results.

The qualitative aspect of the condition known as *emotional disorders* is influenced by many factors, one of which is the very definition by which children are so labeled. A point of major disagreement among the contributing authors is how "broken" the system is and what it would take to "fix" it. Of greatest agreement is that education alone, that is, educators working alone, primarily in the area of academics, cannot provide the breadth and depth of services and programs to meet the needs of children with E/BD. One remedy to this problem has been the creation of the National Mental Health and Special Education Coalition. Forness, a member of the Coalition, recognizes that there is much this group can do, particularly if it will take a proactive stance. While national-level coalitions are needed, there also is a vast need at state and local levels. Forness identified many sources of resistance, such as lack of effective parental empowerment and professional reluctance by both educators and agency policymakers, to name a few. He also noted that while the percentage of those who are receiving any treatment continues to be quite small in comparison to those who receive no services at all, the quality of services remains an unresolved issue.

The quality of programs is another issue of major concern. Coleman pointed out that children who are not in school cannot be educated. Children with E/BD are earmarked by high rates of absenteeism, and they remain one of the first groups to be pushed out of school even before age 16. One solution that Coleman called for—one shared by many of the contributing authors—is a vast amount of social competence training. A rather unique, but noteworthy, concept that Coleman supports is vocational skill development.

Haring believes that schools must not attempt to go it alone. He would design specialized curricula that teach social interactive skills using positive behavioral support in tightly structured behavioral management systems. Paul reiterated what many others have written: that the problem is more complex than just education. He, in fact, sees children with emotional disturbance as part of the deterioration of our current sociocultural constructs. McIntyre believes that this is the best of times and the worst of times for our field. He expressed that, today, the education system for children with E/BD is impersonal and nonsupportive. But he also believes that something is being done about it, particularly in the area of cultural awareness and cultural diversity.

Townsend, Noll, Braaten, and Yell all strongly asserted that the symptoms seen in children reflect what is occurring in the larger society. First-time divorce rates have soared to over 40%, nearly 60% of this nation's children are living with one parent, and nearly 80% are living in blended families. The only conclusion is that the nature of the home in the United States has changed dramatically in the past 50 years. Reported cases of domestic violence have increased dramatically, and the incidence of neglect and emotional and physical abuse also has increased. One clear aftermath has been the amount and type of emotional disturbances displayed by children. The natural conclusion is that one cannot fix the child without fixing the family and turning attention on society's ills.

Rhodes believes that changes at all levels of society are needed. This notion also is supported by Evans, Simpson, Webber, and Guetzloe. There was practically unanimous agreement that the children themselves are changing rapidly. And while the severity of their problems is increasing, the schools themselves also are changing but not in the same direction. Webber and Zabel pointed a strong finger at the early 1980s, when this country, under the Reagan Administration, drew the nation's attention to its failure to compete with the industrial work output of the Japanese. The culpability was placed on the country's schools, summarized in a governmental report called *The Nation at Risk* (National Commission on Excellence in Education, 1983). The solution for this nation's return to world industrial status was to place its educational emphasis on academic achievement. Social curriculum was viewed as a needless frill. The intensity and severity of children's emotional problems and the social and family complexity surrounding the children became and continue to be much-neglected concerns.

Townsend and Johnson, supported by McIntyre, recognize ethnic, sociocultural, and linguistic differences, particularly as they are found in the inner-city family and schools, as continuing, unresolved problems. Do those who make policies and provide service delivery structures place the blame for system failure on the very children and families they are to serve? The result is a denial of support services to black children and their families. Blame is substituted for failure to understand those critical cultural differences that affect children growing up black in modern urban America. McIntyre and Webber have spoken about other cultural considerations, such as those experienced by Hispanic and Asian peoples new to the United States, and the continuing difficulty to obtain social mobility within this nation. The relationship between emotional relativity and changes in the character of the culture was discussed by almost all of the contributors. As McDowell pointed out, society does not know how to respond to the increasing social complexities observed in children's behavior. Simpson asked a most poignant question: Where does the child with emotional disturbance and behavioral disorders fit into all the educational and social reform? Maybe this is what Wood meant when he observed that "we know a lot, but what we do not yet know is vast." Webber and McDowell referred to the many relevant social contributors and how they are affected by race, poverty, parental social standing, and cultural–linguistic variances.

Kelly also defined the many contributors to social blindness as he argued for recognition of a socially relative definition. He believes that "holistic reconsideration" of the many contributors to social–emotional problems must be undertaken by viewing the child's total environment. Tompkins described boards for children in trouble. He called for the sharing of information across agencies and begins a cry for collaborative services. This is in support of the term *wraparound*, connoting the involvement of the child within the various service providers, rather than a single agency providing one-shot assistance.

Rhodes defined a new period: post-modernism. He pointed to apathy and traditional practices as root causes of current ineffective educational practices, which he likened to lines in the dirt that dare children to cross them in expressions of their social/personal and educational needs. Many of these authors wrote that punishment not only remains a prevalent practice in the minds of too many educators but also is the foundation, the cornerstone, of their belief system, upon which the behavioral control issues of children in today's schools continue to be based. Punishment and its use as a control continues to create a social belief, and therefore a bias, that all children must be able to control all of their feelings all of the time. Rhodes provided a splendid example of a point offered by many of the other authors: Even in the presence of space-age behavioral scientists in the school environments, it is inherently difficult to provide state-of-the-art services when the policymakers will not relinquish traditional practices.

Traditional practices that convey punishment, exclusion, expulsion, and placement in alternative schools without psychodiagnosis remain a modern-day nightmare. Punishments that did not work effectively in the past will not work effectively tomorrow because they are based in a dehumanizing process. Morse, Rhodes, Johnson, Long, and Haring see the schools as a closed social system, a social organizational structure that requires beginning teachers to conform and one that reminds all of its members that if they cannot control their classes they have failed as educators. The pressure to obtain behavioral control is part of the social organizational structure and appears to be a direct challenge to many of the contributors. And while they agree that external control of children's behavior is required, they do not agree that it is the goal. They therefore see it as a threat to the more important development of personal autonomy and identity, which contains internalization of impulse and self-control.

There is a strong belief running consistently through these chapters that educators' attitudes toward human beings permeate buildings and can be observed and experienced as school building climates, more specifically the prevailing attitudes of adults toward those children who express feelings in unwanted and inappropriate manners, those who either act out or are depressed and withdrawn from most social interaction. Wood seeks an awakening of state-level policymakers across agencies to coordinate forces and to generate changes. He noted that criticism is popular in contemporary society, which inherits the blame for that which it cannot do. Center believes that special education services for children with E/BD have not been effective. He also believes that education is not driven by fact and must constantly respond to social pressures.

Most of the contributors agree with Morse's request for a Full Service School, a focal point of community (interagency) treatment efforts. A Full Service School would provide teachers support systems with immediate on-the-spot know-how when it is needed. Tompkins examined the system, the very system that provides or denies support to children. His review of the federal role in the development of the educational programs and services for children who are emotionally disturbed identified decisions and decision makers, confusion, and even deceit at the highest policy levels. He bravely examined what did occur and what would have or could have occurred had other recommended steps, as directed by the field, been taken.

There is much agreement among the authors that teachers must be supported with direct services and consultation precisely when they need it. The authors believe that policymakers must understand and support teachers as they constructively engage in therapeutic relationships with troubled children. Certainly, teacher training must be rethought to meet those needs. There is a sense that the hope for the future is an awakening in the schools, that one of the best therapeutic interventions for the child with feeling confusions is a highly tuned and well-trained teacher.

However, Long and Kelly had much to say about the current direction the schools are headed, frequently spirited by special educators who wish every child with disabilities were included in general education settings. These two authors and McDowell would require socially protective environments that are highly structured and that would serve as social learning laboratories to practice new behaviors under close, intensely trained tutelage, behaviors that can only be learned in the times of crisis.

The role of the school is examined in every chapter. Is the school an educational institution, responsible for academic learning only? Or is it an institution that, while responsible for academic learning, realizes that moral development is based on values and that societies do not rise or fall on the basis of knowledge, or artistic production, or scientific achievement, but on their belief systems? Why do children and families have such a difficult time finding the support systems they need when they need them? Why is there such a resistance to providing interventions to children experiencing academic and social learning failure in the public schools?

Central to the unified belief system of the contributors to this text is the fact that this nation will rise or fall on the one social system that interacts with all children and all families. Inherent in this belief is the idea that education, the everyday teacher-to-student and teacher-to-family interaction, has the potential to be therapeutic and that therapeutic means a dedicated and planned effort to improve a condition or eliminate pain. Each given interaction may or may not be an intervention, depending on what is to be taught. Subject matter is information, and conveying information is a form of education. Teaching human interactions and relationship skills, interpersonal communications, problem solving, and decision making based on values that convey reason and responsibility for self, others, and the environment enhances social learning.

When social and academic learning are woven together, they represent therapeutic interventions. If they take place in an educational environment they are therapeutic interventions, if they take place in a family treatment milieu they are family interventions, and if they take place in a mental health center they are clinical interventions. All of the contributing authors agree that the schools cannot fly solo with families of children who are disturbed or disruptive. And all of the contributing authors strongly support the notion that today's complex problems require school–community, private, and public coordination and cooperation.

Today's family with a child who is emotionally disturbed represents a unique but troubled environment. Not one author would have this child and family treated in or by one agency and not have information and experiences shared across agency lines. Yet, while this does *not* occur as the authors wish it would, the future they envision and recommend is a planned and contributed joint treatment effort. Two major recommendations cross all chapters. They are interagency team building and interagency team treatment and a return to therapeutic, sensitive environments where every person having contact with the child is a treatment team member with a role relationship to that child. It is imperative that the bus driver, cook, custodian, and secretary recognize that they interact and contribute to the child's social learning environment.

Interagency experiences will be new for many educators and agency treatment providers. But how else can a sexually abused child's treatment progress? Is the Department of Human Services to manage this problem in isolation from the community mental health providers that see the child weekly or the teachers that interact with the child daily? The contributing authors agree that the most wasteful and therefore expensive treatment form is one that does not provide for interagency interaction from the planning stages. Long-standing territorial and role relationship issues did not provide for enriched treatment in the past and will not provide for it in the future. Who's the boss of a treatment team is not the question. The question is, who is the client and how can that client be served? A team functions as a unit, and a psychiatrist is no more a team leader than the teacher's aide whom the child relates to the best and who works with him 5 hours every day. Role relationships in the team may be and generally are described by the role relationship of the team members with the child.

Who is emotionally disturbed? Forness and Kelly presented two excellent but diverse positions for the inclusion and exclusion of children with conduct disorders into and from the current efforts to revise the federal definition. While it is only a working definition, as a new response to the limitations in the current one is being sought, several authors seemed to be seeking broader freedoms in the reduction of restrictive policies, providing local treatment providers the right to classify and serve children who are emotionally disturbed as they see it. There is sentiment that the schools use language such as *seriously emotionally disturbed* to describe children without emotional disturbances who are acting out or manipulating. There is general agreement among the authors that *emotionally disturbed* and *behaviorally disordered* are not merely interchangeable terms, despite the fact that some states use one term and other states use other terms. There is disagreement among those who discussed the problems of definition on adapting or using the language in the *Diagnostic and Statistical Manual of Mental Disorders–Fourth Edition* (DSM–IV; American Psychiatric Association, 1994). However, this position seems to be softening, and from both sides.

There are those nonclinical educators who believe the mental disorder descriptions in DSM–IV are simply too clinical and therefore not practical. The American Psychiatric Association's committee on nomenclature has been very sensitive to the many shortfalls in the past, and the new DSM–IV entries for children include many of the criticisms from educators to DSM–III. If educators seek team membership they must turn to the *Diagnostic and Statistical Manual for Mental Disorders* for common communications and an entry point agreement for scientific study of treatment effects. Gabel and Evans presented strong cases for moving from nonscientifically declared "best practices" as a 1980s construct to data-based decision making, and for good reason.

There is yet another area of surprising agreement, in fact a shocking level of agreement. Each author at some point acknowledged that there is much to be done and much that can be done. However, any intervention effort in any setting or environment will cost money. Extra-educational and experiential requirements are needed in the preparation of the quality of well-prepared professional service providers sought. Not just everyone should or can work with children who are emotionally disturbed. McDowell, Guetzloe, Noll, Braaten, and Wood all argued strongly that not every person has the emotional durability to serve children who are emotionally disturbed. Support services are critical if we are to achieve the full service schools that so many of the authors have argued for now and in the past. And it must be said that anything less than a full service school will not meet the requirements that are being placed on educators today, requirements by society and requirements by children and families.

Everyone has heard the argument: Increase mental health and special education budgets today or build more prisons tomorrow. There is less than 20% of the funding for children's mental health services available today than under the Carter Administration, and yet more children require services today than yesterday. P.L. 94-142 receives less than 40% of full funding.

In retrospect, our response to this project of the major contributors to this field, the pioneers in the treatment and education of children who are emotionally disturbed, has been a very enlightening experience, indeed an uplifting experience. However, if the needed resources do not appear, the future as predicted will occur. Must we believe in the resiliency of the human spirit, or can human effort make a difference, and will that difference be made now?

Maybe we too would have missed this message, until last Friday, when we both were confronted with a 17-year-old boy who had been expelled from school for the year. His custody had been taken from a rejecting mother and a neglectful father and given to grandparents 13 years ago, and he had grown up emotionally hurt and angry, internalizing his rejection as his unworthiness to be loved. The boy years ago had been labeled as seriously emotionally disturbed and had received treatment on two occasions in a special school program (day school), where in fact he had done very well. Now he is expelled for the year because, having been returned to regular school without any advocacy, any school or mental health supports, any crisis-intervention structure, he swore at a high school teacher. He swore at her because, upon entering the room and finding the class in an uproar, she singled him out as the villain. Interestingly enough, he is socially withdrawn and generally isolates himself from social interaction. You see, common to early rejection, he has a dissociative identity disorder. And while he finds himself unworthy of acceptance, he tries hard to find means to engage in peer interaction, seeking peer acceptance.

In one stroke, a teacher undid all the positive efforts that had gone before. Finding control and redeeming one's social position was more important than being responsive to hurting humanity. The principal supported his content-oriented secondary teacher and ordered the student out for 1 month without a change in placement meeting with anyone. The school board upheld the principal and without any additional data, current psychological evaluation, or current intervention record of any type ordered him expelled for the year. You may view this as an illegal act. We view it as an immoral act.

This occurred in a poor rural county school system that needs all the resources it can obtain. Yes, it was only 2 years ago that a new 1,000-inmate prison was completed in this county. It is true that a pie has only so many pieces. How can school programs be justified in returning normally intelligent youth to the streets in the face of being classified seriously emotionally disturbed? How much does it cost to form a positive attitude toward oneself? How much does it cost to alter professional attitudes? Not one educational administrator in the state of Tennessee (simply to pick on our own state) is required to take one course in special education in order to become a principal or superintendent.

It is our sincere hope that we have brought you a worthy contribution in this text. If we have, we wish to ask a favor in return. Please consider, when you have finished with this book, sending it with a personal note to a policymaker. You will know what to say in the note.

To all our contributing authors, we wish a long and continuing prosperous and productive life.

To all our readers, may we borrow from Long and wish you well in "the continuing struggle."

To those we serve, we thank you for the hope and resolution you have given us.

REFERENCES

American Psychiatric Association. (1994). *Diagnostic and statistical manual of mental disorders* (4th ed.). Washington, DC: Author.

National Commission Excellence in Education. (1983). *Nation at risk*. Washington, DC: U.S. Government Printing Office.

ADDITIONAL READINGS

Bower, E. M. (1981). *Early identification of emotionally handicapped children in school* (3rd ed.). Springfield, IL: Charles C. Thomas.

Braaten, S., Kauffman, J. M., Braaten, B., Polsgrove, L., & Nelson, C. M. (1988). The regular education initiative: Patent medicine for behavioral disorders. *Exceptional Children, 55*, 21–27.

Bullock, L. M., Zagar, E. L., Donahue, C. A., & Palton, G. B. (1985). Teacher's perceptions of behaviorally disordered students in a variety of settings. *Exceptional Children, 52*, 123–130.

Cullinan, D., & Epstein, M. H. (1985). Adjustment problems of mildly handicapped and nonhandicapped students. *Remedial and Special Education, 6*, 5–11.

Edwards, L. L., & O'Toole, B. (1985). Application of the self control curriculum with behavior disordered students. *Focus on Exceptional Children, 17*, 1–8.

Faulkner, W. (1930). *As I lay dying.* New York: Random House.

Gable, R. A., & Laycock, V. K. (1990). *Regular classroom integration of behaviorally disordered students in perspective.* Unpublished manuscript. Norfolk, VA: Old Dominion University.

Gable, R. A., McConnell, S., & Nelson, C. M. (1986). The learning-to-fail phenomenon as an obstacle to mainstreaming children with behavior disorders. In R. B. Rutherford, Jr., (Ed.), *Severe behavior disorders of children and youth* (Vol. 8, pp. 19–26). Reston, VA: Council for Children with Behavioral Disorders.

Gartner, A., & Lipsky, D. K. (1987). Beyond special education: Toward a quality system for all students. *Harvard Education Review, 57*, 367–395.

Grosenick, J. K., George, M. P., & George, N. L. (1987). A profile of school programs for the behaviorally disordered: Twenty years after Morse, Cutler and Fink. *Behavioral Disorders, 12*, 159–168.

Grosenick, J. K., George, M. P., & George, N. L. (1990). A concept scheme for describing and evaluating programs in behavioral disorders. *Behavioral Disorders, 15*, 70–73.

Haring, N. G., McCormick, L., & Haring, T. G. (1994). *Exceptional children and youth: An introduction to special education* (6th ed.). New York: Merrill.

Hendrickson, J. M., Gable, R. A., & Shores, R. E. (1987). The ecological perspective, setting events, and behavior. *The Pointer, 31*, 40–44.

Hobbs, N. (1966). Helping disturbed children: Psychological and ecological strategies. *American Psychologist, 21*, 1105–1115.

Horner, R. H., Diemes, S. M., & Brazeau, K. C. (1992). Education support for students with severe problem behaviors in Oregon: A descriptive analysis from 1987–88 school year. *The Journal of the Association of Persons with Severe Handicaps, 17*, 154–169.

Horner, R. H., Dunlap, G., Koegel, R. L., Carr, E. G., Sailor, W., Anderson, J., Albin, R. W., & O'Neill, R. E. (1990). In support of integration for people with severe problem behaviors: A response to four commentaries. *Journal of the Association for Persons with Severe Handicaps, 15*(3), 145–147.

Kauffman, J. M., & Pullen, P. L. (1989). An historical perspective: A personal perspective on our history of serving mildly handicapped and at-risk students. *Remedial and Special Education, 10*, 12–14.

Kerr, M. M., & Nelson, C. M. (1989). *Strategies for managing behavioral problems in the classroom* (2nd ed.). Columbus, OH: Merrill.

Koegel, R. L., & Koegel, L. K. (1990). Extended reductions in stereotypic behavior of students with autism through a self-management treatment program. *Journal of Applied Behavior, 23*(1), 119–127.

Morse, W., Bruno, F., & Morgan, S. (1971). *Training teachers for the emotionally disturbed: An analysis of programs.* Washington, DC: University of Michigan School of Education and U.S. Office of Education, Bureau of Education for the Handicapped.

Muscott, H. S. (1988). The cascade of services model for behaviorally disordered children and youth: Past, present, and future perspectives. In R. B. Rutherford, Jr., C. M. Nelson, & R. Forness (Eds.), *Bases for severe behavioral disorders in children and youth* (pp. 307–319). Boston: College-Hill.

O'Neill, R. E., Horner, R. H., O'Brien, M., & Huck, S. (1991). Generalized reduction of difficult behaviors: Analysis and intervention in a competing behaviors framework. *Journal of Developmental and Physical Disabilities, 3*(1), 5–20.

Polsgrove, L., & Rieth, H. (1979). A new look at competencies required by teachers of emotionally disturbed/behaviorally disordered children and youth. In F. H. Wood (Ed.), *Teachers of secondary school students with serious emotional disturbance* (pp. 25–46). Minneapolis: University of Minnesota, Department of Special Education.

Rizzo, J. V., & Zabel, R. H. (1988). *Educating children and adolescents with behavioral disorders: An integrative approach.* Boston: Allyn & Bacon.

Rhodes, W. C. (1967). The disturbing child: A problem of ecological management. *Exceptional Children, 33*, 449–455.

Rhodes, W. C. (1970). A community participation analysis of emotional disturbance. *Exceptional Children, 36*, 309–314.

Rutherford, R. B., Jr., & Nelson, C. M. (1988). Applied behavior analysis in education: Generalization and maintenance. In J. C. Witt, S. N. Elliott, & F. N. Gresham (Eds.), *Handbook of behavior therapy in education.* New York: Plenum.

Shores, R. E., Gunter, P. L., & Jack, S. L. (1993). Classroom management strategies: Are they setting events for coercion? *Behavioral Disorders, 18*, 92–102.

Simmons, J. L. (1969). *Deviants.* Berkeley, CA: Glendessary Press.

Tannenbaum, A. J. (1968). *Education and mental health. Unpublished paper by the ad hoc Education Committee.* New York: Teachers College, Columbia University.

Tompkins, J. R. (Ed.). (1970). *Report: Joint special education study group regarding the report of the joint commission on the mental health of children and youth.* Washington, DC: TREC.

Tompkins, J. R., & Allen, M. G. (1985). *National needs analysis and related issues in behavioral disorders.* Lexington, MA: Ginn Press.

U.S. Department of Education. (1987). *Ninth annual report to Congress on the implementation of Public Law 94-142: The Education for All Handicapped Children Act.* Washington, DC: Author.

Wood, F. H. (1979). Issues on training teachers for the seriously emotionally disturbed. In R. B. Rutherford, Jr., & A. G. Prieto (Eds.), *Severe behavior disorders of children and youth* (pp. 12–13). Reston, VA: Council for Exceptional Children.

Wood, F. H. (1982). Defining disturbing, disordered, and disturbed behavior. In F. H. Wood & K. C. Lakin (Eds.), *Disturbing, disordered or disturbed? Perspective on the definition of problem behavior in educational settings*. Minneapolis: University of Minnesota, Department of Psychoeducational Studies.

Wood, F. H. (1987). Issues in the education of behaviorally disordered students. In R. B. Rutherford, Jr., C. M. Nelson, & S. Forness (Eds.), *Severe behavior disorders of children and youth*. Boston: College-Hill.

Zabel, R. K. (1993). The special education initiative: Responding to changing problems, populations, and paradigms. *Behavioral Disorders, 18*, 303–307.

Library
St. Joseph's College
Patchogue, N.Y. 11772

LC 4181 .P47 1995

Personal perspectives on
emotional